FOR GOD'S SAKE, GO!

By the same Author

Thomas Hobbes (1922)
The Science and Method of Politics (1926, reprinted 1964)
Preface to Action (1934)
Study of the Principles of Politics (1929, reprinted 1967)
Durkheim's Rules of Sociological Method (1938)
The Story of the Political Philosophers (1939)
The Anglo Saxony and its Tradition (1939)
The Atlantic Community (1959)
Systematic Politics (1962)
The Grandeur of England and the Atlantic Community (1966)
The Atlantic Commonwealth (1968)

In preparation
The Permissive Society

Sir George Catlin

FOR GOD'S SAKE, GO!

an autobiography

Sir George Catlin

COLIN SMYTHE
GERRARDS CROSS 1972

CONTENTS

PREFACE

FOR GOD'S SAKE, GO!

THE title of this book requires some justification. The original title was *Campaign*; but it is here legitimate to ask, "Campaign about what?" It could indeed have been a study of our own times, of the power and the glory. Sir Roy Harrod, in a recent book and justifying his own title, writes: "The title should stress the subject matter of the ultimate culmination." There is much described in this book which I would wish to see go. However, the book begins with a question. Much of my life has been concerned with arriving at an answer. Maybe a search for the region most like-minded and powerful for peace. The book ends with, on the one side, an affirmation and, on the other, a repudiation of the wrong way in the life of our peoples.

In its original draft, made during the Second World War, this book assumed a different form, more like a Faust-and-Wagner performance or a *Gulliver's Travels* among the political fauna of our day, deprived of autobiographical egotism. It was, to me unexpectedly, T. S. Eliot who advised me to write straight auto-biography which, whether in the world of ideas or of practice, meant political autobiography. It was Frank and Elizabeth Longford who persuaded me to take up this script again. And it was at a birthday party at Victor Gollancz's house that, as we looked over the balustrade, I promised Elizabeth Longford to finish the book. To both of them I record my debt.

I wish also to express my sincerest thanks to Lord Louis Mountbatten for reading the pages on India and for his suggestions made to me at Romsey; to my friend of many years, Professor Ernest Jacob, of All Souls, for reading the Oxford chapter; and to many others, including C. H. Rolph, for reading the text in whole or part. Also I am indebted to Professor G. P. Wells, for permission to quote from writings of his father, H. G. Wells; to Mr Philip Willkie for like permission; to Dora Gaitskell for permission to quote a letter to me from Hugh; to Lord Moyle for like permission to quote letters from Clement Attlee; to Mrs Indira Gandhi for permission to quote a cable from her father; as well as to all those who have allowed me to quote their own correspondence.

FOR GOD'S SAKE, GO!

I

THE GREAT WAR

IN 1967 a book of mine appeared with the title *The Grandeur of England*. How that grandeur was to be maintained, in world affairs, in peace and war, was indicated in the sub-title: "and the Atlantic Community".

Having spent most of a life-time concerned with the problem of war, itself not only "the sport of kings" but part of the history of the aggressive human animal since the days when the Assyrians executed their captives by spiking them on spears and maybe since the days of our ancestral cousin, the carnivorous African ape, my sub-title provided a provisional clue to an answer.

If not yet world peace—and this was not utopian—at least regional peace. If not "the Roman peace", *pax romana,* then at least (as in the later days of Rome itself) a peace maintained by the joint dominion of two—or should it be three?—super-Powers, ruling by law and arms. "By law and arms", centuries ago, had said the great Emperor Justinian. We could say it again today. And the clue lay in the study of power and the power-game. Who wills utopia must will the necessary means.

The trouble was that brother man, call him "common man" or "the mass", was (despite Tolstoy) far more interested, after bread, in circuses, in cheering his boring life by entertainment, in the brothel of a permissive society, than in the dull problems of war and peace which could be left to the élite corps of diplomats. Once actually involved in the adrenalin mood of war he could enjoy the flags, the music, the risks, the slaughter of the gladiatorial show. It is not for nothing that most heads of state are generals or *generalissimi.* But in the West, up to the verge of August 1914, the masses did not believe, such was the liberal euphoria, that there could be war. Business, pleasure, progress and prosperity went on as usual. I recall my father turning the pages of his diary and saying, "This is now the Twentieth Century." And the slogan of those Victorian days was "Peace, Progress and Prosperity."

Mr Ralph Lane, Nobel Prize winner, under his happy pseudonym of Norman Angell, used his wings to fan even the intelligent into the same comfortable belief. That nationalism is not controlled by economic advantage alone, that the Marxist explanation here is also weak, was overlooked. War came upon them all like a thief in the night, the thieving yet not planned even by the "all-highest" rulers of Russia and Germany. Why then did this "happening" become for me more of an aching problem and preoccupation, a choice of answer between free human will and predestination, than for the next man, so that life became one long campaign to provide the answer?

In the winter of 1918 two battalions of the British Rifle Brigade had taken up quarters in Fay-le-Franc, on the French-Belgian border. They were in Normandy, in Rouen, when the Kaiser abdicated. Myself, I heard the news outside the portals of the great cathedral. We heard of the Armistice as we came up to the railhead at Soumain and then marched to what had been the final front lines near Bouchain. The Eleventh of the Eleventh. The regiment itself had many battle honours to its credit, acquired at Le Cateau, Neuve Chapelle, Ypres and elsewhere.

There had been quite recently a "false armistice", a rumour having spread, chiefly among Canadian troops, that a "cease-fire" had been arranged. Canteens had been raided for celebration drinking. There was now another press statement; and the little farms beside the railway line had become beflagged. The Rifle Brigade, as its ranks trudged on for the final lap, remained wary and cynical, whatever mad crowds in London might be doing. Anyhow, they reflected, an armistice was not a peace; and they might not be through with war yet. Who knew what the Boche, the old Hun (the Kaiser's own exquisitely unfortunate term), might not yet be up to?

The troops, shrewd, solid, unemotional, plodded forward, neither "windy" nor exhilarated. They did not allow themselves to expect too much, but packed their kit-bags—"Cheer up, you will soon be dead". The asset of the English, lazy in peace and inclined "to swing the lead", is imperturbable phlegm and humour in war. We are told by pundits that it is their economic defect; they need "arousal." Long live "the common defect"! It was Churchill who said—at least it is ascribed to him—that unlike the orderly Germans who ever march in step, they are members of a piratical nation more reliable in war than in peace.

We were late in arriving at the front because we had been delayed for some weeks to go down to Newport, Monmouthshire, in order to make a *démarche en force* through the streets of Welsh mining villages, where a strike was threatened. It was my first experience of a strike against the Government. It was also a demonstration of armed force by the Government against civilian strikers. Mutiny was later in the air—but not until the war was won. The troops were unsympathetic to the occasional conscientious objector. I recall one, a baker, being called out on parade. "*They* were liable to be shot. Why not he?" The place for conscientious objectors was in work at the front. But "other ranks" were not unsympathetic with the miners.

They also wanted to get the bloody war over. However, these route marches were the Prime Minister's orders. And, for all of Pétain's great resistance at Verdun, the French had not displayed a morale any better than theirs. The French had nearly broken their front in 1916. Many units had defied their officers or went forward crying "baa", like sheep for the slaughter-house. In 1917 there had been open French mutiny under General Nivelle. Nevertheless whatever the cost, victory had come—and the curse of false hopes. The deceptive phantasm shimmered of a land fit for heroes.

The men, on arrival in Fay-le-Franc, were quartered in Belgian miners' cottages, and as the year moved to its end, they celebrated their Christmas feast in the hall of Monsieur le Baron. The place was plagued with the Asiatic influenza which, it is startling to recall, caused as many deaths in Europe as the war itself. I myself had gone down with it and, after being nursed by nuns, I had gone back to lice-ridden Valenciennes and then joined my own battalion where it had moved forward, at Asquillies, eleven kilometres from Mons, dominated by its great Tour d'Auberon.

There, a kilometre away, the Guards had begun their retreat in 1914 and we used the food utensils they had left behind. The winter was bitter and we broke the ice to wash.

One of the greatest of English historians, Bishop Stubbs, upon whose writings I had been brought up, maintained that the French, with their vainglory, had been at the back of every European trouble from the Middle Ages to Sedan. That English outlook prevailed throughout the days of Victoria and until the French attempt in equatorial Africa, which ended at Fashoda. In 1896 the especial preoccupation of the diplomats and defence experts of the Franco-Russian Dual Entente was with the dangers of British machinations. Sir John Tenniel's cartoon in *Punch*, about Fashoda is still worth looking at, with its indignant John Bull and its diminutive but presumptuous Gaul. "Look here, my little friend—come off that flag."

There followed a time when Edward VII, smarting under suppression by his parents and heartily resentful of his nephew, the Kaiser, in whose arms Queen Victoria had died at Osborne, encouraged the new Francophil policy of Entente Cordiale, which was indeed initiated in subtle suggestions and asides at the old lady's funeral. Funerals are especially auspicious moments for

secret diplomacy. It was pursued, although Lord Rosebery,
sometime Liberal Prime Minister, expressed the view at the time
that it was "much more likely to lead to complications than to
peace". The lush Edward was awarded the title of "the Peace-
Maker". His nephew, who was entitled to the uniform of a British
Admiral, he greeted in his heavy accent with the words "the
shtripes on your trousers are far too vide". Peace was to be promoted by private military staff discussions, which later spelled
public commitment to war; and democracy was to be promoted
by the alliance of the Liberal Powers, fortified by the French
association with the Autocrat of All the Russians. To have Nicholas
in was, on the chess-board of power, a prerequisite for victory—a
prerequisite means for the human good of liberalism, anti-mili-
tarism and peace.

The Kaiser and the Big Navy organisations, pushed forward
by Admiral Tirpitz and the fire-eaters, with incredible folly
wrecked the old Anglo-German relationship and plunged Germany
into a war which strategists may have planned on paper but
which, on the available evidence, even the Kaiser had not wanted.
The romance of sabre-rattling had ended in the reality of firing
guns. "Peaceful change", despite Haldane, had become impossible.

Edward Grey, Francophil, more correct in his diplomatic
righteousness than aware that European power would be wrecked
for centuries, had seen "the lights go out". The unforgivable
offence lay here. Grey was in some respects like a locomotive
driver who excuses himself for a train crash on the ground that
he kept strictly to the rules. For him wars still lay in the immemorial tradition of history, as politics pursued by crude means.
He was shocked. But he was not surprised. The crucial decisions
for Britain before August 1914 were taken by Asquith and Grey
alone, without wider Cabinet consultation. This is an important constitutional matter (of the kind that has recently preoccupied George
Brown) with which, twenty years on, I was to concern myself as a
member of the Executive Committee of the Union of Democratic
Control and, later, to discuss with the present Lord Salisbury.

Localised and so-called "colonial" wars apart, the Century of
Peace since the admirable Congress of Vienna, guided by the
genius of Talleyrand, had unbelievably come to an end. *Après la
guerre finie*—after this European civil war—four empires would
fall, with another, the British, to follow. The effect of the fall of
the Hapsburg and Turkish Empires was to be, on the whole,
deplorable and the consequent extension of nationalist fever a
curse for mankind. The cause of democracy was committed to
alliance with the black and plotting reaction of the Czardom.

Cambon had cashed the cheques issued (however privately by Asquith and Grey) on British credit. An accommodation could have been reached with Germany. It was not reached and Europe suffered. Although Port Arthur and the Russo-Japanese war had offered a sign, it was now that, for the first time since Marathon, Europe receded from the foreground of the stage of history. America, Asia and Africa emerged.

In the first volume of his *War Memoirs*, Lloyd George wrote: "In looking back upon the incidents of those few eventful days one feels like recording a nightmare, and after reading most of the literature explaining why the nations went to war, and who was responsible, the impression left on my mind is one of utter chaos, confusion, feebleness and futility, especially of a stubborn refusal to look at the rapidly approaching cataclysm." Despite this damning condemnation of the statesmen, at a lower level of contingency everything was prepared in the logistics of war and army entrainment, even down to Cooper's marmalade and the places where the troops would take coffee—all the detail and none of the decisions on the great affairs of State.

The Great War had begun. John Bull's famous placard, which as a schoolboy I saw myself at Richmond, "To Hell with Serbia"— the country then of a dirty, bloodstained and scandalous dynasty with a dirty network of conspirator assassins—was a mere bleat of protest, far too late. For example, who knew that Austria alone at the time, before 1914, had liberally allowed local nationalist vernaculars to be used in school and law court? In London the Austrian was merely an imitation German.

It nevertheless still seemed incredible, in that hot August of 1914, that the long summer of peace which stretched from the days of Napoleon, unbroken save by localised wars, should have come to an end. Jaurès also protested. The war-party was indeed then a minority party in France. But Jaurès likewise protested too late. Jaurès was shot.

To call the war off in 1916–17 and to negotiate, as proposed by Sixte Bourbon and Benedict XV, supported by the British ex-Foreign Secretary, Lansdowne, could have meant the end of Lloyd George, whose personal power rested on doing the precise opposite. Worse things could have happened. Nevertheless, Lloyd George was not unprepared to consider negotiations. It was Haig who was uncompromising, supported in the War Cabinet by, of all people, slim Jan Smuts. Compromise would yet have involved negotiation with a Germany still massively confident of its power, a Germany still in possession of almost all Belgium and much of France.

Anyone who studies the war reports of the 1914–18 war, republished fifty years on by the *New York Herald Tribune*, will be astounded that the Allies did not enter Berlin, not indeed within the six weeks expected with euphoria in quite distinguished quarters, but—so unvarying is the contemporary press report of military success—within the first six months. On 30th January 1916, indeed, it was announced that "the sky-murderers" or Zeppelins had killed all of twenty-six persons in Paris. I myself saw the one which went over London and ended its days at Potters Bar. Under 17th March 1917 occurs the entry: "The most qualified Russian authorities in Washington declare that the [Russian] revolution is a very happy event for the Allies." All this, however, only provides its own commentary on war reports.

Oddly enough, it was the death of Kitchener, the British magic mascot, which wrongly but really shook the public about a certain victory. The military actualities up to the great German March offensive of 1918 told another story about those who responded to the call for arms. With the Russians crumpled, only American power could compel satisfactory terms. The French and British alone certainly could not.

In 1916 at the Somme, 50,000 men had died in a day—although what impressed Haig, according to his diary, was that his horse had reared when the troops were being inspected by the King. I still marvel that the docile citizens do not haul down his statue in Whitehall along with that of Smuts "skating" in Parliament Square, and use the bronze for the next issue of devalued currency. Of the little town of Inveraray, county town of Argyll, one-seventh of the inhabitants had been killed, most of them in the earlier battle of Loos. Still "the mincing-machine" had gone on mincing the bodies of men, including "the Contemptibles". Haig (of whom Beaverbrook commented that, by his published diaries, he was the only man known to commit suicide twenty years after his death) with more imagination could have done his share in winning the war with far less cost. The brute fact remains that Haig won. Moreover, Pétain had saved the day at Verdun. "They shall not pass." Foch, Haig and Pershing achieved victory, and the Recording Angel will yet note that, the slaughter over, Haig expended himself in pleading for a decent recompense for his veterans.

The Great War, the first great European civil war, was over. It was Marshal Foch who commented, with fatal prescience, "It is an Armistice for twenty years." The problem would be the consequences of the peace.

We defused the hand-grenades, oiled our rifles, and waited.

There was so little to do in Asquillies that I taught an occasiona
army class, since the authorities in their wisdom had decided
that the deboshed soldiery must not be too idle or only occupied
with fornication. Nor could we clean equipment all the time.
Awaiting recall to Oxford, where I held the Open Exhibition in
History once held by Harold Laski at Wykeham's ancient College
of the Blessed Virgin of Winchester in Oxford (as the charters say,
"vulgarly called New College"), in these winter quarters, I spent
the idle hours writing jottings on philosophy in what had been a
civil service ledger, as René Descartes had done in earlier days,
writing his *Discours de la Méthode* in front of a German stove in
army winter quarters in Bavaria.

This was not, for me, an entire novelty. As a school boy of
sixteen, in Kew, I had lain on my bed reading Descartes' *Discours*,
and had been spell-bound, as by a new Euclidean revelation, by
the *Ethics* of Baruch Spinoza. (Years later I was to edit and to
arrange for the translation, which ran into many impressions, of
Emile Durkheim's *Rules of Sociological Method*.) I was certainly
not unaware of the importance of method in answering a scientific
problem. My second book was to be called *The Science and Method
of Politics*. My notes have probably been lost, but they were concerned with the cycle of good and evil, the good of yesterday,
undeveloped and negative, becoming developed as "the evil"
in the development of tomorrow. Years later, these ideas entered
into my Kierkegaard lecture in the University of Copenhagen.

Unless I got them from a library at Mons, I had no books with
me save a miniature, leather-bound copy of Lucretius' *De Rerum
Natura*, "Concerning the Nature of Things", which I carried
with my kit. I still have it. Anyhow I was interested in the nature
of things; and the great poem made good, slow reading.

We were a strange collection in those winter quarters. Most had
been dug out of civilian life, some of them Durham miners or
Bermondsey lads, in the final desperate recruiting call to meet the
disasters bred of the German offensive of the spring of 1918. A
member in succession of two Officers' Training Corps, I had been
rejected by the Artists' Rifles, the ordinary infantry, the Royal
Army Medical Corps, and even by the Army Service Corps,
being so far damaged in health that I had fallen by stages to the
rock bottom of "totally rejected". I have no doubt that this
passion to be in the army was very fine, but I had ended up in the
civil service.

Later I had been "rehabilitated" by the doctors and even drew
pay as a "first class shot". Although I had been advised to try for a
commission, I was rapped on the knuckles by the War Office for

following their own official's instructions. Bluntly, it would have
been most improper at that stage of the war to begin with a
commission. Perhaps this saved my life for at one time the
expectation of life of an officer at the front was about six weeks.
Indeed, during my period of service I was not even a sergeant.
(Neither, for that matter, was cadet de Gaulle. . . .) Once I was
called out on parade to give orders and, smartly switching my
swagger stick, I chanced briskly to catch the regimental sergeant
major a crack across the fingers. This parade exercise was not a
total success, but at least I was not the target of the comment of my
sergeant major: "What we want here is more dis-ci-pline."

Evans of the *Broke* had tried to get me into the Navy, but the
available jobs were technical and I was rejected there also. Hence,
for me the London Rifle—later, just Rifle-Brigade, with its double
quick step (parade purposes only) and its regimental tune, to
which the soldiery appended adequately obscene words. Leaving
Blackdown Camp before dawn one morning, we had entrained and
taken boat for Boulogne, now to find ourselves near snow-bound
Mons.

Of the others in our group there was the fair-headed Welshman,
Williams, a Jesuit novice. There were several Customs and Inland
Revenue men—my good companion-in-arms and my friend until
his death, George Simonds, and Tucker, later to be Sir George
Tucker, head of the Death Duties Section at Somerset House. . .

Among the ranks there were also "Dad", the elementary school-
master, and fortyish black haired "George", a blacksmith, a
reserved and sober man who vindicated Aristotle's approval of the
common man in democracy, a man who commanded my unfeigned
and even reverent respect for his shrewd practical and political
wisdom. To this day "George", a good man, remains my touch-
stone, even in moments of blacker disillusion, of what I mean by
the democratic citizen. Maybe I romanticised him—but I don't
think so. At least we lived in a real world, unlike that of some of
the Oxford society which for me was to follow.

If we are to distinguish between "citizen" and "mob", between
the solid and sober democratic citizen, good judge within the
limits of his experience, the man of common sense, and the raw
human animal, with its hysterical and mob demand for the instant
satisfaction of its wants, rampageous with discontent (as Freud
said he must be) against the inhibitions of civilised life, it was clear
where George stood. It had nothing to do with money, financial
status, love of profit or, yet more, of publicity and noise. It had
much to do with individual dignity. It also became clear where I
stood. Later I was to develop the notion of sound politics as being

the defence of the honest man, and later still my attitude towards the sensation-hunting *avant-garde*, and their commercial profit-hunting exploiters and producers, became one of undisguised hatred. "With it." With what?

I am in no position to be an authority on the relations of the British troops and the higher command, which I would suspect to be effective but not subservient. However, a story which admirably illustrates it circulated among my comrades-in-arms about a certain Brigadier General Sir Hunter Blair, known to the troops as "Hunty-Bunty", much given to conscientious inspections and not devoid of pomposity. In a large hay-filled barn on a winter evening, members of the oppressed infantry were resting, some on and some behind the straw bales. Abruptly the barn door was flung open and a voice of command proclaimed: "General Sir Hunter Blair." From behind the bales a sturdy voice replied: "And if you was the (sexual) Prince of Wales, shut the (sexual) door."

The bored soldiers, awaiting what was bizarrely called "disembodiment", gathered together in smokey *estaminets* to drink coffee and *vin ordinaire* and to tinkle a piano. On route marches the ruder soldiery sang songs so far unprintable that "Mademoiselle from Army'n-tears" was the song of a pure maiden by comparison. Or, maybe, it was "I love my wife", etc. They were coprophilous; not aristocrats in any known sense; but earthy men of the old Adam. They "packed up their troubles" with some gusto. One lusty corporal especially distinguished himself with full voice; and later committed fornication with a French tart who had climbed on board the troop train on the way back to Calais, preferring to consummate this simple act of nature under a blue gauze wrap she thoughtfully provided in a corner of the crowded army truck—"horse-room for eight". My impression, be it said, was that for free transport she provided her services free. Doubtless the angels cast no stones. As for the language then current in the lower army ranks, on present trends its four letter words will doubtless soon travel upwards, including *le mot de Chambron*, to reach the debates in the House of Lords in a permissive age.

Army life had done me immense good, as a relaxation from what had gone before in England. I had so far been lucky in my late "warfaring" that I can say I enjoyed it. Indeed I had met little of the war in France beyond the shuddering boom of the guns at the front, as heard from Boulogne. For good or evil, I did not have to make the decision central to the work of Albert Camus, "to kill or be killed"—and on which he perversely states that, to judge the answer, one must first kill. The surgeon, for a valuable experience, must first be operated upon; the lawyer must appear in the dock.

In the "Khaki Election" of 1918, which we discussed around the iron stove as we drank cans of tea, I voted without hesitation for Labour and Ramsay MacDonald and against "the goat", Lloyd George.

Really I voted for Woodrow Wilson, for the implementation of Wilson's Fourteen Points, as a pioneer attempt, however crude yet made in good faith, to stabilise peace. What mattered was that, the victory won, the peace should not be lost. It was Winston Churchill who wrote, in 1929, in *The World Crisis*: "The prevention of another great war should be the main preoccupation of mankind." But he had also written, in the first volume of that work: "One rises from the study of the causes of the Great War with a prevailing sense of the defective control of individuals upon world fortunes."

I had no confidence in the detestable Clemenceau. Talleyrand, representing the defeated enemy, with Metternich and Castlereagh at the Congress of Vienna had done a much better technical job in peace-making than was likely to be done at Versailles. I did not then know that Georges Clemenceau, *le Tigre*, the main cause of so many of our later disasters, had said: "Monsieur Wilson is worse than *le bon Dieu*. *Le bon Dieu* has only Ten points, while M. le Président has Fourteen." But I loathed the old suedegloved atheist and all his mood of secular vengeance—as Lord Northcliffe's supporting newspaper chose to put it, "squeezing the Germans until the pips squeaked". I expected no good to come of it; I preferred a God-fearing Presbyterian, such as Wilson.

I do not, of course, deny the sardonic quality of the wicked old man. "Monsieur 'Ughes," he is alleged to have remarked to the wartime Premier of Australia, "ven you vas a young man, I learn that you used to eat human flesh." "Monsieur le Président," replied the Premier of Australia, "the report is greatly exaggerated."

Might there, then, not be yet another equally great war? Were Lloyd George and Clemenceau or the Russian Czar and his court the men to prevent it? "Willie" had indeed now gone and the wolves of revenge, yapping around Dorn, howled "Hang the Kaiser". "Nicky" had gone. By now he was a corpse in Ekaterinberg. The immemorial Hapsburg Empire, itself the last relic of the Roman Empire, had gone. Would the less immemorial British Empire last? What would the French, the French of Napoleon III and of yesterday's Delcassé with their diseased desire to fight over filched Alsace, do next? As for martyred "little Belgium", the local Belgian farmer had told our colonel, in Fay-le-Franc, that he "preferred the Germans" to us; and had been told that, if he were not careful, he (a Walloon and not even a Fleming) would be locked up. What, in fact, Belgium did try to do later was to remain neutral in the Franco-German feud and to decline to complete the Maginot line.

How often, over these battlefields, were to be intoned the lines "They shall not grow old as we that are left grow old." They fell— in this war—my brother-in-law, my late wife's close friends, of which she wrote in *Testament of Youth*. Professionals of the Guards, at Mons, volunteers of the Somme, men who according to their lights fell for freedom and for the credited ideal that this might be (as the politicians and H. G. Wells said) "the war to end war"—they will not die so long as we, who survive, keep fresh their memory in the intransigent battle for internationalism against the ever-resurgent tribalism and chauvinism—even provincial and "little regional" chauvinism—which is with us to be fought at this present day. That was and is, at least, my own belief and my assigned contribution.

I now sought to know *de rerum natura*. Now, in Hainault, south of Flanders, east of Picardy, I wanted to know the real causes, the profounder causes of recurrent war, such as that in which, just now, so many had perished, first inspired by the romantic patriotism of a Rupert Brooke, and then in swinish mud. The consequences I could see for myself. I declined to think them a matter of the motivations or obscure intentions of individual statesmen or just a matter of diplomatic fact added to diplomatic fact and piously recorded by assiduous historians. Nor were they, I thought, an affair only of some anonymous Tolstoyan movement of the masses or of an occult Dialectic of Matter, for which human beings were mere flotsam and jetsam of an eternal fate.

Perhaps one might be the theorist, the philosopher, the scientist of power—the power with which the world was obsessed. Not corridors: but stairs and triumphal arches. Corridors are straight and on a level; the pursuit of power is neither. The stairs of power. The sinews of ascent in politics are power. To the very young man, quartered in Belgium, a science did not seem so absurd. There was no one around to ridicule him; and at least it was clear that no one else had given the adequate answers.

Seeking, however, to observe power on the world scale, as yet I failed to observe that, whether I liked it or not, I was involved in its contests on the personal scale also, as men were involved, so Freud contended, in sex and, Marx said, in wealth and ownership. The scholar was not detached by his ideas from the human condition shaped by power. Ideas may have immortality and win victories—

as witness the Koran and the Gospels. But ideas march—on *our* feet. The common soldier knew the consequences of the power struggle among the mighty. But could the soldier voter do anything to shape or alter it? Could he, undistinguished, talk with—persuade—the mighty? Incidentally, Lance Corporal Adolf Hitler —not even a German but a mere Austro-Czech—on the other side of these same battle lines, thought he could.

II

OXFORD

MY mother's family were Ortons, from Atherstone, in Warwickshire. My handsome grandfather had, in the great days of railways, patented a brake which was reputed to be better than the Westinghouse brake—but more expensive. Westinghouse beat his invention out. On my father's side, the Catlins were Bedfordshire folk, schoolmasters, small yeomen, tracing back to two churchwardens in about 1620. There was a pleasant belief, so far as I know unproven, that they could trace a connection with two brothers, the squires of Raunds and Newnham, places a few miles away from Bedford. Of these brothers, the sixteenth century squire of Newnham had enriched himself from church property, cheap on the market, and from the practice of the law. Here Sir Robert had the craft and not small political skill to be Chief Justice, not only in the last years of Mary Tudor, but in the first two of Elizabeth Tudor. It is, however, not myth but fact that he married off his daughter Mary, with a fat dowry (the money travelled that way!) to the aspiring Spencers, into which family in turn the newly arrived West Country family of Churchill married.

Between 1900 and 1904 we lived at Stourbridge in Worcestershire. The poverty of one district, Lye, was such that the borough's official record states, of the local comment in the 1850's, that the Registrar of Births had not much business in Lye, since unwanted babies were "thrown to the pigs". The four storied house "with turret", of the Anglican curate, my father—unexpectedly a keen Gladstonian Liberal—was rather different. I recall the green Venetian blinds; the speaking tubes from floor to floor. To me as a child what was real was not the myths of Spencers and Churchills but the pages of my fat, illustrated copy of *The Arabian Nights*. An only child I was also a most happy one, wandering in the garden with its large display of flowers from dahlia to marigold, delphinium and Canterbury bells; its central mulberry tree; its fruit trees and shrubs; white, red and black currant; gooseberry, apples, pears both "Sweet William" and bergamot; damson, greengage and luscious red plums. In the house itself, there was a nursery, each wall of which was, for papering, covered with cut-out illustrations of every nursery rhyme, from "Polly Put the Kettle on" to "Cock Robin". Clearly someone sometime had loved the

place. I have no nasty memories of a nasty childhood such as
Graham Greene records.

The later years were more clouded. There was indeed a glorious
holiday in Cornwall, when I became an addict of Kingsley's
Westward Ho and *Hypatia*. (I was convinced thenceforth that
philosophy was a beautiful woman and shocked Sir Alfred Ayer by
this confession.) And there were schooldays at Warwick, the
school founded *tempore Regis Edwardi ante Conquestum*, and at the
great school of Colet and Erasmus, St Paul's, myself one of the
scholars numerous as the miraculous draft of fishes. The renowned
High Master, Walker, "Monty" Mackenzie and the other
"Monty", the Field Marshal, were still remembered along with
the distant Milton and Marlborough. Ernest Raymond's "Mr
Elam" was still there. The characteristic of the school, founded
"for the children of all nations" in grand Renaissance style, was
that, unlike Winchester, it left no common character upon the
boys. They were all very much individuals.

My adolescent years were distraught by the incessant quarrels
between my parents, he (although a liberal in theology) a profound
believer in Moses and Queen Victoria and she an earnest supporter
of Women's Suffrage. (I have distrusted orthodox Judaism, the
Old Testament and that brand of Protestantism ever since.)
She would not herself have put burning paper into the local letter-
boxes or set fire to the Kew pagoda; but she did not condemn
those who did. He, now the Vicar of "the other Kew parish", was
always afraid that, crusading for so good a cause, she might
ignite the letters, if not the pagoda. It was the sad story of the
almost inevitable Greek tragedy. Each was right according to their
own lights, although neither the Mosaic indignation of the one
nor the ingrown refusal "to communicate" of the other was
blameless.

My bitter memories of Kew were softened by the kindliness of
nature amid the follies of man and the tensions of behaviour
"ancient" and "modern"—the standards for a decent English life
as against the cause of women's liberation. But the vicarage and its
garden (which at one point abutted on that of Mrs Swanick,
champion later of the League of Nations and sister of Walter
Sickert) and, above all, the gracious spaces of Kew Gardens
provided solace.

At last my parents separated. There was little joy. He broke
down, resigned, and faced, along with a nervous collapse, pretty
harsh poverty. Desperately seeking to be loyal to both, my
physical condition deteriorated despite a reliable constitution,
and so remained until I was put on Army diet. Psychologically I

was left with a horror of unnecessary quarrels. I became, not indeed unpopular at college, but shy, far too sensitive and preoccupied intensely with my own ideas.

By Easter 1919, I was back in Oxford. I was free to recall in peace how, on a dark November day in 1914, I had sat for the scholarship examinations in Balliol Hall, with a vast fire burning near High Table and the imposing row of the portraits of past Masters lowering down at me. To one face indeed I was accustomed, that of Benjamin Jowett. Before the upturned nose of Jowett's bronze bust at school I had for years said Latin prayers—the vowel stress had to be right—in honour of much greater men, the school's founders, Erasmus and Colet.

Jowett's name is irretrievably associated with the rhyme, in one of its many versions:

> I am Benjamin Jowett, Master of Balliol College,
> What's worth knowing, I know it;
> And what I don't know isn't knowledge.

Admittedly Tennyson's poem on "the Master" was more kindly. But here lay, neatly expressed, what Wykehamists tended to regard as all the Balliol arrogance. I use so stern a word because I recall Geoffrey Faber's comment that Jowett—not an unexcelled scholar—owing to his father's business incompetence had "a lasting contempt for worldly failure". Scholarship "had to lead somewhere"—preferably to the ranks of the Treasury or elsewhere in the Civil Service. In this shrewd but vulgar and corrupting philosophy he educated the young men. It is, of course, true that a conspicuous absence of worldly success, where such is sought, also corrodes character. Impotence, too, can corrupt—as much as power.

I was also free to look back and to recall the brief joyous moment when, having been told by my examiner, the historian Ernest Barker, that he proposed to recommend me for an Open Scholarship, I went whistling down New College Lane, towards the cobblestones of the Radcliffe Camera Square. Beyond lay the two colleges, Lincoln and Jesus—as one Fellow remarked, "the names frequently, I find, confused by American visitors". Barker subsequently demoted this Scholarship to an Exhibition because he thought I had plagiarised his own ideas; a belief four-fifths false—I had revamped my own school Truro Prize essay. So well I still remember the points; the historical, political, economic and psychological causes of war, and also the biological. Incidentally, I owed no small debt to Dr Hillard, the High Master of St Paul's, for his glowing comments and good-will.

Above me, between the forbidding walls strategically built to control storming townsmen mobs, towered the Entrance Gate with the Founder's statue kneeling in perpetual supplication to the Blessed Virgin. William of Wykeham, Chancellor of England— incidentally not a university man—had founded "the new college", and had also built anew Windsor Castle. On the latter's walls, tradition says, were inscribed the words: *Guil. de Wyck. hoc fecit.* "What is this, Chancellor?" said King Edward III. "You made it? I made it." "Sire, you mistranslate. The inscription means 'Windsor Castle made me'." What was "to make" a scholar of New College? "Manners"? "Manors", said the cynical Bentham. What was meant by "being made"? Wykeham is "part of history"; he was "made". He had a certain quality of immensity, of the awesome—like Wolsey but maybe better. Nevertheless, what was central on the Gate statuary was not William of Wykeham but the Virgin Mother of God.

A scholar of the College in Natural Science, Leslie Ward, of a Birmingham theatrical family, a most promising poet, a lad of great charm and the closest friend of my first schooldays, asked me to his rooms that good evening for drinks. As I left he remarked, "There are ghosts in the College tonight." The following morning he was to report for the call-up. I never saw him again. Dead in France. I survive. He did not. A poem of his is recorded in his school.

The was the decade of the Waugh brothers, from Alec's *Loom of Youth* in 1917 to Evelyn's *Decline and Fall* in 1928. Of that remarkable writer, Evelyn Waugh, I was to learn a little more later. He suffered from a temperamental persecution complex. Except in the company of known friends, he was convinced he would be attacked and was under an unhappy compulsion to be rude first. Nevertheless, he left us himself inadequately honoured.

The university was enlivened by the presence of N. A. Beecham, a meteorite who began to fall from the unfortunate moment when, sitting next to the very source of Liberal patronage, Margot Asquith, and asked about his life's wish, he is rumoured to have replied that what he really wanted to be was Lloyd George's secretary. There was silence. I myself met Margot, only once. She enlivened her conversation by patting my knee. (Years later I met Violet Bonham-Carter, Megan Lloyd-George's "Lady Violent". However, by this time she was mellowed and was not unwilling to be talked to.)

Not less was the University flattered by the contemporary presence of Beverley Nichols, President of the Union.

Beverley entrapped himself, as have many others, in an

impossible situation. As "embodied youth" he could not escape by claiming that the so-called "generation gap" was a foolish psychological myth, bred of the "Oedipus complex" dogma, the observable facts being only the characteristic arrogant inexperience of youth; the confusions of adolescence; the merry ways of the next in line—the "teeny-boppers"; and (latest discovery of group habit) the aggressiveness of the "ankle-biters". He was condemned, with time, to find himself in the ambiguous situation of "elderly youth".

It was the epoch when students were occasionally dazzled by the apparition of Lytton Strachey, falsetto-voiced, master of wit and of the "debunker's art", who misled a generation of historians by his success. I recall his visit to St Mary Magdalen College and all the novel jests (now forgotten) which, in sudden squeaks, he put into circulation about the Immaculate Conception—not, of course, of the Magdalen. It was the epoch of *Chrome Yellow* and the emancipated titter.

The "political generation" of the College, Hugh Gaitskell, Dick Crossman (sometimes my generous host when he was later Dean), Frank Longford, Douglas Jay, was to come later. Three of these I came later to know well, although in diverse degrees. Frank Longford and his charming wife, Elisabeth, provided me with the steel of determination to write this book. Also there was my sometime host, A. L. Rowse, who belonged to a younger generation, a most exciting man of vigorous opinions who later much enlivened, for my wife and myself, a trans-Atlantic voyage.

The chief honours of the immediate post-war generation were academic. 1919–20 was what is called "a vintage year" for the College. Maurice Bowra, later Warden of Wadham, David Keir, who took over my college rooms and was later Master of Balliol (when Balliol needed a Master it had turned to New College), Ernest Jacob, later Chichele Professor of History on the foundation of All Souls, Dermot Morrah, also of All Souls and of *The Times*, Henry Price, who had rooms beneath me and was later Wykeham Professor of Metaphysics, Roy Harrod, direct from school and later Student of Christ Church, Idris Deane-Jones, who went as Fellow to Merton, Robin Snow who went to Magdalen, Cyril Radcliffe, Scott Stokes, Henry Andrews, whom I later introduced to his future wife Rebecca West—all were on the roll-call of my contemporaries and most of them personal friends. Julian Huxley and J. B. S. Haldane were seniors in residence, as was that remarkable man and boisterous musician, Sir Hugh Allen.

Haldane advised me against joining the Union, as a waste of time. I was a member of the Canning Club, where I met Sir

Valentine Chirol; and of the Philosophical Society—almost inevitably called the Jowett Society. Later I was for a while a member of the Aristotelian Society but found it dull.

The jewel of all clubs, however, was the select College Essay Society, where one drank mulled claret and listened to papers. Maurice Bowra, Ernest Jacob, Roy Harrod, J. D. Woodruff, Henry Andrews were members. I still recall with pleasure the paper on Flecker, *risqué*, phallic, but polished, by Maurice Bowra. Other clubs might enjoy the arrival of W. B. Yeats, with his large bow-tie; but this club was the best.

Going up College stairs to Hall it was the future banker Andrews who, quoting *Hassan*, called to the future Vice Chancellor of Oxford, Sir Maurice, ahead of him, "Lead on, O Master of the Caravan." The reply was unhesitating: "Lead on the merchant princes of Bagdad." My life-long friend, Henry Andrews, is however associated in my mind with a recollection of long-after-college days—indeed the Sixties. I had an invitation to view an Exhibition of opals in Bond Street. The numbering of premises in Bond Street, Old and New, is complex, running up one side and down the other. Only the number I sought was in my mind and, having met Henry in the street, I asked him to join with me in the search and to view the Exhibition. He agreed, while explaining his own preference for diamonds, with their curious particularities of superior interest to the connoisseur. We seemed to stray further from the right street number. A second inspection of the invitation revealed, at the top, the one word, "Cartiers". "Ah!" exclaimed Henry, "George Catlin in Bond Street, seen hurrying north in pursuit of Cartiers." It was a truly Proustian remark. I am confident that for the rest of his life, I was socially placed with exactitude by Henry as "the man who went north in Bond Street to find Cartiers". No breakfast at Tiffany's (today, in London, merely the ex-Trocadero) will provide a compensation. Who "breakfasts at Tiffany's" anyhow? However, the not less Proustian remark, made gazing into a cup of enriched cold soup, "I never know what to do with my red caviar", came from Henry's wife, Dame Rebecca West, herself.

University Fellows had nervously expected a flood of brutal army majors, spilling the white ichor of dons on the cobblestones of Carfax. They found to their surprise a very mature and hard-working crew, if more critical than the usual schoolboys. I was supposed to be fortunate in having as my tutors Ernest Barker and H. W. B. Joseph, who were reputed to be the best then in Oxford. I was certainly fortunate in having as Warden that truly remarkable human being, Archibald Spooner.

Warden Spooner, an albino, in the course of time has become a centre of legend. Not that those who went before him were not formidable men in their own right. The time had not yet come when an adventurous undergraduate would shoot a golf ball through the Warden's window. In days when all undergraduates were supposed to wear, not only the academic millinery of gowns, but also college caps or "mortar boards", Dr Spooner's predecessor, Warden Sewell, proceeding across Old Quad had detected an offender. "Young man, why do you not wear your college cap? I can give you thirty reasons why you should do so. The first is that you can raise it when you meet me. Good morning." There is something splendid and uncompromising in such a Confucian display of authority. These were the days when discipline as such was thought to be "a good thing" and somehow connected with a painstaking excellence, a deliberate civilisation, a shaped and purposeful culture and humanism. It was left for Spooner's successor, H. A. L. Fisher, to immerse himself in politics and to refer one surprised French audience, with pride, to the days (as he unfortunately put it) *"quand j'étais dans le Cabinet"*.

I myself recall being in Warden Spooner's ante-room when, unnoticed by me, he had entered. His quiet voice broke in on my meditations. "Ah! I see that you are looking at the coats of arms of my predecessors. There are thirty-nine of them. A lady was in here the other day and asked me how many there were. I said, 'Thirty nine'. And with that love of round numbers which some people have, she replied: 'Oh, Mr Warden, what a pity there are not forty!'"

The initiative was more often the Warden's own, as when he startled a commoner undergraduate of New College who had, nevertheless, been guilty of also acquiring a scholarship at Balliol, to which College he proposed to go, with the phrase: "Ah, well, it will be Balliol's loss and our gain." Or when J. D. Woodruff, newly elected President of the Union, was told, "Well, Mr Woodruff, you will now no longer have to think up your jokes before Union meetings."

Whether most of the well known Spoonerisms were indeed authentic I would not venture an opinion. Did he, as told, in Egypt delight his daughter by his pleasure in "seeing the minx by moonlight"? For one interchange with his wife I can vouch. "I must now go and change for chapel before dinner." "I don't think you mean what you say, Archie." "Oh, no. I mean that I must now go to change for dinner before chapel." That, having lectured on Virgil, he then assured his divinity class "Of course, wherever I said 'Virgil', I meant 'St Paul'," I will not vouch for. The so-called "true Spoonerism" is illustrated by the remark to an elderly lady in a shady corner of the garden, "Oh, what a nosey cook." At least Spoonerisms are less boring than Joyce's relentless puns, regarded by the *cognoscenti* as "so clever".

The most revealing Spoonerisms were perhaps those of thought, as when he had to "rusticate" a young undergraduate, whose family he knew, and when he was deeply troubled about the pain which would be given to the young man's parents. The astonished undergraduate received a notice of rustication, concluding with the signature of the Warden, inscribed as "Your affectionate son, Archie".

If the world is to be gay, and not only of sweat and strikes, noise, greed and competition for cash and of grim Marxism, then even among the learned the likes of Warden Spooner will be a joy forever. If one's hourly preoccupation is with malnutrition, poverty, war, then of course one might turn elsewhere than to this kindly man. But one can think of the great Confucius, another exponent of manners, being happy there and again producing to a disciple who said "Before acting I always think three times", the immortal reply, "Twice is enough."

Certainly, with the Warden, the unexpected was always liable to happen. On the occasion of a dinner, with many guests, there was a sudden lull in the general conversation. The voice of the Warden was then clearly heard to remark: "Of course, when we were first married we were not very happy" ... The guest sitting next to Mrs Spooner quickly began a new conversation; but no one, to this day, has recorded the full context of the Warden's remarks. I shall, however, always treasure the more serious comment: "There is a great difference, Mr Jones, between intellect and intelligence." Today the great succession of Oxford "characters" is well continued by such people as Sir Isaiah Berlin, recently elected President of Wolfson College and not less, until his recent death, by Sir Maurice Bowra himself, who once remarked on the occasion of his resignation from an academic post, "The time has now come for me to retire and yield place to an older man!"

As M. de Talleyrand observed: "Life is tolerable save for its organised pleasures." It was John Pennycuick, scholar of Winchester, now Mr Justice Pennycuick, who said: "I like this college—it is like a hotel: one need not know anybody on one's staircase." In reminiscence, there were yet, I recall, mellow communal fooleries, *menus plaisirs*. I did not, however, find all the days to be so pleasurable in fact. At least such pleasures as came one's way were mostly not organised.

There were warm afternoons canoeing with Arthur Gaitskell on the Cherwell. I myself entertained at a succession of tea-parties, which Father C. C. Martindale, Bowra, Arnold Lawrence (T. E.'s brother), Roger Stamford (later best man at my wedding), James Laver, James Mann and others honoured.

In the 'Twenties I crossed the Atlantic eastwards with Arnold, who had a store of disconcerting anecdotes. I also recall his off-beat remark to a young English girl who, on first view, enthused about the glorious Cornish coast. "It seems to me much the same as any coast." "You would not say that if you had been away for four years." The early offensive-defensive cult of the harsh voice and of the compulsive anti-hero was authentic Lawrence. It is now the television interviewers' fashion. I thought it a detestable "show off".

Bede Jarrett, Provincial of the Order of Friars Preacher— Father Bede, whom I knew; he was my reply to Laski's query "Have you ever come across any cleric capable of the least intellectual influence?"—came to Oxford only later. But his book *The Social Theories of the Middle Ages* was the first to confirm my distrust and dislike of the "profit first" (or usury) principle of old-fashioned capitalism.

Sir James Mann (as he became; Keeper of the Queen's Armoury in the Tower) I recall not least in terms of his emancipatory remark: "Why are you so impressed by these dons? They are mostly of lower middle-class origin." I last saw James at his funeral—in the Tower Chapel. The Constable of the Tower, the Warders, the ravens, all were there. It could not have been better arranged had James written the scenario himself.

I cannot conclude these casual comments on long ago without a bow to "George" (typically I was never told his surname), Steward of Junior Common Room. Eyeing the "younger generation", newly arrived in College, with laconic humour, he would comment: "Not, Sah, quite the kind of young man we used to have before the war, Sah." It has ever been thus, and is called "the generation gap" by the mythology minded. Listening, we could see the point of the advice given by one parent to his son, about "to come up": "Make friends with Churchill, the College Porter: he has some influence with the Warden."

I spent precisely three-and-one-half terms (the other half being exclusively in my rooms preparing for examinations) in Oxford, since Ernest Barker hoped to shuffle off some of the seniors—too old as he said in his heavy Manchester accent, to be "good Orxford men". "We like to moold them"—into the civil service and, specifically, into the new Ministry of Labour. It was an endeavour in which he was mistaken. Cyril Joad had, in 1914, entered that Ministry (then still a department of the Board of Trade) and had become "established" by consent of the Civil Service Commission, "under the umbrella". By my day the umbrella, exempting distinguished graduates from routine examination, abruptly collapsed over my head. I was indeed asked whether I would care to go into the Colonial Service, but, rightly or wrongly, I declined. I was never sorry to have avoided the post-war Civil Service—although Barker's attempt to lodge me there meant taking Schools prematurely, which could have been disastrous. (I should add that I did not go to school until I was twelve, thereby being spared early brain-washing. Learning is an individual matter. I later continued the practice of breaking all rules by acquiring a doctorate on one year's work.) I took my degree "with distinction" and also acquired, in three and one half effective Oxford terms, three and one half Oxford University prizes: to wit, the Chancellor's English Essay Prize on Aesthetics; the Gladstone Prize on Second Chambers and the reform of the House of Lords (about which more later); the Matthew Arnold Memorial Prize on Thomas Hobbes; and a *proxime* for the Lothian Prize on the Knights of Malta—which, in total, I modestly believe to be probably an Oxford record without precedent. It profited me little.

I was interviewed at Oriel for a Fellowship; but since I was too preoccupied with conversation about the Crusades to notice that the "scout" was removing the table-cloth, Provost Phelps, he of the spade beard, remarked: "First time I have come across a man who did not finish his wine"—and that was that. This was very Oxford. The man elected later left for Merton. I also applied for a research fellowship at Exeter but, foolishly misguided, thought it my duty to withdraw when I learned that I had an American offer from Minnesota (which I subsequently did not take). A Fellow of that College later told me that, if I had persisted, I should have been elected. The unhappy man who was elected was later drowned in the Aegean.

At New College the Warden told me, in his voice like a tinkling silver bell, that "I don't think the College would elect another Catholic." (The other was Professor Francis de Zulueta.) I perceived that I had committed the greatest *faux pas* in the English Establishment. I had yet naively supposed religious belief to be irrelevant to academic promotion. On the contrary, it might indicate a dangerous tendency to be an uncomfortable person. The spiritualities were a minor matter, but "getting on" in the club was a very major one. In Oxford I have heard the cynical comment that Anglicanism was "established" there, "in order to save us from the ravages of religion." I think the remark was Bowra's.

I recall the story of some simple evangelical soul coming to evening service in Magdalen College and joining in the singing. An irate organist stormed at him afterwards. "But," protested the visitor, "after all, this is God's House." "I don't know whether it is God's House or not, but it is Magdalen College Chapel." True that Jack Haldane was an announced atheist who, surpliced, attended chapel because, as he said, singing the Psalms was "good for his lungs". As one Lord Chancellor later informed me over dinner, "it shows poor judgement for any man to change the religion in which he was born." The Chancellor himself had indeed been a Liberal and had rather abruptly become Labour, not without advancement—but this was, of course, a different matter, indeed a gesture of conformity well rewarded. As an undergraduate I took my religion rather seriously. I still do. Lord Chancellor Jowett shocked me.

I had made my first great error, it seemed, on the road to Success. It took me long to realise how severe the blow was. Maybe it was also a salvation. I decline to judge.

I sat for the so-called "blue ribbon" All Souls Fellowship. The major three-hour test was an essay on the one word "Aesthetics." One also had to read any page of a classical author (in this case Thucydides, in Greek) at sight. As Warden Sumner observed: "Here every year we elect two men, one a historian and one a lawyer—one a scholar and one who will get on in the world". For their law fellow, Cyril Radcliffe (later Viscount Radcliffe) was elected. A most able man, he got on.

I am told that I was placed *proxime* for the other. I am in no position to check this but my informant, a Fellow, is an honest and distinguished man who had no motive either to deceive or to flatter me. He added that my only defect was that my papers contained "perhaps a slight shortage of undergraduate wit". I hasten to add that this need not necessarily have been fatal. It depended on the examiners. One aspirant, seated next to the eminent commentator on Norse sagas, W. P. Ker, had sweated with corruscating brilliance in dinner-table conversation. His only reward from Ker was the gruff comment: "I hate wit." In my year the successful candidate, presumably owing to overwork, was found a few months later hanging from a beam in his college room, dead.

His immediate fate was that the college gates shut him in. Mine was that they shut me out. I had already become that atrocious

C

thing in the adventure of English life, an "outsider". *Mene, mene, tekel, upharsin.* Beyond seemed to lie for me the uneasy world of Red Brick. It would be dishonest not to admit that I was envious of my contemporaries who became Heads of College. Three did: Bowra of Wadham, Keir of Balliol, Last of Brasenose (who had been with me at St Paul's and for whom I was to secure a useful invitation to Cornell).

Nevertheless, it may be as well that I did not stay in Oxford. Much would not have been done that was done. The correct adjective for Oxford is "pleasant". As for this last, the maxim that manners are the heart of civilisation happens to be true. A "pleasant" Oxford could lull to sleep. But its message may be the final one of civilised life.

My preoccupation with the problem of "good and the causes of evil", of my Mons days, receded. Nor did I, for better or worse, take the Oxford philosophical "Greats" school as had originally been planned. I merely broke away to listen to some of the lectures. The change to History was not irrelevant, since I became increasingly absorbed in the question of the uses of history. However, this was but part of the wider problem, which stemmed from war-time experience, of "why war?" History revealed resort to it as immemorial. It was an endemic disease. But why just did it occur?

I cannot say that my obsessive interest in some scientific reply to this was helped at Oxford. Maybe it bored—a mortal sin. I don't think I discussed the problem much. That privileged paradise, with its embattled College walls inscribed with the words *odi profanum vulgus et arceo*—"we hate the profane vulgar and fend them off"—and its central fortress keep at All Souls, fortress of a detached liberalism such as, at Cambridge, attracted the Epicurean "love of friends" of E. M. Forster—offered many-coloured pleasures. "Oxbridge" had its Rupert Brookes, its golden and its gilded youth, its dilettantes mostly already becoming, no less than in Harvard, a style outdated and anomalous. I recall the happy observation distinguishing the two ancient Universities: "Oxford believes itself to be the centre of the world; Cambridge does not believe that it is the centre, but believes that it ought to be." Frankly, I cannot say that my unOxford preoccupation and subversive curiosity received any encouragement there. The great Professor Harnack in Germany wrote in 1914 for the German cause; the distinguished Sir Ernest Barker and others wrote against it. It did not go deeper than learned propaganda. Nor did it improve with time.

I declined a university post at Newcastle and accepted one, in medieval and modern history, at another provincial university, Sheffield, where Dame Margery Perham was my colleague in the Department of History, although absent in Somaliland when I arrived. According to my immediate chief, the Professor of Modern History, she was junior to me; according to the Professor of Ancient History, his predecessor, I was junior to her. We neatly solved the matter of protocol after a brief period by both leaving, she for St Hugh's, Oxford, and I for Cornell.

I enjoyed, during my northern sojourn, the kindly patronage of J. B. Black, later Professor in Aberdeen. I also, in addition to teaching history, assumed the responsibility of teaching philosophy to a Workers' Education Association class, chiefly of miners and railwaymen, at Woodhouse Mills, a place a few miles out of Sheffield. There I was paid one of the compliments I have prized most in life. One member of the class arrived a few minutes late. He explained that he had come straight in from his night-shift signal-box work. "What about breakfast?" "I did not wait for breakfast; I wanted to be in time for your class."

I was preoccupied with laying bare the fundamental factors making for peace or war. This also I do not regret. I have left to others that study of the page of history which gives immortality to the very few, including numerous criminals. No subject is more snobbish than history, in which, as Mussolini remarked, ambitious men seek "to make their scratch". I was still very young and preoccupied with ideas which I thought to be for the advancement of learning and, in the long run, perchance for the benefit of man. As Faust's apprentice scholar said to Faust: "How shall our counsel serve to lead mankind?" Recently A. J. P. Taylor has commented: "If I were ever fool enough to draw any lesson from history, it would be that mankind will blow itself up in the fairly near future." Professor Barraclough maintains that the prudent historian will study "consequences". I was concerned, along with Machiavelli and Hobbes, to study "factors and causes"—what Rousseau described as "not How but Why". To put it briefly, practically and politically I did not "move in" in those days and obtain as others, including Hugh Gaitskell and Dick Crossman, did elsewhere, a party constituency nomination in the Sheffield area.

A contributor to the *New Statesman*, Mervyn Jones, writes of "this inability to question and to innovate, undoubtedly *le vice anglais* in our times". Hence there is an efflux (which in the past has perhaps contributed to the development of Empire) which is called "the brain-drain".

Over this so-called "brain-drain" there has been much futile

and occasionally hypocritical hand-wringing and much totally
irrelevant patriotic orating that offers no remedies. In the days of
the Renaissance, Leonardo and many another Italian unpopular in
Milan left for patrons north of the Alps. It is frequently alleged
that the cause is financial. This is not true. The answer has been
put better by Mr Secretary McNamara: "Brains, like hearts,
tend to go where they are best appreciated." The major causes are
in terms of facilities, prestige and a friendly, not hostile, environment. Britain does not lack able men. The trouble is that the
island is too small; the jealousy too acute; the insular complacency
of those who hold power too suffocating. There is no room to
take wing.

I left for Cornell, one of the so-called Ivy League Universities of
the Eastern United States, for very specific reasons. Some of my
friends, such as the subsequent Chichele Professor of History,
made a second run for the All Souls Fellowship. I mentally decided
that I had spent enough time and that I did not propose to have my
life hung on a thread by any judges—myself in suspense—sitting at
All Souls high-table. I chose emancipation from these rules and
judgements of the academic cloister. Enough was enough. My
attention was on this issue of the meaning and uses of history. I
believed it to be important and novel. I already had a script.
I wanted a year to work over it.

Sheffield then gave me a year of absence which, be it put on the
record, was most generous. J. D. Woodruff took my place for the
year. I had, at the time, no intention of staying away longer.
Thanks to friends, Harvard offered me an Austin Fellowship.
This was yet tied about with restrictions concerning attending
lectures—which indeed was more than I had done at Oxford itself
(although there I had, most unorthodoxly, attended lectures on
Philosophy, my first love, in the "Greats" School, as well as
lectures in History). Incidentally, my godfather, Dr George
Gordon, uncle of a later President of Magdalen College, Oxford,
was an Overseer of Harvard and incumbent of the New Old
South Church of Boston, Mass., the cathedral of New England
Independency. In Boston, if others were Brahmins, so was I.

In the circumstances I accepted the much freer offer of the
White Fellowship at Cornell. I owed this to the historian Wallace
Notestein and to my dear friend, Ernest Jacob. Later David Keir,
then at Harvard, both took me along to meet President Lowell
and told me he could procure me a tutorship at Harvard, if I
wished it. (A shrewd Scot, he added that Harvard would have
to pay more if it wanted good tutors.) But by that time Cornell had
with American warmth and generosity, I being aged twenty-eight,

already offered me a professorship there. As Notestein said: "Why not have it young, while one still enjoys it?" I therefore declined this Harvard suggestion. The Cornell offer, I may add, came to me "by luck" (or was it?) as something entirely unexpected and entirely unsolicited. We were not in the graceless world of "written applications in triplicate".

I was, then, in America. I asked my English university whether, on my return, I could study and also teach political philosophy and science. I was firmly told by the Vice-Chancellor, Sir Henry Haddow, that they did not teach it and did not intend to teach it. I was paid to teach History. I had memories of teaching the work of that solid historian, Bishop Stubbs, and of Professor Haskin's (American) book on the Norman origins of the jury system. I failed to see why I should teach, or why my students should meticulously learn, about the possible Norman origins of the jury system. More to the point was whether one must *have*, as of local venue, a jury system. It often worked to frustrate justice. It did so in Ireland and in the Southern States. And, indeed, was "trial by jury", under the Anglo Saxon "two adversary system" of pleading before a jury, so sacrosanct compared with the preliminary judicial examination of facts of European Continental law? Did it inevitably "do better justice"? Historians, as has been happily said by Professor Trevor-Roper, tend to be like small allotment holders, each jealously guarding his "strongly-fenced small-holding". Did I want a small-holding?

When at long, long last Oxford started to teach politics, as the Cinderella partner in the Philosophy, Politics and Economics School, they did not display active interest in inviting me back. I remained in America. "The drain" did not work in reverse. Also my love affair with Oxford was over. Anyhow the true first love affair was with my childhood's Hypatia and with philosophy, still thought of as "the love of wisdom". Like Faust I became preoccupied with the study of power.

III

THE PROHIBITION YEARS

At Cornell I found that I was a member of a staff of two, the Chairman, Robert Cushman, a constitutional lawyer, and myself. Additions came later. In effect we started up the department from scratch. I had the honour, as I regard it, of sharing in the appointment of R. A. Mackay, Canadian constitutionalist and later head of the Canadian Delegation to the United Nations.

A. E. Zimmern (later Sir Alfred Zimmern), the distinguished author of *The Greek Commonwealth*, sometime Fellow and tutor of New College, had been teaching there for a year when I arrived. However, there had been differences. For one thing Lady Zimmern, herself of Alsatian provenance, on the day the French troops went into the Ruhr, had insisted on playing the *Marseillaise* on her piano in their rented rooms for most of the day which cast, wrongly, some doubts upon Alfred's detachment as a teacher of politics. I was asked to take over his work and students.

Since I only joined the faculty in 1924, even now in retrospect it remains for me an amazing thing that, by March 1926, I was invited to take up a post of some national responsibility and to make a report involving the text of the Constitution of the United States itself—and, for that matter, affecting the daily behaviour of millions. I was invited by the Rockefeller Foundation and by the Social Science Research Council to head a national study of Prohibition. Its virtue was that it was to give me an unrivalled experience of one aspect of American life.

In America what is new is thought to be good, unless it is pragmatically found to be bad. One welcomes change and hopes that it is progress. In England what is new was *a priori* thought to be bad, unless by chance it was found to be good. And there is a certain inertia, not least among those who are already blessed in the enjoyment of established power. For myself, I favour tradition. Without tradition there is no civilisation. What matters is to distinguish tradition from prejudice, and to decide what tradition merits conservation.

I have reason to think that I owed my actual selection to a very eminent statistician, a senior Cornell colleague, Professor Walter Willcox, a man especially preoccupied with that redistribution of Congressional electoral districts which has since come. Nearly forty years afterwards I still made pilgrimages to his house, to find him alert and of a dry wit. He was a man who punctiliously walked two miles—or at least, when over ninety, a mile—every day. In the leg of his trouser he had a kind of plummet device, a pedometer, which appealed to his statistical soul. It provided an exact yard measurement of the day's walks. He was a prize subject for geriatric study by the medical faculty of Johns Hopkins University. He visited India at the age of ninety-nine; visited Stockholm, being aged one hundred; and died at the ripe age of one-hundred-and-three. For me, he was a great patron, the kind of active friend whom I had hitherto lacked. To an apologetic or inert friend a plain enemy is sometimes better. Anyhow, so says the New Testament about those who blow neither hot nor cold. Willcox blew hot.

The technical mood of the country inclined Americans to the view that a thorough sociological survey was required, to show what were the actual consequences of Prohibition and, if reform were needed, what shape that reform should take. Today we face the same kind of problem—in part one of mere ignorance—about drugs (and, for that matter, about tobacco), a closely comparable field.

First, then, a pilot experiment was needed to indicate whether so vast and expensive an undertaking would be fruitful. Hence the Rockefeller Foundation, using as its agency the Social Science Research Council of America—neither Foundation nor Council having their counterparts then (nor, with the Council, until as late as 1965) in Britain—decided to establish a nation-wide Study of the Operation of the Eighteenth Amendment to the Constitution of the United States. Of that study I was invited to be national director, in charge of a staff network stretching across the continent from coast to coast.

I was naturally honoured by the proposal; was pleased by feeling so promptly liked and appreciated; and accepted the offer with alacrity as a distinction. It was a prize sociological and administrative undertaking for me—what M. de Gaulle called *une chance*. The explanation of the offer is logical enough. The Eighteenth Amendment to the American Constitution, generally called the Prohibition Amendment, was patently running into grave administrative difficulties. Did the virtues of restraint of alcoholic addiction by absolute methods outweigh the debit of contempt for the courts, the heavy costs of enforcement, the enrichment of the criminal underworld? The patriotic enthusiasm which had enabled Prohibition to be pushed through towards the end of the War and of the Wilson Administration had waned.

Even Repeal, despite all the cumbersome institutional difficulties, was very tentatively being mooted. "Changing the Constitution." A big job indeed—a maze of power pressure groups. Emotions ran high and impassioned. Somebody likely to be detached and dis-interested, an "outsider", was required for the study. Liquor Prohibition was not the only issue on which the Constitution might be due for change—and "change" is good Jeffersonianism. The Right to Bear Arms—to have them when *not* in the militia—was and is another. But Prohibition was the issue of the moment. I had assumed the very Aristotelian title, of which I have always been excessively proud, of ranking Professor of Politics at Cornell. I had also some trivial qualifications for the post of Director, and hence there was a certain logical causation in these events, a feather-stroke of fate. It was not solely "just luck".

It is necessary here to go back for a few years to explain this complex web. My mother, who spent the last years of her life, during the First World War, working in the impoverished East End of London, in Hoxton and Bromley-by-Bow, had there met the wife of (later) Sir Harry Batterbee, who became British High Commissioner in New Zealand, herself the sister of Sir Edward Harding, later Permanent Under-Secretary at the Commonwealth Office. . . . (I last heard from Sir Harry in 1967, when he was engaged on the delicate and fascinating job of sorting out which of the State papers connected with the Abdication of Edward VIII were to be kept, and which "disposed of"). I was just due to leave school and my mother explained my medical and military position, Sir Edward accepted me onto the staff of a newly established Governmental Board.

Lloyd George, a Baptist, had become—probably rightly—con-vinced that excessive drinking in the factories (where workers, many of them Irish, were receiving uncustomarily high wages) was interfering with the wartime production of munitions. His Free Church friends certainly emphasised this danger. On principle he favoured, although no Socialist, the nationalisation of the liquor traffic. This had always seemed to me to have the admirable merit that an industry would be nationalised that would bring in profit to the Treasury and the tax-payer, instead of one that was bankrupt or "in the red". It is unfortunate that, in 1971, the present Conservative Government in the United Kingdom has reversed this decision. (Incidentally, the nationalised public houses were to supply a better beer than most.) However, the Baptists and teetotallers in no wise approved of having official dealings, except in a punitive capacity, with the accursed thing. I have always felt that all teetotal chapels throughout the realm should be under compulsion, every second Sunday, to read aloud the Gospel story of the miracle of the wine of Cana and not to be more pious than the Guest at that feast. I am disinclined to think that He changed water into fruit-juice, a most un-Jewish act.

By a compromise, a Control Board (Liquor Traffic) was set up for the United Kingdom, which nevertheless experimentally "nationalised" (but only locally) licensed premises in Carlisle—the town where Woodrow Wilson's grandfather had been Presbyterian minister—and also Annan and Invergordon. Sir Edgar Vincent, later Lord d'Abernon and British Ambassador in Berlin, became chairman of the Board. Philip Snowden, lame and acid, and Lord Leverhulme were members of it. Of Lord Leverhulme, a business man, it was said that, having been asked by Augustus John a price too high in his view for a portrait, he cut out the portions other than the face and paid John in exact area proportion for the remainder.

Sir Edgar Saunders, Liverpool solicitor, was director and I, for a while, became his secretary. Incidentally, I am always grateful to Sir Edgar for destroying for me for ever the misleading doctrine of old-womanish philosopher Kant about "good will" and "intentions". "I am not interested", remarked my fellow Liverpudlian, when I failed to whip up somebody else to be competently on time, "in your reasons. I am interested in *results*." Along with the remark of my college friend Henry Andrews to me, "One should always treat others as great men, and demand that they treat you as a great man", this is an apophthegm that I treasure as a pearl of great wisdom.

It was, therefore, on the basis of these modest apprentice qualifications that, with the quite admirable staff aid of Vera Mikol (now Mrs Robert Livingston Schuyler), I set up an office in New York and resided there for about six months. For most of the time my wife and I were at the Westminster Hotel, now the King's Crown, opposite Columbia University campus, which boasted a magnificent six-foot six Negro head-waiter and where Bruce Bliven, editor of *The New Republic*, was also a denizen. I wrote a few articles for that most worthy, if slightly dull, journal, and also for *Harper's Magazine* and for *The Nation*.

Later, when my wife returned to London, I lived in rooms at a University Settlement house, approved of by "the Twenty Second Street crowd", as it was called, of earnest social workers, whose journal was *The Survey*. At *The Survey* office I first met that remarkable matriarch, Jane Adams. In the same connection I also met Dr Alvin Johnson, editor of the *Encyclopaedia of the Social Sciences* (to which I contributed) and Director of the New School

of Social Research. I recall him (later) sitting, as Director, in front
of an alcove of Pompeian red with, rising behind Alvin's Middle
Western bulk, the white marble form of a statue of the Venus de
Medici.

The Settlement was on the border line, near Harlem, of the
Negro and Italian racial blocs. Those in charge went in for high-
mindedness and low (or, rather, austere) living. Race relations
were less than perfect. During the four or five weeks I was around,
a policeman was shot dead at the street corner. It gave a vivid
insight into New York City life.

In the course of my administrative duties of coordination, I had
to travel as far as Chicago, St Louis and Salt Lake City. I went
down to Atlantic City, city of the St Valentine's Day gang, where
I purchased a treasured music-box for my wife. In Chicago I did
a night tour of the "flophouses" and "skidrows", where the out-
of-work drunks congregated, saturated with liquor, not least
methylated spirits. As the formidably bearded police physician
who was my guide remarked: "They would murder you for your
boots here." His cheery remark to the denizens as form of greeting
was "You ought to be dead, oughtn't you?" It met a grunted assent.
He also had ferocious views about prostitutes, the maligned
under-bitches of our supposedly tolerant social life. Paid pansies
fare better.

One journey to Madison, Wisconsin, I recall vividly. The issue
was a trivial one of office organisation: the expense of a supplementary secretary in connection with the preparation of the report.
It may interest those academics who spend solemn hours on the
grandiosely styled "studies of decision making". I received telegraphed instructions to catch the night train, the "Wolverine",
from New York to Madison. The structure of the Social Science
Research Council was such that, under Charles Merriam of
Chicago as chairman, there was a committee *ad hoc* of which the
chairman was Professor Gillin, an eminent sociologist in the
University of Wisconsin.

I arrived in time for the executive lunch and, in the course of
discussion, pointed out that the expense of my return journey to
and from Wisconsin was slightly larger than the sum I had set
aside to pay the additional secretary during the brief time she
would be needed. "I think you have made your point, Professor
Catlin, and I don't think we need discuss this further." We had
reached this stage by the salad. Then there was a pause in the
decision-making process. At last the relevant committee chairman,
later President of the University of Oregon, exclaimed: "Well,
has anybody got any further ideas to suggest?—because I often

find that some of the most damn fool ideas are the ones that work out best." Perhaps, as I said earlier, the most outstanding difference between the British outlook, with its cosy inertia, and the empiricism of the American outlook lies here. The Wisconsin chairman had flamboyantly expressed that illuminating distinction.

The execution of statutory prohibition under the Volstead Act and the prohibition itself of alcoholic drinking under the sumptuary law, now ratified in the Constitution, raised problems vast, complex, fascinating.

Some people were manufacturing their own illicit liquor by various devices, ranging from illegal stills in the woods to "bathtub" gin. Down South the stills had always been there, producing "white mule", so called because it had "a powerful kick to it". The problem in those days was not one of hashish among the young, but of maudlin drinking among the middle aged. It could be that they were alternatives. I recall that eminent sociologist lawyer, Dean Pound of Harvard, telling me a story of would-be drinkers crossing the border of one State (dry) to another (dry but less effectively such). The second State—I believe, South Carolina —had "blue laws", prohibiting also Sunday trading. The companions obtained their bootleg liquor from an ostensible seller of soft-drinks; and found the product powerful strong. "Any soft drink to wash it down" ? "I can't sell you *that*", replied the vendor, "it's Sunday—against the law."

Dean Pound added that in Stranraer, Scotland, when the Irish boat arrived late, he had watched the passengers flock up one street and turn sharp left. The local policeman was on duty. Dr Pound followed and found himself behind the inn bar; the time was 2.40 (the licensing hour terminated at 2.30). Having had his drink, the Dean left and casually enquired of the policeman the time. The officer solemnly produced his turnip watch. "It is now," he observed, "2.25 precisely." Other lands, other manners of law enforcement.

Even members of what considered itself to be respectable society in America were, by 1926, onto dodges. The problem of "pot" is that it may inaugurate the deadly reign of heroin. But respectable society, the normally law-abiding establishment, was and is most unlikely to move over to methylated spirits. Merely it demanded the civilised drinks of its forebears. The distinction, valid in the West if not in the East, is important. Needless to say, some of the "boot-leg" liquor was of most dubious quality, even despite reasonable precautions. Some years after the events recorded, I recall taking along Henry Noel Brailsford, who was due for a public forum debate at Town Hall, New York, on the following day with Philip Guedalla, to the apartment of my wife's charming cousin, Standish Chard, attorney and stockbroker, in the Crillon Building, Park Avenue. I felt quite hale the following day; but I chanced to meet Brailsford and asked him how the debate had gone. His reply was lugubrious. "The trouble was that I had such a headache that I saw, not one Philip Guedalla, but two Philip Guedallas."

Some people, who declined private chemical experiments, patronised the omnipresent "speak-easies", all of them liable to be abruptly shut down but many of which continued to remain open, on a basis of mutual blackmail, by virtue of "considerations" conveyed to the police. Very big money was involved. Elected persons, the juries, the police, even the local judiciary were corrupted. Amid the wealth (and it was such in both senses) of little mean bucketshops and back-street places, some "speak-easies" flaunted their existence and had elaborate gadgets for confounding the prohibition enforcement officers. Incidentally— and this is relevant to like mistaken proposals in dealing with the drug traffic—these were members of a specialised agency, quite separate from the local police, with whom the police in some great cities by no means always cooperated. The policeman in some towns, conscious of public opinion, might direct those in need to the nearest "speak-easy".

Around West Fifty-Second Street, New York, it was readily possible to find luxuriously appointed "joints", which almost paraded a device (I wonder how often used) whereby, far transcending the miserable expedients of secret doors and escape hatches, by pressing a button the entire bar-shelving could be turned over and the contents would crash into the basement as broken bottles. There would be "no legal evidence".

Disrespect for a law regarded with disapproval or contempt, issuing in corruption or connivance, spread to the highest ranks. It is a perennial problem. Judges of the high courts did not hesitate, in their private cabinets, to slide back a panel and treat their personal friends to a high-ball or "old fashioned" from bottles they kept back there for their convivial purpose. Even conscientious law-observers were put under pressure.

I recall a tale told me by Walter Lippmann, who was present on the occasion. The highly respected and personally abstemious editor of *The Forum Magazine*, Henry Goddard Leach, was acting as host to the visiting lecturer, Count Keyserling. Keyserling (not Count Keyserlingk, President of Palm Publishers, Montreal) a Baltic baron and suspected of being a sad adventurer, at one time had a reputation as wide as Oswald Spengler's, with whom he indulged in mutual dislike and competitive notoriety. Like many continental Europeans (and some Englishmen) apparently he went in for calculated rudeness in his treatment of admiring Americans, as being good for their souls. In fairness it should be said that he did not limit his habitual and calculated discourtesy to the Americans, here differing from Evelyn Waugh, whose son recalls that he punctiliously wrote replies to all correspondents, "except of course obvious lunatics and Americans". Of Waugh it is told that, munching his luncheon sandwiches alone in an *Express* office, he was suddenly accosted by the visiting Lord Beaverbrook. "Whotsch yer name?" enquired Max. "Woh." "Wot?" "Woh." "Yer sack'd." I have always thought that sacking, whether by a Canadian such as Max or by an American, could have been good for Waugh.

Keyserling had been recommended by A. J. Balfour to address that solemn body in London, Chatham House. As Esther Murphy (Mrs John Strachey) once said to me, "Let us go down to Chatham House to hear the accents of the ruling class." Keyserling sent his usual pretentious notice about how he wished to be received. The perturbed officials passed the Count's letter over to Balfour for advice. It was returned, marked very appropriately in the margin: "Tut, tut"!

At one dinner Keyserling so far insulted his hostess, Mrs Thomas Lamont, that, as the ladies rose from table to go down-stairs, she exclaimed to her husband: "Tom, if you bring that man down before an hour, I'll never speak to you again."

One of Count Keyserling's little ploys, communicated through his agent, was that he must have one or more glasses of champagne before he would condescend to lecture. (After the lecture the baron was prepared to attend a dinner where, it was added, the men could be labelled "intelligent" and the women "good-looking".) Poor Leach, Keyserling's host on the present occasion, was on the spot. Host and guest of honour adjourned to an inner room, while the other distinguished guests, including Lippmann, sat at table sipping water as by law ordained. The sound of a popping champagne cork could be heard from the sanctum. The guests, as Lippmann said and as I can well believe, did not feel charitable towards their visitor.

Incidentally, I may perhaps here mention another incident affecting the Leaches, in which I personally was involved. As a boy I had read, with sturdy and persevering admiration, right through two volumes of *Furthest North* by my hero, Fritzjof Nansen. At this later time in New York I had been invited by

Mrs Goddard Leach to a tea where there was only one other guest besides myself. The conversation was somewhat dull and perfunctory. The chief concern of my fellow guest, who was staying with the Leaches, was how long it might take to get his pants pressed, a prosaic, unromantic subject. Suddenly the grey-haired old man, standing by the window of a Fifth Avenue apartment and looking down, meditatively remarked: "My daughter tells me that if I go to the Antarctic, it will kill me—but I am just as likely to be killed here on Fifth Avenue." (Winston Churchill nearly was). Abruptly the penny dropped in my memory.

The anonymous old man was indeed Nansen—Nansen of *Furthest North*. The moral of this is that hostesses should never mumble introductions. And the bold American custom of saying outright, good and clear, "What is your name ?", is best. I did not again make the error of "registering a blank" about the immortals. I took trouble. Pavlova I went to see in *Swan Lake* at Covent Garden. Chaliapin I went to hear, and much later, Edith Piaf. Paderewski, magician of my childhood (even if Jan Smeterlin did tell me that he expected others to kiss his feet), I drove sixty miles through a snowstorm to hear.

The true menace of the situation, which confronted Prohibitionists and anti-Prohibitionists alike in the summer of 1926, but which can apply also to drugs today, was the breakdown of law enforcement; the excessive burden placed upon the administration of justice, especially in connection with legislation so unpopular that respect for law was being brought into contempt; and the threatening growth of wealth in the hands of millionaire chieftains of the underworld who had turned from their normal pursuits of the drug traffic, the white slave traffic, counterfeiting and straight burglary and mayhem, to a lush new quarter, where money was to be made. There was an unholy alliance of moralists and teetotaller prohibitionists with bootleggers, both enemies of the hitherto legitimate trade, an alliance which perhaps neither party sought but which "objectively" existed. More than one great commercial empire of today, based on gin and the like, began with successful liquor-running across the Great Lakes by smugglers chased by law-enforcement officers. The founders are now honoured men of great wealth, seeking admission into the best society or an "Oscar" for humanitarian beneficences.

Prohibition was perchance, in the words of President Hoover, "a noble experiment". Even in 1921 the estimated annual profits of the "boot-leggers" was placed at $500 million. The issue was whether it was a successful experiment. Law, of which the rule is vital to civil society, depends for its enforcement upon a modicum of popular consensus. The problem recurs in the case of the drug traffic. Shall one, for example, prohibit medical prescription of the amphetamines? How shall one not enrich the underworld? Idealism could become an undemocratic tyranny of "the saints" when, as in Calvin's Geneva, it sought to impose its blueprints for goodness upon an unwilling and resentful population. Here for once Lincoln's dubious rule, that no man is so good as to be entitled to instruct another man how to be good, seemed very much to apply. "The permissive" is not to be acclaimed as "the civilised", but this is not to approve of the bigot on drinking, smoking, even on medically prescribed or allowed drugs. What matters is that the social discipline shall be socially respected and the law enforceable. There is what Mr Justice Brandeis called "the right to be let alone"—but, for man in society, not entirely. However, these Prohibition regulations in many areas were illogically not felt to conflict with American individualism. As one Middle Westerner remarked to me: "Where I come from individualism is the custom: everybody has, by God, to be an individualist—they had better be."

As an exercise in applied sociology, a major task of the Study was to break up the problem, emotionally regarded as a unity, a confrontation of "the demon Drink", into its component factors. The same rule holds with drug taking, hard and soft—and (more obviously a private matter) with tobacco smoking, cigarettes *versus* pipes. "Drinking", which here spelled "excessive alcoholic drinking", is itself, sociologically and psychologically, of different kinds, affecting differently the statistics of different avocations. In the case of journalists and, oddly enough, hairdressers it seems to be an occupational risk—in the case of journalists a matter, apparently, of long hours of waiting followed by brief spurts, often nocturnal, requiring almost superhuman energy and the need to "be with it". The temptation for the hairdresser may be bay rum. . . . There is the convivial drinking, at holiday seasons, of good fellows together; and there is the far more dangerous solitary drinking of the mentally and economically depressed, where the object frequently is stupefaction, "to be blotto" and "to find the quickest way out of Manchester" in the gin-bottle. Contrary to British Parliamentary practice (for example, on "street offences"), I am convinced that there cannot be sound social legislation without prior sociological investigation (with a budget) and 'probing for the facts'. We need what the Fabians called "more facts" and more disinterested research. Here the Wolfenden Report, from lack of such investigation, was at fault. This was a weakness.

That a member of the Wootton Commission on Drugs, before publication of the Report, should announce to the Press his personal bias—that "he would rather have his son smoke 'pot' than drink whisky"—seems both insolent and irresponsible in the circumstances. This does not mean that the use of the appropriate drugs under the appropriate conditions in medical prescription should be prohibited.

Americans who, unlike Latin peoples, are untrained in the civilised art of moderate drinking and have a strong sense of guilt, seem peculiarly apt to go all out, first "to raise hell," and then for stupefaction to an extent which shocks even hardened Italians. The Japanese, a neurotic people, have the same tendency. The more neurotic, "trendy" and over-stimulated the pattern of life, the greater the danger. In America, too, there is the warfare between the pattern of life in rural areas and in great cities, full of drink and sin and allegedly only concerned to corrupt poor farmer boys, newly up from "the sticks". Rural areas tend to be "dry" by consent and option.

Although California and New York both produce an excellent wine, in some quarters wine, to one's surprise, is not popularly identified by Americans with the immemorial custom of high civilisations but with the degraded desire to drink "red biddy", a deadly combination of cheap wine and methyl alcohol. It is not a view shared by cultured men. On one of the most cheerful Christmases of my life after the Second World War I was the guest, in Davis, outside the Paradise city of San Francisco, of Dr Amerine, California's Professor of Viticulture. We made a pre-lunch selection of the best wines from the University's vast cellars and appraised the product. It was a Christmas Day I shall not forget.

In other quarters there is the Phariseeism of "being holier than thou" (in some sects total abstinence being a condition of church membership and, allegedly, of admittance to Heaven) or the hypocrisy supporting legislation that keeps liquor away from the Negro, whereas adequate provision is made for one's more opulent and respectable self.

Engineers tended, in 1926, to regard the whole problem from the specialised angle that anything which interfered with the efficient driving of cars at high speed was a patent evil, the automobile itself being regarded, not as a pollution agent but as a sacred virile bull, a symbol of modern progress, with its use— even to commit large scale murder: more slaughtered than today—superior to criticism.

The medical profession, equally specialised, regarded the good

life as finding its key in a timed avoidance of all health risks—
automobile accidents apart. An exclusively medical research
committee, looking into the liquor question, would have been of
no use at all. Enthusiastic physicians displayed even more coloured
pictures of rotted livers than are now displayed of rotten lungs by
medical experts who (contradicting other experts) insist upon
regarding all forms of smoking as equally deplorable. The real
issue is what the public opinion of a particular society is prepared
to tolerate, or, alternatively, to condemn, whether by social
ostracism or by regulation or criminal law. The over-valuation of
efficiency in health can lead to the undervaluation of free
choice.

Medical campaigns shift from decade to decade. It might be
well today to direct such campaigns not so much against all
tobacco smoking (including pipes), where the evidence, according
to the highest expert opinion (that, for example, of Sir Alex
Haddow, of the Chester Beatty Cancer Research Institute) is
weak on pipe and cigar smoking, and the moral choice one very
much for the individual, to the far graver problem of drugs,
where some of the consequences are patently both serious and
social and where, in some cases, use may merit, not only persuasion, but prohibition with all its risks to respect for law obser-
vance.

Do those who take drugs stop heavy drinking and smoking?
Are drugs supplementary or alternatives? Who are the drug-
takers? Does the cannabis ("pot", hashish) smoker statistically
become a heroin (opium) smoker? Do these classes over-lap or
are they—for which there is some evidence—sociologically
distinct: the one "middle-class student" and the other "near-
criminal" or, like the "meths" drinker, "drop-out"? What exactly
are the medical and sociological effects of "psychological addiction"? And when does this become "physical addiction"? Is the
remedy punitive (with black-markets and high prices), or by
seeing to it that these different species of traffic do not pay the
profit-hunting boot-legger or "pusher", or rather a matter of
stringently enforced and restricted medical prescription?

The answer is largely that at this moment about drugs as once
in smaller measure about liquor—the one a custom of the East
and the other of the West—we do not know all that we could
know. Is legislation now to be based on ignorance or even on
mis-information? Are, for example, Royal Commissions in
Britain, without sociological expertise and in the habit of sum-
moning witnesses already committed in their answers, the right
way to find out the truth or merely a cheap way for the Treasury,

D

which can end by being expensive? More profoundly, is the root
of the matter the despair of the human "inadequate", the desire
for stimulus or tranquilliser, the nausea about competition and
"progress", or the revolt of a neurotic civilisation which has been
taught by its psychological *gurus* that all codes of manners, all
discipline, all authority (even, as Sartre says, that of reason) is a
bad thing, whereas "free" anarchism—"freedom" being a moral
absolute, instead of morally a neutral—or ecstatic Bacchanalianism
and Leary neo-paganism offer an alternative.

One interesting point about Prohibition and the Hoover era
is worth notice, since it affects the whole issue of the genuine
character of Congressional or Parliamentary democracy. Normally, for Party reasons, the maxim of Randolph Churchill
holds: "It is the duty of an Opposition to oppose." But not always.
It did not hold with the Abdication of Edward VIII. It did not
hold (as I shall tell) in all matters with Willkie. And again, however vital the issue for the nation, it does not hold where politicians feel that their own Party can be rent in two. This has
hitherto been the difficulty in Britain about the promised "national
debate" on Entry into the Common European Market. It was true
with Prohibition. There was a temptation to sweep the inconvenient issue "under the rug". Only when it was known that, for
quite other reasons, the Republican candidate would be Herbert
Hoover, "a dry", and the Democrat candidate Alfred Smith, "a
wet", could the lines be drawn—and, even so, diffidently.

To get advice on the broad issues involved I went off to see
Havelock Ellis, who was then living near Brixton Bon Marché in
London. Thanks to the hysterical D. H. Lawrence cult, there was,
at that time, a boom in Ellis. I found the old patriarch, with his
venerable beard, sitting amid a shoal of books reaching from wall
to floor. He offered me a choice of subtly different varieties of tea,
just as a connoisseur of wines might offer a selection of vintages.
I discussed with him liberalism and drinking, and the views of
John Stuart Mill—and then led on to the more marginal issue of
restriction on drugs and of addiction to them. I missed the chance
to discuss obscene literature, so much supported by publishers
who are apostles of freedom and quick money.

Havelock Ellis was *a priori* against all restriction. Permission
and civilised living were much the same. All sumptuary laws were
an interference with a quite fundamental value: the free choice
of the individual. Here Ellis was a kind of proto-Sartre. Such
laws were totalitarian. "If a man is weak enough and foolish
enough to become a drug addict, in the end he will kill himself.
Let him. It will be for the good of society." In brief, a Darwinian

selective agency against the unfit. The burden for society, before the addict poisoned himself, Ellis did not discuss. I recall the sometime Director of the London School of Economics, Alexander Carr-Saunders, father of Nicholas Carr-Saunders, abruptly standing stock-still near Carfax, Oxford, and addressing me with the words, "I venerate that man." But I went away from Ellis, unsatisfied that I had got adequate answers.

The final question with Prohibition had little to do with alcoholism.

The underworld is always there, just below the surface. The modern Mafia has made its own technological improvements, even in the astute use of new numbing gases. One chief purpose of law enforcement is to demonstrate pragmatically that crime does not pay. It is comfortable to regard this as a platitude. It is true that "Crime does not pay" for the weak, incompetent, "inadequate" or, again, for the young and rashly emotional. For two millennia, since the days when Plato so profoundly explored the issue, it has been clear that, in pecuniary and power terms, crime does very much pay for determined and able men, skilled egoists, who lack all social conscience (save maybe in their own *cosa nostra*).

The liberal educationalist wastes his time in painfully demonstrating what for the master criminal is a mere pious humbug of the weak. He can only be met (if and when caught) by a firm "aversion psychology", which might be tried out more systematically; by the ostracism of a homogeneous society; and by what Thomas Hobbes sardonically called adequate "weights and pressures". No anarchist or "trendy" can, of course, agree with this. Maybe only Socialists can . . . The Communist Party does. The "virgin lands" of Siberia always come in useful to teach good citizenship.

At least one can state that the police merit more support from the citizenry than they receive even when they patently merit it— although how far one can enhance their authority without conflicting with the Whig principles of the two-century old American Constitution is another story. One cannot defeat the tactics of the Mafia by choking it with cream—or patronage. The only man who defeated it effectively, in its Sicilian homeland, was Mussolini. This said, it is necessary to reaffirm the need for cool discrimination, alike in the treatment of criminals and in detecting the different categories in police statistics—and, be it said again, for much more sociological research in the analysis of the very diverse causes of crime.

A Government needs to be ever vigilant against the growth of the power of the underworld to intimidate—recently so well demonstrated, not in Chicago but in Durham, England, in the plan to release "the train robbers" by force of arms. Under certain lax or over-tolerant social conditions, the criminal, as Plato saw, makes a perfectly intelligent and correct calculation, from which no liberal education will shift him, about where the road to financial success lies. He must have it made clear, beyond per-adventure, that force lies with the other side. The pieties of unenforced law obstruct this.

It is encouraging to note that, whereas in Al Capone's day over two hundred gangster murders could take place in Chicago in a year, today it is one of the world's great cities in which crime is fairly firmly under control and is consulted by the London Metropolitan Police about how it is done.

Since vice is news, some journals hope for a murder a day— preferably with a torso in the Thames. The pathological desire for publicity, the lust to be gawped at, has to be confronted as one of the facts of life and factors in crime. Although outdistanced by pop-singers and sportsmen, the second group among those statistically known to the public and with most publicity consists, in Britain today, of "criminals and senior statesmen".

If indeed there be, as we are told, psychiatrists who can iner-rantly predict the types and even the individuals (and I doubt this) who will commit particular crimes, then let preventive measures be taken accordingly. Preventing this stock from breed-ing—some gentler means than castration—might be one technique in an epoch when human population is so excessive as to upset the natural balance of the Creation. Further, in the case of the more atrocious members of society, "baby-bashers", parents who stand little children in front of electric fires until they die of the burn, unfit to be parents, sterilisation may be the right retribu-tion in an already over-populated world.

The surest refuge for the criminal today is to commit a crime so atrocious that his lawyer can plead insanity. It can be so for de Salvo, the Boston Strangler, with his odd plan of predestina-tion: "I meant no one any harm. Why did it happen to *me*?" However, if a Richard Speck, who murdered eight nurses, can carry tatooed on his arm the phrase "Born to raise hell", it cannot be supposed that he was born mad. It can be supposed that he was always a potential criminal who should never be a parent. It is noteworthy that, as with the assassin Oswald, so with Speck, his declared wish was "to be somebody"—what our popular educationalists and artistic corrupters call "developing all the powers of his personality"—with pride in criminal success.

More soberly, let us say that law-enforcement involves an adequate, well-paid, and well-supported police; a modicum of courage in an often cowardly and petty-selfish public (it is not in long-range police interest to discourage good citizens "having a go"); and a swift, efficient and impartial justice. Above all, to cope with any growing social evil (and Prohibition almost certainly involved a false, "black-or-white" emotional diagnosis), it is necessary to act quickly and massively while the criminal organisation of the evil is still new to the game. It should also mean, first, impressing on our school teachers the importance of authority, which is not a species of evil but the polar complement of freedom; and, then, teaching respect for authority and civil manners in the schools. Major violence, however, has to be met by violence; illegal violence by the austere force of the law.

My Report was presented to the Council in late August, 1926, in Hanover, New Hampshire. I may add that, as an immigrant to the country, and not a native-born American (although a resident holding a responsible position), I did not feel it any part of my assignment, while professionally presenting or summarising facts, to advise or recommend policy. This would have seemed to me an impropriety. I find it an impropriety in others. One had had the privileged opportunity of watching, in a Continent-wide society, the counter-forces of law, of crime and of perfectionism; of the claims of free choice, of natural freedom and of uncontrolled indulgence and of freedom to satisfy wants which, forgetting Aristotle's maxim that "desire has no limits", have no such authority. One watched the collapse of authority unbacked by adequate educated opinion.

The Conference, for reasons of which I shall tell later, was also memorable for me because Professor Charles Merriam, of Chicago, there introduced me to a young political scientist, also from Chicago, Harold Lasswell. "He is working along the same lines as yourself." Arthur Schlesinger, snr., the Harvard historian, discreetly enquired whether I was thinking of becoming an American citizen. If I had accepted Schlesinger's suggestion, my children would have been born as American citizens. I "kept my options open" and gave him no commital reply. Perhaps I then made another great mistake. The English are among the slowest to take out other citizenships: they tend to assume that they will be accepted in any society. Perhaps I felt myself already a world citizen. I have never yet felt tempted to feel that I was other than English. The best patriotism is not grounded rootless in the soil. It has pride of ancestry. Nevertheless, the Anglo-Saxon world stretches to both sides of the Atlantic.

As the years of the Depression and bank moratorium passed into the gallant and memorable years of the New Deal, I widened my circle of contacts beyond those concerned with the Eighteenth Amendment. My first meeting with the great President, Franklin Delano Roosevelt, "the Squire of Hyde Park", had taken place in the Executive offices in Albany, N.Y. This followed a letter, dated 5 March, 1929: "I was awfully sorry I did not see you in Ithaca, but I hope to have the pleasure of seeing you in Albany if you come here at any time. Very sincerely yours, Franklin D. Roosevelt." After that I never had occasion to wish to see him without being able to do so.

He was the subtlest politician I have ever met. He also had a pervading sense of humour. The unkinder critics said that, so courageous in meeting his polio affliction, he therefore thought that, because he could move his big toe, he could also move the world. He did more than move a big toe. I recall that, when we met about three years later in the White House, he picked up the conversation where we had left it in Albany. It was a remarkable feat of memory, but it was also the manifestation of another gift which goes with personal greatness. When he spoke to you he was entirely "present" and talked as if you were the only person he wished to meet at that moment. I can count on the fingers of one hand those with the like gift of personal projection, Pope Pius XII and Earl Mountbatten among them. There was none of the busy "snip-snap: I have only a few minutes to spare" of the newly arrived business man.

Franklin Roosevelt was a great gentleman, a quality which he could yet combine with a popular out-going geniality. That he was the patrician was one factor in his success. Americans prefer their President respectable, in the tradition of the great Virginian dynasty. It also explained why, in Republican quarters, he was detested to the point of apoplexy. He had "betrayed his class".

Another fact was that, following a liberal policy in the early Albany days, he was also able to assemble support among minority groups, recent immigrants, even (despite their Republican tradition from the days of Lincoln) the Negroes. Aiming to get support —going all out for "support", the key factor in quantitative politics—from any likely quarter, he felt no need to be excessively scrupulous. The Democratic city bosses were prepared to support him, since they did not regard "the Squire" as, at that stage, any danger to themselves. This chameleon "adaptability" is well illustrated by a reputed conversation. Jones, expounding a proposal, was greeted by Roosevelt with an expression of his keenest interest and sympathy. The same interest and sympathy was extended to the next man, Smith—who happened to be expounding the opposite view. Eleanor Roosevelt, outraged, remarked "Franklin, you shock me; two men with opposite views and you tell both of them that you agree." A pause; then: "Well, yes, my dear—I entirely agree with you."

However, arrived in the White House, "The Squire" of Albany became "the Chief" in Washington, surrounded by admiring aides whom he held well in balance. "F.D.R." was the supreme political exponent of the tactic of "holding his fire until he saw the white of the opponents' eyes". In Albany, disliked by few and liked by many, he limited himself to benevolent generalities and progressive reform. Once established in the White House, the President declared himself—and had, in fact, a unique four terms of office ahead of him.

Vice-President Henry Wallace, still Secretary of Agriculture, with a conspicuous hole in his sock and earnestness in his voice, told me of his Keynesian plans, so cardinal to the New Deal against unemployment, for "priming the pump" of the economy by the direction of public expenditure, adding that he had been a subscribing member of the Fabian Society. I visited the Supreme Court, then adorned by Mr Justice Holmes, who, asked whether he "liked the human race", commented: "I have not much hope for it, but I wish it well." (Incidentally—a warning to puritans—the liberal Justice used to visit the Washington Strip-tease Burlesque Theatre once a week, presumably to keep in touch with the common man.)

I visited the Senators—Swanson, Nye, Borah. The two last were self-consciously plain men from the Mid-West (if Idaho can be called Mid-West). Citizen Borah, of the bushy-white hair, isolationist and neutralist, save where Mexico was concerned, once produced the remark: "How can I visit Britain. I might meet a duke—and what should I do?" This robust posture of the plain man from the pioneer log-cabin always has its admirers, but complicates diplomacy.

Another time I took a bus to Winston-Salem, amid the hills, and then over to Tennessee to see the Tennessee Valley Authority at work ("creeping socialism", some called it) on the Norris Dam. Indeed it was a subtle and creeping legal construction of the Constitution, which gave the Federal Government power over navigable waterways and over all areas where material for explosives, such as nitrates, were to be found and extracted. Later—in India—I was to find this legal construction very relevant. What interested me then was that, in contrast with Russia, here the management and the construction workers on the job shared the same canteens and ate at the same tables. It was America that was socially "more proletarian." Decades later, it was to be in such places as Spartanburg, South Carolina, that a genuine mixing together of Negro and White, in predominently white schools, was most conspicuously to take place.

It was in these Southern parts that the Negro butler confronted the visiting professor, Harold Laski, with the happy remark: "Easter Morning today, Mr Laski. A fine day. Lord rose today, Mr Laski, and I feel like rising myself." And there was the large Negro chef at Cornell who greeted a most distinguished professor from Edinburgh, who had strong and expressed views against racial discrimination, with the words: "And what do you want, young man?" The eminent man was not amused. There might be no case for discrimination, but there was a case for status—his.

All these things I have described in chapters of my pseudonymous book of the time, *Face of Revolution*. These were the "Dancing Years", and the days of Frank Sinatra and "of all that jazz"; after the gloom of the Depression a new spirit was in the air. "Happy days are here again." If the Republicans did not think so, a new popular majority did. And in compliment to the sometime Under-Secretary of the Navy, Franklin Delano Roosevelt, at every political gathering the signature tune rang out:

> "Roll up the score, Navy,
> Anchors weigh."

Some, such as John Strachey, at one time the associate of Mosley, thought that the New Deal was not merely American but, worse, proto-Fascist ("properly understood", of course.) I thought and said that this was doctrinaire twaddle. (However, President Hoover had the same views on the Roosevelt régime). Strachey merely meant that he, in his Communist phase, had to disagree.

The background indeed of the Depression of the Thirties in the United States and in Britain were not entirely the same; and both, international in causation, differed from the more national situation of the 'seventies. (It can be argued—and I have flown this kite—that in the latter case a remedy could be found in taking the joint rises of dividends and of wages, balancing these against production; and then, not politically but by computer, devaluing or revaluing money accordingly.) In Roosevelt's America the trades unions, just then beginning to depart from the Gomper's principle of party detachment and to attach themselves to the Democrats, were yet weak.

The problem was not primarily one of wages or prices, but of rash speculation on boom, loss of financial confidence and a plague of bankruptcies. And the remedy was not found in decreasing expenditure in the public and private sectors, but in increasing public expenditure and putting more to work with a view to renewing expenditure, confidence and production in the private sector, itself a sector of salary and wage cuts. Forty years later President Nixon, in 1970, was to announce his conversion, unlike Prime Minister Mr Edward Heath, to the economic philosophy of John Maynard Keynes. Certainly, unlike Hoover, Franklin Roosevelt did not believe that progress was to be made by reversion to *laissez-faire*.

Strachey fortified his charges by industrial statistics. In the course of my explorations of the New Deal I received a letter from Harry Hopkins:

"In regard to Strachey's assertion that the core of the New Deal recovery program was the depression of real wages, it is evident that Mr Strachey failed to consult the available statistical material bearing on the problem. . . .

If these data can be taken as indicative trend of real wages, then Mr Strachey's first point is clearly unfounded. His second point, that the only prescription of recovery given by the New Deal is to depress real wages, cannot be sustained. As shown above, the factual data do not bear him out."

Ithaca, home of Cornell University, steep-cliffed goal of my "Ulysses" adventure, was not far from New York. Many times a student would run me over there in a few hours—although one commented that the speed could be increased. His friend, he added, for speed "always drove at night", a veritable demon driver. There was our modern Babylon—although, with its one-third Jewish population, also our new Jerusalem. There I explored through the canyons; saw Empire State a-building; visited Rockefeller's Radio City, half expecting to descry under the plain paint of one entrance hall the outlines of Diego Rivera's mural, with pictures of Lenin and all. I enquired of the door keeper: "Mr Rivera?" "No, sir, they chipped it out. Mr Rivera, he kinda crabbed his borse."

Manhattan remains one of the greatest expressions on earth of human technical power. The New Yorkers, often so sad, have their merits. But it is New York which elevates the technical mind, even if its beauty—unlike San Francisco's, which redeems the ways of America to God—is a cruel beauty with its ziggurats and Aztec pyramid roofs. One drew breath with astonishment as one saw, from one alpine height in the offices, the white snow on the black cornices of the buildings opposite. To adapt the words of Dr Samuel Johnson, "the man who is not excited by New York has lost his appetite for life".

I recall visiting that great photographer, Margaret Bourke-
White, in her studios, high up below the needle-top of the Chrysler
Building. One went out on to the projecting buttress of the tower
and viewed cars in the street thirty floors below looking like
remote lady-birds, red and yellow and black. I would have moved
more freely had not the cramped roof-space also been occupied
by young alligators brought by Margaret from Florida. The Web
and the Rock.

These were the days of the New York of George Gershwin.
These were the days, also, of the great intellectual stir. But the
view on Manhattan Rock left a more lasting impression than all
the lunches in the Algonquin with Heywood Broun and the rest of
the great American novelists. These were the days of the absorbing
view of the New America given by Scott Fitzgerald in *This side of
Paradise*, although the fantastically exaggerated cult, comparable
to the Joyce cult in the smarter sets, of "Scott and Zelda" and
others of the Riviera set, including Ernest Hemingway, later to
become "the jet set", was not yet. Gertrude Stein and Alice
Toklas were yet the vogue. Now they are all embalmed in doctoral
theses. Nor can I think any man a whole man who, coming in
towards Lower Manhattan on a summer morning on an ocean-
going liner, is not stirred—does not feel that something is wrong
with him if he is not stirred—by the first sight of the great towers
shining through the early haze and has not wept with delight, as I
have wept. Even New York on "the Great Night of the Blackout"
(so strategically disturbing) of September, 1965—and I was there
in the eerie moonlight—was not more stirring.

The Rockefeller Report was followed by the Wickersham
Commission. I had many friendly opportunities of meeting
Mr Wickersham, of the great legal firm of Cadwallader, Wickersham and Cadwallader. The Commission was followed by Repeal
and by a change in the American Constitution. I myself had not
expected that change would go beyond the Supreme Court
holding beers and light wines to be *boissons hygiéniques*. "Not
alcoholic for the purposes of the law." I was wrong. Public
opinion was prepared, in its reaction, to go further than I had
anticipated. The People was prepared to change the Constitution
itself.

I published a little "Home University Library" book on the
subject. I understand that it left some impression on new legislation in New Zealand and Manitoba. I was later summoned by
Nancy Astor to a luncheon at her St James's Square house, to give
her guests a report on the success of Prohibition. My report was

not excessively well received. Occasionally, the People is aroused in its indignation and, laying hands on the sacred ark, changes the Constitution. In that change *pars minima fui*—I had a very small finger in changing the American Constitution. At least I had learned much about America and its people. Later this was to matter a lot when I turned from the ideas of politics to the practical application.

IV

SCIENZA NUOVA

THREE things have chiefly concerned me in life: the development of the Atlantic Community; the independence of India; and the establishment of a systematic Political Science. Since the establishment of an effective Political Science is demanded if there is to be any fully valid insight into the root causes of war and peace —what Machiavelli called "the effectual causes of things"—and since, in my judgement, the integration of the Atlantic Community is the longest proximate step to stable peace in contemporary politics, these concerns are not as disparate as they might seem. Both alike sprang, logically enough, from my wartime meditations of 1918.

Nor can peace be stable if one uses power to flout what vast masses of human beings, for example in India, regard as their legitimate aspirations. This issue of power, even more than that of wealth or population, is the prime issue for mankind. For whom is the benefit? It is the still unresolved problem of what the philosopher Kant called *Ewige Friede*, "Lasting peace". Let those regard it as dull, or boring, who will. The "Yahoos" of Swift's tale will always so regard it. Swift himself did not. The world— even the democratic world—is full of Yahoos in search of a circus, an entertainment, a "happening" and no more; and full of those prepared to provide the circus for profit and their own publicity in Vanity Fair.

To the warning words of the *Dies Irae*: "the very heavens shall be dissolved in fervent heat", let us add *The Tempest*:

> "The cloud-capp'd towers, the gorgeous palaces,
> The solemn temples, the great globe itself,
> Yea, all which it inherit, shall dissolve,
> And, like this insubstantial pageant faded,
> Leave not a rack behind."

Should this chance, the fault is mankind's own.

> "Rex tremendae maiestatis . . .
> Juste Judex ultionis
> Donum fac remissionis
> Ante diem rationis."

"The day of the adding up of accounts." To those who would wish to meditate further upon this theme with a wise guide, I would commend Sir Solly Zuckerman's book, *Scientists and War*. "Let us use true scientific method as an aid to human judgement and not as a hindrance."

In discussing the technicalities of Political Science I must ask the indulgence of Virginia Woolf's "common reader". The matter is literally one of life and death, of peace, war and revolution— but it is not readily brought within the book salesman's requirement of a good yarn.

The subject is too close to the core of what I have sought to do for me to pass the matter over. Engels, with some slight immodesty, maintained the view that Marx had done in the social sciences what Charles Darwin had done in the biological sciences. It is a pity that Darwin never chose to reply to Marx's note to him indicating the same comparison—one which some would hold to be quite complimentary to Darwin. The massive work of Marx is yet far too propagandist of a particular point of view for it to be regarded as a triumph of disinterested science, however original his insights. My contemporary task was and is to put the scientific discussion on to a new and more acceptable basis. In political science something has been achieved since the 1920's.

As to Marx, incidentally, I recall making a pilgrimage to his sometime residence in London's Dean Street, Soho. It is now a restaurant. I remarked to the waiter, humble spokesman for the masses, "Marx lived here, did he not?" "I don't know about any Mr Marx, sir—but the boss upstairs will probably know." And yet the Dialectic did not strike that waiter dead. Another of the *Lumpenproletariat*.

The great Utilitarian school of philosophy, one of the major glories of British intellectual life, had always entertained the view, throughout the Nineteenth Century, that there could be a political science, in the strict English language usage of a coherent corpus of empirical knowledge, capable of test and verification. It was a view which had been entertained earlier by Machiavelli, Spinoza and Hobbes and even, many would say, by Aristotle himself.

To the philosopher must be left the continuing discussion of the *ends*, the goals. The science would be of the *means*. The issue has been very well put by Aldous Huxley.

"About the ideal goals of human effort there has existed in our civilisation, and for nearly 30 centuries, a very general agreement."

The practical problem is that of the appropriate means. Humanity, for example, states that it wants peace. But just how does it get it?

It is not enough that some Italian Renaissance prince was concerned with the efficient means to the agreed or "given" ends. The problem is with us here and now. Nor did Machiavelli, or Cesare Borgia, in choosing their means, sufficiently reflect that such morally shocking methods do not win friends and support. Gandhi himself, not to speak of Lenin, had to consider the appropriate means for the time and place. Even youth, struggling to free itself from a civilisation of commercial or profit technology, has to discover the effective means or be condemned to futility. There may indeed be moral impropriety in the political scientist commending the method of the advertiser or "hidden persuader" to those who wish to be deceived, or of the lawyer defending the guilty party. But this is a different issue. We must ourselves evaluate the ends and our own free choice of them.

Said Hobbes, of the pattern of politics, this "consisteth in certain rules, as doth Arithmetique and Geometry, not (as Tennis-play) in practice only." President Harry Truman thought the opposite; and so do many British politicians and even academics who should know better. Machiavelli, Hobbes and also the Utilitarians thought one thing. The defeatists, full of the conceit of their own negatives, have thought the opposite—with consequences that I shall indicate.

Hobbes' statement, natural in an age obsessed by developments in geometry, algebra and physics, goes indeed too far. I recall President Truman, in a speech in London to the Pilgrims, explaining that, of course, politics was *not* science, but an art, presumably to be learned in Kansas City with the Pendergast family, who bossed that remarkable town, as tutors. Later in the same year the ex-President addressed the American Political Science Association in Washington, where again I was present. Here he admitted to that particular audience that there *could* indeed be a political science, the task of which was to comment upon political practice "objectively". He then added, with humour, that no one who did this could remain a Republican; and forthwith proceeded to deliver a vigorous party speech in terms of the ideals of the Democratic Party and the practices of Kansas City. Needless to say this form of approach to the matter did not command enthusiasm among Republican members. Almost they felt there might be a case for detached science.

I have referred to the Utilitarian philosophy, often Radical Liberal but yet Hobbes' legitimate successor, of which the influence lasted to the end of the last century. Brisk logicians, neo-Hegelian and post-Hegelian, of the succeeding century showed up the crudities of poor Bentham's "hedonistic calculus".

Unhappily, much that was worthwhile in the work of these earnest fustian evangelists of utility was thrown out at the same time. Economics was now too well established as a science to be discarded; but the very assumptions of a political science were felt to be no longer worth even examining by those who aspired to be in fashion. Any claim for it was presumptuous; and the search for systematic concepts was abandoned.

I did not for a moment believe that political philosophy was unimportant; or that any adequate political theory could be shaped which disdained to discuss issues of values and choices. Here Max Weber was wrong. To this theme of political philosophy—its methods so different from those of political science—I shall return. Marx, as Engels rightly asserted, was primarily a revolutionary, even if chiefly a revolutionary on paper while a good bourgeois at home. His philosophy, economic in stress but, as Kautsky had to confess, in the last analysis materialistic, was probably inferior to that of Hegel—just as the Hegelian philosophy in range was inferior to that of its begetter, the Fourth Gospel.

I did, however, think that these speculations on values were likely to continue indefinitely, with multiple liberal dissents, in the endeavour to arrive at ever new syntheses, whereas an empirical political science might arrive at some few objective conclusions. Modest conclusions, perhaps, but not sterile—in my own view revolutionary—about which cumulative corpus of knowledge all serious students in the field could concur, as in the other sciences. I favoured the pioneering of that advance, together with, not the divorce, but the very clear distinction between science and philosophy, seldom here made by British writers. One of the great contributions of Sir Isaiah Berlin has been to re-emphasise the distinction. However, I wrote on both subjects.

As I have said earlier, my concern was a very practical one—nor did I feel ashamed to assert, with Marx, that no divorce of theory and practice was laudable. The purest science, which rightly moves by hypotheses, abstractions and models, yet arises, like geometry, from the ground of practical needs and, having completed its arc, returns again to the applied and practical. I put the most practical of all questions: What were the anatomy and the physiology of the body politic? If wars, as a malfunctioning thereof or as diseases, were to be ended, what contribution did history or did philosophy make? Was history, I asked again, just for "fun", as A. J. P. Taylor later said? Should it, according to Professor Barraclough, only concern itself with "consequences", after the event. Even for the historians, looking into the crystal ball of "the future in general" was a most dangerous occupation. What contribution could political science, if there were indeed an authentic (and not a misnamed and bogus) political science, make to the benefit of mankind?

I had a sentiment or a "hunch" that psychology could make a contribution to fundamental insights. So also could the study of animal societies—of that superlative, totalitarian and functional technologist, the bee, and of our baboon cousins, so repectful among the young of seniority and of leadership. As Aristotle remarked, the cruellest of animals was man. Human nature, asserted Machiavelli, remains always the same. It was the basic assumption on motivation of his great *Discourses on Livy*. But what useful conclusions were we to draw from that? The worthy, if heavy, Lord Bryce, Laski's bugaboo, had suggested a clue in the relation of psychology and politics, but he had not followed it up. (Laski himself held that politics was solely "a branch of ethics", and a fit shield for social and ideological propaganda.)

At a much later stage in my career I had the privilege of seeing something, although all too late before his death, of my good friend and mentor, Graham Wallas who, at the London School of Economics, brought an almost anecdotal treatment of psychology into play with his studies of politics, based not least on his own local government experience. For few men had I more respect. His *Human Nature in Politics*, which so keenly influenced his distinguished erstwhile student, Walter Lippmann, along with his *Great Society*, will not readily be forgotten. He was a founding father of the Fabian Society indeed, with the Webbs and Shaw a member of its founding trinity, and very proud of it. But my contact with Wallas was too deferred to be seminal to my own thought, although I dedicated one of my books to him. Wallas endeavoured to get me back to London University, as he had done Laski (who began with a part-time appointment in economics). He failed. Laski very clearly indicated that I was not wanted and, although he himself owed so much of his recall to England to Wallas, in conversation habitually removed him from a share of the limelight by referring to him as *passé*. I have always aspired to deliver, some day, a lecture commemorative of Wallas's teaching and person.

By the merest chance in 1920 the venerable University of Oxford had offered the Matthew Arnold prize for an essay on the topic, baldly worded, "Thomas Hobbes". I had read (approximately) the nine volumes in English and maybe as many in Latin of that author; and won the prize. The essay, my first book, was published by Basil Blackwell.[1] Moreover, I chanced to come across the work of Alfred Adler. That great historian, Sir Lewis Namier, held that Freud contributed a deeper understanding of political action than Marx. I doubt it. However, Adler seemed, as a psychologist, unlike Freud and Jung, to confirm clinically what Hobbes, as a philosophical adventurer of genius, had propounded nearly three centuries earlier. With Hobbes (who was here talking of Euclid) I could exclaim: "By God, it is true!" I married Adler to Hobbes. *Eureka!* I had the needed working hypothesis.

I chanced to have met the psychologist Professor William McDougal on a committee of the Liquor Control Board, along with Sir Charles Sherrington and Dr William Sullivan. McDougal later told Dr Lowell, the famous President of Harvard, that he de-manded promotion in that University and, in the alternative, he had an offer from Duke University. "I congratulate you, Professor McDougal," was the laconic reply. McDougal was perhaps not a very good psychologist; but he had suggestive ideas. Before the vogue of Freud, he stirred my interest in psychology.

With some timidity I consulted my Oxford philosophy tutor, H. W. B. Joseph, about the scope of the contributions of contem-porary psychology to the study of politics. "You will find much better things in Plato," was the sour and not entirely helpful answer. True, Plato's genius anticipated by centuries the close connection between "hippy" music and "hippy" politics... But that was not the question at issue. It was indeed a murderous reply which nearly killed my groping and hesitant hope. I vividly recall a discussion at an Oxford High Table—whether New College or All Souls I cannot recall. It ran to the effect that a science, a "logy", must be objective, whereas the "psyche" by its very nature was subjective. It followed that psychology or any science of the psyche could not exist. Q.E.D. More important and practical conclusion: there was no need at all for Oxford University to have a chair of psychology.

That eminent and internationally renowned University did not have this chair for many years. As for Sociology, it had not heard of it, except as being some discredited fantasy of Comte's, about which Mill had said a few words in the authorised texts, which had "settled Comte's business". Oxford remained undisturbed by these novelties of the New Learning, as of old it had been undisturbed in its verbal scholasticism. Cambridge, in those far-off days, did better for Erasmus. One practical danger in the Oxford attitude of my day lay in its inclination to brush aside all

---

[1] *Thomas Hobbes*, Blackwell, 1922.

E

tentative groping for truth—which, incidentally, is very much a scientific method—in favour of what can be stated with lucid, logical articulation in words, even if the premises might prove to be inadequate or false in context.

With no less diffidence I went to see Bradford Titchener of Cornell, a red-bearded and fearsome man, in appearance like a modern Jehovah, a president of the American Psychological Association. I explained to him my problems and hopes. "All this discussion by Freud and others has in it a great deal of froth. But there will be a residue that will endure. I think your line has great possibilities. I advise you to follow it through." I was encouraged to the depths. Oxford had never begun to encourage me. The chief and ambiguous encomium I had received from Ernest Barker was that I had "a soobtle moind". I was emancipated. I was launched. It might after all be—it could be—that I was on the right road.

Hypothesis followed hypothesis. The world seemed well lost for the sake of the adventure and of the elegance of the theory. I can well understand why Bertrand Russell, with a like joy, decided that suicide was not worthwhile so long as there was mathematics to explore. The vision came, just as a man abruptly sees an optical pattern in tiles or on wallpaper which has been there all the time, which he had never noted before, but which, once seen, could never be forgotten. Aristotle calls this the precise test of the scientific genius. It comes not by logic but by incubation—sometimes in a hot bath and sometimes on a solitary walk. There was a beauty of intellectual discovery. I recall the exact point as I walked by Cascadilla Gorge, in Ithaca—magic name—New York, in 1923, where one new piece suddenly fitted into the jigsaw puzzle.

Why was it that Economics had so well matured, even quite recently, whereas Politics, much the older discipline, the glory of classical thought, Plato's architectonic study, had hitherto failed in prognostication and solidity? The economists, I noted, had precisely defined their terms. The politicists (my own word; but later I found that Seeley had used it) had not. The clue in Economics lay in the axiom of the law of Supply and Demand. Incidentally, this involved stress upon quantity and units. Much later the "psephologists", especially at Nuffield College, Oxford, developed this emphasis. But they did so in detachment from any systematic General Theory of Politics. (Even the historians admitted statistical techniques to their studies.) Had the logic of Supply and Demand a political equivalent? The then current, even if recent, academic view was that this was pretentious nonsense. History, the photographic study of institutions, neo-

Hegelianism, an emergent (Bentham-based) Logical Positivism feeding on the Hegelian corpse, soon Marxism as a popular philosophy after 1930, then the abstruse forefathers of Existentialism —these were the fashion. I yet remembered that the great Dr Caird had said that history itself was "not a suitable academic subject" —not being "scientific".

Was not the clue in the polar, but indissolubly connected, relation of Freedom and Authority? Though the politicians regarded "Freedom" as a word of blessing and "Authority" as a word of disrepute—yet this emotionalism carried us nowhere in analysis. To obtain some desired freedoms men had to obtain the securities offered by an authority; but, for this, reluctantly, they had to pay the price. *To pay the price?* They had, moreover, in their quantitative units to support that authority. The law of the Political Market was born. Of the theory of the Political Market I think I can say, with some assurance, that I initiated it. (If not, then certainly I do not know from whom I learned of it). The old Social Contract school had never said this quite so clearly or so systematically. However, the basis of all—the analysis that could go deeper than Marxism—lay in the Political Science of Power.

So my Oxford essay on Hobbes and my little essay written in Sheffield on the Utility of History, grew. In Cornell, uninterfered with, I worked over it for a year and, as *The Science and Method of Politics*, presented it as a doctoral thesis in 1924. In 1965, forty years on, it was reprinted.[1] My Cornell doctoral examiners searched in past records back to the case of the philosopher Dr F. C. Schiller for a precedent, and came up with the award of a doctorate after one year's residence. (The regulation period was three years.) The document, revised and elaborated, was published in 1927 by Knopf, and C. K. Ogden arranged (not very advantageously) for its publication in Britain. I was thirty-one.

On the book the great John Dewey, whom I occasionally met, the Engels (or should I say the St Peter) in the chair of succession, after William James, in the leadership of pragmatic philosophy, expressed friendly sentiments. The *American Political Science Review* wrote: "The impression left . . . is one of wholesomeness, like a refreshing breeze blowing through a close atmosphere." My friend-to-be, for many years, the historian Charles Beard (after whom a lecture is named and delivered in Ruskin College, Oxford) was equally encouraging. It was refreshing for me. They were all so generous and unstinted in praise. I took courage.

---

[1] *The Science and Method of Politics* (Knopf, Routledge), 1927; (Archon), 1965.

Later, no little of my encouragement, in days of great discouragement, has come from my dear and admired friend, Chancellor Robert McIver, the dean of American sociologists.

The *American Journal of Sociology* commented: "The work has the distinction of offering the sole constructive suggestion of recent years in the methodology of Politics." A book, introduced by Albert Einstein, said, a few years later, that I was "one of the first in our time to treat systematically the question of linking theory with practice in politics." A young author would be exceptional who was not flattered by all this, although at the time I was too diffident and respectful to my betters even to grasp the full implications of the judgements.

Professor Harold Lasswell, to whom Charles Merriam had introduced me, against the background of Middle Western isolationism and in the 'Twenties, had written a significant analysis of wartime propaganda—some of it what Lord Ponsonby called "Falsehood in War-time"—and then, himself a student of psychoanalysis in Vienna, had published in 1930 his pioneer *Psychopathology and Politics*. I do not think that he would wish to claim that our philosophy has always been the same, but in political science we have maintained an unbroken partnership. Recently, however, he has turned his attention rather to the theory of law. However, we shared the same idea. And men live by the idea. We found political science a chaos. We left it tidied up.

To our enterprise Charles Merriam, while scarcely living long enough to enter into the promised land himself, yet like Moses lifted up his arms in blessing over the young men, a blessing not uninfluential. Chicago University, its name then associated with John Dewey, became very much a centre for these studies. On its very buildings, cut for all time in stone, was the sentence of Lord Kelvin about the quantitative nature of scientific knowledge. It is perhaps a mistake to cut things in imperishable stone. "When you can measure ... you know something about it." Indeed I myself usually referred to the new revival of political science as such, as the work of "the Chicago School". I dare to say that a little of the work—my own—was done at Cornell. Ironically under President Robert Hutchins, who got rid of Bertrand Russell, there was a vigorous reversal of policy and a new stress on classical values. (Subsequently, however, at Santa Barbara, in the Center for the Study of Democratic Institutions, Chancellor Hutchins' contribution has indeed been impressive and regarded by some as revolutionary.)

Hence Lasswell himself, like Bertrand Russell, left Chicago to wander for some years in a twilight wilderness, until he was at

SCIENZA NUOVA 59

length rescued by the Yale Law School and became there a professor of law. (His chair there was, until retirement, in law and political science.) Rumour has it that he owed his post to an admirer who declined to transact business in the Law School until he was appointed. If true, this shows a professional determination which I commend as both courageous and unusual in detecting and even utilising near-genius.

Lord Russell, as it happens, I represented with some vigour to H. H. Price, at Oxford, and through him to Professor Broad, should be recalled to a fellowship at Cambridge. He was; and for this I received the written thanks of Patricia Russell, although I certainly claim no exclusive credit. His first wife, Alys, I knew well in Chelsea. She was of the opinion that Bertrand was making a lot of money in America and quite enjoying himself. I did not think this to be so. I persisted despite her opinion, and was in the event perhaps contributory to success. This is how opportunity ought to be opened and the consciences of sluggard or timid electors (who may prefer cosiness) stirred.

Russell's book *Power* followed Lasswell's and my own, in 1938. I nearly had a quarrel with Charles Merriam, the dean of American political scientists at that time, for paying it undue honour. I disagreed with Merriam's hostility—and won thereby his disfavour. Bertrand de Jouvenel and other eminent workers followed along in the line of power study. I told Jouvenel that I hesitated to read his books, often so similar to my own thought, to avoid the danger of plagiarism; but that most courteous man replied (I am sure untruly) that he had been "plagiarising me now for twenty years".

It is not my task or intention here, in this autobiography, to present a discourse on the nature and use of political science or even of political philosophy. I hope to rehearse these matters in a later volume. Anyhow, is not the process written out in the books that I have written—in *The Science and Method, The Principles*,[1] and *Systematic Politics*,[2] in the last of which I summarised it all? To these I may add my *Applications*. Both these last have now been translated into Japanese.[3]

[1] *The Principles of Politics* (Allen & Unwin, London; Macmillan, N.Y., 1930; Russell & Russell, 1968).
[2] *Systematic Politics: Elementa Politica et Sociologica*, (University of Toronto Press, Toronto; Allen & Unwin, London, 1962; also in Japanese, translated by Professors Y. Takehara and K. Kamiwagi (Horitsu Bunkasha, 1971).
[3] *Political and Sociological Theory and its Application* (University of Michigan Press, Horitsu Bunkasha, 1966).

We distinguished the empiricism of political science from the speculations of political philosophy; we stressed the fundamental and methodological identity (of some administrative importance) between political science and political sociology; we emphasised anew, aided by Stuart Rice and Jacques Rueff, the challenged importance of a quantitative approach, today commonplace (thanks partly to Dr George Gallup) but then dismissed with contempt; we denied that political science was "faulted" because the dogmatists "knew" that it could not be quantitative; we found quantity (even if "compounded" by organised persistence and durability) in units of support, primitive and military or "conventional" in votes; we reflected on the efficient cohesion and duration of "the vanguard" or party; we insisted that students should turn their attention away from rhetorical ideologies or superstitions and textbook *clichés* to look at what men actually did and how they behaved in the widest political world, including churches and industries and unions. We understood Politics in the sense that Aristotle understood it.

With the Pluralists, we deposed the sovereign national state to study the politics of Society itself, as well as States and municipalities; yet, unlike the Pluralists, we did not evade the problem of sovereignty and of final political power; we asserted that the great revolution in thought was to be made, not by minute textual critiques of the deductions of earlier "classical" writers—we were our own classics (as were Marshall and Keynes in economics)—but by re-examination of what they might uncritically have taken as axioms (such as the eternity of the modern State as datum); we defined our terms with precision.

We defined again what we meant by "power", not only dominative (as the Germans thought)—even the Master, Hobbes, here himself had erred. We took note of the contributions of psychology. We found in this Concept of Power the central hypothesis of our science, and around this construed our conceptual system—as economics had done around the pursuit of wealth—our abstractions and our models. Marxism, we noted, had never within its cramped economic framework answered the problems of unprofitable nationalist passions. As for Lenin he had provided not a conceptual answer but a red apocalypse.

The impulse that shaped affairs came not only ultimately from the dialectic flood of material factors without, as Engels held, upon which material flood human creatures were but flotsam and jetsam. In politics the impulse also lay, biologically and psychologically, in the act and the actor and the man within. The two might not be divorceable; but each counted and each deserved study. Whatever man's ideal (or sordid) ends, we insisted that the study of the available means thereto was important and could be disinterested and objective (which certainly did *not* spell that these politics as a whole could be a valuationless study).

Freedom is tinged with an essential goodness biologically since, without it, there is neither health nor life. However, the absolutely free, unsocial, can scarcely survive a week. Freedom without authority has only a brutish worth. We examined Freedom, which we distinguished from (civil) Liberty, and Authority for their exact meaning; and found that neither had a value except in terms of their purposes and functions. But we found them to be not contradictory but complementary, freedom arriving but slightly to its ends without the power of recognised authority to guarantee achievement. Authority without supporting recognition was but Force, itself needing (as David Hume said) support. Why then, we had to ask, was support given more, on the voting figures, to a tyrant than to a parliamentarian? How far did the pleasure and equity of reason prescribe peace? Or how far was peace enforced by rewards, bribes, fear and terror—*armis legibusque*? Who drove Plato's chariot? What could be expected from man without grace? In a realistic assessment, how much power, by reason or terror, did it require to turn the original egotism of man, the ape cousin, and nations; and to uphold the tribunal of justice without producing, with peace, a desolation? What objective justice (as Kant asked) can there be, enthroning reason, above the law? What is a powerless justice?

As, some years later in 1956, the UNESCO Report on Contemporary Political Science commented: "Two decades of the continuous advocacy of the view that power is the central concept of political science—as wealth is of economics—have had an effect both on founding the 'politicisation' of political science and in determining its nature." It is no small thing to redetermine the nature of a science. We had done what our predecessors had not done. We had done what our successors were to elaborate.

Taking, not the modern states established in the seventeenth century, and their vainglorious sovereign pretentions, be it of Luxemburg, Mali, Egypt or even France, or the routine terminology of the textbooks, but the more fundamental theme of Aristotle himself, "Master of Them that Know", as the basis of our studies of the social structure and network of control and of the meaning of politics, we discarded prejudices.

The relation of political supply and demand was discovered, and the theory of the political market enunciated—in one sense liberal, in that the nature of the democratic or free market, and the pressures of common men, and their coherence or organisation, more competent or less, for the fulfilment of their uncensored demands, was explored; but this was not to the exclusion of other forms. Equally, the theory could be regarded as revolutionary, insisting on the need for the underprivileged many, of all peoples, to attend to reality and to assess their power against the few.

A quite new approach to political behaviour was taken, seeing politics as a business to provide, for the political consumer who contributed his votes and support, the efficient goods of legislation and of government and rule, rather than as a football match between competing parties or as an all-in wrestling event between champion political leaders. As philosophy, the right of diverse educationalists to shape the character of common demand was not denied, but affirmed. Aristocracies, whether so called or not, had their function. And we examined what that structure of power might be, in a world of power politics, which was best calculated to provide lasting peace. In stable peace and the end of war, I never forgot, were the practical goals of the effort. Further, unless one comprehended the necessary operations in the safeguarding of peace in the international world, how could I judge the future shape of Europe, the relations in the Anglo-Saxon world of America, the chances of world government, the true policy of England?

As the theory was pieced together for the advancement of learning one got from this adventure a remarkable sense of exhilaration, an aesthetic sense, as in mathematics or Newtonian physics, of the elegant solution.

We set the style of quite a new language in talking about politics, although those educated in, and who gained their prestige by, the use of the old language of law or history or philosophy in this area of empiric science, are likely to persist in it until they die off. This obduracy will not apply to the younger men coming on or to those eager spirits who are prepared to distinguish between the language appropriate to the social sciences and that best suited to the discourses of philosophy—or that, again, suited to the party hustings. I do not go to such an extreme as Professor Sir Isaiah Berlin, in saying that the sciences are the "matricides" of their respective philosophies; but there will be no advances for the sciences unless the distinction of their subject matter of "means", not "ends", and the consequent distinction of methods, are noted and digested.

An argument has been put abroad, intellectually improper and in general nonsense, that all this was part of some "American science of politics"—the word "American" implying its patent absurdity, if not its suspect or charlatan character. As to myself, far from being developed against some peculiarly American ecological limitation, my thoughts were shaped in Oxford (as I have said), although elaborated in Cornell. Thomas Hobbes was not a tree which first grew in Brooklyn. I here certainly do not wish to imply any snide criticism of my good friend, Professor Bernard Crick, who has done and will do excellent work. This error is widespread. Merriam and Lasswell were able to defend themselves. It is not proper to judge any science as "American", any more than French or Tibetan or Eskimo. The sole issue is whether it is valid as science. Our argument was not indeed Marxist and we maintained that it was not less, but more, fundamental than that of Marx. This became a stumbling block to many for whom Marx was inspired by the Holy Dialectic. Perhaps this was one reason why G. D. H. Cole and his circle were against us. One recalls the comment of Einstein about his General Theory of Relativity: "If my theory proves to be true, the Germans will claim that I am a German and the Jews will claim that I am a Jew: if it is disproved, then the Germans will say that I am a Jew and the Jews say that I am a German."

In 1930, when I published my *Principles of Politics*, the *Political Quarterly* (London) was good enough to say that it marked "a fresh chapter in the history of political science in England". Much later still, in 1962, when I published my *Systematic Politics*, the *Political Science Quarterly* (New York) wrote in superlatives that "not since Spinoza in the seventeenth century has there appeared a study of politics so comprehensive in scope and so rigorous in analysis"—clearly a magnificent exaggeration but at least showing a resolute determination to "sound a bell and call attention". I got my work compared with that of the great economist, Alfred Marshall. A distinguished dean of Göttingen asserted that I was "one of the most influential of the political theorists of our age". Maybe. They did not think that in Oxbridge or Portland Place.

In these much later years, the *Yale Review* was good enough to say that my little "follow-up" book, *Applications*, was "apt to move the reluctant reader to make the unwonted judgement that great *homines politici* may exist somewhere, after all; here, just possibly, are the thoughts of a great man". I blushed and read with mixed feelings, in *Mens*, the Amsterdam professional journal, that I was "een der 'grand old men' van der politicologie" —whatever this may be; and the journal *Key*, of the distinguished society of Phi Beta Kappa, wrote that the book—really far too hasty a production with some sad slips in it—was "a summing up by one of the leading political philosophers of the day". Perhaps, in the immortal words of Garfield St Auburn Sobers: "The critics may be right."

All this did not prevent one don, a commentator on the comments of Locke—whom indeed that great scholar, A. J. Carlyle, maintained was "only a second-rate thinker"—from what one colleague had named "the fenlands" of Cambridge, describing any suggestion that my work was of any importance as "intolerable". I perceived that the desire, if possible, "to kill me off" was still not dead in some academic quarters in Britain. A very small group held a power of perpetual blackball. I could confront the comment by that stage, however, with stoicism, even recalling the Olympian flourish by Freud: "I do not discuss; I expound."

Even the master, Hobbes, was in his day excessively unpopular. It is stated that he suggested the Royal Society to Charles II, which, so founded, returned thanks by blackballing him, thanks perhaps to the forgotten mathematician, Professor Wallis. Incidentally, it was a social scientist, Sir William Petty, the statistician of "bills of Mortality", who got the Royal Society on its feet after some delay. Maybe I found compensation in the fact that, a generation on, my daughter addressed the Royal Society—I suppose the first woman to do so—at its three-hundred and tenth anniversary Dinner. But although ironically satisfactory, this was not quite the same thing. The Warden of Nuffield College, Oxford, is said to have observed of himself, when taking office: "The stone which the builders rejected has become the head-stone of the corner." I cannot allege the same.

There is a certain vulgarity and a fault in good manners in giving, without provocation, such a recitation of comment. Such a blowing of trumpets may justifiably be held to be, not merely defensive, but indefensible, conceited, offensive and execrable. I excuse myself by reflecting upon how many, over the years, have confidently affirmed the opposite judgements to mine (and to these) and have published them. Also this recitation appears to be necessary in view of what happened later, which I shall recount.

My only remark could be that, whatever might be thought in North America, or Europe, Israel, India, China or Japan (where my work was, as I have said, translated), I wished that I had had, at that time, any like influence among my own countrymen. I did not observe it. However, recently one Pro-Vice-Chancellor has been good enough to call me "the dean of British political scientists", after many years during which I was certainly not thought to be such. Things change and opinion with them.

Hobbes, tutor to Charles II, claimed that, in one of his books, *De Cive*, he had laid the foundations of the systematic study of politics. As a consequence he was denounced as *irritabile animal* and as having "the brags of a mountebank . . . lately dropped down from heaven". In the slow perspective of history Hobbes was perhaps not wrong. Machiavelli was not systematic. There was indeed a man called Aristotle, a predecessor—but he, in turn, was unpopular at the time when Hobbes wrote. Briefly, it could likewise be said that, as a matter of the chronological record, in my *Science and Method* I had, with Lasswell, Merriam and Bentley, assisted in refounding political science as much as ever Hobbes had founded it. And to do this had been one of my three purposes in life.

I did not in fact say this. First, at the time of its publication, I did not grasp the full implications or significance of what I myself had written. The fuller vistas only became clear as I continued to write. Secondly, claims similar in effrontery to those of Hobbes (even if later shown to be well-justified) offended against my own sense of good manners and of good Confucian style. Further, Arthur Bentley, so brusquely dismissed at the time by the leading professional journal in a few lines of notice, also had claims. It seemed to me it was for others to pass these judgements, not myself. I did not accept the thesis, even in the McLuhan and Madison Avenue Age, that only noise and publicity communicate ideas. Here, maybe, Hobbes was more shrewd than myself.

One New York colleague in my own field, Professor Lindsay Rogers, accepting a copy of the book, explained that he did not expect to read it since it was not in his subsectional field of the subject. I wondered why I troubled to write at all. The thought inclined me to practical politics. Mankind is singularly deaf to new ideas unless patently profitable or coming with the sound of trumpets and the battle-cries of dispute. I limited myself, perhaps leaning over backwards, to emphasising the work of what I called "the Chicago School"—which, taken literally, would have included Merriam and Lasswell but not myself. I merely insisted, as an adequate slogan, that political science, as science, be "taken seriously". In Gianbattista Vico's phrase, we could contemplate *scienza nuova*.

In his Inaugural Lecture at Cambridge later (1946) the new Professor of Political Science, Denis Brogan, a sometime junior colleague and protégé of Harold Laski, remarked: "we may doubt today whether any such academic discipline as political science exists." He did not rebut the doubt but continued to hold the chair and its emoluments. The issue was squarely set. Although it goes on all the time, I hold that the sharpening of knives of academic conflict is a petty and contemptible occupation. This yet does not mean that I do not hold that the professor of any subject should believe in his own subject. I confess that it made me angry. I was not forgiven for being angry.

As I have mentioned, one of my theses was that of the identity of political science and political sociology—a thesis not without significance by avoiding the unnecessary administrative expense of having separate departments, as well as intellectually useful by persuading sociologists to think it, perchance, worthwhile to read the writings of political scientists and political scientists to cease to regard with less ill-concealed contempt the works of sociologists. While making this point I do not wish to quarrel with my school friend Sir Roy Harrod in his assertion, in his *Sociology, Morals and Mystery* that sociology, as usually taught, is far too ambitious, if not pretentious, to be authentically scientific; is amorphous hitherto in definitions; lacks "laws" in the sense used by economists; and hence needs radical pruning and clearer basic concepts before it can be called a science.

Since the early days so many distinguished scholars have followed the track that the very word "power" (which is not dominative; can be cooperative), that occurs in all the titles of their books, once again stands in need of critical scrutiny. David Truman, of Columbia—who indeed exhumed the all too neglected body of work of Arthur Bentley, a veritable Grandma Moses of American political science, a man of the same mental mode as Lincoln Steffens and Veblen-Easton in Chicago and Robert Dahl in Yale have made quite especial and distinguished contributions, as has Professor Downes and such an eminent political sociologist as Seymour Martin Lipset. They are later than my own work and probably much more sophisticated. I must leave the work of further development, as it should be left, to others.

My years at Cornell, until 1935, I look back upon as quite the happiest in my life, as well as the most creative. I was surrounded, in a delightful society, by colleagues friendly and helpful—men of international distinction in history such as Carl Becker, Wallace Notestein, George Lincoln Burr, Preserved Smith, Bancroft, himself the grandson of the great American historian, later to be followed by Mommsen, grandson of the great Theodor Mommsen; psychologists such as Titchener; economists such as Davenport and Willcox; lawyers such as Charles Burdick, all famous men in their day—as well as a philosophy school which published its own journal and has recently set about the critical analysis of Professor Ayer's work. Cornell was even more distinguished in physics. I had a generous chief in Robert Cushman and warm personal friends in my junior colleagues, R. A. Mackay, later Canadian Ambassador to Norway and leader of the Canadian Delegation to the U.N., and Herbert Briggs, editor of the *International Law Review*, in whose appointments, as I have said, I had the honour of sharing. "Bert" Mackay described me as "Machiavellian" but this comment, perhaps unfortunately, applied to my theory and not to my practice. I lectured in the hall dedicated to Goldwin Smith, the historian who had quit Oxford for Cornell and later for Toronto (where he was stripped by his colleagues of his honours for suggesting the union of Canada and the United States).

I had indeed certain reforms to suggest—the lifting from students' necks of the excessive burden of lectures for credit; the need, without abolishing fraternity houses or always establishing collegiate halls, that faculty members should reside, so far as practicable, in the same new residential buildings as the students and be in contact with them. In this way the alleged curse of "alienation" (a later modish word) and of "impersonality", in tutor-student relations in the larger universities, could be avoided. Here I had so far the enthusiastic support of my President, Livingston Farrand, that he was accused of "rail-roading through" the proposals.

In the 'Thirties we were joined, in the Philosophy Department, by Professor George Sabine, hitherto of Ohio State University. Since he wished especially to work and to take seminars in the field of political philosophy, on which I was lecturing, I had to be consulted about his invitation as academically his senior. My view was that the stronger the university became in certain subjects the better. He was, therefore, duly invited. His work in this field, pervaded with Humean detachment, is widely and deservedly known. Indeed he remained on after I left, became an Academic Vice-President of the University, and quite outshone me in his own chosen field. More recently, Professor Andrew Hacker has become a third of those, in Cornell, who have contributed in this area of the history of political ideas. To my own *History* (or *Story*) *of the Political Philosophers* I shall return. In it I endeavoured to express my personal philosophy of an absolute aesthetic—beauty is objective and the basis of absolute values, however much logic may elaborate—and also my philosophy of history as providing, by its record, a probabilism in detailed civilised values and a "grand tradition" which the individual could only challenge at his risk.

Among my contemporaries, in my first year, I found Keith

Murray, later Rector of Lincoln College, Oxford, and now Lord
Murray of Newhaven—and also, following Adolph Menjou,
Franchot Tone, the film actor. I recall with pleasure and pride my
students, Harvey Mansfield, sometime editor, later, of the
American Political Science Review, Francis Wormuth, sometime
editor of the *Western Political Quarterly*, K. C. Hsiao, now of the
University of Washington and author of the excellent book,
Political Pluralism, Eliot Janeway, who has, as finance expert
made "a corner in bears" and who, in August, 1971, advised
President Nixon on his novel "dollar policy", Raymond McKelvey
of California (who facetiously chose habitually to address me as
"maestro"), Andy Biemiller, lawyer to the C.I.O., Val Lorwin,
President Ludlum, Simpson of Brooklyn, Sarah Solovay and
John Mueller, translators of the little book by Durkheim, which I
edited, Mark Hellinger, of the Hellinger Theatre, New York—I
hold an inscribed book from him—the Friedenbergs, Ted Adler,
and Fred Reinhardt, for so many years the distinguished Ambassador of the United States in Rome. Young Langdon was around,
into whose family Mark Twain had married. So was Bob Treman,
who married Irene Castle, partner with Fred Astaire in *Dancing
Years*. Later she married a Chicago textile merchant and Bob was
to be found by a window in the University Club, New York,
looking across to that merchant's Fifth Avenue shop display.
"Sometimes I like to look at my step-husband's store." The
residence in Cornell of Professor Vladimir Nobokov, chaser of
butterflies and inaugurator of a new sub-species of literary *erotica*,
was after my time.

I was happy with my students so that, in time, I acquired a
certain *mana* or legend, as "Catlin of Cornell", such that trivial
little episodes of my alleged exploits were told of from mouth to
mouth and became part of the tradition. They had also the
required undergraduate veneer of slight obscenity. I found to my
surprise that I could scarcely, it seemed, put a foot wrong—perhaps a dangerous impression. How dangerous indeed was this
warm atmosphere of approval I discovered abruptly when I
moved into a more frigid climate. Certainly I had far more
academic freedom, in that campus of Andrew White and Ezra
Cornell, than I had ever had at Sheffield, which was not guiltless of
nervousness about "political clubs". Cornell indeed is so concerned for its academic independence from pressures of any kind
that it confers no honorary degrees. Whatever temporary dis-
contents my diaries or letters may reveal, I was never happier
than I was in those halcyon years.

The place itself, the little county-seat of Ithaca, was a magic autumnal paradise. Below spread, glittering in sunshine amid the yellow maples and scarlet sumach, the waters of the fifty-mile Cayuga Lake (of which Theodore Drieser tells in his dreary story, the first of the "documentary novels"—which Mr Truman Capote claims to have initiated), one of the Finger Lakes in these lands of the Seven Iroquois Nations and of Fennimore Cooper. On either side were the gorges and waterfalls. In midwinter we toboganned—the Willcox and Bancroft girls, Morris Bishop, and the rest of us—on to the ice of Beebe Lake, while the Fraternity Houses amid deep snow kept high festivity.

Even the University bells deserved, for the sentimental, better comment than that of the first President of the University, Andrew White, to the President of the United States, Theodore Roosevelt: "You have fine bells here, Dr White." "What did you say?" The remark was repeated. "I'm sorry, Mr President, but I can't hear you because of these damned bells." In front of the Library was a stone bench on which was inscribed a quotation from Goethe: "Above All Nations is Humanity." Later I was to take this as the title of a postwar joint book of my wife and mine and of Sheila Hodges, which sold about forty thousand copies and was translated into German.

In England, on long summer days, one plays cricket. In Ithaca, in long winter evenings, beside log-fires in the stone-built houses above the lake, one played bridge, and some of the men played poker. However, there was no need to join in with these innocuous contented pursuits of professors and their ladies on the upward round of academic promotion. I didn't play bridge—I had played too much in the army—or poker. Sometimes I rode and fenced. Discussion in the Faculty Club, wooden, white-painted, New England style, was not bad. Late at night, in Ithaca, there was little sound of the busy world save the wail of the train, coming up the valley amid the wooded hills to where sparse lights, amid the maple trees, like fire-flies marked the enchanting small town.

Visitors from the outer world, Tagore, George Trevelyan, Kühlmann (who negotiated the Brest Litovsk Treaty), Alexander Wolcott, followed in quick succession. In Wolcott's case I was taught for a life-time the duties of a chairman, which are to study his man, stand up, speak up, publicise with skill the speaker and efface himself, and sit down. It was all too clear that I did not know much about who "the Man Who (later) Came to Dinner" was. He was not pleased. He was right. It was, at least, kind of the local university club to invite me to take the chair.

The steam locomotive of the Twentieth Century Limited, in those days with cow-catcher and with search-light blazing, still puffed fire and smoke as it ran through the main, snow-packed street of nearby Syracuse, while the glory of New York City was not too distant. I recall the story of how a local magnate, Judge Blood, late to catch the train, ordered his car to follow it and of how the Negro porter lowered the platform for the chauffeur, so that the sixty-year-old judge could move across from the car to the train. Almost, the judge made it. Last moment traffic frustrated the gallant judicial enterprise. Unless it were the fair city of San Francisco, beside the Golden Gate, I cannot conceive of any place on earth which could make a young man more contented than this tranquil scene. Nevertheless, driven by the ambitious desire to join action with theory, I left. I went home. God! how cold I was to find it and its academic world.

V

MACDONALD AND MOSLEY

I DECIDED to return to my own country. I decided, that is, to plunge into the politics of action. If the final decision was abrupt (and due to the caprice of the British electoral system), what had led up to it had been a matter of some years. Having voted Labour in 1918, I became an active party member in 1926. I was later to be a constituency vice-chairman, chairman and, for many years, member of my local executive committee. In conjunction with a like oligarchy on the Conservative side, we came near to running—democratically—the borough where I resided. To avoid misunderstanding be it said that I have also knocked on doors in tenement buildings and distributed party circulars; and have stood outside school doors and polling booths and checked voting returns as late as 1964. These are the routines of humble party duties which I have not sought to avoid.

Following the example of the Olympian academic, Dr Hugh Dalton, the man with the loudest voice in Parliament, I presented myself to the electors—with better right than many physicians—as "Dr". An unhappy, somewhat deaf elder once called to "Uncle Hugh": "Speak up!" The roar came in reply: "What I was saying was that there is far too much dead wood in the Party." For voice his one rival was Ernest Brown, on whom, speaking to his co-Scotsmen in the Central Lobby of Parliament, Stanley Baldwin commented: "That noise is only Mr Brown talking to his constituents in Edinburgh." Dr Dalton was prepared betimes to consider me as a member of his seminar.

It is sometimes absurdly said that one cannot—no, not even a political scientist—combine academic and political life. Bryce and Laski did, without being in the Commons; and quite successfully. Spinoza was perhaps merely an agent or spy. Francis Bacon did better—but came unstuck. The great Goethe was poet, playwright and Minister of Finance and Mines. Admittedly Weimar was a small Duchy, but perhaps what we want are more small duchies (or states of Connecticut size); more Goethes; more courage to seek to be the whole man. And there was also Marx, the natural British Museum academic, the great revolutionary, who raised the union of theory and action into a principle.

I yet do not know anybody today who has sought to combine

F

fundamental political theory with conventional practical politics. Marx's politics were certainly not conventional. Professor Woodrow Wilson—who outdistanced in popularity his own Party—and Masaryk the elder are no longer with us. Erhard and Salazar have been economists. Washington indeed is full of academics and ex-professors, to the great advantage of Washington. But most of them are there as advisers. There are a few ex-professor senators. Thomas More's advice, in *A Man for All Seasons*, to future Chancellor Rich was "be a teacher." But neither followed the advice. It is yet my judgement that America gains greatly by that fluidity in occupations which enables her to utilise to full stretch the services of a Schlesinger—however much President Kennedy claimed he was kept awake o'nights by the sound of Schlesinger scratching away at the historical record—a Bundy, a Galbraith and a Kissinger. Such men provide a balance to the influence of overpowerful bureaucrats.

It is open to any critic to say that this combination of theory and practice is too ambitious, and that I have not myself succeeded. Luck plays a part. Item, I did not entirely fail in administrative practice in North America. Bryce, Laski and Dalton all made a try at the politico-academic combination. The Labour Cabinets of 1964 and 1966 were almost entirely all "Dark Blue" teams of ex-Oxford dons.

I myself first approached active political life from the angle of quite specific academic interests. I was interested, not in the pseudo-religious conventicles of the party devout and in the pretentious enthusiasms of ideological commitment, close kin to a poisonous fanaticism, but in efficiency and sound legislation for what some would call "the good society"—something, be it added, significantly different from "good Society". I wanted to see legislation—hitherto traditionally shaped by men who still prided themselves upon being amateurs (no harm in that, as representatives), even if good at the hustings—based upon a more adequate study of the facts. Actually many Members of Parliament were not amateurs but professional lawyers, with all the bias of the legal profession for fighting their brief and for chicane. It is a bad tradition. Good lawyers seldom make good statesmen. Although not deliberately such, mine was indeed a very Fabian, "Webbical" notion. My purpose was to push research—academic research, party research, governmental research. A Three Point programme. Politics, political science and research interlocked. There was no profit in legislating in the dark. The consequence could be appalling waste. It is a point which Richard Crossman has emphasised.

I also wanted to see a magazine that would "communicate"; that would interest and enlighten the public on the newly explored world of science and its contemporary ideas, and stir a healthy curiosity. Like the great Bentham, immodestly I never doubted that I had as many original ideas to communicate as most people, indeed rather more, some of them worth examining and some worth fighting for.

Some senior Members of Parliament, such as Wedgwood Benn, later Lord Stansgate and father of the present Member for Bristol East, were concerned with the issue of Party research and felt that something ought to be done. I had been introduced in 1928, through Quaker channels, to Charles Roden Buxton, an M.P. whose brother was later Minister of Agriculture and who had a library and bureau of his own up in the Victoria Tower of the Houses of Parliament. There was, he told me, a young and even brilliant Labour Member, with the same concern, who was rapidly coming on in the Commons. He had married no other than Lord Curzon's daughter. Incidentally, when the young man's secretary had written to the sometime Viceroy a letter, as he himself told me, beginning "Dear Lord Curzon", the son-in-law had got the abrupt comment: "Why does your damned secretary write to me, 'My dear Lord'? I am not his 'dear lord' anything." (In an age of excessive informality I have some sympathy with Curzon.) I can imagine Lord Gladwyn writing the same thing.

This Member would certainly be interested and Buxton suggested that we should all meet. His name was Oswald Mosley. To his political friends he was "Tom". Later he was to be thought of, quite seriously, as a possible Leader of the Labour Party and future Prime Minister. He was rising like a rocket.

In due course and with commendable speed I received a courteous and cordial letter from Sir Oswald Mosley, Bt. He had a house in Smith Square, in a favourite residential area for M.P.s under the very shadow of the Palace of Westminster which houses the Mother of Parliaments. Would I come to lunch? It was a lunch in some style. I found there Benn and Buxton, and also John Maynard Keynes and Douglas Cole. I was not unimpressed by this galaxy of talent.

The discussion was about research. It was agreed that some new party research agency (the Fabian Society being then somewhat moribund, with Galton as its ageing secretary) ought to be set up. Number One point in my programme seemed to be on its way to fulfilment. Hitherto, in the words of Dick Crossman over thirty years later, there had been "a scandalous absence of information on which to base Government policy".

Thanks to the outstanding generosity of Cornell University I had reached an arrangement which Cole and others held to be enviable under which, after 1927, I taught there for only one semester in each year. The other semester was devoted to travel and acquainting myself with the political world about which I taught. It was an admirable, generous and far-sighted arrangement. It is my judgement that, if I had pulled all available political wires, I could have got myself selected as parliamentary candidate in at least a marginal constituency in time for the General Election of 1929, with its Labour victory. However, I did not pull these wires and was too new a man to be invited spontaneously. I did not feel in a hurry. The vacation over, academic duties drew me back. This was a mistake which neither innocence nor dedication excuses.

Before I returned to London again, the Election of 1929 was over and the second Labour Government under Ramsay Mac-Donald was in office, although scarcely in power. Actually the popular vote at the Election, as distinct from the Parliamentary vote, gave the Conservative alone a 300,000 advantage over Labour, which had yet greatly increased its own vote.

On my return to London in 1930 I resumed contact with the Party. It had gone into office in the high hope of developing the welfare of the community as that of "one nation", not of the two of which Disraeli had spoken. The stress was upon health and social insurance. This was the theme of R. H. Tawney's election pamphlet *Labour and the Nation*. Arthur Greenwood and others, on so many platforms, held forth upon what could be done for hospitals and schools in the war on poverty and neglect—although, unlike the Soviets, not so much for defence. Democracy likes defence on the cheap.

Unhappily for them a thundercloud had arisen, a far-ranging atmospheric depression in the economic sphere, quite beyond the powers of individual politicians or even of national parties of any colour to cope with. The threat was international. The response still could only be national.

By an uproarious irony, in the end the economic depression flung from power in ignominy MacDonald's Socialist Government ("Socialism is the trouble!" cried the people) and Hoover's Capitalist Government ("Let's have a New Deal!" cried the people. "The bankers are the trouble!"). What mattered to the electors was not indeed the bankers or the political "bakers", whose problems they scarcely understood, but "the bread". It was tasting bitter. The people, said Aristotle, are not the cooks but judge the cooking.

The Great Depression was, in some respects, a delayed consequence of what Keynes called "The Economic Consequences of the Peace," a French-contrived vindictive peace. Astronomical reparation figures, despite General Dawes, produced instabilities in international credit. In part, however, it was the consequence of excessive optimism about the rebuilding of Germany; ill-considered investment there; excessive private speculation back in America, with elevator boys betting on margins—boom and then sudden alarm and crash.

I discussed the crisis with ex-Governor Al Smith, of New York, high in the Empire State Building, where the wind whistled through the unoccupied office suites. A sound man of business unique, so far as I know, in his ability to address a political audience as if it were a shareholders' meeting, while holding their attention, he had no ideas to offer. More production: "If only the retailers would put more in their shops." Production. Expansion. Growth. But who, among those laid off, was to buy the goods? On the international scene (and of the essence of the situation that it *was* international and beyond the power of the most "industrious apprentice", as virtuous individualist, to command) financial aid which might have been given to that economic purist in orthodoxy, Chancellor Brüning of "Weimar" Germany, was not forthcoming. The Bank of France was especially restrictive. How reminiscent it all sounds today. *Le plus ça change.*

Clarence Hatry, a small but dangerous financial acrobat, was caught in mid-swing between flying trapezes on the 29th September, 1929. Something far greater than the earlier Florida crash came on "Black Friday", 25th October, 1929—the Stock Exchange crash in New York. Soon everyone there was on the run.

The unemployed later walked the streets or pathetically tried to sell apples on Fifth Avenue to keep body and soul together under "a free economy", where relief was only local, uneven and inadequate, not national. They trudged to Washington in hope of a remedy or of better chances. American artisans who had never begged before stood and begged, while frightened Levites passed hurriedly by.

The economists, like my friend Wesley Mitchell, studying the business cycles (and nobody had given these expert gentlemen more encouragement than the unlucky technocrat, Herbert Hoover), were caught between wind and water. They did not know whether unemployment was only to be expected under "natural economic law", the saving surgical remedy in a capitalist society, or whether it was not.

My wife's cousin, Standish Chard, staunch Republican, whom

I had known as a stockbroker living in Park Avenue—I owe to him my introduction to that great actress Katherine Cornell—lost all his own fortune and most of his clients' in a few weeks and was, at last, happy to pick up a few dollars a night as a watchman of stage properties, gritting his teeth as he realised that he was down on Federal Aid given by the Democrats.

A prudent man will always reconsider each year the qualifications of his physician, his lawyer and his stockbroker. But how should a stockbroker examine his own qualifications? Chard clung on to some patent he partly held in a never-never monorail system—just as my grandfather, Richard Harding Orton of Leamington, had sunk his money, in uneven competition with Westinghouse, in a railway-brake patent in the Railroad Age. ("Railroad" was the earlier English word.) Standish Chard died, desperately poor, thanks to the natural laws of economics; but remained to the last the charming man he had always been. As for myself, I lived, during the week or so of the bank moratorium, on dollars peeled off her roll by our Negro cook, who had learned prudence about banks in the Florida crash.

Amid the international financial chaos, in which irresponsible speculation and most pious thrift suffered alike, it was inevitable that there should be a backwash reaching the shores of Britain, which any Government, regardless of party, would have to meet. The manual workers who had voted Socialism in, complained (not for the last time) that they, betrayed by a Labour Government itself, were being made the first to suffer. And had they, victors in the Great War, not expected steady rises in wages? What point in being "a victor"? But the economic mills, international, impersonal, ground on and ground small.

Mosley by now, in 1930, was Chancellor of the Duchy of Lancaster. Serving under the National Union of Railwaymen's chief, Jimmy Thomas, David Low's "Lord Stuffed Shirt"—but for all this a man of earthy wit, popular alike with trades unionists and with George V—Mosley was deeply involved along with Tom Johnston, Secretary for Scotland, and George Lansbury, Minister for Public Works, in economic plans to meet the growing crisis. It was logical that I should go along to his private offices in Grosvenor Gardens Mews North, off Ebury Street, to see what aid I could give.

It was, I thought, highly significant that the walls carried two large-scale maps, not of Germany or Italy, but of the British Empire—and of the Soviet Union. I was surprised but did not necessarily disapprove. I became involved in studies of markets and of whether widening "the bottle-neck of bullion-production" might not be one clue to reform.

Douglas Cole wanted to have a double-currency; one for home and one for abroad. Every economist had his own plans, usually contradictory. As early as January, 1928, the *New Statesman* wrote, with some self-righteousness: "The nation is living on its capital. That way lies national collapse. Yet neither the Government nor the great employers appear to have an idea in their heads for any plan of national reconstruction." (And who else did?) A recent editor of the *New Statesman* appositely pointed out, in 1966, that the problem still has an up-to-date look. Britain is still searching for a clear vision of its future role and for a lucid statement of the demands which can be paid for and met. At least today the economic charts and plans are considerably clearer.

Interestingly enough, the *New Statesman* has recently recommended an emphasis upon "national sovereignty", which would have pleased Tom's heart, and has used precisely the very Mosleyite word "insulation", i.e., let the sovereign electorate of Britain make its own economic choices and to hell with international policy and opinion. It may be "true socialism for at least one country" (as they said in Stalin's Russia); but it won't work. Like many Socialists of the time, Mosley was the advocate of policies of import-controls, quotas, bulk purchasing. Today it all still sounds very contemporary.

The issue was also raised, as it has been since, of a small Cabinet of super-Ministers, relieved of a department's day-to-day responsibilities and with time to plan. It had its difficulties then and still has. A Minister with no departmental civil service is like a boxer who has lost an arm. The "over-lord" Minister either has to run the department himself or tends to be a *roi fainéant*, as Greenwood was to find later, even when he brought in Frank Pakenham (now Lord Longford, K.G.), as a Beveridge economist, to help him.

Having to go to Norway and Sweden I was asked by Mosley to report upon the Scandinavian grain trade, not least the Norwegian farmer subsidy, which central planning alone enabled (as was nationally and socially desirable) any sizable population to be maintained in the north of that country, partly as fishermen and partly on their farms. The talk, amid the economic storm, was of "insulation" ("isolation" was scarcely practicable for a food-dependent, trading nation) and, in effect, of a Schachtian policy, such as enabled Germany in the 'Thirties to weather its storm.

J. H. Thomas, who had risen to influence as a trade union chief, later moved to the Dominions Office. ("The Mother Country!" he is said to have remarked. "The Dominions would bite off the tits of their mother, if they could.") He was well out of his depth in economic matters. Also he had the usual practical trade unionist's distrust of economic experts—experts in other fields than his own. ("Go upstairs; see what the experts are doing; and tell them not to.") George Lansbury and Tom Johnston, who were assigned to work with Mosley, were in little better case. Fred Pethick-Lawrence (later Lord Pethick-Lawrence), as Financial Secretary to the Treasury, worked on his own on the financial aspects. With some background in the so-called "Birmingham Programme", which Mosley, John Strachey and a few others had put together, and in Lloyd George's economic research policy, Tom Mosley turned his attention more specifically to the threatened unemployment issue, in that year of 1930, as the blizzard became fiercer.

Most of the points of what became the "Mosley Memorandum" have since become accepted or acceptable Socialist policy. They involved reducing the number of unemployed by raising the school age and lowering the old age pension limit, so that thousands would be taken off the industrial market. It involved deficit financing, already advocated by Lloyd George. It profoundly shocked the soul of Philip Snowden, ex-Customs and Revenue officer, a rigidly orthodox economist and ardent Free Trader, who was in the key post of Chancellor of the Exchequer. Snowden's ideas, like those of Brüning in Germany, belonged to an earlier age. To put the matter quite simply, by and large Mosley's policy was right and Snowden's wrong.

The crux of the economic situation then was the same as it is today; Britain was suffering from the heritage of Adam Smith. We suffered the present nemesis of our very past success, which had in it an element of luck and of merely transitory opportunity. Spain, Sweden, Holland had all, for diverse reasons, had a like mischance. The country was just too small, although its empire was not. This is, of course, a bitter pill for the electorate and something which the ordinary voter and worker found it difficult to accept. "After all, we have *won* a war, haven't we?" Management, on the other hand, remained lazily complacent, encouraged in obstinacy by the anodyne memories of past success. One of the problems which throughout my adult life has beset me is whether some new setting—yet one not inconsistent with her tradition— could be found whereby the prosperity and indeed the grandeur of Britain could be maintained, and this in peace rather than war.

The graining of the entire economic structure of the country to Free Trade, which was the secret of Britian's prosperity in the days of the Industrial Revolution and exporting initiative, was the clue to the vulnerability in the Twentieth Century. Mentally she still lived in the great Age of Coal and Rail and Cotton. However, contemporarily, not only had other countries achieved a measure of economic self-sufficiency (advocated in Germany since the days of Fichte), but Britain had also so rashly increased its population that it was dangerously dependent upon imported food and had the habit of demanding cheap food. Nobody, not even Jack Haldane, actually advocated killing off potential mothers. But the problem was there.

No one can reflect on the economic crisis of 1930–31 without being impressed by the comparisons that can be made with 1966–71. In 1931 there was the same demand for import controls and for reduction of imports by home production of necessary goods and the same dismay over the threat—still greater at that time—of unemployment. There was the same run on sterling and the same diversity of counsels among economists about how to stem it. It is an ironic thought that, in 1931 also, the Bank of France was found to be not entirely helpful.

At home, especially among the manual workers, there was a tendency to look for a scapegoat, not indeed in "gnomes of Zürich", but in the evil *genii* of "Wall Street". The consequences of London being now the second and then the first financial centre of the world, the brute fact that Britain, as a trading nation, in terms of population is grossly dependent upon exports and upon international credit (even in terms of dealings with the Communist bloc) tended to be overlooked or deliberately ignored. Courses in elementary economics and civics, which impress the distinction between a worker's nominal and his real wage, even today are not given in the schools.

As to the role played by the habitually Anglophil firm of J. P. Morgan, I had the opportunity of discussing this with Gordon Wasson, of Morgans, some years later. His case was that Morgans had been asked to report on the actual prospects of American aid in loans and credits and had done no more than give a professional objective report. The only alternative was that kind of Schachtian "insulation" which is almost impracticable for the British economy, which has to learn "interdependence" the hard way. Today, even instant "Entry into the Common Market" assuredly provides no unconditional reliefs.

Assuredly there are certain marked differences between the situation of 1930–31 and the situation today. The crisis of "the Great Depression" was emphatically international and not primarily British. Ultimately it stemmed from the terms of the Versailles Treaty and secondarily from the refusal of the banks to sustain Brüning in Germany. Today the crisis is especially national.

Admittedly, "international credit" has a subjective aspect of, for example, dislike of specific socio-economic items, held to be financially relaxed, in a political programme. (However, the bankers detested Schacht, who was assuredly not "a Socialist".) Here the attack on the Government in 1930, for "gross mismanagement", by the Opposition was perhaps less patently a matter of trying, with tedious and biased regurgitation of charges, to score party points of dubious patriotism, patently weakening national credit, than in 1966.

In a remarkable article in the *Daily Mail*, entitled "When Will They Ever Learn?", Bernard Levin has recently written of Ian Macleod's partisan attack:

"For the majority of our politicians . . . have reduced themselves, through the exigencies of the present party system, to a condition in which they literally do not know whether they are telling the truth or not, and some of these seem to have gone further and rendered themselves permanently incapable of finding out. . . . It is now time that our politicians began to understand that making faces at each other is no substitute for hard work."

I have mentioned that I had not only a plan for Party research and for academic research but, also, for a National Economic and Social Research organisation. This was my Point Number Two. We needed to utilise, to the maximum and in focus, all the economic expertise, as distinct from doctrinaire political rhetoric, that we could command. I distrusted, and always have distrusted, emotionalism in the quest for solutions. At a quite early date Mosley asked me to write a memorandum on this research issue, which he wished to take up with MacDonald. I worked most of one night to complete it.

In effect this recommended a strong research staff to prepare the ground for special and economic legislation ahead of time by adequate research into the facts. Any department without a staff is impotent in Whitehall. We wanted to know what we were about (not only in transport and the like, but more widely) and to know it quantitatively. The national statistical agencies were quite inadequate. We wanted relevant statistics and yet more statistics, instead of legislating in the dark—and providing perchance the *wrong* political product. Unlike Mr Gladstone's "experts", whose habit (as he said) was to say "no", their work would be positive, without failing to report on technical difficulties. The staff would be headed and guided by a small Council.

What was required then is required today; along with the Registrar General, a Statistician General, with a cluster of computers, working up-to-date along with a National Social Survey.

MacDonald, I gathered, discussed the matter with Mosley and a few others at three hasty breakfasts. There emerged from the bacon and eggs something it is the damning burden of all Civil Servants to bear (and hence my early decision not to be a Civil Servant) to wit, the vital distortion of the original reasonable plan. The fruit of the hasty consultations was indeed a National Research Council, headed by Sir Hubert Henderson (editor of *The Nation* and later Warden of All Souls) and staffed pre-eminently by Colin Clark. There was little other senior staff; the days of Lords Balogh and Victor Rothschild were not yet. It was "on a shoe-string", and it had loaded on to it a top-heavy Council of distinguished pundits, not elected persons, including Keynes and Cole.

The inevitable happened. The experts differed. Some economists were exponents of the thesis that the current economic disease was "over-production"—there was need for a cut-back. Others (such as Fred Henderson, in his *Economic Consequences of Power Production*, published in 1931, and J. A. Hobson) were "under-consumptionists", here anticipating the New Deal. Henry Ford's High Wage thesis, that the highly paid worker himself expanded the (home) market, had scarcely made any impact as yet in the United Kingdom with its competitive Free Trade, cheap-labour prejudice.

Philip Snowden took up the cudgels for Parliamentary responsibility by elected persons against a body, not so much concerned with objective research as with giving subjective and very opinionated economic advice. If, as Snowden said, Acts of Parliament were to be passed, it was he who would have to take the blame for any failure and he must be in full charge as Minister.

The Council, not unexpectedly, languished on the vine and withered away. The long-range arguments for it, that I put forward in my memorandum to Mosley, yet remained. In recent days we have seen their revival—although more in the form of a case for arbitration in a national wage plan through the various National Economic Development Boards or "Neddies" than as chiefly research investigation prior to legislation. But, today, they are firmly under the control of a Minister able to argue his own case with the Chancellor of the Exchequer.

Jimmy Thomas, although a disastrous failure in a year of bitter crisis, became notorious in fable. At a dinner, not given by Lady (Nancy) Astor but when he sat next to her, he is alleged to have said: "Lady Ashtor, this is a wonderful country to be born in,

where a man can begin life as a locomotive counsellor and end
life as a Privy Cleaner." When the so-called Mosley Memorandum
came up for Cabinet discussion, from one of his own junior
Ministers, tradition says that Thomas commented: "All I know
is that Tom Mosley come to me and said, 'I've been thinkin'.'
'I'm glad to 'ear it, I says.' And then 'e 'ands me a sheet of paper,
and that is the horigins of the no-tor-ious Mosley Memorandum."
Since Thomas dropped his aitches chiefly for vote-catching
purposes, and not because of incapacity to speak the King's
English, I am sceptical of the record, but the mood is probably
captured truly enough. Of such bluff, casual men, little was to be
expected. Also Philip Snowden, in his professional mood of the
ex-Customs and Excise officer, was dead-set in opposition to
radical economic reform.

Not all the politicians were in like case. Although Arthur
Henderson personally distrusted Mosley, whom he regarded as
"this wealthy pusher", MacDonald was not unfriendly. Aneurin
Bevan, the young Welsh miner, was a very close *confrère*. So were
John Strachey and Dr Forgan; so was the powerful miners'
leader, A. J. Cook. Mosley, Bevan and Strachey indeed constituted
a political trinity.

Moreover, certain Conservatives in the Opposition were known
to be interested in the Mosley economic proposals, especially
Harold Macmillan and Bob Boothby. Aneurin had the ear of
Lord Beaverbrook, who later counted such well-known men of the
Left as Sydney Elliott and Michael Foot among the editors of his
Evening Standard. An influential section of the Press was not
unfavourable, especially Massingham of the *Observer*, the present
Hugh Massingham's distinguished father.

David Low told me of one occasion when Mosley's circle was
more unusual. Four of them (the late Sir David being one) had
gone to the famous Mrs. Maybrick's "joint" and had succeeded,
not only in gaining admission, but in being served with drinks
after the closing hours even for "drinks with food". Within a
matter of minutes a detective inspector entered the room and
"proceeded in the course of duty" towards their table. He looked,
paused and turned back, muttering the words, "too big a job for
me". The party consisted of Low, Oswald Mosley, Winston
Churchill and Lloyd George.

One newspaper alleged that Mosley had a collection of eminent
experts working on his plan in his private office. Mosley read the
statement blankly and then turned to his assistant, Allan Young:
"Experts in the office ? Whom do they mean ?" Then a pause, and
a laugh. "They must mean Catlin." Once Harold Laski, who was

not in touch with Mosley, asked me whether I "ever penetrated beyond the periphery of his consciousness?" Mosley was a great egotist. I do not know the answer but maybe I did penetrate. At least he acted on some of my suggestions. (Also he had the imagination to recommend me on to a Royal Commission on the Liquor Traffic, but Home Secretary Clynes thought otherwise. He also introduced me to Franklin Roosevelt). Some of the suggestions were Strachey's. Most proposals were his own.

Further, Mosley was capable of being popular. The prize honour of the Labour Movement has always been that of being invited to speak at the Durham Miners' Gala. In 1929 the speakers were Ellen Wilkinson, the young Jennie Lee—and Tom Mosley. Well I recall attending a trade union luncheon in Oxford Street. Tom was the guest of honour. I had to leave early, and as I descended the stairs of the restaurant I heard, echoing loud, the chorused voices: "For he's a jolly good fellow . . . a jolly good fellow; and so say all of us."

It was in May 1930 that the Cabinet discussed the Mosley proposals to cope with the economic depression. They were rejected as too drastic and expensive. Mosley then carried them to the Parliamentary Labour Party, where his speech was remarkable. But loyalty to the Cabinet decision prevailed. According to my information an *eirenicon*, a compromise formula, was put forward at some stage by MacDonald, so drafted that it could satisfy Henderson. It was offered to Mosley. Mosley turned to his satellite moon (whom some would hold to have been his evil genius) John Strachey—later, ironically, the author of *The Coming Struggle for Power*—to consult him about acceptance. Strachey's counsel was to refuse. "What the people want is Action." In those days the phrase smacked of Lenin. "Action", repeated as a slogan as late as the Election of 1966, is a dangerous catchword. "Judgement" can be better. Mosley refused. The crossing of the Rubicon was nearly reached—but not yet.

The appeal on policy was carried one stage further. The Labour Party Conference, in 1930, was at Llandudno. The Executive Committee of the Party stayed at the Grand Hotel, just behind the pier, overlooking the sea, where I stayed also. Once, as I walked from the pier, I met John Strachey and Aneurin Bevan coming on. I told John that I was just off to see my father's old friend, Henry Woodall, whose brother, Sir Corbett, had been in Gladstone's Ministry. "Well, bring him along here—or better not. He may find us far too reactionary."

The great day was to be when Mosley made his speech before Party Conference. MacDonald had delivered his speech earlier in the week, and there had been a standing ovation to "the First Socialist Prime Minister". Then MacDonald and his Ministry had gone off to be photographed. It was Laski, quoted by Malcolm Muggeridge, who said of MacDonald at one time, "no one could be long in his presence without feeling that he had the magnetic gift of leadership"; and blandly, at another time, that there was "no abandonment of principle he has not been prepared to make". Years later I was present at a lunch when Harold Wilson delivered a speech on MacDonald's birth centenary: "The most difficult speech I have ever made in my life."

James Maxton, I.L.P. leader, had spoken later, his black locks reaching almost to the Clydesider's shoulders. He spoke like—he visualised himself as—a Tribune of the days of Robespierre, although he was indeed a most gentle character. His memorial speech on Speaker Lowther deserves a place in any anthology of the great Parliamentary speeches of the century. With long, thin forefinger extended, he indicted the platform, who should speak for the people, for their lethargy and conservatism amid growing unemployment. He sat down to roars of the comrades' approval. It had been fine, heart-stirring rhetoric. Moreover, "he cared".

On the day for the discussion of the economic crisis, I sat in the public gallery next to Cynthia Mosley, all taut with anticipation about Tom's speech. The whole Conference awaited it. It was a triumph. Oswald Mosley was ever the dark, handsome baronet, master of fencing, but he was more. Force of words and that confident, arrogant, dominating personality were given body in argument by citation after citation of effective statistics at the expense of the platform's decisions. Again a long, standing ova-tion. Then the vote—the card-vote carrying the unions' millions. The vote was reported—it was "against", by a narrow majority.

A rumour goes that A. J. Cook's train was late and that no taxi was obtainable. An unlucky triviality and a massive historical con-sequence. Cook was late for the vote and it was stated that had he, the miners' leader, been there he might have turned it. I have not been able to check this, although it may have been one of those little incidents that could have altered history.

Of Sir Oswald's policy A. J. P. Taylor writes, in his *English History, 1914–45*: "His proposals were more creative than those of Lloyd George and offered a blueprint for most of the constructive advances in economic policy to the present day. It is impossible to say where Mosley got his ideas from. Perhaps he devised them himself. If so, they were an astonishing achievement, evidence of a superlative talent which was later wasted." To one, at least, of his ideas—a National Economic Council—it is a fact that I contributed.

An "objective Life" of Mosley would certainly be fascinating—
but also anti-climactic. Doubtless it will be written. Taylor interestingly compares his career and his error with those of Lord
Randolph Churchill, another "actionist". He believed himself to
be a patriot and I do not doubt it. Whether he was ever a democrat
I doubt; certainly he did not believe in "democratic committeeism".
What sticks is that he came so near to reaching the highest power
in the land by constitutional means. He remains as "The Man who
might have been Premier". Nevertheless, his miss of the leadership was that of a hundred miles. Indeed he was to choose to be
merely chronologically second to Mussolini in the list of would-be
dictators in the West. The little man, the Austro-Czech of the
Munich Bierhaus *putsch*, was later to go further. Lord Snow talks
of "the Corridors of Power". The pursuit of power rather carries
men, as I have said, if not through *couloirs*, yet up the stairs. These
are the Stairways of Power, and those who leap up them may fall.

The pursuit of democratic power, however, can also lead into
closed hotel rooms and executive suites. On the night after his
speech, Mosley was sitting late at his table in the almost empty
dining room of the Grand Hotel, conning over and discussing
press comment, some favourable, on his speech. John Strachey
left early to escort Cynthia Mosley to a theatre. Aneurin Bevan
was not there—as Allan Young said: "A good thing, or he would
have quickly told all the rest." The reputation of Bevan at that
time was of a politician, able, even brilliant with the Welsh *hwyl*,
but frothy. That was Mosley's view. As Minister of Health, years
later, this was shown to be a wrong estimate. Allan Young was at
the table and less than half-a-dozen others. I was one. The dessert
had been cleared and only the coffee remained.

Mosley continued his analysis, of the voting and of the press.
Suddenly he pulled himself up. Those were the days of Lenin and
Stalin; and the days when the I.L.P., at least, liked to talk in
flamboyant terms of "revolution". "This means a dictatorship."
I still recall the *frisson* when my singing ears heard the remark.
A short talk more and we left. A dictatorship in Britain? It could
not happen here. Cromwell was long dead and gibbeted. And
what had Mosley in common with the Puritan dictator? Russia,
China, Italy, later Germany, Spain, France were to fall to dictatorships or to semi-autocrats. But surely not Britain. Or could it?

H. G. Wells, feeling himself to have been insulted socially
by the Mosleys on the Riviera, attacked him in *The Dictatorship
of Mr Parham*, oddly enough hinting that he was a Jew and called
him "Mr Moses". (Mosley did indeed look Jewish; but it was his
wife who was half-Jewish.) Once I expressed my regret to Laski

that I had ever been brought by Buxton into association with Mosley even in his Socialist days. "I blame no man," was the reply, "for having become secretary to a future Prime Minister." Incidentally, I was neither secretary nor paid—but this is by the way.

In December 1930 Mosley issued a Manifesto, which a dozen or so M.P.s signed and also A. J. Cook. In the following February he broke with the Labour Party and founded the New Party, here emphasising the Randolph Churchill analogy and folly. The "activist" had forgotten the character of party life—although, many years later, he was to admonish (and who knew better?) Enoch Powell on the matter. But he became convinced that, to hypnotise his public, he had to convert himself into a political fanatic—which, by nature, he was not. It is a danger of which our present Enoch Powell, not yet carried into heaven in a fiery chariot, has also to beware.

Mosley collected around him a strange menagerie. Aneurin Bevan—himself no mean master of Parliamentary resignations—with (as Allan Young told me) an old mother and dependent on his miners' trade union subsidy, refused to join. This wrecked the proposed political balance of Left and Right. Mosley was left with some politically useless Ulster M.P.s. He acquired, however, such ill-assorted bed-fellows as Harold Nicolson and Cyril Joad. I never joined it, but supported the Party line—and also that line against MacDonald. An internationalist by strong conviction, I was disturbed by the incipient chauvinism in Mosley's "insulationist" programme, with anti-American overtones which I deeply distrusted. From America that winter I asked him for clarification on this issue. I received no reply. I quit.

Many who had early been associated with Tom took a speedy opportunity to clean themselves with scrubbing brushes. Others, such as Hugh Dalton, not devoid of jealousy, said that they had "always seen through him". Even to this day his name remains poison and he is like one of Gandhi's "untouchables". Horrid tales were retailed of his bullying conduct at Winchester, which the gossips had quite recently discovered. As to his occasional affability, it was turned on and off as by an electric switch. Just as MacDonald was to produce a major trauma in the Labour Party, which lasts until now and equates coalition with betrayal, so Mosley produced a minor trauma of suspicion of adventurers of wealth and brilliance, converts to the Party but not rooted in it. Nevertheless, the cult of the humdrum can become excessive.

Later Dalton was to deliver a calculated attack upon his rival Stafford Cripps, Beatrice Webb's nephew, in a speech at Party

Conference, as a man using his wealth like Mosley to acquire power. It was, of course, a lie. There have been (and perhaps are still) bouncing men who aspire to buy themselves a high position in the Labour Party. "Money can achieve anything." Hitherto they have never succeeded. Mosley's early career was a *tour de force*, a study in personal power and its limits. But this particular charge, which was not in my view even fully warranted in Sir Oswald's case, was assuredly grossly untrue of that dedicated Puritan, Sir Stafford.

I was a devoted admirer of Maxton (Jennie Lee, seeing us together on the Terrace of the House, described us genially as "two conspirators") and an admirer of the I.L.P., although I declined, along with Frank Wise, to abandon loyalty to the Labour Party and to follow the I.L.P. into secession at Bradford in 1932, at a conference which I attended. I was also, like Barbara Castle, an enthusiastic if uninfluential member of Cripps' Socialist League, of which Dick Mitchison (later Lord Mitchison of Carradale) was treasurer.

Many, especially Cripps, but also (quite surprisingly) Attlee, in writings in succeeding years talked about the need for a Labour Government, once elected, to "complete its job", against possible Tory insurrection (as in the Ulster days and at the Curragh Camp), by prolonging statutorily the life of its Parliament and by use of Orders in Council. Harold Laski was frankly sceptical that the necessary social changes would be permitted by the wicked ruling class to be carried through peacefully. His philosophy was one of sorrowful, but firm, pessimism about civil peace. I vividly recall Douglas Cole, in our house in Glebe Place, Chelsea, explaining to me that, if we were honest, we had to admit that dictatorship was superior to democracy as more efficient. I was not favourably impressed.

The Great Depression encouraged this "activist" mood and caused a revolutionary, if temporary, change in Socialist thinking in Britain. Marx, until this date a figure almost as obscure to the British worker as he had been sixty years earlier, suddenly became quite the academic fashion as well as with "active party workers". The old gradualist formulae did not seem to meet the critical requirements. The Webbs, patriarch and matriarch of the Fabians, the Methuselah arch-Fabians, had produced a book on Social Research which adopted the sound view that it was scientifically dishonest to beg a question before the research had been done. They were acidly dismissed as *passés*, in a *New Statesman* review.

The comment was current that these old people were now

sterile and withered fruit, due to fall from their vine. Suddenly, flattered by the Russians and after much research, chiefly in blue books (by Beatrice not least from a bed in a Soviet hospital), like Moses and Miriam they produced their new version, *Soviet Communism: A New Civilisation?* Later, after the highest consultations in Sinai, they removed the question mark. Old Fabian opposition to revolutionary Marxism, and belief in "the facts" and in evolutionary progress, slow but sure, the characteristic doctrine of English and even Scottish socialism, became *démodé*. Mosley's decision at the time—when he still hoped for Aneurin Bevan's help—was disastrous, even privately for himself, but explicable in terms of the then current mood. But he might have moved either Left—as Strachey did—or Right. Later, in the light of events, his movement became publicly disreputable and a focus for bully-boys and flash followers. It was well perhaps for Cynthia Mosley, whom we all loved, that she died.

Mosley's movement in due course developed into full-blown Fascism, obsessed by commitment to "Action". Lord Rothermere's slogan, "Hats off to the Blackshirts", became an intolerable public stance—for which, it is stated, Rothermere was rebuked by the future Edward VIII. The Mosleyites moved on to rallies in the larger public halls, followed by violent clashes with the Communists—and with the police, whom the Communists, falsely but habitually, described as being "Fascist" themselves.

One of the greatest of the rallies was at Olympia, in 1934. I excerpt from a record, made by me at the time:—

The 7th of June, 1934. Yesterday the giant Union Jack flying from the tower of the Fascist headquarters in the King's Road, Chelsea—King Henry VIII's royal road to Hampton Court—was replaced by an even more gigantic black flag charged with the signs of the fasces and the thunderbolt. Today the greatest Fascist mass demonstration, hitherto, is to be held in the Exhibition Buildings at Olympia.

To Olympia, with an architect, Clough Williams-Ellis, my wife, Storm Jameson and an hereditary enemy of the House of Hapsburg, Countess Katherin Karolyi, who incidentally is a very beautiful woman. Long before we reach the great Exhibiton Buildings, the broad Hammersmith Road becomes congested with cars and taxis making for the entrances. The huge building looms up, like some greater railway terminus.

Amid the crush of people we present our tickets, push through the entrance and across the large, cement-paved passage ways that surround the building. Already we can hear the stir of the crowd and the blaring out, through loud speakers, of the Fascist anthem.

As my companion remarks, "This is the biggest bear-garden I have ever been in."

To me, it has other associations. The whole place, even though built of steel and glass, rather resembles some amphitheatre of ancient Rome. I half expect to find the games in progress; the animals loose in the arena; Caesar and the Roman mob, *populus Romanus*, applauding. The impression is if anything heightened when, at last, directed by black-shirted guides wearing their military ribbons, we enter the auditorium.

The great space, larger even than the Albert Hall where Mosley held his last meetings, has seats for fifteen thousand. It is full. Whether it is full with sympathisers or critics—and I can see, in whichever direction I look, the faces of Socialists I know well—it is an amazing demonstration. And Youth—there are lots of "Youth" in evidence. The Horst Wessel song roars out through loudspeakers—the music, but not the words. "*Es schaun aufs Hakenkreuz voll Hoffnung schon Millionen.*" A vague association takes sudden shape in my mind. Last time I heard that music, under like circumstances, was in the *Sportpalast*, in Berlin. Göring was speaking, on the eve of the 1933 poll.

The speaker of tonight is late in arriving, owing, it is stated, to the congestion outside. A newsboy goes around selling cricket news. At last the march of the British Union of Fascists is played. Flags are dipped. In slow procession the Leader, preceded by his banner-bearers and Blackshirts, comes up the length of the main aisle, ascends the carpeted stairs to the high dais, turns and salutes until the music concludes. His officers are ranged around him. Mussolini himself could not have staged the matter better. After an interval, during which the applause dies down, Oswald Mosley begins to speak. He is to be the only speaker.

The speech begins on lines that are familiar to anyone who studied Mosley in his Socialist days. I can almost see the typescript of the old speeches and memoranda with their marginal notes. Britain is in peril. In a machine age we have learned how to produce untold quantities of goods. But machine production neutralises the craft skill of the world's best craftsmen, the English workman. Economic nationalism closes—and it is impossible to put the clock back—the markets of the world to our goods. Our industrial policy has been founded on the supposition that the world market is ours for ever. The old gang of politicians, concerned only with the party game, do not confront the unpleasant facts or encourage the electorate to do so. What is required is to confront with courage the situation; to maintain and raise the standard of living by developing the home market; to turn out the old politicians. . . .

But before the speech has reached this stage, uproar is already loose. As the speech begins, there has been a protest from the stalls, on the middle right. Attendants converge to eject the interrupter. The interruptions come quicker and faster. There is no reasonable doubt that, in many cases, the interruptions are organised. It was so in the Women's Suffrage days. An interruption; a convergence; blows.

Women, with hands clapped over their mouths, frog-walked out. Men flung out. Free fights. Most of the audience standing. I find that I am standing, shouting, and somebody (very properly) tells me to keep quiet; they want to hear the speaker.

Mosley, during the interruptions, is silent, content to bear spectacular protest to the infringement of his right to free speech. "It is our Blackshirts who protect free speech in England." ("Does Hitler stand for free speech?" cries an interrupter.) A few words on India—and on peace. "No Englishman shall ever fight save in defence of these shores."

In the passageways outside, other scenes. Gerald Barry, sometime editor of the Conservative *Week-end Review*, the following day broadcasts what he saw. "Not in any case which I witnessed did the violence originate with the members of the audience. But the use of force did not end with the ejection of the interrupter from the auditorium. . . . I was curious to see what happened to these people when they disappeared from the arena, so on several occasions I followed the ejectors out. On one occasion I saw a man lying on the floor, obviously powerless and done for, being mercilessly kicked and horribly handled by a group of, certainly not fewer than eight, and more probably ten or twelve Blackshirts. On another occasion I saw a set of Blackshirts kicking and manhandling a miscreant in the stomach and all over the body more brutally than anything I have ever seen in my life, short of the war. It made me feel physically sick to see." Later Barry's report was embodied in a pamphlet, to which my wife also contributed.

Barry's evidence is corroborated by the sometime Dean of Canterbury. "A young man who had been ejected," the Very Reverend Dick Sheppard writes to the *Daily Telegraph*, "was showing signs of the way in which he had been handled. I was horrified at the monstrously cruel treatment to which he was now subjected by the Fascist in charge of him. He was bleeding on the face, and was gasping for breath. He was being chased down the corridors by a horde of Blackshirts. Some collared him by the legs, others by the arms, and held in this way he was beaten on the head by any Fascist who could get near him."

The violence used was unprecedented and unjustified. As

A. J. Cummings wrote in irony, "It was a noble English spectacle for an Englishman to watch." The interruption, as I have said, with the cries of "Does Hitler stand for free speech?" was in large part organised. It was not entirely so. One young man in whose veins flows the blood of a ducal family will be convalescing for several days to come, in the feudal mansion of one of the proudest families in England, after his injuries tonight. The protests in the press come from Conservative Members of Parliament, including the private secretary of the Lord President of the Council, Mr Baldwin.

Still the tireless figure standing after two hours, carrying the title role of the drama unrelieved, goes on speaking; denouncing the Labour and Coalition governments for a record of buffoonery and betrayal; asking for the spirit of 1914, of determination and sacrifice. Sir Herbert Samuel is "a difficult John Bull". Sir Samuel Hoare is "both silly and dangerous". A very able man, a new Sulla, is trying to justify his conduct both to himself and to his audience. He is relying upon the fact that a great country is on the stir, determined to play a less nerveless role than it has done for ten years.

In a little office in a mews, which saw the obscure beginnings of what is now the British Fascist movement, but which was then the office of Oswald Mosley, Socialist M.P., there used to hang on the wall two maps, one of Soviet Russia, one of the British Empire. Those things were a symbol. Significantly, the song of his men, the song they sing tonight in Olympia, runs:

"Proudly we mass for the struggle,
The Ranks of Reaction are swept before us!"

"Down with Mosley!" A voice from the sky. "Mosley is a millionaire." "Down with Mosley!" Knots of the audience standing. Fingers pointing, up into the dimness made darker by contrast with the glare of the spotlights on the speaker—up into the spaces under the glass roof, high as a railway station. Someone up there, calling, from among the steel rafters that span the great auditorium. Blackshirts start to scale the lattice of the steel pillars. "Down with Mosley."

Suddenly the great eyes of the searchlights, that remind one of the air defence in war-time, turn round and upwards, move uncertainly, then come to rest on the red-painted steel beams. At last one descries a man sitting up there with his megaphone, calling. If he loses his foothold, he is dead.

A few minutes and, from the edges, where the cross rafters join the supports of the immense glass roof, Blackshirts, four, five, six

begin to swarm along the beam towards him. Quickly one's memory
runs back to the comparable incident—in H. G. Wells' *The Sleeper
Awakes*, the flight in the dark across the roofs, through the snow,
over the great Babylon-City of the Future.

The stewards converge; a last call down; and then a hurried
struggle, legs astride, to reach the roof edge before the pursuers;
out through the glass roof itself. There must be some door. A few
minutes. A crash of glass. "There is no cause for alarm; this hall
is adequately protected by Blackshirts." The speaker's remark
sounds ironic. No more crashes. Perhaps the escape has been
made good.

The great audience streams out into the Hammersmith Road,
and into the congested streets. All are talking of the meeting.
Cars are getting away slowly through the crowd. Some Communists
are explaining how they got down three or four Blackshirts before
they were turned out; others how they had observed Blackshirts
using knuckle-dusters or seen the gashes made by razor blades.
The Blackshirts, on the other hand, had astutely paraded down the
central aisle of Olympia a tough looking fellow with handker-
chiefs, perhaps concealing knuckle-dusters, over his fists. The
technique of revolution—of making an "incident"—is becoming
a matter of form, these days.

I am talking to someone who has led the interruptions. "It may
be well," I say, "that the international press should report that
Mosley's big advertisement meeting was not an ovation; that it
did not go off without protest—but if this is repeated, public
opinion will swing round and say, 'Let us hear the fellow'." The
Fascists and Communists alike are getting ahead with what, for
them, is the good work of producing "a revolutionary situation".
Only one thing can make Mosley—and that one thing is the
Communists.

It is late at night, the same night, and outside Sir Oswald's
headquarters in the King's Road. The large stone and brick headquarters, with the barbed-wire entanglements on the walls, were
oddly enough once a theological college. Unexpected Gothic
crosses gleam in the lamplight. To many readers of the popular
press it is perhaps best known as the address given by a witness
in the case of Tony Mancini, alias Noytre, chief hero-villain of
Trunk Murder Case No. 2.

Two men are standing about, talking business of their own,
on the other side of the street opposite the entrance. A Blackshirt
steps across and tells them to move on. The man addressed says:
"I had intended to walk on in a minute, but now I'll be damned if
I do." The Blackshirt threatens him with the police and calls one.

"No, sir; he has no right to tell you to move on. Hi! you; move on yourself."

Outside Olympia, as the crowd moves out, the police stand motionless, shoulder to shoulder. They have scarcely entered the building that night. One of the queer principles of English liberty is that the police may not enter a hired hall, which is a private place, except on invitation of the chairman of the meeting or on evidence that a breach of the peace has been committed. My last sight as I walked away was a uniformed Blackshirt vigorously protesting, and a mounted policeman telling him to go—quickly.

In connection with this rally Dorothy Woodman, a close friend of Kingsley Martin, editor of the *New Statesman*, asked whether she could use our Glebe Place house as a centre for the distribution of anti-Mosley pamphlets. We agreed.

The strung-out processions, to and from Trafalgar Square, always a manifestation of democratic London life, with their banners, their slogans and bands, their red and black shirts, their youths—all too like the Komsomols and *Hitler-junge*—became more in evidence. They have their excuse in the apathy of the common citizen unless there are circuses—something to get adrenalin into the blood. Some of those who demonstrated were just out for fun. Some were engaged upon more serious operations, black or red, where knuckle-dusters and razor blades were to be discovered. One of the few good acts of John Simon, as Home Secretary, was to outlaw the wearing of all party or para-military uniforms (which would have included the Ku Klux Klan, if around and maybe the Orangemen). Democracy itself was under challenge.

After 1931 I saw Mosley personally only once again, when I attended a debate between him and the Socialist rising star, William Mellor, editor of the *Daily Herald*. He expressed regret that I did not speak. On one occasion I used his associates as a method, by introductions, of learning more about what was really happening in Germany. As a member of a crowd I did indeed view "the Leader", standing on a dray in Upper St Martin's Lane, in 1939 on the eve of war, when he was speaking to the slogan (not unheard elsewhere) "Mind Britain's Business"—keep out of the war. Years later I was to find that he and I were both involved in a documentary broadcast on the life of Franklin Roosevelt.

As the Hitler menace grew, the Blackshirts moved into heavy trouble. When they paraded into Hyde Park for a meeting, Sir John Gilmour, then Home Secretary, arranged for more police to escort the procession than there were marchers. When Mosley addressed his followers in Hyde Park, the police disconnected the microphone—"free speech but no mikes". One way of coping with demagogues, prison apart, is to rob them of glamour. Gilmour did that. Even "the red shirts", hissing in chorus songs about "the Muss-ssolinis and the Hitlers", came under the ban against political uniforms. I loathed the lot of them. Animal spirits are not the best servants of justice.

I had returned to England in the hope of conjoining political theory and action. It might seem, by hindsight, that I had obtained more experience than I had bargained for. At the time, however, the collapse of the I.L.P. was not yet; the B.U.F. had not yet emerged; and Mosley seemed simply to have moved over, be-friended by some of the *intelligentsia*, into yet another group of rebel Labourites, called the New Party. For myself I was far more gravely concerned in 1931 about the conduct of the Prime Minister, Ramsay MacDonald.

One afternoon I walked along to Party headquarters and, as a protest, I "came to the aid of my party" and put my name down as a possible Parliamentary candidate. For all this, I more or less forgot about my gesture—my wife assured me that I never even told her—and took her on a long-delayed holiday to St Raphael. (It was on a later occasion, I think, that we visited Bayonne and I went to look at the Watteau cartoons in its art gallery. I enquired my way from the elderly concierge, who disappeared into a cabinet and reappearing, waving a duster, indicated a toilet. I expostulated. "Mais, monsieur, vous avez demandez les 'waters'!")

In St Raphael I suddenly received a message from Winifred Holtby. The Brentford and Chiswick constituency party was much interested in my possible candidature, and had consulted her. Would I return to London immediately, for the early selection conference? My wife expressed no optimism whatsoever about the result of my dash to London. She thought I was quite mad to go. However, in haste I caught the night train from St Raphael; appeared, a day or two later, at the selection conference along with several others; spent half-an-hour in a back room sweating it out with them—Stafford Cripps, as would-be candidate, had had an even longer experience of waiting in Bristol—and, lo! found that I was "the Prospective Parliamentary Candidate" for John Wilkes' old Parliamentary division in Middlesex, where once, at the hustings, the streets had "run with blood".

My constituency chairman assured me that my style of speaking reminded him of Ramsay MacDonald's own—in the circum-stances a dubious compliment. A by-election owing to the probable bankruptcy of the Member, Colonel Grant-Morden, was expected, and this I had been promised; but, as it eventuated, the General

Election came. Harold Nicolson records that he also had thought of being a Parliamentary Candidate for this expected by-election. It was, he writes, "important" and would attract "national attention". Had he so decided, I should have been the Labour candidate and he perhaps the Conservative (or maybe New Party) candidate.

In the darkening autumn evenings we campaigned, Winifred Holtby and my wife, Vera Brittain, assisting, in and around the Brentford and Chiswick High Streets. My opponent, now departed from these shores to reside in Ochos Rios in Jamaica (where taxation is less), was a wealthy mine-owner with mining royalties behind him. Harold Mitchell was stung quite heavily for local party subsidies. Described in *Who's Who* as a "big-game hunter in Canada and India", he later became vice-chairman of the Conservative Party. He was an amiable man with a slight stutter. What, however, determines elections is mathematics (today revealed in opinion polls) and the party trend.

As for myself, perched on rickety steps, soap-boxes and like rostra on pavements, in the cold October evenings, I preached, with quotations from Arthur Greenwood, the values of constitutional democracy; the importance of welfare plans; the discrimination of the means tests, which broke up families; the error of unemployment relief being regarded as a charity and not as a right; the iniquity of regarding unemployment as a healthy medicine in the economy, to correct the patent consequences of the rash speculations of foreign or native speculators; and, in the style of William Jennings Bryan, on the sacrifice of British workers on "a cross of gold" to maintain the orthodox gold standard.

The last point was indeed not so ill-taken and was more than demagogic rhetoric. MacDonald, having sworn in July that the gold standard was essential to the credit of sterling, proceeded, when himself returned to power, to abandon it in September. Devaluation proved neither, on the one hand, a disaster nor, on the other, any final remedy. (I have since come to the conclusion that devaluation should not be party political but computer-automatic, according to the rise and fall of conjoint dividend and wage rate. There would be no gain in inflationary demand.) When the golden calf fell down no plagues followed, and even Winston Churchill had no success in restoring it to its pedestal. Credit had been hurt moreover by quite unnecessarily injurious alarmism—as it can be today. The crisis had been exacerbated by the (Sir G.) May Report, published in July, about the financial situation, a document ill-based and described by Maynard Keynes as "the most foolish document I have ever had the misfortune to read".

For the rest, for those who were to trek, unemployed, from a stricken County Durham—in Jarrow, 72.9 per cent were unemployed as late as September 1933—the vision of a mining-royalties owner, some of whose associates worked managerially and some of whom enjoyed wealth from royalties as the lilies of the field, was scarcely appealing. However, it is electoral mathematics, seldom personalities alone, which decide these things. I later attended Brentford police court when the unemployed Durham marchers arrived and some were arrested. When you are on "the dole", the Webbian doctrine of "the Inevitability of Gradualness" loses some of its appeal. However, suburban Chiswick was not Jarrow.

The area itself I recalled as one where I had spent most miserable weeks in early wartime, with my dear father, very ill, almost bankrupt and very, very bitterly poor. We had contrived to live on £112 a year between us. I found milk, bread rolls and rice an economic diet. It was a time when I was ashamed to meet a school-friend on a wet day on London Bridge because my shoes leaked. I sold my leather-bound school prizes—Plato's works in Greek —to repair them.

The tragic choice, which is with us to this day, between schools or hospitals and rearmament and maintained armament, had not yet to be feared. It was still the age of the Spirit of Locarno. My social philosophy was one that I had acquired in boyhood, and I was sceptical about all doctrinaires who held forth concerning political means. But I was sure that the common citizens who had volunteered or been called upon to fight the country's wars should not be left, the crisis over, to the tender mercies of *laissez-faire* (even according to Enoch Powell's later version) and to beg in the streets.

Although my assignment in the States had been with a grave social problem, so grave that in the end the United States Constitution was changed, my major political preoccupation was with conditions of peace and with international affairs—issues which scarcely arose in the 1931 Election, apart from the reiteration of homage to the League of Nations. In 1918 the war, Wilson's Fourteen Points and distrust of Lloyd George had decided my vote. In 1929 I had indeed been involved in technical economic issues, although it was precisely on the internationalist issue that, abjuring chauvinism, I had refused to secede from the Party. I was convinced that the pragmatic road to peace, my fighting concern, was by the integration of "the widest possible areas" of the globe. It was not Mosley's line.

Some profound and early social convictions, behind all the brouhaha, arose from the past to come into play in my campaign in Wilkes' constituency in 1931. Internationalist as to peace conditions, I yet believed profoundly in the national community—and in the national community as one, not two. I could not, with *The Times* in the days of the General Strike of 1926, readily identify "the community" with the possessors, "the establishment", "the top people". It was much too smug.

Vividly I recalled seeing, as a child, old soldiers, authentic veterans of the Boer Wars, selling matches in the gutters of the streets, soliciting the alms of passers-by. Increasingly I was outraged. These men, so praised at the time and despite A. E. Housman never called "mercenaries" then but "professional soldiers", were discarded as nobody's responsibility once they ceased to be useful to the economy, commerce and trade.

Every constituency has its own peculiarities. Brentford boasted a traditional Philanthropic Fund which gave away puddings and the like at Christmas. It was primarily administered by Conservative ladies and it was tacitly (and correctly) assumed that it enhanced the chances of a Tory vote. Nevertheless, as a municipal benevolence, the Labour candidate was solicited to subscribe. It must have been one of the few cases where (as the Marxists put it) the candidate "objectively" contributed to his opponent's funds. "Eatanswill" indeed lay in the past; but Brentford was still not far removed from the association of free beer and votes.

The candidate had to take prudent precautions lest over-enthusiastic supporters inveigled him into going around in a car for which the licence was out of date. One admirer was a retired middle-weight boxer, who insisted on accompanying me to out-of-door meetings. A rival light-weight boxer felt it incumbent on him to complete the bodyguard, and I did not like to offend them by refusing unwanted aid.

I made a habit, from the outset, of going straight on to the platform of my indoor public meetings. The supporting speaker soon desisted, and I flung off my overcoat and entered the ring to speak. "Desisting" did not indeed apply to Harold Laski in a supporting role or to one Commander Reginald Fletcher, ex-Liberal M.P. However, at least the electorate did not see as their candidate some grey-haired and donnish professor. It was good campaigning—but it was also fun if conducted with adequate panache.

At last came the day of the declaration of the poll. On the basis of the heavily adverse figures I did not seriously expect to win, nor did my admirable agent—although we little guessed how many heads of eminent Labour Cabinet Ministers were to roll in defeat that night. The declaration was late. I stood in an illuminated porch of the Chiswick Town Hall, London, looking over the fog around the elm trees of Turnham Green and, amid the fog, the crowd stretching away. The gowned Town Clerk, the recording officer, stepped forward amid uproar below to make the announcement: "And so I declare the said Harold Mitchell to be duly elected." I shook the victor's hand and he stepped forward to speak. The uproar was deafening and I was in the peculiar position of having to demand silence for my opponent.

It was over. Rather prematurely the Tory Agent commented to me that I was an able young man and would undoubtedly win if I went elsewhere, "since you can't hope to win here". In the Party offices, some of my dear and so hard-working, loyal "active party workers" wept. I made appropriate remarks. I then went home.

And, as always on such occasions of defeat, I started a new book, not one of my best, *Preface to Action*.[1] Like Walter Lippmann, in his *Public Philosophy*, I gravely tried to base political principles upon Natural Law, reason and fundamental instinct. I also tried to make the argument popular. I failed.

I had, at least, the mild satisfaction of learning that, apart from seats earlier held by Labour, we had got the best Labour voting result in Middlesex. I was clear in my own mind that I would fight again.

[1] Allen and Unwin, London; Macmillan, New York (1934).

VI

H. G. WELLS AND "THE REALIST"

I HAVE already mentioned that, fresh from directing a national investigation in the United States into the operation of one clause of the American Constitution, I came back to the United Kingdom with the idea glowing in my mind of a quadruple operation. There was to be a national advisory research body, especially economic and sociological. Although, until thirty years later, it was a weakly growth, thanks to Ramsay MacDonald's action it was actually established. I had also wanted to see an efficient, and not merely superficial, party research bureau, more official than the Fabian Society. I have already described the strange consequences of my pursuit of these particular benefits to party and country. As the American Ambassador, David Bruce, was to say many years later, I "sparked off ideas like the sparks from an emery wheel". Perhaps there were too many, and sparks alone are unharnessed energy, achieving nothing.

In a four-pronged plan, the third proposal was to establish an institution like the Social Science Research Council of America, with which I had worked in its very early days, which should be an organ neither of the State nor of the Party but would enjoy all the prestige of entire academic detachment in social investigations. On the advice of Sir Percy Alden, I raised money from the Halley Stewart Trust which enabled a committee to be set up with a paid secretary, Alexander Farquharson, of Le Play House. This was in 1930. With William Beveridge (Lord Beveridge) as chairman, Josiah Stamp (Lord Stamp), A. C. Pigou, Graham Wallas and others on the committee, it was a body of some weight. So far as I am aware, the only person around today who has read our Report (because he once worked with Beveridge) is, according to his statement to me, the recent Prime Minister, Harold Wilson.

The conclusion of Farquharson's Report was that something similar to the American S.S.R.C. should in fact be set up, although, as to its governing body, there was the difficulty that, at that time, the various disciplines often had no professional organisation which could appoint academic representatives on to the council. This immaturity was later corrected but, at that time, both political scientists and sociologists were still unorganised. Our ultimate misfortune was that Lord Stamp had the prejudice that only the economists were really "scientists".

It happened that the policy of the Rockefeller Foundation at that time was all in favour of a multi-disciplinary approach. Nevertheless, Lord Stamp succeeded in persuading them, as a fruit of our investigation (and without mentioning the matter to me), to endow a National Institute of Economic Research (to which the words "and Social" were later added), in due course to be headed by Professor Noel Hall, now, as Sir Noel Hall, President of Brasenose College, Oxford. I was left contemplating the rump of my project with the economic studies excised. I discussed the matter with John Buchan; but it soon became clear to me that scientific sociological research and social investigation into welfare and benefits meant the same thing to him.

I revivified the proposal during the Second World War, with the helpful collaboration of my good friend, American-born Professor Philip Sargant Florence, of Birmingham. Sir Alexander Carr Saunders, Sir Richard Gregory and Morris Ginsberg were members of the new committee which, in 1943, met in Burlington House on several occasions. I was encouraged by the good wishes of the Royal Society and of the British Academy, expressed to me by their Secretaries. The committee was that quite unusual thing, a special committee of the British Association, and a report was published by the Association. However, it was held, finally, that the British academic world did not wish to have research "Americanised" in Britain; that our fine tradition was that of the quite individual and even solitary research worker; and that every other problem could be adequately met by the Vice-Chancellors' Conference. "New problems are not easily solved in the first instance", as Professor Hugh Trevor-Roper has remarked, "by old societies." The scrutiny of research priorities and their impartial co-ordination; the canalisation of funds into the most important projects; the overall survey of needed research; the improvement of the status of the social sciences, such as the Royal Society now gives (it used to have a far broader membership) to the natural sciences—all this could be passed by, its importance overlooked.

In 1965 I presented a statement, chiefly for the historical record, to the new Heyworth Commission on the subject. At this time of writing, forty years on, the Council has been reconstituted. The task requires, and has perchance found, an administrator of genius, appropriately salaried. My information is that at one early stage the Council was more preoccupied with minutiae of scholarship awards than with the academic strategy of putting the social sciences on to the national map, precisely as the Institute of Physics is concerned to do for the physical sciences, and with vindicating the importance of their results. This is how England is renovated. It is not remarkable that she lingers in the technical race. The race itself imperatively requires a sense of proportion in research investments.

I entertained no doubt that the work of the political theorist and the technical studies of the social and political scientist were not only as important as, but more important to mankind than, those of the physical scientist. He is much or more entitled to recognition and renown. Perhaps comparisons of "importance" are irrelevant but not entirely. It is political studies Plato held to be "architectonic". Much of the demand for the physicist and engineer is either, fundamentally, a military demand for newly devilish instruments of war "and defence", or to increase production by an over-swollen human population which that population, to sustain the affluent production, might then be pressurised into buying. The labouring, troll-like "boffins" produce for profit, all in a day's work, the toys of science: "sonic bangs"; aerial buses for many hundred passengers which will fly at supersonic speed and crash; "unsafety" belts which tie air passengers into a burning plane; insecticides which will poison the birds; "warfare germs" that will indiscriminately kill off men. As I told Robert Oppenheimer (who did not like it), at the Reichenbach Conference of the Organisation for Cultural Freedom: "The physicist as such has no more qualifications for judgement in political and social matters than any other lay citizen" (except so far as he might hold, with Einstein, his own inventions to be in danger of being perverted). Lord Attlee later commented that, in his experience, the physical scientists, Cherwell-types, had *less* judgement than the common voter. The physicist provides men with power over nature. It is for the political theorist to consider and advise the public about the best social order in which to use that power without disaster.

In 1971—forty years on—our daughter Shirley Williams, recently Minister of State for Education and Science, in a much praised article in the Saturday Supplement to the London *Times* (27th Feb.), developed the theme of the importance of this research in the physical and social sciences, which spells in the latter case the professional training of research workers.

My fourth proposal was of a more popular character. I had been impressed by the high quality of the articles published in America in *Harper's Magazine*, (to which I had contributed), *The Atlantic Monthly*, *The Forum* and the bright *American Mercury*, which escaped from the Victorian stuffiness of such magazines as the *Fortnightly*, to which I also contributed but which were, I suspect, chiefly read in dentists' ante-rooms. These latter had a magnificent history but no adequate bulk of readers. This remark also applied to the politically minded *Contemporary*, then edited by my much revered friend, Dr G. P. Gooch, but now under the keen editorship of Rosalind Wade. At one time I expressed interest in buying up the *Fortnightly*, perhaps backed by Foyles, but in fact it was privately sold to its printers and later ceased independent publication.

My enthusiastic hope was to see a British magazine which would make the common citizen of some intelligence and curiosity aware of, and alive to, those issues of human importance with which the social, medical and physical scientists—in this pragmatic sense members of one culture—were concerning themselves. I wanted to have this said in a language not so much "popular" as intelligible to the layman. Even the world of letters and the world of politics were not to be divorced. The Soviets today are right, with Plato, in recognising that they cannot be divorced; wrong in their "gun-shot" marriages.

Stephen Spender, sometime co-editor of *Encounter*, once remarked to me at a P.E.N. meeting that no editor should direct himself to any particular audience. I thought it a foolish statement. We should, I held, give our contributors full freedom of opinion; but we should yet choose them because they could state a theme of interest to the particular audience. I had the bank clerk (the man who had made Hogben's *Mathematics for the Million* a big seller at a time when publishers were sceptical), the trades union official, the small professional man as our target. Their interest would connect research at the heights with the life of the country. And, in this scientific enterprise, men of letters and humanistic culture could collaborate.

In 1928—I was thirty-two at the time—I discussed the project with Archibald Church, M.P., assistant editor of *Nature*, a Parliamentary Private Secretary to Sidney Webb who was later to hold a like post in the 1929 Government, and a business collaborator with Baird and Jarrard in the very early days of television. (On their yacht off Fire Island, New York, I saw a great deal of Jerry Jarrard and his attractive wife who, in her early days, had been a friend of Wilfred Hyde White. There was an occasion when, being invited by a clergyman to meet him at the Athenaeum and then proceed to lunch, she invaded the sacred portals, dashed up the grand stairs to greet her host—at which point she lost a garter . . . *Honi soit.*) Church told me that Julian Huxley had had a very similar idea and, further, that he was sure that Sir Richard Gregory, the editor of *Nature*, would be much interested. He was. The problem was to find a publisher—and here we were fortunate in getting the help of Macmillans—and a financial backer.

The first Lord Melchett, sometime Sir Alfred Mond, was something of a rough diamond. It is alleged that, in a speech in the Lords, having run out of notes more speedily than he had intended, he concluded with the words: "And vot is more, there is money in it." The report ran that Clemenceau had declared with a shrug: "Je connais le monde et je connais le demi-monde mais je ne connais pas un monde comme ce Mond." A member of the great firm of Brunner, Mond, later incorporated as Imperial Chemical Industries, he was both very wealthy and certainly not lacking in enterprise or a desire for public service.

We approached him and he was interested enough to provide the necessary, if quite modest, subsidy. He chose, moreover, to appoint his own private secretary, Conway Davies, a minor poet on the side, as chairman of the business board, along with Professor Dunham, connected with I.C.I., Alexander Carr Saunders, Julian Huxley, Church and myself as co-directors. We were even so high-minded as (very foolishly) to decide initially that we would need no advertisements. Church was to be general editor and Huxley, for some obscure reason, wished a newly noticed writer Gerald Heard, somewhat *tief* and (in the pejorative sense) mystic—withal a very pleasant fellow and a friend of Dick and Naomi Mitchison and of Aldous Huxley—to be literary editor.

The crux of the matter, however, was to gather together a strong editorial board. Here indeed we showed what I shall venture to claim as remarkable enterprise. We assembled a group which would be a veritable galaxy of talent in any epoch. In the end our editorial board, apart from the directors, consisted of Arnold Bennett, H. G. Wells, Julian's brother Aldous, Harold Laski, J. B. S. Haldane, "Bruno" Malinowski, Richard Gregory, Eileen Power, Rebecca West, Herbert Read as an art critic, J. W. R. Sullivan as a music critic, Milne Bailey as a trades union authority, the Metropolitan magistrate J. A. R. Cairns, Naomi Mitchison, Sir Percy Nunn, the educationalist, and two or three others. Five at least were later placed, by the editors of the *Sunday Times Supplement*, new archangels, salaried by Lord Thomson and (in lieu of God) come to judgement, on the Calendar of the Immortals and in the dubious company of the so-called "Makers of the Twentieth Century"—along with Alistair Crowley and some eminent criminals.

Arnold Bennett led off in April, 1929, with an article on "The Progress of the Novel". I contributed a lead article in the May issue on "The Next Step for Democracy", followed by one on Julian Benda by Herbert Read. Aldous Huxley had two on Pascal

and, in this second issue, there was one on the finances of broadcasting. "Is Science Credible?" was the title of an article by
Herman Levy. Julian Huxley, R. G. Collingswood and Winifred
Holtby all contributed to the first issue; and there was an article
on "Has Labour to Fear Science?" We paid a flat rate of £20 to
all contributors, well-known or less well-known—which was an
exceedingly good rate in those days.

The Realist was decided upon as the title for the magazine.
Contact was suggested; but Naomi Mitchison, in her Freudian
way, objected that this might cause embarrassment to girls behind
book-stall counters. We got an excellent send-off from the Press;
and to this day I come across people in remoter parts of India or
Canada who treasure copies of the magazine.

Other names were discussed for the Board—those of Lord
Russell and, I believe, of Cyril Joad, who did not receive many
suffrages, although he became a contributor. J. B. Priestley
should certainly have been invited. His name was, in the particular
milieu, more obvious than that of T. S. Eliot who was mentioned.
Eliot had his own outlet in Criterion and we did not desire to
overweight the literary side.

Some years later T. S. Eliot was my guest at our Cheyne Walk
house and I became greatly indebted to him for his rather unexpected advice. (I recall reading the words of a review, in The
Sunday Times, of Eliot's After Strange Gods: "He is one of about
ten people writing in England today who are worth reading."
I wondered who might be the other nine. Then, as I meditated,
there was a tinkling of memory. I went upstairs; pulled out the
review copy—and found that I had written the words myself. Nor
was I so far wrong.) His advice had to do with an early draft of this
present autobiography. At that time my chief obstacle in writing a
straightforward autobiography was that it seemed to me to be a
style of writing which was almost inevitably egotistic. Indeed, at a
large lunch Rose Macaulay, sitting next to me, had ventured to
comment, dismissing St Augustine and Rousseau, that autobiographies were "always vulgar". I could not help but note that
this was intended as a hit at my wife's Testament of Youth, then
just published, and I thought the remark was extremely bad
manners. By irony it was Rose Macaulay's misfortune to have her
own very confidential letters published posthumously.

At this earlier time, I had thought to avoid all this by basing
myself on Montaigne's maxim that there is something of all men
in every man; by concerning myself with the lasting concerns of
the condition humaine; by using myself as a mere Quixote or
Faust-like illustration or symbol—the scholar concerned with the

magic of power and its transcendence, tempted by the Average Adjuster, who showed to him the kingdoms of wordly success. As full of allusions and symbols as Eliot's own work, the result would have to be judged by the high standards of literature. It was Eliot who (as it then seemed to me, paradoxically) advised me to write straight autobiography, egotism or not; and this advice I took, when at long last I had a sudden inspiration about treatment and climax. The immediate result was to lead me to put the script in a bottom drawer for twenty years. Incidentally, Eliot's views on the intolerable vulgarity of the waste land of our days were much my own. He became an unmerited target for "per-missivist" abuse. He detested anarchism. So do I.

Arnold Bennett, we are told—and it is worth mentioning—interviewed Kingsley Martin with a view to Martin's appointment to the editorial chair of the *New Statesman*, where he attained a great mundane success by turning it from Clifford Sharp's small affair—the interim acting editor C. M. Lloyd, I knew quite well and counted as a personal friend—into a prosperous com-mercial venture. Assuredly Martin was far too shrewd to be just the "flibberty-gibbet" he was adjudged, according to his own modest statement, in the austere eyes of the Webbs. If he could be accused of being a pacifist on Mondays, Wednesdays and Fridays and a Marxist on Tuesdays, Thursdays and Saturdays, this Hamlet quality had definite editorial advantages. It widened his public. Nor have many very able men possessed any more coherence of judgement, granted their cursed fate—however Trotsky might sneer—to live in such times as they did.

The high standard of *New Statesman* articles, the eminent literary reviews, but (perhaps above all) the exploitation of a certain universal factor in human nature explained Martin's journalistic achievement. This universal factor, like sex, curiosity about cruelty and crime, and vanity, is—as Marx knew so well—a general human characteristic, more virulent because usually dissembled, which I choose to call "left-handedness" or, for those who prefer mechanical analogies, psychologically the screw-spiral that goes in reverse. It is not "anti-Establishment" for any rational or logical reason but, as Alfred Adler implied, for reasons biological and almost of the genes. It inspires revolutionaries in search of a revolution (which will make them feel good). More simply, the instinctive driving appeal was that of identification with resentment, assiduous, acidulous. As Martin himself tells us, he suffered from "a flaming inferiority complex"—that was "the way his head was screwed on"—although it is difficult to attack a man who so frankly, in his autobiography, buffets his own qualities.

His feeling that his admiration for his father (whom he describes delightfully and movingly) was some kind of drawback—that one ought to "cut the umbilical cord" by quarrelling with one's parents —I admit seems to me to be psychological and neurotic foolery. If he believed it, then one can only say that he is not the only man today corrupted by brash psychologists. The man who indeed suffers from "the flaming inferiority complex" should rather seek a physician or a psychoanalyst's couch than be let loose upon an innocent public. In the severe words of the great Professor Conrad Lorenz on this precise subject: "I would recommend suicide at his earliest convenience."

There has always seemed to me to be a marked similarity between the "K.M." of Britain, Kingsley Martin, and his friend, Krishna Menon, the "K.M. of India", who has something of the same characteristics. Both have burned with too often misplaced resentment. It was perhaps precisely because of this complex and insecurity that Martin would betimes fail to recognise one's existence, even if seen by him at no great distance, were one masochist enough to tolerate such exhibitionist arrogance. To an old acquaintance in the welfare field he observed: "I did not introduce you because I could not recall your name." It was the defensive "snub calculated".

I recall that one Liberal hostess, anxious to please her distinguished guest, Clement Attlee, is reported to have placed by his bedside a copy of the *New Statesman*. The following morning she got only the gruff comment: "Never read it." I would add that recently, under a later editor, Paul Johnson, the *New Statesman* seems to me to have taken a marked turn towards stability and to be less characterised by what Peter Shore has called "hysteria" and Clement Attlee the characteristics of "an undergraduate newspaper". Perhaps the chosen organ of disgruntlement, its responsible judgements yet merit attention, and its literary reviews have become indispensable. (It has to be added that occasionally, without ceasing to be the Grouchers' Gazette, it reads like a more inhibited edition of *Playboy*.) Under the firm hand of Dick Crossman, a man of outstanding ability, this change to responsibility is likely to become yet more pronounced.

As Priestley records, whether or not it was "all *mihi* and Kingsley Martin", "K.M." got sadistic and jocose pleasure at any social gathering, between the salad and the luncheon coffee, in depicting all civilisation as going up in flames. The habit led to the unkind, and on the whole unjust, remark that "he hurried to hire a crown of thorns at Moss Bros.". A certain schizophrenia or mental ambiguity actually helped him (as I have suggested) as an editor, to have it both ways.

However, his strong attack on the monstrous experiments in biological and chemical warfare alleged to take place at Porton commands my unstinted admiration. It seems to me essential at times for the political scientist to condemn the activities of certain physical scientists as traitorous to their own vocation.

But I cannot recall that Arnold Bennett, Martin's patron, ever put forward his name to us, and on reflection I wonder why he did not. Perhaps he was thought too young and unproved. Perhaps the board felt like Harold Laski, who could do a work of demolition even at the expense of his most enthusiastic admirers and who remarked to me: "Kingsley Martin is the luckiest man in Britain today: he has only just been sacked from the *Manchester Guardian* and has now been made the editor of the *New Statesman*." Laski likewise treated Bertrand Russell, a greater man than himself, as not only embarrassed by shortage of funds but (most mistakenly) as a lightweight. Jealousy of his near equals was, with Harold, a major characteristic. He disliked having other lights burning too brightly near his altar.

Arnold Bennett was, in those days, the Lord Grand Panjandrum of letters, the boss-cat reviewer, pontificating from the top of the column in the *Evening Standard* and deciding for his countrymen what was good and what was bad; making and breaking, almost like the BBC in later days. He once commented to me, in the 1917 Club in Gerrard Street, about a most distinguished, still living, writer: "The trouble with —— is that —— c-c-can't wr-write." Just as my wife had a complex about provincial middle-class towns, so Bennett, in his drab, flat way, liberated old ladies from the Potteries and Five Towns and sent them to enjoy the culture and cuisine of Paris; to hear the thundering wheels of the Grands Exprès Européens bound for Vienna, if not Stamboul; and to catch a glimpse of the Ritz-Savoy hotels, complete with gilt and plush. He had a certain vulgarity in values—the age of Madison Avenue was on its way—defensively covered by the bright journalist's "cockeyness" and by the provincial *arriviste's* desire "to show 'em how". It was not unexpected that Virginia Woolf should display aversion to his work as "superficial"—an aversion reciprocated. Indeed his discovery as a writer of stature was first due to American reviewers, and it was his misfortune that his last big work, *Imperial Hotel*, (the Savoy Hotel being his laboratory) was rather deflated by Vicki Baum's *Grand Hotel*.

Imperial Hotel was, as a theme, very much Bennett's cup of tea. So was *Lord Raingo*, a study of Thomas, first Viscount Rhondda, the kind of "self-made man" ("Sir, you relieve the Almighty of a great responsibility") he fully understood. But his reputation stands on *Clayhanger*, *Riceyman Steps* and *The Old Wives' Tale*. Here he is the "Man from the North", from Mr Enoch Powell's Staffordshire; the philosopher-emancipator from its puritanism and its grime; kindly to the frustrated, be it provincial reader or struggling young author; progressive; even privately diffident. "Emancipation for what?" To become a member of the Beaver-brook-*New Statesman* set, well-publicised mixture of the brash and the sour?

Bennett was to become the metropolitan "card", with his quiff, pleated shirts and private yacht; the "Success". It is Malcolm Muggeridge, a "sour", who writes: "It was brass he wanted from the beginning; brass he got; and brass he became." Here he was precursor of a yet more vulgar age to come, in which excellence was to be acclaimed in terms, not aristocratic, but of cash. But he was also the member of the board of the anti-capitalist *New Statesman*, the patron of Kingsley Martin. He tried for the best of both worlds and seemed to both worlds to have got it. The author of well-paying little books on "How to Achieve Success", his sad death-bed words to his common-law wife were "It's all gone wrong, my girl." Some indeed of the grit and grime of the Potteries remained. An unhappy man, the business man in letters adding up his accounts, he was more vulgar than Wells, for I doubt if Wells would have been guilty of the calculating cynicism: "Posterity wants too much and will pay nowt for it." However, Bennett in the good sense was supremely the master of *haute vulgarisation*, the communicator. Also, unlike the Marshall McLuhan school, he did not write pretentious jargon. It would have been fascinating to read a review by Bennett on McLuhan. Because he could so communicate, Bennett was needed by *The Realist*. It was a pity that he died too soon to make more than one contribution in print.

It was entirely in keeping that, on Bennett's suggestion, *The Realist* group held its inaugural dinner in the Hotel Splendide (since disappeared) in Piccadilly when Bennett, cockatoo-quiff nodding, gave us our send-off and our instructions about what to do and think. Later we moved to Jules in Jermyn Street and, afterwards, to Kettner's Restaurant where Jack Haldane, later of the Communist *Daily Worker*, told us that the food was better.

Owing to Bennett's early death from typhoid, as a result of a typical confidence in things French (including the tap-water), H. G. Wells became the dean of the group. If we did not get anything from his pen, it was thanks to characteristic querulousness. He undertook to write an article on the economic future of the country, if Melchett would reply to it. Melchett, who was anyhow finding the money, showed no inclination to pledge himself to reply to the indictment; and a dangerous quarrel started to open up. I had many opportunities of meeting and talking with "H.G.", at the "brains-trust" Club in Gerrard Street, of which Leonard Woolf was a founder member; at the Athenaeum; and in his apartment in Chiltern Court, where, one New Year's Eve, he, ourselves, Malinowski, Lancelot Hogben and others met together. I was able to test my memory against his, since he swore, with no little petulance, that he had never referred to Harold Laski in any of his novels. His secretary and his *maîtresse en titre* of the moment said the same. I affirmed the contrary; I won. However, the best occasions were at *The Realist* dinners themselves.

We had agreed on the quite excellent and Hellenic scheme of meeting monthly for a veritable symposium ("a drinking together") or dinner, to discuss plans for the next issue. I commend the procedure for all future "magazines of ideas"! We got to know each other well. Sometimes the discussions were grave, if brilliant, sometimes were not so grave. I recall one occasion, in the upper room at Kettner's, when Wells entered with J. B. S. Haldane's arm around his waist, in a charade of Anthony and Cleopatra—Jack, proud of his descent from the earl or Jarl, Halfdan the Black, a very Vikingesque Anthony; H.G. a somewhat pregnant Cleopatra. It was the only occasion I remember when Harold Laski (in the midst of one of his usual tall stories of what King George V said to him and he said to George V—"Let me see, Mr Laski: what university are you at—Oxford?") was put off his stride. The counter-attraction was too great. Laski, a mighty name-dropper, turned off to discuss how he had found Henry James to be the great bore of Rye.

Wells desired to be a Diderot. When, in those later days, he was not preoccupied with his encyclopaedia of history, science, work and welfare, his mind was occupied with his Open Conspiracy—what today would be some eclectic revolutionary society of intellectuals for Open Communication.

True "world citizen", *Weltbürger*—and here lay one of his prime claims to eminence—he was preoccupied with reflection upon who were the right men with the technical capacity to set up a World Authority. Having quarrelled with the Fabians, he decided it would not be they. The politicians were in no better case. Business men, *samurai*, Rothschilds, new Machiavellians, technocrats, who? He irritated men such as Shaw—who maybe looked back to "Good King Charles" but also had some very dangerous contemporary ideas of a very practical order—because of this cocky confidence, which his enemies called vulgarity or

insensitivity. He was even more incapable of understanding a
Newman than the worthy evangelical Philistine, Charles Kingsley. He was a "sitting duck" for the satire of little Beerbohm,
"the divine Max", in *A Christmas Garland*. Tens of thousands
gasped over *Ann Veronica* and were grateful. Wells sincerely
sought, and more honour to him, to be the Man who Made Tomorrow—although thanks to petulant conceit and a certain, not vulgar
but commonplace provinciality, he failed in the eternal qualities.

Wells had an immense following—wider than Arnold Bennett's
but for the same reason. He was often a flat writer, but with less
grime and more sunlight than Bennett. Their common virtue was
to take people whose lives—more lower middle-class than
"manual worker", as with D. H. Lawrence—had been trapped by
petty social fears and very real hardships; and to show them vistas
of health, happiness and strength through joy a bit better than
Morris-dancing on the green. Fantasy, of the civic kind that
inspired Herbert Morrison's happy Festival of Britain, and the
lights that still hang on the London Embankment and Lansbury's
Lido, was balanced by a solid, respect-worthy honesty—even at
times when his social anti-flunkeyism was being shared by that
other anti-hero, his friend Beaverbrook, and had become a pose.
As Malcolm Muggeridge has said: "No one is more fanatical a
snob than the anti-snob." However, Wells, like Bennett, was a
"literary tycoon", who saw to it that he moved in good, or at least
wealthy, society.

Wells claimed to be a journalist, a man of the *journée*, writing
for and of the day. In this special sense he was a *novelist*, writing
of novel horizons. In the phrase of Michael Foot he regarded
earth as a "footstool" (or Tower of Babel), from which man
stretched his arms—and this was felt to include Wells' readers—
up to heaven. Despite his own occasional modesty, his remark to
Maugham about his books, "dead as mutton", was a false modesty.

He was angered by the popular demand that he, the seer,
should "write another *Mr Polly*", although he compromised with
The World of William Clissold. Unfortunately the folk who gathered
to the standard of the open conspiracy, a few high-minded
"progressives" or "personalists" apart, were bearded and "permissive" young men and their mates, nudists and others whom
Cyril Joad, the *ur-mutter* of all permissivists, was able to
manage better, by taking them on rambles to drink beer and reshape
the brave new world's future with the aid of contraceptives.
Cyril Joad, the rambler and nature-lover, the awful example
to the present decade of what comes of the man determined
to be "a trendy", was once reported as being seen with

knapsack on back and complete with new beard, "travelling fast in a taxi across Hampstead Heath".

On the campus of Washington State University, Pulman, Wash., there is a statue called "The Nature Boy". It would have pleased both Wells and Joad. Wells' film, *The Shape of Things to Come*, with Sir Cedric Hardwicke in the leading role, was not a success—although it says something for it that I can still recall parts of it. One was left too much with the impression that the Light of the World belonged to "boffins" in slacks or "Oxford flannel bags", God Almighty being really a superior boffin. Incidentally, the word "boffin" is used to reassure the inferior-feeling "common man" that the scientist is not a superior fellow but just as common-place in his tastes as he is.

As a vice-president, I regret that the H. G. Wells Society was not even competent to arrange for a bust in his honour at the Imperial College on the occasion of Wells' centenary. It discussed "power" and lacked money. It did inaugurate a plaque on Wells' Hanover Terrace house and put together a fine bibliography. Even the Wells Memorial project, under Beveridge, came to nothing, like the Shaw memorial, partly from lack of family enthusiasm and partly from disregard for the tax rules which condition the charitable donations of wealthy men and bodies. If we had appealed for Wells in the context of a dog-home, we should have done excellently. Tax-wise business men of wealth insist on a "charity".

Wells was often unlucky in these chance ways. On the celebration of his seventieth birthday at the Savoy Hotel, which should have been an occasion of *bonhomie*, those responsible were led by an evil genius to ask Bernard Shaw to respond. At various tables sat members of Wells' family, both legitimate and natural. "My old friend H.G.," said Shaw, "has always been noted as a devoted son" (pause), "a devoted father" (pause), "a devoted" (long pause) "friend—and, altogether, a very fine fellow." There was belly-mirth over Shaw's wit, but the moment was not happy. To use the fashionable language of that day, it was a little "shame-making". Shaw had an inhumane streak. He was good indeed for Wells, as a gadfly that saved H.G. from confusing himself with divinity; but the gadfly could sting too often. Nevertheless, a note of real tenderness, of nostalgia for things hoped for, was struck by Wells himself. "And then Dame Nature comes and says, 'Well, Master Herbert, pack up; the time has come to put away your toys.' " Poor Wells, he had outlived his fashion but, although not a great man, he was a rather greater man than the times, even yet, allow for.

Wells had a profuse mind, but not always a consistent one. I well recall one talk at the Athenaeum Club when, before lunch, he expounded the theme that the supreme virtue of a civilised man was tolerance. After lunch, the talk having turned to denominational schools, he promptly asserted that "Superstition has got to be suppressed." What he really meant was that others who disagreed with him had better learn tolerance—and quickly. For natural science, most amoral of the idols of our age, he had an unrestrained and Victorian veneration until near the end. By definition, knowledge is good. The trouble lies with its application, and as we increase the diameter of our knowledge we increase the circumference of our ignorance.

The winning side in his character was a fundamental, optimistic belief in reason and a hatred of tyranny (not least Stalinist). His weakness was an impatience—not merely with the other members of the Establishment as represented in the Athenaeum— but temperamental, which in the end, with the coming of war, plunged him into the angry pessimism of *Mind at the End of its Tether*. The Royal Society, of which he deeply longed to be a member, kept him out because those sedate elders felt that he was "too much in touch with the press" and, hence, not "an insider". It was his misfortune that, like Herbert Spencer, so many of the novel things that he said had become so far accepted commonplaces by the end of his life that his public had come to wonder, being themselves Wells' children, why anybody should be impressed by papa. An anti-Edwardian, he was limited by being also an Edwardian.

Despite its faults, perhaps the most significant of Wells' books and the nearest to his heart, as the new Diderot, was *The Outline of History*. It was such because, despite all its early optimism about revolutionary change, it affirmed, as a central thread, the value of the study of history as such; the continuity of civilization; what, in my *History of the Political Philosophers*, I have called "the grand tradition"—on which, incidentally (and ironically for Wells), all the great religions of the world rest their orthodoxy. It was and is an affirmation which confutes the contemporary neophilia for change, any change; for a Heraclitan fire of destruction; for "a burning of the books"; and for an anti-culture where "Chaos is king". There is indeed, not only cultural modification, but technological change in the social infrastructure. But the change, as such, carries no guarantee of progress as human benefit. Above all, Wells never fell for the sick, anarchist, Sartrean irrationalism that "reason is a tyrant".

Wells' personal life, recorded in his readable autobiography, was unconventional in a middle-class way. I always recall his telling me with glee how one of his mistresses, Odette Keun, had really learned her English in the port of Marseilles. The Grenfells of Labrador, heroic missionaries of the Great Arctic North, were visiting and the talk chanced to turn on Casanova. "What", inquired Sir Wilfred Grenfell, "did Casanova do?" Madame Odette explained in simple Anglo-Saxon. There was a silence. "Ah! well", replied Lady Grenfell "we don't know much about literature." For all of this, when myself being entertained in Grasse by the remarkably attired and turbaned Odette (who by then was engaged in a vituperative quarrel with H.G.), I found it sad to see inscribed on the fireplace of their house—alack! in stone, *et verba scripta manent*—the words, "This House was built by two Lovers."

Until nearly the end, and the Second World War, Wells had a sure and certain hope of predestined human progress. God Himself was retained by him as a kind of Super-Wells—Wells saw only "humanism", not a philosophic impertinence, in the suggestion—the Deity aware that all was not in nature quite as it should be, but sweating along, as a "force", with H.G. and the other good companions.

I must not call this a pantheist (or "enpasitheist") "Life-Force", since this was the despised, emotional and "intuitive" thesis of his "unscientific" rival Shaw and of *his* rather inferior mentor, Samuel Butler. "Wells's God", with whom occasionally he carried on, in his role of world-prophet, a theological flirtation, was rather a Progressive and Aspirant Rationality, immanent in the better sort of men but visualised (as "H.G." himself blandly explains) as a kind of Personal Incarnation of the Soviet Five-Year Plan. In brief, not dissimilar from Herbert George Wells, the onlie-begetter of the Open Conspiracy and consubstantial with its paternal Creator. A kind of Fate, in the form of "the ruthless impartiality of Nature" (which threatened man's damnation), kept Him in check and produced a Manichee dualism (no better theology than that of the original Manichees). Wells was a fanatical believer in "Education" (an interesting Victorian touch here) and "Enlightenment", which were somehow to hold the ferocities of disinterested Nature in check. Whether Wells ever asked himself what precisely he meant by Education, beyond the worship of Facts and more Facts, I doubt. He had the weaknesses of the autodidact. His was an all-too-human kind of God, all bent to follow along the open road towards the horizons of the future.

One may laugh, but "H.G.", part republican and egalitarian, part thinking of himself as one of the *samurai*, the Platonic rulers—no one asked what Plato or the *samurai* would have thought of *him*—in his own quite courageous way sought what he chose to call "the smile of approval" from his fellows. Sincerely he laboured for the good of humanity. As such, he merits its gratitude.

His essay of 1945, *The Happy Turning*, deserves reading along with that final outburst of prophetic rage where, in *Mind at the End of its Tether*, Wells warned mankind, including the Rationalists and the Progressives, that Nature had no redeeming bias in favour of the anthropoid apes and their naked cousins, any more than in favour of the pterodactyls and like creatures who only exist as fossilised remains.

To compare Wells with Leonardo da Vinci offers a yardstick which shows how far "H.G." fell short. Yet there is in *The War in the Air* (1908), in *The World Set Free* (1914) with its atomic bombs, and in *The First Men in the Moon* (1901), an almost Leonardan touch. Nothing would have irritated him more than to be described as "Not a great man but a good man." Nevertheless, despite patent faults of balance and manners, I think this dictum would be true. He was not of the calibre of an Erasmus or a Goethe or such of the greater Humanists. He was not even a Schweitzer. Not vulgar like Bennett, he was yet almost proudly "common", the archetype of the Common Man with his Problems. It was not entirely false modesty but a certain nagging insight which led Wells to sub-title his Autobiography, *Conclusions of a Very Ordinary Brain*. He was yet a very good and needed worldcitizen.

Before leaving the subject, it is interesting to notice, in his late and little known *A Contemporary Memoir* (1942–44), Wells' vivid comment on a contemporary with us until recently. After all (as I have said) he had singular gifts of prophecy! The target of his wrath was Capitaine (later Brigadier) Charles de Gaulle, conscripted for wider service by the British General Spears—and chiefly known for his monomania about tanks. (It was Lloyd George who, in the First World War, decided that Generals of Brigade should be gazetted in Britain merely as Brigadiers.) General of Brigade de Gaulle had been professor of Military History at St Cyr; and the professor had written a book, *Vers l'Armée de Métier*.

That Wells chose to entitle his article "A Sample Adventurer" may be thought both ill-mannered and blind. After all, the ex-Marxist Mussolini was that (whom Churchill had praised in an unfortunate moment, as he did Hitler). Wells writes:

"He seems to be an artlessly sincere megalomaniac. . . . He

becomes, like Hitler, a 'leader' who has succumbed to the temptations of his position and got out of hand. . . . All liberal-minded Englishmen have a profound admiration for France . . . and equally do they detest imperialist and reactionary France, which must ultimately degrade that country to the level of a Balkan state. All these speeches of de Gaulle are the quintessence of aggressive imperialism."

Then Wells goes on to make almost *verbatim* the mistake Laski, in the *Daily Herald*, made about Hitler. "He may be cured by his deflation. Somewhere a voluble old gentleman may sit and explain and explain. He may become a second Kerensky." Nevertheless the truly damning part of Wells' indictment comes in his quotation from de Gaulle's *Vers l'Armée de Métier* (which, like his *Fils de l'Epée*, so few read—even the later Lord Alexander of Tunis told me he had not read it). It is the soldier, known to his youthful contemporaries as "The Big Asparagus"—actually no taller than Lyndon Johnson—who writes:

"A man made for great deeds. . . . Shaped for heroic feats . . . grim impulse of ambition to spur him on . . . for glory gives herself only to those who have always dreamed of her. . . . For the sword is the axis of the World, and greatness cannot be shared. . . . A leader will have to appear."

That is what Mosley, Curzon's son-in-law, thought. But he was not built up, at political need and from junior rank, by subsidy from a foreign Government.

In his explosive indignation against de Gaulle, Wells failed to note that his opponent had been useful in achieving victory for Wells' own country. In refusing to recognise that others also might be no less genuine enemies of Hitlerite neo-paganism and terror, he was guilty of the same lack of perspective when he delivered his shrill and unmeasured assaults on Catholics and Christians. He was an unrestrained denouncer of those who disagreed. In this, of course, he is not, and was not, unique.

It is alleged by statisticians that, in the State of California alone, there are hundreds of potential geniuses. However this may be, even on a more restricted use of the term I would have no hesitation in describing Naomi Mitchison's brother, "Jack" Haldane, the nephew of Viscount Haldane of Cloan, as a genius. Those who care can see illustrated in his case also the drawbacks of the Goethean-Leonardo model, the disaster of the "rounded man", *l'uomo universale*, unsuited to our mediocre bourgeois-departmental-computerised civilisation. Haldane could begin an argument in the field of philosophy with obvious brilliance; make an excursus into theology, which would show unexpected erudition; illustrate the point with an accurate quotation or two from Homer; and then end up in that field of biology where he was now an acknowledged master. I have never met his like—not even in my very dear and admired friend, "the Dante of Modern China", Dr Hu Shih. It was a matter of chagrin to Haldane that, nevertheless, he had no memorable discoveries and achievement in biology to his credit. By the damned chance of fate these were much less than those of the simple Abbé Mendel; and scarcely vindicated those potentialities about which he was seldom modest.

Of Viking stature and one of the most aggressive of men, he ended as a pacifist in India. An announced believer that human beings are not equal and that the preachment of it is the damned hypocrisy of the democratic bourgeois age, he became chairman of the Board of the *Daily Worker*, a position which, as an aristocrat to his finger tips (with very bad manners), must have given him peculiar satisfaction. He departed from the camp of the comrades on the Lysenko issue confident that, were he but one tenth of his own size, he would still know more than Lysenko. Immensely personally courageous—the kind who strides around, bombs in hand—he was a very dangerous man, the sort who makes human civilisation worthwhile.

It is odd that he is likely chiefly to be remembered by a little essay in the "Today and Tomorrow" series, *Daedalus*. In this it was indicated with malicious joy that, in time to come, much of the human race might be hatched out of Leyden jars. Today, thanks to the progressive advances of a natural science which may be regarded as either, like Frankenstein, sinisterly brainless or all too menacingly purposeful, this bizarre suggestion for the twenty-first century appears singularly practicable. We can even go further and hold it to be possible to take a Harold Wilson, a de Gaulle, a Hitler or a Mao and so ingeminate or twin their cells that we could have to lead us a thousand identical Maos, indistinguishable even in their finger prints and glorious doctrines. At length, per-chance, the identical plastic flowers would bloom but need no breeding, and sex itself be put under.

In his unusual book, *The Inequality of Man*, this eminent Communist (fully in the tradition of Marx and Stalin) maintained, as against "bourgeois idealism" and the follies of the French Revolution, that this inequality between individuals and stocks—something, be it noted, totally different from *bloc* inequality between races, mostly mixed—should be so far accepted that, in time, people would come to regard it as being inevitable, like variations in the weather. All men are by nature born unequal. (He should have added the reservation that our medical commissars might get to work, providing twinned equality, as much as superiority, from their own Leyden jars.)

The human race being quite excessive in numbers and yet not endowed, like the lemmings, with a periodical impulse to mass suicide, Haldane would have bred the future families artificially from the better stock—an embarrassing issue for any democracy— if not sterilizing or castrating the more deficient. As a Darwinian, he would have reflected that the human animal, like any other, requires selective breeding and "pruning out". On this issue of "equality in general", as against Rousseau perhaps the wisest maxim is that propounded by Edmund Wilson: "The equality that people fight for is really the chance to excel." Edmund Wilson, however, perhaps forgets that many men are congenitally lazy and (as Marx knew) both resentful and vain.

Julian Huxley was seduced, by Wells, from his post as a professor of biology at King's College, London, into becoming Wells' collaborator in the encyclopaedic *Science of Life* series. The venture was not quite such a financial gold-mine as had been expected. Also Huxley, as a biologist, had his severe and explicit critics in such biologists and sociologists as Sir Alexander Carr Saunders, in due course Director of the London School of Economics, with whom I once took walks around Cumnor Hill, Oxford, and with whom I stayed in Liverpool. Sir Alexander was a master of silences. Julian found himself in the somewhat incongruous position of becoming Secretary of the London Zoo and famous with the populace as, along with Joad, an "original Brains Truster". It must have been a martyrdom, although not without gratifying compensations in publicity.

Sir Julian, like the Haldanes, Arnolds, Forsters, Butlers, Trevelyans, Darwins and Stevenses, belongs to one of those very few families which constitute the recognised hereditary intellectual aristocracy of Britain and to which the closest analogy lies in the Boston Brahmins. His distinguished intellectual powers he dedicated to building an altar to his grandfather, Thomas Huxley. The incense-perfumed cult was called "Scientific Humanism", its name an interesting contradiction of Lord Snow's dichotomy of "the two cultures".

The Rationalists—for a large part, according to Laski, very rich but very old—were aware that in the Twentieth Century their name did not exactly attract converts or proselytes. I myself, on S. K. Ratcliffe's suggestion, occasionally addressed meetings of the Ethical Society which, although the meetings were flavoured by musical solos and Wordsworthian hymns, I thought to be just what the name indicated. Actually it was closely tied in with the

Rationalists. Busts of Paine, one of their *avatars* (more pure than Comte), and memories of Ingersoll might have warned me. On the occasion of one of their international conferences they were good enough to invite me to speak. I replied, accepting, but adding that I was not of their persuasion and would speak accordingly. They replied that, of course, they believed in free speech but that this would not be a suitable occasion.

A more popularly attractive name than either Rationalism or Secularism or even Positivism, for this slightly antique school of thought was now being found in "Scientific Humanism". Even this worked no great miracles of popular persuasion and, in due course, the noble and historical name of "Humanism", adjectivally unqualified, was shamelessly stolen for the doctrinal sect's purposes. Apart from the grand tradition of true Humanism (which for me is a sacred name, not to be blasphemed), from Pico and Erasmus to Goethe and on, there had of course been minor conventicles of philosophic thought that had used the name, one led by F. C. S. Schiller and another by a certain Dr Babbitt (not to be confused with the ineffable Babbitt immortalised by Sinclair Lewis). The British Humanist Association, E. M. Forster among its distinguished departed, is a very vocal association—remarkably so, since its total membership is around only 3,000. The Secretary has recently explained its principles in the *Daily Mail*. It is true that, of these, Mr Lindsay Barnet remarked that there were such—"but, off-hand, I can't remember what they are". However, non-humanists, he held, have debased themselves. "They have placed themselves in a secondary position to God. . . . Humanists recognise that the driving force of man is emotion." Since it is not to be supposed that Mr Barnet is a first-class comedian, we must construe his remarks literally, not least in the age-long contest of Reason and Passion (or emotion). A hearty atheism, approved by a *nil obstat* from the most popular professors of philosophy, is however genuinely encouraged among the faithful. In America, when campaigning, members occasionally emerge under the enigmatic banner of "Protestants and Others [*sic*] United".

At some stage—I did not notice and cannot recall when—at a time when the title of *The Realist* was being discussed, the subtitle must have been slipped in, "A Journal of Scientific Humanism". Its significance escaped me at the time. I was all for "science". And, as the product of a famous school itself in part founded by the great Erasmus, I was a pious Erasmist and an unreserved believer in what he meant by "humanism". This was the catholic association of Christianity with the broad stream of classical culture and a repudiation of Lutheran dogmatic, or even of monkish, provincialism. Luther, an Augustinian friar, was a fanatic for the more excessive notions of Augustine of Hippo. The Humanism of Erasmus stood opposed to such protestant rejection of humane culture as was later to be illustrated by sects like the Anabaptists and, today, by the Primitive Methodists and those Exclusive Brethren who find it intolerable that other men should be saved. This catholic humanism was indeed to be the precise philosophic theme of my own later *History of the Political Philosophers* with its demonstration of a "grand tradition" in values from Confucius onwards.

I later discovered that "Scientific Humanism" was rather to be regarded as the formulation of a new religion than the mere sub-title of a magazine. I confess that it had never occurred to me that Huxley (among my acquaintance master of the finest collection of *risqué* stories, not least about the phallic qualities of Nelson's statue in Trafalgar Square, when viewed from the right angles— although I confess to finding his articles in *Playboy* rather unex- pected, allowance made even for high-brow frivolity) should be regarded as a religious leader, with or without the relics of the immortal Thomas Huxley placed in some ostensory under the baldachin. I recall the story of a French abbé being entertained in a Cambridge combination room. "You see that man going out there," remarked his host of an elderly don from that foggy university, "he is founding a new religion." "Ah!" quizzically replied the abbé, not without memories of Voltaire: "Pour cela il faut être crucifié." The notion of Sir Julian being crucified still moves me to mirth. The London Zoo provides no adequate precedent ex- perience; he should be left in peace as a fairly good liberal and "a great intellect".

The conclusion of the matter, it seemed, when I came to think about it, would be some kind of revival of the Comtean religion of Positivism. The basic and insufferable fault was that religion would become detached from the immense universe in which our so-small globe revolves and under whose skies our ape-related race, *teste Darwin et Sigmund Freud*, exists. It would become an intellectually intolerable affair of little men, as in the Tower of Babel story, worshipping other slightly less little creatures. We should find ourselves worshipping Albert Schweitzer, Winston Churchill, Napoleon, H. G. Wells—and, of course, T. H. Huxley. We should be trapped in the intolerable "success snobbery" of recorded history.

In fairness to Julian Huxley it should be said that he would almost certainly repudiate this and call attention to his recent

J

syncretism with the stimulating views of that remarkable Jesuit, Père Teilhard de Chardin. Whether Barbara (now Baroness) Wootton, also an eminent scientific humanist, would here agree I just don't know. So far as I have heard her broadcast views, they seem to be a re-expression of old-fashioned Utilitarianism, "the greatest happiness of the greatest number" here and now; and are open to all the well-known objections to that useful but uninspired philosophy. It has its common-sense merits; but it is no accident that its basic belief was hedonism. And the suggestion of hedonism, ever welcome to the natural man, is not what our civilisation requires. I prefer Confucianism. Confucius was my sound kind of Humanist. However, I may perhaps owe an apology here and an explanation to Huxley. He is quite other than a mere utilitarian or, for that matter, a neo-Ingersollian or neo-Comtist, or flamboyant about No-God in the manner of A. J. Ayer. In his later writings I probably agree with him more than I have here made apparent.

The risk seemed to me patent that we should end with just one more elect sect—of which there are too many already—and, moreover, an intellectual snob sect. That what for a century has been called "the reconciliation of science and religion" is a laudable pursuit I do not, of course, for a moment deny but affirm. Later I hope to discuss it. As Pope Leo XIII said: *Nulla unquam inter fidem et rationem dissentio esse potest.*

Thanks to Julian and *The Realist* I met Aldous Huxley. The days of *Chrome Yellow* and of the confections typical of the brittle, witty and almost professionally disillusioned mood of the early, after-war 'Twenties already lay in the past. The fashion had changed. The 'Thirties (in Quaker language) "had a concern". They were also more violent. Aldous Huxley was moving onto the kind of Quaker "simple man" declaration of religion and philosophy of life which one finds in *After Many a Summer*, oddly comparable with the philosophical summing-up of the importance of living in *The Razor's Edge*, with its wise taxi-driver. Aldous Huxley, Maugham, Hemingway and Thomas Wolfe were among the few writers whose books could always hold my enthralled attention—but, if *Brave New World* was the best known of the later Aldous's books, *The Perennial Philosophy* was something which moved me to a greater measure of sympathetic agreement.

Aldous Huxley indeed was not above compelling attention by the shocking incident. However, he was a friend of the mystic (or should I just say Irish) Gerald Heard, himself a protégé of my good friend Naomi Mitchison. Julian Huxley, slightly to my surprise when I offered praise but with the umbrage of the less well-known elder brother, dismissed one of Aldous' ethical studies as "just a torso"; but with glee described Aldous' precocity as a child when he exclaimed that he "did not like gooseberries because they tasted like babies". My own memory is chiefly of a lunch à deux at the Ivy Restaurant and of Aldous exclaiming on the architectural beauty of the Charing Cross Road Welsh Methodist chapel. I confess that hitherto I had not been conscious of this. However, as the Lord said of the dead dog in the street, "he had beautiful teeth."

Of "Bruno" (or Bronislav) Malinowski I was to see much. Graham Wallas apart, he was about my only close friend in the London School of Economics and I was responsible for his being invited to deliver the Messenger Lectures in Cornell. He was also a good friend of that excellent historian and delightful human being, Eileen Power, also of *The Realist* board; and I found for myself a loyal companion as well as an enjoyable conversationalist; indeed he perhaps put into conversation the energy which he should have put into books. His conversation was usually *risqué* and often unprintable. It had unfortunate disadvantages. When I arranged for Bruno to be invited to Cornell, I knew that the President, Livingston Farand, himself an anthropologist, was prepared to get a chair founded in anthropology to which he wanted to invite Malinowski. However, Bruno was in a strangely nervous condition, so that he had been unable to prepare his text, and, desiring to be popular, he served up so highly spiced but light a *soufflé* of *erotica* that academic eyebrows were raised and the invitation was never extended. It was the more pity since Yale University did later capture him.

As he was one of the world's leading anthropologists I noted with interest his judgement that 90 per cent or even 95 per cent of homosexuality was not due to any physical character but was a matter of smart fashion, as in the Prussian army and in the British public schools—ex-public-school headmasters may make good archbishops but are scarcely the best impartial judges about homosexuals. Homosexuality was more a fashion, which in some vocations conduced to success in life, than a disease to be cured or wept over. True that the Greeks went in for "the love of young boys", but even the brightest reformers were scarcely prepared to say that this was "just a private matter". I am not competent to say whether Malinowski's opinion was right.

While we were in Cornell Malinowski warned me about Harold Laski as no friend in life's competition. He expressed his views in brief Anglo-Saxon monosyllables. I had myself only recently been responsible for inviting Laski to deliver a lecture in Cornell (in which he had remarked that "a hemisphere being too small for both of us, we divided the globe between us"); and I discounted these warnings. I did not know that Harold, having given me high praise for my "mental sweep" in his earlier letters to Mr Justice Holmes, had subsequently damned me—probably having forgotten what he had written earlier. It was not until, as acting chairman of department, I had occasion to go back through official files that I discovered that, at the time when he was calling me by my Christian name and walking with his arm around my waist, he was writing to my chairman in terms that a lawyer could have called damaging in law. The possible explanation, offered to me many years later by Ellen Wilkinson, was straight jealousy. At the time, such was my admiration, it would not have occurred to me that he had anything to be jealous about.

The final awakening, from my condition of intellectual worship of Laski, came when he read out private letters of mine, in which I had unguardedly poured out my hopes and fears, in the common-room at Yale. What he did not allow for was the fact that a some-time student of mine, later a professor at Columbia University, was present, who warned me that I had here a fairly dangerous and unscrupulous enemy. I had a sudden and shocked sense of betrayal.

I still remained at a loss to discover the reason for the enmity. I know (because he himself told me) that he had threatened Ernest Barker with a libel action. What I did not recognise was the initial weakness of Laski's position in the London School of Economics to which, under Graham Wallas' patronage, he had returned on a merely half-time appointment from no more than a lectureship at Harvard. I did not know that he and the Director, William Beveridge, were very much at daggers drawn; and, until much too late, when he had ceased to be Director, I failed to exploit the fact the Beveridge's Webbian views on political science were very much my own—and not Laski's. Like the Webbs and Beveridge, and as against Laski, I was a believer in the very Fabian slogan, "measurement and publicity", to a degree not usual in those days!

Laski resembled Picasso in one respect. His work fell into definite periods. Following those very early days when he had been a (not too successful) biology student under Julian Huxley and inspired by the eugenist Galton, there was "the Blue Period", when this son of a Manchester merchant, a very orthodox Jew commemorated in Israel, was a disciple of John Stuart Mill in his more socialist mood but, nevertheless, remained an individualist or, at least, a "group" protester against the increasing power and alleged absolute sovereignty of the State. Laski being himself a leading member of the Pluralist School (the history of which, as I have said, has been written by my excellent student, Professor K. C. Hsiao, in C. K. Ogden's International Library), I have indeed often suspected that Laski's political philosophy of the state was influenced and given dynamism by an Oedipus complex. When he said "the overbearing State" he really meant "my father Nathan". (In the same fashion certain contemporary philosophers have become unrelenting critics of theology maybe precisely because they were not so much logicians as the sons of bishops.) During this period Laski wrote his little "Home University Library" book on Communism, which provided a useful "alibi" when he was accused of being too friendly to Communism and also earned him boosts, as the real intellectual autocrat (along with Cole) of the Labour Party, from Stanley Baldwin and Mackenzie King. (R. H. Tawney was overlooked by these gentlemen.)

There followed his "Red Period", when he declared, in the columns of the New York *Nation*, that he was a Marxist and attracted, like Herbert Marcuse, crowded student audiences for his novelty and courage—not least because it was publicised that his very appearance caused reactionary university governors in the American North-West to think that he ought to be banned. There was also his "Pink" or cautious period when, as a preferred member of the Labour Party National Executive Committee (until Nye Bevan came along) he had to watch his words and to defend policies which personally he might have shaped otherwise. He was certainly no friend of the minuscule-dimensioned British Communist Party; and between them there was no love lost. His maxim, in this phase, was "no enemies to the Left". He described the small British C.P. to me as "quite impossible". But he did better and held, like Kingsley Martin, that there was much forgotten good to be found in Stalin, the powerful, the great, world champion of the workers, merely reserving for himself the right to compose footnotes suggesting how the Red Czar might perchance, properly advised by himself, have done things in an improved way. The Moscow Mecca he visited with pleasure.

Remarkably generous in material ways to poor students who could be his feudatories, there was a certain waspishness, a streak of vindictiveness and even treachery in his nature towards possible rivals—a characteristic quite lacking in his courageous and admirable wife, Freda, now Vice-President of "War on Want". Personally ambitious and, according to Felix Morley, discussing in his early days whether he should or should not go into the Lords, he was (in the words of Clement Attlee) in a letter to me, "an intriguer" for power. To a mutual friend, Dr Gilkes, sometime High Master of St Pauls, Attlee added that Laski was "strangely disinterested in truth". A political chess-player, few steps were ever taken without calculation.

For all of this, he was the most brilliant conversationalist that I have known, a stimulating teacher and a remarkable thinker. It is no small tribute that, for a couple of decades, few political conversations could be started up in any university common-room in Britain, America or Java, without his name, and anecdotes about him, being recalled. Sir Alfred Zimmern once told me that "nobody reads his books any more." Poor Zimmern, however, had been supplanted in two posts which he had hoped to hold, first by Laski and then, at UNESCO, by Huxley—on the steps of the Athenaeum Club it was settled that Huxley, not Zimmern, should head UNESCO. It was Lady Zimmern who, according to Laski, remarked to him: "And now that you know you are holding the post designed for my husband, I hope you will resign." I don't think Laski's early work on sovereignty will be forgotten. He did much to demolish the academic error that "politics is about the State".

He had indeed one well-known weakness. It was Sainte-Beuve who wrote of Chateaubriand: "M. de Chateaubriand, it is understood, is writing his autobiography and those who know him will be aware that this will then omit everything that matters most." I recall beginning a review of a book on Laski with this quotation. Harold Laski's sins were not indeed of omission. He had, like Lloyd George, an almost congenital incapacity to speak the exact truth.

His defenders will say that this Baron Munchausen tendency was due to his delight in a good anecdote and a tall story. Yet one could not help but note that these stories were seldom at his own expense but so magnified his importance among Top People that simple-minded visitors were quite taken in. It was indeed his calculated defence, as an "outsider" in two hemispheres—and as an outsider myself I could sympathise. As was said at the High Table of his own college, when he became Party chairman: "Laski will now be meeting some of the people about whom he has been telling us for so long." "Now that we have gone into the Rühr", ran the story about Poincaré, "tell me, Laski, what are we to do?" However, the point was that thanks to his very technique of intimacy, real or fictitious, he *had* in fact met some of these people and would surely meet more. He acquired that invaluable asset among worldly men, "a name"—in today's jargon called "identity". "The cult of personality" is always with us, even in the land of Chairman Mao.

Nevertheless, the techniques produced irritation, as debasing the currency of honest conversation. H. G. Wells told me, on one occasion, that Laski had related a story of some alleged incident. "So I rang up Sybil Colefax who knows all these people and she phoned me back, 'There is not a word of truth in it.' Now you may be able to get away with that kind of thing in a big country like America but, in a small country such as this, you just can't do it." Wells' voice rose high with indignation.

Conversely, Laski gathered to himself not only the credit for non-events, but the credit for things really said and done—but by others. The epigram, said in humour, "What has posterity done for me?" I have seen attributed to him. Arnold Bennett had a variant. Actually it was a note taken by Addison over two centuries ago, quoting the saying of "a testy old Fellow of a college": "I wid faine know w't posterity ever did for us." An aura is one of the qualities of those who attract a legend, true or bogus; but the beginning of a legend is a requisite for any magnetic aura.

Laski judged affairs from the angle of power. I learned from his technique the importance, if one wishes to implement a policy, of going direct to the top and of never lingering at lower levels. (There, nevertheless, is where indeed one's concern should lie.) It means that the snobbery of those jealous in possession of power, and bureaucratic obstruction, have to be struck at there—and hard. What matters in politics, as I have always told modest students, is the *entrée* and the two-page memorandum sent to the top. Patronised from his early stages, first by the admirable Professor Max Cohen of New York University (after Laski quit his brief residence in McGill during the war), then by Felix Frankfurter, and then by the Webbs, what Laski superbly had was the technique of access. On the other hand, he once told me with irony that the T.U.C. thought it to be its job "TO PUT YOU IN YOUR PLACE." They were the great unimpressed. He had, for them, all too many ideas.

Two things irreparably damaged him in the end. His private doctrine, unshared by other members of the Party Executive, that the chairman of the National Party Executive Committee was thereby *ex officio*, like the Pope, its public conscience, and the tactical error of a letter to the Party Leader, Clement Attlee, telling him that he should resign. That temperamental bounce was met by a laconic communication saying that his letter had been noted.

It may seem odd, but nevertheless I would record that if he could be found in a mood when his personal ambitions were not concerned, there is perhaps no single person to whose judgement

I would rather entrust my reputation than to Harold Laski. One's early uncritical admiration of his own work would not, I think, interest him save as a possible pawn in the game. His scholar's estimate of one's own work was what would interest him. We both were absorbed in the same subjects; we both believed in the marriage of theory and action. He had an almost feminine intuition (which made one seek his company) of what the other person was really thinking—as well, be it added, as of what they would like to hear said—and a realistic judgement. Not until after he died did I learn, from those near to him, that—wounded by indications of exclusion from election to the Reform Club—he had a conviction that he was being persecuted by anti-semites. I would suppose that this was merely not true; it was rather his own weakness of character and exhibitionism that made him a target.

So far as I was concerned, he told me with engaging frankness that I suffered from "frustrated ambition". I can say with sincerity that at least he had weighed me and not made either a false or uncomplimentary estimate. If we were enemies (which I would not fully accept), at least we had considerable mutual respect. He paid me the compliment of making my *Science and Method* compulsory reading in his seminar although, as one of his students, Thomas Cook, informed me, he did not approve of Cook's excessive enthusiasm for it. Whatever he may have written to Holmes, at least in *Time and Tide* he wrote: "Professor Catlin attempted to outline a science of politics which is really scientific." I would wish for no better comment. For the rest, his figure, like the Shadow of the Brocken, still strides abroad, larger than life among the students in the market places of Ghana and in the plantations of Malaya. It was a brilliant spirit, a bitter spirit but, for all of that, not an ungenerous spirit. I wish he were still around to talk to. He was a refreshing contrast to some members even of the Left-Wing establishment.

It would be tedious to direct a telescope on every member in turn of the galaxy of an editorial board. There was the brooding quality of Naomi Mitchison; the scientific adventure of Sir Richard Gregory; the wintry charm of Sir Herbert Read. There was Dame Rebecca West, mistress of the elaborate sentence, the chiselled phrase and the jewelled, ruby adjective. Every member was a person, remarkable in his own right. (Incidentally almost every one of those still living has earned his or her honour or decoration.)

The Realist grew and flourished. Then the Great Depression came. Melchett lost heavily—about two million sterling in speculations. For much of this loss he blamed his secretary, Conway

Davies. Davies departed from England for a variety of reasons, and everything he had done became anathema to his lordship. Melchett himself had insisted on Davies as our chairman and the channel of our funds. Now our subsidy dried up. Archibald Church was too busy with his politics to give his whole attention to the matter. I tried to get Waldorf Astor and then Leonard Elmhirst (whose family, including Dorothy Whitney, I had known in Cornell) interested; but failed.

In our various issues we had carried articles (members of the Board apart) from Sigmund Freud, Solly Zuckerman, Robert Lutyens, "Goldie" Lowes Dickinson, Bertrand Russell, Julian Benda, Lord Adrian, John Galsworthy, Charles Singer, Vera Brittain, G. C. Coulton and Havelock Ellis. The last number carried an article by a Premier of France, Paul Painlevé, on "The United States of Europe". The total of the issues must be a most valuable collector's item. They should be reprinted.

Cyril Connolly's later *Horizon*, and the Leavis journal and similar literary journals were more specialised. I was acquainted with the assistant editor of the Paris-published *This Quarter*; but that again was a bird of a different feather. Much later still our plan was in some measure adopted, with a narrower circle of contributors, by *Encounter*, with Spender, for long, the co-editor and with support from the vastly opulent Ford Foundation. It carried articles in my view intolerably critical of Britain by such writers as Malcolm Muggeridge. Nevertheless *Encounter* has been inspired by something of the same idea, although only *The Realist* fitted neatly into my four-fold plan. There was yet no help for it: our subsidy having ended, we folded up. I could wish that I had the opportunity to edit another such journal. Its critics said it had been a zoo of all the talents. At least it had been a gallant endeavour.

Nevertheless I felt that something at once more specific and more massive had to be done in public affairs than individually these British men of letters and of science had had the resolution to attempt. A war cloud was growing in the sky and would not be dissipated. My environment, living in Chelsea, even at a literary level, was not only that of *The Realist*, and always I preferred action to words or to writing. One had to return to the problem of international power.

VII

CHELSEA AND BLOOMSBURY

NOT all one's life was lived at the level of public affairs. If pre-occupation with political means, and with the power play in the achievement of this or that reform, preoccupied the pundits of Bloomsbury, in Chelsea, where I lived for over twenty years, we had our direct enjoyments, our *menus plaisirs*, our domestic life. Any autobiography lacking this chapter would indeed be arid. It would omit most of what interests the run of human beings who are not politicians, and who do not even regard the theatre of politics as the only *grand monde*.

Besides the world of party conflict and the colder world of academe there is also the great world of art and letters, although Plato maintained that, even in dreams, these worlds could not rightly be divorced—not even the spheres of politics and music. And also there were the little domestic worlds, with their own gods of love and of the hearth, private under the arch of Heaven.

After my Oxford days my sense of vocation changed or was changed by circumstances. My post-war preoccupation of 1918 I have explained. On board ship going to America I passed the time reading Conrad's *Nostromo*, where one character is drawn by Conrad as *catholique et gentilhomme*. I felt sufficiently young, adventurous and romantic to send copies of my recently published small exercise in *belles lettres* to two women: I admired the poetry of one, and the newly published Oxford novel of the other had moved me—a book rather in the spirit of Wells' *Ann Veronica*. It expressed a kind of new attitude towards women, both gay and courageous. To my pleasure and a little to my own surprise at the success of my daring, I got a pleasant letter of acknowledgment from Edna St Vincent Millay, and also one from Vera Brittain. My correspondence with the second developed. We met in 1924, when I was already the young professor; and we got engaged in about ten days. We married in the following year when I was on vacation from America.

Since my wife has fully described her own life's record in two autobiographies, her immensely popular *Testament of Youth*, perhaps the great book of woman's experience in the First World War, and her less well-known, less emotionally appealing, but perhaps even more important, *Testament of Experience*, there is no need for me to add commentary to what already stands in its own right.

Testament of Youth in fact was saluted in 1964 by the sometime Director of the B.B.C., Sir William Haley, as "the war-book of the women of England". It was also, oddly enough, coupled by one commentator with Field-Marshal Ludendorf's *War Memories*, as together being the most important books directly issuing, within a decade, from personal engagement in the war itself, as distinct from either history or novels. Except on the point of direct experience the comparison with the Field-Marshal's Diaries would seem to me more obvious in terms of difference than of similarity. The book ran to twenty-three impressions and had a vast, widespread and lasting emotional appeal. Of my new parents-in-law the curious will find a sufficient description in *Testament of Youth*, and of their house which was a house of ghosts.

In those days Vera was an ardent campaigner, in the suffrage tradition, for women's rights. Later, after speaking around the country (once as a guest of Sir Alec Douglas-Home's father) for the League of Nations, she turned to the newer and more uncompromising phases of the peace-movement. Although our answers were to become different, in our absorbing concern we were at one. She wrote in *Testament of Youth*, "It's my job, I thought now, to find out all about it. . . Perhaps the careful study of man's past will explain."

My mother having been a suffragist along with Lady Willoughby de Broke and others of that group, I was clear that women, in British (and indeed world) society at the turn of the century were getting very much less than the legal and civil rights to which they were fully entitled. Even today, although the Women's Liberation Movement (for example in America) often lacks judgement as well as dignity and tends to endorse the "trendy" theme that the public is too stupid to attend to anything unless there is some kind of violence or at least political strip-tease, I do not regard the Movement, compared with those of race liberation and class liberation, as being quite so stupid as some people suppose. Here Plato and I happen to agree.

Actually the women's rights movement came only just in time. It was primarily middle-class and our daughter was not a little shocked to discover that the suffragettes, led at this stage by Christabel Pankhurst, not only demonstrated their patriotism by work in munition factories in war-time but, towards the end, became remarkable as strike-breakers when the male munition workers went on strike for better wages. After the war the manual workers' organisations gained impetus, and both men and women factory workers achieved higher pay. Domestic help in Britain became almost as unobtainable as it had earlier become in America (save for the core of Negro cooks and domestics who arrived, as daily helpers, in their automobiles). The mass of middle-class women returned again to the sink, from which they had just—and only just in time—emancipated themselves.

So far as there was emancipation it was in terms of machines, electric washing and cooking apparatus, and the incoming of new methods of providing almost all food out of tins. In France the intransigence of the cuisine-loving male slowed this progress. However, one change of no small class-importance for women, certainly not to be underestimated, did take place. On the sidewalks of New York it became difficult to distinguish at a glance the dress of the daughter of a docker and of the daughter of a millionaire and, by implication, to which class each belonged.

I myself went so far as to coin certain slogans (one, I recall, much treasured by Dorothy Woodman), and to write a fairly thorough introduction, at the request of Ernest Rhys, for the Everyman edition of John Stuart Mill's *Subjection of Woman* and of Mary Wollstonecraft's *Rights of Woman*.

It would be idle to suppose that marriage today is easy between people with a developed sense of their own powers. The solution is to be found in reason, patience and commonsense. I have never accepted the paradox maintained by St John Ervine that the happiest families are those that have the biggest rows.

In 1927 writing to my wife (a passage quoted in *Testament of Experience*), about the intimate companionship of shared experience, I said: "Of our short play upon the stage, so short before the actors are gone, the scenery decayed, the pretty dresses in rags, the players dead and dust, this is the best, the climax of it." One could have "the proud joy that the act was well-played. ... This is marriage".

There were difficult times. After the publication and *réclame* of *Testament of Youth*, I was to deliver a lecture in a large Canadian town, Hamilton. At dinner before the lecture my host's wife remarked that, with my wife's publicity, I must feel "like a hat with the rim knocked off". I had to restrain my impulse not to rise and quit. There was nearly no lecture in Hamilton that night. I have often been impressed by the sheer malice of human beings, a malice not bettered because their ill-mannered remarks probably spring from unconscious impulses of jealousy, scarcely measured by themselves. Television interviewers, salaried for their gladiatorial toughness and "abrasiveness", are not the only culprits. Dame Rebecca West once told me of a certain eminent knight and county court judge whose feckless hostess introduced him as "the husband of *The Constant Nymph*". Sir David Davies turned on his heel, picked up his hat and stick, and walked out. "And quite right too," added Dame Rebecca. I recall the present Lady Pethwick-Lawrence rebuking, with imagination, her husband for the same kind of discourteous and insensitive introduction.

That Elizabeth Taylor and Richard Burton, or Dame Sybil Thorndike and Sir Lewis Casson, are "married" expresses the correct formula. In a commercialised democracy where publicity is king, the fact that a scholar is at a disadvantage compared with a well-known writer is merely one of those facts of life which one has to face with good grace.

For myself I had not yet recognised that mankind is divided into "men" and "women": and I continued to regard them all as "human beings". The world of power preoccupied me and only subsidiarily that of erotic escapades. There are others who, as Muggeridge remarks, find in sexuality "the mysticism of materialism". I did not find mine a dull world, whatever it may seem to the vulgar and to readers of *The News of the World*. In so far as I was attracted, it was to women of elegance and breeding who, like myself, regarded with contempt the roll-about world of sex and blood of the pre-fascist D. H. Lawrence, the blatant world of its current spiritual mentors, Tynan, Lennon and nihilist Beckett, conjoined in *O Calcutta*, the world of Eros and Priapus.

Far from being hypocritical, I was very clear about my views, some of which I have already indicated. When a lady of charm takes the initiative by saying "Perhaps", it could be ungallant not to compliment her—and no small loss amid life's rarer joys. But this does not equate the conduct of life with graceless bundlings in the nearest bed and then, in the style of admired contemporary literature, making anatomical notes for some future "work of literary value". I leave Henry Miller, Mr Burroughs, Mr Selby, of *Last Exit to Brooklyn*, and the baboons on Ape's Hill to others. I am content to have kept all my friends as dear friends this thirty years or more.

My wife, shy and withdrawn, preferring one or two friends to many acquaintances, was one of the most single-minded and conscientious women I have ever met. As time went on our affection grew even deeper, in the companionship of a long life-time. Before her death she recorded that she died having had a life full, happy and satisfying. Of the later years I can say, with Sir Winston about Clementine Churchill, "We lived happily ever after." Since such comment is usually merely conventional, I will add another which has its own unimpeachable veracity, the veracity of dreams which, whether or not inhibited, assuredly do not express a feeling that is not there. For the last eleven years I have kept a nightly diary of dreams (as, for thirty years, I have kept a day-to-day one) which collection is deposited, by request, in the library of Sheffield University. In one of these I recall a dream which ended with words of mine: "Good night, my love." I am content to leave the record there. Vera chose that it should be repeated in her obituary notice.

One of my late wife's closest friends was Winifred Holtby. The record of their friendship is to be found in *Testament of Friendship*, and in their published letters. At a time, at Somerville College, Oxford, when Vera was under great emotional stress, Winifred had provided an invaluable stabilising influence. I was fortunate, thanks to the tolerant liberality of Cornell, to be able to live in London during part of each year but, in our earlier houses, Winifred was always there also, renting rooms—and indeed easing the household financial economy.

Of Winifred, Rebecca West said: "Her writings always seemed to me to be a kind of Yorkshire home-spun." The remark was not entirely complimentary but I do not think it to have been unjust. Winifred Holtby's quality as a human being was her transparent honesty (which won for her the almost fanatical loyalty of friends and admirers) accompanied by a disrespectful Yorkshire wit which was given to puncturing not only the pompous and portentous but also the ambitious. The wit comes out in *Mandoa, Mandoa*, although it was a mishap that this book appeared at almost the same time as Evelyn Waugh's *Black Mischief*. Her gift as a durable "regional novelist"—later commemorated by my wife by endowing the Royal Society of Literature annual Winifred Holtby Prize for the best young "regional novelist"—was that of being able to put into writing, in her great posthumous volume, *South Riding*, the earthy description of the Yorkshire countryside and even to infuse with human interest the no less earthy but authentic record of local politics with its foibles, follies and hopes. If local affairs can have an epic, this is it.

Alderman Mrs Holtby, her mother, not unnaturally far from enjoyed the depiction of herself as "Alderman Mrs Beddows"—although, equally humanly, she later relented when she had to confront the fact that the book, along with the film (in which Edna Best and Ralph Richardson starred), had been a success which immortalised her. This change of attitude was yet so late that my wife, an executrix under Winifred's will, had a full load of trouble in getting the book published at all or without the expurgation required to conform to the Alderman's sense of propriety.

Thanks to the organic effects of a childhood bout of scarlet fever, Winifred Holtby, by all medical calculations should have died at least three years before she did. She was kept alive by a brilliant medical man and by the dedication of her friends: and her best literary work was done, under the luck of things and due to her own resolution, during precisely these years.

She owed indeed no little to Margaret, Viscountess Rhondda, for keeping her in circulation as the hard-working co-director of *Time and Tide*. This had its disadvantages. Not only was Winifred overworked during the last years—one reason why her Yorkshire boy friend, Harry Pearson, a Cambridge scholar and intimate of T. E. Lawrence, found her too little responsive—but those who disliked Margaret Rhondda spilled their distaste over on to those whom they thought were associated with her.

It was largely thanks to Winifred Holtby that we ourselves were drawn into a circle of another and political kind, that of (to his friends) "Jon" Creech Jones, Carol Johnson, Leonard Barnes and —after my day—Dame Margery Perham. There was a small group called "The Friends of Africa", of which I was for a while treasurer. When Creech Jones became Colonial Secretary he had to deal, not only with Palestine (and here his papers, now in Oxford, will be of interest to students), but with issues affecting such persons as Seretse Khama. Our young family, in early days in Nevern Place and later in Glebe Place, Chelsea, grew accustomed to seeing distinguished Africans, including Paul Robeson, coming up the stairs to visit Winifred. Veteran Glasgow trades unionists, thanks to her financial and political efforts, were sent out to make their names, as did William Ballinger (later Senator), in South Africa and to organise, along with the Senator his wife, multi-racial trades unions in that former Dominion. It was indeed chance that William Ballinger went there and not Arthur Creech Jones.

It was perhaps especially Winifred's literary friends and acquaintances who became ours and whom we found dropping into the Chelsea house—Stella Benson, E. M. Delafield, Violet Scott James (the beautiful mother of a beautiful and accomplished daughter), Jan van Druten, Cecil Roberts, the Jan Smeterlins, and Desmond MacCarthy. (The Smeterlins were good enough to invite me to be their guest at their Monte Carlo flat, my co-guest being the great Mary Garden's sister.) It was from E. M. Delafield that I heard the doomed story of the Charlotte Yonge papers. She had called on the family to see what material there might be for a biography. "Oh, grand-aunt Charlotte's papers ?— they were up there in the attic. Quite a lot. So we burned them a few years ago!" Dear Phyllis Bentley, from Halifax, was a close friend—although sometimes treated by Vera far too brusquely—and a frequent visitor, who stayed with us. Formal lunches, to heavyweight economists such as Sprague and Cole, I gave myself: these others came rather to tea or cocktails. Vera and Winifred were busy writing and I do not recall many formal dinner parties. Perhaps I went to far too few, since I like the friendly circle and draw ideas from it. Indeed, hard literary work was only possible thanks to an efficient and loyal staff, the Burnett family, husband, wife and (at various times) the two sisters, whom we were fortunate enough to bring to our aid.

There was the "Chelsea" world of Gwen Farrar, Syrie Maugham with Beverley Nichols (better recalled from college days), Peggy Ashcroft, Sir Francis Rose, Diana Wynyard and Sybil Colefax—the opposite number in her Chelsea *salon* to Lady Ottoline Morrell in Oxford; but her place (known to the malicious as "The Lions" Corner House) to be found centred just at the end of the street. Much later, the painter Pietro Annigoni made 26 Glebe Place his headquarters. The work of Gaudier-Brzeska one could discuss with Gerald Hamilton, who lived just opposite, by Glebe House. Also just opposite, owned by Henrietta Leslie, was the international headquarters of P.E.N. Henrietta's amiable husband, Peter Schutze, after her death committed suicide at the Reichenbach Falls. All those whom I have mentioned were much more than a list of names. They just happened to be the people we would meet, in the Chelsea "village", within a street or so. They added, as "neighbour children", to the colour and the pleasure of the place.

In Swan Court, so short a distance away, were our dear friends of so many years, that noble figure Sybil Thorndike, with her warm generosity and unforgettable voice, and Sir Lewis Casson—among our friends none more treasured. We also paid our occasional visits to the Café Royal, in its great age of plain marble top tables and beer, when for conversation it held a lamp to the Savoy Grill. There I recall with amusement "Nye" Bevan holding forth in a spate of dogmatic Welsh monologue and my wife, under that influence, falling asleep at the table from sheer boredom.

My world was not entirely Vera's, although they overlapped. Further, except as an amusing *hors d'oeuvres* I do not think that either of us was greatly interested in Chelsea café society. Although "amusing"—the open sesame to all society in those days, as "exciting" is today—for anyone of a resolute vocation it was not a good milieu.

My own obsessive and even austere interest was in watching the play for power, the pursuit of interests, in the international scene. Excepting maybe on some trivial *salon* level, Chelsea came nearer to Paradise in being interested in the direct pleasures of art, transcending the machinery of political power. Later "The King's Road", the royal road passing the place where, tradition said, Charles II made merry with Nell Gwynn—Henry VIII's royal road past Thomas More's garden to Wolsey's Hampton Court—was to mirror the antics of the American student campuses I knew so well. In the days of which I now write, Chelsea Village rather centred around its decorous and *Cranford*-like Arts Club.

A decent Establishment, an amusing Counter-Establishment, the houses starred with the blue memorial plaques of the literary immortals, George Eliot, Thomas Carlyle, Whistler, Turner, Mrs Gaskell and the rest, current politics did not bulk large, whether in Old Church Street or under the leafy bowers of Cheyne Walk.

Of this Chelsea group (rather later, when we had moved to 2 Cheyne Walk) I saw most of Sir Francis Rose, the painter, a friend of Dennis Conan Doyle and his Georgian princess wife, one of "the marrying Mdivanis" who, with her fur-trimmed clothes, gave the appearance of having only just alighted from a Russian sleigh. Sir Francis' wife was then Frederica Dorothy Carrington. At Sir Francis Rose's apartment I met Dorothy Fellowes and Serge Lifar. The Conan Doyles I saw at Maria von Neurath's, whose husband Willy, son of the sometime head of the Vienna *Credit Anstalt*, was a joy to all his friends. There I would occasionally wash up party dishes with the exiled Hapsburgs— all four of the Archdukes out of five.

Of Sir Francis Rose—one of whose paintings, done on the balcony of 2 Cheyne Walk, for long adorned the Embassy drawing room of Mme. Wellington Koo—the unkind tell a story which is yet not out of character. Not unconscious of the aura of royalty, on one memorable occasion he had prevailed upon Queen Mary to visit his Cheyne Row studio. Wicked fellows, with a misplaced sense of humour, were aware of this. In a room above the studio they awaited the solemn moment with pails of water. Her Majesty having arrived and been centrally seated, and Sir Francis having begun to display his wares, all was thrown into embarrassed confusion by drippings from the ceiling which increased in volume. I was never told whether Queen Mary's sense of humour rose to the occasion—she was a stern lady, with a long knobbed umbrella which she was capable of using—but that Sir Francis himself was thrown into a condition of near-panic I do know.

Oscar Wilde's son, Vyvyan Holland, with his white, flower-like

K

face, I met at Eve Kirk's flat—she "The Yellow Lady" of Augustus
John's picture—along with Sir Allen Lane. It was many years
later, in the Cheyne Walk days, that at the Garrick Club I again
met Lane and also "Monty" Compton Mackenzie—once an out-
rageous name at my school—and Alan Herbert, genius, reformer
and scalliwag. With Herbert we later adjourned to Pratt's Club
and were joined at a table by Lord Hinchinbrooke, who later
ascended to being Earl Sandwich (of sandwich fame) and then
descended to being Mr Victor Montagu. "My boy," began Sir
Alan Herbert. He then, in an unforgettable phrase, corrected
himself: "My lord and boy. . . ."

Chelsea was indeed a self-contained "village"—and even now,
absorbed into the amorphous and stucco-housed Royal Borough
of Kensington, it probably still is. That is what those who lived
in it for over two decades loved about it. It defied the efficiency of
modern computer bureaucracy, *laus Deo*. It was a community.
(Hatred of bureaucrats and Jacks-in-office is one of my most
ingrained characteristics. I count that day well-lived when I
frustrate them.)

Even the local politics were equally parochial in the *Cranford*
style. I was vice-chairman of the local Labour Party, and later
chairman, with the brother of the Liberal Leader, Lord Rea, as
my vice-chairman; and about a dozen of us managed the opposition just as another dozen, on the Conservative side, managed the
municipal administration. Even today, when Chelsea and Kensington have merged, the joint Royal Borough is so decorously managed
that the Tory chairman is elected to the housing committee by
proposal of Labour Alderman the Hon. Thomas Ponsonby,
General Secretary of the Fabian Society, the Tory councillors
having been too idle to turn up in sufficient numbers (being a
majority) to elect their own man. Truly a remarkable and cosy episode. By her twenty-first birthday our daughter "Poppy" (now
Mrs Shirley Williams) became local party agent for a General
Election.

There the family grew up. Of our son John, I shall never forget
a remark he made as a small boy: "Daddy, do you like me?" It
displayed all the heart-rending vulnerability of childhood. Preoccupied with real estate, he subsequently acquired a taste for
eating up castles—that on the North Foreland of the wicked Lord
Holland, uncle of Charles James Fox—leaf by leaf, just as Cavour
ate up Italy. The place, later broken into freehold suites, was for
long in the hands of the Lubbock family, whose present descendant
is Eric Lubbock, Lord Avebury, famous among hopeful Liberals
as their then victorious Member of Parliament, "Orpington Man".

The poem *Impromptu*, by Thomas Gray, is about the place.
"Here sea-gulls scream, and cormorants rejoice,
And mariners, though ship-wreck'd, dread to land."
As for our daughter, Shirley Williams and her husband, Bernard, now Broad's successor as senior Professor of Philosophy at Cambridge and occupying Maynard Keynes' old rooms (with their indecent paintings by his male admirer) at King's College, their exploits are sufficiently publicly recorded and need not be elaborated here. As a baby the young politician's phrase of approval was "Ain't it nize?" and of diplomatic disapproval, "Bye-bye". What I recall is an under-ten poem, printed in the local paper, about the old street-seller of violets, who had impressed, as a kind of "call of London", her sympathetic mind.

Thanks to *Time and Tide* we saw something of the St John Ervines. I shall always be grateful to Ervine for telling me, with Ulster bluntness, that I had a fault of speech and recommending me to see Elsa Fogarty about it. That great professional on dramatic speech auditioned me. Her only comment was: "There is nothing at all wrong with your speech, except that somebody has made you nervous."

I also conceived a reverential admiration for Henry Nevinson, father of C. W. R. Nevinson, an Elizabethan born into our present age, an outstanding figure of Quixotic gallantry and panache and one of the noblest men it has ever been my honour to meet. He was president of the P.E.N. Club and of course much more. As a young man the friend of Thomas Carlyle, who was in turn a disciple and expositor of Goethe, Nevinson was in the great apostolic succession.

In my admiration I tried to get a knighthood for him, in his old age, through John Buchan and Lord Lothian. From Evelyn Sharp, I knew that he would have accepted it. With his usual Quixotic gallantry, he had declined a knighthood awarded to him earlier, as a foreign correspondent, on the grounds that such honour should go to the fighting men. His campaign against slavery in Portuguese possessions from which the Liberal and Quaker Cadburys drew no small part of their fortune, while typical of his valiance, had not made him popular in high Liberal quarters. The P.E.N. headquarters being in Chelsea, I appealed to its secretary, Hermon Ould. I received in reply a prim and chilly note to say that, being "a democratic club", they did nothing to support honours. It is a disgrace to England that I failed. Later Ould, I believe, accepted some very minor French honour for himself. I never forgave Ould. To P.E.N. itself I was elected, after their 1938 Conference in Prague, on H. G. Wells' nomination.

Bernard Shaw approved of Winifred Holtby and she saw quite a lot of him at Malvern. Had the old man been wise he would have left his relics to be buried in the quiet Abbey Church there, instead of leaving them (when both Westminster Abbey and, certainly, Dublin and St Paul's waited for an approach) to be pepper-potted around by the Public Trustee in the garden of remote Ayot St Lawrence. Relics produce pilgrimages. Distant Kansas tourist agencies would have seen to it that Americans, paying to visit "the Shakespeare Country" around Stratford, would have added "the Shaw Country" around Malvern, to the great profit of that municipality and of the Malvern Festival. If a *son et lumière* could also be arranged at Warwick Castle—and, having been brought up around there, I have piously worked for it—it would be better still. (After three years work, much discouraged by the Earl, who regarded it as an impertinent intrusion on private property, and a mayoral sub-committee established, I am gratified to hear, as I write this, that such a *son et lumière* does in fact take place to the advantage, cultural and financial, of the Warwicks, of the local citizenry of Warwick and Leamington and to the pleasure of the world.)

Shaw impressed H. G. Wells, when he first met him at William Morris's house in Hammersmith, as "a raw, aggressive Dubliner". He was never quite as impressed by Wells as Wells thought he ought to be. Hence "H.G." developed the extraordinary notion that he could count Shaw (along with Conrad and Henry James) "uneducated". Needless to say "H.G." had here invented a special use of the word "educated" which enabled himself, the sometime South Kensington biology student on the Prince Consort's benefaction, to count as highly educated—that is, trained in a systematic, factual and somewhat narrow fashion, especially useful in the physical sciences. "H.G." suffered un-fortunately from the vanity, arrogance, dogmatism and social resentment of many largely self-educated men. It was he who was too "raw" to be fully civilised. As he remarked, in his *Experimental Autobiography*, in a luridly revealing passage: "I eschewed dignity."

Shaw had more dignity and more panache, although not (odd in Irishmen) more humanity. His prentice masterpiece which he put into competition to match and overreach Shakespeare's *Anthony and Cleopatra*—his *Caesar and Cleopatra*, more suitable for a philandering dialogue, if not a Platonic one—falls sadly short. His weakness was his Butler–Nietzsche–Ibsen cult of the Life Force, expressed in the Superman, who showed that he could be *führer* and who had no objection to cracking a few human eggs in order to make the efficient social omelet. It was a view later expressed, about Mao's China, by that very Shavian, robot-dry and exhibitionist character, Field-Marshal Montgomery.

I myself came across Shaw on several occasions—at Fabian meetings and elsewhere. At one such meeting, Shaw having spoken for an hour and a quarter, I found myself yawning. No souls are saved, even by genius, after half an hour. On another meeting with him, thanks to the Richard Pagets, we talked about *The Realist*. Shaw did not lack generosity. He was seen, pink-faced, slinking away from Buckfast Abbey, after having deposited a note in the Benedictine monks' collecting box. But his generosity was spasmodic. A group of young literary hopefuls having approached him about the founding of a new magazine of ideas, his sole response was: "You have *The Realist*, haven't you?" All I got out of him however, was the laconic, "It failed, didn't it?" Not very helpful.

The occasion I chiefly remember was a Fabian Jubilee celebration in the mid-Thirties. Alderman Hubert Humphrey of Birmingham and all the other most worthy and devoted people were there. At the Fabian Executive Committee Laski had already told us that "he found Shaw, these days, very difficult to deal with". Shaw and Nancy Astor had gone off for a junket to Moscow, and Shaw had jubilantly announced that food given to him by friends had been "thrown out of the train window". According to him, the Soviet Union was full of food—almost as in the days of Lloyd George's "bursting grain-bins". I have forgotten how many thousands of Russians died of famine that year. The fact was that Shaw, in the name of efficiency, loved a dictator wherever he saw one. Maybe it was "the Irish in him"; a bit of bloody revolution was good. He did not much mind the dictator's political colour—better than nothing, he'd take on the Merry Monarch Charles II, who at Dover sold us out to France. Hence he was inclined to think that Hitler, on the whole, was a good fellow. He was not, of course, alone at the time. Even Winston Churchill added his encomium about how good Adolf was for Germany.

Among the correspondence which I keep is one of Bernard Shaw's well-known cards (in this case in an envelope), dated "16.8.37", addressed to me. It is in his usual jaunty style, which irritated many (as it was intended to do) and infuriated some who reflected upon the implications of "Alternatives to Parliament":

"I am just off to Sidmouth (Hotel Victoria) for a few weeks at the seaside. This postpones all personal contacts until

October.

"The article on the Fabian Society in Chamber's Encylopedia is by me. Up to its date (1925) it holds good.

"What has happened since is the final achievement of a Labor Government and its complete failure, due, not to the sensational 'apostasy' of Ramsay MacDonald, but to the obstructive power of party parliament as an institution. The F[abian] S[ociety] has now to invent some other instrument.

"I return [Eugene] Lyons. No case: abuse the plaintiff's attorney.

"No introductions necessary.

                        G.B.S."

At this high Fabian Jubilee celebration were the Webbs themselves, patriarch and matriarch. Shaw was there, clad in blue serge, with pink face and white beard (as Wells commented, no longer with white face and red beard). He ascended on to an impromptu rostrum, composed of chairs and a table. He held forth on the New Jerusalem which true socialists, not timid men, wished to see. It was not just a Heavenly City. It rested on what today we call an infrastructure. It needed roads and local government. Certainly it needed a good sewerage system. Drains. Efficiency must be the real collectivist watchword. And (entirely in the mood of the early 'Thirties) we must not be too squeamish about dictatorships.

I made a note at the time of his remarks. Why not try competence, Shaw suggested, for a change. What did they want?—to put in a new Labour Government no more competent than its predecessor? "My friend, Oswald Mosley, is a much better Socialist than most of them. A lady came to ask me to lead a campaign against Fascism." But "Why do socialists fight each other, and let the reactionaries in?" (His remarks had, at least, the merit of showing that those who accuse Labour Governments of not being "really socialist" tend to keep strange company.) Shaw continued—and then paused. "But perhaps I have said more than enough." He had indeed. The Superman got down, with a bearded grin, from his perch. As he left the hall, he passed a young man, obviously much knocked about, who had been engaged in a fight with the Blackshirts the previous night. Shaw doubtless thought him a misguided fool.

The faithful shrugged, partly in apology for the ancient Methuselah, partly in consternation. Had he no sentiment, no party loyalty? What would he say next? Wit and "the shocking"— à épater les bourgeois—was all right and indeed progressive. But in its proper place. Not at a Fabian devotional meeting.

Emil Davies was along. So, I recall, were the Woolfs at this gathering and solemn feast-day—both Virginia, to whose "lucubrations" H. G. Wells referred with ill-concealed irritation, and Leonard. Winifred Holtby wrote a short book about Virginia Woolf and noted the slightly rotten apples about their rooms which served to give a pleasant smell, like that of ancient medlars. The Woolfs themselves impressed me as being like two cards, the King and Queen, from some Alice-in-Wonderland pack. Virginia's dress, severe but stylised, almost like Edith Sitwell's, heightened the impression. They did not talk much to the comradely throng. I did not see them talk at all. Leonard trembled and Virginia looked afar off. In *Orlando* I never could make out why she gave Old St Paul's a dome. So eccentric. So Bloomsbury. This was, as reviewers have noted, not the sole such instance. I suspect she liked the feel of the deliberate error. It permitted esoteric explanation, not least in the subtle era of the literary triumph of Proust and the stream and waves and wash of self-consciousness. I tried hard to be an admirer but failed. However, I have to recognise that the Bloomsbury arrogance or *hubris* has always aroused primitive emotions in me.

Leonard Woolf was an opinionated man, although his *Principia Politica*, which I reviewed was, despite its pretentious title, of no great weight. I never found him a friendly man. Whatever his friends may have thought in the circle of that Bloomsbury with which he was connected by marriage, he impressed me as a drear fellow, a man of the conventicle. Another of his books, *Quack, Quack* (1936), expressed all too clearly his judgement on the opinion of those who ventured to disagree with him. (At least the geese saved the Capitol.) For some time I assisted Morgan Jones, M.P. on the Public Accounts Committee of the House of Commons of which he was chairman. It gave me a green card of access to the House. ("Why assist Morgan Jones?" remarked Laski. "He can't help you. He can't even help himself." But I liked Morgan.) As Morgan Jones's assistant I occasionally attended meetings of the Labour Party Advisory Committee on International Affairs, of which Woolf was secretary, just as, in my own right, I attended meetings of the Educational Advisory Committee, of which that dedicated and admirable man, R. H. Tawney, was factotum. In the former committee my opinion of Leonard Woolf was confirmed—a scrupulous and somewhat doctrinaire civil servant, a critic of other men's orthodoxies, conscientious and patient but of little warmth, who had chosen to become a theorist and also a man of letters. A man of measured wit without humour, very different from the admirable Tawney, a tobacco-smoking, most human man, who delighted to tell against himself stories highly typical.

During the Great War, and registered as an army sergeant, Tawney was sent, sick, to hospital. He received routine attention. He was then called upon by his close friend, the famous Bishop Gore of Birmingham. After the bishop had left, the sister-in-charge remarked, in rebuke and with some umbrage: "Why didn't you tell me you were a gentleman?" A new instance of "a class-stratified society", about which the good soldier Tawney would chuckle. Had he lived in the new-class-dominated Soviet Union, he would have had even more cause for comment. As the revolutionary Yugoslav Djilas has commented from his own especial angle of vision, there always have been, are and will be, class divisions in any functional society with wage differentials. An underpaid clergy, very platonic, is the major exception to the rule.

The so-called "Clapham Sect", the very embodiment of early Victorian liberalism and Puritanism, found its last expression in the fulness of time in the ex-clergyman, evangelical Sir Leslie Stephens, Virginia's father, who produced the three volume history of Utilitarianism. (It is interesting that, to this day, when the "Scientific Humanists" express their ethical creed, it will be found, as in the case of Lady Wootton, to be fundamentally utilitarian.) The apostolic succession then passed from Clapham to Cambridge and to Bloomsbury, with a bridge-head in the *New Statesman* and the London School of Economics. With some bureaucratic exceptions (for the Webbs were scarcely members of this sect any more than of the comparable "Souls", Cambridge "Apostles" and "Heretics", spawned on the banks of the Cam), they were less Socialists and far more permissivist, individualist Liberal bourgeois than they recognised themselves to be.

Some, profoundly "Cambridge men" such as the venerated E. M. Forster—and not politically preoccupied—disseminated an almost traditional Epicurean philosophy of "the friends" and "the garden", although maybe Epicurus was more heterosexual. Forster indeed, during the Second World War enunciated the distinctive but unsocialist belief that "if I had to choose between betraying my friends and betraying my country I hope I would have the guts to betray my country"—a counter-doctrine perhaps excused by the abominable Bolshevik (and Maoist) indoctrination of the duty to "sell one's parents out", but which yet seemed to enjoy the starkness of a paradoxical alternative which indeed was due to a question wrongly posed. Silence is always possible. However, this did not seem to occur to Forster.

Despite the early founding work of the Fabian Webbs and the

frequent clashes between Keynes and the new editor, Kingsley Martin (about one of which I had a personal letter of comment from Keynes), after the fusion of the *New Statesman* and the *Nation*, the "Bloomsbury" spirit, committed, sectarian, highly "intellectual" but not unconscious of native superiority, dominated the *New Statesman* and found a medium of expression through it. It was a spirit too party-sectarian, too lacking in judgement, too negative, cantankerous, acid and intolerant, and too arrogantly conscious of its own intellectual infallibility—even when it hovered between two opinions—for me to find it sympathetic. Its circle was frequented by young men "who know that they know"—the kind against whom John Locke had warned us.

Apart from my plan for a journal such as *The Realist* of popular range, I had played with the notion of a more strictly professional journal. The old Oxford-centred *Political Quarterly*, to which Sir Ernest Barker and others had contributed, had unfortunately folded up. I thought it should be revived. In 1929 I, therefore, called on the Warden of All Souls, G. W. R. Adams, as a likely person to take the initiative. The Warden received me with geniality and much sympathy and tea. He himself lay full length on cushions in front of a blazing fire, its glow illuminating the fine aura of his white hair. I stated my case and benevolence radiated in his every feature. I thought, "We have started something." Not for the first or last time in my life I was to discover the sad and time-wasting experience of taking at face-value the benevolence natural to a man who has spent his life in the warm air of popularity by being all things to all men. Nothing happened. The *Political Quarterly*, the revival of which was an excellent idea, was indeed started again in 1930—but by a London group, including Woolf, William Robson, Martin and Laski, whose publication, it seems, did not mention its predecessor of the same name. I was not invited in. It sadly ended by being, not an eminent journal of political science but, under Robson and Crick, a philosophico-propaganda journal of mediocre weight, preoccupied with savage personal attacks on Harold Wilson, Leader of the Labour party—a sorry affair.

Later I entered upon another publishing venture which was rather more successful and twice edited symposia. The first was called *New Trends in Socialism*.[1] I got together as contributors all the younger men of my acquaintance and a few others who had something to say. Among the contributors were Douglas Jay, Hugh Gaitskell, R. H. S. Crossman, Ellen Wilkinson, John

[1] *New Trends in Socialism*, Lovat Dickson, 1935.

Parker, Evan Durbin, Ivor Thomas, Leonard Barnes, Robert Fraser and Milne-Bailey. The first seven all became Ministers of the Crown. I got Arthur Henderson to write the introduction. Crossman later told me that he knew Gaitskell at Winchester, but had lost contact with him until we were all associated for this book.

Richard Crossman, Wykehamist, son of an eminent judge, at one time Dean of New College, and sometime Lord President of the Council, I had known well since those days when, on more than one occasion, I was the guest of himself and his then wife, a vivacious German. He threatens, like myself, to publish a diary or autobiography. May I yet, without *arrière pensée*, say that Dick, "out-going" and truly interested in ideas, was and is in my judgement one of the ablest men of my time—an ability shown in an early study on power, which he showed me in script; through the period when, frankly concerned to survive, he was engaged in war-time propaganda to erode enemy morale (about which I heard from Fitzpatrick, his slightly alarmed Foreign Office chief); on to his House of Commons career, and to the time when he found a strategic position for his gun-emplacements in the fortress (aimed at since Martin's days and only temporarily occupied by John Freeman) of the *New Statesman*. In the Commons, according to a letter to me from Clem Attlee, he was not popular; but then Attlee was probably not popular with him. He should, in my view, have been Minister of Education; he would certainly have been a revolutionary one, "a stirrer up". A fascinating conversationalist full of very new ideas, abrupt, dogmatic, egocentric, never suffering fools gladly, his character resembled in many respects (more probably than either would have been willing to accept) that of Maurice Bowra. Both, in such very different ways, looked out beyond Oxford to a wider world, the one in Chinese poetry and the other up the stairs of power at Westminster. Successful and unhesitant men of the world, I liked them for the same reason. They expected results.

Adding Durbin as co-editor, I later produced another volume in 1938, called *War and Democracy*.[1] Jay, Crossman and John Bowlby were among the contributors. I attempted to confront the problem of Labour's dual interest, on the one hand, in peace and, on the other, in restraining totalitarian expansion. The problem was most real and so remains to this day. But I should have been wiser had I spent the same energy in acquiring the practical power for these ends that goes with being a Member of Parliament.

[1] *War and Democracy: Essays on the Cause and Prevention of War*, (Kegan Paul, 1938).

Outside Oxford station Carr-Saunders had asked me, years before, what I would really want to be. I had replied, "to be in the Cabinet or to write a book that will be read a century hence". Although two books have been reprinted after forty years, I run the great risk of doing neither the one nor the other.

Hugh Gaitskell made a very long contribution and, as editor, I had the most unfortunate obligation of passing on the publisher's message that he must either cut it or Routledge & Co. would not take it. He declined to cut and I suppose it remains among his unpublished papers. However, a "Hugh–George" acquaintance-ship remained between us up to the time of his premature death. His elder brother, Arthur, had been one of my closest Oxford college friends. A few years later Evan Durbin died in a heroic attempt to save a child from drowning, an act typical of the man.

There were indeed less depressing episodes. On a wartime Sunday, in front of the rain-beaten panes of the windows of a Settlement House, overlooking the Pool of London, I recall reading, for review, one of Bertrand Russell's latest books. Both mind and heart were cheered by reading the work of so brilliant an intellect. It was not for nothing that, on his Richmond mantel-piece, Russell kept a bust—quite inevitable in logic—of Voltaire. What people forgot about Russell was that the Earl Russell, O.M., never himself forgot that he was the grandson of a great Whig Premier of England—Lord John, in whose four-wheeler carriage the standards surrendered by the French at Waterloo had been driven through the streets of London. Russell did not regard himself as the inferior of politicians living in some other world; but looked on them as juniors to himself in the same political world.

Later, after the war, he was my guest at 2 Cheyne Walk. He reminisced about being left alone as a young man, when the ladies had risen from dinner, to entertain Mr Gladstone. The G.O.M. said nothing. In the end he made one observation. "Good port: pity they served it in sherry glasses." More philosophically, Bertrand Russell then made a confession of faith. "There is no value I believe in more passionately than liberty." He paused. He then added sadly: "But the trouble, you know, is that I can't prove it." He yet continued, surely interestingly, that one could not live by proof, and that most of practical life had to be lived on faith in the authority of the word of somebody else.

As I have said I have always kept a diary of dreams. One, of an *Alice-in-Wonderland* type, is on record. Russell was to dine with us. He arrived and we saluted each other on both cheeks. Then, amid domestic confusion, he sat down on the floor and, in ap-pearance like the Mad Hatter, in complete tranquillity began to read a book. I trust the noble earl, if he learns of this in Heaven, will not take my dream amiss; no psychoanalytical explanation can I offer. But at least it demonstrates, from the unlying subconscious, my veneration for him. Not the least part of that veneration is due to the fact that, in an impassioned article, he has recalled our Schoolmen philosophers, from logic-chopping and verbalist cross-word puzzles, to their traditional duties to humanity of evaluation. (I here assume that, in our philosophy schools, the word "value" still has meaning. . .) Even when very wrong, Russell is still magnificent.

I do not pretend that I always agreed with him. In the encomium, to which I contributed what the Indians call "a garland", on his ninetieth birthday I worded my contribution with truth and considerable care. But, in the tradition of a great Whig nobleman, he always displayed intelligence, wit, courtesy, some tolerance and (especial joy) an open-minded respect, when you had him privately and alone, for the opinion of the other person. He liked to discuss his cousin Odo, and his Monsignori friends, with his usual humour. One of the greatest men, in his own way, of this century. Often self-contradictory but, as much as Churchill, if so unlike him, a great Englishman, a great eccentric Whig, and a great *Weltbürger*.

In these last years, however, what is called "Russell" has too often seemed to be his ubiquitous American anti-American secretary, Mr Schoenman. Russell himself, in a memorandum printed in the *New Statesman*, has put us right on that score. Also the mathematician's inhuman callousness, revealed in his auto-biography, left me feeling unhappy. In some volume I shall expect to read an account, candid, frank, of the famous Sicilian fish-fry episode, with the "spiked" wine. A lady of great charm, a Sicilian resident from Taormina, sitting on a couch in a psychoanalyst's parlour in Maida Vale, told me the story. I advised her not to try to marry Russell. It is all very well to have, as Russell's publisher (a very old hand at inexpensive advertising) emphasised, an agonising pity for all humanity. Rousseau, as he put his children into a foundling home, doubtless proclaimed the same. But what matters is, not the universal and abstract, but the individual treatment of other human beings.

One more organisation, in those pre-war years, I did become involved in. I have had long experience of avoiding becoming the "front" or "stooge" for any man or group. The Nazis, however, were increasing their mischief. Among other follies they were busy with a purge, publicly burning all the books by authors of whom they disapproved. Dorothy Woodman put forward the notion of a committee, a "Nazi Burned Books Fund". Subscriptions were to be invited, so that copies of all these books could be purchased and put on exhibition in some library, to be located in Paris. Would I become treasurer? Professor Bernal and other eminent scientists were interested. I agreed. Among those who sent subscriptions were H. W. B. Joseph. The sums collected were sent on to Paris. My trouble was that I could never get a Paris accounting. I appealed to Charlotte Haldane, the chairman, later strongly anti-Communist. But it was made clear to me, in other quarters, that my persistent enquiries were rather a nuisance.

Little did I then know that this, along with the London Dimitrov Counter-Trial—which has its fascinating parallel today in the Russell–Schoenman–Sartre Counter-Investigation in Stockholm of "imperialist" America—was but one among many of the brilliant propaganda ideas of that remarkable international Communist Willi Muensterberg, centre of the Communist propaganda web, but later himself "liquidated" by the Kremlin. The design was to rouse the righteous ire of the British *bourgeoisie* —but without telling them too much. Our money, I suspect, ended up in Communist Party coffers. Assuredly I got no accounting. I was irritated. If I was to be embroiled in practical politics I preferred it to be to some purpose and that of my own choosing.

VIII

RUSSIA: TO MOSCOW WITH EDEN

I was, and am, totally a political being. Politics has been for me meat and drink. It is arguable, however, that I made the mistake of being concerned to know what I was about, before I acted. What had impressed me was that, in 1914, emperors and statesmen had plunged into war with only a cloudy notion of what would be entailed—consequences involving, in the case of at least five great empires, their own downfall amid miscalculations of power. In the striking metaphor of David Lloyd George they "backed their machines over the precipice". In the words of Winston Churchill, in *The World Crisis*, already quoted: "One rises from the study of the causes of the Great War with a prevailing sense of the defective control of individuals upon world fortunes." It has been well said that "There is always more error than design in human affairs." *Quantula sapientia.*

Nor did it seem to me that scholars and historians, surveying these affairs in tranquillity, threw much more light on fundamental causes and consequences than was vouchsafed to the actors themselves—unlike Marx, who had at least made a massive attempt. Lowes Dickinson was a noble exception to this generalisation. Bertrand Russell gave answers fundamental but diverse. Norman Angell, not an academic, gave answers lucid but wrong. What indeed were the fundamental causes of war? Was one the unwillingness of man to pay political costs—the effective costs of peace? Were the Roman Emperors, who made desolation, yet right? Did peace, to be kept, have to be imposed by force? Did peace only come thanks to terror? Was "justice" without a tribunal, as Kant thought, merely "subjective"? Must not an International Tribunal, confronted with rebellion against a world government, be superior to any question of asking the consent of the no-longer-sovereign and indeed (like the barons of old) rebellious local states? The major conclusions I had reached and to which I was to adhere were that the ultimate peace of the world required a world authority; and that what was needed immediately was the widest practicable regional integration. This yet left the problem of some pragmatic understanding between these regions—between East and West. Even between those who shared human aims, the issue was primarily one of power rather than of ideology. Ideology became not goal but propaganda. Any nationalistic disruption of that West by men of overgrown ambition was a threat to lasting peace. As to the East, a common ideological faith does not produce an end of the power conflict between Russia and China.

Incidentally, Walter Lippmann, draftsman of some of the earliest schemes for the League of Nations desired by Woodrow Wilson, in his last years seems to have drifted into a profound defeatism, a kind of *accidie*, of which the logical consequence is the revival of the international anarchy, its banner-bearer de Gaulle. Profound although my respect for him was and remains, I could not here disagree with Walter Lippmann more—nor shall I be persuaded by those who dress up defeatism and call it "realism".

As one political organiser, Allan Young, remarked to me in the 'Thirties—I am glad that it was not his Stracheyesque advice I took—"The time has come to act and not to write 'prefaces' to action." He ended in the New Party. I was not even obsessed by the desire, commended by Beaverbrook to his journalists, to be able to say: "I was there." But I adhered to the principle I had followed in the case of Prohibition: before one generalised, it was well to go and look at the facts for oneself.

For a couple of years in the late 'Twenties, during the long vacations, I had acted as occasional leader-writer for the *Yorkshire Post*, then under Arthur Mann, a great editor. My wife also sometimes took over. I may add that it was my sole activity of which my father-in-law expressly approved. Unlike the young—and not then very successful—de Gaulle, I could not count on financial support as he was able to count on his wife's kinsmen, the Vendreux. Later I sometimes acted as special correspondent for Reuters. It was a useful exercise to have to prepare an editorial, of which one might not know the topic until 6.30 or 7.00 p.m., and to get the product, information collected and decisions made, over the wires for better or worse to the Leeds office by 11.00 p.m. zero line.

The *Yorkshire Post* gave me the opportunity in 1935 of accompanying Anthony Eden as its correspondent on a mission to Moscow where, having earlier joined with Sir John Simon in exploring the situation in Berlin, he was to pursue negotiations with Stalin. Having a book in mind, I accepted with alacrity, proposing to stay several extra weeks in the Soviet Union. The position was not quite that later attributed to Sir Victor Gollancz: "Gollancz goes to see himself." I went as a modest observer on what was yet a privileged and (after the assassination of Kirov) a highly critical occasion, indeed a turning point in the "purges"— as good an occasion to see Stalin at work as any.

The Friedrichstrasse Bahnhof in Berlin. March 1935. Jules

Sauerwein, A. J. Cummings, my good friend Norman Ewer, and other eminent journalists on the platform. Vernon Bartlett was not with us this time, but others were of the group which used to meet, along with Archie Church, at the *Taverne* (where I kept my own pipe in a rack), near the Kurfürstendam in Berlin. Red-haired Knickerbocker, of the *Philadelphia Public Ledger*, had given me some last minute suggestions in London. I had leave from my ever generous university to take time on these investigations.

The train for the Polish frontier. Subtle Sir John Simon had just been bluntly told in the Wilhelmstrasse by Chancellor Adolf Hitler that Germany had now as strong an air force as Britain, a nemesis on the do-nothing policy of Stanley Baldwin and on all the staunch supporters of disarmament, even unilateral disarmament, in order to save money for the home economy and for a more affluent life for all. Incidentally, these advocates, despite 1939, are still amongst us today: they never learn their lesson. (To protest against nuclear dissemination, instead of economic tactical centralization, is another story.)

The reason the history of most democracies is glorious but brief is, first, their tendency to disarm beyond the danger point; and, secondly, their sovereign refusal, as in ancient Hellas, to federate in time and to set up a common federal government, adequately *armed* by them. If, of course, all major powers would agree to disarm to the level of their contingents required for use in an international police force then I, for one, would be, within these terms, a pacifist except as to that international force. But this was not the announced proposal, the then popular short-view of the electorate which rested on an optimistic judgement. Russia, allegedly concerned with the well-being of the masses, did not want to fight. Germany, her own generals and industrialists alike proclaimed, was in no condition to do so. However, from that view Eden, the Galahad of the internationalists of the decade, now differed.

While sly Sir John made his suave speech afterwards to the Press in the German Chancellery, Anthony Eden sat twitching his fingers. Actually both had just received a blow in the solar plexus. Hitler was busy with a hustled policy of force which, ultimately indeed a Pyrrhic victory, would forge an iron ring around Germany quicker than could have been believed. A slow policy of calculated advance, it could yet be argued, would have deprived him of the strategic asset of surprise. This was Hitler's boasted "success", one more "success" of *Realpolitik*. It repeated, as Churchill points out, what had been the strategic error of 1914—oddly enough an error of "the two fronts," with which Hitler had charged the Kaiser in *Mein Kampf* and had insisted must not be repeated. Unlike perhaps Russia, Hitlerite Germany had not the manpower or the bomb-power (nor did the pseudo-romantic Hitler conscript his women until too late) to make an effective success of a policy of Might, whatever its morality. (France only the other day, under the atavism of the obsessive de Gaulle, equally lacked manpower and bomb-power to impose its will; it bluffed its way up with a toy atomic establishment.)

The British Lord Privy Seal, Anthony Eden, was now on board the train for Moscow, along with Lord Cranborne (now Lord Salisbury), and William Strang of the Foreign Office. Under the naive belief that because the *Yorkshire Post*, owned by Eden's family connections, the Becketts, had asked me to go to Moscow, therefore I must be the especial controlled mouthpiece of Eden, the Russian Embassy in London, under Ivan Maisky, had loaded me with every courtesy. Mr Vinogradoff, of that Embassy, had stood me good lunches. No work I have ever done for Anglo-American relations in my life has received a particle of the acknowledgement I got from the Russian Embassy in recognition of possible favours to come. Who works for Anglo-Soviet friendship, in my experience, will secure Press plaudits and invitations; who works for Anglo-American friendship will merely bankrupt himself, although there will be few who do not offer, for his virtue, tepid praise.

Since vanity is a universal human characteristic, in this the Russians, children of this world, with their subtle (and not-so-subtle) bribes, are yet sometimes very clever. It is amazing how highly intelligent people will "fall" for bribes of even overcoats or oriental rugs which keep them with the feeling that they are "appreciated". It is well to recall that the union of England and Scotland was achieved by unblushing bribery of the influential. Communism, here like Naziism, battens on the ambitious, inferior-feeling people who think that their importance has never been enough appreciated.

At this time, in the mood of the 'Thirties, I was myself pre-possessed by the notion that the Russian Revolution could be a great "workers' movement"; that it should, therefore, like the terrorist French Revolution, always be given the benefit of the doubt; and that its successes must be stressed in public and its weaknesses understood in the light of Russia's history and of revolt against the autocracy of the, until recently, serf-holding Czars. (Serf-tenure ended for salt-miners in Scotland only in the beginning of the last century.) To the outsider revolution is always romantic. The abject misery of millions of the peasantry, since 1933, especially in the Ukraine, under the despotism of Stalin—

L

"the Peasant Slayer"—was then unknown to me and, I suppose, to Eden. Edward Crankshaw's *Russia and the Russians* (1947) is worth reading in this connection. How much he has changed since. "One cannot make omelettes without breaking eggs." What did a few massacres matter—even if one chanced perhaps to know about them.

Past white Warsaw on the Vistula. Across the Bug and Neman. Past the swamps and shacks of the dismal Polish landscape by Bialystok and north of the Pripet marshes. Fir tree and birch and the gleam of snow. On to the frontier, with its newly built reception hall, smelling still of sawdust, at the railway station. All in *remont*—"under reconstruction". Triumphal arch: "Communism abolishes all frontiers." This was inspiring—or was it? Bolshevism everywhere. Here, at Negoreloye, we changed from the western European narrow-gauge railroad tracks to the—for strategic reasons—Russian broad-gauge. On to the crack Trans-Siberian train. An elaborate dinner with vodka in the ornate and lighted wagon-restaurant, as the *élite* and flattered guests of the Russian Government. Unfortunately all lights go out in the midst of dinner. We continue by candle-light. It was my first experience of something characteristic of Russia—the combination of great ceremony, quite strange to proletarian America, with unexpected breakdown. Outside the windows night falls, as the train goes through the Russian forest, so that memories come back of the novels of Seton-Merriman. Birch and fir, such as one expects at any moment will spring into a wood of lighted Christmas trees—which indeed would be very appropriate in "Holy Mother Russia", eldest daughter of "the Rome of the East", about which we heard so much propaganda and dishonest pseudo-mysticism in 1914. The "land of the true Christians"—also of the Czar-Caesars, of Pan-Slavism and the pogroms.

The chance came for a few words with Lord Cranborne. Perhaps the Great War would have been avoided, I suggested, if Asquith and Grey had been allowed, by the state of opinion in pacifist Liberal Britain, to make it harshly clear in time just where Britain would stand in the event of war. To this plea indeed Winston Churchill, in *The World Crisis*, has given the reply. No such pledge to France could have been given in 1914 by the Liberal Government, since the majority alike in the Government Party and the Cabinet, until the very verge of war, would have denounced it. They distrusted the French agreement. They would have denounced even more vehemently the secret Anglo-Russian naval agreement, had they known about it. They felt, as against the efforts of Edward VII, who personally detested his nephew, and, in the words of Lord Rosebery (to which I have referred) about the 1904 Anglo-French agreement, that the French were too egotistic ever to be good allies and that "this agreement is more likely to lead to complications than to peace". Actually in 1914 the majority of French parliamentarians, although not as emphatic as Jaurès, were disinclined to war—but not so the decisive and determined minority. The error of the Liberals was the usual one of well-intentioned but ineffective men, not fighters.

I might have added that, instead of excessive commitment to Delcassé and Cambon, Britain for her own interest might have negotiated with Bethmann-Hollweg, instead of leaving this proposal too late—to her sometime Foreign Minister, Lord Lansdowne, and, in 1918, to General Maurice. It remained true that, in the case of a clear declaration, the Germans might not have chanced war, the first European civil war. Cranborne agreed. As to the League of Nations, it would be better, he thought, either for it to declare itself speedily against this new threat of aggression or for it to be clear that it could not; and for it to be "wound up" as useless, so that we knew where we were. No talk, now, of making the League (like the United Nations later) merely "a forum for debate", where there was no hope of all being like-minded. The need was for decision, not for a "forum of debate".

Morning and the Baltic Station in Moscow. Light snow. Literally the red carpet rolled out for Eden, who had come to build up some military safeguard against Hitler. Whether Eden yet knew that Stalin was at this moment in receipt of a loan of 200 million gold Reichmarks from the Reichsbank or that he would much prefer an understanding with "a real dictator", which he was already trying to negotiate, rather than with the "bourgeois democracies", is another question. Eden was an admirable lieutenant but a poor general. (The man who in fact would succeed and achieve a treaty was called, not Eden, but Pierre Laval.) Not yet had come the snub to the mission led by the fantastically named Admiral Plunkett-Ernle-Erle-Drax, scarcely the name for a "comrade"!

Immense Red Guards, the red star in their caps, stood stiffly to attention as the diplomatic cavalcade bustled out to its cars. Bolshevism "in at least one country". A long way from the humiliating defeats of the Pripet Marshes or of the Peace (which I had personally discussed, in Cornell, with Baron von Kühlmann) of Brest-Litovsk. On the contrary, the success of the Stalin policy.

I went to the National Hotel. Opposite was the Kremlin, with its high red-brown fortress walls; with its unused cathedral of the Archangelski, in which lies buried Ivan the Terrible who

murdered his son; with its white ghostly towers, among them that
of Boris Godunov, their distinctive architecture unlike anything in
the West. Beyond was the other, then unused, cathedral of St Basil,
turned into a show-place for tourists, with its onion-shaped
domes in diverse colours, where connoisseur visitors tap the ikons
with their sceptic finger-nails, searching for genuine gold; and also
the black polished block of the Lenin mausoleum where, surrounded by red flags, the little man with the flaming beard,
lighter than in life, self-described (and accurately) as of *la noblesse
de la robe*, lay mummified.

One of my refreshments at night, at one in the morning, before
turning into bed, was to walk around the Kremlin walls and to see
how many seconds I could remain outside one of the great draw-
bridge entrances before an armed sentry would come in my
direction, grunt and indicate that I should move on.

Of our Intourist guide in Rostov, an excellent, high-minded
ex-school teacher, I asked why I could linger outside Buckingham
Palace or even drive my Ford car into the driveway of the White
House (and once I could, before everybody got security-minded),
but that these democratic habits were *verboten* in Moscow. The
reply was: "We have to defend our liberties, *svoboda*, against the
class enemy." The enemy, not of 1917, but of 1935, twenty years
on. (Interesting that Stalin's daughter found *svoboda* in the
United States.)

I asked the same thing about the men with guns in Moscow
factories. This was during my first days in Moscow and I was
surprised and, indeed, shocked. "Protection against saboteurs and
the class enemy." "But, how, after eighteen years of the Revolution,
is it that you still have an internal class enemy? Why men with
guns in textile factories?" A foolish question, since one of the
greatest purges in Russian history, after the assassination of Kirov,
in Leningrad, in December 1934, was just getting under way.
Armed men, again, on the staircase of the Press building, as we
went up to see Radek in *Izvestia*. The Dictatorship of the Proletariat over the proletariat. (No wonder Mrs Sidney Webb wrung
her hands and deplored the extraordinary sort of idiosyncracy of
actually liking to talk about "dictatorship" in what was really
"a fuller industrial people's democracy".)

A real enthusiast, English-speaking and I believe English,
wanted to show me over the wonderful *Moscow Daily News* works.
He returned red-faced. It was not permitted. Security. Even in the
Garden of Culture and Rest, where we could read the inscriptions
on the gravestones now used as paving stones, in the Home of
Mother and Child, I found an old bearded gentleman with a

rifle, presumably to protect this pleasure garden against looters and the class enemy. After all, the woman conductor on the train in Sevastopol station did tell me not to leave my luggage unattended inside the train while I paced the station platform, since the risk of theft was too great. Shade of Tolstoy—Communism and the risk of theft.

I saw Eisenstein's famous *Gulliver* film—of the Hapsburg-like monarch and the right proletarian Enceladus-Gulliver—in Moscow. I talked with Eisenstein in his apartment, with a futuristic Saturn-like object hanging from the ceiling in his bed-sitting-room, his portmanteaux piled in a corner and a foetus in a bottle on the window ledge. Very modern, these decorations.

I met Gordon Craig, whose enthusiasm was for the puppet theatre, and suggested that he should see the remarkable puppets of the Eisenstein film. But Craig, the spoiled child of the European Theatre, did not demean himself by seeing films. I chiefly recall his telling me in Moscow that Mussolini had offered him the Colosseum for a production. Gordon Craig was riding high, an artist among the dictators, munificent patrons of the arts. And, after all, *il Duce*, the once Marxist revolutionary, had been the first of all to recognize the revolutionary Soviet State—so why not go to Rome? In a basement café, I also heard Prince Mirsky discourse very sincerely on a new way of life. Although capable of deviations, this admirable man—even if Leonard Woolf found him frightening ("not quite the best Bloomsbury")—was a show exhibit. Later he left for a concentration camp.

In another film I was hugely impressed by, there was a close-up of a serving man of the old régime with bare foot in some kind of clog-polisher, polishing his master's floor to and fro, to and fro. Let us have a higher standard than this, I said. The Revolution perhaps had given it. It was, therefore, a shock when one morning, coming down from my room in the National Hotel, I found a hotel worker busy, with bare foot and clog, polishing to and fro, to and fro. An old Russian habit, I presume.

Some of the staff there, I learned, regretted times past. One good woman, an official, told me that she was soon going into hospital and that she hoped she would die there. It showed the passion of courage for her to dare to make the remark. Nobody had in fact told me as much as that in Berlin, not even the grandson of Field-Marshal von Moltke, who was so much in revolt—nor indeed any industrial workers. Most of them were, in their own way, riding too high or marching twelve abreast. This does not mean that some of Hitler's victims, who failed to get away, were not going to die— indeed six million German citizens during the Second World War, and more in Poland. (Ultimately, however, seven million Germans were expelled by the Soviets from the Eastern provinces.) But Stalin, of course, liquidated a couple of million, chiefly by starvation, in 1934 alone. (Slavophil Professor Bernard Pares declined to name even an approximate number; he pooh-pooh'd the matter.) The Civil War had taken twice as many. Good Uncle Joe boasted that his total, shot or starved, was ten million. He took sardonic pleasure in counting them up on his fingers. The mind boggles at the barbarism. The Nazis possibly accounted in all for about a million more; the figures, astronomic, lack statistical accuracy, but the latest figures, provided by a Russian Academician, make Stalin accountable for about twelve million Russians, and some students make the total twenty million human beings.

Beside the tragic side of the brave new world, there was the amusing side. At another hotel, the *Nova Moskaya*, even the morning newspaper could only be paid for by getting a chit from the vendor; paying for the chit at a pay desk; and then, third, collecting the paper. Alas! The plan produced a great wait, which at last became insufferable. One consulted the manager; there was no one less who could do anything. He would, he explained, take the money, because maybe the young lady had gone to the toilet.

However, in the great Hotel Metropole one could sit until two in the morning listening to thirteen fiddlers playing, clad in full evening dress in the best Vienna style—that is unless one preferred to spend the time travelling up and down the grand new Moscow metro, where even the spittoons and waste paper or garbage baskets were of marble. As was stated frankly by one official: "Something cheaper might have been more useful but we can't afford to do anything less striking here." The great Soviet building, "like a wedding cake", to be surmounted by a vast colossus of Lenin, had still—has still—to be built: but everything had to be either the "greatest in the world" or "under reconstruction", *remont*. What money went on rehousing the abominably overcrowded workers among all this marble show was not so clear.

Outside I walked in the streets amid the crowd of human bundles clad against the Moscow weather; found my way past puddles; stubbed my toe against the guttering from the houses which ran higher than the ill-made pavements (doubtless now re-made); and looked at the bookshops. There was a fine copy exhibited of *Engels on the Housing Problem*. My attention was distracted by an insistent tinkle. I turned to find a little boy holding a beggar's tin cup, begging for kopecks. I was horrified by all these beggars and asked my Russian friends about them. It was, it seemed, all very sad and criminal. They "should be punished". "But, you see, they make more money that way."

Anna, my Intourist guide in one place, told me, *inter multa alia*, that her chief, the Intourist hotel proprietor, was also a murderer; that there were indeed very wicked men about. There had been thousands of small children orphaned during the Civil War. Those times had been such that men had eaten potatoes mixed with clay to satisfy their gnawing hunger during the Civil War, and even cannibalism, as among those shut in the German concentration camps, was not unrumoured. The orphan children were very wild, but "the social workers were trying to do what they could for them", although not nearly enough. When the soldiers got drunk, she added, they would go out and club them on the head.

It was in April, while I was in Russia, that *Izvestia* carried the announcement of a new regulation under which, even for petty larceny, those over twelve became liable to the death penalty. The decree was signed by Vaycheslav Mikhailovitch Scriabin, *alias* Molotov, an execrable man. In the 1939 trials, confessions were made by some accused of torturing children over ten to get admissions: those guilty got a ten years' sentence. I seemed to recall a story by Dostoevsky of a drunken moujik beating a horse to death. Turgeniev's mother did the same to a serf. An old Tartar custom, I concluded: "Scratch a Russian and find a Tartar." Doubtless there were and are innumerable exemptions to that rule—sensitive Dostoevsky characters. But still it was one country.

Perhaps there is no better guide than Leo Tolstoy to the Russian mind. And even sensitive Dostoevsky characters could commit very macabre murders; and Gorki characters be revolting in immoral brutality. The world's High Civilisation is of extremely limited extent—and even Germany, one discovered, did not always conform to it any more than did the French in Algiers. As Arthur Miller has underlined, in *Incident in Vichy*, the French majority did not revolt, even against like atrocities in their own midst. (Were the British and Americans—the Anglo-Saxons—always exceptions? "It never happens here.") Hitler's Germany, I remembered, had concentration camps for "politicals"; and of Russian concentration camps I had not then heard one word—I had seen atrocity photographs indeed of the Civil War, but had put them on one side as unchecked propaganda, and hence omitted to ask. Item: such inquiries would not improve Anthony Eden's chances. Later I was to reflect upon a remark of Madame Pilsudski, that she would rather be the prisoner of the Gestapo than of the G.P.U. For myself, I would rather be gassed quickly than work on in the long Arctic night, to be sure of dying slowly. Perhaps Swift was right about the human race.

I mentioned the name of the Intourist guide, Anna to a certain aristocratic British politician. My friend Morgan Jones, M.P. described him as given to leaning over backwards towards "advanced" views by way of compensation for his aristocratic descent. This eminent man, Charles Trevelyan, told me that at the time of the General Election of 1935 in Britain he had just completed for Gollancz a little pamphlet on Russia. "I hadn't time to write it really but, since the publisher was pressing, having four days on a boat on the Volga, I wrote it then. It sold"—and he quoted a number in thousands. "I wrote Gollancz back, 'You must mean ——hundred copies'. But he telegraphed 'No:——thousand copies.'" I told him that this was very interesting and then asked whether he had ever by chance met this Intourist guide, at the town I mentioned.

I remembered her vividly because we had travelled together in a car; the driver, she explained, was a Czech who knew no English. She was a pleasant little woman, much like a school-teacher or church worker. She was certainly frank. During the course of the journey she not only explained to me the state of Russia but also added that she fully expected to be shot at any moment. She had talked too much to visiting sea-captains, it appeared. Could I suggest any means whereby her children could get away?

I did not, of course, explain to her Eden's hopes of a great alliance for freedom and democracy (with Christianity thrown in) against the Hitlerite menace; but I did counsel caution. Sir Charles Trevelyan's reply I no less vividly recall: "Oh, yes, I remember. She talked to Lady Trevelyan, I think. Rather a bore, I thought; rather a bore." Certainly she was a bore. She upset the distinguished baronet's tidy views about 'the new civilization'. The trouble lies in that there are also human beings as well as abstract civilisations. I could have expressed my own views with great vigour but I refrained. The world is full of Sir Charleses. They think they understand the real nature of politics: "No omelettes without breaking eggs." Pleasant fat gamester, Charles James Fox, and the French Revolution with the green-eyed, inhuman metaphysicians making the omelettes. (At Cornell I met Sir Charles' brother, George—the one who advised Lord Moran to publish a medical history of Churchill, in the interest of "future historiography"—an abrupt, arrogant man.)

A. J. Cummings, of the *Daily News*, glowingly described Kharkhov in the guest book as "a city of cheerful faces" (he knew little German, no Russian, and the brother-in-law of his Intourist guide was a G.P.U. official). An honest-faced railway worker asked me how many train smashes we had in Britain. "We get much advice here and a lot of discussion and self-criticism, but the smashes still go on." However, without being an engineer, I surmised that the great steel works at Dnieproges or rather Zaporozhe, with their electrically fed furnaces, compared most favourably, as up-to-date, with the hand-fed furnaces of Messrs Dorman Long, in Yorkshire. They compared well with Krupps. What chiefly impressed me, however, was the earnest remark of my serious young guide (who was not best pleased because I beat him at chequers): "Before the Revolution we had fourteen different classes in this country." "Ah! yes." "And now we have only seven." I do not know precisely what he meant, but I could see around me the truth of what he quite unintentionally implied—or was it Russian humour? Great technological advance. Great human frustration.

I gave full marks to the schemes for industrial insurance; some to the schools with their two or three shifts of children a day (with whom the hard-driven teachers had to cope without complaint), where they were taught to read what was good for them—nothing of course to indicate that Trotsky had ever played a great role, but something about England as faithfully revealed in *Oliver Twist*. I gave the highest marks to the hospitals, better yet in blueprints than in practice; many to the free polyclinics for medical advice, in the days before a national health service in the West; more to the children's crèches for the infants of mothers engaged, whether for good or ill, in manual work, sometimes very hard manual work, with a doubt whether so many women needed to be so employed to keep up any tolerable family income on low wages. (Incidentally, in the photographs of the Kremlin ruling group, one never at that time saw any women included, whatever might be said about advanced feminism. There were of course eminent Russian revolutionary women, such as Vera Zazulich, and one eminent woman ambassador. The Russians did better than this, at least for the few, in the days of the Czars and the great Czarinas.) But I gave few marks indeed to the new workers' tenements of a poor workmanship, so far as I could judge, which no public authority in the West would have dared to provide as part of any slum replacement scheme.

An ex-bellboy from the Grosvenor Hotel, London, now a sub-commissar for Food, took me round, remarking incidentally, as a piece of philosophy, that as one grew older one recognised that one could not possess all the pretty girls one met, but only some of them. I joined his family in their apartment, one of solid middle-class comfort. I have not been speaking here, as touching housing, only about over-crowded Moscow, where one tap could serve a courtyard and where families lived three (families, not persons) in a largish room. But the apartments in Moscow for the civil servants were quite a different matter. Here, amid the rags, was the new aristocracy. Perhaps this was what my young man at Dnieproges meant.

In Yalta I asked one of the Russian journalists who were on show—and I knew that the actors or other representatives of "art and culture" and, also, the technician-journalists were the darlings of the regime—what a man should do with money in Soviet Russia. He shrugged. I knew that Stalin, in an ever-memorable comment, had quoted Marx and had said that he "stood by Marx and Lenin and not with the bourgeois egalitarians". That, at least, was refreshing and honest. "Do with money? Why, one can always find something to do with money. Travel or buy a *dacha*." That many of the higher-ups, especially in Moscow, had their *dachas* or country houses I knew, although not all were as closely guarded by police as Stalin's. A famous one was that of Maxim Gorky, whom the G.P.U. chief Yagoda was accused, at his trial, of attempting to murder. Yagoda was shot.

It is this kind of thing which provided the basis for Trotsky's—and later Djilas'—not unjustified complaint about "the Revolution Betrayed". This was indeed the theme of the book which started the great disillusionment. Those by Gide, by Orwell, by Djilas, by Koestler followed. One unexpected consequence of Soviet Communism ceasing to provide, thanks to"totalitarianism", any tolerable ideological refuge for the utopian progressives, in the fight against "the Hitlerite hell", was the post-war surge of protest movement, of which the fundamental philosophy was no longer Leninism or even Trotskyite but anarchist. For Western liberals, nurtured on individualism and "fundamental civil liberties" (or "natural rights"), its appeal was peculiarly powerful. After all, the United States came into being from "anti-executive, anti-government" revolution.

The way to rule in Russia under Stalin was to shoot the Left-wingers, as Lenin had shot the Kronstadt sailors—and then to adopt part of their policy. The firing-squad, "for the good of the Revolution", was never far away. The hedonistic liberal bourgeois is almost mentally incapable of coming to terms with, and recognising as fact, the "steel" (or "Stalin") grimness of the Russian answer. He does not count Dostoevsky among his ancestors. During the Civil War after 1917, shooting "Anarchist dogs" was as commonplace as shooting rabbits. The Soviet Comrades then, and today, although they may find them convenient allies in negative subversion (as even the Nazis were found to be), have a way of dealing with the young followers of Bakunin and of the black—or "black-and-white" or "black-and-red"—flag which lacks nothing in ruthless thoroughness and which demonstrates the ultimate in antagonism in social philosophy. In the exemplary words of Lenin: "Revolution is authoritarian." Contemporary Western youth has yet to face up to this. The enemy to be shot is the Anarchist.

The cynical structure of dominatory power showed itself once again in politics, as it had done in earlier revolutions. Although the Party line emphasised the difference between the French and Russian Revolutions, in the minds of almost everybody in the outside world the comparison was present. Hence Liberals must, of course, (so ran the argument), support the Russian Revolution as Charles James Fox had supported the French, even if it did end in "the Terror" of Marat and Robespierre, and in Napoleon confronted staunchly by Pitt, and in Waterloo. Moreover, "this is the Workers' Republic". And all the workers must obviously support the Workers' Republic. The logic of the propaganda had the authentic hypnotic quality. And the conclusion was that democracy should betray itself to oligarchy. Maybe Kerensky, if he had been given a chance, could have democratised Russia. His fatal error was to be too deeply committed to the Allied military cause, with its purpose "to make the world safe for Democracy". Today Democracy has perforce to shake hands with Stalin's successors, unless it prefers Chairman Mao.

I have almost always noted among Communists of my acquaintance that it is precisely the oligarchic or tyrannical-aristocratic element in Bolshevik Communism which appeals to them. They feel that, whatever their birth or social status, they can join the "politically conscious vanguard", the clerisy, the directing oligarchy which is united to the masses by an inspired mystique of collectivism; and they, by strange coincidence, always think of themselves as future commissars and seldom as Siberian labourers. I can think here of individual Britons. This hope appeals to secretly ambitious and frustrated men, burning with the resentment of an inferiority complex. It may well be that there is a proper aristocratic rôle which bourgeois democracies overlook; and that the world should be guided by a diversity of educational aristocracies or by Mandarinism (or plurality of mandarin advisers). But this is not quite the kind of aristocracy that one finds in Party quarters in Russia or in contemporary Communist China.

It is easy for a Communist to say, in discussing feminism, that what is determinant is "class, not sex". Equally one might say it is not "colour" or "nation". That the answer to these issues of discrimination is indeed more difficult; that it lies in the psychology of the man within, questing for recognition and status, more than in external institutions (for all that Hume said); that it lies in child education; and in whether men are trained in democratic fraternity and co-operation or have early concluded that the human race is, to a significant degree, one of "snollygosters" and "bastards" to be met aggressively with expectation of violence—this the Bolshevik vanguard (not at all the same thing as the communist, with little "c") refuses to recognise, as being "unrealistic". Even today the Russians think the socialist governments of the West "too soft". Lenin's prescription for dealing with insurgent workers, such as the Kronstadt sailors, was in the last resort the same as Napoleon's: "a whiff of grapeshot". This is otherwise known as the Terror. Leon Trotsky was frank about this. He defended rule by terror.

The gravest error of the mentally bewildered West has been to fail to see that, practical or not, desirable or not, there is nothing morally wrong with communism with a small "c", with the *kibbutzim* of Palestine or with the Oneida Settlement in New York, or, for that matter, with St Peter's early Christian Church in Jerusalem. It was indeed a pretty tough Church. St Peter's methods with Ananias and Saphira were scarcely of the "voluntary order", when they defaulted in their contribution. We must not be misled by what General de Gaulle truly calls "ideological patter". What is very wrong is the aggressively "dizzy-with-power" Bolshevik or Maoist oligarchy. The clash is not one of uncompromising ideology, taken as gospel, not propaganda tool. The essence of power is the core of the evil, just as with Hitler's shirted men and new élite of violence. The one oligarchy, spreading fear of foreign devils to keep its own neck safe, stimulated into new violence the other oligarchy. By its very nature tyranny had to *encourage* fear, in order to provide ground for its own survival. As today the insecurity of Russian tyranny declines, the prospects of cooperation increase—not rapidly but encouragingly; not today in Prague but perhaps tomorrow.

As I left on the train for Rostov I was cheered to see seated together in the plain restaurant car serving endless *chai*, tea from the samovar, somebody who looked like a miner and also a highly polished uniformed official. "This", I said, "is fraternity", the newer Democracy, the Russia I had come to see. An hour afterwards I walked through the train. My worker I found on the wooden ledge bunk, where most of the "hard" passengers lay with their boots on, sleeping, often feet to head. But my officer I could not find, even in the "soft" compartments where I was myself. However, persistency and willingness to brave the obvious suspicions of the conductor, who viewed me as a low-class intruder, rewarded me by the discovery that, attached to the train, there was a special car, comparable to those on the Paris-Lyons line, with apartments second and first class. Here, well ensconced with feet on the seat opposite, was my officer. Maybe he was a railway official.

On my boat on the Black Sea the experience was the same. I sat inside in a saloon lit by red-shaded table lights. Outside, the proletariat lay like baggage in their sheepskin coats, full length on the deck. One may say, if one likes, that this is Asia; but I did not note those things in the admirable pre-Communist Shanghai–Hangchow express where they served, free, endless tea and little hot towels to wipe one's hands. Even India wore a difference. For the rest, I noted the Moscow slogan: "Be cultural: spit in the can."

The same thing I observed again in the railway station waiting-rooms and platforms. Of course I did not travel in millionaire American Ambassador Joseph N. Davies' luxury launch on the Black Sea, from which vantage-post he was able to discover and 'reveal' in his book that all things, or so very, very, many, were good, unlike conditions in the world of "imperialist" Winston Churchill.

Nobody perhaps converted more ordinary readers to the feeling that, making all proper allowances, the Bolsheviks were on the great highroad to freedom than Roosevelt's Ambassador Davies, a very convenient man. For some time I was almost another such, deceived by the philosophy of "taking the long view". Doubtless the Revolution did some good. The industrial progress of Russia, already under way before 1917, shaped later by a social democratic constitution under Kerensky, would also have done good, with less violence. But the Revolution did not do all the good that the devout pretended, and it inaugurated an epoch of despotism. The same applies to China today.

In Moscow the party with which I had come from Berlin to Russia was given quite unusual facilities. This, of itself alone, made my journalistic opportunities well above the ordinary. One entered, welcomed, by the Borovstsky Gate into the gigantic fortress. One saw inside the Kremlin—the vast, more recent halls; the strange, small, Oriental, older rooms, decorated as in some Persian miniature, not marked by the Westernised brilliance of St Petersburg, but utterly Muscovite, from which one could see in imagination Catherine and Orlof, or the mad Czar Peter with his boyars, appearing at any moment from a drunken rout. To be honest, some of the ornately painted smaller rooms also reminded me of the lobby of the Randolph Hotel in Oxford, sharing a common barbaric quality. One saw the assembled jewels of the Scythian Czars.

One did the tour of the theatres; saw a beautiful production of *King Lear* at the Jewish Theatre; and *Swan Lake* at the Bolshoi Opera House. The heads of the aristocrats were paraded around on the stage of the Bolshoi Theatre on pikes, for the present Earl of Avon's better edification. Josef Stalin and his entourage sat well back—unlike Lincoln, out of firing range—in their box. The *corps de ballet* and the scenery were admirable although, of course, traditional and not quite so good, I was told by connoisseurs, as under the Czars. It impressed all visiting groundlings and tourists. At least the red curtain, of a gorgeous silk with the gold hammer and sickle upon it, was new.

Later in the evenings there were the parties. Fortunately I had brought full dress, "hammer tail" coat (as in America it is irreverently called), white waistcoat and tie, all very protocol. What I had not realised was how often they would be strictly required. The Russians, as is well shown in the play *Tovarich*, are very protocol-conscious. American informality they take as a sign that one is not quite "of the vanguard"—American "immaturity", in fact. American army car drivers, accustomed to pleasant informality with their generals, were to discover this abruptly. They were directed to an entrance "below stairs". For the Russians a general is a very great man. The head of the Union of Soviet Socialist Republics, bank-robber, ex-seminarist Stalin, was to be Generalissimo.

The first of these expensive parties I went to was given by the Russian Foreign Office, then under Litvinov. Oddly enough one wall of a reception room of the palatial premises in the Spiridovna Ulitza was decorated with the royalist blue and *fleurs-de-lis* of France—as I said to a neighbouring French journalist, I presumed *pour encourager la République de la France*. The coffee cups still bore the imperial monogram "N", for "Nicholas II".

The British Embassy reception was a stiff and chilly affair, with local claret; a soloist from the opera; a very bored-looking Commissioner of Education present, the brilliant Lunacharski's successor, Bogdanov. It began at eight and Lady Chilston extended a cold hand to say goodbye to her guests at eleven. All very British. Only the representative of the London *Times*, the journal of the Top People, derived the advantage of a major interview from it.

Moscow, however, is a late city. Hence the reception given at the American Embassy, by William Bullitt, to celebrate his return to

Moscow, beginning at eleven, was more in accord with the general tempo. Odd though it may seem, there is something congruous in the American and the Russian temperament, a character the English have lost since the days of the first Elizabeth or the second Charles. Given a chance, Americans and Russians are both uninhibited. The men are strong; the manners share some of the qualities of the later Roman Empire. There is a Senatorial quality to any first class American performance, just as there is definitely a Byzantine quality to any first class Russian one.

Slowly the ball of crystal network, suspended from the ceiling, turned and the reflected spectra of the lustres kaleidoscoped on the polished floor of the Embassy hall. Immaculately attired, coming from their cars in the snow without, the guests arrived. Orjonokidze, the czar of heavy industry, bushy-moustachioed and all broad smiles, was there; Lazar Kaganovitch, Stalin's brother-in-law; and Bogdanov, Commissar of Education.

Litvinov also was there. Many "with-it" London hostesses thought him—and Ivan Maisky—"such a dear", although, if one looked at him closely, the wreathed smile of the cartoonist became something set in folds of flesh, made more emphatic by heavy glasses. The error of those, in London or Geneva, who took his dicta—"peace is indivisible"—as "the voice of Russia", was that they forgot that he, not in the inner circle, only gave expression to *one* of Generalissimo Stalin's several alternative policies. He understood the value to a diplomat of dancing, since not only can a dance step enable one to get through a diplomatic cocktail crush but a partner can provide one with protection for the evening from inconvenient questions. One merely takes the floor. Marshal Clementi Voroshilov, hero of the Soviet Union and later its President, medalled with those badges of distinction and rank which the proletarian Soviet Union likes, was also on show, along with Bukharin, Radek and innumerable smaller fry. Almost the whole diplomatic corps was along.

By one o'clock in the morning the party adjourned to sup with the aid of Russian wines. At one table one could see Radek, of *Izvestia*, and the eminent fellow-travelling American idealist, Anna Louisa Strong. In the corners of the hall little brown bears, brought from the Moscow zoo, were in cages. Some guests stood them alcohol. Nobody put Anna in a cage.

Borodin—"Borodin of China"—I lunched with at Voks: I cannot recall whether he was alone among the eminent on this occasion. When I asked him questions at the lunch he expatiated on his love for the green lanes of Cumberland. He was the agent intended to fulfil Lenin's dictum, "the way to Paris lies through

Peking"; but he was the agent who failed with Chiang. When I
persisted he replied in Latin. Abruptly I noted the emergency uses
of Latin, which is a language everyone should be taught. "*Clericus
clericum non decimat*," he muttered—to be freely rendered: "One
journalist does not cause the liquidation of another."

Having feasted itself adequately, the brilliant and decorated
company in the Embassy arose to dance again. As I watched, a
quiet voice observed: "Somebody ought to make a record of this."
"Perhaps somebody will." "But discreetly. . . ." The speaker, clad
in the exquisite Chinese national costume, high in the neck, close
as a glove and slashed to the knee, was Hilda Chen, the very
beautiful daughter of the Chinese Ambassador. I watched the
gaiety until 4.00 a.m.; but many, not least the Russians, were
clearly determined to stay it out until breakfast. I left, for the sake
of the air walked back through the snow of Moscow and got to my
hotel in time for a few hours of bed. I could not help reflecting
upon how precisely one might define a "decadent capitalist
society" and how identify a "fine, young, vital, democratic one".
I did not attend the Marquis de Cuervas' ball in Biarritz, which the
Vatican's *Osservatore Romano* alleged to be vulgar and ostentatious
but, costume effects apart, I cannot suppose that the pleasure
given to the guests can have been very different from that on this
occasion.

However, the Russians are a cheerful folk, whose unvarnished
virtues and vices have never been better described, as I have said,
than by Tolstoy, the elder—I do not refer to the incredibly
chauvinistic Alexei Tolstoy, who wrote apparently to save his neck.
They like parties and lots of drink. A little vodka thaws a lot of
Marxism. Unfortunately, although it may aid a Prince Yousoupoff
in assassinating a Rasputin when his guest, it does not lead to the
overthrow of a truly Muscovite police terror such as Ivan the
Terrible might have viewed with deferential respect. But, in colder
blood, a police-chief Beria, because his works are evil, follows a
Yezhov to execution; and a Yezhov, because his works are evil,
follows his predecessor Yagoda to execution and the grave.

Ivy Litvinov I met later for a luncheon *à deux* in her apartment—
an intelligent and sincere woman. Where she now is I do not know.
Much of our conversation turned on education. She was very frank
in her condemnation of "modern progressive methods" in Russia
and on the need for more "discipline". This was about the time
that the permissive enthusiast, Dora, second Mrs and first
Countess Russell of that creation (or generation), was trying out
advanced "new education" methods at Telegraph Hill. Ivy
Litvinov complained that some of the pupils not only thought

themselves equal to the teachers but, even, that it would be more democratic for the taught to provide the rules, if there were any, for the teachers. We also discussed her enthusiasm for Ogden's Basic English as world language. It is sad that no permanent niche in Soviet life could apparently be found for a woman of this ability.[1]

I also, as I told Ewer of the *Herald*, had an introduction to the girl friend of one of the Red Army generals. In fact, I had been asked by her kinsfolk in London to see her, and I tracked down the address and presented the note. She was out of Moscow but her old mother welcomed me to the comfortably, if not elaborately, furnished room. Soon she suggested that we moved into another room. Those who knew Russia better than I did would have suspected that the room was "bugged". Our conversation was about her family details and trivialities, but there were, she said, several people in the house and we might be overheard. It was well to be careful. When I left—I was new to Moscow or I should have remarked it when I entered—I noted that a police detective took regular turns up and down before the window. I had earlier presented introductions in Germany; but it only gradually occurred to me how very unkind it is for people coming from the democracies to present introductions to friends in totalitarian countries. However innocent this only builds up evidence against them when it comes to the next purge.

On May Day I stood in the Red square, close enough to the Lenin Mausoleum to see on it clearly Josef Vissarionovitch Stalin, with his reassuring Baldwin pipe, and also his brother-in-law, Kaganovich. Little Constantine Oumanski, a Bessarabian by birth, the hated Press officer, who later went as ambassador to Mexico and "had an accident", was all over the place. The great military masses marched past, big men in magnificent order. The aeroplane demonstration was overhead. The old Cossack officer, Budyenny, although he was maybe already militarily a back number, put the magnificent cavalry through its paces. The implication was that cavalry could still win victories—a strange illusion which was the curse of the Poles. Later followed columns of factory workers. It was a species of lynching party. Some bore banners denouncing one more ex-hero of the people, Zinoviev—"Zinoviev, thrice traitor." Zinoviev and Kamenev had already had one trial this January: they would both be shot in 1936.

It was all part of the show, maybe rather a sinister show. Others

---

[1] As I revise this paragraph, I learn with joy that Ivy Litvinov is not only alive and alert, but is about to produce a book with the significant and typical title, *She Knew She was Right* (Gollancz).

M

had been lynched in their time, including the great trades union leaders of the Soviets. The ruthlessly ideological intellectual Lenin, as much a "metaphysician" as Robespierre and more, had little patience with trades union thinking. He showed them "where they got off". Always there was some high-placed traitor being denounced—presumably there was a lot of treason about. Muriel Draper, Ruth Draper's sister, was standing next to me: "I always think," she said, "that fear is the hall-mark of savagery." To this day I do not know to what Muriel referred, but from other remarks I conjecture it was to German National Socialism.

It is worth noting that it was Budyenny (whose obedience to orders from Stalin overrode those of his commander-in-chief, Tukhachevsky) who was responsible in 1920 for the Russian defeat by the Poles who had captured Kiev that May. Upon the causes of this Pilsudski commented. Tukhachevsky was unwise enough, in his book, to place the blame where it lay. The ever-jealous Stalin, the successor of the Czars, "the genius of geniuses of the workers of the world", never forgave Marshal Tukhachevsky. He had seemed to challenge the infallibility of the Great Necromancer. In the end Tukhachevsky too was shot. Some of the evidence against him was apparently obtained through those who had enmeshed the Czarist émigré, General Miller in Paris. Miller later was kidnapped and disappeared.

More immediately relevant to this May Day was the demonstration I was watching against the veterans of the Revolution, Kamenev and Zinoviev, sometime President of the Comintern. The liquidation was in progress of the Old Bolshevik core whose prestige Stalin regarded as a potential challenge to himself. Already the great George Dimitrov, hero of the fight against Hitler, was receding into the shadows. He was not alone. Security precautions following the assassination of Sergei Kirov, Soviet boss of Leningrad on 1 December 1934, were the excuse for this purge of 1935. New regulations had set up a secret tribunal for trials within ten days, and for immediate execution on conviction. But the interesting thing is that the investigation into this murder of Kirov was conducted by Stalin himself. Yagoda, head of the G.P.U., was excluded, was nearly the victim of an "accident", and his fall from favour dates from this time. "The best Chekist of all the Chekists is Stalin himself." He began life as a seminarian; he graduated as a bank-robber. Who knows where he might end?

The assassination of Kirov provided an admirable excuse for the removal of difficult colleagues and rivals, who could be popularly regarded as heroes of the Revolution—what Leon Trotsky, later to be assassinated, called *The Revolution Betrayed*. But whether this assassination of Kirov, which led to the liquidation of thousands of Party members besides Zinoviev and Kamenev, was not itself Stalin's "Reichstag Fire" is open to question. It would have appealed to his sense of humour. As President Truman later remarked in an unguarded moment: "He is quite a good fellow."

It is significant that Kirov's alleged assassin had already been arrested two months earlier by Kirov's men, and then had been released. It is also relevant that during the Civil War Kirov had ordered Beria's execution; and that Beria's rise to power begins from the date of Kirov's death. There was mystery about the investigation; and the esteemed Mr Vishinsky, the Fouché of the Russian Revolution, whose watchword was "shoot the mad dogs," (and whose memory the United Nations saluted with piety as a "valiant fighter", in the words of M. Mendès-France) at Yagoda's trial, in 1938, did not permit the matter to be brought up by Yagoda. After all, in 1931, Kirov had gone on record, to Stalin's annoyance, in opposing a change which allowed death sentences for Old Bolsheviks, if brought to trial as part of the liquidation of the Leninist heritage. However, there was no London counter-trial, aided by Denis Pritt or others, to the trial of Kamenev and Zinoviev, "counter-revolutionary traitors". Mr Pritt, Q.C., M.P., wrote a pamphlet to explain that such things were all quite just. As Stalin said, "Europe will swallow it all." Europe did. The autocrat of All the Russias won.

When I was taken across the Dnieper Dam by its assistant engineer, we paused to talk in the middle. A sentry came up and said something to my guide. With some embarrassment he apologised. It was, it seemed, contrary to the regulations even for the assistant chief engineer and his guest to pause. There might be sabotage. Senator Joseph McCarthy might have noted this as a suggestion or, maybe, the anti-McCarthyites might have noted that the Senator had not in America got round to this form of charge yet. However, I had, experience of another incident, illustrating Soviet suspicion and spy-mania in their police state, which might have been more unpleasant.

I had helpfully suggested to Oumanski that, if he wished to be a good propagandist, he should not just keep open the Anti-God Museum—housed in a former church which I visited—but also cme of the churches and, moreover, give the utmost publicity to his liberality. The visits of the Dean of Canterbury (and indeed officially of the Anglican Archbishop of York) were not yet. This seemed to strike Oumanski as a novel but dubious idea. After all some churches, about ten per cent of the original number, were open.

I was aware not only of this but that some of them were crowded to suffocation. But I wanted to see what happened on the great occasion of the Orthodox year, Easter Eve. Stephen Graham's sentimental books about anti-German Holy Mother Russia who was to regenerate the world, books which did much to corrupt and confuse Western opinion during the First World War, had at least acquainted us with this custom.

That an important minority of the common folk of European Russia are sincerely Christian, even if the policy of the Caesaro-papalist Orthodox Church has always been to associate religion with national patriotism and with the leadership of the Master of the Russias, is a consideration never to be overlooked. But it must be added that, under the direction of camouflaged police, the Russian Church, as was well recognised by the American Orthodox, can itself become a spy-network and a Soviet recruiting agency abroad. Some of the new Russian Orthodox hierarchy were suspected of being police spies, including the Orthodox Patriarch of Jerusalem. I knew that a previous Patriarch of Moscow, Tikhon, had abominated the Bolshevik régime. Reconciliation was to come later, with the approach of war and on the nationalist basis of defence of Mother Russia, between Generalissimo Stalin and Tikhon's later successor. The story goes that the ex-seminarian Stalin accosted the Patriarch Sergei with the words: "Well, your Beatitude, this is quite like old times. I hope all goes well." The Patriarch assured him that it did: the young seminarians would no longer be admitted at twelve, but only at twenty-one. "Ah, well, Beatitude," Stalin replied, "I hope that the Holy Ghost will still descend upon them as late as that . . . !"

There had been no difficulty in finding the way to the church. I followed the trickle, which became a current, rushing to congregation. They were by no means only the old. (According to slick journalists it is always "the old" who frequent Russian churches: presumably, being eighty in the 'Thirties, they are now mostly one hundred and ten years of age. According to a few pressmen, however, they have now been joined by the deviant young.) Not only the lighted church, a furlong from the Nova Moskaya Hotel, but the dark churchyard was crowded, although workmen were busy putting up a fifteen-foot-high billboard image of Big Brother Joe, which overlooked the place where the faithful were gathering

What I did not realise (for to open the churches at all was a new and unorthodox experiment) was how many of those present among the crowd were police detectives finding this a very convenient occasion to make a check. A competent dictatorship, a tyranny, passes up no opportunities, even on the occasion when the faithful have assembled to say "Christ is Risen" and to light their Easter candles. The trouble with the Germans was that, as I observed with old Herr Bunge, the Judge President at the Reichstag Trial, they had too many centuries of civilisation and decency behind them to provide the assenting basis for a thoroughly efficient and total tyranny. It became unstable, hysterical and inefficient. In both countries there were, of course, devout "suckers" for propaganda. (Concentration camps in Bavaria, although not camps in remoter Poland, were more open to inspection or public curiosity than those in Siberia, from which the press can be kept well away.) By comparison with the older Russian tyranny it was deplorably amateur. I was shown over the Gestapo headquarters in Berlin by officials. I was certainly, and perhaps fortunately, never shown over the Lubianka. In a burst of benevolence I decided to go back to my hotel to call a young American student from Texas who would not wish to miss this. All excited, he came. I did not note that, innocent-student-wise, he had brought his camera.

He went his way and I mine. A few minutes later I heard a call: "They are taking me away." I came over to where he stood with the police, and explained that he was only a student who meant no offence. Large, green-grey, with the red star in their police hats, the uniformed men indicated that I was arrested too—guilt by association. Up the street we went, a quarter of a mile; and down on the benches of the police station we sat. Only Russian was spoken. The American lad's courage was clearly at a discount; he visualised that—who knows?—he might end in Siberia. For myself I had decided that it was one occasion when I would enjoy myself. It is the kind of situation, sniffing of danger, that I like. I insisted that we must see the police chief. What was the offence? We could identify ourselves. It was already past midnight. Nothing seemed to happen. They would, they said, have to check.

I produced my ace. I had on me my Press card. The consequence was that the whole matter seemed to assume a new, even alarming, importance. They were trying to telephone police headquarters. It took time, much time. The officer was not there. Odd, I said, that the telephones to Moscow police headquarters took so long to get a connection. Anyhow we could not leave Moscow. Why not summon us in the morning? The desk officer and his two assistants were unimpressed by the suggestion. We continued to sit on the white scrubbed wooden bench, in the small room, as the clock ticked on into the early hours. At last, as the plotting Faust, I was summoned up to see the police chief. The room was small, with naked electric lights. The chief was polite, German-speaking, elegant, Mephistophelean, black-bearded. We had been identified. He regretted the delay. We were free and could go. I bowed— replied: "Gute Nacht, mein Herr, aber nicht auf Wiedersehen." Our enquiries about the Lubianka Prison could still be strictly detached investigations and made from the outside.

Or perhaps not so detached. With some others I went along to a late-night party at *Izvestia*. We had taken cars and, I crowded in along with Radek, had driven to the *Pravda* printing press. I still have a stick of the type with which they presented me. By what odd chance I do not know, it carries the word *Cheka*. At the *Izvestia* office I had sat for supper at the table next to Nikolai Bukharin, the great exponent of Marx-Leninism, the co-author with Radek of the brand-new paper Soviet Constitution which, among other things, guaranteed the rights of the conscientious objector. Subsequent enquiries, incidentally, by British pacifists such as Stuart Morris, revealed that, in the great land of Tolstoy, no known person apparently had been so courageous or so much an "enemy of the people" as to venture to apply for exemption from military service on this ground.

For some facetious but (it seemed to me) less than kindly reason Karl Radek would always greet Bukharin with a Hitler salute and the word "Führer". The conversation turned to the relatively safe topic of Spenglerism. Bukharin, in entertaining the guests, was expected "to do his stuff". The bearded but mild Bukharin, once described by Lenin as "the favourite of the entire Party", explained the doctrine of Spengler, in a mixture of German and French, as pessimism, but "the doctrine of Marxism is optimism". "*Moi, je suis optimiste.*"

A few days later I was invited to attend a conference at *Izvestia*. We had expected Bukharin, as editor, to be there to answer questions; instead his chief leader writer performed this function. While it was going on I went out of the office but opened the wrong door. Behind it was Bukharin. I put a question or two to him, not too seriously, but he would give no direct answer. Seldom have I seen a man look so frightened. He did not look an optimist. He had just four years to live. Involved in the next big purge, along with Police Chief Yagoda, Beria's predecessor before one, who was shot on 13th May 1939, and Rykov, Lenin's successor as Premier, he was prosecuted by Vishinsky, so well-known for his decent contributions in United Nations circles. Bukharin was duly executed. The conscience of our age is corrupt and, for reasons of state, salutes all kinds of accomplices of murderers.

If one asks what was the response of "public opinion" in all these matters, it is like asking what was the response of "public opinion" in Germany under Hitler or in Italy under Mussolini. I have little doubt about the issue of a massive "democratic" vote. It would have expressed love of the dictators, Saviours of the People.

Coming up through Donbas I met an elderly man who had been talking to his son before he got into the train. As we stood in the corridor, he said that his son had got such a fine job as assistant engineer in charge of the new works. "And what are you?" I asked. "I? Oh! Before the Revolution I was a banker"—this with a deprecatory smile. He then added hurriedly: "But this man Litvinov is doing a fine job, don't you think?—putting Russia on the map." On the other hand I talked in a cinema in Odessa to a shop girl—there are no prostitutes in Russia—little Miss Lili Shenko, vivacious rather than pretty, but marked in protruding hip-bones with the signs of some recent near starvation. "The Bolsheviks are wicked men, politicians; they make women work." One can take one's choice.

In a recent press survey, a very small boy, asked about his notion of Heaven, added that "there would be no politics". Human nature has something lovable in it to whatever country one goes and, assuredly, not least among the fraternally-minded, if pawky, Slavs, who yet have their full measure of peasant suspiciousness. The rulers of men are often less pleasant, especially when they have murdered so many human beings that their own necks are in danger of being wrung should there be change. It should always be borne in mind that, be it Ky or Ulbricht, literally they are fighting for their lives. (Of some, one can remark, as Roosevelt did of Trujillo: "A bastard? But *our* bastard.")

What I did get the chance to observe were various methods of achieving a labour speed-up such as the emphasis on piecework; the allocation of a production quota; the grading down of those who "could not make it" with the threat of being publicly listed in the factory, if not actually charged with sabotage (I looked at the lists); the system of "brigadiers" as foremen promoting production; and the factory photographs of those Stakhanovites who were making top grade in a production which was stimulated also by the "socialist competition" of one factory with another. It would turn an Anglo-Saxon trade unionist's hair grey. However, Western socialists and capitalists alike should bear in mind that this is one way of "increasing production", our current god.

Were I a "hard-faced stone-hearted capitalist", I would most seriously consider living, not in the United States, but in the Soviet Union. I should indeed have to come to terms with the Party. But that done, granted managerial ability I should receive a differential reward greater proportionately (in relation to that of the average manual worker) than I should get, as a median case, in America; I should have no need to fear strikes (illegal); obstructive workers and "unofficial strikers" would be deprived both of their work card and (until recently) of their card permitting them to move elsewhere; and their subversive leader would be sent, "for the community's good", to break stones in the virgin lands of Siberia. I should get my *dacha*; and my wife would have the advantage of "directed" domestic labour. I should do fine. I might get some distinguished decoration to wear in my coat to pick me out from the herd that had not given equal service. Ardent "red" left-wingers might gladly consider this. And, of course, this captain of industry or politics would have the immense satisfaction of seeing the cloth-capped proletarians standing on the sidewalks applauding (to order) the heroic work of the *tovarich*. What could be better?

Incidentally, the Soviets to this day have their own methods of dealing, not only with crime (I recall the squealing farm woman being arrested in a Moscow market) but with youthful "hooliganism". In 1966, we were told that such hooligans, beatniks and young louts will "have their heads shaved and be put on a bread and water diet". In one place four drunks, arriving in a football stadium, were not only fined on the spot but "the fact announced over the loudspeaker" and this was "received with applause by all present". This should bring cheer to the hearts of Celtic and Ranger fans in contemporary Glasgow. The Soviet is a bracing civilisation.

Of no less interest to true left-wing socialists interested in criminal reform is the Soviet way with those who profiteer from old army stores or who sell public property for private profit. Comrade Rabinovich recently made a fortune of £360,000 in this way, it was reported in *Trud*. His associate got twelve years' hard labour and loss of his property. Comrade Rabinovich—in August 1966—was sentenced to be shot. It is one way of dealing with forms of Rachmanism in the People's Republic, *pour encourager les autres*. It is certainly one way of dealing with the criminal classes. The criminal deviant may, of course, say: "One must live." The reply by the Soviet authorities is the brief one of Napoleon: "*Je ne vois pas la nécessité.*"

Since it seemed to indicate a future social re-stratification, such as Trotsky accused Stalin of, I was not uninterested to observe, in connection with some of the great heavy industry concerns I visited, the establishment of a training school taking on students at about fifteen. I enquired what function this fulfilled. It was to supply experts and management. What chance, then, would a young man of ability in the shops, a factory hand, have of rising to management on the basis of that "practical experience" which I had heard so much about ? "He would probably have to go through the school." "Beginning at fifteen ?" "Yes." In brief, he would have almost no chance. The Yugoslavs seem to have got further with industrial democracy, although how far they can make this run in harness with industrial efficiency is another question. I recommend (here with the Liberals) experiments in Britain. It might give a sense of common interest.

Admittedly many of the factory workers may have been peasants only the year before. Nevertheless, "equality of opportunity", owing to specialisation, tended to mean opportunity, if they inherited ability, for the *next* generation. The worker's son, at least for the moment, until the new managerial hierarchy was well established, might become a boss. What in fact appealed to the plain folk of Russia was, as one old couple explained to me in their little apartment, not that they could rise, but that, as a new thing, their sons could rise into the privileged ranks of the civil bureaucracy, army and police. The structure, including that of the Communist Party, five per cent of the population, is profoundly aristocratic.

In the retrospect of over three decades, I would only wish to say that, despite the hopeful days of the rumbustious but very human Khrushchev, the Soviet Union does not seem to have changed much. There has been slow but not over impressive improvement in human standards; but this has been subordinated to technological advances as good as any a boasted free capitalism can produce, but advances primarily for military advantage or for that of heavy industry. The maniac quest for private advantage or for that of heavy industry—the maniac quest of private profit and notoriety, alike in commerce, show-business, "sex-ploitation", the arts and culture, will not help the Soviets' opponents—or the triviality and vulgarity, the corrupt and *louche* quality, of Western civilisation today. Here Saul Bellow, in his all-out attack on the "trendies", is justified. Here, at least, the Bolsheviks have, like Plato, stood no nonsense. The greedy little pelf-hunters can end under the tread of tanks. But so will the anarchists.

The life in the Soviet Union of the deviant "militant" trade union leader, and above all of the militant "wild-cat" striking shop steward, in so far as such exists, remains nasty and short—which Western militants do well to remember. A bullet is their reward. The non-conforming extremist has no place in the land of the sovereign Dictatorship. His shrift is short. I applaud this within

the limits of natural justice. If a Revolt comes in the West it will
not be a fascist one. Moral issues apart, this is too narrowly based.
It will be Communist; and, in this sense, it will be by diplomatic
power, rather than by direct military action, that Khrushchev's
boast will be justified. Doctrines may change, but power will
prevail. An anarchist infected and undisciplined West, if bourgeois
democracy can produce nothing better, is sure to go down. And a
Communist régime, of square Victorian conservatism, will be
established, in which protesting youth, "viewey" liberals and the
exhibitionist *avant-garde* of art, both "guys" and "dolls," will have
a tougher time, being put under heel, than they ever dreamed of,
even in their wilder drugged nightmares. It will provide sadists
with something to enjoy, like the vision of sinners burning in hell.
I would say that the present odds on this conclusion are about
fifty per cent, although a ruthless social reform in the West, well
cognisant of the limits of "pure toleration" and of permissiveness,
may by a new confidence save the day.

What did and does impress, with the Soviet Union, as indicating
the shape of world things to come, is the extreme severity of its
criminal law; its emphatic methods of treating the trade unions, if
deviant; and its reversion to Victorian morality and to community
standards which make no attempt to dicker with the permissivism,
even when called "liberty", which comes to easy terms with the
anarchistic philosophy characteristic, not just of "Left-Wing
infantilism", but of large segments of Western civilisation.
Authority and freedom are basically treated as complementary.
Even if I personally may have no vocation for it, I can see no moral
objection to what Marx called the "utopian" Communism of the
monasteries or, indeed, of the Early Church. However, I have at no
time been a member of any Marx-Leninist Communist Party; I
detest the murderous tyranny of Stalin; and I regard Marx, whose
messianism was not as good as that of the Fourth Gospel and whose
sociology (hooked to the economic clue) I regard as inferior to my
own, as primarily greatest as a paper revolutionary (Engels' view
also). But I shall, nevertheless, stand by the summary above. The
fundamental issues between East and West are those of power,
not ideology. Nevertheless, the ideology of pure Communism can
win the world unless the West radically revises, without ambiguity,
its own egoistic philosophy.

At the time of the London Conference of Foreign Ministers
in 1945, Mr Molotov, a master exponent of Great Power politics,
reversed a decision already agreed upon, although his own
appointee had taken part in the communiqué about it. "My
actions," he observed, "cannot be controlled by my secretary or

representative on a committee." He decided. Still less were decisions to be shaped by any mere public opinion, a vague, uncritical notion. While in Moscow in 1935 an occasion arose for me to talk, in the Soviet Foreign Office, with Mr Rubinin, head of the Western Section. The question was the live one of a German military reoccupation of the Rhineland. "What should be done?" I asked, "You believe in collective security?" "Yes, realistically." "You mean that the armies should march?" "We believe in collective security realistically." "But what if public opinion, in France and Britain, was opposed to the armies marching?" "Is this," said the head of the Soviet Foreign Office, Western Section, "a matter for public opinion to decide? Governments decide." To hell with the interfering electorate, the impertinent citizenry.

While in Russia I met Alfred Cholerton, a sometime don of King's College, Cambridge, who, like Malcolm Muggeridge, had gone in search of the New Jerusalem after the World War. For the most chivalric reasons he had married a White Russian lady and had then turned in realistic reports which had distressed his Liberal employers, the *Manchester Guardian*. Cholerton was now correspondent for the London *Daily Telegraph* and kept visitors critically informed about the weak points of the régime. Indeed most of the resident journalists took a pitying interest in the official process of duping unwary but much flattered visitors—or, as was said of the Webbs, "feasted, filled and birds ready for the plucking." Most of these visitors had no background and were as devoid as babes of experience in sociological research. Unless *a priori* ideological capitalists, they were just "thrilled", the poor devils, to be there at all.

Malcolm Muggeridge I did not meet in Moscow, but later in London. The son of a Labour M.P., after a most worthy period as an enthusiastic teacher in India, like Cholerton he had gone to Moscow as a *Guardian* correspondent. As was said of a Minister who had left Congregationalism for Unitarianism: he went to see Jerusalem without the walls but found the walls without Jerusalem. Muggeridge recorded his experiences in *Winter in Moscow* (1933). Here again, the despatches had not pleased his worthy paper which both hoped for, and insisted on, more roseate reporting. He later established himself as editor of *Punch*.

In those early days he impressed me as a straightforward, honest and very likeable fellow. Later, it seemed to me that the commercial world and its editors had discovered in him a quality called "abrasiveness" and, to succeed and "maintain his image" in that world of "pleasing the great beasts", "abrasive" he had to be. He joined up in television surrounded by ill-mannered, ruthless

interviewers ("that is our job"), the hard-faced, harsh-voiced men.
For punsters, he was "the mugger"—and woe betide the mugged.
Recently he has undergone a remarkable change. Along with
melancholy, compassion, idealism, authenticity, a sense for the
lacrimae rerum has returned. Independent to the point of perversity,
again he commands my affection.

Caution in forming judgements and reporting from Moscow
was the more necessary since some of the eminent correspondents,
including the Grandees of Fleet Street—such people as A. J.
Cummings, of the *News Chronicle*—were being very well fêted by
official Russia. The trouble with most eminent correspondents is
that they tend to make their name by being specialists about a
particular country. If their reports are favourable, like those of
Walter Duranty on the Soviet Union, they have "all the contacts"
and build for themselves private empires. Thus Cummings was
not a little annoyed because he was not able to have a personal
interview with Stalin (just as, much later, Joseph Alsop failed to do
with Sir Alec Douglas-Home), especially as Ward Price, of the
Daily Mail, always claimed that he could count on seeing without
delay all the Nazi "top brass", thereby "scooping" all the other
journalists. Like princes, they expected the "red carpet" treatment.
Edgar Snow, author of *Red Star over China*, was to have the same
kind of personal empire, much to his advantage and to the world's
confusion. They "understood the ropes."

As Gordon Lennox, of the *Daily Telegraph*, later explained to
me in San Francisco, those of the new career of special correspondents, with their voice heard by the public, were more important
than ambassadors, who were now mere bell-hops at the beck over
the telephone of their masters at home. (Admittedly Gordon
Lennox was not a bourgeois like most British ambassadors, but a
kinsman of the Duke of Richmond and Gordon.) However, if their
reports were unfavourable, the dictatorships found ways and means
of seeing to it that even these top journalists were "through".

Balancing Cholerton who had been in Moscow for years (as
Ebbutts of *The Times* had been in Berlin) was, for the benefit of us
visitors, Barnes of the *New York Herald Tribune* and also the
representative of the London *Observer* (and, I believe, of another
London journal as well). He seemed a good little man, anxious to
please. He handed out what were more or less the routine Soviet
apologies; but also provided interesting "slants" of his own. I
went on the principle of adding his comments to Cholerton's,
dividing by two and then supplementing the result by some independent investigations of my own, forming my own judgement.

Many years afterwards—after the war—I met the London

Observer man in the concourse of Grand Central Station, New York. He was charmingly engaged in buying toys for his children. This was at the time Ernest Bevin was Foreign Secretary and Palestine was still administered by Britain under United Nations Mandate—British "law and order" being tempered by Stern gang assassinations. I asked my Moscow acquaintance what he was doing these days. "The same now as usual." "And that is now?" "Lobbying for a Hollywood concern—in Washington." I expressed interest. Then an abrupt moment of truth came—that strange, almost aggressive desire to confess which overtakes people. He looked at me and said: "I was in Palestine in the First War. I fought along with the British troops. I believed it was all for the liberation of Palestine." He paused; then added with flaming passion: "The British deceived us. And I looked forward daily to the downfall of the British Empire." Odd, loyal fellows we sometimes have as British correspondents or cartoonists, instructing the poor British public (as well as their fellow correspondents) about what is what in politics.

Anthony Eden left Moscow in the spring of 1935, without his Anglo-Russian treaty. Four years later Sir William Strang was sent to resume negotiations. There was some criticism because some higher officer of the Crown was not sent. In that disastrous period of "appeasement" of tyranny, for which Neville Chamberlain is so generally censured, it has yet to be said to the credit of the British Foreign Office that it refused to initiate the events of "a war for free nations" by acquiescing, as the Russians asked, in the murder of the independent national life of the three Baltic States, from which 4,300 people were deported—and it was not the only one, or worst, case of mass genocide—in 1941. (After the war the Russians seized half of Poland and then, with Machiavellian skill, incited the rump Polish State to deport no less than seven million Germans from the sometime German lands, Herr Ulbricht concurring.)

It was left for the Soviet Union to start a further war (without even the formality of a declaration) against another of the small states, Finland, in November 1939, for which aggression, since "peace is indivisible", it was expelled from the League of Nations as almost the last act of that august body—which was, interestingly enough, not even brought in to adjudicate in the Second World War. This was indeed embarrassing. However, having offended the Communist régime owing to certain mishaps in Switzerland, it was the Geneva League of Nations, not Lenin's successor, that was liquidated.

As for the treaty of agreement which Eden unsuccessfully sought to negotiate, a similar treaty was in fact negotiated by the French shortly afterwards. The name of the signator and successful negotiator in precautions for democracy against the fascists was, as I have mentioned, the well-known democrat Pierre Laval.

In mid-May 1935, I returned on a Soviet boat from Odessa to Salonika; took a plane to Athens; and then went on, through Bari, to Rome. There I was invited to the memorial service to Marshal Pilsudski, the man who routed the Russians at what was so wrongly called, by enthusiasts, one of "the decisive battles of the world", that of the Pripet Marshes. I met Beatrice Pignatelli and—later—Moravia, enjoying in Capri his fame as anarchist. I also met the head of the Holy Office, the Grand Inquisitor, with the enchanting name of Cardinal Caccia Dominione—"the Hidden Dominion". I was present in the Senate when Benito Mussolini effectively declared war on Abyssinia. On the national day of commemoration of the battle of Vittorio Veneto, I watched the King, Vittorio Emmanuele, and the Duce descend the glaring white marble steps of the National Monument in Rome, the Duce displaying his equality of status by keeping strictly in step with his sovereign. A military *aide-de-camp*, who appeared to interfere with this technique, was pushed to one side. In the Senate House it was fascinating to note how the Duce's gestures, with his slashing motion of the right hand, contrasted with the Führer's habit of gesture with hand to breast. The one emphasised like a dictator; the other appealed like the Tribune of the People, the Wagnerian Rienzi, which as a schoolboy he had dreamed himself to be.

The British, be it added, were highly unpopular in Italy, especially Anthony Eden. "Was it for the brigand retired from business, who had acquired an empire, to rebuke Italy for avenging Adowa? What about the Stresa Front? Was it not more important, British along with the Italians, to resist this Teutonic madman, Hitler?"

In Rome I was entertained to lunch by the Scottish Press attaché of the British Embassy. Anne Hare McCormick, of the *Chicago Tribune*, arriving late to the distress of her hostess, was one of the guests. Sir William, the host, placed me next to a lady, of partly Russian descent, since she would want to hear my report on Russia. However, the conversation turned to the proximate canonisation of Thomas More, the associate of my early heroes, Erasmus and Colet. In so many ways Thomas More seemed to me to be extraordinarily relevant—a man for all seasons in days of tyranny. I expressed a desire to be present, and the question was whether I could get tickets. The lady, who had her own tickets, told me to telephone her if I could not.

As it happened, neither the British Embassy nor the Legation to the Holy See could provide tickets. I had meanwhile learned that my co-guest was the wife of a sometime Liberal Minister, a kinsman of Sonino's, and herself a grand-niece of Cardinal Antonelli. I rang up and was told that she had only two tickets, and had one guest—"But we will see what we can do: come along, in full dress, at eight tomorrow morning." I explained that if we could not get into St Peter's, I personally would be happy to depart and enjoy a modest breakfast near the Piazza. In fact we took a taxi, the tickets were examined, but their number not checked, when we entered the Piazza. Again the luck held when we got into St Peter's. Alack! we had come in on the wrong side. I felt that the luck would scarcely hold three times—and what were diplomats for? At the other door I handed the tickets over to my co-guest, a junior Embassy Secretary and, seizing my hostess, plunged in deep.

The great cathedral was crowded to the doors and even on the pillar bases. There was nothing for it but to sit on some stairs on a drugget carpet. (As a Roman born, and Roman-mannered, thoughtfully my hostess had brought sandwiches.) Later a chamberlain, in black silk with ruff, appeared. "How long do we have to sit here?" "My dear Duchess di Cesarò, you arrive late. What can we do? There is indeed a space because Alfonso of Spain has made two reservations, one at the apse and one opposite the High Altar. I have told the Secretary to the Cardinal Secretary of State that he cannot go in. But I'll see what I can do and return." I pricked up my ears. "Cesarò" meant the *nobili neri*—meant the Colonna. In twenty minutes he returned. "All is well. Alfonso goes to the apse. You can, all three, go to the reservation by the High Altar."

Incidentally, some years later I suggested to the remarkable parish priest in Chelsea, Canon Alfonso de Zulueta, a great initiator, that a statue to the saint should be put up by the Thames in Chelsea, the "village" which he had done so much to develop. The financial chances were indeed all against it but we could make a try. A little later a modest committee under Sir Arthur Richmond, encouraged by the Mayor of Chelsea, Lord Cadogan, and with one lady honorary secretary, was set up to erect such a statue. The citizenry, the Archbishop of Canterbury—even the Holy See—contributed. In the end the Appeal was—a miracle!—oversubscribed... Inscribed to Thomas More, that Man for All Seasons, as "Scholar, Statesman, Saint" (I chose the words myself), the statue was, after all, unveiled by the Speaker of the House of Commons, the ceremony attended by Cardinal and Archbishop. More, that admirable and brave man, can now be seen gazing across the waters of his Thames, to be looked upon by all who choose. I won on that one, as I had won at Warwick Castle and hope, in 1976, to win with Chatham's statue outside Washington's White House.

On the day following the canonisation, the Rome Press announced that, among those present, were the "Duca e Duchessa di Cesarò. I was "il Duca". I still correspond with that quite remarkable woman, Nina di Cesarò-Colonna. (Later her daughter, Simoneta Visconti, the couturière, and her sister, were imprisoned by Mussolini in the Lipari Islands.) The ceremony over, I had sped, white-tied, through the streets of Rome to lunch with Roberto Michels—whose son-in-law, Mario Einaudi, son of the future President of Italy, was by odd chance to become my successor in Cornell.

The Duca also I met, an invalid. Later I stayed with them at their summer residence near Leghorn. As an ex-Minister of eminence I asked him how, in this summer of 1936, he thought things would shape. I got my reply. He was a sage man, and almost any topic from Communism to the Pope would be discussed by him, with an aristocratic detachment, quite freely. "The national characteristic of the Germans is that they always make some massive psychological blunder sooner or later. We must wait for them to make it." With Jewry, with the "fighting on two fronts" which he had himself condemned, and with the Ukrainians, Hitler made that blunder.

IX

SPAIN: THE CIVIL WAR

THE distinctive quality of the Spanish Civil War, for those who lived outside Spain, was that it was a symbol, just as the Greek War of Independence, when Byron fought at Missolonghi, was a symbol. Hitler's Nazis intervened; Mussolini's Fascists intervened; Stalin's Bolsheviks intervened. But for the young men of France, of Britain, even of America, it was not so much one more round in the game of Great Power politics—which, however, in fact it was. It was, for them, an idealistic challenge, a conflict between Republican Democracy and military Junta Dictatorship.

However false or true the picture, this is how the poets and the writers saw it. Quite recently that distinguished and elegant British writer of *belles lettres*, Cyril Connolly, has restated the position, in reviewing the published life of young Cornford and his colleagues, the logically minded but more "actionist" and committed children of a Cambridge-Bloomsbury upbringing. Unlike the Bells, Clive and Vanessa, and their circle, including Julian Bell who died in Spain, young Cornford was capable not only of repeating the strict Communist Party line but of the gross anti-humanism of justifying any Soviet massacres or atrocities against actual human flesh and blood with which he might be confronted. It would all be in general and in the mathematical abstract, "for the good of humanity in the long run".

These young men, the romantic and the sentimental, Mr Connolly still praises as the brave and idealistic youth who illuminated the confused years of the 'Thirties. All, I suggest, that one is entitled to say is that some of them died for what they believed in. Of itself mere courage—as Confucius well said—is no excuse for bad judgement. As Confucius also said, even brigands have courage. And it is no good suggesting that those who differed from these impassioned black and white judgements were somehow themselves morally deficient or eunuch.

It is yet true that the Spenders and the Philip Toynbees and Jordans, the middle-class and guilty-feeling youth of the time, assuredly saw the war as a noble challenge to personal courage, an act of international courage *pour l'humanité* (if not *pour l'Humanité*), refreshing after the cynical and even frivolous disillusionment of the immediate post-war generation of the 'Twenties. For some

N

indeed the kind of chivalric spirit, which had been so submerged bodily in the mud of Flanders and spiritually in the army under Haig, seemed to come alive again. For nearly thirty years, to the misfortune of Spain, Spain was to remain a symbol. Not only "true Socialists" but true Liberals here felt at one.

Those who wished to see a popular front in Britain against Hitler in actual political organisation, such as there was in the France of Léon Blum, and those who hesitated about the consequences of such a step, felt a personal challenge "to get off the fence". There were refugee camps for children, orphans of the Civil War (Republican), in Paris. I myself went over to Paris to visit them, along with Ivor Montagu, a kinsman by marriage of the Liberal Leader, Sir Herbert (Lord) Samuel. Incidentally, Ivor was himself a Communist.

Isabel Brown, an announced Communist leader, for whom I felt no small admiration as "quite a comrade", and Dorothy Woodman, whom at that time I thought not to be a Communist, whether card-carrying or of the "recognised non-card-carrying" variety—and would have so assured others—urged me on. I was very popular with the Communists at that time. Later I regret to say that Dorothy and I were scarcely on speaking terms. She could indeed be a generous hostess and had an alive social conscience. Whether later she was supporting the Russians against the Chinese, or for that matter the converse, I really do not know—it is all part of the dilemma of contemporary Communism—nor do I think it important enough to enquire. Her connection with Kingsley Martin and the influential *New Statesman* was what chiefly mattered.

I was anxious to commit myself personally, provided the situation was as stated to me. I was not so rash as to wish precipitately to commit myself politically, "sight unseen". As usual I wished to go and look at the facts for myself. Here at first hand one could see not only the power clash of liberal democracy and military nationalism but, in the wings of the theatre, the rival figures of Stalin and Hitler. Could Faust, studying power, ask for more? There was yet one issue on which it seemed to me that decision could be quite clear.

In the Civil War thousands were going to be orphaned, refugees, short of food, famine-struck. Already the Red Cross under Dr Marcel Junot, a Swiss, had recognised this need. The conviction came to me that what was needed and should be initiated was some kind of Nansen Commission for the impartial relief of hunger. I was prepared to go to any part of Spain for the purpose— the executive phrase was "relief of hunger"—and indeed to encourage such an exploratory delegation on the Franco side. Thanks to the views of the official Spanish Embassy in London, my immediate facilities were on the side of the Spanish Government. I organised a lunch at our Cheyne Walk house, to which I invited the Spanish Ambassador and an old and appropriate acquaintance, Philip Noel-Baker. I also brought along a Liberal M.P., a connection by marriage of Gilbert Murray, Wilfred Roberts, and Dame Rachel Crowdy who had held a most distinguished position in the International Red Cross. My proposal was discussed and approved. I decided to go.

The night train through South France, past Toulouse. I had travelled down with the Spanish Ambassador in Paris, Louis Araquistain, who had told me that the Republic could "clear up the Franco-ists in two weeks", if the Germans could only be made to withdraw. Across the frontier into Spain by breakfast time. Port Bou, January, 1937. To a little *estaminet*—with faded pictures, unbelievably "last century" in character, of Spanish worthies, one gathered revolutionary in politics, the frames decorated with the colours, purple, red and gold, of the Republic. In front, the cobblestone quay and the lazy water of the little Mediterranean harbour. Then back to the small frontier station to ask for the return of my passport. (I little knew how valuable passports were then in the black market.)

"But I have not got it, señor." "But I gave it in at your request half an hour ago and certainly you have it. I must have it back. It is essential." "But, monsieur, we will search," exclaimed the little, agitated, bearded man in control, "*mais nous sommes en pleine révolution, monsieur, en pleine révolution.*" In a gesture, indicating the immensity of "full revolution", he lifted his hands above his head. Later I was to discover that it was the pre-beatnik habit of Spanish Anarchists to wear beards, perhaps out of respect for the memory of Bakunin. The erstwhile Oxford undergraduate game of counting "beavers"—ten up for a red beard or "royal beaver"— had not reached Spain or it would have had great hunting. At length, I obtained my passport.

I had come to Spain, after long discussions, by the arrangement of the Spanish Ambassador in London, Don Pablo Azcarate y Flores (who earlier held the eminently respectable post of Assistant Secretary of the League of Nations), stopping off in Paris on my way to visit the Spanish Embassy there. Before leaving London I had had a talk with the British Foreign Office and, later, I was to have a brief and apparently very helpful session with Lord Cranborne—"Bobbity Cecil" to those who claimed to be his intimates. Indeed so pronounced were his family Cecil characteristics (including voice) that, outside the Chancellery in Berlin, I was able to identify him in a crowd and to speak to him, without having seen even his photograph. Of his family I occasionally told students—it is no longer true today—that Britain was governed by the House of Cecil or Salisbury and by Transport House. (The House of Cavendish or Devonshire and Mr Harold Macmillan put an end to that one. As for Anthony Eden, he was connected with the House of Warwick, whereas Winston Churchill was kin to Marlborough—such, for better or worse, was England.)

The British Foreign Office, under Anthony Eden, was then in the full tide of the doctrine of "non-intervention". A century before, the immortal M. de Talleyrand had defined non-intervention as "a metaphysical term used by diplomats—signifying the same thing as intervention". But experience was to show that this was not entirely true. My later view was that the Foreign Office was precisely right for reasons that I shall make plain, although the attacks, for example by my esteemed friend David Low, on Eden as a spineless appeaser were at maximum then. In retrospect these cartoons are of vivid interest. Incidentally certain principles of peace-time search of vessels on the high seas were adopted, which were also not without interest during the Second World War in terms of American policy.

At the time two considerations influenced me in my views. On the one hand I had, as I have said, come to feel that, on the analogy of the Nansen Mission after the First World War, there was a compelling case for the establishment in Spain of something comparable to an International Red Cross mission, but with wider terms of reference, for relief of the victims of famine, irrespective of party but in accordance with need. Dr Marcel Junot's account of his Red Cross mission here is relevant. It appears in his book *Le Troisième Combattant*, translated as *Warrior without Weapons*. Herbert Hoover's post-war Relief Organisation was also in my mind. Let me admit that, to the outside observer, all this plan has a patent resemblance to the Medical Relief for Vietnam (primarily Northern), where again the well-remembered names of Stephen Spender and Dorothy Woodman recur; but I do not regard the analogy as more than partial.

I was, of course, not unaware that, with the Franco-ist forces holding the agricultural areas of Spain, the chief benefit was likely to accrue to the "Constitutionalist" or Republican masses. This was within my calculations. My temperament, however, was almost deplorably sociological or judicial. The issue was precisely to aid the sufferers under conditions of war. And, if it had been feasible to obtain a visa from both sides—as it was not—I should have been happy to visit the Franco side and to report objectively on the actual situation there. Without doubt the first claims in my mind were those of humanity, although I was aware that the Constitutional Government viewed with impatience the suggestion of negotiation with rebels found with arms in their hands—an attitude later taken, with equal legalistic warrant, by Chiang Kai-shek in China and by the British in Kenya and Malaya. But I was not, even mentally, a combatant and I was not tied to these considerations.

Secondly, my personal sympathies, when I arrived in Port Bou, admittedly were on the Constitutionalist or "Loyalist" side as that of "democracy, freedom and law". So were those of people I respected. What yet were these words going to mean? Clement Attlee had visited Spain and a fighting battalion had been called after him. But I can only speak for my own case.

I felt that fascism, which I had seen in its Italian and its German forms—and indeed in its English form—at close quarters, was an instant menace to the values of human dignity, the final fundamental values, by which even "reason of state" must ultimately be judged. The cause of humanity cannot be arrested at frontiers, even by sovereign rulers. True, for me, the gilt was off the ginger-bread of "the great progressive workers' movement, for freedom against autocracy", of the Socialist Soviet Republic. The red dawn, when it was bliss to be alive but "to be young was very heaven", of the second great Revolution of European history had faded into the livid, stormy skies of Joseph Stalin's monstrous dictatorship—the rule of the New Red Czar, with his twelve Politbureau Apostles. I had hourly fewer illusions on that score. But fascism impressed me as tyranny; the Russians had not yet fully shown their hand in Spain, and my opposition to tyranny was free from opportunism.

If the penalty of opposition to tyranny was war, then the penalty must (it then seemed to me) be paid—at least wherever the tyranny had international implications, although I had never enthusiasm for avoidable wars. So far I was on the way to agreeing with Patrick Henry—whose "liberty", however, was for Virginia, not for the United States. The logical and indeed scientific answer to wars themselves and their multiplication was an international authority so soon as practicable possessing force to ensure law—and, to use Kant's ancient term, to make it practical was a categorical imperative.

Here in Spain it seemed to me that we had something liberal, popular—and, above all, a democratic régime, defending its clear legal rights against a rebel military junta. After Russia, it was a spiritual relief to have what seemed, at that moment, to be such clear issues. The Basque nationalists at least, and many of the Catalans, were pious Catholics. My "sword and pen" were, subject to a prior commitment stated above, at the movement's disposal. Many others felt the same. If I did not volunteer, it was because I felt that there was another function, more my vocation, which I could perform better; and which did not involve interfering militarily in the internal affairs of Spain.

However, I should add that the naive and simple enthusiasm very common among chest-slapping men of letters and of the arts, not guiltless of self-display, which says "this principle is right: I do not care with whom I am associated", was an attitude of which I was already suspicious. I recall the grand simplicity of a certain venerable British peer who said that he associated his name "with anything that contained the word 'peace' in its title". The question was not only with what principles and faith one began but, thanks to one's associates, with what practice and works one would end.

Things indeed were perhaps not quite so simple as they seemed, although an enthusiastic journalist, one Duff, had posted me with all the Republican case. Since the almost unnecessarily precipitate departure of Don Alfonso XIII, the last of the Bourbon-Hapsburgs, no one could claim that any of the elections, being Spanish, had been quite above suspicion. And assuredly the majority which had put the then Spanish Government in had scarcely been so large as to warrant a ruthless treading under foot of the natural rights and the established habits, founded in Spanish tradition, of the minority. The curse of political fanaticism had fallen on the land and many of the pro-Government crowds assuredly, *en pleine révolution*, were (like their opponents) ruthless fanatics if the Liberals and Federalists were not. "The gods were athirst"; and there was no lack of that detestable type, *les buveurs du sang*, the partizan men whose lust for victory had run away with humanity and mercy, not to speak of political judgement.

The Spanish Republicans whom I had met, such men as Azcarate, who had dined at my own table, and de los Rios, later Spanish Ambassador in Washington, whose guest I was to be, were yet far from ruthless and obviously quite good liberals. The admirable da Madariaga, if not Unamuno, was in the same camp. They seemed to me, at the time, men of about the same type as d'Olivet, whom my good Liberal Party friend, Sir Geoffrey Mander, in reply to my slightly suspicious enquiries, had told me was "just an ordinary French liberal". (D'Olivet, afterwards, was discovered to be, at the relevant time, quite clearly pro-Communist or, as it was put to me in Paris with delightful but unconscious humour by Isabel Brown, of the British Communist Party, "our peace man".)

These men, of course, were anti-clericalists. But with Latin Liberals one had to take this secularism for granted. The Basque nationalist supporters of the Republic were Catholics in good standing. It was up to democrats to support the democratic cause against military juntas. I did not like dictatorships; nor had I divided between those dictatorships which had world schemes of expansion and those, like the Yugoslav, which had not. At that time I had not made the distinction; they were alike dictatorships to me. And anyhow all the world seemed to have a finger in Spain.

The train moved out of Port Bou station for Barcelona. On arrival I went to the Hotel Oriente in Las Ramblas, the broad thoroughfare which distinguished the town. I reported myself to the local authorities; and Señor Battista y Rocca, later known as a Catalan exile in London and member of its P.E.N. Club, took me in charge, himself another patent liberal and, incidentally, a Catholic. What preoccupied Barcelona was, however, the local problem of *España Unida*—"United Spain". Was the Republic, like the Monarchy, to be united in the sense of being centralised and Castilian-dominated—or was it to be federal, with full regional rights for Catalans, Galicians, Basques? My sentiments were federal; but it is not so easy to fight a desperate war on strictly federal principles, especially as understood by the Anarchist Party, adherents of the black and white (or black and red) flag; nor had the Republicans of Castile any especial enthusiasm for these decentralising principles.

Before I finally left Barcelona, I saw President Campanys of Catalonia, fiery and with cavalier beard. Most of his complaint was that the Federal Republic centred in Madrid was not giving, the Madrileños were not giving, Catalonia the co-operation which it desired and deserved. The truth was that the federalists, and the social revolutionaries, and the legal constitutionalists and such trades unionists as Prieto, if not Largo Caballero, were fighting three different wars, each fighting his own war.

It did not take long in Barcelona for me to grasp that the whole situation was indeed at sixes and sevens. If the Republicans held the industrial quarters of Spain and the few munition factories, Franco held the food bins and had considerable peasant support. The Anarchist Party was stronger in Spain than in any other part of the world, including even Mexico.

I had a talk with that one of the Cabinet Ministers, Señor Garcia Oliver, who was an Anarchist. He had been a Paris bookseller. He was an amiable idealist, addicted to the Left Bank

Parisian rhetoric of abstractions about freedom, such as is today greatly exploited by Sartre. It is a sad pity that our contemporary professional philosophers fail to apply their logical analysis to the vague—and, because vague, disastrous—words of the political vocabulary. Politicians will resist but philosophers, going beyond scholastic verbalism, have their duty. Fine words about "freedom", such as Oliver used, were gaseous but highly explosive and cried out for deflation. What it came down to was that he believed in the spontaneous co-operation of peace-loving and benign humanity ("flower-power") to be achieved by anarchic violence. A good early Rousseauite man, a Prince Kropotkin man— but a very dangerous muddle-head of the kind the tough Bolsheviki just shot in the woods.

He explained that, for the moment, his party would co-operate in the Government; but that the fundamental differences of view remained. His party were believers in "Liberty", not in "the State". Of the last there should be a real "withering away". Liberty spelled a spontaneous, syndicalistic, advanced co-operative society—if not, with Bakunin, opposition to "God and the State". Human nature was naturally good; and the Government and priests were, by a strange paradox, naturally bad. Spain and England, he said, stood by an individualist tradition, but most of the difference between Bakunist and Marxist was an issue of the past. In Spain they were fighting, on the basis of international law, for a new civilisation (I had heard the phrase before) in which any valid authoritarianism and true libertarianism would somehow be reconciled. The culture was, anyhow, that of "freedom". I admired the man but thought the argument piffle. However, it was at least "in good faith".

Nevertheless, the conclusion was clear. Europe must aid and demonstrate a *solidarité morale*; for the moment, the task was *lutter et vaincre*. Later Willie Gillies, of Labour's Transport House, was to tell me how Anarchist leaders in Barcelona had shot those of the trades unions (U.G.T.) in the back as they were going upstairs. Down with bourgeois "honour" and romanticism of the Pimpernel type. Maybe Oliver did not know or could do nothing, or salved his conscience, like Robespierre, with words.

Up in the hills one was told a community was to be found which was living out these Anarchist principles. Perhaps its pattern was not, in practice, so different from some of the settlements in Palestine, which called themselves communist and lived under rule. But suggestions that one would like to visit it met with no response. After all there was a civil war on. Nearer the truth was possibly the explanation that the Socialists and Catalan nationalists were not so anxious to advertise Anarchist activities and the black and white flag. (It would be forty years on before I saw it—now black and red—paraded in a London "demo").

There were other groups in Spain, not least in Barcelona, even worse off than the Anarchists. The Communist Party of Spain was Trotskyite in its political coloration. At the beginning of the Civil War, the Stalinist section was a minority—in Catalonia indeed a minority of two hundred or so members, and about three thousand for all Spain.

One of my great regrets is that, having an introduction to Leon Trotsky in Mexico from his translator, Max Eastman, and passing through El Paso, I did not get off the train and go down to Mexico City to see the man Lenin preferred to Stalin. A brief while afterwards he was assassinated, according to the best evidence (for it has never yet been settled), by a Spaniard who, disguised under the false name of a Belgian, Jacques Mornard, had wormed himself into Trotsky's confidence and who was for long incarcerated in a Mexican jail. The Spanish police have the information about his life history, and whether he is indeed Ramon de Rio Mercader. His mother was a Stalinist deeply involved in the Civil War, and seems to have had the responsibility of sacrificing her son for the cause by urging him to take the immense risk of being torn to bits by Trotsky's guards. (It was Leon Trotsky who insisted that he should be kept alive for examination.) She, the effectual assassin, was honoured later by a high Soviet decoration. She lived in Moscow.

Likewise the long hand of murder, in Molotov's international conspiracy, had stretched out and assassinated Krivitsky, sometime chief of Soviet Military Intelligence in Western Europe—in his Washington hotel of all places in the world. It is Krivitsky who gives the eye-witness account of his friend Sloutski at the purge trial in 1935 of the Old Bolsheviks, including Mrachkovsky. Before he was brought to "confess", Sloutski, who was then the examiner, relates that Mrachkovsky said to him: "You can tell Stalin that I loathe him. . . . They took me to Molotov who also wanted to bribe me. I spat in his face." Examinee and examiner were both liquidated. I mention these things, these incredibly fierce enmities in the revolutionary Left, because they explain much of what went on in Spain. It is an unlucky commentary for bourgeois, comfort-loving Anglo-Saxons upon the kind of world in which it is their misfortune to live. Some are not indeed bourgeois, but intellectual Hamlets. In Trotsky's own immortal phrase: they are "unfortunate in the times in which they are born". Spain toughened me, first and foremost against Anarchists.

Beside the Republicans of liberal colour, such as Azaña, the Federal President, and the socialist trades unionists following the lead of Prieto, and the provincial nationalists, Basque and Catalan, and the Communists of two kinds and the Anarchists, there was also the party, much in evidence in Catalonia, which was the opposite number to the British I.L.P., although of more Trotskyite leanings, to wit, the *Pardido Obrero Unificado Marxista*, P.O.U.M. However much the other parties might quarrel, even with the battle on, among themselves, they were all prepared to be at one in savaging P.O.U.M., if the opportunity occurred. Some admirable young British socialists ended their lives in Spain, thanks not to Franco's bullets but to this vendetta among "the comrades". They hated a heretic more than an unbeliever. One learned a lot about the structure of power and politics in those days. The Anarchists preferred (like some "true Socialists") to be doctrinally pure rather than to win the war. But War, as Lenin said, is authoritarian.

It did not require great wisdom to see that, with such a political structure, the Republic was bound to fall. It suffered the nemesis of uncontrolled liberalism in war-time or in that almost more difficult time which is not war but wears a deceptive appearance, favourable to conspiracy, of peace. The people were being betrayed by the politicians, not from malign intention, but from party egotism or from the sheer heterogeneity of the various party philosophies. They could not pull together. Their very principles forbade it. Each was out for a glorious adventure in emancipated living and "happy warrior" partizanship. As Dr Marcel Junot records, the Anarchists, the F.A.I., were even prepared to announce in posters, "We are out to disorganise organisation, and to organise disorganisation!" The damned enthusiastic, pathetic fools! They have their like today, especially in the United States among romantic adolescents looking for "the Greening of America".

The people who realised the danger best were the Communists, the Stalinists. The Soviet Union had no illusions whatsoever. It sold munitions, with cold Kremlin cynicism, to the desperately fighting Republic for Spanish gold, cash down. Later Araquistain and Caballero were to make this clear—although one can argue about how much bullion there was. The purpose of the ruffian Stalin was to see that, whoever became involved in war—and the more the better—Stalin emerged a winner. But Russia took the opportunity to use Spain as laboratory material for a wonderfully successful experiment in propaganda. Compared with this what happened to Spain was unimportant. One scarcely realised, at the time, that it was a very bloody war in which, not thousands, but hundreds of thousands died. Not since the Moorish Wars had Spain had such a blood-letting; and not even Goya in the days of the resistance to Napoleon had had so great an opportunity as this Civil War provided for the study of atrocities which man can work on man.

Most of the Stalinists in Spain were not Spaniards. They were German Communists, or German-speaking Poles or Russians, even people like Marshal Tito, then plain Comrade Broz from Croatia. An amazingly large number of the key men who later manned the pro-Communist "underground" in Europe, got their training here. That was the Soviet purpose. In Buda-Pest, in 1926, I was told: "If you wish to win a revolution, occupy the telephone exchange." In Barcelona the Anarchists had done just this. But with great skill, having only limited numbers, the Stalinists installed themselves in such key positions as the various passport and visa offices, so that they had control over all travellers coming into or going out of Spain. They also came to control the War Ministry. (To compare the small with the great, the parallel with recent events under President Arbentz in Guatemala is interesting.)

When the time came for me to leave Spain I proceeded to the Barcelona passport offices and, braving all queues, I went through to the inner office where the comrades sat. I explained that I had to be in Paris within forty-eight hours and, as a guest of the Spanish Government, required an exit permit from them. I already had no less than two others, one from the provincial Catalan government and one national. I needed all three.

The security officer in charge said that they would require three photographs. But where could I get them? He passed over the address of a photographer and thither I went. I asked the manager of the studio how long it would take. "Mañana," he said optimistically; but he was, he explained, very full of work. It might take perhaps three or four days. In Spain, and in revolution, I foresaw the worst. Probably he meant a week. I had to consider how to cope with the situation.

Calculating that the security comrades were probably German and proud of it, once again I walked past the hesitant and confused Spanish guard and took the offensive. "Do you believe in efficiency?" I asked in German. "Certainly." "Why then, when I have to be in Paris within two days, do you send me to a photographer who can do nothing under three or four and, this being Spain, if he says three or four days, what does that mean?" The comrades looked. They smiled. The senior, with a shrug, issued an order. The visa should be given. The passport and exit card would

be mine, "und ohne Photographieren, mein Herr, ohne Photographieren. Guten Morgen". (Agreed: no photographs).

In Barcelona, on my arrival, I was attached to a party of British
who were going by Government car to Valencia. Cars were
usually almost an hour late in arriving to begin their journey, but
this one was punctual. My companions were to be Cyril Connolly
and his wife, and an Irish peer, Lord Antrim, much later to be head
of the British National Trust. Although he did not take this
journey with us, several times in Barcelona I met another member
of their group, Wynstan Auden, the poet, who for a while was
married to Erica Mann and about whom I was to hear so much
later in Philadelphia. Antrim had also been along to the security
and passport office where he was asked what his interests were and
he had replied "agriculture". The comrades had failed to see just
why a British aristocrat, chiefly interested in agriculture, should
wish to come to revolutionary Spain. They thought his intentions
were probably sinister. It had, it appeared, been a very unpleasant
time and, according to his own account, Antrim had emerged from
the office a pale and much shaken man.

Little did the comrades know the liberality of the British
aristocracy. To be "slightly Communist" was to be intellectually
chic, not least in Oxford and Cambridge colleges, although only a
choice few among those who instruct youth as college dons were
card-carrying Party members. Also it was one of the quickest ways
to be able to call a Countess by her Christian name. Indeed in these
undergraduate quarters to discover that somebody was a Communist was to think that he must be an adventurous fellow of
courage or, at worst, "rather a joke". One must always allow for the
vast fecklessness of youth—and of the "arrested adolescent".
"Such fun."

I myself first heard "The Red Flag" (a very mild affair) played
by an earl on a grand piano before red damask curtains. A direct
ancestor of his had signed the death warrant of Charles I and a
more remote ancestress had been the Bessy Wallis Simpson of
the days of Edward IV—and, as such, damned by Shakespeare.
The great Whig families of the Russells and the Greys expect to
direct politics, not to be directed. To be pro-American was of
course to be "farmer-boy" and dowdy. Virginia Woolf, an
intellectual snob of pure vintage, was sure that the Americans
spoke a language which was not English—what the Canadians or
Australians spoke was not clear. I personally ended by regarding
such people as cultural traitors, dividers of an English-speaking
world that was united, in order to keep united some literary sect.
I was, and am, a fanatical believer in the English-Speaking Union—

except that its interestingly entitled English-Speaking Union "of the Commonwealth" did not much believe in me. I was perhaps too pro-American for them. To be too pro-America was very suspect.

In a more representative but still typical form, the head of an Oxford College was heard to observe with enthusiasm: "Why, *of course*, we must support the Revolution." The Master of Balliol, "Sandy" Lindsay, gravely assured me that Marx was "a seminal thinker" but that Thomas Aquinas was not. He meant "revolutionary". Politics became not a matter of a scientific social hygiene, a skilled adjustment, but was associated with a kind of euphoric, glandular discharge, as cathartic in effect as a boxing match or gladiatorial show. This secular Salvationism was not in my temperament. Precisely as a political scientist, I was "against".

What soon struck me about this particular set of innocents abroad in Barcelona was that almost all the men I met were Etonians and a group of old friends together. They were not unrepresentative of the young men of the time, mildly "leftish", some more adventurously so than others. The Lynds' daughter was of this circle. So was Stephen Spender. Some of them were for a while members of the British Communist Party who subsequently were appointed junior intelligence officers during the Second World War. Others regarded what was happening as an interesting political phenomenon. Of those who came from across the Atlantic Louis Bromfield writes: "Most of the kids . . . were filled with ideals or seeking adventure and I don't think many of them were Communists. When it came to helping them to get back home, the Communists wouldn't lift a finger. That's when I got an education, dealing with those sons of bitches."

On such members of the exhibitionist élite as André Malraux and Louis Aragon the limelight of attention shone more brightly. Malraux, the laudator and mentor of de Gaulle, claimed it as his ambition to "leave a scratch on the face of the earth". Morally the same ambition—here called "to leave the scratch of a lion's claw on history"—was expressed by the immoralist, "sawdust-filled" adventurer, Benito Mussolini, ex-Marxist revolutionary.

Somewhat unkindly—for such young men as John Cornford, Julian Bell (Virginia Woolf's nephew), young Carritt, and, in his way, Churchill's nephew-by-marriage, Esmond Romilly, were sincere enough—Arthur Koestler describes the fashionable young Englishmen as engaged in "a revolutionary junket". Some died, not unwilling to be Rupert Brookes of twenty years on. A few, be it added, such as Bob Smillie, the son of the great miners' leader, were done to death in a Spanish prison by Big Brother's henchmen.

Others, although they had in a sense been "in the Spanish Civil War", did not impress me as being likely to make themselves profoundly uncomfortable about it, although they may have had vivid literary reminiscences of Byron at Missolonghi. They were prepared to have their hearts bleed. Maybe they preferred to suffer in spirit. One of my more vivid memories is of a night club in Barcelona, the floor filled with dancers, professional and otherwise, and of Auden presiding at a quite lordly table above the balcony where the wine flowed from a bottle of adequate size. But, after all, the scene is not unusual in any war. And for Auden, as a poet who has changed his views, and for Connolly, as the editor of *Horizon*, now defunct, I have a wry admiration. As George Orwell reminds us, Auden once wrote:

"Tomorrow for the young, the poets exploding like bombs . . .
Today the deliberate increase in the chances of death,
The conscious acceptance of guilt in the necessary murder."

This attitude and attitudinising is something to be damned. It is to be deplored whether the murders are in Spain, China or Kenya, and it was, in those days, a view all too typical of the arrogant Etonian Communist young men—what Etonian George Orwell calls "public school, Oxford and Bloomsbury"—the breed which later produced Burgess, Philby and MacLean, son of a one-time Leader of the Liberal Party. In retrospect this moral light-heartedness and hypnosis by some supposed determinism of history, this deterministic immorality, seems very difficult to forgive. The first thing that youth needs to be taught, in politics, is modesty. "Is war any better?" some will ask. I will endeavour to reply later, when we ask "War for what?"

Old Etonian Professor J. B. S. Haldane also came out to Spain about this time and, himself indubitably a man of courage, was good enough to instruct the fighting comrades, with great panache, about how to conduct themselves. As I have mentioned, he kept pinned grenades in his pocket or tossed them around like cricket balls. He was held to be rather a nuisance. About Eton he only said that he hoped a slow drum fire might pass over the place.

Having travelled with Lord Antrim and the Connollys through Tarragona as far as Valencia, I reached my hotel. There I found a group of exploring clerics led by the Dean of Chichester anxious to learn, and themselves a political exhibit of some importance, as displaying the concern of the unimpeachably respectable demo-cratic world for the Republic. Later, the Canons of Chichester forbade Bishop Bell, their bishop, to preach in his own cathedral lest he might denounce the "mass bombing" of German workers.

I also saw in Valencia another sometime member of my Oxford

College, Basil, son of the Nestor of my undergraduate days, Professor Gilbert Murray, and of Lady Mary. Basil was an aesthete who had wandered from post to post in flight from boredom, and then had suddenly found himself, like so many of the gilded and avant-gardist youth (although less rumbustious than Sir Winston Churchill's nephew, young Romilly), existentially "committed", exhilarated, elevated, purged, indeed "saved" from a sense of insignificance in life, by involvement in the Civil War and in a desired baptism of blood, instead of the old quest of seeking what would "amuse". Although he died from a sudden appendicitis (or some like cause) and not, like the Spanish lads in the hospital I saw, from wounds, yet it can truly be said that he gave his life for the democratic vision which, in those days of mixed idealism and cynicism, seemed to float over Spain. He also went to Spain "to defend freedom".

Pacing the streets of Valencia together, before he went to Malaga, he said this war for him gave to life—not hitherto a very satisfactory life—a satisfying purpose. Did I not think the same? The cause of Liberalism? I remembered the days when undergraduates said he chose his guests according to whether they would look elegant sitting in this or that corner of his rooms in the College of the Blessed Virgin Mary of Winton in Oxford.

His was another case of that frequent phenomenon of the decade, the young man of a wealthy or aristocratic family (Basil was a Howard through his mother) who had a bad conscience in terms of all that his class had not done for the manual workers; who wanted to be assigned some "purpose" or motive for self-sacrifice to drive out cynicism, having lost any other faith; and who sought a sacramental identification with the proletariat, about whom his views were yet grotesquely different from those of Messrs. Stalin, Molotov and comrades. It all has its parallel among the students of Yale and elsewhere in America today. Similarly, the admirable Naomi Mitchison, Lord Haldane's niece, walked about among the trades union chiefs at a Party Conference, clad like a mill-girl in a shawl and gnawing an apple. It was pathetic; it was admirable; but it was not politics and it provided no guidance to sound judgement. I never saw Basil again. There were many like him, the next crop of youth to the so-called "lost generation" of "the Great War", who there sought to vindicate in arms their own right to survive.

From Valencia I took car with others, across the Ebro and over the parched, tawny, California-like land, to Madrid. The following day, accompanied by Philip Jordan, another typical "man of the 'Twenties", journalist and later public relations officer to the British Premier, I went on to the University section of the city.

William Forrest, of the Tory *Daily Express* (later of the *News Chronicle* and then its Moscow correspondent), was out there at the same time, although I certainly did not realise that he was (but is not now) a card-carrying Communist Party member, any more than I realised the significance of my brief meeting with Otto Katz, *alias* André Simon, in Paris. (Such is the proper freedom of the Press that the Madrid correspondent of the ultra-Tory *Morning Post* of London at one time was credibly asserted to be a Communist Party member. "And why not?" What better coverage could he have—or give?)

At this time the front-line trenches ran through Madrid itself and indeed through the University grounds. The local transport still ran, although humourists suggested that if one did not get out at the right stop, one might end behind enemy lines. I walked on to explore the trenches on that slope which had been captured from the Franco troops the previous day. Jordan struck me as pretty pale and admitted that he did not find the situation healthy. It so happened that one major hospital was quite near to my hotel, the Florida, and I saw the wounded being taken in the evening on stretchers into the wards. During the day we were taken along to see the general commanding the Government forces in Madrid in his headquarters in the railway tunnel at the back of the del Norte station, and drank Spanish brandy with his staff.

Superficially indeed it seemed to be a very gentlemanly war. Many of the inhabitants of Madrid had been painfully evacuated by the authorities; but the Madrileños refused to abandon their homes and returned. The cinemas were full and the shop lights were still full on in the main streets of Madrid. The artillery barrage would start up at a given hour each night. We were told that the shells would pass between the hotel Florida (where most of us, including Sefton Delmer among the journalists, were staying) and another larger building. There seemed to be a polite agreement that the Florida should not be hit—it continued to operate with full staff—and rumour said that the large building also was not hit because it was owned by one of Franco's generals.

Comparing their experience with what came later, I would say that the international journalists, writers, social investigators and other thirsters for knowledge had a fairly light time in Spain and even in Madrid. This could yet produce misleading impressions. A thousand were killed and three thousand injured—petty though these numbers now sound to our horror-numbed minds—in a month in Madrid alone, the first great city to be bombed, soldiers and civilians, men and women alike, from the air. As Koestler observes, "Spain caused the last twitch of Europe's dying

conscience." Guernica and Lidice, Coventry, Lübeck, Hamburg
and Dresden came later and provided a brutal culmination to the
refusal to distinguish military and civilian and possibly even to the
retrogression of our civilisation since the eighteenth century.
Russian slave camps in effect caused no sentiment save irritation
at the reminder. When the final count was made the Spanish
slaughter, not so much in battle as in civil massacres, was a toll of
one million.

One party of thirsting questers for news was shepherded round
schools in the villages to be shown what the Republic was doing
in the way of an edifying new approach to education. There was
something very pathetic in this, since the Republic was fighting
for its life; and how good the new approach might be in training
little children for the future was something beyond the competence of visiting journalists to assess in a hurried quarter hour.
I retain also vivid memories of the orange groves of Spain bathed
in sunshine which matched the colour of the fruit even so early in
the year, where one could, by invitation, help oneself to any variety
in accordance with one's taste. If the blood of Spain was shed, the
sunshine and the orange trees remained. One was also introduced
to several ministers by whom one was to be impressed, including
one lady in Valencia, Señora Montseni, Minister of Health, a kind
of blonde Bessie Braddock, square, muscular and masculine. The
oranges were bitter.

Almost we had a surfeit of ministers. But somehow I felt myself
to be more in touch with the spirit of the real Spain in the orange
groves with the lazy hum of their heat, the Spain of slow movement,
of great cruelty and of great courage. Spain, where life is not so
cheap as in the East, but where yet honour and passion matter
more than life, the land which is filled with scarcely tolerant
contempt for French ideas and for France, the soft erring youngest
sister of the Latin people—Spain, wrapped in the pride of her own
fierce crusading history, almost as murderous as that of Scotland,
but with a Lucifer-like grandeur of her own; not for nothing,
although Cervantes mocked, the land of Don Quixote.

Fat-cat, secularist Europe has forgotten how in Castile, as well
as at Malta, Lepanto and Vienna, the Moslem Arab onslaught on
Western civilisation was turned back. That is something Spain,
asking no favours, yet does not forgive. The European debt to
the House of Hapsburg is incalculable, even for ungrateful egotistic
France (though Louis XIV did weep when news came that the
chivalry of Christendom had saved Vienna from the Turk) and so
it is, the Spaniard thinks, to Spain.

The people whose vanity was flattered by free trips to Spain got

o

too often the wrong picture of the war. They wrote their dispatches or comments about it as one might write about a party conference or, at best, as if they were seated on the Olympus of Printing House Square, shaping the cold Ionic columns of a *Times* dispatch on international affairs. The extent to which Spain suffered in this affair was little known by the outside world and when at length the news came through it was too late for the world, full of its own affairs, to care much—although even to suggest that the Republicans were being defeated could bring a storm of protest upon the offender's head, as Norman Ewer mournfully told me.

Hitler was becoming Europe's all-obsessing headache. And yet this massacre in Spain, provoked by the bitter passion of Spanish fascist and Spanish secularist, sharpened by the poverty of the confused masses who clamoured for more humanity, the deafness to humanity and common sense of the infuriated leaders on both sides, the cold exploitation by the sinister figures of Stalin, Hitler and the little Duce, is something of which the record should not be forgotten.

Let me admit that Faust left Spain less sure on which side he would find Quixote fighting than when he went there. He had started out in something of the same mood as the young enthusiasts of the Left who had seen a clear crusade, and as those undergraduates of Oxford and Cambridge who, in their more excessive mood of utopian vision and under the influence of Joad, Strachey, Laski and others, were prepared to vote that they would not "fight for king and country" but only for a "cause", and that one of revolutionary humanity. The young Faust, in his curious enquiries into the nature of power, was already too old to follow these calls to arms for a cause, without reservation or caution.

Nevertheless in the complex world of politics the Spanish Civil War had looked like a very plain case of principle and of the ideological alliance of democracy and the underprivileged against dictatorship and great wealth, which abused privileges, now devoid of social and moral justification. There might be a strong case for the constitutional restoration of the Bourbon-Hapsburg monarchy. But even eminent members of the Catholic hierarchy, such as the Cardinal of Tarragona, had quit Spain for Italy rather than support the Caudillo.

A better acquaintance indeed had shown me that the facts were not quite as I had once supposed. The eminent respectability of the Republican Embassy in London, headed by Azcarate, a "good Geneva man", had deceived me. Madariaga, a sound liberal, supported the Republic, but it was interesting that Miguel Unamuno had declared that its side was "not that of civilisation" although, a lonely figure, as Rector of Salamanca he had before his death uttered his protest against the Falange. At the time I could not conceive why he stood so alone, and thought that Unamuno, one of the greatest figures in Spain, must be more reactionary than I had supposed.

At the Spanish Embassy in Paris, when Araquistain was the Ambassador, I had had my first shock. With some others, mostly journalists, I had been looking over photographs of the Civil War. One journalist picked out as striking for publication a photo of robed friars, with rifles in their hands, in a church tower firing down on people below. It could, of course, have happened; but it was not exactly a pleasing picture of these men of God. A member of the Embassy staff looked at it. "It is all right," he remarked, but "of course, that one was posed—posed by actors."

This remark came immediately to my mind when, in the Press, I recently read of a sergeant returned from imprisonment in northern Korea, and how the Communists in England had got hold of his bride in his absence, and had plied her with pictures of atrocities committed against the northern Koreans and Chinese. "And after all, photographs can't be faked, can they?" said the poor woman. Can they not? Would photographs alone tell us whom to identify as the organisers of the monstrous Katyn Massacres?

I knew in theory all about "Falsehood in War-time". I had read Arthur Ponsonby's book and had burned with indignation about the false "cadaver story" of the Germans who boiled down human bodies for fat, and about the priests who (by a distorted report) were alleged to have been used by the Germans as human bells in the belfry of Antwerp Cathedral. They were "black propaganda", dishonest and dastardly methods of rousing popular anger. They were deeply anti-human, anti-civilisation, a deliberate debasing of the currency of truth, barbaric, Hunnish—just as the mass damage to Rouen and Dresden, and the demolition of Monte Cassino by Freyberg against Mark Clark's orders, were vandalistic.

This was yet the first time that I had seen, used for precisely the same purpose, a deliberate and admitted fake. The generosity in my heart froze and my whole system seemed to shrink and grow taut. Was I concerned to back this? Or the men whose minds, without excuse or shame, turned to this kind of thing? Those who were in, or interested in, the Spanish Civil War had all seen the leaflets with the figures of small children, gashed and bloody with bullet wounds. How was I sure that these were not faked too? It was well that liars should know the consequences on opinion of their lying; and I took a few quick resolves.

Later, I found myself again in Barcelona. We were all taken along to a "Popular Court". Some of the eminent foreigners of "sound views", who had been brought to Spain to look around and report, were all lined up there, in due course, as "observers". The virtues of a court of popular justice, where plain men, taxi-drivers and the rest, were judges were explained to me.

I know that Denis Pritt, K.C., was always ready to defend this procedure. But, the longer I observed, the more I became ashamed of myself and the less I liked the look of this kind of thing. These Popular Courts seemed to me to be obscene. Frightened men without a defence lawyer were brought up, according to Continental practice (a little modified), before popular judges of interrogation. It was clear, perhaps not at first glance at the human bull-ring but on reflection, that their case was lost before they began to speak. It was enough to be identified as a fascist. They were there, as were aristocrats in the days of the murderous French Terror, to provide a revolutionary spectacle as touching the way to deal with traitors. They were guilty unless they could show themselves innocent and, in the mood of the court, with the war raging, their chance of proving the latter was small indeed.

One wonders what could have been the fate, even before a British popular court so constituted, of German airmen in 1941— or of British airmen in Hamburg before a like German court in 1943; or of some American airmen in North Vietnam. "War criminals." Doubtless it was all something better than a drumhead tribunal in the France of the Terror. It was better than what was going on elsewhere, where men were shot without trial or shot by mistake for others. But it was filthy, inhuman and revolting. I swore that, as God was judge, might God do so to me and more also if I lent my pen or support to such proceedings. The excuse was always in the catch-phrase: "They punished those who did them wrong." So do the cannibals. The question is: how?

Suddenly the blackened churches of Barcelona, burned out by the Anarchists before I had arrived (although alleged to have been burned in air-raids which did not take place), acquired a new meaning. Let us admit that, with less physical and mental suppression by the old Spanish State and Church, more tolerant indifference to eccentric views, there would have been less violence. This was yet not the great pure cause of liberty and parliamentary democracy. It was all too like what I had seen, and what had turned my stomach, in Russia and Germany. It was the Terror in action.

There was, of course, no particle of reason to suppose that the Whites, in their turn, in the cruel country of Spain were behaving any better. The record to the contrary is too clear. Guilty, half guilty, innocent, they were all being driven over the precipice by an animal passion, masquerading as the august figure of Justice. The filthy horror is well on the record—after the event. It is a record of the baboon-cousin, the naked ape, in action.

The Bell tolled also for me. And, as one powerless individual, from the depth of my heart I registered a protest against the evil—not against Azaña, not against Prieto, not against de los Rios and the rest, good men enough, men as civilised as Madariaga himself, but against the dictatorial terror, the utter evil of unrestrained inhumanity, be it of the Right and the Franco-ists, or of the Left and Yagoda or the Communist henchmen in Spain. To fight this was the real fight. I felt that if human beings had got to be shot, the best thing would be, with concentrated attention, impartially to shoot bullies and terrorists. The first loyalty was to decency. Down, down with the Fanatics. Down with them.

One little trivial incident dwells in my mind, as such things will. I have referred to my visit to the trenches in Madrid. I was crossing the road, which was still under occasional rifle fire—on the crest of the ridge below which lay the University park and the front trenches of both the Government and the Nationalist troops. I was going down to their trenches. I noticed an object which caught my eye. I stooped down and picked up a head—the head of a large doll dropped by some child in flight from the battle area. I took the trouble, I do not know quite why, to bring it home with me.

A stupid battered little doll's head, with the unmoving blue eyes and fixed smile on her face, dropped by some frightened child in flight. And yet it seemed to me the symbol and epitome of all that was wrong. The inrush of war and especially of cruel civil war upon the family life; the hurried explanations to the child; the rushed flight and the cherished possessions left behind; the total helplessness of little people in the clash of great forces, on the whole quite evil and yet unnecessary forces, avoidable forces, parading as "just", a negation such as evil in essence always is. These forces found their focus, not even in impoverished Spain herself, but in the *Reichskanzlei* in Berlin where a rabid monomaniac shouted, and in the painted barbaric halls of the Kremlin where, not in any degree less sinister but more slowly, Stalin plotted, guarded by his silent Georgian guards from assassination by his closest colleagues.

Before I left Valencia, on my return from Madrid, I saw del Vayo, Foreign Minister of the Republic, who spoke of his cordial relations with Cranborne and recalled that he had been president of the League of Nations Commission on the Chaco war. Spain, he asserted, was passionately a believer in the League and the enemies of the Republic were not conservative, but reactionaries. The Government of the Republic was precisely one of the Popular Front and neither of Anarchists nor Communists. As for my Nansen Relief proposals, they commanded his support and they should be fitted in with those being discussed in Geneva (later Azcarate was to tell me that these had become "a farce"). Others assured me, however, that Franco would never agree—but this was not my problem.

Not without difficulty I got myself into the train which still ran from sun-drenched Valencia to Barcelona. Some passengers sat on my suitcase, some boarded the train at the last minute by being thrust in by the window. In Barcelona, as usual, confusion reigned. Bakery shops in the narrow *calles*, like canyons between the high tenement houses, bore the legend "no bread"; there had been bread riots by the infuriated housewives. But still, in the squares and in *Las Ramblas*, the loudspeakers dinned out their tinned martial music and their endless propaganda speeches. Political Party politics. Tinned music broadcasts, flooding the streets with noise as sailors might swab decks with hoses, this and no toilet paper, had become everywhere the outward and visible sign of revolution, whether in Berlin, Moscow, Madrid or Barcelona.

On the other hand, the great Ritz-like hotels, the Grand Excelsior, the Oriente, remained as oases amid the chaos, although in days of full revolution taken over by the Headquarters Staffs. And doubtless in the Metropole at Moscow the thirteen violinists, in white waistcoats and white ties, were still fiddling well into the middle of the night and the early hours, while murder went on in the near-by Lubianka. It was against that murder that the world's generous youth must be aroused, against all the cold murderousness of the "reason of state" of ambitious men; in the name of humanity itself.

New conscripts were still paraded through the streets, there (like Chinese peasants later) because they had no choice. Although a few were technically veterans having actually fought in Madrid, these boys were marching with irregular unmilitary step towards that guerilla fighting in which chivalric show is soon lost, and only the human animal can survive amid the sort of unspeakable atrocities depicted by Goya in Napoleonic times. "It is better to die on one's feet than to live on one's knees." So said Dolores Ibarruri, "La Pasionaria". It is magnificent; it is heroic. Nevertheless, in the name of principle I declared war on "principle"— the "principles" of blood. There is usually a worm in the apple.

The transport as usual late (in Germany, on the other hand,

they said they were punctual to the second, "because it is war-time"), at last, escorted by my good Catalan friend Señor Battista y Rocca, I reached the airfield, boarded the plane which skirted the high Pyrenees and flew on to Marseilles, and so, in due course, reached Paris.

I got into Paris late on the Saturday with an appointment to see M. Léon Blum, recently the Premier of France, and advocate of the Popular Front, on the Sunday. The concierge seemed to be not a little uncertain where, on the Ile de St Louis, the particular Quai might be, in which M. Blum had his residence, and I decided that it would be best to go and see for myself, ahead of the time of appointment. I discovered the lovely seventeenth-century house on the Quai Bourbon, overlooking the quiet cobbled street, the plane trees, the Seine flowing around the islet and dividing it from the Cité.

I spent the intervening time reading *La Vie Merveilleuse de Mrs Simpson*, based on material from which Mr Bocca, described as an Englishman, has since made a fortune without having met the lady involved. I gathered from Stephen King Hall that evidence of telephone calls made from a hotel in Evreux showed conclusively that Mrs Simpson had sought to persuade the King not to abdicate and to forget her. Harold Nicolson had the same story, which was to her credit.

At 5.30 p.m., I called on M. Blum, tall, broad-shouldered, short-sighted, with wispy moustache and the *pince-nez* which give an air of intellectuality to many Frenchmen. In Léon Blum's case the air corresponded to the fact, for like M. Mendès-France he was as much the wealthy man of letters as he was Jewish and the French politician. Instead of stiffness and what has been called "Spanish court protocol manners"—not that I ever found them there, even with undoubted members of the Spanish court—such as one occasionally meets in England among minor officials, his manner was relaxed and affability itself. He received me, without any indications of haste, in his small but charming panelled study, lined with the works of Chateaubriand, Saint-Simon, Jules Romains and, unexpectedly, his own writings on women and sex. Incidentally, he was the intimate friend of Elizabeth Bibesco who, for a while, had resided at 2 Cheyne Walk, the Elwes house at this time occupied by ourselves.

We discussed the Spanish situation and my proposal for an international relief commission which could be compatible with non-intervention. He was interested, approving, and volunteered that he would himself write to M. Bonnet, the French Ambassador in Washington, on what I had in mind. However, when we parted, moved by I know not what politician's impulse, he gave me the clenched fist salute. For once, startled, I lost presence of mind, and, to my own surprise, found myself shaking him vigorously by the hand.

I returned to London; briefly saw Lord Cranborne at the Foreign Office in order to acquaint him more fully with what I was doing and left, on 20th February 1937, for America to see whether I could enlist the sympathy of the American Red Cross. The International Red Cross under Dr Junot had already done much in the matter of interchange of prisoners, but only at the end and with very limited resources had addressed itself to the issue of food and medical supplies, which steadily became more desperate.

I had also engaged myself to deliver a foundation lecture at Yale and one at Princeton, the former purely academic, the second on international affairs. Mr Colston Leigh was my agent for lectures elsewhere. My entire stay was a matter of days, most of them in Washington.

Owing to the speed with which I left London after arriving from Spain, the renewal of my re-entry permit as an American resident had not come through and the most the American Consulate in London could do was to issue a visitor's visa. The day before I left Southampton the permit came in. Having been cleared by the immigration officials on the visitor's visa, I told them about the recent permit. Immediately there was a grave debate whether they could admit me. Being told about my Princeton commitment for the following day, they relented but with the consequence that when I next came into America a year later, on the S.S. *Ile de France*, the immigration officials threw up their hands. I had *two* valid grounds for entry; who knew what my status was? I must go to Ellis Island. However, they courteously allowed me to go to my hotel over the weekend.

In Washington, as arranged with Lord Cranborne, I called on the British Ambassador, Sir Ronald Lindsay. Rumour said that Arthur Henderson, when Foreign Secretary, had shipped him over to Washington because he could not come to terms with him as Permanent Under-Secretary in London. He received one sitting sideways on and gazed impassively into the blank wall whilst one talked. He probably regarded me as a dangerous Red. Never yet had I failed to see President Roosevelt when I wished, so I rang up Ernest K. Lindley, his biographer, told him the situation and said I would like a brief chat with the President. He promised to arrange it as he had done before. Hence I did not trouble, as M. Blum suggested, to see M. Bonnet first.

The day before the appointment Lindley rang up. There were

difficulties. I could see the President but only at his general Press interview—which I did—and I must ask him no questions. I walked over afterwards to the Department of State and asked them "For why"? The reply was disarmingly frank: "Since you went to your ambassador, who said he had no *objections* to the President seeing you, it has all become so protocol that we can do nothing." I swore.

I returned to London by boat, meeting a certain Dr Hövel (if my memory serves me, of the German Foreign Office) with whom I drank a few beers while he discoursed on the Diktat of Versailles, and also the worthy Dr Sallet, later of the post-war Civil Service in Bonn. So as to keep abreast in information, I was then a member of almost every international society producing periodicals, friends of Soviet Union, friends of Germany, and all the rest. Since no concern was nearer to my heart than how to assure peace, I not only told Hövel, but wrote to him afterwards, saying that there was no desire at all in Britain for war and that it was fantastic to think that the country was plotting "encirclement"; on the contrary, a sincere desire for peace would be reciprocated. It was an indiscreet thing to do, rather like writing to somebody in the Soviet Embassy a decade later, and no doubt some clerk put a copy of my letter on to the security files of M.I.5. Hence I was not "a Red" but "a Nazi". These risks have to be run.

In London I got together a luncheon group at my house which included the Liberal M.P., Wilfred Roberts, Rachel Crowdy, some of the Secretariat of the League of Nations, Philip Noel-Baker, later Secretary of State for Air, and Don Pablo Azcarate. Dumbfounded I heard Azcarate, who had been largely instrumental in sending me to Spain, declare that the Spaniards were "not Abyssinians" in need of charity, and that there was no shortage of food in Eastern Spain. The situation, he added, was "very delicate".

Admittedly the Communist interest was not international intervention to relieve Spain's needs, but the presentation of an intransigent opposition to Franco. But in view of the ambassador's declaration, I felt that I was wasting my time and personal money endeavouring to do more. Years later I met Battista y Rocca and went over the story with him. "Azcarate's decision was a historical catastrophe," was his comment.

The Republic continued its forlorn fight until the final collapse in 1939. Not least hunger brought it to its knees. Earlier in New York, I again saw Ernst Toller, the dramatist and major figure in the Bavarian Soviet Revolution of 1919. One would not describe Toller as even Trotskyite, although both Trotsky and he were

Jewish, and not at all Stalinist, but rather the messianic type of Communist. Indeed Toller was rather I.L.P. or P.O.U.M. in sympathies than Communist, in any sense that the word is used outside the Vale of Esdraelon. Perhaps the last book that kept me awake until two o'clock in the morning was Toller's *I was a German*, with its insight into why the revolutionary outlook has always appealed to what I will call "left-handed" youth, to all youth that, for whatever reason of upbringing and antiparental revolt or of pride of intelligence, is in revolt. Christopher Isherwood, "Herr Issivoo", who knew this German group, has written a sympathetic study of him.

Toller described what he had been doing; the long fight he had had with the authorities, the unexpected backing he had received for his relief proposals, from such people as Archbishop Temple, then of York. Toller was suffering badly from asthma. He sat in his small bed-sitting-room on the fifth floor with an inhaler by his side, and told me the tale. My heart sank as I realised that it was all going to be a repetition of my own experience, the same people, the same approaches; but tried out a little later in the game and, therefore, a little more hopeless. I was not, then, so surprised a few months later, when I read in the Press that Toller was a suicide. It was the end of what could rightly be called a noble experiment in living in the true Central European revolutionary tradition of Kossuth, Hertzen and the rest, gallant if unpractical. If not guiltless of the romanticism of violence, at least they loved liberty, not tyranny.

General Franco consolidated his position. By 1939 he had won and the world was too busy to trouble about what was happening in Spain. Like Hitler he painted the picture of possible Russian triumph and, like Stalin, he ran a dictatorship of which the principle is always distrust and fear. His régime in principle is no more dangerous to civilisation than that of the South African Boers, of Strijdom and Donges, Verwoerd and Vorster—and of Smith's right wing, "boss" Lilford and the rest. It is much less so. I have always favoured a Hapsburg-Bourbon restoration and the re-entry of Spain into the mainstream of Europe. The Spanish people are one of the great historical peoples of Europe and less vainglorious in leadership than the French. The re-entry will come. Moreover, one can today discuss the régime in the cafés of Madrid fairly freely without being arrested.

If British shipping rode at anchor in the northern bay beyond Gibraltar, and if Gibraltar was not taken by force during the Second World War, it was on General Franco's sufferance; it was due to his refusal to enter into a full military alliance with Hitler, as distinct from action against the Soviets; it was thanks to his determination to sit on the fence and to keep his independence. We have solid grounds for being grateful for these diplomatic manoeuvres.

Nevertheless, if anyone seeks today to organise labour in Spain other than as the régime desires, he will land in jail and will be lucky if he escapes a charge for which at least the nominal punishment is the death penalty. If there is no resistance, it is because, having bled so deeply, at all costs the Spaniards wish to avoid the resumption of war. Like General Mao in the East but much less ambitious, General Franco is where he is because the great mass of the population first and foremost has asked for peace and the end of civil war. Still I salute Spain.

The Spanish Civil War in many ways was a local affair—but not entirely. At the level of ideologies and ideals, the clash had an effect on the youth of the Thirties not incomparable with the effect of the Greek War of Independence. I am sure that Auden was well aware of the comparison. It seemed to symbolise the clash between liberalism and democracy, on the one side, and military revolt of the Carson and Curragh type, and dictatorship, on the other. This was how it was presented to the world. This was how it had been presented to me. I had seen Berlin and Moscow and had few illusions; but here, it seemed to me, was something different.

It was the increasing violence and insensate fanaticism that repelled me, as it impressed Hemingway. Hemingway wrote *The Old Man and the Sea* in 1937 in Madrid. His *For Whom the Bell Tolls* memorably depicts the Spanish scene. In words from *Encounter:* "Now perhaps we shall no longer be plagued by the rhetoric of a messianic arrogance of the spirit which has blithely perpetrated so many hideous crimes against the flesh." One has to welcome sinners to repentance.

There was certainly something more to the war than the simple plan of burning churches in order to reach a new heaven. Despite the idealism of Toller and P.O.U.M., Anarchists and Liberals and the rest, it was indeed a very nasty and cruel war in which many good people perished to no purpose, not least because passion was preferred on both sides to reason, fury to humanism, the evil irrationalist nonsense of the Century of the New Tyrannies expressed by D. H. Lawrence, to the wisdom of Cervantes. What temporarily issued is not the system of the Spanish Cortes under which social and political advance was at least conceivable, but the system of a dictatorship, for long admitting no opposition—but now, perhaps, mellowed.

On the more sinister level of *Realpolitik*, the Spanish Civil War was neither local nor idealistic. It must have been in that same year I saw Toller, before the Second World War, that I had a talk about the matter with Ellen Wilkinson, who in her time played with many groups from Communist to pacifist. I still recall my startled shudder as she made one of those remarks that throw a flood of light into dark places, as if one had turned on an electric switch in a charnel house. "Of course," she said, "it was just a try-out for the show-down later."

To put it briefly and bluntly, it was Kremlin policy to get the world to take sides; to get the common man "blooded", suffering losses among his own kith and kin and thus ready for war; to get the West well and truly implicated and (to use the Existentialist jargon) "committed" in spirit to war, so that Stalin did not bear the attack alone in the anti-German clash which was likely to come— the war which could threaten, in power terms which the Kremlin quite especially feared, the security of the regime, the tyranny, in Soviet Russia. It was not Stalin's only plan. In the end, of course, he found what seemed a better and even more Machiavellian alternative, the partition of Poland and the Ribbentrop-Molotov Pact. However, in the earlier phase Spain was in some ways singularly apt for his purpose. It affects the whole problem of peace and war—and it is what bourgeois hedonism likes to forget— that some peoples (including the countrymen of the Maccabees) from honour or conviction evade being killed less readily than others. They are fighting peoples. And those near them get killed also.

In Arthur Koestler's striking phrase, "It seems to be almost impossible to mobilise public emotions for an ideological two-front war." This is one of the dilemmas of liberalism, as distinct from dictatorship, unless it can state a case at once positive and apocalyptic and also anti-totalitarian. The agreement with Hitler was no part of Stalin's original plan, deep as was his respect for the armies of Germany as distinct from those of the democracies which he held in contempt. The fundamental plan was Stalin's usual one: to let others do the fighting for him and become committed, while he remained militarily uncommitted. It seemed to him idiocy that the Western powers would not wish to do precisely the same thing. The intelligent policy, which clearly a statesman would follow, was that of Neville Chamberlain. It was difficult to persuade him that this, logically, must not be the West's plan. But the temptation for him of despoiling Poland was too strong. And the paradox of an understanding with Hitler must have amused him.

The Kremlin was mortally afraid that it might be left to face the more recent but no less tyrannous Reich alone—so horribly afraid that Bukharin had staked his life on plotting for negotiation. Stalin, while executing Bukharin, had still been coming to terms ever since 1936—had come to terms in 1939 with Ribbentrop. The result was their Pact of mutual flattery, to the clinking of champagne glasses (Ribbentrop's champagne?), which damned the West as "the aggressor" against a peaceful Reich, and of which the words still stand as a blistering indictment of themselves.

The words of Vyacheslav M. Molotov (to use M. Scriabin's revolutionary *alias*) on this occasion are worth perpetuating. In his speech of 31st October 1939 to the Fifth Extraordinary Session of the Supreme Soviet concerning the Molotov-Ribbentrop Pact and the partition of Poland, he said:

"Instead of the enmity that was fostered in every way by certain European Powers, we now have a *rapprochement* and the establishment of friendly relations between the U.S.S.R. and Germany. . . . One swift blow to Poland, first by the German Army and then by the Red Army, and nothing was left of this ugly offspring of the Versailles Treaty which had been created by oppressing non-Polish nationalities. Today, as far as the European peoples are concerned, Germany is in the position of a State that is striving for the earliest termination of the war and for peace, while Britain and France, which but yesterday were declaiming against aggression, are in favour of continuing the war and oppose the conclusion of peace."

To the accompaniment of champagne toasts, Molotov and Ribbentrop were photographed, having jointly signed the abominable Pact which stands in their name and which the pathetic Communist Parties of the world found themselves committed, by whatever sophistry, to defend. The theme was stated even more succinctly by Stalin himself: "I know how much the German people loves its Führer. I should, therefore, like to drink to his health. . . ."

It was inconceivable to Stalin that the British Cabinet would not try to play the game he would have played himself. At all costs the West, if war came, must be involved in war also, must be committed, must not be allowed to be neutral and undamaged. At little cost to Russia the Spanish cause could be used as an instrument to bring liberals and democrats, for all their traditional and temperamental pacificism, into such commitment. There lay grave danger for Stalin in the traditional pacifism of the Labour Party which could even, in individual cases, feel grateful to Chamberlain (as some expressly did) when he spoke of "peace in our time".

It so happened that this was a game of "hotting things up"

which the Nazis and fascists were as ready to play as the "Commies" and Bolshevik Party. Also, as an official of Imperial Chemical Industries, returning from Franco's Spain, explained to me on the plane to Paris, some would think it quite good capitalist business to make profit on both sides. It was enough to get the Germans out of Spain again. But it was left to the men of the Kremlin to make profit from the bleeding Republic and gold from the blood of its own supporters.

Nearly thirty years on, I chanced to see Cyril Connolly, now one of Britain's most famous men of letters, in the Rivoli bar of the Ritz Hotel in London. He was with two others whom I did not instantly recognise. He greeted me and introduced me to a figure from that past—Lord Antrim. I sat down and remarked that I was just going back, for the first time, to Spain. "We have just come back." "A rather remarkable thing has happened", I said. "I suspect I owe it to my college friend, Santa Cruz; but the Spaniards have invited me to become what is termed a Member of Honour of their Instituto de Estudios Politicos de España. It is a remarkable gesture and I have much hesitated about accepting; but I find that William Robson, that pillar of the *New Statesman*, has accepted. Why should I be more rigid than the Pharisees themselves? Under Fraga Iribarne there is a movement on foot to liberalise the régime, vigorously encouraged by the Spanish Cardinals. If they want me, I see no reason why I should not help in a good cause." "Ah! well," remarked Cyril Connolly, "the Spaniards are very forgiving." I looked him in the eye. "Cyril, it is *I* who am very forgiving." (Lest this be thought a snide remark, I hasten to add that, as with Rommel's chivalry, I thought and think Fraga's action most magnanimous in its courtesy.)

The situation had indeed a delightful irony. Naturally I would have preferred such an honour from my own countrymen; but I had not got it, and that had its own element of the ironic. Doubtless my acceptance would cause annoyance to certain academics who were concerned to suffocate me; but such annoyance I could only hope would be acute. I was indeed most dubious about my own decision, while deploring mere gnawing over of old bones. It is seldom good politics for any country to multiply enmities to gratify ancient emotions, and I confess I was agreeably surprised by the rare generosity of those who could, naturally enough, regard me as an ex-enemy. I had not concealed my support for the Loyalist cause and even, later, for the monarchist one—although I had authentically gone to Spain to study a human problem, this time of hunger, and to propose relief with, so far as the relief was concerned, an impartiality proper in a sociologist.

I went to Madrid and there received my honour in a company of eminent Vice-Chancellors and distinguished hidalgos. It was a pleasant occasion without bitterness. Recently, when a group of Basque nationalists were condemned to death by a military court, I drafted a letter resigning the honour. But when the sentence was commuted, I did not send it. I hope that the Gibraltar issue, perhaps by a condominium or an Andorra-type solution, satisfying honour on both sides (instead of having a smuggling den in Gibraltar), may be settled with equal amity. The treaty of Utrecht says the King of Spain (and, presumably, his successors) have an option if the British leave; and the United Nations in its infinite wisdom and opposition to the yoke of what is wrongly called "colonialism" have requested the British to leave. The model I would propose is a Free City (like the Hanseatic towns) displaying a large Gibraltarian Flag. Further, as with Andorra, there would be two "sovereign princes" and the flags of these too, those of Britain and Spain, would fly beside it. Honour would be satisfied. A Gibraltarian Minister recently assured me that it would be acceptable to the Gibraltarians. Certainly, instead of empty fights for prestige, it would correspond to political realities. It may be that this Andorra-type solution will not be acceptable to Spain, although much to her advantage; but this is no reason against propounding it and being seen to propound it. As an alternative, I personally would not be sorry to see the Members for Gibraltar and Malta in the British Parliament along with the Members for Belfast.

At lunch in Madrid with Señor Fraga and a representative of the Spanish Foreign Office, I suggested that one tactic for a restoration of good relations could be in getting the trades unions of Spain and Britain together, especially the miners. The especial concern of my hosts was to bring Spain into the main current of European unification. I could only applaud this, although whether Spain and Britain should soon join in "the Unity and Identity of Europe" is a different and highly ironic question. Westminster closer to Madrid than to New England or Toronto? Surely only a cultural maniac can believe this. I record again my profound respect for Spain and its people as, in terms of *Hispanidad*, one of the greatest countries of the European tradition, the elder sister of France. It is a country, incidentally, which has played, not too great, but too small a role in the stabilising of Latin America where, as usual, the new *colons* and rich exploiters have played an all too dubious and self-interested role. The history of Spain is not an ignoble history.

X

GERMANY: FROM LEIPZIG TRIAL TO NUREMBERG TRIAL

30 JUNE, 1934. A dinner at the Ivy Restaurant off Soho, London. I was waiting for my guests, H. G. Wells, Ernst Toller and Vernon Bartlett, the distinguished foreign correspondent of the *News Chronicle*, along with Stephen King Hall, one of the last Independent Members of Parliament. Vernon arrived late, apologetic and clearly excited: "Hitherto in reports from Germany, I have always tried to be strictly objective. But this is the end of it. For the future I shall attack the bastards."

Actually I had already heard the news from somebody who had got in from Berlin at 7.00 a.m. that morning. Adolf Hitler had personally arranged for the shooting down, that previous night, of Brownshirt Leader Röhm and his homosexual friends—had arranged for what was known as "the blood bath". General Schleicher also was dead—one of the series of generals and admirals, ending with Beck and Canaris, who it was hoped, might save Germany from Hitler. Personally I was not as greatly stirred as Vernon Bartlett by the Walpurgis-night shooting down of these Nazi sodomites. As for "H.G.", he turned to the discussion of civilisation and the fall of the Roman Empire. He thought the Romans of, say, the time of Honorius, probably felt just about as complaisant as Londoners did at the moment. (I may add that Rome had, in name, still ten centuries or more to go in some form of rule or other.) "H.G."s' own inclinations, made plain in the film *The Shape of Things To Come*, were towards some kind of dictatorship—even over the "Passworthies" and "Common Man"—by natural scientists with the aid of "peace gas" ... "Boffins" *versus* "Blimps". In terms of forty years on, this would have meant Soviet planes flying over Tel Aviv or American planes flying over Cairo (or Belfast) subduing the fanatical and contumacious into involuntary slumber.

John Gunther had fairly well apprised me of the kind of thing that was going on in Germany. Nevertheless, the affair made it pretty clear that the German dictator, the *Führer*, had now come into the open, in contempt of the usual proceedings of law and order. As such it not so much marked as made apparent a turning point. The days when the little Czech-Austrian lance-corporal had only 10,000 registered members in his Party, the days of 1928 when he only got 2.8 per cent of the vote in local elections were of the past. Incidentally Stalin was, for the first time, really impressed. Here, he felt was a man to be reckoned with—a real dictator.

I had some measure of background. To learn more of the language I had visited Hanover (where Hindenburg was still to be seen), Brunswick and Lübeck in 1922. In the gardens at Brunswick one could see the statues thrown down and broken during the Communist rule there. It was a brief rule—but not forgotten in Germany and one significant item in explaining what was happening. Not Hitlerism but a room, empty and garnished, waiting for Hitlerism, was to be found in sober, middle-class towns, not merely humiliated by a defeat where the Germans had suffered calculated humiliations, but afraid to their bones of what a native Communist victory (did not Marx come from Trier?) might spell for them. Inflation and unemployment were other factors, traumatic for the German memory, even the memory of the German workers. The fantastic inflation of currency broke while I was there. Later my host, poor man, a retired civil servant, died of starvation. One had to shop with a basketful of paper currency. The moral life of Germany, whatever the merits of the liberal democratic Weimar Republic, was (as well depicted by Isherwood) more rakish and permissive than attractive.

I was to visit Germany fairly frequently from then on until 1938, when I did a final round-up for information, including in my tour Vienna, Prague, Budapest and Rome. In 1926, in the hey-day of the Locarno spirit, I had seen Herr Dr Stresemann jubilantly invited to take his seat at the League of Nations Assembly in Geneva. I had heard Gustav Stresemann and Aristide Briand there speak together. "C'est finie, la guerre entre nous."

On a gloomy September day in 1933, I had taken a Czech plane to Leipzig, stopping off at Essen where, as in the rest of the Ruhr area, advanced unemployment was rife. Brüning, as Chancellor, for lack of Allied financial co-operation at a critical moment (as he later explained to me one afternoon in his New England refuge), had failed to cure it. In retrospect the conduct of the Western Allies during the Weimar period, and especially of the ever-egocentric French, was, to put it briefly, clearly criminal. Briand was an honourable exception. The Nazis, as largest party, had just come into power and President Hindenburg, who regarded the ex-lance-corporal as about fit to be a postman, had reluctantly agreed to his becoming Chancellor.

Henry Noel Brailsford had suddenly fallen ill. And I, largely

P

thanks to Dorothy Woodman, had been asked to replace him on the second day of the trial at Leipzig, 22nd September 1933, as a correspondent to cover what came to be known as "the Dimitrov Trial". Since I wanted to write a book on contemporary Europe as well as to lecture academically on these matters, I agreed. Cummings, of the *News Chronicle*, Norman Ewer, of the *Daily Herald*, and most of the more eminent British journalists were to be along. Of Ebutts, of *The Times*, and of Elizabeth Wiskermann, we saw something, later, in Berlin. The peculiarity of most British journalists at this time was that, sharply unlike the new American breed of Gunther, Mowrer and the rest, they did not move about gaining an over-all political view but remained, like Ebutts, for years in one place, with the danger that they regarded this as their local empire and, indeed, tended to become involved in its national politics.

There was indeed arising, as I have said, a new breed of international journalists who regarded themselves as moulders of public opinion and—as they did not hesitate to say—more important and no less responsible than ambassadors. (They had a point: many embassies today, including the million pound sterling one at Brasilia could arguably be closed down without disadvantage or reduced to delegations—or in the case of Brasilia the ambassador be more cheaply accredited to all South America.) As for myself, by chance I was not inexperienced in major trials—the one at Flemington Court House, New Jersey, about the kidnapping and murder of Lindbergh's baby; at least three obscenity *v.* censorship trials; this Reichstag Fire Trial; and, later, the Nuremberg Trial, when Ribbentrop and others were hanged.

Leipzig, the dull German university city, the home of Johann Sebastian Bach, the church still standing where he was organist—and the home of the annual World Fair—did not seem to be unduly disturbed. The solid citizens went about their ordinary life; they registered massive apathy. The bookstalls carried booklets explaining the rise of the Nazis—but were chiefly about the Nazi-inspired "German Christian Movement". I was later nauseated to hear German Christians singing hymns about "black is the night, white is the cross, red is the blood"—*schwarz-weiss-rot*—in Berlin's Lutheran Cathedral, with Hackenkreuz standards around and presided over by a "German Christian" bishop in brown jack-boots.

I had always distrusted "national churches". Here they seemed to me to reach the pitch of blasphemy. According to Alan Bullock, Hitler himself was a rationalist and a materialist, most impressed, in Wellsian style, by physical science. He at least was spared personal association with this buffoonery.

I also watched Midsummer Day pagan revels above Heidelberg, with fires and solemn oaths "to the soil of Germany". It pleased the youth. The Lutheran pastors, ever nationalist, "discussed the matter". The pre-beatnik *wandervögeln* were among the seeds of Hitlerism; contemporaries of the followers of D. H. Lawrence, the prophet, they fell into step with the rise to dominance of irrationalism and mass barbarism. As no other than Lenin said: "God has ordained that the young should be stupid." Perhaps the caustic remark of the great ironist and revolutionary goes too far; but that today's youth, instead of attending "demos", should stand in sack-cloth doing penance for the atrocities, spurred on by the cheering youth of yesteryear, seems to me only just. It is the old men, the Churchills, Adenauers, and Pope Johns who have been the saviours.

The Germans had not yet achieved the Soviet perfection in running state trials. There was a sprinkling of placards and of streamers, telling the citizens of the risks of a Communist rising and how the Führer had foretold it in April. In the Ruhr I had learned that, of the ten thousand recent Communist voters, most had become passive; some had joined the Nazis, because what they really wanted was "action"; and some had gone underground. What especially urged men to new and dangerous ideas—precisely as in Britain, but more so—was heavy unemployment, due to a financial crisis which had already hit Germany once and bitterly only ten years before, and which terrified those who had been through it, especially small men on fixed incomes. Recent detailed investigation by sociologists has underlined this.

On entering the High Court, there was a brief search for arms, courteous enough. The courtroom was crowded with every correspondent of eminence from Rio to Istambul. The judges entered; the chairman Herr Dr Bumke, white-haired, red-faced, unfortunately named. All stood. The German journalists gave the new Hitler salute. The foreign journalists did not. The judges did—but perfunctorily. This was a preliminary examination according to the Continental juristic pattern, allowing greater freedom of procedure and, in this case, public. The German Parliament House was burned on the night of 27th February, 1933—who was responsible? Were the prisoners before the court? All stood again for the administration of oaths.

The prisoners were Herr Ernst Torgler, chairman of the Reichstag Communist Parliamentary Party; the law-student Popov and the shoemaker Tanev, both Bulgarians; Georgi Dimitrov, also Bulgarian and outstanding Communist leader; and Marinus van der Lubbe, Dutch. Torgler, in almost bourgeois

style, recited the list of the Reichstag committees of which he had
been a member. He bitterly complained that he, a Deputy, had
been kept manacled. Herr Torgler amazingly survived the Nazi
régime and was still alive (and free) after the war ended. In Russia
the odds are that a similar deviationist would have been shot.
The rigid and formal Popov, the unhappy little cobbler Tanev,
darting looks about like a frightened hare, were minor characters.
Van der Lubbe, drivelling, his head almost between his knees,
seldom answered questions. Bargehand, waiter, plasterer's assistant,
mixed up with the Anarchists, four times a member of the Communist Party and four times having quit it—on his own statement,
a damaging one, associated with Nazis before the fire—was he in
the late stages of degenerative disease or was he drugged?

To the question, "Did you burn down the Reichstag building?"
he gave no answer. But, after arrest, he had been loquacious
enough, claiming the glory of it. He also boasted that he had once
been in France, "to swim the Channel". "There was a great
prize offered." Was he just another Dutch Anarchist *provo*, a
beatnik-type of which, even in 1966, so many have been in
evidence? The new Red Guy Fawkes—but with fewer principles?
An exhibitionist, who will be disappointed if he is not in the forefront? Probably an arsonist, who will associate with anybody for
the sake of a blaze?

The real question here is: Could he have done it alone; and, if
not, who were his associates? During the Great War, at a time
when Scheidmann made an anti-war speech in the Reichstag in
1916, there had been an attempt to fire the building. A corridor
led from the house of the President of the Reichstag to the
Chamber. The President was Hermann Göring. But there was
some evidence that this little-used passage was blocked by junk
furniture and remained blocked. Who egged van der Lubbe on?
For the Government the answer was: "The Communists." For the
Communists the answer was: "Göring". According to "Putzi"
Hanfstaengl, as he informed me, he himself had noticed smoke
from the Reichstag building and had rung Hitler, Goebbels being
with him. They registered surprise but Goebbels had exclaimed:
"I knew they would do it." Who were "they"?

Fundamentally this was Dimitrov's trial. Availing himself of the
court's rules and of its opportunities, so that he, not his counsel,
could hold the floor, in effect he consciously addressed himself,
over the head of the court, *urbi et orbi*, to the world's journalists.
It was great propaganda. His business, as with Black Panther
leaders in the American Courts, was not to keep the court rules but
to defy them. No British Court of law would have tolerated it.

Busy with objections, Dimitrov was on his feet again and again, electric, gibing, under the bush of grey hair a triumphant, indicting face. He fought for "freedom of speech", "the rights of man" and class victory. All were speaking at once. At last the exasperated presiding judge addressed him. "It is said, Dimitrov, in the foreign Press that you are conducting this trial, not I. This must cease." Dimitrov even had the effrontery to refer to an event in his native Bulgaria. He had, he said, been wrongly accused and wrongly imprisoned. Few of us realised at the time the full significance of this.

There had been a bomb explosion in Sophia Cathedral on 16th April 1925. The bomb had been placed with extraordinary skill. The king and cabinet members had been wounded, when attending the funeral of the assassinated chief of staff. During the memorial service the bomb had exploded—from behind the high altar. Fourteen generals and many others, including pressmen, were killed by the explosion. It was a typical Balkan atrocity in that accursed region of political murder. Perhaps it was done by some "deviationist" break-away group from the official Communist Party. Nevertheless, Dimitrov did not fail, in Moscow later and in his *Selected Speeches*, to make clear that it was not, as he had said in Leipzig, the work of police *agents provocateurs*, but was the work of Communist Party members, even if of uncontrollable *ultras* on the rampage. He took credit where credit was acceptable. Dimitrov's brother, it should be added, had been killed by the Bulgarian police as had Lenin's by the Tsarist authorities.

Cui bono? Who stood to benefit by the Fire? There is a story told of Hitler going to the gates of Heaven and demanding to see a reluctant Moses. "Do not be alarmed, Moses. I only came to ask one question. Now, tell me, that Burning Bush—did you set fire to it or did it catch fire of itself?" According to the landlady of my Leipzig *pension*, clearly the Communists were responsible. "Would the Government set fire to their own property?" A popular and general answer, but naive.

One often has to ask *cui bono?* There was, a few years ago, an attempted assassination of M. Mitterand in France, making that politician a martyr and hero. But did M. Mitterand arrange for the little affair himself? There is the mysterious kidnapping matter of Ben Barka of Algeria, in Paris. Does a Minister of the Interior go to a foreign country to carry out an assassination in person? Who finally stands to gain? In Berlin did the Communists stand to gain by some violent uproar? Constitutional democracy indeed went up in a blaze; the fire finished the chances of von Papen and Hugenberg. Assuredly those who did gain were the

Nazis, but the Communists might have gained also. The charge stuck however, that the Communists, not for the first time, were bent upon violent measures.

The Communist Party having been excluded, as violent subverters of the constitution, from the German Parliament, the Nazis became numerically the majority Party in the Chamber. Hitler became formally the constitutional ruler—unlike Lenin. That he was "constitutional authority" was going to warrant the commitment of appalling atrocities by many dutiful Germans. "Theirs not to reason why." This was Eichmann's defence. Be it added that, whatever one may think of rigging in the Elections or of tough pressures, there seems little reason to doubt that, in the years after 1933, the German people on a democratic and free vote would have given a large popular majority to Hitler, as the Italians did to Mussolini—although maybe not quite so vast as that which Hitler (and also Stalin, with 99 per cent) was later recorded as attaining.

The trial was moved, temporarily, to Berlin. The final judgement, given in Leipzig, did not altogether surprise me. Van der Lubbe guilty and to be executed. Torgler to have a prison sentence. The Bulgarians, interestingly enough, acquitted—including Dimitrov. The German High Court, it must be recorded, subjected to those terrific party pressures before which courts of justice in South Africa and Ghana have been forced to bend, conducted itself with an integrity and—as Göring's outburst was to show—even courage greatly to its credit. The ebullient Göring committed his memorable *gaffe*. "Dimitrov, wait until I get you outside this court." It was the Nazi Government which itself had, not nationally but internationally, come to be on trial.

Would that Government allow Dimitrov to get away? In fact, for whatever reasons of diplomacy or second thoughts, it did. Dorothy Woodman went off to see "Georgi" in prison, where she outwitted the Nazi guards and gained access. The problem was to arrange quick asylum for him. The Bulgarians, perhaps naturally, were not so anxious to receive their son. John Strachey's sister, Annabel, and Catherine Carswell went along to the Soviet Embassy to make a plea for the martyr. In the event Dimitrov was accorded Soviet citizenship. I saw him a couple of years later in Moscow's Red Square, still a hero. But already he was fading into the shades, and finally, like many an Old Bolshevik, he "disappeared" in the late days of the Stalin tyranny. Stalin, at least, knew how to deal with deviant heroes.

Actually one day before the Leipzig Trial opened, on 20th September, a so-called Counter-Trial began in the respectable premises of the Law Society in London. H. G. Wells, young Dodds, the son of the American Ambassador in Berlin, and many others were along. Maître Moro Giaffery, with all the resources of French legal rhetoric, assisted by M. Gaston Bergery (who much changed his tune later, in the days of Vichy), led for the defence of the Leipzig prisoners. The formal title of the gathering was "The Committee of Enquiry into the Origins of the Reichstag Trial." Ellen Wilkinson organised it; Pritt, K.C. (later expelled from the Labour Party for Left-wing deviation) presided and the Secretary of the German Communist Party, Thalmann, gave evidence for the defence. The purpose was to take the initiative from the Nazis and, before the bar of world opinion, to put them, not Dimitrov and the others, on trial by exposure. That purpose it fulfilled. The Committee, not unexpectedly, held the Nazis or their agents to be the probable criminals, not the Communists.

I went along to view the proceedings, but for years I did not know that the idea of this Committee of Enquiry originated with the World Committee for the Relief of the Victims of German Fascism, of which one of the master minds was Herr Willi Muenzenberg, that key Communist who, by an odd coincidence, had left Berlin on the very night of the Fire.

This so-called "court technique", invented in the fertile brain of Muenzenberg, has now become classic. Only the other day we had the "inquest" set up in Stockholm, on the initiative of Bertrand Russell, by his then secretary, Mr Ralph Schoenman, along with the detestable M. Jean-Paul Sartre, to indict the American and Australian, etc., Army (but no others) as "war criminals" in Vietnam. It is wonderful propaganda—as has been said, with rather heavy humour, "for the proper goose". More recent news is that a group of Eastern European émigrés has been demanding that an ever hospitable Sweden give like facilities for a court enquiry on the Katyn Massacre, to put the Soviets in the dock.

The Brown Book of the Hitler Terror, published by Gollancz, was chiefly compiled by Muenzenberg's partner, whose *alias* was André Simon. His real name was Otto Katz, who once had worked under Leopold Schwarzschild. The Counter-Trial and the *Book* together had a far from negligible influence upon British public opinion. It can quite legitimately be held that it had an entirely beneficial influence in arousing the British to their danger, in awakening them from pleasant sleep, by telling them about the internal affairs of Germany at that time—just as one might properly insist today on studying the internal affairs of the prisons in the far less powerful country of South Africa.

The subsequent careers of Willi Muenzenberg and of Otto Katz were indeed interesting. Muenzenberg was found hanged in 1940 (during the period of Soviet-Nazi *rapprochement*), allegedly murdered for "deviation" by Communist Party associates. Incidentally, Muenzenberg's "common law sister-in-law", Greta Thuring, a Party member and later author of *Under Two Dictators* (1949), did hard labour in Soviet concentration camps for three years, was then handed by the Soviet G.P.U. over to the Nazi Gestapo under the 1940 agreement and did five years in Ravensbrück, which she survived.

There is one comfort for the bourgeois: to no one is "the Party" more brutal and faithless than to its own members who serve it with dog-like devotion and the laudable and religious idealism which philosophically they deny to exist. Even the most clever remained, in Leninist terminology, still as much "nature's idiots" as their own dupes. Otto Katz was "liquidated" by the Communists—shot as one of the accused at the Czech Slansky trial in 1952—on the preposterous ground, *inter alia*, that he was a British spy. Stalin, as I recall Borkenau emphasising to me in conversation at Rebecca West's house, had repeatedly ditched the German Communists. What they had failed to allow for was that the Georgian bank-robber, Stalin, would ditch them by declaring, to the clinking of champagne glasses his profound friendship with Hitler—against "the aggressive, Western democracies".

This whole story has a somewhat James Bond quality, which the ordinary Anglo-Saxon finds difficult to believe and is still inclined to disregard. Bond techniques, however, should not be regarded as unexpected in the case of men living so dangerously as to be in daily fear for their own lives. They also had the exhilaration of the expectation of power. The contest, to which I referred later in discussions with Sir Percy Spender and Eisenhower, was on for "the minds of men". In his *The Invisible Writing* (the world's finest spy story), Arthur Koestler writes:

"It taught me that, in the field of propaganda, the half-truth was a weapon superior to the truth; and that to be on the defensive is to be defeated. It taught me, above all, that in this field a democracy must always be at a disadvantage against a totalitarian opponent. My years with Muenzenberg have made me sceptical regarding the West's chances of waging 'psychological warfare' against opponents like Hitler and Stalin. For to wage effective psychological war the West would have to abandon precisely the principles and values in the name of which it fights."

I do not necessarily agree with Koestler's argument. Indeed

his own book, precisely by himself "telling the whole truth", in the long run defeats it. But what about the short run? John Milton's over-simple dictum against censorship, everlastingly quoted by liberals, is misleading. Everything turns on the key phrase (usually ignored): "on equal terms". Truth will not be defeated—when fighting on equal terms. When is that? Let us, nevertheless, admit that to fight a war on two ideological fronts, as also on two military fronts, was almost intolerably difficult and ended in the demotion from great power, first of France, and then of Britain. The British Empire ended and we live, for better or worse, in a new epoch. What we make of it rests not with our fates but with ourselves.

A succession of German generals—Schleicher, Hammerstein, Blomberg—were going to save the country. From von Hindenburg down they distrusted the upstart Hitler from Braunau and Linz— no more a German than Napoleon was a Frenchman. They thought his plans impracticable. Until recently, they recalled the little man chiefly in terms of the failed Munich *Bierhaus Putsch* and as a protégé of the great, but eccentric and neo-Gothic, General Ludendorf. The bankers and respectable businessmen in Germany steadily preached, at home and abroad, that he was absurd, that not too much should be made of him, that he would never come to power. Many accepted this view. President Hindenburg, we were assured, would never consent to the lance-corporal becoming Chancellor. However, Field-Marshal von Hindenburg was now pretty old. A Prussian peasant, we are told, coming to visit his President and local squire was told to wait in the ante-room; like a sensible man he unrolled his little parcel of sandwiches and *Wurst*, began to eat and deposited the paper on the floor. Said an *aide:* "You had better pick that paper up or the President will come in and sign it."

Even Harold Laski, in the *Daily Herald*, drew a picture of Adolf Hitler as an old man drinking beer under a tavern beech-tree and spinning stories of what he would have done had he ever become Chancellor. As some of his early Linz school friends could recall (as recorded by August Kubizck, in a most revealing book, *The Young Hitler*), inspired by the Wagner opera and dedicating himself in an all-night vigil in the wooded Bohemian hills above Linz, Adolf had aspired to become a Rienzi, a People's Tribune. A very devoted son, they added. That was, "to his mother". His father, it has been suggested, was perhaps, like the Nazi persecutor Heydrich, partly Jewish; but in Vienna the son had fallen out with his Jewish employers. Anti-Semitism had become part of his cult. Blood and Race.

Although there was some belated talk about "the death-rattle of capitalism", it was utterly contrary to Marxist dialectical orthodoxy in the immediate post-Lenin age to hold that there *could* (at least north of the Alps) ever be a great popular movement *against* Marxism. Likewise, the top people, capitalists, sometimes felt that they might use the little corporal. It was incredible that he, or the upstart National Socialist Workers Party, N.A.S.P.D. could use them.

Some of Hitler's early supporters, such as Feder, were pretty Left-wing. Some, such as the Strassers—Gregor's brother I met in New York—were theorists. Others, more unpleasant, such as Rosenberg, had dreams of some racial resurrection. Spengler's alleged "work of genius" (even Brailsford fell for that) offered a popular philosophy of "fate-with-exceptions". Some of the top people, however, were inclined to think that Adolf Hitler was possibly "quite a good thing". Eminent names in France and Britain were not guiltless.

Since most of my connections were British, Jewish, even Communist, to get a detached view I got some introductions into Nazi quarters, including the Berlin P.E.N. Club. (In like fashion in Russia I had used "The Friends of the Soviet Union", to which I even paid a subscription.) These associations were chiefly useful to get tickets to public meetings. Hanfstaengl I saw and—he having a temporary grudge against Goebbels for banning a "Horst Wessel" film of his—I found it intriguing that, in a Berlin restaurant, he spent his time whistling the *Internationale*. Very deviationist. I also went down to Wedding and talked to workers in the Koeslinerstrasse, once the centre of a German workers' rising. They seemed to view the parades with detachment as a circus. However, Frau Marie von Hindenberg and the cousin of Field-Marshal Earl Haig I also saw, a Scottish lady married to a some-time State-Governor of Saxony, Graf von Nostitz. She was sure that Hitler merited support. Some of the workers—even the commissionaire in their own block of flats—were becoming very Bolshevik. And certainly Soviet Russia, with its vast armaments opposed to a Germany disarmed, was a menace. It was clear as daylight.

Not in all quarters did I get a reception so tolerant of Hitler. In the Herren Klub, in what was now the Hermann Göringstrasse, Berlin, I met members of the great North German family of Puttkamer. Hitler was quite intolerable. "Why, then, the situation?" Nobody respected von Papen. "But Prussia, at least, has a great military tradition. Why do not the German army men rally against him?" *Querelles allemandes.* The army generals quarrelled among themselves, and were chiefly united by traditional obedience to the State. Moreover, the Prussian junkers depended upon *Ost-Hilfe*, Federal aid for their farm estates. Ex-Minister Treviranus, that intelligent man, was also along. He hoped for the best. He mocked at a German professor there, who declared himself a liberal but concluded each sentence with the words "But nevertheless. . . ." Treviranus later escaped from Germany in a car, with bullets whistling around him. There was no centralised, organised and popular opposition. From the British Embassy as usual I learned nothing; it had "sealed lips". From the American Ambassador a lot. Hitler was prostituting Germany.

Later I called upon a young man bearing one of the most distinguished names in Germany, young Helmuth von Moltke, grandson of the old Field-Marshal. He was reading Heine. That poet was the only author, he said, for a civilised man in Germany to be reading at the time. However, as he said to me, to express Heine's views at the moment could spell the concentration camp as penalty. Later young von Moltke (whose letters, published by the Oxford University Press, all should read) became involved with the Catholic Mayor of Munich, Dr Karl Goerdeler, in the German Resistance to Hitler. They did not regard themselves as traitors to their country but Hitler as a traitor to the Germany of which they represented, in their persons, the tradition.

These dedicated men—none Communists (the Communists began, in 1939, be it remembered, as Hitler's allies)—were executed, in some cases with torture. It is well that their courage and their principles—in the particular cases mentioned, their religious principles—should be remembered. They did not get over-much support from Eden and the British Foreign Office, whose light does not shine brightly in these matters. (Not long before 1939 the Foreign Office had regarded the persecution of the Jews as "an internal German matter", an attitude indeed warranted by a moribund international law). As has subsequently emerged, if the generals had succeeded against Hitler, one of the Hohenzollern princes, such as Prince Friedrich of Prussia, was ready to take over.

It is the historian, A. J. P. Taylor, who writes: "The man who came closest to embodying Rousseau's *volonté générale*—the popular will—was Hitler; and he is not much of an advertisement." Stalin, for that matter, was also an embodiment—with one important reservation. Communism, with its "politically conscious vanguard", its doctrinal "clerocracy" of "those grounded on Marx" and its willingness educationally to select the more able, is an aristocracy. This is its strength in contrast to all forms of extreme anti-authoritarian anarchism, which is the parasitic pest of the West.

The Nazis, however, did not get as far as having any principle (victory apart) save one: race-theory—race-theory at the expense of Jewish, gypsy and even Slav minorities. Today the same theory, under the explicitly Nazi-minded Verwoerd and Baltha-zar Voerster, flourishes in South Africa. It is this theory which pin-points the distinction of Naziism from other fascist police states, its peculiar brand of Cain. Personally, I would ban by law all contributions in support of fascist or like organisations, including the K.K.K. and American Nazi movement, as subversive and threatening violence in substitution for State law. However, not inexplicably, this idea does not appeal to the Communist Party, so eager for the defence of civil liberties and the full rights of the individual.

"Wir sagen Ja." Such were the election placards carried on the trains as they steamed into the Friedrichstrasse Bahnhof on the eve of the German Election of 12th November 1933. I had come over again to observe it. It was a massive popular victory for Hitler, the common man had overwhelmingly expressed his views, and the days of electoral ambiguity were over.

Earlier, as I came in by train to Berlin, I had noted a considerable crowd gathered, saluting somebody in our train. Even the train-driver of a neighbouring train, some solid trades unionist, was saluting. A small airplane with red fuselage flew in circles overhead, like a heron with spread wings. I decided to explore. I walked along the corridor. Helmeted *schupos*, black-shirt S.S. men—Hitler's praetorian Guard—stood about, the more tight-packed as I went forward. A turn of the corridor and I was on top of a group of three. One of them, in crushed felt derby hat and military raincoat, flushed, alive with excitement, was unmistakable. The Premier of Prussia, Hermann Göring, after speaking in Hanover, was returning to Berlin. I could have shot him with ease. The Gestapo may be brutal, but I was impressed by how very much less efficient in security it was than the G.P.U. It lacked the centuries of the black, suspicious background of the Czars and of Scythian Russia.

Earlier I had gone down to Munich. There I heard the news that Hitler had decided to undo Stresemann's work and to quit the League of Nations. He had offered a proposal for general disarma-ment which Sir John Simon, not himself one of the most straight-forward of politicians, had (probably rightly) regarded as dishonest and anyhow, without further exploration, had dismissed with contempt. What exquisite pleasure it must have been for Hitler, in 1936, in the *Reichskanzlrei*, to be able, on an occasion when I was present, to tell Sir John that he, Hitler, had a larger air-force than Simon could speak for. I told the Germans I met that, in the matter of the League, they were making a diplomatic blunder and by their own act, putting themselves *hors de la loi*. I got in return a display of Teutonic anger from a member of the family of Admiral von Spee. The time for such compromise was over. *Wir müssen mehr einfach sein: wir müssen durch und durch Deutsch sein.* More simple, more downright, more German. More foolish. Stalin made no such simple error.

It was early in the morning in Munich. The Führer was coming to lay the foundation-stone of a Palace of Culture and Art. Through my bedroom window I heard the sound of marching and songs, and I could see the brown-shirt columns coming, not four but twelve abreast. (The last photo I saw of men goosestepping was in 1954—para-military police, in the Soviet Zone of Berlin, part of the People's Democratic Republic. . . .)

> "Zum letzenmal wird nun Appell geblasen!
> Zum Kampfe stehn wir alle schon bereit."

The Horst Wessel song of one of the so-called "martyrs of the Nazi cause", shot by the Communists in March 1930.

S.A. and S.S., Brownshirts and Blackshirts, converged on a field. The Blackshirt Security Staff were "a pacific, non-military organisation" that had their military caps decorated with a roccoco silver skull as a badge. Here and there were companies of Stahlhelm men, in their grey-green uniforms, and of students with their bright corps colours. In the field large wooden tiers of seats had been erected. By ten o'clock those on parade were all assembled.

There must have been ten thousand men in uniform, to honour Culture; and yet more spectators in the seats. At the back, behind the platform for the speakers, were immense pennons of red, dropping twenty feet to the ground. On the red, the white and black of the swastika badge—the badge of the Hooked Cross. The legend varied little from that in the Berlin Lutheran Cathedral in its colour hypnosis. "Red for the blood, and white for the spirit, and black for the soil of Germany." I had seen a like scene, with the same mob emotion, when Göring spoke in the Sport-Palast in Berlin, and had denounced "the red rats" and the clericalists, "the black moles". (Did I not also see something like it in Olympia, London?)

The platform protruded into the open-air auditorium, like some fantastic portico of a pagan temple to Power. Black pillars of wood supported the awning of the black roof, and at each corner of the roof vast black braziers had been filled with fuel and sent up columns of black smoke. It looked like a scene from *Aïda*. I was witnessing

the Rebirth of a Nation if one liked to call it that; certainly the
founding of a new religion—of the sword. Like Leninism, a new
Islam. This time, not Stalin's thugs, but Hitler's thugs.

The Leader came forward to speak. The little lance-corporal
already had Crown Prince William of Prussia, heir of the Hohen-
zollerns, in his entourage. In his appearance there was nothing
especially operatic, as with Mussolini; nothing even very impressive
—the khaki raincoat, the high voice, the faintly ridiculous
moustache. Even as he decisively struck the foundation stone, the
unlucky ceremonial hammer broke. He was yet the Little Man
incarnate. The waiting crowd was ready to be hypnotised by its
Mahomet—to himself a Rienzi, tribune and emancipator.

"It is glorious to live in an age which confronts the men who
live in it with heroic problems. Need and misery have overwhelmed our people. Germany finds itself without protection
and without rights. Destiny sets us the grand task, to fight in
these straitened times, to fill with faith and trust the hearts of
our crushed fellow-countrymen, to give work to millions of
unemployed, to build up a new society and to check its enemies
with an iron fist, to protect the nation, its material, moral and
cultural goods from the elements of destruction. It is a bold and
proud mission."

It was intoxicating rant. Enigmatically the Papal Nuncio commented: "Hitherto I have not fully understood the purpose of your
movement." It is perhaps not wholly remarkable that Winston
Churchill spoke of Germany as having been fortunate to find such
a leader in the days of its extremity and of miseries due to "the
purblind victors" of 1918. In his *Great Contemporaries*, a book
always fascinating for the historian to reread, before referring to
Hitler's "subtle personal magnetism", Winston Churchill wrote
(1935) that Hitler, for all his "stern, grim and even frightful
methods", might yet be regarded as one of "the great figures whose
lives have enriched the story of mankind." In retrospect, how odd a
passage. But yet how illuminating as to the mental ambiguities of
even the greatest men in 1935.

As I examine myself I ask how far would I today be prepared to
go. My reply is that, were the West actually confronted by the sole
alternative of Anarchism—even a decadent anarchism manipulated
by clever men with a driving desire for quick personal advertising
profit—then, and only then, might the Communist Party, as an
available party of order, however perverted—and its world prevalence
does not rest on thin air—have my vote and, I believe, that of
many as little Marxist as myself. Let the Catholics make a concordat
who can. As for a rakish civilization, I am against it. Anarchism,

not Communism at all as such, not even Marx-Leninist Communism, is today in the West the greater menace.

That same night I was in the Munich Opera House. The Führer was in the front row. The opera was Beethoven's *Fidelio*, in which the prisoner-hero (who, on this occasion was he?) declaimed much about that most ambiguous word *Freiheit*, "freedom". By some strange irony the prison-warders were clad in brown shirts. I don't think this was the symbolic intention of the producers. Or was it?

Adolf Hitler was an obsessive. Thanks to his obsession, within a few years he was to conquer more of Europe in less time than the Genoese-Corsican Emperor of the French. But, like the Corsican adventurer, his campaigns and his obsessions were to end in disaster. His first obsession was hatred of the Soviets. In *Mein Kampf* he explained his plan—to humiliate the presuming French, with their belief that they were patently entitled to lead Europe; and then to defeat the Bolshevik armies. He condemned the Kaiser for fighting on two fronts and for not coming to terms with the British—who, indeed, should remain in India. This was also the view of Rudolf Hess, whose chief fault, for all parties, was that he knew too much. (The unhappy man remains in Spandau prison because the Americans and the others choose to crawl to the Kremlin instead of arranging an accidental escape.) Hitler's second obsession, acquired when he worked in Vienna, was the Jews. His assistant, Heydrich, was partly Jewish, and it may be (as I have said) that in his own mysterious descent there were Jewish ancestors—although I doubt it. But he regarded the Jews emigrating from Poland and "international finance" so opposed to Schacht's plans, the internationally minded Jews, as the peculiar enemies of Germany. (Incidentally not all the German Jews, whose lasting and pathetic hope was to be good German patriots, loved the Polish Jewish immigrants. As usual in such matters, it was the numerical proportions that mattered.)

Hitler appealed to the unemployed, damning Brüning's orthodox finance. He appealed to Germans against the military encirclement of disarmed Germany, especially by Stalin's Russians. To attack Russia he needed power; he needed manpower. This meant consolidating the whole German folk. According to A. J. P. Taylor he was an opportunist who played by ear, and who discovered that to frighten the comfortable fat-cats of democracy was to succeed. Others have maintained that he had a vast plan. It seems most probable that, in the long view, he had a plan, early set out in *Mein Kampf*, and that, so far as German advantage was at stake, it was a mistaken one. When he opportunistically departed from it, it became more mistaken. He tried bullying for a while. It succeeded beyond belief. Then it failed. Before marching out East on crusade, he made the error of deciding that he could not afford to leave his Western backyard unsecured. He had to teach France a lesson; and Poland became his trip-wire.

To appropriate the Rhineland and then Austria was, for an Austrian, not difficult. At this point he should have paused, realising that to succeed he would need the tolerance, the rally of support, even the trust of other Western nations—and their indifference to the fate of the dubious régime in Poland. However, he believed (probably wrongly) that he might soon die of cancer and he impetuously wanted early war. Slowly the West, even the British, had to accept this fact. Moreover, it was a quite decisive fact, even for those who would have preferred to explore "peaceful change". He was in a hurry. He ceased for the moment to look East. Hence it was he—for all the policy, grasped at by Neville Chamberlain, of "letting the dictators fight each other" and the Germans, like Napoleon's Grande Armée, get bogged down in the depth of Russia, tied in holding the Russian peasantry down—it was Hitler himself who threw away this plan and compelled the West to fight.

Rather Hitler gambled on Czechoslovakia and on regaining the Sudetenland—and won. He gambled on Danzig—and won. He gambled on Poland, Eastern but assuredly not pro-Russian—and, by an indirect but almost inevitable sequence, he lost. The West, at last, had reached sticking point. The actual sticking point was, in fact, the Polish post-boxes in Dantzig:—"Polish sovereignty." To uphold post-box glory the Poles technically crossed the frontier. The foolish, brave, romantic Poles, who thought their cavalry invincible, lost; and were disgracefully betrayed by those intimidated or deluded by the power of Stalin. But Hitler's opponents won. In the end, with inadequate man-power, demagogic foot-stamping ceased to avail him, and his world-image became a thing of horror. Some said that he was mad; some that, however mad, capital punishment was too good for him, he was worse than "Boney".

I was to leave Berlin with sloganed streamers decorating the streets: "We refuse to be a people with inferior rights." "The German people demands Peace, but a Peace of Honour and Equality." "With Hitler against the world's armament madness." "Fight for Hitler and Peace against a World gone mad." "Work and Bread with Honour and Freedom." "It is not Germany that threatens the peace of the world: Germany has disarmed." "Lloyd George says that Germany has a moral right." "Lloyd George says. . . ." One could not but recall the slogans about Freedom and Peace in the Soviet Union. The essence of propaganda is to look the opponent in the eye and go one better. How wonderful are the ways of propaganda liars. How wonderful are the follies of the dupes among mankind, and how little their understanding of sheer power.

In the spring of 1936 I revisited Berlin, along with my wife. Hitler had left on the Saturday, for Cologne. Having acquired the requisite tickets of admission, we also left by train for that great city. General Blomberg, already in disgrace, was staying at the Dom Hotel. The crowd was so dense, awaiting the Führer's arrival outside the Bahnhof, that we had some difficulty in getting across to the Excelsior. Since Hitler was speaking that evening in the Messe-Halle across the Rhine bridges and time was short, we took a taxi and hurried there. The hall was packed but we got seats about five or six rows behind the speaker's rostrum. The German Army had re-entered the Rhineland, and the Chancellor was to defend his policy. Guards beat the tapestry behind us lest some enemy, more dangerous than any Polonius, could have been lurking there. I suppose that on various occasions, I could have assassinated most of the important figures in Germany if I had felt inclined. (The execrable but astute Stalin, when at the theatre among his faithful people, sat too far back for a pistol-shot.)

Hitler had no difficult task in convincing a German audience of the rightness of his policy. At the Congress of Vienna, after the massive defeat of the French dictator in 1815, Talleyrand had been present not only to represent France but to shape the Treaty. It was a very civilised and an eminently successful piece of diplomacy, a triumph, not for peoples, but for diplomats; neither press barons nor soldiers had a say. It provided the concrete framework for a century—1815–1914—of world peace. The Germans had had no such representation in 1918. That had been the Treaty of old Clemenceau "the Tiger", and of the narrowly intransigent Poincaré, both detestable characters. Hitler's argument was simple therefore. Was the punitive *Diktat* of Versailles to stand unchanged for ever, with Germany in a position of permanent inferiority? Conditions had changed. "Woe indeed to the conquered"; but Germany was no longer weak. Was the Germany Army never to be allowed to show its face in a vast area, the Rhineland area, of the German Fatherland? It was intolerable.

The Führer's speech was less staccato, more measured, than usual. He could not have been unaware of the doubts of his own General Staff, of the Army's fear that the Allied West would take military action to which no adequate resistance was practicable. But the applause of his Rhineland audience, for their hero of deliverance, was deep-throated and massive. The meeting over, the crowds, ourselves among them, poured back over the beflagged

Q

and illuminated Rhineland bridges, dominated by the cathedral, the Rhineland's glory. What, I reflected, was going to happen next? On the following night, under rain in the Market Square, from loudspeakers, I heard the voting results come in—a massive endorsement for the Führer and canned applause.

We went on to Strasburg in Alsace (where I noted with amusement that the French election notices and appeals were printed in the language of the people, German) and so on, for the Saturday night, to Verdun. Here the German offensive of the Great War had been stayed by Pétain. On the Sunday morning there was to be a *rassemblement* of veterans of the earlier war, to be addressed by Deputies from the Assemblée Nationale in Paris. Little medals (of which I still have one) were handed out. And the theme, the conclusion of this gathering a thousand strong? *Jamais la guerre. Jamais.* We returned to London.

The problem of 1936 is recurrent; it is a contemporary problem. When should one undertake a preventive war? The war of 1939 was to end as a world war. By hindsight we think we can see that the spring of 1936 would have been the right time for the statesmen and armies of the democracies to strike. The German High Command was resentful of being ordered about by the little Czech-Austrian corporal, distrustful of the success of his plans, and prepared to withdraw under a show of force. Yet might not the same German demand have recurred later with increased resentment?

At the time decision was not so easy. In 1952 there seemed to be a strong case for authorising General MacArthur, one of America's greatest generals, to cross the Yalu River, not in order to get bogged down in the mainland of China, but to attack the massed Chinese supply forces and force Stalin to make a choice, at a time when he was militarily unprepared either to desert his Chinese allies or to lose Vladivostok. (From the British point of view, if war there was to be, it would be better in Asia than over Berlin in Europe.) It could have been the end of Chinese pretensions to expanding military power, which beset us two decades later. It might have exploded Stalin's prestige. Would it, then, have been supremely wise? In 1952 Truman and Eisenhower both knew of the grave depletion of American armed forces. On both occasions the democracies were affected by their inherent weakness: the popular objection to their boys serving in the wars. There was popular demand for rapid reduction in the armed forces. Power is not force; but power involves the potentialities of force.

In 1935–6 Arthur Greenwood and many others—I among them—had stood on platforms pleading the cause of schools and hospitals.

All the electorate wanted was both to keep their cake safe and also to eat it. As to the French both then and later, under M. Cot, their air-force was in a deplorable condition. A democracy always likes to sweep unpleasant things under the rug—until a day of reckoning comes when it is aroused by the smell of the rot. More solidly: "Was not the Versailles Treaty sadly in need of revision?" and "Was the case for war to be to prevent the German authorities from 'going into their own back-garden'?"

It is easy enough to talk—and most weighty men, such as E. H. Carr, at that time talked—about "Peaceful Change". Even to revise frontiers, in some equitable way, yet relates to the realities of power. Before long the Roumanians announced that all such talk, translated into action in Transylvania or Bessarabia, would be regarded as a hostile act. I have come across few people with deep respect for the Roumanian national character (reluctant although I would be to indict a nation); but what the Roumanians said other small countries, with dubious territorial gains, might have been prepared to act upon.

In 1938 I visited Prague, on the invitation of Czech students of mine. Czechoslovakia had been so called (first in America) by an act of propaganda. It was patent that the Slovaks and the Czechs, united in disliking the Hapsburgs who had endeavoured to rule them, cordially disliked each other. Beneš, with his Czech National Socialist Party, it was pointed out to me, headed a minority government. Czechoslovakia, indeed, with the highest tariff barriers, largest military expenditure in proportion to population and, in Skoda, biggest munition works, boasted about its democracy. But the largest single Opposition Party, the Agrarians led by Beran (with whom I talked), officially sought good relations with Germany for reasons of trade and geography. Reports of this situation were suppressed in most of the British Press by direct request of the Beneš-controlled Czech Embassy in London. Munich provided "a correction of frontiers", a change; it was not a successful one. Annexation went on.

By 1938 the situation was out of hand. Just as the tall General of Brigade de Gaulle, for the greater glory of France, was "an old man in a hurry", so the little lance-corporal Hitler, for medical reasons, was in a hurry. Although the gas-chambers, "the ultimate solution", were still to come after war started—and, indeed, might never have come without war—the attacks on the Jews had become blatant since the Nuremberg Laws of September 1935, and particularly with the breaking up of the synagogues on *Kristallnacht* (the Night of the Broken Glass), 9/10th November, 1938.

No one more outstandingly attacked the régime than American

Ambassador Dodd—with whom I talked freely—who rhetorically compared it with that of a Caesar, "seduced by the wiles of a lewd Cleopatra". Martha Dodd, his daughter (who later changed her mind to its polar opposite), was bitterly criticised by John Gunther for being seen with Nazis in the very streets where girls were being led, shaven-headed for having relations with Jews—just as French girls, shaved "co-operators", were later led by the Communists (earlier themselves "co-operators" with Ribbentrop and Molotov) in the streets of liberated Paris. For many Jews a fight was on to the death between "the Germans" and the House of Israel—including those Jews who would earlier have been only too glad to be accepted as loyal Germans. War came and by 1942 Himmler and his fellows were working out that "ultimate solution" which Germans will not be allowed to forget for generations. Nevertheless, under Adenauer, a conscientious man, vast financial compensation was in fact paid—as it never was by the miserable East Germans of "the People's Republic".

Very eminent citizens joined, as I have said, in parades in the streets of London, with placards: "Call Hitler's bluff." Many of us—although we did not suspect the abominable treachery of Stalin and Molotov, inspired by cowardice or calculated from intelligence (as by Bukharin) about their own weakness—were dubious that Hitler's plans were indeed only "bluff". They seemed rather graver.

So reliable and informed a man as R. C. K. Ensor assured me (despite the experience of Napoleon) that "the Germans would go through Russia like a knife through butter". Maybe he had never read Tolstoy or studied the story of Napoleon's Retreat. Military intelligence, wrongly based on the Spanish and Finnish Wars, seemed to confirm his view. (It is an odd thing, suitable for enquiry, that Intelligence is so often wrong.) A victorious Hitler would then, having demolished the one country, "find all the dominoes falling before him" and would turn to crush the West.

For myself I was well aware that the old conspirator Stalin's earlier plan had been to involve Germany and the despised democracies in war, having "bloodied themselves" and committed their emotions in Spain, and to remain, if he could, triumphant on the side-lines. The British Communists, of course, at that early stage in the late 'Thirties, did not accept this. Stalin, the Great Emancipator, would staunchly fight for fuller democracy. However, in view of Winston's past "black imperialist" reputation, I was slightly surprised when Dorothy Woodman remarked to me: "It looks as if we shall have to turn to Churchill." Soon the *New Statesman* advocated this editorially. Few statesmen's stock stood at that time lower than Churchill's—how low, it is today so easy to forget. As Lloyd George had remarked, with his bitter cynicism: "Winston is finished; only a war can save him."

Winston Churchill is one of the greatest men whom Britain has produced, far outplacing in character the Prime Minister of the First World War, Lloyd George. In retrospect the extraordinary thing is not his late success and popularity as a national hero, but his earlier marked unpopularity. It was an unpopularity that endured and that reached nadir when the affair of the Abdication was managed under wraps and Stanley Baldwin was saluted by the incredible Hannen Swaffer as "standing like Cromwell". On the day before *The Times* editorial on that crisis, Dawson, the Editor, received a phone call in formal style from Baldwin. "A message from the King. If you are publishing an editorial tomorrow, His Majesty would like to see it beforehand to comment." Baldwin then added his own words: "That shows how the little man fails to understand how things are run in this country"—an odd comment for an allegedly "loyal subject". It was Baldwin's hour of glory, so soon to end.

Arthur Greenwood described Baldwin to me as "one of the greatest parliamentarians". I myself was not involved but I sent on to Ernest Bevin, for information, the volume of the Charles James Fox correspondence in which that leader of the Opposition advised the Regent that if "Prinny" would only wait until he became king, Fox would get Parliament to legalise his marriage to Mrs Fitzherbert. As Lord Attlee wrote to me, it was popular opinion not in London, but the North and Knox's Scotland, that was decisive.

It is not remarkable from a party point of view that Winston was unpopular with the Conservatives, when he early left them for the Liberal Party and campaigned against the House of Lords with the slogan "Refer-and-end-'em"—Churchill clearly holding the referendum to be constitutional as did others. "Never a good Party man." Nor was it surprising that the Labour Party opposed his later imperialism and "hard line" on India. In politics, Winston Churchill was the great outsider, the man who did not make good.

These yet are judgements in politics, not on character and quality of personality. But "opportunity" alone does not explain the change in these judgements. Thus one finds an eminent and influential (if somewhat self-important) courtier, Viscount Esher, writing in 1917 to Sir Douglas Haig: "To me he appears not as a statesman, but as a politician of keen intelligence, lacking in those puissant qualities that are essential in a man who is to conduct the business of our country through the coming year." How exquisitely fatuous a judgement. And yet, how many shared it?

What more fascinating than this *volte-face* in opinion ? A certain
piratical rumbustiousness, almost an Edwardian insensitivity, does
not explain how the rejected by all became the character acclaimed
by all as the hero of the Second World War. Lord Attlee's judgement
I shall quote later. Sheer hatred of Winston's personality explains
no little of the (highly profitable) Sikorski libel. Against all this one
sets Sarah Churchill's filial tribute: "He epitomised for many
people the kind of father you'd like to have."

What explanation ? I suspect that the answer must be that offered
by John Stuart Mill: the eternal human fear by the mediocre of the
outstanding—the alarm of placemen, in all walks of life, lest their
sweated-for prestige may be undermined and their hollowness
exposed. The powers that be preferred Inskip to Churchill. It was
not until after the Battle of Alamein that Churchill's position became
secure against domestic attack.

Incidentally, I recall talking at some social gathering with Mary
Churchill, Mrs Soames, and asking whether Graham Sutherland's
portrait of her father, the ill-starred House of Commons gift to
Sir Winston, was still stored in the cellar. She replied that it was.
I chanced to recite this story to a fellow guest as I went up in an
elevator to a lunch. He drew himself up. "I am Graham Sutherland's
brother-in-law." I excused myself as a mere reporter of fact, but
my story drew a most revealing explanation. He said that the
painter had found Sir Winston, when he sat for him, in his eyes just
a sullen and unpleasant fellow—and he painted what the subjective
eye saw. In brief, he "did a Moran", although his resentment here
involved no breach of professional etiquette. Sutherland was
obviously the wrong man to commission here, although clearly a
master in handling "crinkled brown wrapping-paper men",
leathery men, like Max Beaverbrook and "Willy" Maugham.

For myself I could, at this time, see only this: that if the rational
pursuit of peace had now run its course and there was going to be
war, the imperative urgency was to win it. I pushed—it is the only
term I can use—my children out of the country to America where I
had so many friends, in order to keep my own hands free for the
war; and notified the Foreign Office of the date of my return—a
date which I kept. In honesty I should add that I had some fears
that, if war came, my wife might be locked up as Bertrand Russell
had been, as a known pacifist. She certainly did not trim her sails,
as some did.

As Harold Macmillan said, when he lunched privately with us in
Cheyne Walk, about Neville Chamberlain: "Many of us are very
ashamed of what happened about Czechoslovakia." Chamberlain
had made his throw for peace or, if there was to be war, to let the

Germans and Russians fight it out and keep the democratic power, intact, on the side lines—a plan indeed so far rational that Stalin remained utterly convinced that (since he would have done the same) it must be British policy, dishonestly concealed.

Strictly from his own point of view, Chamberlain, less militant than his father, Joseph, should have ordered a general election instantly after the Munich pact, so as to confirm his mandate. In this event not only would Chamberlain have had the applause of a majority of the House of Commons, including many Labour members, but in the General Election, Churchill, Macmillan and Boothby, even Eden, could all have lost their seats. Left-wing trades-unionist Mr Jack Jones, recently re-affirmed to me this same electoral judgement. The Hitlerite troops, upsetting the post-boxes in Danzig and marching in, would have confronted the Soviet troops on their own frontier. They could well (as was feared) have defeated them and embedded themselves deep in the steppes of Russia. Certainly Hitler might have detected the trap and made sure of France first. In the alternative he would have had to consider how many troops he could spare, depleting the home army, to hold down the obdurate Russian people as Napoleon could not. Both dinosaurs might have died in each others' jaws. Halifax, who was later considered as a possible Prime Minister instead of Chamberlain, advised Chamberlain against any such electoral *coup*.

For myself, I did not share with R. A. Butler the alleged view conveyed to the Swedes (and, perchance, itself a diplomatic manoeuvre) that "the last-ditchers" should be ditched. In 1938 I was approached by Katharine, Duchess of Atholl, sometime Conservative Parliamentary Secretary for Education, and M.P.— "Red Kitty", to her critics—about a certain committee or group which she invited me to join. My memory is refreshed by reading a memorandum she sent me shortly before her death. Arthur Koestler, in his *Invisible Writing*, recounts that at the time of the Spanish troubles, before offering co-operation in providing an introduction to his *Spanish Testament*, she asked whether he was a member of the Communist Party. "I had no choice but to answer 'No' out of a constricted throat". She said, "Your word is enough for me." It was this kind of regulation lying which in the end caused Koestler's conscience to revolt.

Katharine Atholl's invitation was to join with others in what was in effect a pressure group to get Winston Churchill into the Cabinet in view of the national danger. It looked as if it might not be so easy. Even when he was brought into the Ministry, he was not initially put by Chamberlain into the Cabinet. The days had not quite come when the Labour Party wished urgently to forget its campaign for disarmament and the collective-security-for-all Peace Ballot (in which half the electorate took part) of 1935; or the Conservatives to strip their memories of all allegiance to Neville Chamberlain, who became the scapegoat for the sins of others.

Already another group existed—"Focus" (of which Eugene Spier, later disgracefully treated by the authorities, has documented the story). It was largely responsible for providing Churchill with a forum in the large Free Trade Hall, Manchester; and—at a time when Churchill felt himself to be totally abandoned and when Lord Derby, who had first promised to do so, had later declined to be present—it had substituted for Derby the popular then Lord Mayor of Manchester, Alderman Toole. The prominent members of our own group, apart from Kitty Atholl, were Randolph Churchill (who had, in effect, disappeared before I came in) and Duncan Sandys. I do not believe that I have ever been a member of a committee which so rapidly saw its purposes achieved—although the issues of the Premiership and Party Leadership were still to come. Our major objective achieved, the residue of our programme was taken over for a while by an association, of which I was a member, called the Active Democrats, guided by Lancelot Spicer.

Despite the support of the local agent I had failed (for reasons later given) to be selected as Labour candidate for Rochdale. Owing to the death in an automobile accident of my successor at Cornell, that University, with its habitual generosity, had invited me to return there despite my resignation of 1935. I had declined, stating that it seemed more than likely war would break out and this did not appear to be a suitable occasion to leave the country. After the visit to Rochdale, I spent the week-end in Manchester, and on Sunday morning, 3rd September, 1939, outside Manchester Public Library, I heard Neville Chamberlain's voice on the radio telling the country that, owing to the absence of any German reply to his ultimatum, a state of war existed. The Second World War had begun.

There is an epilogue to this story, an epilogue of seven years later. Hitler, Goebbels, Himmler, possibly Bormann, were dead. So, for that matter, was Roosevelt. I was officially invited to visit Nuremberg. In a public building, allocated for the purpose, a trial was going on. With an ironic sense for the fitting, Nuremberg had been chosen for the purpose. The aim of the trial was to write an unforgettable epilogue to a criminal chapter of history, to spell out a Radamanthine judgement. From the public gallery, I saw (surrounded by white-helmeted American soldiers) the banker Schacht, keeping himself to himself; Keitel, Ribbentrop, Hess in a group and, nearest to where I sat, the remembered figure of Hermann

Göring. The Field-Marshal was in a plain white uniform. Here I saw the end of the gospel of "Action". Facing these men was the judicial bench—an English presiding judge, Mr Justice Lawrence, and British, American, French and Russian assessors.

The accused were all guilty. No one doubted it. They were guilty before trial and no one was going to find them innocent. A French officer, who had been in a Nazi concentration camp (British officers alleged that he was a little unbalanced by his sufferings) had a large exhibit of Nazi atrocities in the court buildings. Lampshades of human skin; shrunken heads—proofs of sadism. I looked at some of the photos and noted that they were all stamped in Cyrillic characters as from Russian sources. I asked him whether the court had certified the exhibits, but he didn't like questions. He was providing a service for which it was the duty of visitors to be grateful. It was a foolish and improper performance to be on show in the premises of a court of law. The case was strong enough anyhow. But the dedicated propagandist understands no limits.

What yet was to be done with the criminals? Were they to be treated as prisoners of war? As Winston Churchill grimly remarked, the time was soon coming when anybody who lost a war would be shot. This, after all, was the tyrannical Twentieth, and not the civilised Eighteenth Century. Lucky if they were merely shot. Should, then, the army shoot them? I recall the story told to my father by an old Devon coastguard about the suppression of African slave-runners: "We'd captured the Arab captain, sir. What were we to do with him? No capital punishment in Zanzibar, sir; no capital punishment in Zanzibar. But he'd been wounded. So the surgeon, sir, amputated a leg and an arm. Died the next day, sir. No capital punishment in Zanzibar." The thing to do, it was decided, was to establish an international court "to manifest humanity's justice"—Stalin's judges would be along on the bench—to try the criminals and to put on record the convincing evidence.

Later on, in California, I talked with the American professor of psychology who had been professionally in charge of Göring at the trial. Patently he had a considerable admiration for the old brigand. Göring, he said, was *not* a drug addict. He medically used drugs to alleviate former war wounds. He had a sense of humour. His comment on Eisenhower was: "I raise my hat to him: only he could have kept such mavericks as Montgomery and Patton together in one team." The man who could produce the ever-memorable phrase, "When anybody mentions the word 'culture', of course I reach for my Browning," did not lack wit. However, the stink of Belsen and Auschwitz was in all nostrils, so that Katyn itself was to become insignificant. And Göring was almost as guilty as any. (He committed suicide: I do not know who was responsible for this act of grace.)

There were indeed only two courses open to the defence. The first was to plead that the Court itself was incompetent in international law. This, when later he was kidnapped, was to be the plea of Eichmann, the miserable little civil servant who regarded massacres as a "duty". The Court took it upon itself to overrule this defence. The prosecution case here was stronger than for Eichmann, since some of those at Nuremburg had themselves issued orders on behalf of the Sovereign State. And, in effect and without precedent, it was the absolute Sovereign State itself that was on trial.

The second course was to plead degrees of crime and extenuating circumstances. This succeeded with Schacht and others, including (rightly) Hess. For others it was unavailing. Ribbentrop, for one, was hanged and whether from professional blundering or sadism he took a long time a-hanging. There was capital punishment in Nuremberg. *Vae victis.*

Certain high members of the American judiciary involved at the time have since stated that the whole trial was a mistake. They well might. Certainly the international court was *ad hoc*. It had no connection (as it should have had, especially had it been a permanent Criminal Court) with the United Nations Court of International Justice. Today, if an officer commits "a crime against civilisation and humanity", on the Nuremberg precedent an international court could hang him. I do not doubt that Stalin or Mao (who has liquidated millions of "class-enemies", Chinese subjects, as Hitler liquidated Jews) would both be hanged high as Haman by such a High Court. On the other hand, the same officer if (like William Douglas-Home) he refused to carry out orders, might be court-martialled and shot by his own national authority.

On reflection, however, I do not agree with the judgement that the trial was a mistake. I think that the Nuremberg Court, although highly irregular since it was not a Permanent Court of Criminal Justice, was right. I would favour hanging Hitler and Stalin, if caught. What the Nuremberg Trial established in international law was something very important—and very unpleasant for certain national authorities (such as the Gaullists) with their archaic and dangerous chatter about national sovereignty.

Incidentally, at the time I was attending the trial of the German criminals, I was shocked to read an excerpt, published from a writing by M. de Gaulle, reiterating what he had earlier said in his *Métier des Armes*: "History turns on the sword." I read no Allied condemnation of his atrocious Mussolinian sentiments.

What was established in Nuremberg was the precedence, on principle, of "the laws of humanity" (and indeed the international laws of war) against all national sovereign claims whatsoever to the contrary, even in the case of that sovereign country's own subjects. The principle that other states must not interfere with how governments treat their own subjects in internal affairs, save within approved rules of jurisdiction, is hereby voided. The consequences for South Africa and even for China are plain, whatever Lord Montgomery (the apologist of Mao's methods), the revolutionaries and the *buveurs de sang* may say to the contrary. The need for a World Authority is plain—an Executive and Judicial Authority itself holding the Sword, the Scales, and the Bomb and prepared to use them or, maybe, H. G. Wells' "Peace Gas".

The hanging of Ribbentrop and his associates in Nuremberg did something to avenge the liquidation, as the war went on, of the Jews and others in Europe. But before this was possible it had been necessary to corner Hitler, an operation which required a six years' war. The prospects for victory in 1939–40 were assuredly not over-promising. Just as at the time of the mutinous mood of French troops in 1916–17 and the collapse of Russia in 1917, so, at a time when France was occupied, the Communists supporting Molotov, and Germans and Russians were dividing under their pact the spoils of Poland, everything turned upon what the United States would do. For the second time, here lay the issue. Having declined to return to America in 1939, in 1940 I found myself suddenly and unexpectedly involved.

XI

WAR AND WENDELL WILLKIE

§ i

In 1936 I had a talk in the House of Commons with John Buchan, author of *The Thirty-Nine Steps*—steps to be seen at Broadstairs —and later, as Lord Tweedsmuir, Governor-General of Canada. I wanted to talk frankly with a politician who also understood the American scene. I told him (as indeed I had already written in an earlier book) it seemed to me that war-clouds were now fast approaching and it would be only prudent if we could be allocated, at least provisionally, the posts we could most usefully occupy if war came. My own qualifications, I suggested, were chiefly in the Anglo-American field. He was friendly, helpful, and told me to get in touch with the most relevant Minister under Mr Baldwin, Sir Thomas Inskip. I wrote to Sir Thomas but the reply, without being chilly, was negative; I detected no sense of urgency. The theme was that we should all beware of alarmism. I suspected that I was regarded as another alarmist; I was what might be called "prematurely prepared".

As for the Labour Party in opposition, the pacifist members were still very much to the fore, although less certain of themselves than they had been. The Fascist ex-Marxist Mussolini had made an attack to revenge Adowa and to extend "the Roman Empire" over what was then called Abyssinia. This had indeed shaken them. The pacific resort to economic sanctions, the alibi to arms, had patently failed as usual—as it had against the Japanese in Manchuria. The Japanese had bluntly said they would treat such sanctions as a hostile act. Sir John Simon at Geneva had stated their case for them, as they embarrassingly remarked by way of compliment, whatever Secretary Stimson in Washington might say to the contrary. The advocates of economic sanctions, the "wrist-slappers", had then run away from their own shadow. The Hoare-Laval Pact had been an attempt to preserve the Stresa Front, including Mussolini, against Hitler; but to supporters of the League of Nations it had seemed a gross betrayal, a cynicism symbolic of the Foreign Office at its worst. That the League itself was a paper tiger with false teeth was less stressed.

At the Brighton Conference of the Party in 1935, at which I was present, Ernest Bevin had indeed made his famous and ruthless attack upon "Uncle George" Lansbury, so that Lansbury had quit the Leadership of the Party. But a large section of the Party, here the heir of shop-keeping Nonconformist Liberalism, wrongly never liked spending much money on defence. It was like spending money on liquor. As Dean Acheson later said of George Kennan, this section had "no sense for power". I recall a Party Conference addressed, to cheers and with the full force of the Welsh *hwyll*, by Rhys Davies, M.P., protesting against arms expenditure.

However, the mood of the Conference delegates had now changed, thanks to Mussolini, who had revived the old pre-1914 German theme that war is "a medicine for mankind diseased". Instead of the pacifist repudiation of all war, Conference had voted for arms increase. This did not later prevent Members in Parliament voting against an increased arms budget—strictly, as we were assured, as "normal Parliamentary procedure" and as registering Opposition disapproval of the specific Government technical plans. The public did not quite understand the "procedure". As I stood next to my friend Morgan Jones at Conference he turned to me and said: "I have never before voted for arms in my life—but what else am I to do?" But the campaign against the Air Minister's "bombing planes" went on. There was at this stage a still legitimate doubt about starting up "an arms race", when there appeared to be a clear Western superiority—in fact a misestimate.

Arthur Greenwood continued to preach the benevolent claims of the welfare services, health, housing, education. Stafford Cripps took the line, with his Socialist League even on Abyssinia, that "the true socialist" should concentrate his attack on capitalism at home and not make "imperialist" war on imperialism abroad— even on *il Duce*. Others escaped from the unpleasantness by refuge in a formula, blessed by Litvinov, "collective security". *If* all acted together, *then* there would be peace. Its critics alleged that this meant: "Every war becomes a world war." In practice it rather meant that each country "passed the buck" to its neighbour.

The League of Nations Union massively rolled up its "Peace Ballot", not pacifist by intention or logic but pacifist-supported and clearly seeking instant "peace". A few Labour leaders, such as Hugh Dalton, whose determinant experiences were those of the Great War, were firmly and loudly anti-Hitler and anti-German. However, my friend John Wilmot, who had got his first job of importance as an adviser to the Soviet Economic Commission under Krassin, won the Fulham by-election on the peace issue— and "collective security". To some this spelled that "appeasement" (until then a word of praise, spelling readiness to compromise) was not out of order. To others Litvinov provided a new and hypnotic slogan: "Peace is indivisible." He meant that we must all co-operate with the Soviet Union, not least in Spain. It was reserved for Stalin to demonstrate that "Peace" was strictly divisible. What dupes we were!

Collective security, "realistically", meant collective arms among those like-minded; and the willingness to use them. But who were like-minded? As for the League itself, its Assembly in 1938 chaired by de Valera, its preoccupation (technically a correct one) was with Finland. Consideration of the factors of power was pushed under the rug. "All politics is power-politics." For many orators this was a wicked thought. But I had not spent twenty years on the study of power-politics for nothing. The greatest power bloc was the United States-British Commonwealth, if indeed it held together as one.

Through the years 1938 and 1939, the British mood hardened. The Jewish community naturally became more explicit in alarm and outrage, whatever might be said about the sovereign right of states to deal with the domestic affairs of their own citizens as they might sovereignly see fit. Groups paraded in Whitehall, with banners demanding "Call Hitler's bluff". Little did they under-stand the man who was to conquer more of Europe in a briefer time than Napoleon ever did. The traumatic experience of the Molotov-Ribbentrop Pact followed.

Philip Kerr, later Marquess of Lothian, I had been in touch with since the days when he was connected with Rhodes House. His letters to me were characterised by that quick interest in new ideas, that geniality and lack of starchiness, so rare in the England I knew, which were a large part of the secret of his singular success (save with Roosevelt) in the Embassy in Washington. Later when he was Under-Secretary of State for India, I saw more of him in connection with Indian affairs. He was a man of singular charm although, as Gilbert Murray once remarked, he not only wel-comed new ideas but was liable unexpectedly to change his own. He was likely, as he himself said to me, to prefer an efficient dictatorship with which one could (he thought) negotiate, but one likely to be short-lived, to a less efficient, but more massive one, likely in terms of the Russian autocratic tradition to be longer lived. In the end Lothian was to make the error of judgement that Churchill did not make. Although not a pacifist, he was to become "an appeaser" of Fascist, rather than of Stalinist, tyranny, in what he thought wrongly to be the cause of peace—Dick Shepherd approved of him. Churchill's hope, as later emerged, was to appease neither.

As war approached—and I followed through the line I had suggested to John Buchan—Lothian recommended me for a "foundation member" post in the Ministry of Information, probably to be established. I was in touch with Sir Stephen Tallents on these terms. Whether, in fact, Lothian's recommendation was helpful or unhelpful when Winston Churchill had achieved power is much more open to question. Clear about what I wanted to do, I looked to those quarters both friendly and immediately available. At least, having been a Minister of the Crown, Lothian was maintained by Churchill as our Ambassador in Washington. Roosevelt himself had little use either for him or for his successor, Halifax—who yet, surprisingly, went down well with the Senate.

I well recall being in Broadcasting House on the evening of Halifax's appointment and hearing the fury of my friend, Ed Murrow, about the appointment of "this Municheer" and the B.B.C.'s refusal to permit Murrow to broadcast his views. He regarded the appointment as an insult to the American people. (Incidentally, Halifax in his autobiography, made no mention of the excellent work done during the war in New York and Washington by Professor Sir Isaiah Berlin, which assuredly merited full comment.) I myself hoped, both now and earlier, that Gilbert Murray would be appointed to succeed Lothian in Washington, where he could have been another Bryce. Nobody could have been less fortunate than some of the ambassadors we sent, such as Sir Ronald Lindsay, allegedly posted there, as I have mentioned, because Arthur Henderson wished to get rid of him from London, where he found him unmanageable.

Arthur Greenwood, with whom I had been in closer association than with any other Labour Minister, had never been in the United States (so far as I am aware), knew few Americans and less about American affairs. On the outbreak of war I offered him my services and he asked me to keep him in touch with such American information as I might have or be able to obtain. (According to Laski he had asked others to do the same—perhaps Laski included —and some at least had, according to Laski, abused his confidence.) When the wartime Coalition Government was formed and Clement Attlee, Leader of the Party, became Deputy Prime Minister, Greenwood became Deputy Leader. I would not presume to say that he attended very much to my advice but occasionally he broke out into very satisfactory encomia about myself as "a sound fellow". He stayed with us, on at least one occasion, in our gamekeeper's cottage in Lyndhurst and he was many a time a visitor along with his charming wife at our Cheyne Walk house.

§ ii

I must now turn—at least briefly, for it is recorded in many other of my books—to the strand in my thinking, my action, my life which had been more important than all else... It was the answer to my question of 1918 and my searches at the university and later. All the evidence points to the fact that, apart from Election gladiatorial shows, in technicolour, the great mass of people are bored stiff by politics and international affairs and "switch off". As the new media well know, one "must give the market what it wants"; and this is entertainment, sport, circuses. He who wants to "make a million" is well advised to sell "genuine British fish 'n chips" to the locals of San Francisco. As one publisher remarked to me, "people don't buy books on politics", even although affairs of state and power are going to shape their lives—and their deaths. This is the apathy factor which encourages dictators and is the key criticism of democracy. The time comes when men prefer an élite "vanguard" to democracy. However, these issues happen to be my métier and hence I persist in writing on them. Every man must go to hell his own way.

As political scientist I wished to see, as normalised, the concentration of power in the hands of an international World Authority, maybe with a World Tribunal (apart from which, as Kant said, there is "no objective justice")—anyhow Executive and holding the Bomb. This is the logic of sovereignty. "If two men ride upon an horse, one must ride in front." Unless democracy can face this successfully, then there is a strong case for the reconstruction of that Roman Empire, which Gibbon admired—a Roman Empire of the East and the West.

This World State was yet a "horizon idea". Mishandled, it could so far provoke local patriotism as actually to produce war. Pragmatically, what was required was the integration—or, to use the phrase I myself coined, "the organic union"—of the widest practicable and like-minded area, from which basis to build yet wider if one could without becoming what Aristotle called "a watered-down community". To "Make the World One" required more than one step. As a practical politician I thought of this in Anglo-Saxon terms of a "special relationship", but never in racial terms—hence in terms, initially, of the United States and the effectively *multi*-racial British Commonwealth, especially India. I viewed without applause the long history of Vienna's foolish jealousy of Berlin.

Later, in the 'Sixties in an expanding world, I put with emphasis in the forefront the possibility of a Russo-American *entente*

("They never fought a war") as "next step" towards "one world". It was on this issue of *Weltbürgerschaft* and of internationalism— "ending the International Anarchy"—that I parted with Mosley while he was still nominally, along with Aneurin Bevan, one of the leading lights of Labour.

On the internationalist issue I fought the Elections of 1931 and 1935. Amid the choice of immediate things, I was and am concerned before all with the grandeur of England. But where I differed with passion from the earlier fascists and today's Gaullists was in abjuring all forms of chauvinism, whether called "the glory of France" or "Fortress America", neo-isolationism or "little Englandism". No great nation can be rootless or tear itself up from its roots. The lethargic English tend to forget this. Later on de Gaulle saw to it that the French, themselves in far worse case, did not. The grandeur of England lay precisely in her expansion and development, first into the United Kingdom and then westwards to the lands overseas; this apart she is a negligible country. The United States was the greatest of all England's colonies, and as the eldest daughter she is the prime heiress of the heritage. On this depends the power, prestige, and world-rôle of the whole. Great statesmanship lies in the realistic recognition of this fact; it does not lie in turning our backs, with Edward Heath, on the history of great nations.

Way back in 1925, before my marriage, I had written an article on Anglo-American relations. It was written, on the mere chance of publication, one Sunday morning in Ithaca. It was the first piece of paid journalism I had ever done, as distinct from magazine articles for *Harper's* and others, and to my pleased surprise it paid me enough to cover my fare across the Atlantic. It was published —perhaps to indicate the malice of British machinations—by the Hearst *Boston American*.

The theme was geo-political. I was impressed by the different shape the world took when regarded, not in the perspective of the meridian of Greenwich, but of Chicago or Winnipeg. This gave a quite new outlook. Like Thomas Hobbes, I "fell apouring over mappes".

The first thing that impressed me, from the new view, was that the United States, like the new moon in the lap of the old, was three-quarters surrounded by the (then) British Empire, curving up—how strange it now seems—from South Africa, through the African colonies and Great Britain itself, over across Newfoundland and Canada, down by Oceania to Australia and New Zealand. Apart from the United States it was indeed "absent-mindedly" scattered; with the United States included, it was not strategically scattered at all. From the geographical phenomenon of an English-speaking bloc on the atlas, I drew one not unimportant geo-political conclusion: that strategically and for defence the Panama Canal was more important than the Suez Canal (so important to Anthony Eden) with its "red line" of communication via Gibraltar, Malta and Aden, and with focus on India, conspicuous on British maps. At the time my judgement was eccentric. How right it was appeared thirty years later.

I was indeed already acquainted with the somewhat exotic "English-speaking" views of Lionel Curtis, of *The Round Table*. Curtis had been a member of Milner's "kindergarten" and shared responsibility for the, in the end, misconceived South African policy, which did not allow for the ideological obstinacy of the Boer Broederbund. It was an illusion that the Boers, who trekked from Cape Province to Transvaal because of their fanatical distrust of British policy towards the Negro, were going to change their faith under the sunlight of a little Liberal tolerance. Curtis's views were indeed eccentric, tinged with similarity to "Anglo-Israel" prophesying, and with dangerous anticipations of a new religion of which the standard-bearers were to be "God's Englishmen" (as, with quite singular Protestant provincialism, Milton had called them). Indeed Curtis had sent me the proofs of his book, called by a somewhat pathetic plagiarism from St Augustine, *Civitas Dei*. He had not liked my criticisms; he wanted, not critics, but devout disciples. However, his ideas were, although disfigured, far from entirely foolish. He was the first prophet of Federal Union, and he was in some respects a great man. But he was jealous or suspicious of those who did not accept his views holus-bolus. His work impressed on me the need to turn my attention from purely geo-political and strategic insights of power to political and cultural ones of common values, if support was to be obtained. Later on, Clarence Streit, author of *Union Now*, had the same defect as Curtis. Unlike Jean Monnet, he had no political flair, and although a worthy, dedicated and kindly man, even a great man with a right grasp of principles, he nevertheless damaged his own cause. However, I pay him homage.

An *obiter dictum* of that sage man, Gilbert Murray, gave me further food for thought. All the *savants* were enthusiasts for the attack of the Pluralists, Maitland, Figgis, Cole, Laski, upon the traditional views of state sovereignty. As I have said, a student of my own, Professor Hsiao, now of the University of Washington, had written an admirable history of the movement. We had digested Lowes Dickinson's critique, in *The International Anarchy*. We were hopeful supporters of the League of Nations—which yet, for me, seemed never to have confronted the real problems of power. We wanted to see a Sovereign League of Free States rather than what Austen Chamberlain had called "a free league of sovereign states". But as Murray wrote: "There can be no pooling of sovereignty except among like-minded societies." We had not yet begun to talk, with easy facility, about a United Nations which should be just "a forum of discussion". We hoped to see an organisation "to maintain peace". Were the states, members of the League of Nations, indeed "like-minded"? And if we wished to see a "pooling of sovereignty" and "erosion of frontiers", had we not better begin with those nations who were like-minded? This would be a big enough task for the present. It had taken all of a bloodstained millennium, since "the fall of Rome", to establish civil and domestic peace. To establish international peace by power and consensus could take as long, if mankind could afford that time.

I turned, therefore, to those fundamental cultural issues of national tradition which shape true communities. In 1937 I was invited by the Graduate School (under Dean Ernest Griffiths) of the American University, Washington, in convenient conjunction with—of all things—the U.S. Ministry of Agriculture, to deliver in the halls of the latter a series of lectures. These were published, by Macmillan of New York and by Unwin in England, under the title of *The Anglo-Saxon Tradition* and, in the States, under the more startling title, a fit target for criticism, *Anglo-Saxony and its Tradition*.[1] (Winston Churchill later talked of "Anglo-Saxondom".) I appended "An Open Letter to H. G. Wells".

The whole, which endeavoured to provide some common grounds of British and American thought, was itself set against the attempted vindication of a "grand tradition of values" in human civilisation, a vindication humanistic and *Weltbürgerlich*, set out in my *History of the Political Philosophers*,[2] which had taken me three years, after 1935, to write.

I sent Wells copies of both books. He was good enough to praise my *History of the Political Philosophers*, writing that he gave "full marks" to certain portions—the mediaeval. (In the title I deliberately had used the word *Philosophers*, since the philosophy cannot be entirely divorced from, or even understood without, the parent philosopher.) I now received from "H.G." the following letter:

[1] *The Anglo-Saxon Tradition* (Unwin, 1938); *Anglo-Saxony and its Tradition* (Macmillan, N.Y. 1938).
[1] *History of the Political Philosophers* (Unwin, McGraw, N.Y.; Editiones Penses, Buenos Ayres, 1938).

13 Hanover Terrace, Regent's Park, N.W.1.
April 24 '39

"My dear Catlin,

I don't know whether I like your title. The English tradition
is only partly Anglo-Saxon. I'm *very* English, but I suppose I am
celtic to a large extent. I shouldn't be surprised at a remote Jew
or so. My wife was certainly one sixteenth or one thirty second
Jewish. I had a grand time blaspheming in Australia but God has
since got back at me with shingles and spastic colon. I shall look
forward to the book anyhow.

All my best wishes.

H. G. Wells."

The convenient word "Anglo-Saxon" (I include the Irish . . . and
refer to the historic nucleus of the English-speaking world),
itself always evokes one of two comments: either "the creature
does not exist and never did" or, alternatively, "he exists so
precisely that I must insist that one eighth—or sixteenth or
whatever figure—of my ancestry was non-Anglo-Saxon". I prefer
to accept common usage—and then stress the values of the multi-
racial Commonwealth. These books of mine came too late, in the
sense that the second great Civil War of Europe, the Hitlerite
War of 1939, was already upon us.

§ iii

It chanced that I had had some slight experience in meeting
Presidents of the United States. In 1924, as a member of the
American Political Science Association and a very young man, I
had had the opportunity of meeting President Calvin Coolidge,
who succeeded to the White House after the strange death of
Warren Gamaliel Harding. We were ushered into the Presidential
presence by Charles Evans Hughes, sometime Cornell law lecturer
and now Chief Justice of the Supreme Court, a dignified bearded
figure who might have been President of the United States instead
of Woodrow Wilson had he not failed to carry the key state of
California. Political pundits asserted that it was the vigorous
campaigning of William Randolph Hearst, "Citizen Kane" (who
had ridiculed Hughes' style as that of "an animated feather-
duster") which lost Hughes the vote of the Golden State.

President Coolidge's manner of greeting guests was that of a
turnstile. It was indeed characteristic of this man who, sometime
Lieutenant Governor of Massachusetts and catapulted into office
from the Vice-Presidency by the death of Harding, had been
"made" as a public name as Professor Harold Laski was in part

"made" by the Boston Police strike—the one by suppressing it
and the other by supporting it. The President gave his right hand
to those on his left, with a decisive movement swung them past
him to the right and redirected his fingers to the next figure.
It was, in its way, as laconic as his famous comment on the preacher
whose sermon was on sin: "He was against it." My chief memory
is of the gracious figure of his wife, Grace Godahue Coolidge.
Calvin Coolidge was, however, immensely popular, a veritable
symbol of security and soundness to the smaller business men, and
he remains of interest to students of the secrets of democratic
popularity. After retiring he preached the philosophy of silence
in many writings.

Herbert Hoover I met on New Year's day, 1935, at his house on
Leland Stanford campus in Palo Alto, California. A heavy man
with an eczemic face, he was still smarting, even so late, from his
political defeat and feeling that the world, the electorate and the
fates had done him an injustice. An engineer who had translated
a Latin work on metallurgy, the successful organiser of Belgian
Food Relief, he was a pioneer of the technological age, the father
of the U.S. Bureau of Standards and patron of the U.S. Commission and Report on Social Change. His economists, he felt,
had let him down, at least in plans acceptable to the Republican
Party. The natural economic law (in which he believed) of "boom
and bust" had, unseemly, hit him in the face. He it was who was
"busted". Quaker and business man, he was a divided person:
"Thee should not do this, Herbert" confronted "This is the
efficient thing to do". His passion for technology and standardisa-
tion merits respect, even in today's still under-standardised Britain.

An affable enough host, he retold me the old story that America
knew no class division "until that man Roosevelt came along to
stir it up." I tentatively indicated that there were institutions in the
South which suggested, not merely class divisions, but the even
greater rigidity of caste divisions. He objected and, unconsciously
following Marx, averred that all these tensions were "economic"
—the prejudiced attitude of "the poor white trash" concerned
with their small jobs. I raised my eyebrows over a phrase bolder
than I would have dared to use. With the years, time was to be
slightly kinder to Herbert Hoover, recognising, beyond his ill-
luck in a world misfortune, his limited but honest merits and even
his industrial insight.

Before we parted, however, after a long morning talk, President
Hoover presented to me a copy of his capitalist-Quaker testament,
American Individualism, inscribed "To George E. Catlin, with the
kind regards of Herbert Hoover." This autograph later had some

very practical advantages. On the only occasion I ever had my pocket picked, in a New York night club, it was helpful when I reported to the precinct police. The club owner paid the sum over without demur. As we parted the detective officer remarked: "New York Police—always happy to be at your service."

The little book also enabled me, when detained one morning on Ellis Island, nevertheless to keep a luncheon appointment in Manhattan. Having two valid entry permits—but in different categories, which (as I have already mentioned) was the cause of the trouble—and assured by the French Line that there would really be "no problem", I had the prescience, practising the American tradition of individual initiative, to supply myself with credentials, the President's book and a letter from Mrs Roosevelt, before proceeding from my New York hotel one fine morning to Ellis Island.

I found myself seated next to a stout Jamaican lady. Far from rapid movement, there was complete immobility, without an official in sight. So we remained. I felt that the time had come for action. A sharp look around discovered an interpreter. I intercepted him, stated briefly that the issue was purely technical and deftly flashed the credentials under his nose. He departed. Ten minutes later he returned to report. "The Court has risen for the morning. However, the chairman was Mr Hoover's *aide* in Belgium, so you are lucky. The Court has decided to sit again." The court sat. It unanimously validated my entry. This must be something of a record.

My relations with the Roosevelt family I have already largely described. As I have said, whenever I set out to see Franklin Roosevelt, from the early days when he was Governor in Albany onwards, I always saw him. I lunched in the White House and, after his death I spent a week-end at Hyde Park with Mrs Roosevelt and two of her children, and kept up correspondence afterwards.

Hence, although the Party connection was unexpected—in the United States I "had no Party"—it was not unexpected that, when war came, an invitation should come to hand. It was only the manner and form—and the almost unique consequences—which were surprising.

In the spring of 1940, to an unexampled degree a critical time, I received a laconic message from a Harvard friend, Professor Raymond Buell. It only said that he had, by consent of Harvard University, been seconded to act as expert in foreign affairs to the Republican Presidential Candidate, Wendell L. Willkie. But it concluded with the imperative words: "Please advise on Britain's needs and powers to resist." It was possible to put so sweeping a request into the waste-paper basket as fantastic. Or it was possible to take it seriously. I chose to do the second. Moreover, in order to keep my hand in on American affairs, and having been invited to deliver an Inaugural Address and subsequent lectures in Kansas City, the heart of the isolationist Middle West, I accepted an offer from President Decker, of Kansas City University for June 1940.

Losses of ships on the vital sea-lanes to Britain from the Eastern American sea-board were heavy. They could prove decisive and fatal. Winston Churchill had a strange prejudice in favour of relying on aircraft to cope with submarines in the Atlantic and for too long neglected the importance of convoy. His belief was proving to be not only risky but wrong. Convoy was desperately required. But where to find the ships? The United States had indeed old destroyers "in moth balls" in the naval ports. But in view of the constitutional situation under the Neutrality Act, with the United States not yet at war and a Presidential Election pending, could they be made available? Here, at least, I thought I could be of use.

Raymond Buell I had known for some time. He and his wife had dined with Vera and myself, the Laskis and Winifred Holtby, in early days. He had produced a two-volume work on Africa which rivalled for thoroughness Sir Malcolm Haley's (Lord Haley's). He was a solid man, like Denis Brogan of wide and monumental scholarship. He and I had also spoken on a platform in Central Hall, Westminster, arranged by the National Peace Council, when we had A. J. Cook barracking in the rear of the hall and following the Strachey line against Roosevelt.

I decided to do what I could to provide Raymond Buell with the decisive information he wanted. I went out to collect a dossier from Grigg (later Altrincham) at the War Ministry and from my personal friends who were Ministers, Arthur Greenwood, A. V. Alexander at the Admiralty, and Hugh Dalton at the Ministry of Economic Warfare. The dossier I got from the Admiralty was of the first importance.

The situation was critical and the American constitutional position delicate. For Britain, 1940 was the most vital year of the war and many, including most of our French allies, had small hope of our political survival after the German successes save on Hitler's terms. The control of the Atlantic was scarcely of less importance than the air victory "of the Few". Owing to disarmament we had too few destroyers for convoy service and yet economic survival, food itself, depended upon the security of the Atlantic supply lines.

Could, then, the American destroyers be made available?

Franklin Roosevelt, who hated Hitler to a degree as yet un-shared by the majority in Congress or the nation, was prepared to lend them. But the opposition, Republicans, isolationists, paci-fists, had hitherto successfully tied his hands statutorily by the Neutrality Act, still in force. The legality of such a loan, to put it at the lowest, was dubious. Assuredly in an Election year, Roose-velt was highly vulnerable to attack from his opponents. If the new Republican Candidate, Willkie, chose to attack, the situation could be difficult indeed—and not only for F.D.R. Fortunately Willkie, promoted by "Willkie Clubs" from the floor of the Republican Convention, had been selected as their Presidential Candidate rather than the worthy but strongly isolationist Robert Taft, the "machine" choice, son of President William Howard Taft.

I took one of the old "Clipper" hydroplanes, a technical marvel in its day and immeasurably more comfortable than the modern mass Jumbo jet, to Newfoundland. The only general store there was run by a Chinaman, who sold out-of-date New York maga-zines. I went on to New York and found that Buell had already started out on the Presidential election campaign, which began in Indiana. I could see him, I was told, in Chicago or Kansas City. I left that night by "stratosphere plane" for Kansas City, break-fasting with President Decker in the morning. A telephone call brought the message that Dr Buell was not too well but would I see him at noon. Noon found me in the lobby of the Hotel Muelebach, Kansas City.

A further call elicited the disturbing information that "Dr Buell has gone to hospital and Mrs Buell has gone with him." I had with me the dossier, most highly confidential. I was sitting in a red arm-chair in the main lobby meditating upon what next to do, when I noted a sometime student of mine, Harold Metz, crossing the floor. "Why are you here, Metz?" "As you know, I have always been a keen Republican. I am an official of the National Committee, in charge of files", he replied. "Then you can help me"—and I explained my problem. "You had better see the Campaign Manager, Russ Davenport." The lobby was full of the campaign crowd, local politicians with their Stetson hats, State senators, some national figures on the campaign train. "Harold, I know him a little. Can you get me through all these and up to see Russell Davenport?" "Certainly."

Russell Davenport was slightly deaf and wore a hearing-aid. I made my report to him but what he heard I do not know; his mind was on other things. Suddenly he said: "Look here, we are rather in the soup. We had been relying a good deal in this cam-

paign on foreign affairs—Roosevelt's handling of the Monetary
Conference in London with Cordell Hull and Moley, and the rest.
But Buell, who was our foreign adviser, has gone sick on us. Can
you take on for the moment?" I had to think very quickly. I had
no desire to interfere in American electoral affairs, certainly not
against F.D.R. But I had acted as a professional consultant before
on a matter even more delicate, the American Constitution.
"Yes." "How long can you give us?" "My young children are in
Minneapolis and I was on my way to see them. But I can give you
four days." "Well, if you can only give us that time, give us that."
"Who pays?" "The Republican Party pays; but don't discuss it."
"Good." "On to the campaign train, then, 9.00 tomorrow morning. Kansas City station."

Monday 9.00 a.m. found me on Kansas City Station platform,
boarding the Presidential Campaign train as back-room boy and
foreign affairs adviser, to the sound of "America"—which happens
also to be the tune of "God Save the King". The precious dossier,
including the Admiralty file about convoys and destroyers, was
safely deposited in the campaign files.

The beflagged train went on to Coffeeville, Kansas, where
Wendell Willkie had once been a football coach in the local
college. The candidate spoke on the open football field, on that
hot day, to a packed crowd, not least of college students. Then on
to Tulsa, Oklahoma, for a large evening meeting, and so to
Amarillo, Texas, blooming with flowers. I watched Willkie at
innumerable "whistle-stops".

One coach was full of Press-men, from whom I learned what was
going on. An ex-Professor of Politics from Cornell was always
acceptable. This extraordinary kind of assignment could indeed
only happen in America. Its occurrence, to this day, would be
inconceivable in the more constipated and establishment-con-
stricted constitution of British life. I saw a little of the candidate
and more of Mrs Willkie. "This is the first time I have been in
New Mexico in my life." "This is the second time, Mrs Willkie,
that I have been in New Mexico this year." With a visit to Maine,
later, I had been in every State of the continental Union and had
stayed in towns from Portland, Maine, to Portland, Oregon, and
from Pocatello, Idaho, to the self-advertised "old Victorian hotel"
(good for Victoria!) in Oshkosh, Wisconsin.

One of the Rockefeller sons-in-law, Brooks Emeny, who had
been President of the Council of Foreign Affairs in Cleveland,
joined the train in Arizona as the incoming adviser. I had once
been his house guest in Cleveland. We had a talk. I had spent my

time on the train drafting memoranda, chiefly on foreign affairs, for possible speeches, just as I had once done in London years before. I left the campaign train at San Bernardino, California. Willkie gave his major speech on foreign affairs at San Diego, the great naval station on the Pacific. It included most of what I hoped he would say. It solidly and militantly supported the cause of democratic liberty against Hitler. The job had been done.

Throughout the campaign Willkie harped on the danger of giving a third term to any President—later it was to be constitutionally vetoed. "Why not, then, a fourth?" (In fact, F.D.R. got it.) The United States would end in some kind of monarchical system, with an overbearing executive. Both candidates explained that it was no aim of theirs to involve the United States in war— F.D.R. used the cautious, subtle phrase, "a foreign war". What then was "a foreign war"? One in which American interests were in no wise involved? Willkie did not criticise the President's foreign policy in opposing Hitler. He looked to the defence of freedom. A challenge to a loan of "the Fifty Old Destroyers" (some ships doubtless in San Diego naval base; most in Boston, Baltimore, or Norfolk, Va.) was never mentioned.

I went on to meet my wife in Los Angeles. (We tended to travel on separate trains, each on lecture tours, and to meet at intervals. Once, from a taxi, I saw her on a Chicago side-walk and picked her up...) I had been there before; had visited the Four Square Temple where Aimée Semple Macpherson had presented me with a rose. "Where have you been?" asked the bus conductor from whom I enquired my direction. "The Four Square Temple." "Ah! they are always confused when they come out of there." Later in Hollywood I met Greer Garson, Sir Aubrey Smith, and Maureen O'Sullivan, with her delightful, beautifully mannered children (one of whom is now well known as an actress in her own right), and even the formidable Hedda Hopper. On an earlier occasion I had paid a call on Upton Sinclair for whom I had the deepest respect, friend of my friend Norman Thomas. We were to sustain a correpondence over years. He suggested that we should go to visit Charlie Chaplin. We nearly missed him but on the way out of the studio encountered a young damsel clad in brown rags. "See how they treat the Hollywood actresses." "Hello, Paulette, where's Charlie?" "In the studio but they are keeping it quiet." We returned to the studio to watch the filming of *Modern Times*. "Don't watch your feet, darling", observed Chaplin, "or there must be something wrong with your face." Paulette Goddard, to whom Gershwin also was devoted, presented me with her lipstick. I next saw her at Hyde Park, Eleanor Roosevelt's week-end guest there. Thornton Wilder I spent an evening with, on another occasion, in New York.

On this present occasion Vera and I went out to see Upton and Charles at the Green House hotel but, underestimating the vast distances in Los Angeles, arrived at least an hour late. They had waited for us and after a joyful dinner Chaplin himself drove us back to the Biltmore. He talked all the way. Seldom have I come across so zestful a conversationalist. He talked of his visit to Vietnam; of walking along roads there with Annamese padding along the road behind him—"strong, silent men". Somewhat sinister men one felt, with Charles a waif. I met him on one later occasion along with Lord Chancellor Jowitt, at a Pickwick dinner in London. He made some bitter, and certainly not Pickwickian, remarks about America in his speech that night. Some of us knew enough of his past history to realise why. It was then also that the Chancellor, in response to my question, told me how he had made his patronage appointments to Anglican livings. "Easy enough. There was a major in the War office who was interested in all these things. He advised me. Fine fellow." He added, as I have mentioned (which was not so good for the primitive Christians), that no one should change the religion of his birth—it showed an unstable character. Lord Jowitt had indeed changed his own political affiliation, but that was, of course, a different matter.

John Buchan, Lord Tweedsmuir, on this visit had invited me up to be his guest at Rideau Hall, Ottawa, after he returned from Halifax, "where I have to go for a naval review". Alas! he fell in his bath and died. The visit never took place. However, I saw no little of his later successor, Vincent Massey.

With a couple of weeks to spare before my next commitment, I went up to Santa Barbara and booked myself in at the old and modest Margaret Baylor Inn. I began work each morning at a quarter to nine and ended at four-thirty, dining most nights with Cynthia (now Lady Corry), daughter of Sir Arthur Bliss's stepmother. I wrote fifty thousand words in ten days, five thousand a day. I published it, almost as written.

If it owed something to the stimulus of Cynthia, and something to the paradise of California, it owed yet more to Wendell Willkie, who had so far encouraged me as firmly to crystallise my own ideas. The little book was published by the Macmillan Co. of Canada and was to have been published in Britain by Secker and Warburg. However, Warburg wanted to tell me how to re-write it, so our ways parted. Andrew Dakers had paper and he published two impressions in 1941 before his paper ran out. It was entitled

One Anglo-American Nation: The Foundation of Anglo-Saxony.[1]
Eighteen years later I re-read it, decided that I agreed with everything I had there said, added a new chapter bringing it up to date,
and republished it under the title of *The Atlantic Community.*
About that book, written in a passion of conviction, I shall have
much more to say. It was my testament. As to the provocative
challenge of the sub-title I have already explained my internationalist position. The problem was not of the possible periphery, but of the immediate nucleus of world power.

Before leaving America to report home, I visited the American
Federation of Labor Convention in New Orleans. I entertained
Gertrude Lawrence who told me, in her husky voice, that she felt
she ought to be back in England—what did the authorities advise?
—and of all that she was doing for "Bundles for Britain" and in
creating good opinion. With David Dubinsky, of the Women's
Garment Workers, an excellent friend of Britain, I dined, if not
"at Antoine's", at least at the next best restaurant and signed the
book.

Returning to Washington I lunched with Lothian, whom I had
met when I came out. The occasion remains vivid in my mind
owing to a *gaffe* of my own—shall I say a consciousness that I was
about to shoot rapids but an amnesia as to what the rapids might
be? At the full Embassy table we were discussing the World Fair
and whether the British pavilion should be continued into the
second year. I suggested that this advertising would be good:
Britain always under-advertised—although the Chicago Fair had
only avoided debt in the second year owing to the attraction of
Miss Sally Rand, fan-dancer of the Paradise Club.

I added, parenthetically, that I had met Miss Rand; she had
let me out of her Club herself—with her own hand, in the early
hours of the morning—and then, rather defensively, I continued
that she was really quite a nice girl. (At least her conversation
was more exciting than dancing, as I did one New Year's Eve, with
Carmen Miranda or being told by young matrons how much I
resembled Leslie Howard...) We had talked for over an hour
over her supper; she had spent the time telling me why she had
become a Christian Scientist. Had a pin dropped at the table it
would have been heard. A flash of memory enlightened me on the
situation; but I hope my face only recorded the application of the
telescope to the blind eye. Lothian bore no malice and none was
intended.

Instead he carried me off to his study and (although I several

[1] *One Anglo-American Nation* (Dakers), 1941.

times rose to go) detained me in talk for over an hour on political affairs, to the patent annoyance of his Counsellor, who wished to consult him on papers. So far as I was concerned, he was more than friendly; he was benevolent. That afternoon I was guilty of a folly too habitual with me. One caller, while I was there, was asking him on the telephone for a post for her son. I had known him for several years and I should have taken the chance to ask for a job; it did not occur to me. As one lady wrote to me some months later—although I feel guilty and smug to quote it—"Never mind about the public causes; what are you doing to look after yourself?" One has to train oneself in brashness by an act of will. I do not doubt that something of public utility would have been forthcoming. As it was, within three weeks, Philip Lothian was dead. I read of it in a news flash on my way home—for which unnecessary death it is more than possible that his Christian Science (which he owed to Nancy Astor) must take a share in the responsibility. I prefer Lourdes, if anywhere, for unexpected faith cures.

Incidentally, in Baton Rouge, La., I had seen the Willkieite committee rooms shutting down, rolling up their placards. At least, on the vote, Willkie had given Roosevelt the closest fight for the Presidency of any candidate earlier or later in F.D.R's career. I had watched Willkie grow in stature. Later President Truman remarked to me, "We always regarded him as a good corporation lawyer." One cannot, however, dismiss a politician outright because he is a lawyer. Neither a Senator nor a Governor; breaking all rules; nominated from the floor of the Republican Convention thanks to local Willkieite Clubs and against the wishes of the Republican platform and machine—Willkie cannot be labelled "a machine politician". He was quite a considerable human figure—and one of America's few defeated Presidential candidates to be remembered a decade or more on. Alfred Smith and Adlai Stevenson were the others and we must today add Hubert Humphrey.

In January 1941, Willkie came to London. I knew that he would be arriving and called on him at the Dorchester Hotel—in fact in his bedroom before he had got out of bed. A vast bear of a man, still physically the football coach, one foot protruded from under the blankets. Whom should he see in London? With some pride in his literary interests, could he see Rebecca West? I happened to know both her and her husband, Henry Andrews, well. Could I arrange a meeting? I took up the bedroom phone and there and then arranged it. At a dinner, put on for him, they and others were his hosts. Those were the days before he published his best-selling and highly important booklet, *One World*. The slogan was his. But that January, in the Beaverbrook Press, he made a statement, to be balanced along with "One-Worldism", which I do not forget.

Still titular leader of the Republican Party, he there had the temerity to propose, apart from educational interchanges and such items, a common citizenship of the British Commonwealth and the United States and what he called "a social and economic union". These, it must be recalled, were days when Germany and Italy were enemy powers and when France was already under Vichy and Nazi-occupied. To think, and write, in terms of the Washington-Westminster-Ottawa Triangle was inevitable. Winston Churchill, in a last minute effort, had himself proposed on Jean Monnet's suggestion—nor must we suppose his proposal to have been disingenuous or dishonest—common citizenship of British and French. In the climate of those days, Willkie's proposal was not preposterous. Nor today, when we are invited to "have faith" in being good Europeans, can it be so regarded. It involved no vaster change. It was to be construed as an aim in the context of his own "One World" plan, highly significant. Thirty years on, it can still hit some critics and defeatists on the head.

The notion of a common citizenship, as between England and Scotland, is not to be dismissed out of hand. Certainly if the idea of a world government is not to be merely an escape wish or a pious dream, unfulfilled since the days of Isaiah (although most closely approached under the iron rule of Rome and the Caesars), then this notion must be taken seriously. More immediate practical politics is that 'organic union' of mutual confidence and personal interchange from which can spring a common foreign and economic policy. It is for the United Nations to cultivate an effective internationalism which can be world wide. This was the thesis of Willkie's *One World*. A common foreign policy is yet more capable of achievement between peoples like-minded, in an open-ended regionalism which the U.N. Charter itself recognises. I do not say that a common foreign policy of all Europe, or part of it, perhaps in relation to Israel, is impossible. I do say that a consensus on foreign policy and effective joint executive action among those historically like-minded peoples who together constitute the nucleus of the Atlantic Community is much more likely, and here too Willkie pointed a way that merits a vowed and dedicated service which does not know how to compromise, sell short or yield, made this advocacy mine.

At one time I played with the notion of writing Willkie's biography. It has never been done adequately. However, the talk at the time of an official biography checked me. On April 12th 1944, I received a letter which ran in part:

... "I want you to know how much I appreciate your interest throughout this period and the many helpful suggestions which you sent along to me.

"Although I am sure you understand fully, I want you to know directly from me that the major reason which prompted my decision to withdraw was based upon my belief that I could better do the job which you and I know must be done if all suggestions of personal ambition or reward were eliminated.

"As you know, I am thoroughly convinced that, unless the United States adopts a forward-looking domestic policy and wholeheartedly cooperates with the other nations of the world, now as well as after the military phase of this war is over, there can be no hope of permanent peace.

"You may be sure that I shall continue to work and fight for the realisation of those things in which we believe so strongly.

Again, many, many thanks.
Sincerely,
Wendell L. Willkie."

There was another letter, concluding: "Do keep in touch with me, Cordially, Wendell Willkie." However, exhausted by his primary campaign in Wisconsin, Willkie went into hospital with one illness and died of another, a hospital infection. America was much the poorer for his loss. A man from the much abused Middle West, he was a great American—and much that he advocated was profoundly true. I was honoured, thanks to the oddest of chances, to have known him.

Meanwhile my own book of 1941, so very much inspired by American experiences and to which I have referred, was published. A written note of acknowledgment from Winston Churchill apart, it drew comment which to this day is not without interest, as illustrating the mood of those war-days. It carried a stirring preface from my old Staffordshire friend, Colonel Josiah Wedgwood (Lord Wedgwood), sometime Chancellor of the Duchy: "Go step by step no doubt; but start now." (In the transcript I have here as I write, this phrase by a pretty irony is rendered in typing: "start nowt".) Leopold Amery, Secretary for India, Ernest Brown, Minister of Health, Leslie Hore-Belisha, sometime Secretary for War, George Gibson, President of the Trades Union Council, Walter Monckton, Director of the Ministry of Information, Salvador da Madariaga, J. A. Spender, even the *New States-*

man, all contributed their encomia. It received indeed one adverse review, commenting on its pseudo-Jeffersonian style, from a some-time assistant of Harold Laski's, Dr Denis Brogan, of Cambridge.

A correspondent in *The Times* even alleged rather erroneously and misleadingly that, until he went to Washington, "Lord Lothian occupied a place in the Federal Union Movement some-what similar to that now held by Dr Catlin." (Actually my advocacy was of "organic union", my own formula, which was rather different.) Maurice Fanshawe, of the League of Nations Union, compared me rather drastically to Streit, unfairly to my advantage. So did the *Yorkshire Post*. The *Manchester Guardian* wrote: "Mr Catlin is the founder in this country of the idea of a close union of the United States and the British Empire. He first proposed this policy sixteen years ago."

However, the comment which I especially valued came from such men as Gilbert Murray. "I have read your little book with very great interest and almost complete agreement." A. V. Alexander at the Admiralty, wrote: "I feel that only good can come from the wise and temperate advocacy of many of the broad ideas which you put forward in your book and I wish you success in your endeavours." This was balanced by Max Beaverbrook: "It is an immense project and Lord Beaverbrook is happy to think that it is getting such powerful advocacy." Archbishop Temple was not less kind: "I have now had the opportunity of reading your book and found it extremely interesting and, I think I must add, very persuasive." The High Commissioner for New Zealand, Jordan, expressed the hope that I would be present at the Peace Conference and make a contribution. The "punch-line" was, however, provided by sometime Lord Chancellor Sankey:

"It is a book that should be 'chewed and digested' by all who can influence the shape of things to come. . . . Your scheme holds the field. I wish it well. It may want the hammer and the anvil, but, if it succeeds, you will have deserved well of two hemispheres."

I painstakingly recite these encomia because, as I shall show in a later chapter, their practical effect was, in the short range, almost nil. I awaited some such invitations in London as I had received from Buell and Davenport. I failed mercilessly to harass Govern-ment departments with publicity about my campaign. However, the Kingdom of Heaven, one has to learn, is taken by violence and importunate conduct. In retrospect I can only conclude that I should have made it my business to conquer hesitation and to go direct to Churchill.

Any human being is important to his times, not only in terms of the life that he lives, but in terms also of the idea that with simplicity he embodies. The idea alone, however, will wither unless there is courage and determination behind it. This fight, one has to recognise, makes initially for unpopularity. I was yet convinced that I had shaped an idea—that of an Atlantic Community with a clear nucleus, whatever the periphery—to which I desired, and was determined, to dedicate myself.

XII

SHIPWRECK

FROM Minneapolis, after leaving Willkie's train, I returned to
Kansas City and spent a very brief time there, completing my
commitments. My effigy, in that short stay, was painted, "for all
time" on the University walls, as a cardinal, in a mural display of
the characters in *Don Quixote* by the Mexican painter, Quin-
tinella.

One pleasant Sunday afternoon I spent with the Archduke
Felix of Hapsburg, also lecturing in Kansas City, who gave me
introductions to his brothers. The Archdukes Otto and Robert
were wartime refugees in London, where they received many
kindnesses from Queen Mary. Years later my wife and myself
were guests at a reception and lunch given at Pöcking by the
Archduke Otto, who maintained a little court there—an entirely
good-hearted, admirable and singularly well-informed man.
Of the Archduke Robert I was to see quite a lot, and all the
brothers, save Rudolf, were visitors at our Chelsea house. In
conditions of humiliating difficulty, these brothers of the greatest
of all Imperial Houses maintained themselves in exile with admirable and modest dignity, despite being the bait of cheap
journalists, some of whom thought that "His Imperial Highness
is taking lunch in the soda-fountain" was shriekingly funny. I did
not. (For one thing, the Austrian Hapsburgs were poor because
they had been too patriotic, unlike some royal houses, to stow
away money outside Austria.) I preferred to recall the Titian
painting of the Emperor Charles V, wrapped in the melancholy of
an empire not dishonourable.

From Kansas City I hastened back towards New York and
London. In the port of New York I picked up a boat, homeward
bound, *The Western Prince*. Incidentally I noted (as could any
other bystander in the docks) that its decks were crowded with
airplanes, destined for the British fighting forces. On board was
the remarkable correspondent of *The Manchester Guardian*,
James Bone, and a powerful commission from Canada, concerned
with armament supplies and led by C. D. Howe, later one of the
most influential of Canada's Liberal Ministers. There was also a
British vice-admiral—in charge, I believe, of something no
more dashing than "stores", and Sir Cecil Carr, a constitutional

lawyer of some distinction; and also some nuns, with their Mother Superior. A strange but not uncongenial company.

The month was December 1940, and the seas were rough. However, the passengers were cheerful, the food and wine good and the journey as far as mid-Atlantic, like my outgoing voyage, uneventful. Although the American "fifty old destroyers" had already been released for much-needed service, there was as yet no full convoy system but, for some hundreds of miles out from the North American coast, there was air protection. This ceased in mid-Atlantic. The navigators' calculation was that the speed of the merchantmen of this class, could always exceed that of any known German submarine in pursuit. So it could—unless the submarine happened to be coming the other way, which would not be remarkable for a submarine from a German port.

The night of Friday, 13th December 1940, was reached. *The Western Prince* was about 200 miles off the Icelandic coast. It was a cold, singularly clear night at sea, with high visibility. I noticed, as I took a final turn on deck, that the moon was so full that the shadows of the rigging could be seen reflected in the sea's white foam, churned up by the ship's bow as she cut the water. There had been some kind of ship's dinner—Christmas still twelve days off—and a young honeymoon couple had toasted in champagne the fact that they had successfully got through a day so ill-omened to the superstitious as Friday the Thirteenth. There were the usual light-hearted paper-cap fooleries and the usual after-dinner dance. The clocks were re-adjusted to the hour. Outside, the ship was blacked out, as it moved silently on its course, the wash of the waves whitecapped but almost inaudible.

My cabin was small and shared with another Englishman, who was connected with some Far Eastern bank in Shanghai. Many years later he was to ring me up in that city and we were to drink together in the once famous Long Bar. (I wonder who patronises it now.) I slept well but not heavily. Six hours must have passed when some subconscious awareness warned me that the ship had changed pace, moving faster and faster. I listened. Although the night had been clear, the mid-winter sea was now rough and it was not surprising that the ship was struck, as it seemed, by the thud of a heavy wave. What did surprise me was that the ship changed pace yet again, first slowed and then stopped. I thought it wiser to rise and rouse my companion.

Gingerly I opened the cabin door. There was nothing to be heard save the distant ringing as of a passenger's bell, such as might have been heard at any time. I remarked that we "didn't want to be windy" or to show a light from our cabin door; we were at the end of the corridor, next but one to the deck-door on B deck. Against emergencies, we each pulled on a suit and over-coat over our pyjamas. Next door I looked into the doctor's cabin, a physician who had more reputation for medical skill than conventionality. It was empty but, with the doctor, this proved nothing. Nevertheless, despite the deadly quiet in the corridor I suggested to my companion that it might be prudent to explore.

There was no time, nor did there indeed seem to be need, to look for jewellery, such as the platinum and gold fob which had been my father's wedding-present to me. But my prized diary I thrust into one wide overcoat pocket and a passport, just to hand, I casually put into another. Three (in every sense weighty) volumes of Professor Arnold Toynbee's *Study of History*, which I had with me for review, I did not think would be popular in a life boat, and those went into Davy Jones' locker—the review was eventually done from memory.

It would not, I think, be inaccurate to say that my mood was fairly cool. I remembered, and passed to my companion, the advice originally given by the Duke of Wellington to an aspiring subaltern, and to me by Graham Wallas—"Whenever there is a toilet available, use it." We took the advice, which was indeed wise, for one man who did not, but was afflicted with modesty or with fear of freezing in his nether quarters, was subsequently the victim of kidney trouble for many days.

The doors of the next few cabins were shut. Perhaps they had never been occupied. But then I saw that the further cabins, their doors open, were empty, the sometime occupants fled. Along our deck and up the companion-way we quickened our pace; hastened up what were the main stairs and, pushing a door, came out onto the apparently deserted upper deck, where the night wind blew keen and cold. At first glance only the capstans, the various ropes and chains, the securely fastened airplanes, were to be seen. Dawn had not yet come but even the bright disinterested moon had gone, leaving December gale and darkness.

We hastened to the ship's rail. It was true then. We had been torpedoed. I could just see the black shapes of three lifeboats, one at the ship's side, and two stood away. I called down. "Abandon ship," echoed back a shout. A rope dangled down the ship's side, ending in the Atlantic Ocean. *How*, I muttered, *does* one abandon ship? "Try the other side."

I crossed the boat deck with haste amid the encumbrance of ship's tackle. Two life-boats still hung on their davits. My com-panion hurried ahead and got into the first. I took the further boat. A petty officer, stalwart and to attention, handed me over the gunwale. I took seat on a central plank, without premeditation but fortunately, since others then sat on top and kept me warmer. Those about to be shipwrecked should bear the advantages of this sacrificial act in mind. In a shipwreck in northern climes one must decide either to be able to swim or to be warm. It is better to choose the latter. Luck in Atlantic swimming is not great. However Bertrand Russell, at an advanced age, decided to do both and swam successfully off Norway, as he told me, in an overcoat.

Sir Cecil Carr, our authority on Statutory Regulations, only sixty but tall, thin and drawn, by their own prior choice was with his wife at the stern, too near the waves for convenience. By good fortune the Commodore of this merchant fleet, travelling privately, was also at the stern and at the tiller. The over-crowded boat was lowered. The sea was white-tipped above its blackness, the sky still that of night, with as yet no flush of dawn. A minute with the ropes and, lowered, we touched water.

A sudden new problem arose. How to uncouple the pegged metal hooks and, in the rise of the wave, to release the boat? This should have been automatic; but the automatic sometimes, and with deadly effect, fails to "automate". Maybe the routine boat drills had failed to ascertain the defect, and I thought that, on shipboard, perhaps it was not the passengers' boat drill but the ship's management that merited checking. With each high wave the boat rose, then sucked away; rose and slammed, held by its ropes, into the towering side of the abandoned liner. I found myself whistling.

This present experience was not quite new. I had nearly drowned in the desperate undertow of the coastal waters off Ostia, when I had gone along with my hostess Nina di Colonna on a summer outing. Oars were got out (there were not too many) and used as staves to push the boat away. They broke like matchsticks. Regarding the matter with a kind of personal detachment but muscular tautness, which I had experienced before, I speculated that a few more crashes and we would capsize. "For God's sake release her." With one violent tug the Commodore got the hooks loose—we were away. The boat then started to flood.

Hat-bailing, as one man tried, was an absurdity; one could not bale out the Atlantic Ocean with a trilby hat. It was the bung, clearly, that was out of place, but no one knew where the bung-hole was. What one saw was a collection of oars, broken or whole, some canvas for a sail, passengers' legs, bodies, small belongings. "Bung half out, sir; fixed now." That fear was surmounted.

As we began to stand away an officer, I was told the second engineer, dived from the deck, having stayed on duty to release the boats—whether he had a life-belt or not I do not know. He was in sight within a few yards. Hands and oars where held out to reach him. One could see the man threshing the water, his body as a swimmer half-turned. I can still see his face, that of a desperate swimmer. Another high wave and boat and man separated. We saw no more but circled a while to see what we could pick up and, finding nothing, hastened to get clear of being sucked down by the sinking ship. The sea, ever untamed by man, be it wine-red or black-green, is an element treacherous and cruel, lifeless parent of all living things and, like Uranus, their devourer. I do not commend its dark mercies in December off Iceland.

"What happened—I heard no bells?" "Didn't you hear the ship's siren, the blasts?" "I was awake and stirring but I certainly did not. Anyhow, what happened to the bells? In our corridor there was no constant ringing of them." "The bells only ring in the event of fire." "The bells only ring—what?" At 6.30 in the morning *The Western Prince* had been struck in its steering-gear by a submarine's torpedo. Now it was 7.15. Slowly, slowly dawn was coming.

Some in the lifeboat said that they had seen her—the submarine, the periscope. I did not. Maybe the Germans would open fire on the open life-boats. Who knew? Most of the passengers seemed to be accounted for. Howe and his delegation were in the lifeboat which, if all had been according to routine orders, as it never in fact is, should have been mine. In the confusion, it was not. It alone had a covered cabin. A few, such as the engineer, might still be on rafts or bits of wreckage. It was best to suppose this. The honeymoon couple? Alas, they had come out on deck, then had turned back to collect some wedding treasures. They were never seen again. The captain also had remained on the ship, deciding to go down with her. Dame Rachel Crowdy later laconically explained to me that many sea-captains have unhappy married lives, and don't mind going down with their ship, but I have no reason whatsoever to suppose this explanation filled the case here.

7.15. Abruptly the noise of explosion. One had seen, of course, the placards picturing the submarine peril; giant ships breaking their backs, each end tilting and then quick descent beneath the waves. In the still dim but better light we could see *The Western Prince*, sharp-lined, black, static. The expected second torpedo had followed. There was the bright explosion, the slow, inevitably quickening, then breaking amidships. A sudden final blast on the siren—"The captain's?" Fateful, sure, precisely as on the placards, the ends rising, from moment to moment sharper angles, then slowly, quicker, utterly sinking, sunk. Gone: it was over. A gurgle of waters; a wallowing of the boats. And then, nothing in view but the gloomy dawn horizon and the little boats with their crowded cargo, the waves, with a cold wind. And it began to sleet.

One young sailor—although most of our "sailors" were plain stewards, more accustomed to serving ham and eggs or even *crêpes suzettes*—was so sick with fear that he looked near death's door. A paternal morale-booster from the Commodore. For the rest, women and men alike, little said, little movement. One man thought they should put up the sail. The stern realities of longitude and latitude were pointed out to him; so many hundred miles from Iceland, so many from Scotland. "If you put the sail up, all you will do will be to overturn the boat."

The boat was not equipped with radio. I saw no sign of iron rations, and could not escape one damning, unpleasant thought, which yet left one detachedly, coldly amused. In peacetime every merchantman ploughs at full speed through any weather to the aid of a wrecked ship. But in wartime? In wartime every merchantman would be under warning to hasten from "submarine-infested waters"—to hasten *away*. A soldier on land, whatever the luck of the "poor bloody infantryman", has yet his feet on the mud. He is not at the mercy of the waters.

It wouldn't look too good for older folk when the December night came on, although the depressing thought was absent from my mind at the time. My overcoat was warm and the waves worth looking at. I had a brandy flask in my pocket but reflected that this had better rest untouched for another day. I have always enjoyed being in ships in gales, seeing them "shipping the green" —big ships, admittedly. Nothing is more fascinating than to watch, from a great Cunarder, like Lucretius' landsmen, some tramp ship wallowing; nothing more fascinating on a smaller boat, to stand in storm at the protected bows and look, as the Atlantic wave, tons of water, rises up and over—white froth and green water. Anyhow it was wartime—not my first war—and one took things as they came. One had better, as Thomas Carlyle said in another connection. The dawn grew lighter, the sleet stopped, occasionally the clouds parted and let in light to heighten the wave crests. One youngish man in the boat was a director of the line, and was in a confessional mood. Hitherto, he said, he had always opposed metal life-boats as too expensive. Now, "having seen how wooden boats can be staved in", for the future his vote would be cast at the directors' board for metal.

Noon came near and passed. The "wild doctor" got his sailors and stewards to put out their oars and, in the now watery sunlight and flatter seas, to row in competition "just like an Oxford and Cambridge boat race". Perhaps the fun boosted morale; but physical exertion is not to be recommended to those who may have need to harbour all their energies. Anyhow what was important was for all to keep together. At one stage occupants were transferred from the overloaded life-boats to those which lacked full complement. There was complaint about absence of radio sets from other boats—after all it was these which sent out the, admittedly weak, S.O.S. signals.

The day wore on and became overcast again. Perhaps we were in a main sea lane and could expect to be picked up. Perhaps not, when "main sea lanes" were not at all routine. High waves, dark on the horizon, had a habit of looking like ships coming to our aid. Quite a few were counted, perhaps too many, since all were disappointments, and expectation was running a little too high. "Would ships pass us by?" The cool obstinacy of survival has few emotions and little speech. It even forbade reflection on a night at sea in an open boat. *Che sarà, sarà:* what will be, will be. Why worry?

Eventually it was the feeble radio signals of the life-boats that had sets which were picked up. A small collier standing out from Glasgow, New York-bound, heard them. Democratically the skipper summoned his company. There might be some salvage-money. There was very clear danger, and there was the comrade-ship of the sea. The Scotsman decided to move in.

14th December, 3.30 p.m., towards dusk. A wave as high as the high ones; higher, indeed, and black. However, this time the wave did not fall. It was perhaps—it was in fact—a ship. Little noise for fear of new disappointments. Slowly, we drew in. Now we saw the details of the collier, two decks at either end on a level, and low amidships. Closer still and we were almost under the ship's rusty sides, wave-washed with scuppers gushing sea-water. Some of the other life-boats were nearest, and the rescue work began of getting the people up and in, by aid of rope and loop. A low-lying boat but, even so, it seemed a long way up when one was along-side. Steel plates provided no toe-hold, were one caught by a wave.

Yet there was humour in our situation. The collier's coal-buckets were brought into use. One was filled up with the Reverend Mother Superior and two nuns who were, without ceremony, hauled up like coal sacks. The life-boat with cabin and radio, in which I might have been, drew alongside. In it were the members of the Canadian official commission, Howe and the rest. Many crowded to its side waiting for the lowered ropes. The waves were still running high. A wave and a flush from the scuppers; the water caught them, the lifeboat overturned; flung into the sea, they were swimming for their lives. For those in the cabin it was a death trap, and the end of them. Howe's adviser and friend and others died—drowned within yards of safety.

Up and finding our way to such crowded quarters as there might be. Hot drinks. Sitting on plank benches, with our legs on the cabin table, trying to get a spot of sleep. Turned around and heading for the Clyde, with three days and a half to go. My cabin companion was apologetic. "I should have let you get into the life-boat first." "Forget it: I didn't even notice it." He was a little mentally shocked, and developed a persecution complex, most solemnly warning me that there was a conspiracy against us. If anything happened, we would be left. Not quite balanced, but with only two life-boats on the collier, he had a case. Indeed, from this time on in life I felt that I lived "on borrowed time". It had the merit of adding to one's energy, pertinacity and determination —of putting both time and ambition in perspective, and refusing to be deflected.

Once there was a heavy thud. The mate rushed out, hurriedly adjusting his life-belt. But, praise God, this time it was only a wave. The ship carried one gun. After the first night and preferring sleep on the next, I betook myself to a more distant, empty and quiet part of the boat, across the mid-ship planks and to the bow. I slept on the space on top of an eight-foot locker which, I was told, contained all the ship's ammunition and explosives. No one else seemed to want it. I slept exceedingly well. If anything happened, one was as safe on top of an ammunition dump as anywhere else. The vice-admiral-in-charge-of-stores made himself comfortable in the captain's cabin. With skill, in the morning, one could get a shave.

Off the Hebrides, down the Kyles, and into the Clyde. The vice-admiral and the official party got off in a launch at Gourock. So did I. There was some fuss but I had my passport. The rest were to get off at Glasgow and a wise man avoids queues where there is no need. Although I had been unconscious of it, some ship's hook must have struck my temple. That night, in an overcoat and lounge suit over my protruding pyjama suit, and with a black eye, I was admitted, first with scepticism and then with full service, into the Dorchester Hotel, London, as my wife had arranged, and there I spent the night. I was glad on reflection that in future ships would go in convoys. It was on that night at the Dorchester that I met that remarkable man Chaim Weizmann. Later, in such distinguished company as that of Lord Halifax, I spent some nights of bombing in the Dorchester's cellars. I eyed with suspicion the boiling water-pipes above. It could be extremely unpleasant if they broke.

The "fifty old destroyers" were surely useful. At least I had had a finger in that pie, and perhaps a grateful Government would record the fact. Not every Englishman had acted, in foreign and war affairs, as private adviser to the would-be President of a United States still officially neutral. Some constitutional and statutory restrictions had been waived; and the waiver had remained unchallenged by the Republican Party and Candidate.

In a recent book, *Fifty Ships that Saved the World*, the writer, Philip Goodhart, makes a report. "On Sept. 4, 1940, as the Battle of Britain raged towards its climax, eight destroyers sailed from Boston Navy Yard for Halifax, N.S. They were ugly ships—four funnelled, herring-gutted, awkward in a sea-way and liable to every eccentricity known to old and time-worn ships—but their departure marked the end of isolationism in the United States and the effective beginning of the Anglo-American alliance." Maybe, with my dossier for Willkie, and the avoidance of what could have been very unpleasant trouble, I had made a contribution. Constitutionally the position was so tricky, the President's orders to release "the old destroyers" so insecure, that the decision of the Opposition Candidate not to oppose—to support—was assuredly nothing negligible. Bluntly Roosevelt had broken the Neutrality Act as it then stood, by executive action.

I will add one small footnote. I turned in a report to the Admiralty that, with skilled men scarce, it should be an Admiralty instruction that the ship's captains must leave sinking ships, not go down with them. I also naturally reported my Willkie adventures to the Foreign Office. They guffawed genially about the oddity of it all. I heard no more from them. Nothing at all. Maybe they were nonplussed. What I had done "was not done". Maybe Roosevelt would be annoyed. In fact, as Mrs Roosevelt was later strikingly to demonstrate, he was not. Perhaps the Foreign Office miscalculated.

Quite recently, I have had a letter expressing a seaman's sorrow and fellow sympathy over the death of the captain of *The Western Prince*. I had decided to learn more about the captain of the submarine, and whether he was still alive, and I wrote expressing appreciation of the chivalry, to which we owed our lives, thanks to which, contrary to strict orders and with risk to his ship, his men and himself, he had delayed for three quarters of an hour putting in the final torpedo which sunk *The Western Prince*. I had indeed broadcast for five minutes on the B.B.C. about the sinking, but had been instructed to omit this reference.

From Norfolk, Virginia, came back a reply. Yes: he was alive, a merchant sea-captain sailing from Hamburg. "I remember exactly *The Western Prince*, observed the life-boats lowered and separating in the twilight." He was glad so many of the passengers and crew were saved. He was "sorry indeed for the captain's fate. Signed: Lehmann-Willenbrock." So ends this story of the sea.

Although it was almost a miracle that I survived drowning in the sea off Ostia (as I learned later: "Two drowned there last Sunday"), I do not think that I am given to panic—or afraid of death as such. Indeed when life, as is not infrequently the case, takes the character of purposelessness and dry sand, death is, in my judgement, to be welcomed. Without hypocrisy or reservation one can welcome the lot of those "who fall asleep in the Lord". Nor, despite Shakespeare, do I fear to dream. Have I not for fourteen years recorded nightly my dreams? No nightmares. The metaphysical *angst* about death which afflicts some of the circle of Sartre, I can intellectually understand, especially for self-centred individualists, but I do not share it. I am content with such immortality, and in such fashion, as Providence may allocate.

This attitude may give a certain humour and courage. Some may call it the courage of indifference. It would be better phrased as the courage of detachment. To feel no concern for others would be inhuman, but a man is entitled to regard the degree of anxious concern for himself, as distinct from mere foolhardiness, as being strictly his own business. Torture (such as Goya depicted and such as even the French exercised against the guerillas in Algeria) and extreme pain are, of course, very different matters, which I am not discussing here. The bravest man fears these abominations.

There is a coda to my brief epic. A few months later, by arrangement made by Captain Reginald Fletcher of Admiralty Intelligence, Member of Parliament for Nuneaton, I went out as observer on a destroyer, one of two charged to convoy a group of ships coming up from South Africa. This was done. Meeting them off the Mauritanian coast, we turned and stood north towards Cape St Vincent. Again the journey was uneventful, although we were told as we reached home that there were submarines off Galway. Since the next day we would, God willing, be in Belfast Lough, I spent some time on the bridge with the Captain of H.M.S. *Verity*, a pleasant fellow who enjoyed the life on the sea. Indeed I spent the first watch, that night, on the bridge, feeling disinclined to turn in; and also the second. I drank good thick, hot cocoa with the third watch and went down to my cabin, lying down in my clothes. I must have slept.

Abruptly a thunderous noise. The metal fan fell on my bunk. "Another one," I reflected. Sea-water started to pour in. I arose; put on my thick overcoat and beret; picked up my white pig-skin attaché case; and climbed the iron stairs. There were flames on the deck (I knew the destroyer carried depth-charges there) and the destroyer was leaning at a heavy angle. I went up to the bridge but found the captain in a mood which led me—it was also a sound security calculation—to move off, keep close to the sailors on deck and to watch the next act.

After a while I discreetly enquired what had happened. No: it was not a submarine torpedo. Unhappily, in a pre-dawn sweep around the convoy, the *Verity's* sister-ship had run athwart and rammed her. Her ram had penetrated the cabin next to mine. If the mate had been in his bunk, he would have been decapitated.

It was just one of those unfortunate mishaps of seamanship which occur even in the Royal Navy and are most properly not given wide publicity. I was assured that I myself had appeared on deck, overcoated, hatted, case-carrying, "just as if you were going to catch the 5.30 from the platform at Victoria". I was allowed to possess myself of (and still have) the White Ensign of H.M.S. *Verity*, which I kept for a memento. However, when I later went out with a mine-sweeper down the Thames, as far as the Nore, I did not tell the skipper about my past, lest he should think me a Jonah.

XIII

THE BOMBING OF LONDON

§ i

Only for one year since I left Oxford had I not been a tax-liable resident in Britain. From 1929 my re-involvement in political affairs at home had become more insistent. My formal resignation, after eleven years, from my American academic appointment, was in 1935. For seven of these years I had been implanted in two worlds, only part of each year in Cornell. Unlike American elections, British national ones are decided, as to date, between the Prime Minister, God and the pollsters. I felt that a time of decision had been reached and that it was important not to repeat what perchance was my error of 1929—it was important to find a constituency, not merely as a "standard-bearing" venture, but one likely to enable me to achieve something worthwhile in Parliament. One would move from the chiefly theoretical to the chiefly practical life—and had not Marx said (not that I unduly worried about what Marx said, except when he chanced to be right), that it was our duty to conjoin the two? "He who can, does", said the teacher, Shaw. The politician, indeed, can be the slave of the vote that empowers him. The teacher is not: he has perhaps influence, but he is without power to get things done.

When I saw Herbert Morrison in London County Hall, he told me (a) that "there was much good in Marx" (but was there enough?) and (b) that, if I chose to come into London County Council work, he would give me support but if my real interest was "in that place", then he could not. Herbert Morrison, the political boss of London, did not lack a certain sagacity well illustrated by his remark about the desire of Edward VIII to make an independent broadcast after his abdication. "If I disagree with my Party on seven points and agree with them on three, I talk about those three—and the sooner the young man learns to do the same, the better." And the future Home Secretary and Foreign Secretary, wiggling his stockinged toes under the desk, gestured with total detachment towards the Palace of Westminster. After all, wherever his ambition was to end, he had begun as mayor of Hackney. ("What about little 'Erb here?", the tea-drinking mayoral electors, in search of a candidate, had said). I was left with the impression that Herbert could not have cared less about

Parliamentary ambitions. Fundamentally, the advice was dishonest. It was not meant to apply to himself. However, thirty years were to pass before Clement Attlee was to write: "I did not dream that this little man had so much ambition to become Foreign Secretary."

Before I was thirty I had been put in charge of an investigation which, on the major social problem of alcoholism, could and did affect the Constitution of the United States. It had been performed perhaps not unsatisfactorily. I was profoundly convinced—and this was one base of my Parliamentary interest—that needed reform in complex social questions meant not only legislation, but legislation based on knowledge and on expert research. The alternative could be appalling social waste. "Scientific socialism" or not, a new range of social legislation demanded a new expert range in social and economic research, not amateur jabs at legal remedy. In the light of experience gained, I thought that in Britain I might be put in charge of some study like that which I had already done —for example, of the drug traffic—or at least put on some Royal Commission. It seemed to me that it would be an eccentric failure to use technical and administrative experience if this did not happen. It was what the Americans call "logical". Instead, I made my first chill contact with the deep freeze.

In America I had the choice of either pursuing my first love in political theory or of moving over to the administrative side. I was indeed later interviewed by trustees with a view to my possible appointment as President of one of the Claremont Colleges, in California, a useful beginning. I recognised that, in contemplating resigning my academic chair, I had also to contemplate losing a not-inconsiderable academic income. It was a most grave decision. It was perhaps a very foolish one, but I decided I must be prepared for the sacrifice. Indeed my early expectations were most modest. A dozen years earlier I had been a W.E.A. tutor, simultaneously with being a university lecturer. It was a worthy Labour cause. I decided, inspired by Tawney, to begin again in England. I made the error, which any billed actor will appreciate, of supposing that, because I could hold a major job, I could readily acquire a minor one. How wrong I was. All personal prestige and *mana* were gone. "Who are ye?"

Although I was a founder member of both the British Sociological Association and the British Political Studies Association, I was never invited to address either, but left merely to address the respective International Associations. After all, if I was right in my definition of political science, they were wrong—and they would have to start reading a literature which many had never read. It was intolerable. The eminent professor of Göttingen who acclaimed me as "one of the leading political theorists of our time" may have been deplorably wrong: but I was perhaps not as negligible as they supposed. As for myself, willy-nilly I had to achieve the position of, "at least, unconformity". It was many a year later that, when the question arose who should write the over-all article for the *Encyclopaedia Britannica*, entitled "Political Science", I was requested to write it.

After inquiring about the W.E.A. I was referred to Barbara Wootton, a talented young economist then in charge of London area tutorial appointments as director of studies. I explained my modest hopes and needs. It soon became clear that I should get no change. Entirely unimpressed, she made it clear that it was London University graduates, newly fledged, who would have first claim on whatever was going in her bailiwick. American commendations (painstakingly cited, as relevant, earlier in this book) left her quite unmoved. I got the dusty answer. As she modestly records in her autobiography, *In a World I Never Made*, she herself nearly lost one job because, as Hugh Dalton commented, of her "apparently cold-blooded and pompous intellectualism". I have never thought her pompous—but perhaps this was one of her bad days for cold-bloodedness.

Since I had acquired a professorship at twenty-eight, "full ranking" three years later and acting-chairman, almost unconsciously I moved on a level of equality and I had had no reason to come up against subtleties of hierarchy. Even at Harvard, certainly at Cornell and subsequently, invitations had always come to me; and there seemed to me a certain commercial vulgarity in making applications for "jobs" and displaying one's virtues, whether in triplicate or sextuplicate. I had left for America rather than attend for another year to await the judgement of the High Table at All Souls. I made a resolution, right or wrong, which I firmly kept, to make no academic applications. I had some claims in original scholarship. Robert Cushman had, with exaggeration, described me as, in his opinion, "one of the best teachers that Cornell had." I decided to wait.

I broke my rule twice. Ernest Barker wrote suggesting that I should be a candidate against Denis Brogan, Glaswegian and sometime assistant of Laski's—a man who regarded the religion of his forebears as "that superstition"—for his own chair at Cambridge. (I suspect Barker also supported Michael Oakeshott.) I was not known in Cambridge but I applied. Supported by my old friends Ernest Jacob, Chichele Professor of History, and

Robert McIver and, since practical experience seemed relevant, by Lord Louis Mountbatten, I also applied against Isaiah Berlin for the Oxford chair in political theory. I had written a few books on the subject. However, Roy Harrod rightly warned me that the latter application was a forlorn hope. I felt it to be no damage to my prestige to lose in both cases.

Although I received invitations from the United States, India and Canada, I received no invitation from any British university, ancient or recent. Maybe they waited for me and I for them. There was an echoing silence. Had not the American universities repeatedly come to my rescue I should have been financially sunk. Perhaps I was arrogant. Since my Oxford days, departments of politics or of political science indeed became common. I was told, however, that in Britain there was such a dearth of competent sociologists that there was no point in establishing departments of sociology. Thomas Hobbes somewhere writes that "Mr Hobbes will instruct the young men of Gresham College, London, if they will deal civilly with him." Mr Hobbes was not invited.

When we married, I had given a rather rash and indiscreet promise to my wife to return to Britain (making assumptions beyond my powers) in seven years. Ten years had gone by. Love England I might, but my feelings towards the British academic world ceased to be very friendly. I had to come sharply to realise that one could not always be popular; that I had myself left behind a community full of friends bent on being helpful; and that I was now in a hostile climate where, if one were not to be smothered by neglect, one must attack—if need be, with a battle-axe. The effect on my character of this chill was not beneficial. One had to decide for oneself, quite objectively, what one amounted to and then, quite toughly and uncompromisingly, insist upon it.

Brought up as I had been, I realised as a young man that some people would like one more than others, but the notion of any personal enemy was foreign to me. A reasonable man should not have enemies. It was not until years later I was compelled to recognise that, if one were determined to achieve anything new in life—be it in the field of art, learning or politics—it was neces- sary to go through and endure a period of unpopularity. Those who await "Buggin's turn" will always be irritated. The sooner one confronted this and brought it into the open, the better. And such unpopularity spelled enemies. There was nothing for it but to fight through.

Some episodes were trivial enough and entirely impersonal. I suggested to my *Yorkshire Post* colleague, Charles Davey, by now on the *Observer*, that I might make a little money reviewing for them. He kindly introduced me to Ivor Brown. I told Ivor Brown, *inter multa alia*, that as a Catholic I might be competent to review some of the Catholic literature that reached their desk. Nothing happened. As Davey said to me: "I didn't know you were a Catholic. We have only had, so far as I know, one Catholic to review for us—and he didn't last long." Since those days the *Observer* has nobly reversed its policy. Much later, in Newcastle, its owner Angus Watson asked me whether I would be interested in editing *The Spectator*. However, a chairman is not an autocrat and I heard no more of the matter.

More dangerous and personal, because ill-defined, vague and unanswerable, was the suggestion that I was a considerable bore, especially on Anglo-American affairs. That this rumour was being circulated in London I was informed from California. I am sure there have been many, from General Booth to General de Gaulle, whom others thought bores. A bore may be defined as someone who talks when one wants to be talking oneself or, alternatively, someone who insists on saying what one does not want to hear, at the wrong time and place. One reserves the right to decide the appropriate time and place, the probable answer being "never" and "nowhere".

On things that matter one has to be content occasionally to choose to be not only a bore but a crashing bore—indeed a punching bore. After all it is for the good of the other man's soul. And in politics one must cultivate a thick skin and a firm punch. Politics, alas! can itself be a form of pugilism. *Nemo me impune lacessit*. Dean Inge remarked that the accepted routine in confronting an argument that one does not like is to say, first, that the proposal is impossible; secondly, that it is immoral; and—if these fail—that one thought of it long ago oneself. The Dean omitted a possible first gambit for the defence: that the argument was a bore.

Many years later, during the war, knowing Ellen Wilkinson well, I went along to see her. My concern was primarily political. "Tell me, Ellen, I seem to have got into a rut, but I don't find much aid in getting out of it. What should I do? What is the explanation?" With the passage of time I became ever more impressed by the wisdom of the reply. "I think you much under-estimate the element of jealousy in human affairs." Further, one of the disadvantages of English life is "the team spirit". Excellent under certain circumstances, it can become the clique spirit, its sacred number Eleven (rather more restricted than the Apostles), although occasionally known to reach Fifteen. It is not good

T

for those who do not early "make" the Eleven or the Fifteen.

Be it said in defence of my academic colleagues that they probably regarded me as merely an obscure unplaced Labour Party politician. Those who take the risk of supporting a Party have to recognise that, unless members of the Upper House, the academic world does not love them, regarding them as liable to be derelict in performance of their teaching duties. The cliché is: "One must choose." It is not true, but it is impressive. The real issue is rather one of mere luck. Nor could the Parties themselves care less. (In America the situation is sharply different: Harvard empties out into the White House in order that no talent may be wasted.) My colleagues had indeed full excuse. My son-in-law later moved brilliantly in the accepted and strict *cursus honorum*: student of Balliol, Fellow of All Souls, Fellow and Tutor of New College, Professor in London, Professor in Cambridge. It is a record of uninterrupted success, each move following naturally from its predecessor. On the other hand, I arrived in England conscious of my status in North America and expected to be accepted on that basis. The British academic world, on the contrary, did not know me and reckoned nothing of that status. My closest academic friend, Robert MacIver, the dean of American sociologists, had himself left Scotland for New York. It was an epoch when *The Times* newspaper felt the United States to contain little worth notice save hurricanes and like phenomena of nature. The B.B.C. carried periodic notice of atmospheric turbulences in the State of "O-Yo". They felt me, hence, to be self-assertive, arrogant—in which I was yet, in Oxbridge, certainly not alone—pretentious, innovating. *Cet animal est méchant.*

Power in England, I quickly gathered, is institutional. The day of the independent scholar, from Hobbes to J. S. Mill, is over. That shrewd Scotsman, Robert MacIver, pointed out some of this to me in a letter. "Join an institution and grow with it." All men afraid of danger or novelty, and in quest of security, make instinctively for the bulwarks of an institution.

Incidentally, I also found that among publishers and agents I was now nameless—I had "no name". One reflects that the quickest contemporary way to acquire "a name" or "personality" is to write (as a B.B.C. man said to me) something "really sensational and preferably notorious". Jean-Jacques Rousseau was a political philosopher (not a good one) but his fame he owed to writing about his masturbations, which proved he was human. The author of *The Confessions* had a name. Some even read *Le Contrat Social*. Someone with a "name", not just part of the scholar's underworld, especially if he is a television "personality", may almost expect to rank with the pop-singers, our new social House of Lords, real ticklers of what Plato called "the great beast".

Moves I did make in the world of political candidatures. As Hugh Dalton told me, "One must be 'inside the cage' "—a member of the Parliamentary in-group, "the best club". Before the 1935 General Election I received thirty-six and, after it, twenty-six of those yellow forms which indicated that local parties or their wards would offer me a nomination for candidature. (Morrison commented: "Clearly he needs no aid from us.") Some indeed were for electorally hopeless constituencies. Some were not.

The North-West Leicester executive committee was frankly annoyed with me because I did not accept their nomination to fight Harold Nicholson. I had earlier met him, in a small group of friends including Lothian and Victor Cazalet, on *s.s. Berengaria*, crossing with Vera to New York in 1934. He was engaged on a study of Dwight Morrow. My wife thought he was "a nice man" and it seemed a pity to fight one's friends. Nicolson himself, with a very narrow majority, thought indeed no little of himself. There was an element of silliness in him. His memoirs record that he felt he would be a contemporary Proust, while at the same time dreaming about being a Secretary of State. He was perhaps the last Englishman (or Scotsman) to feel that politics was "run" from the better London clubs.

Consciously *cadet de bonne famille* (his own remark), pondering in sucession on being Liberal candidate for Falmouth, Conservative candidate for Brentford (where he would have been my opponent), Mosleyite candidate for the United Universities, he became in Leicester a National Labour Member. Indeed a nice woolly-bear of a man, and fundamentally a natural diarist rather than a politician of sound judgement—and also, to tell the truth, an appalling snob, over-pleased with himself, who was unhappy in America because "They never listen to what one says oneself"—he was not indeed a universally acceptable candidate. Years later, in one Surrey division—this time as a Labour candidate—he indiscreetly recorded in a weekly journal his low opinion of electioneering. His active party workers were not amused. He lost. I was ten years Nicolson's junior. I should have accepted nomination in North West Leicester and, if selected, have fought the Election. The admirable Sir Barnett Janner (now Lord Janner) the outstanding President of the Zionist Association, became member.

I also had a ward nomination, after 1935, to fight my wife's publisher. The Labour national agent, Dick Windle, recommended it to me—Stockton-on-Tees—but I did not pursue it.

This was an error. Had I been selected and fought it I should have won in 1945. Harold Macmillan, the then sitting Member, was defeated. Maybe I did not realise how weak his position was.

In the spring of 1934 I went up to Peterborough by a lunch train. On the basis of previous experience I thought I was going to meet some small committee, drawing up a "short list" of possible candidates. I found, on the contrary, that I was in full selection conference. I was in fact selected and made the appropriate remarks. However, I subsequently explained to the officials my embarrassment. I had undertaken to go on that very afternoon to meet a pre-selection committee at Nuneaton. I did not expect anything to come of this but, I added, I thought Peterborough should be informed. The Peterborough Party officials very pleasantly expressed their hope that I would come to them.

In Nuneaton I met the chairman, secretary-treasurer and the agent (according to Morgan Jones an excellent one) of the Nuneaton Party. They explained that they would much like me to be their candidate. They added that there was only one other likely candidate in the field, the man who had spoken on my platform at Brentford, Commander Reginald Fletcher, an ex-Liberal M.P. They explained that they "didn't want" an ex-Liberal. After the meeting, as I walked along the Nuneaton station platform, I said to the agent that I was committed in Cornell from September to January 1935. He replied that there would be no election in 1934 and that my commitment would cause no difficulty. We shook hands and I returned to London. In fairness to the Peterborough officials I notified them of my withdrawal.

A couple of weeks or so later I received a letter from the agent. Nuneaton was "safe for Labour" but immediate work would be required to put the organisation in proper trim. What would the candidate contribute? A sum was mentioned. The outgoing prospective candidate, Wynne Jones (who was indeed charged by his critics with not fulfilling his constituency promises), and "Jon" Creech Jones had both represented to me how important it was to fulfil the Hastings Conference Resolution on candidate contributions—which yet the Co-operative Party and certain trades unions flatly declined to observe.

In a critical decision I concluded that I should consult the National Agent, George Shepherd. I did not mind doing as requested but I wanted the whole thing to be above board. George Shepherd's answer was quite clear: "£150 except in election year and not a penny more." In the garden of Glebe Place I sat down and wrote a letter in this sense. Knowing Fletcher slightly I even went to the extreme of sending him a copy of my letter. I had the passion of idealism; what, I suppose, would be called by others a tendency to folly. A silence followed, a chill silence that could be felt. There were off-stage mutterings about the rule of free selection conferences. In September I had to leave for America. No selection conference had yet taken place. In January I returned. Commander Fletcher was, I discovered, now prospective Parliamentary candidate for Nuneaton—Commander Fletcher, later Minister of Civil Aviation, Governor of Cyprus, Lord Winster (happy title). He was succeeded in Nuneaton by Mr (later Lord) Bowles, and Bowles was succeeded by Frank Cousins. I told Shepherd of my dismay. "Fletcher's legitimate political ambition" was the reply. I also told the story to Ellen Wilkinson. "What did they ask?" "£600." "Rather cheap, wasn't it?" I swallowed hard.

In five brief minutes of letter-writing I had killed myself—in retrospect I knew that in five brief minutes I had probably killed my entire political career. At the moment, however indignant, I yet felt that a man who could collect two constituency nominations in one afternoon was sure of a place somewhere. I was in fact wrong. (Years later, it abruptly occurred to me that, of course, Creech Jones could and always did count on a union subsidy for his own party agent.) My friend the Average Adjuster (otherwise the Button-Moulder) has always told me that I was a fool—not even a moralistic fool, but just an arrogant fool to feel that it was up to me to purge the practices of the Party. To this day I cannot decide. Publicly I am glad that I did what I did. As a private individual I consider that, if I regarded what I had to urge in policy as of importance to the nation—and, with the passing of the years, I felt this with ever more urgent emphasis—I had no right to assassinate the opportunity to do this, from petty scrupulosity. The role of "fall-guy" is not a respectable one.

In 1945 Shepherd sent me up to Sunderland, in the Labour stronghold of County Durham. I had some confidence in the selection result. To that date I had never yet appeared before a selection conference without being selected, save once in Derbyshire. There, a mining constituency, they had selected the solicitor to the local miners but even so I had out-distanced on the vote the Labour Party's National Chairman. As "Jon" Creech Jones pointed out to me, the technique of the seven minute speech and three minutes for questions is an extremely imperfect means of selecting a legislator, such as no business house would adopt in choosing a junior executive—but I was, nevertheless, not bad at it. I was selected—but the time before the Election was most dangerously short.

Sunderland was then a two-member constituency, with each elector voting twice and hence a vast total vote. As there was a massive potential Liberal vote, a Lib-Lab coalition was sure of victory, but the Labour Party did not like local coalitions. (Against the grim background of 1938 I was to urge on George Shepherd a Lib-Lab Popular Front, but he demonstrated to me that it was a statistical error—the Liberals, independent, took more votes from the Tories.)

At this time my father-in-law died in very distressing circumstances, and a month or so later my wife was overwhelmed by the death of Winifred Holtby, who had been a very ill woman for some time. A respite was necessary as the guests of Dr Singer, the medical historian, and his wife at Par. In Sunderland we seemed to be "carpet-baggers". What was electorally decisive was that Sir John Simon headed a Coalition Party Commission ("National") which, realising the dangers for the Tories in Sunderland, pressed one of the Tory sitting members, Sir Luke Thompson, to stand down. A Liberal (admittedly National Liberal) was put in his place. Instead of a possible Lib-Lab coalition we had two Labour candidates confronting a Tory and a National Liberal. The result of the future election—and defeat for me—was settled from that moment. I got (anti-feminism being unhappily routine enough) a few more votes than Dame Leah Manning; but we were decisively defeated. Sir Samuel (later Lord) Storey won. As at Brentford, the unemployed on the whole voted against us: they were told the employers would then reopen the factories and shipyards. It was small consolation indeed that we improved on the previous Election vote.

As distraction, on the day after my return from Sunderland I sat down to the writing of my *History of the Political Philosophers*. Robert MacIver said that, although perhaps less scholarly than the book by my Cornell colleague, George Sabine, it was likely to outlast it. Charles Beard showered praise. On publication, in 1938, it alone stocked one window of Brentano's bookshop in Fifth Avenue. It went into eight impressions in English and two in Spanish translation. Even Italian publishers remained interested. It was used as far afield as Jerusalem and India. I hope that some day it will be revised and republished, as its predecessors have been, since in my theoretical work it balances my political science by its political philosophy. As such I think it not unimportant. E. H. Gumbrich writes: "It is a matter of experience that great art needs a great tradition." Although there may be more direct aesthetic ways of arriving at judgements of value, the book, superficially a history, yet carries the theme that there is a grand tradition of values and manners, and that history gives us standards of probability whereby we can assess the enduring standards of human civilisation. This theme of the connection between philosophy and the history of the times—and, be it added, even the biographical history of the philosopher—may be not unimportant. I also, later, wrote a little pamphlet, *Sartre Resartus*.

In the following year my father, to whom I was most deeply attached, died. One minor reason for my return to Britain had been his failing health. At an earlier date he had been prepared to make the adventure of coming out to live in America; but this had not been done. I brought him from Oxford to Ealing to be near me, and he died there. But until nearly the end he had found pleasure in being the honorary secretary of the Oxford Clerical Society, which he had done much to vivify. Quite typically, about the last book in which he had found interest was a two volume account of the monasteries in Mount Sinai.

In his young days, as I have told, he had been a preacher of considerable repute, counting Henry Asquith among his congregation. He was a scholar, even a tolerable Hebrew scholar—he insisted on my learning some Hebrew: *Sh'ema Israel, Adonai Elohenu Adonai echod:* "Hear, O Israel"—but he was a simple man, who esteemed learning above ambition. He came from a long Puritan line in the Bunyan county of Bedfordshire, a firm Victorian moralist, modified and mellowed by deep respect for Mr Wordsworth, *Rabbi ben Ezra* and *The Grammarian's Funeral*: these also he admired—this and Dürer's etching, *The Death of the Palmer*, the elderly pilgrim-sexton in his church tower. Liberal in politics and theology, he was a conservative in morals. But he shared with me a belief in the Roman *pietas*, the piety of things—a belief which inspires with respect—and in the decorum which shapes even the small and daily matters of human behaviour. Religion for him meant very largely this. He did not much like cleverness.

Towards the evening of a spring day he died. Our affection had been unbroken and, although duty had sometimes been hard, the contemporary notion that there is some kind of psychological obligation to resent one's parents had never occurred to me. I was and remain strictly Confucian. The best of his sermons in country places, still so well remembered by me, were on Christ's yoke— "Take My yoke upon you"—and on the Lord's healing of the sick by the shores of Genneseret. I sat waiting by the half-open window—it was a Sunday. The sound of some radio came in. By some coincidence it was a hymn—the hymn that had gone with his sermons at Evensong. "At even when the sun was set, The sick, O Lord, around Thee lay. . . . Once more 'tis eventide, and we,

Oppressed with various ills draw near." He died an hour later. We buried him, near Leamington, in Old Milverton churchyard, in which church he had preached—a country churchyard in the Warwickshire countryside, on a slope above Guy's Cliff Mill, where the autumn leaves fall in the mill-pond. In accordance with an old, not yet extinct custom, as the funeral went there, stray passers-by removed their hats and I was moved to tears by the courtesy. At such a time the noise and ambitions of politics seemed a very small thing.

§ ii

I have mentioned that in 1938, on Katherine Atholl's invitation, I became a member of a small pressure committee to propel Mr Churchill at least as far as the Cabinet. If there was to be war, he was the man to win it. Ramsay Macdonald had been a pacifist in the Great War, and after the débacle of 1931, when even Arthur Henderson lost his seat, another pacifist, George Lansbury, took over the leadership of the party on grounds of seniority. The pacifist tradition, if not fully dominant, remained strong in the Labour Party until the invasion of Ethiopia and indeed took flame for the last time (not that John Wilmot was a pacifist) with the East Fulham by-election of 1933. At the age of six our daughter Shirley ("Poppy") was handing out lemonade to George Lansbury in our Chelsea house. It was inevitable that I should hear the arguments and be aware of the organisations that were of this spirit.

I was requested to become, not only a local vice-president of the League of Nations Union, then guided by Lord Robert Cecil, but a member of the National Peace Council of which the chairman was Reginald (later Lord) Sorensen. I was not in touch with Donald (now Lord) Soper but I was in touch with Canon "Dick" Sheppard of St Martins-in-the-Fields, later Dean of Canterbury before Hewlett Johnson. The National Peace Council was, I will not say a Buridan's Ass, but a kind of eunuch organisation, unable to take a decision one way or another. A confederate body, it contained such pro-Communists as Bridgman; it contained Dorothy Woodman; it also contained many Quakers, "nice" people, indeed definitely "good" people. What I would call "scientific peace research", I would add, was not their line. In a situation where the Communists could regard the war of 1939 as "an imperialist war" all might be well; otherwise a stalemate was clear. One could, of course, still agree to annoy the Government. (I recall one local party member in Chelsea who simultaneously urged that we should challenge Hitler and also that we should not co-operate in civil defence with a Tory Government.) I tried to get something clear-cut in the way of a policy from Gerald Bailey, the N.P.C. secretary—a worthy man, but he reminded me of a rabbit. He scuttled off into a general moral disapproval of lamentable events. I was weary of this pious theme. I became an absentee member. "The cause of humanity" was too ill-defined.

Rose Macauley and Margaret Storm Jameson were among Canon Sheppard's supporters, in the mid-Thirties, in his Peace Pledge Union with its simple abjuration of war. Later, when it came to the crunch of hostilities, many departed, some into the Ministry of Information. Some were fundamentalists, standing uncompromisingly on the basis of the Sixth Commandment, the crucial word being "kill", not "murder". Some were pragmatic pacifists, in terms of war's consequences. I well recall a luncheon in a "sea-food restaurant" in Los Angeles, with Bertrand Russell, Patricia, Vera and myself present, when Russell with impressive gravity canvassed the situation and declared that, in this war, he could not be a pacifist.

The position of that eminent Protestant theologian, Reinhold Niebuhr, was somewhat similar to Russell's. He was a pacifist— but an ardent interventionist against Germany in 1939. He was a pacifist—but only as touching those wars of which private conscience disapproved (and never mind the views of the masses of his fellow citizens who also had consciences but differed). He was "his own tribunal" as to what was "a just war".

Some were pacifists, as they would have been slavery-abolitionists, on absolute moral principles. One trouble here is that slavery was abolished, in significant part, by war. "The claims of humanity rise superior to all national claims." (We have heard it again in the Vietnam war: the context very different but the principle the same.) This was Dick Sheppard's view. War of itself, any war, all war anywhere, any time, was morally evil. The pragmatist, on the other hand, could give different answers in Berlin and in Vietnam. What, then, was "a just war"? (Immanuel Kant said there was "none"—unless there was an international Tribunal. There isn't.) There were also those who were not pacifists but fatalists. In a recent dispatch on the Arab-Israel crisis of 1967, James Cameron writes: "There comes a point when the certainty of disaster becomes so unreasonable that one begins to will it on oneself, as one does in Israel today." There were many such in those days, neurotic people desirous of being relieved of their neurotic tension, wanting peace but wishing war. Very dangerous people to have around.

It would be cruel but not untrue to say that, when Dick Sheppard looked into his shaving-glass in the morning, he asked: "What would Jesus do?" There was a touch of the actor in that good man. However, his real position cannot be dismissed with a grinning gesture of what, in the Sixties, was called "satire". In the First World War an answer was given: "We'll have to put Christianity into cold storage for the duration." Who accepted that answer? On the other hand, how far was the answer in Palestine for the First Century the adequate answer for the Twentieth? And, if one looked at the historical record, Jesus seemed to counsel no "Masada" defiance of the Roman Empire; but to "Render unto Caesar the things that were Caesar's". In the late Thirties the British Government was becoming daily clearer about "the things that were Caesar's". The orthodox Christian reply is different. (It is orthodoxy which especially concerns me—I can do the rest myself.) "What is the word of the Divine Wisdom which is Christ?" What, indeed, is the reply of simple reason in its sincere quest? Reason and morals do not differ.

That veteran American pacifist, A. J. Muste—be it noted, in 1940—put the issue abruptly. "If I cannot love Hitler, I cannot *love* anybody." It was more honourable than that of the demagogue divine in London who made the headlines by preaching hate: "the Banners of Hell". But Muste (who later went to Hanoi in his eighties) surely forgot, apart from the differences between the long-term goal and short-term justice, to distinguish love and permissive indulgence. Does reason demand of good human will that we not only understand but also pardon and spoil even our own children? So long as there is human free will, to know all is *not* to pardon all. It is well that pacifists should exist to balance *enragé* militarists; it does not follow that the pacifist position is right. The case remains—and it is my conclusion—for the force of a police power, which itself should both exercise restraint and yet possess force decisive and overwhelming. Such a police by definition does not wage war. It exercises force. And all national or other "war" is, by definition, other than what such a world police force would wage—even by arms. If yet it does not possess this force (which to rebels will appear as Caesarean tyranny: this being the cost of peace), then the likelihood arises—against which there have been protests since the Second Lateran Council condemned the cross-bow and Grotius wrote against warring on civilians—of the atrocious national use of weapons, culminating in torture. The local State, be it Machiavelli's Florence or de Gaulle's France, becomes the highest good; or the victory of a class, by whatsoever means, becomes the sole test in ethics. The trouble lies with the unwillingness of mankind to recognise their own natural aggressiveness and to pay the harsh cost of world peace.

My own answer I have given here and shall reiterate again. There is a categorical moral imperative to establish a World Authority, sovereign and potent, ruling "by laws and by arms". It is imperative to establish a Tribunal without which, strictly speaking, there is no secular justice in international affairs. Nevertheless, history is in evolution and, in choices of the imperfect, the moral answer of the moment is that which is best adjusted to the moral achievement of tomorrow. Slavery indeed was ended (rightly *not* in the first century); but it was ended by war. "And the last enemy that shall be put under is death that hath put all things under." Later, the World Authority alone will hold the absolute weapon. And, against rebellion, it will not be afraid to use it as a deterrent. Innocent life cries for rational compromise. It must have the courage not to cry against executed justice.

Absolute pacifism, I concluded and conclude, is wrong. (After the war I questioned Gandhi on this.) To some this will seem mere opportunist compromise on principle. It is yet a strict intellectual conclusion. Absolute pacifism ignores justice. The virtue of charity is balanced by that of justice. This does not mean that politically I do not welcome pacifist extremism to counterbalance that disastrous combination of military and industrial interests against which Eisenhower warned us all in his last Presidential speech. (Eisenhower's mother began as a Quaker.) Nevertheless, war *à l'outrance*, for victory without negotiations and insisting on unconditional surrender (General Grant's phrase), is deeply, uncompromisingly, morally wrong—be it centred on Hamburg, Dresden, Hanoi or Saigon. It is fatal to truth, mercy and common human decency. The Emperor Franz Josef was a civilised man, respecting the laws of war. Today, in this moral confusion and amid the popular emotions alike of democracies and dictatorships, we are not. The solution of that paradox I have given. The amoral physical and biological scientists, inventing new devilries with clinical precision, have forced us ever more up against the need of a solution. Humanity cries out for it. It demands the widest union of nations, beginning with those most like-minded. Such is the Campaign. Dick Sheppard, however, in taking the short cut had his excuses.

After his death there was a "smear" movement, led by Hannan Swaffer, who always reminded me, with his sallow face, of a cheese liable to disintegrate. Among the "deans" of journalism no contrast can be more grotesque than that between Walter Lippmann, the immensely dignified dean of American journalism, and Swaffer, "the pope of Fleet Street"—not to the credit of Fleet Street. It is true that, as Swaffer said, Sheppard, "the friend of the poor", left to his family a private fortune of £40,000. There were distressing domestic problems. Dick may well have felt that his family had had to put up with much from his minority view and that, in compensation, he owed to them his worldly assets. It was an anti-hypocritical gesture.

Dick was a remarkable man who possessed that gift which I have known only about five men to possess (Roosevelt, Pius XII and Mountbatten among them)—the gift of "all thereness", the gift of immediacy. One felt that one had known him for years. "Tell me, Dick, what should one do?" He admired Lothian. Stalin indeed was so convinced that the British interest was to throw Hitler, like Napoleon, against Russia and to keep the West intact, prosperous and at peace, that he (and Khrushchev) could never be convinced that this was not the real plan. Later Stalin had to invent the theme that the Soviets defeated Hitler by themselves. The fact remained that Hitler, anxious for war before (as he supposed) he died of cancer, wanted quick war in the West—and feared that Chamberlain at Munich had robbed him of a year of opportunity. But by this time Dick was dead and Lothian's appeasement theorising dead. Hitler had to be resisted. And Stalin? Hitler anyhow, reversing what he had said in *Mein Kampf* about the Kaiser's error of a war on two fronts, was now determined to involve us before turning East (where it was, as I have said, quite wrongly felt in Britain that he would meet with no effective resistance but pass "like a sword through butter". What a folly of misestimation!) The time for decision had come.

It has further to be recalled in judging Dick Sheppard (and is easily forgotten) that—despite the persecution of the Jews ("A domestic matter", said the Foreign Office, comparable with *apartheid* in Nazi South Africa and the smashing up of the synagogues so late as 1938) the "ultimate solution" by gassing of Jews and gypsies, Polish Jews, and German Jews who wished no more than to be good Germans, only came after war had started. Without war many ten thousands of Jews might have remained alive. Only *with* war was this persecution discovered to be not "a domestic matter".

I attended Dick's funeral as I attended the memorial service to Lansbury, after war came, in Westminster Abbey. The funeral procession, of all classes and kinds, from St Martins-in-the-Fields to St Paul's must have been a mile long. I walked the distance in step with Admiral Drury Lowe, along the Embankment, where the men in tug-boats, bare-headed, lined their ships' sides. At least

Dick gave an answer—better than "call Hitler's bluff *but* no arms or war", even if a wrong answer, a "short cut". And he demonstrated to the world beyond peradventure that the Britain of the Thirties had a concern for peace.

Later, indeed, things were to change. There was to be the incineration of men, women and children in Hamburg and Dresden—far worse than anything that happened in Coventry which I visited, where the factories, placed in the green belt, were quickly at work again. Those who are so glib in denouncing what another people does, called to aid in Vietnam, should reflect in sackcloth about what, guided by that evil and, moreover, stupid Alsatian, Lindemann (Lord Cherwell), they themselves did when they had the power.

Vera Brittain, my late wife, put her whole literary standing in jeopardy by her integrity and unwavering stand on the absolute pacifist principle. A chairman of *Peace News* and a foundation member of the Peace Pledge Union, if it had not been for the repercussions on her daughter's career she would probably in the end have gone beyond John Collins to end up with Bertrand Russell's Committee of One Hundred. Her emotions were expressed in *Britain's Hour* and perhaps even more in the booklet *Humiliation with Honour*. On one occasion she discussed with me whether it would not be politically better for me if we had a divorce. We had become more and more closely devoted to each other and I repudiated the idea. Admittedly it is easy to talk about "standing on one's own feet"; but society has an instinct to feel in terms of guilty association. Nevertheless, I preferred to stand by my own reputation and to let the consequences ride. It is odd to reflect that the obscure and despised symbol of the P.P.U. is now world-known and the very banner, since the enlargement of the Vietnam War, for student millions in America, reaching Britain again on a return flood. However, the lack of organisation of the pacifist movement is indicated by the fact that public recognition, commemoration and statues of the early pioneers are still conspicuous by their absence. The Quakers, shy folk, are not given to statues—although the violent suffragettes were. It is the men of war who are commemorated.

After I returned in 1940 from my expedition with Willkie and the mishap of *The Western Prince* and had made my official report, I waited, confidently expecting that the men who had supplied me with *dossiers*, Greenwood, Alexander, Dalton, would find me a new job. I was not dissatisfied with what seemed extraordinary luck in my execution of the old one. There were helpful talks with Noel Hall (later, as he told me, sandbagged by Churchill

and sent to West Africa, and now Principal of Brasenose College).
I made specific proposals (some of them discussed with Sir Harold
Butler and recorded in my *Grandeur of England*). Above all I
thought that I could be most useful in Washington or New York
or at the London end of any Anglo-American organisation, such
as would patently be demanded. After all, I had some background
of experience. Indeed the only comment of mine that New
College High Table recalled (later cited by Kenneth Galbraith),
was that "No one should visit America for the first time." I had
warned Lothian in Washington that too many people were coming
over to talk without background, who would only cause trouble.
It had not occurred to me that, under a new ruling of this kind, I
would be excluded myself.

I saw that great man, Sir John Reith, but only the day before he
left office. (He lent me his official car to run me down for a lunch
with Laski.) Earlier I saw Duff Cooper who asked me, "What do
you want me to do?" I outlined to him public proposals in
Anglo-American affairs. As with Lothian in Washington, I totally
forgot the opportunity of job-hunting or to put to him any private
proposals for myself. It is not perhaps impertinent here to recall
a remark by "Rab", Lord Butler: "I now think I spent too much
time on the merits of the case when I ought to have been thinking
of myself." In one of these Ministry of Information visits I saw
Graham Greene hunched behind his desk in one corner. (Later he
was to go to West Africa on intelligence work, and Malcolm
Muggeridge to East Africa.) On another occasion Harold Nicolson,
who had achieved the level of Parliamentary Secretary, was so
indiscreet as to tell me, almost a stranger, that the British Government might even have to leave for Canada.

Even at this hour Nicolson still chose to back the wrong horse,
the brittle Eden, rather than the man of the hour. That the enigma
of the Dardanelles (although "Jackie" Fisher was probably far
more to blame) dogged Winston Churchill I understand. That
rigid party men could never forgive his party changes and invective—of the Lords: "refer-and-end-'em"—I understand. But as I
have earlier said, I remain at a loss to understand the arrant mis-
judgement of character, the extraordinary judgements (which I
have already quoted) of such men as Esher. Perhaps these gentlemen of elegance could not understand the brigand element
(which even the Duke of Marlborough, John Churchill, did not
lack)—a Churchill but, withal, a Jerome. I here venture to cite a
quite recent letter from Lord Attlee—which also bears on
matters I have still to discuss—which he gave me authority to
quote:

14 Feb. 1967.

"My dear George,

Thank you for your letter. I gather that there is plenty of opposition to the Common Market among Labour back benchers with whom Shinwell is in touch.

Winston was very much a horse for the course. He was very erratic on home affairs. The Tories took a long time to forgive his ingrown radicalism. They did not like his attitude to India and on Edward VIII. Even in the war they took a long time to forgive him replacing Neville Chamberlain. . . .

I see you had an interesting dinner party last night. All good wishes.

Yours ever,

Clem."

I can honestly say that a British defeat had never occurred to me as likely although, before the war began, at a luncheon at Eton, I had heard a high military officer opine that, if we had to take on the Russians as well, we should "be in for the high jump". Cyril Joad had tried to make it a condition for his support on one of his committees that I should register, in those days of the R. A. Butler interchanges, support for a negotiated peace. I had declined any such promise. An alarmed jeweller had volunteered to me that he had been asked to make up a valuable piece of jewellery for Göring and, as I told him, I so informed personal friends at the Home Office. I did what I could in obtaining visas (not easy) for several Jews, desperately seeking to reach the security of British soil; and I gave encouragement to a good Dr Sternberg, who wanted to establish a Jewish community in Australia, and his family. Meanwhile I put in time, with Sir John Mactaggart, in shaping the America and British Commonwealth Association, of which we had secured Sir Clive (later Lord) Baillieu as chairman and, later, Lord Trenchard as president. One would find at Sir John's flat a mixed company ranging from Herbert Morrison (frequently) to the Princesse de Polignac. The serious work the Association tried to do, not least an Anglo-American Cultural Institute for the study and enrichment of the common language I have described elsewhere in my book, *The Grandeur of England*. Maybe also it could have taught the French to understand the English.

Although I had been a member of the Fabian Society Executive Committee, it was not until wartime that I really came to see something of the Webbs. I ought to have made it my business to see them earlier. Both Hugh Dalton and Harold Laski had early established contacts and patronage. Politically and academically,

Sidney and Beatrice (H. G. Wells' "Altiora Bailey") ruled in County Durham as well as, in the early days, in the London School of Economics and the offices of the *New Statesman*. We visited them, under war conditions, on more than one occasion at Passfield Corner.

After lunch one started off on a trot in the Surrey hill country by Hindhead. I well recall Sidney's conversational gambit: "It was our experience in 1894", followed by some uncut jewel of political wisdom. He revealed the startling discovery that they had found somebody better than Laski in a young Fellow of All Souls, Ivor Thomas. I shall spare Ivor's blushes; what it meant was that they had ceased to approve of Harold. I found it difficult to approve of the strong-minded Beatrice sitting on a dumpty in the lounge and, a member of the utilitarian school, exposing not her lingerie but her woollen knickers. I hasten to add that, to Vera, she was quite charmingly gracious, presenting her once with a bunch of flowers which she herself had gathered. A distinguished woman, a great patron, with a side to her character which her detractors overlooked. My chief memory is of Sidney displaying with joy (a) their "Lenin corner" or shrine; (b) a *Punch* cartoon of Sidney with a red flag, walking in front of a steam roller, labelled "The Inevitability of Gradualness". Rather contradictory, I thought, but they were well pleased.

Very different were occasional lunches, in what I believe was the old home of Lord John Russell where Bertrand was brought up, with its marvellous view of Richmond Park, where Mary Oliver, daughter of Baldwin's favourite historian, and the Princess de Rohan were hostesses. They amused themselves with the Tarot cards and discovered that I was "the White Knight". But I did not find this society precisely my wartime "cup of tea". My wife, incidentally, at this time was painted by William Rothenstein and, at his house in Gloucestershire, we met James Stephens, the admirable Irish writer. No less removed from the stress of war was Max Gate which we visited from Swanage, when one of the children was at school near there. Here, behind her blue teacups and silver teapot, presided the widow of Thomas Hardy—maybe and maybe not described by "Willy" Maugham in *Cakes and Ale*.

The conversation chiefly turned on T. E. Lawrence, Fellow of All Souls and historian of the Crusaders' castles in Arabia and Syria, but also "Aircraftsman Shaw" who had shared a regimental dormitory with Harry Pearson, Winifred Holtby's friend, also a "lone wolf" man. A divided narcissistic character, complex as were all the Lawrences, but achieving something of the stature and mood of Elizabeth's Walter Raleigh. According to Mrs Hardy he poured out his problems there, sitting informally, but if a visitor arrived he fled. His view of the human race was perhaps like that of Mr Justice Holmes—to wish them well but hope to see little of them.

After the war we had the real pleasure of seeing something of Louis Golding, so naively and pleasingly impressed by his "Maggie"—his own success in *Magnolia Street*. Since I had to review a book of his, where it seemed to me so much depended on the character of the author, I asked Colin Wilson along as a guest. He was then regarded as a kind of literary proto-Beatle. I was most favourably impressed by his integrity and a certain quite charming naivety, which I found refreshing. Maybe excess of erudition does not help him. We also saw quite a little, in the Chelsea days, of John Brophy, a good novelist and a most pleasant man. His daughter, Brigid, the ultra-fashionable moral reformer cheerily described by Bernard Levin as one of "incomparably the three biggest twits in Britain", we did not meet. Hence I decline to judge her. I can, of course, admit with Michael Foot that many of "the classics of literature" are "bores". *Ulysses* is a bore. But Maugham showed that, for the most part, the authors were not.

My good personal friend and sometime Cornell colleague, the eminent historian, Allan Nevins, then U.S. cultural attaché in London, told me that he had been consulted about who should be adviser on American affairs to the B.B.C. He had, he said, recommended my name. However, Dr Denis Brogan, once a junior colleague of Laski's, was appointed. An official there had arranged a series of four or five-minute broadcasts for me. But these were cancelled. Truly or otherwise, the official privately told me that Dr Brogan was personally reponsible for the cancellation. Let me hope that he was misinformed.

Several years later, I had adequate circumstantial evidence that Dr (now Sir Denis) Brogan was responsible for my being blackballed at the Athenaeum. I told his brother Colm, a friend of mine, that I disapproved of nursing uncharitable thoughts and, if the rumour were false, I should be most happy to be so informed. Colm accepted the challenge but, although we corresponded further, he did not rebut the suggestion. Odd indeed are the ways of academics. Denis may have been persuaded of course, that I was a doctrinaire pacifist or a crypto-Hitlerite. Or, maybe, it was that I was a heretic in political theory. . . . Arguments in theory hit back upon use in practice! (In 1971 Paul Einzig organised a dinner—I there—for a residue: Vernon Bartlett, Chandos, Janner, Salter, Sandys, Shinwell, Snow, Rebecca West and others.

Philip Kerr, as I have already said, told me well before the war

U

that he had recommended my name to Sir Stephen Tallents to come in on the ground floor, were a Ministry of Information to be established. Lothian later became Ambassador; but his was perhaps not the best of recommendations. A Permanent Secretary of one of the great Secretariats of State wrote to me that it made him "hot under the collar not to be in a position to offer you any post, equal to your qualifications"—but there it was. Sir Kenneth Grubb did his best again at Information without success. My friend of many years, Lord Ammon—"Charlie" Ammon—advised me (I think wrongly in view of the career of Lord Franks) not to take up any minor post or I should be stuck with it. Ellen Wilkinson did indeed arrange for me to meet a selection board on the Security Section of the Home Office. I found myself sitting on a small chair confronting three very severe gentlemen behind a table. I walked down the corridor and dropped into the office of John Jager, M.P., Ellen's assistant. He told me that it was merely a routine job, which would give me no satisfaction. I withdrew. The luck was out.

I perceived that, unlike others, this was not going to be "my war". (Such is the imagination of bureaucracy that this was also very nearly the case with Sir Francis Chichester.) It was not, for me, going to be what some people call "a good war"—and what the still almost unknown Colonel (acting Brigadier) Charles de Gaulle, called *la chance*. Six crucial years were to be wasted, and all chance of major war work wrecked. I was (and remain) mystified as to why. Stuart Morris, secretary of the P.P.U. told me that "a man from Scotland Yard" had told him that Federal Union was regarded as being as dangerous as the P.P.U. There may have been the tiniest grain of truth here—in the sense that *The Times* correspondent in Lisbon had got into trouble with the Portuguese Goverment on the issue. I also speculated that the Government might hold that by giving, on invitation, professional aid to Willkie, I might have irritated Roosevelt and that this was a black mark. But this was not enough.

I can only suppose that, on the principle of association, I was thought to be either a pacifist or someone who would work against America's entry into the war or would slow the war effort. This was mendacious to the pitch of absurdity. Certainly I sided with my wife against Cherwell—whose policy, strategically proved wrong, was "to bomb the workers"—in her protest *Massacre by Bombing*. I was outraged by the Dresden mass burning, also without warrant. Wives of men I knew, anti-Hitler academics, were there incinerated by us. I supported Professor Camaerts of Belgium, in his campaign for food for our allies' children; and then

John Collins and Gollancz in their, chiefly post-war, *Save Europe* campaign, from which directly sprang "War on Want", of which I have had the honour to be a vice-president under Frank Harcourt-Munning.

Later John, indeed a doer of so many good works, became also the demagogue of the Lord, a stirrer up of consciences. Victor Gollancz, who received the Goethe medal, always remarkable but since the Molotov betrayal a much changed man, was concerned with "the fight for values". In these connections I met that most admirable Quaker, John Fletcher, and we were not without the early concurrence of Bishop Bell of Chichester. Earlier we gave some encouragement to the admirable pioneer Peckham Medical Centre. (Incidentally, much later, as a co-chairman of a Christian Action Conference, I was responsible for a resolution, sent to the Home Secretary, urging the appointment of a fit number of Negro police on the beat—such as one can find, not only in Harlem but on Fifth Avenue, New York—and, more important for prestige, of magistrates on the Bench.) Before the United States is criticised in Britain on racial grounds it would be well to see a Negro in the English High Court as a Negro is on the U.S. Supreme Court; a Negro bishop in England such as there is in Massachusetts; or a Negro mayor in one British town as there are in seven major cities in the States. The virulently anti-American long-haired youth (not least in America) would, nevertheless, not be likely to be deterred—while also for fair measure denouncing Comrade Brezhnev—from proclaiming the Rights of the Natural Man, and also the "Thoughts of Mao", at what moment President Nixon and the Chairman were supping together. But what matters in these affairs is not fact but belief and opinion.

However, this was, after all, also the public's war—the war endured by men (and women) with "private faces". I became a fire-watcher in Richmond and Chelsea. For these most modest services, added to those in the early Local Defence Volunteers, I acquired, in due course, one war medal. To this day what happened shocks me. But there it is.

§ iii

In the spring of 1941, the Chelsea house being unmanageable in wartime, we lived for a short while in the Athenaeum Court flats off Piccadilly. Michael Arlen lived in a neighbouring building and I recall, one night, hearing his conversation with his taxi-driver, coming from the street below and presumably about his own area. "I'sh not drunk, ish I?" "No, sir." "Name's Michael Arlen. No, I'sh not drunk. All kept women here—all kept women.

Goodnight." Many, if not most, nights we bedded down in the cellars, used as air-raid shelters—under the level of hot-water pipes which I regarded with suspicion. My modest objections to being killed were limited by my extreme objections to being scalded. It was alleged that St James's Park and the west end of Piccadilly were on a routine German bomber flight-run, guided by the Parliament buildings, "the Palace of Westminster", and Buckingham Palace as landmarks. However this may be, on the night of April 16th 1941, the bombs shook down outside. I heard the thud on Piccadilly with the kind of taut interest—I would almost say, sporting amusement—which, I suppose, a gambler has.

About 4.00 a.m. the raid stopped. We went upstairs to look out on the burning horizon of London. It had been a major raid—perhaps in retaliation for one on Unter den Linden. We wondered whether Allan Nevins, whom we believed to have been staying in the Athenaeum Club, was safe.

We decided in the early morning light to explore. Piccadilly was full of shattered shop-window glass, a bric-a-brac collection of shop contents lying about, ladies' black gloves, hats. The shop next to Spinks the antique dealers, a stone's throw from Fortnum and Masons, was in flames. (How nice, I irrelevantly reflected, to be introduced by Mr Mason to Mr Fortnum; or indeed to sit down to lunch between Mr Chatto and Mr Windus—"Chatto and High Windus".)

The Athenaeum Club, we saw, had escaped; but a couple of elderly gentlemen in dressing-gowns had already called at White's to discover whether the billiard tables were unharmed. The roof of Charing Cross Hotel was a bonfire. We returned and Nevins breakfasted with us as arranged (he had in fact spent the night at the B.B.C.) and together we went down for a tour of Chelsea. The tower of the Old Church was rubble and much of the nave, under which, it may be, lie the bones of the headless body of St Thomas More. (As I told Stafford Cripps, when Chancellor, "Every cubic centimetre of it, if found, is worth platinum as relics.") At other times, 2 Cheyne Walk, our Chelsea house, was both hit by an incendiary and had windows blown in.

However, I did not propose to spend the war in Piccadilly or even fire-watching in Chelsea or Richmond. The elderly but eminent divine, Dr Scott Lidgett, was warden of a settlement in Bermondsey beyond Tower Bridge. The London docks were taking an awful pasting. I took a room in the settlement and spent at least weekends there. I could be found behind a coffee-trolley, running it into spaces under Southern Railway arches, where the locals gathered not only as shelter against the lighter bombs and A.-A. missile fragments but also, amid the ghoul wail of sirens, to keep themselves cheerful with harmonicas and the odd piano. The stout citizens of Bermondsey are a tough and cheerful people, mostly dock-workers.

Later in the war, instead of the sight of barrage balloons by day and searchlights at night, one heard the new sound, with the fascinating interest of a horse race, of Hitler's V-1's. One could spot them in the sky, hurtling forward, and wait for the sound of the cut-off. Then, knowing that the bomb would fall, one could make, from the moment of cut-off, a neat thirty-second calculation of just where they would fall—short; or over target; or on you. Kent and the drear expanse of south-east suburban London got many "shorts" on them. In the country one good housewife left the over-bombed Yorkshire coast for a little quiet in unbombed Bury, Lancs. She caught the bomb that night. The moral was simple: "Find the best hole; stay there; and go to sleep if you can" (pneumonia was as deadly as bombs); and "Be content." The peacetime lethargy of the Englishman was his salvation in wartime humour and phlegm. The clever intellectuals sank to their negligible importance, like little dogs yapping. However, the Second World War was not as the First, and the admirable humour of David Low was a full generation more mature that that of Bruce Bairnsfather.

On the advice of that stalwart and immensely courageous soldier, Colonel "Josh" Wedgwood, DSO, the children, then aged eight and ten-and-a-half, had gone to America. We had seen them off from Liverpool, very determined-looking, on *The Duchess of Atholl* (but with the name painted out). Aged now eleven and thirteen, I thought it would be no less psychologically good for them to be back. It was a calculated risk, which Lord Salisbury had the courtesy to tell us might well be taken. We re-opened the Cheyne Walk place. Outside, across the Thames, was a temporary wooden bridge—why I cannot tell, unless it was a decoy or to allow the Germans a more direct route into London. Our daughter I found trying to climb across it—on the underside, holding on by arms and legs. She was that way. I also recall standing with her on the Embankment and once again, in that last year, viewing the London sky-line—a long line of flickering fire from burning buildings. Before the war, Lord Halsbury had prophesied that London would be flattened out; the Government itself had talked about an attack by poison-gas (it had its own little store for possible use in Hamburg) and it was protocol at first to sport a gas-mask. Neither mischance had occurred.

After *la guerre finie*, the "George I" Cheyne Walk panelled house (which I loved dearly until I recognised that attachment to it was putting me in servitude to the property), sprang to life again. Later we looked for a house in Battersea—"What was good enough for Chesterton is good enough for us"—but found the waiting queues such that one could wait two years or more, so we went to Whitehall Court, with the Canaletto view from below Westminster Bridge, which we were able to occupy within a matter of weeks. At No. 2 we celebrated our silver wedding, with Arthur Greenwood, John Wilmot, "Jon" Creech Jones and Vi, Edith Summerskill and Jeffrey, the Fred Bellengers and some dozens of other friends. So many dined or lunched with us there— the Harold Macmillans, the Vansittarts, the Ian Smeterlins, the Hapsburg Archdukes, the David Lows, Sybil Thorndike and Lewis, Rebecca West and Henry and, indeed, Harry Pollitt, national secretary of the Communist Party, who was late for lunch because he thought Cheyne Walk was in Southwark—a pleasing and sincere man who talked with me about the importance and indivisibility of peace. Palme Dutt, part Swede and part Indian, who sought to direct the political fortunes of Britain from King Street, Covent Garden, for the greater benefit of the Communist Party, I did not meet. One of the few personal benefits of my "nursing" of the North Hendon constituency in the late 'Forties was that it enabled us, at much too long last, to make human contact with Clement and Violet Attlee—thanks to my wife and Maria von Neurath, a friend of Violet's.

Just as I had been slow to grasp that my enemies in the London School of Economics were also the enemies of the Director, Sir William Beveridge, and (especially) of Lady Beveridge, so I failed to exploit the poor relations of Herbert Morrison and his ally (for a time) Harold Laski with Clement Attlee. Attlee ruled by the unspoken word and awe-inspiring silence. He was a laconic man, not easy to approach. I failed, from a foolish diffidence or reserve, to make an earlier "break-through" and to approach him. Greenwood never helped. Almost too late, after a Hendon-organised Margaret Macmillan charity show at the old Scala, the Attlees and those golden-hearted people, Sybil Thorndike and Lewis Casson, and others came along in the late evening to Cheyne Walk, where we had the further pleasure of hearing Harriet Cohen playing.

However, what I recall above all is a dinner in 1946, that perhaps restored our political respectability. When the so-called Nazi Black-list of those intended for arrest when the Nazis occupied London (published in part by Peter Fleming) was found in Berlin, our names were on it; the only occasion that I found myself on a list along with "Chamberlain, Neville"; "Churchill, Winston Spenser" and even "Cadogan, Sir". I do not venture to interpret its meaning; but many "personalities" were very peeved by finding their names left off. This event was yet for us less decisive than this dinner occasion of 1946—which cleared up for disbelievers, with some emphasis, my position in the States. It was indeed a distinguished dinner, about fourteen in all at table with others coming for coffee later. The greatest woman of my time, public office apart, Mrs Franklin Roosevelt had decided to honour us and she brought along with her Ambassador Winant. Our daughter, Shirley, then about seventeen, had to replace at table the Dean of Westminster, Dr Delabillière, who had suddenly fallen ill—she was equal to the occasion. As it was a private party we put no notice in *The Times*—a practical mistake since Eleanor herself put it into "My Day".

Later my son and myself were the Roosevelts' guests at Hyde Park; and a delightful tale of how the Emperor Haile Selassie, visiting Hyde Park, reserved a quarter of an hour to take off his boots from his sore feet, was told me by Mrs Roosevelt at her birthday party in St Paul. At least the rumour that we were in ill-favour with the Roosevelts, whatever officials might think, was brained stone-dead. I regarded the episode with melancholy satisfaction. Five years had been lost.

As I have mentioned, I was at different times chairman and vice-chairman of the Chelsea Labour Party, a minority organisation but yet one of the two groups which settled Borough affairs. In the Election of 1951, our daughter became party agent at the earliest possible date, her twenty-first birthday. She had already worked as an agricultural worker—"My desire in life is to be a member of the agricultural workers' association" she had claimed at a tender age—as well as being an hotel waitress in the North where, re-entering her room too late at night from outside, she had astonished the hotelier by falling down the coal pile. She had also been a worker in a London boot-black factory. Short of providing her with a log cabin in which to be born, we provided her with almost every aid within our power.

Middleton Murry, of all people, had established a utopian Adelphi Community; we often stayed there; a kind of after-glow of I.L.P.'ism, a kind of *kibbutz*. An alleged sketch of him is to be found in Aldous Huxley's *Point, Counter Point*. Of the apostolic circle of D. H. Lawrence, he preached human fraternity but was prepared, rather than himself to suffer it in some manual work community, to live in a remote village, discovering the sacramental mysteries of sex, with some assurance that he alone would remain, amid acolytes, the male high-priest. The *kibbutz* outside Colchester was patronised by my wife, and was run, as manager, by the most admirable and honest Joe Watson. My occasional visits to this Adelphi Community were the nearest I ever came to joining a *kibbutz*. Joe secured selection for Shirley at Harwich for a by-election in 1953, the youngest woman ever to fight a by-election as, at Oxford, she had been the first woman to be elected chairman of the University Democratic Labour Club.

She fought the General Election of 1954 at Harwich and 1958 in the Test Division of Southampton, but was defeated in both. Rescued from the fate of journalism in the *Daily Mirror*, not her role, she became unique as a woman on the editorial board of *The Financial Times*. Lord Moore was extraordinarily generous in allowing her time off from this appointment to fight for "the other Party" and economic knowledge gained there served her in good stead as Secretary-General of the Fabian Society, on whose executive committee I had once sat. (There was a time when I had sought to get her to join; but she "didn't want to get mixed up with all those intellectuals".) She became a Member of Parliament for Hitchin in 1964 by an 8,000 turn of votes; Parliamentary Private Secretary to the Minister of Health; Parliamentary Secretary of the Ministry of Labour (taking a seat in the Cabinet during Ray Gunter's illness); and Minister of State in the Ministry of Education and Science, aged thirty-six, and then Minister of State, Home Office. Although her massive majority of 1966 in Hitchin was reduced in the 1970 election to a mere 4,000, itself a fairly decisive figure, in Opposition she became a member of the Front Opposition Bench as Shadow Minister of Social Security, Health and Pensions, as well as member of both the Parliamentary Labour Party Executive Committee and the National Party Executive.

The Daily Mail, *The Sun* and the *Radio Times* have all acclaimed her as a "possible future first woman prime minister".

In these days of Mrs Golda Meier, Mrs Indira Gandhi and Mrs Bandaranaike, this may not be impossible. Although the Orientals are more advanced in these matters, perhaps there will be some vast wave among the voters to demonstrate that the old prejudices have been ripped aside in a new age.

I will rest the case with a charming comment from "Old Moore's Almanack", style of Isaac Bickersteth, by Alan Watkins in *The Spectator*: "*The Daily Mirror* (April) demands a place in the highest Counsels of the Ministry for Mrs Shirley Williams, whose wit, Industry, Beauty, Sagacity and Virtue have been the wonder of all who behold her." However, Mr Watkins' "Old Moore" continued: "*The Daily Mirror* demands a place in the Ministry for Mr Alf Hinds", the famous jail-escapist. Item, she is a Visiting Fellow of Nuffield College, Oxford—but Mr Hinds, not yet.

At least she has one quality not unimportant in public life: integrity. She has also an unexpected austerity and the constitution of a horse within a deceptively small frame. An able intellect and a compassionate heart are characteristics of value. Perhaps it was for these reasons that *The Sunday Times* (Feb. 1967) suggested that in the Prime Ministerial Stakes of 1990 its readers might be prepared "to reach for the 'phone to put a 'tenner' on her".

§ iv

Lord Longford, in his autobiography, *Five Lives*, tells how he was blackballed by an eminent City of London Club. He had, on precedent, expected the election to be a formality. No man could be more personally charming or socially acceptable, but prejudice prevailed. He was blackballed. Of the Athenaeum Club, Leonard Woolf, in *Beginning Again*, records that he chiefly visits it "to go to the lavatory on the way to somewhere else". It is true that what Woolf calls "its distinguished urinals"—Sir James Mann had added, "the largest in London" ("where some can't begin and some can't stop")—have now been moved so that this space can be allocated to the new Ladies' Annexe. Nevertheless, it is a most honourable club and, if I inclined to denigration as Woolf did, I don't think I would wish to seek its fellowship lest I foul my own nest. Without overestimating the importance of clubs today, I have other views on clubmanship.

There were of course past glories that will not return. For years I was a member of the Reform Club, and I recall its vice-chairman, Clement Davies, telling me of their past Head Porter, tall, massive, silk-stockinged and clad in knee breeches. The late Lord Salisbury, the Premier, shortsighted, absent-minded, entered the portals to the Invalides-like hall. He felt that he was in the wrong place and so said to the Head Porter. "Can you tell me where is the Carlton Club?" (then next-door). "Carlton Club, milord, Carlton Club? Never heard of it. But if, milord, you ask in the street, I think they can tell you."

In my fairly early years Gilbert Murray had been ready to propose me for the Athenaeum and John Buchan to second me. However, Buchan went to Canada and the proposals lapsed. Before the war indeed I was to my surprise (since I was not a member) summoned to a gathering to use my influence—what influence had I?—to get the Athenaeum rules, held to be in practice anti-Semitic, changed and Lord Melchett, who had been twice blackballed, elected. Melchett was in fact at last elected but, very properly, declined membership. After the war two bishops were good enough to propose and second me for membership, and my friend, Sir Alex Haddow, at least one High Commissioner and others chose to support me with some vigour. However, I also was blackballed.

It had a most pleasant coda. Admittedly piqued, I promptly sought membership of "the Senior", the United Service Club. I found this assemblage of admirals, generals and others of lower degree friendly and very clubbable, an excellent companionship. It is indeed a most excellent club and, furthermore, more progressive than the Reform, not to speak of others (the Royal Air Force Club apart), in that it admits women to associate membership in their own right. Lord Mountbatten of Burma proposed me; Lord Alexander of Tunis seconded me; and the chairman of the management committee sponsored me. I was honoured—and I felt honoured—by election within about twelve weeks. It was a pleasant salve; and "snaps" to petty fellows. It was a gathering where most members have professionally, not the abrasive mood of competition, but their own station and (as Bradley would have said) their duties.

To revert to politics and to an earlier date: Having talked to a trades union council in St Helens, Lancashire (a solid Labour constituency, carrying recently a 19,000 majority) on international affairs in 1944, I had a note passed up to me by the chairman. Would I be interested in nomination for the candidature in that constituency? Myself a Lancastrian and indeed a Liverpuddlean or Liverpolitan, I said "Yes." The party chairman, it soon became clear, would be my stout supporter. The agent told me that I "was walking in". Arthur Greenwood warmly supported me—but I had yet to learn that Arthur fought no battles. However, Herbert Morrison (later Lord Morrison of Lambeth) had other plans.

An ambitious young law lecturer from Liverpool, Hartley Shawcross, had become Deputy Regional Commissioner for wartime Civil Defence in Kent, under Morrison's Home Office, and when the very popular Regional Commissioner for the North West resigned, Hartley Shawcross took his place.

Doubtless inspired by F. E. Smith's advice to the Labour Party, Morrison was determined to push more lawyers into the House on the Labour side and St Helens offered a safe opportunity. Once again, the cards were stacked against me.

Shawcross was elected for St Helens and became Attorney-

General. His ambition was to be Foreign Secretary but there, ironically, it was Herbert Morrison himself who frustrated him. Now Lord Shawcross, he left the Labour Party, becoming a director of Shell Transport and, amusingly, Chancellor of Sussex University—a post which it had been hoped, in some quarters, a member of the Royal Family would accept. His later views, be it added, on American investment in Britain are intelligent, much to his credit and ground for forgiveness of much. In 1967 he found himself in a position to lecture the Minister of Public Buildings and Works, Charles Pannell and, on the basis of "very active experience of politics at a high level (which Mr Pannell lacks"), to state that "Socialism just did not work in practice." This late revelation had not been vouchsafed to Lord Shawcross—or, one presumes, to Herbert Morrison—in 1944.

Perhaps emotionally stirred by having seen the film *Mr Smith Goes to Washington* on the afternoon of the selection conference, I was furious and blackly morose as I waited that evening for the train to London. I had no particle of doubt about my own competence to make a substantial contribution in Parliament—on issues that concerned me to the vital core. Such a person in America, although not in Congress has openings at the other end of Pennsylvania Avenue—Schlesinger, Bundy, Kissinger have found them—but in Britain "out of Parliament" is to be like an actor addressing an empty hall. Bagehot's comments remain valid. Any citizen, hitherto undistinguished, who is elected to the Commons (unless he be nominated to the Lords), becomes a man of importance, meriting the attention of the "news and television media" overnight. The luck was yet still out. Politics as Plato said, is one of the highest concerns of man. However, it is also—and I suspect necessarily—a cruel game.

Shortly afterwards I was nominated for the Bilston constituency in Staffordshire (with a more recent Labour majority of over 7,000) and, once again, I had a most keen supporter in the chairman. However, so I was told, at the last moment there was an inrush of the Co-operative Party organisation. Fred Nally, a journalist who appeared in uniform was selected; I lost by four votes. Next to me was placed a certain Captain Goacher but, most interesting among the candidates, was a young man of twenty-five (here comparable to Tony Wedgwood Benn), the son of a most distinguished trades union leader, Roy Jenkins, later to be Chancellor of the Exchequer. The chairman was so angry about the result and Co-operative tactics, as he wrote to me, that he resigned. Later an invitation came from Wolverhampton West, a marginal seat, which was declined off-hand during my absence in San Francisco.

(It was won by Herbert Hughes, later Principal of Ruskin College, Oxford). Mr Nally, the Cooperative's choice, abode but a brief time in Parliament as member for Bilston, but my defeat (although I did not realise it at the time) was a disaster, which was to close my mouth in public affairs for twenty years.

This last incident had yet one good effect. Years later, in 1964, my daughter was in the States and then left for the West Indies— typically without leaving a forwarding address. During this time a Labour Party Regional Agent asked me for it: she had a good chance of nomination at Tory-held Hitchin. I told him where, perchance, she might be caught in Washington. Then, moved by the disaster of 1945, I had second thoughts. This at least was not going to happen again. I raised the 'phone receiver and asked whether it would help if I pledged that, if nominated, she would accept selection. "Yes: it would help a lot." I had no particle of authority, but I said: "Good: then I pledge that she will accept." She became Member of Parliament for Hitchin. To remove misunderstanding I should perhaps add that our political views, while amicable, have not in all matters been identical—nor was she always right.

Later, to keep my hand in, I nursed constituencies at Bury, Lancashire (in the square of which stands the statue of Robert Peel, for ever immortalised in bronze with the buttons of his waistcoat the wrong way round) and N. Hendon. The good people of Bury were kind enough to nominate me for the Labour Party National Executive Committee as a "favourite son" candidate. Morrison and Laski still carried influence, but—since a Preston selection conference when I had lost to a younger man with a great name, Lord Shackleton—the National Agent, Dick Windle, had become friendly. He wrote, before retiring, that he had put me "in the pool" for the Lords: a very stagnant large pool, I fear, seldom syphoned off. According to Lord Moyle, Clement Attlee's P.P.S., the proposal was indeed quite serious and, (a) if I had no male heir or (b) if there had then been life peers, "indubitably" I should have been one. But I had a male heir and there were not then life peers. Later, the withdrawal of the Labour Government's Lords Reform Bill reacted to my disadvantage.

In 1966, having come in by air that afternoon from New York and Reykjavik, Iceland (where I had been the guest of a hospitable Government) and having hurried by limousine to the Commonwealth Conference Reception, by invitation of the Secretary-General, Arnold Smith (a Canadian), behind an aspidistra the Prime Minister was good enough to tell me that I was still "in the pool". In a letter I replied that I was not interested in the pursuit of honours as such (not that recognition is not always grateful and comforting) but that, were there a job to be done, especially in Anglo-American relations, I was always passionately interested. I decided in the case of All Souls, and I have so decided since, that I would not want to spend my life looking over my shoulder for some advantage. Nevertheless, I had a sense of appalling isolation, of terrifying loneliness. I wanted passionately to speak and be heard; and not to be condemned, by lack of opportunity, place and invitation, for ever to be damned to silence. This is what matters.

Recently Professor Richard Titmuss, normally a most modest man, is reported in the Press as using, while announcing that he had turned down a peerage, a very different phrase than mine. "I should not accept a seat in the Upper House, unless there were an important (*sic*) job to be done." This seems to me, if indeed the report is correct, to be a most dubious posture for which I recall only one precedent. I have never desisted from the belief that it was my duty to be in Parliament, for reasons I hope to give before this book ends. For a politican it is clearly far more important for the community that he should be of use in Parliament in whichever House, than that he should merely be decorated for services rendered. As no other than Winston Churchill said, decorations are merely baubles compared with the substance of power. Doubtless Colonel Montgomery would be as important a man as Viscount Montgomery or even (had he been accorded the same status as Lord Alexander) as Earl Montgomery. Nevertheless, the nation would not in fact be held to have accorded him the same degree of recognition for work done. And who shall have the impertinence to dismiss such recognition as trivial? Egotism and vulgarity are the attributes of those who do. A nation may, of course, be wrong but, if so, the reference is to the bar of history. Personally I am not averse to the Quaker mode; but, if adopted, it must be international and without reservation—no military decorations, no colonels, no aldermen, no esquires, no misters, no Orders of the Red Banner or of Lenin. . . . Just the naked man, who might be allowed a kilt in honour of Rob Burns. And one hopes the anthropologists will not there discover "the Naked Ape".

On redistribution of boundaries, to some astonishment on the part of my committee, I withdrew from Bury. It could only be won if I chose to reside in the constituency: and I could not afford this. In North Hendon I found again that I simply could not financially afford to continue to decline cabled offers from the University of California. But the Hendon affair brought me, as I have said, into touch for the first time with Clement Attlee.

In 1945 the war was patently coming to an end. I was invited journalistically to go to the San Francisco Conference. It seemed probable that, if not itself the Peace Conference comparable to that at Versailles, at least it would be a Conference of the highest political importance in the century; and I was sorely tempted to accept. Having dealt in terms of constituencies carrying majorities of several thousands, I thought I could take a calculated risk. However, I proceeded with caution and, in March, asked the Secretary-General of the Labour Party, James Middleton, about what he thought I had better do. His clear reply was "Go; it is safe enough; there won't be an Election yet." It is true that, in a tea-shop in Bridge Street, Westminster, my friend Jack Lawson, later Secretary for War (Lord Lawson), warned me: "It may be for your private advantage to go, but it is for the public benefit that you should stay." Despite the brutal rule that a politician, at the first stage, should think about no politics save getting and holding a seat, I accepted.

With his usual delightful wit Claud Cockburn, in his auto-biography, tells the tale of our joint trans-continental tour from Halifax, N.S., to San Francisco—that great city which, to the astonishment of French journalists, provided an Opera House for the Conference but remained superbly unmoved by whether the statesmen of Europe assembled there or not. Travelling, San Francisco-bound, from Halifax I had the advantage of having Cecil King expound to me the philosophy of newspaper publishing. This was to have the genius to ascertain whatever the great mass of the public was going to want, and then to supply it to them more quickly and more amply than any competitor. If the British public wanted to love Stalin, then love of Stalin was the thing which journals should massively hand out.

After Chicago, it seemed probable that Claud Cockburn and a few others, including myself, would be in a compartment separated from the central core of the fraternity of travelling journalists. However, the *Daily Worker* did not lack financial capital. We transferred our reservation to a very luxurious compartment *à deux* at the front of the train. Hence I had the pleasure of Claud's company and, not least, of hearing the story of what happened to him in Nevada in his wanderings. Apparently he reached, without worldly means of support, a small Nevada township effectively of four streets. One was full of brothels, which was not a quarter where a man might expect actually to acquire money. More hopeful was the one where they sold pistols. He had indeed nothing but a typewriter to pawn or sell; and it was regarded as definitely suspicious that any man who was a man (above all, in Nevada) should not have a pistol to sell but only a typewriter—and an out-of-date one at that. However, he raised the cash but was indeed rescued by a visiting Nevadan who, over the drink Claud could now afford, on ten minutes' acquaintance asked Claud if he would like to hitch, in the stranger's car, a mere three-hundred or so miles to the California coast. The fates were kind and Claud so hitched. And still without even a pistol.

I saw there in San Francisco all the great statesmen, including "slim Jan Smuts" (whose bronze statue is to be seen in Parliament Square, looking as though he were skating over thin ice—hands behind back: "Which hand? left or right?"), receiving honorary degrees from the University of California. Vyacheslav Mikhailo-vich Molotov, *alias* Scriabin, "old Stone-Bottom", had declined, on a postcard—"In my country we only honour scholars." I listened in the Opera House to Molotov develop and insist—quite rightly and despite the Latins—upon a Great Power policy: he was interested in power and nothing else. He converted me to the view that not only was nationalism not enough, but that the road to peace lay in accepting, as under Rome, Great Power politics and in seeking their harmonisation.

I heard (Lord) Francis-Williams, as Press officer, explaining that, after the sweat and tears of war, we should not indeed get "a League to Enforce Peace" but would yet enjoy the manifold welfare benefits of a Social and Economic Council. (Incidentally Francis-Williams, as publisher's reader, read an early script of this present book. He did not like it. It was a misfortune—for which I was yet not responsible—that he died the same week. I should hate to feel responsible.) Already one could see the prospects of an organisation of tragic inadequacy—a paradise for "buck-passers"—of which the future might be like the League of Nations, in its then shape, in 1945, a life pathetic and also brief. One reconciled oneself to the theme that the only effective policy for peace would be that of Great Power politics and—however little encouraged by history—of Great Power collaboration. It was necessary to walk softly with a big stick. The oligarchs preserved their veto—with extra ones allocated in honour of the future of China and the past of France. Almost I wept with anger.

For this present century, to reimpose as it were the *pax Romana* (along with "the Divine Emperor") by dominant power and force —"by laws and arms", as said Justinian—although logical, may be the route to the holocaust. The nearest, I concluded, that we could get in our present times to a stable world peace was by the inte-gration of great balancing regions—of the widest possible regions of those adequately like-minded, beginning with the Westminster-Washington-Ottawa triangle but ready to explore any other likely door. It involved support for Great Power politics, not a petty resentment such as ended in the collapse of ancient Greece.

In April Ernest Bevin had delivered a speech which directly precipitated a General Election. But neither Jimmy Middleton nor any other warned me of the total change of political climate. Indeed I then found Fred Bellinger, later Secretary for War, and John Wilmot, later Minister of Supply, almost alone among those active and pragmatic friends who count in life's contests. We have not always totally agreed politically. But on record I put my sincere thanks to these stout friends.

Ellen indeed got me a high priority air-passage back home; but on my return I found that, in the haste, almost every constituency had gone save St Ives, Cornwall. It is true that Clem Attlee so little expected a victory—only Carr Saunders, Aneurin Bevan and the tennis coach on the hard courts in Calcutta ("I found Indian Army gentlemen going to vote Labour") were right. He sent me a message: "See me after the Election: I shall have more time then." Conservative Central Office had indeed a correct report; but Beaverbrook persuaded Churchill to ignore it. The Election came. I sat in a hotel watching the landslide result in an Election—in which I was taking no part. Labour won. I did not. The luck had fled.

I have slept soundly on H.M.S. *Verity*; I have slept in Anderson shelters during the bombing of London; I have slept soundly on top of the ammunition locker of a collier returning to Glasgow after the torpedoing of *The Western Prince*. But now I found my weakness. Everything had turned on achieving something in the policies to which so much of my life had been dedicated—and sleep deserted me. I counted the strokes of the sullen clocks. The words of Sophocles came back: that man is happier who is not born. To go to bed was to confront a nightmare of anxiety and self-reproach. "What a fool. What a fool." At last I reconciled myself to taking sleeping pills to restore confidence; consoled myself with a medical nostrum, "What matters is not sleep but entire muscular relaxation"; and at last awoke cured amid the warm and humid air of Pierre Loti's India—friendly Travancore. By then it was 1947.

XIV

THE INDEPENDENCE OF INDIA

§ 1

The second Round Table Conference on India took place in London from 2nd September to 1st December 1931. Mahatma Gandhi—Mohandas K. Gandhi—attended it. He stayed at Kingsley Hall in Bow (the area where my mother had worked), an "East End" settlement under the direction of Muriel Lester and her sister and under the patronage of the great man there, George Lansbury. There the Mahatma got his goat's milk and daily spun on his spinning-wheel. This had some of the symbolism of a Tibetan praying wheel, but also had the practical purpose of encouraging *khadar* cloth production and of discouraging "the exploitation of India" by Manchester textile manufacturers. The little man, barrister of the Middle Temple, admirer of Tolstoy and Ruskin, the New Testament and the *Gita*, son of a local Indian premier or *diwan*, caused some starry-eyed wonderment among Occidentals. The London journalists floundered in their endeavours to classify the unusual fauna. They had never met an ascetic. Winston Churchill was clear: he was "a naked fakir". Mr Enoch Powell, it should be added, was later to outdistance Churchill in his views on India.

My wife and myself attended a vast luncheon given for Gandhi in a kind of cafeteria or restaurant which then existed in Windsor House, Victoria Street. Before the select audience of that solemn institution, the Royal Institute of International Affairs, the Mahatma had insisted on speaking from a sitting posture, so they arranged cushions for him on the top of a desk, where *guru*-like he could sit and address the assembled civil servants and pundits. He also sat at Windsor House and, much later, at the Inter-Asian Conference in Delhi. The Mahatma's voice, in Windsor House, was distant and his theme seemed chiefly to highlight the importance of a humane vegetarianism and of "keeping the body nice", as he phrased it.

Frankly, my memory is more vivid of the late arrival of Cyril Joad, who sat next to me and who, doubtless, could have expounded the Mahatma's virtues and gospel in terms of it "all depending upon what you mean". He himself, that day, was sporting his new *Wandervögel* beard, for the first time on public view. As Harold Nicolson remarked to me: "I liked to see his faun-like face appearing at Knole." (I hasten to add that Cyril Joad had a more attractive, and indeed admirable, side to his character than most people knew.)

Far more important was a small evening gathering of less than a couple of dozen people on Ellen Wilkinson's invitation and in Frank and Winifred Horrabin's apartment. Pethick-Lawrence was there. So were Wedgwood Benn (later Lord Stansgate), Secretary of State for India, Harold Laski, Muriel Lester and others. I can recall Harold's acid comment upon "Wedgy-Benn" being there at all, in view of his supposedly negative Indian policy. Laski was a fluent conversationalist; the Mahatma was not, nor was he easily drawn out. The Indian leader expected a respectful Quaker-type audience; the Occidental Jewish pundit expected brisk polemic. There was a spiritual hiatus.

So far as I was concerned little came of the evening except recollections of general liberal sentiment and gratitude to our host, that exceedingly nice man who made his living as a strip-cartoonist. My wife, however, maintained a close friendship with Muriel Lester, a remarkable woman whose use of statistics in oratorical speech, however, was as uncertain as that of Winnington-Ingram, Bishop of London, but whose voice was like Sybil Thorndike's, whose heart was pure gold, and whose astonishing collection of friendships ranged from the I.L.P. to Lord Halifax and Stanley Baldwin.

A little later I joined the India League, which owed much to the initial work of a Universalist minister, Reginald Sorensen, M.P., (Lord Sorensen), but of which the Executive Committee meetings, when I attended them, were chaired by Bertrand Russell, with Krishna Menon as Secretary, aided by fanatically devoted girl admirers. Krishna, sometime editor of Sir Allen Lane's Pelican books, lived on black coffee, was very poor, and untiring. He was also himself devoted and indeed fanatical. For many years he flirted with the Communist Party (some to-day would hold him vindicated perhaps in terms of Indian-Russian accord), until he was firmly told that he must choose between this and the Congress Party. Despite some charges he, like Robespierre, was held by me to be "sea-green, incorruptible", although not above self-dramatisation, in the later years at the United Nations Assembly, as an Indian Talleyrand, with his mane of white hair, Mephisto-phelean face and conspicuous walking-stick. In these years he succeeded in arousing the almost speechless distaste of Jarwaharlal Nehru's sister, Mrs V. L. Pandit, but not of Jawaharlal Nehru himself.

Some committees are run by their members and some by their secretaries. The India League was of the latter kind. Academic duties made my attendance irregular. "The K.M. of India" whom I have earlier compared with "the K.M. of Britain", Kingsley Martin, carried an over-size "chip" on his shoulder. He regarded me (as indeed he regarded most people) with suspicion and I, in turn, had no desire to be his rubber stamp. I ceased to attend. Years later, in 1962, I made myself a little unpopular in official quarters in India by testifying to my belief in Krishna's integrity and dedication, at a time when he was politically "out" or—as K. M. Panikkar put it—would have been "torn to pieces" if he had sought the highest office. I did not forget that, remarkably enough, when the critical issue arose whether India should still remain within the Commonwealth, Krishna Menon was in favour, as was Nehru.

My responsible involvement in Indian affairs dates, un-expectedly enough, from the intervention of the Marquess of Lothian, Philip Kerr, who was then Under-Secretary for India. A Scottish Liberal, he was looking Leftwards for people with whom to bring Congressmen, and especially Nehru, into what is today called "dialogue". Visiting Indians of immense but remote distinction I had indeed met earlier, thanks to another member of the Muriel Lester circle, Agatha Harrison, that admirable Quaker. I also met Nehru's daughter, then a schoolgirl but now Mrs Iudira Gandhi. I received a letter from Lothian, explaining his wishes and expressing the hope that I could make some kind of arrangement by which Nehru, then visiting London, could meet some of the younger men of responsible judgement in the Labour Party.

On 8th January 1936, we put on a tea-party for him at 19 Glebe Place, Chelsea, and I believe that I showed some skill in picking Derby winners. Only one of the guests, John Parker, Secretary of the Fabian Society, was already an M.P., but (if my recollection serves) every one of those invited was later to become an M.P. and most of them Ministers of the Crown. In effect I invited my *New Trends in Socialism* symposium group. Apart from Parker, later to be Under-Secretary of the Commonwealth Office, Hugh Gaitskell was along; Arthur Creech Jones, later Colonial Secretary; Ivor Thomas, later Under-Secretary for Civil Aviation; and, according to my recollection, Richard Crossman, later Lord President, and Douglas Jay, later President of the Board of Trade. I hope that these contacts proved useful.

Some months later I saw Nehru again, briefly and with Menon, who was almost his child of adoption, on Nehru's return from a visit to Spain. He was clearly preoccupied with the moral issue of pacifism, and it was equally clear that he was not a pacifist either in

Spanish terms or in relation to Hitler. The notion of a gallant, disciplined band, who would obstinately demonstrate non-violently but who would refuse, until shot down, to take orders from aggressors or tyrants, did not appeal to him. I could offer him no ready-made solution to the Spanish problem, including armed intervention, nor advocate at that stage preventive war on Hitler—although, of course, a case can always be made out for it by those to whom it is given to know that negotiation, be it with Hitler, Stalin, Mao or Ho Chi-minh, is fatuous. Certainly Menon, the Westernised St Pancras Borough councillor, was no pacifist, although precisely with whom he wished to fight in arms was perhaps less clear to this diffused revolutionary and to his ultra Left-wing circle.

With the coming of the Hitler war, Indian issues receded into the background—indeed the Indian Empire had war declared for it by Westminster—but did not become quiescent. Agatha Harrison, a friend of the dedicated Catholic Rajkumari Amrit Kaur and one of that intimate Quaker group, including Horace Alexander, who enjoyed, like C. F. Andrews, the profound trust of leading Indians, asked me to establish contact with a young Indian, recently graduated from Cambridge, Amiya Bose. Amiya, the son of Sarat Chandra Bose, of Calcutta (and, although I did not know it at the time, the nephew of Subhas Bose), and his older friend, Pulin Seal, were intelligent and active young men. I saw, with pleasure, a good deal of them, although even more of a leading member of the Indian journalistic corps in London, Sundar Kabadi. Incidentally, the Indians like the Poles differed fairly vigorously among themselves.

One step proposed for keeping alive public interest in Indian affairs, even in the bombed London of wartime, was a cultural exhibition in June 1944, in the Alpine Club in South Audley Street. Vigorously helped by Dr Codrington, of the Oriental Section of the Victoria and Albert Museum (in the old Imperial College), I was able to assist Bose and Seal in the organisation of this Indian Art Exhibition and Sir William Rothenstein was President of the Council. In war conditions a grave risk was taken with valuable pieces of oriental sculpture but the Exhibition proved an adequate success. I also became the vice-president of a Tagore Society, later replaced by another more closely associated with the India League under Reg Sorensen. Like many cultural concerns, these were on the periphery of political activity, but were perhaps helpful since, as E. M. Forster has shown, even the vast interconnection provided by the British members of the Indian Civil Service had not penetrated far as a leaven into the dough of Western unawareness.

It may be said, as one of the best things on the record of George Nathaniel Curzon, that he was not guilty in this respect. In his own Allah-like way, he took personal pride in the jewels of what he regarded as his own empire and, indeed, regally concerned himself with what too many Indians had themselves neglected. May St Peter remember it to him for righteousness. If the sidesman in the Viceregal chapel did not bow, before receiving the Viceregal coin, he received no coin. I contribute my coin of remembrance.

Far more important, as an affirmation, was the proposal made to me in 1943 as Vice-Chairman of the Council for Indian Independence, by Amiya Bose and his circle, that I should draft a Declaration in Support of Indian Independence, which non-Indians and especially British M.P.s might sign. A copy is to be found in the Library of Calcutta University and doubtless elsewhere, and the text is an appendix to my own book, *In the Path of Mahatma Gandhi* (1948).[1]

It may be that the shape of the document was mine (its Jeffersonian cast rather suggests this), while the general idea came from my Indian friends. However, it is possible that the whole idea was theirs and merely the drafting mine. Whichever is the case, the document received a satisfactory number of signatures, including that of some who were later to become Ministers of the Crown and Privy Councillors. W. G. Cove, a Welsh M.P., played some part in collecting them, and among those who signed, as well as Cove, were R. R. Stokes, later Privy Seal, Aneurin Bevan, George Buchanan and Alfred Edwards. Although Reginald Sorensen was not a signatory, no man worked harder for the cause of Indian Independence, with little personal recognition or reward. Creech Jones, who was going out of London, once asked me to press on Krishna Menon the case for some recognition for him, but I had no immediate success. I merely received an electric smile.

The political attitude towards India in Britain in the Forties has to be recalled to memory. Ultimate Home Rule for India was indubitably official policy. What mattered, as in the comparable Irish case, was the timing. The Prime Minister himself, Winston Churchill, his views on the record, was not only no favourer of Indian Independence: he had even gone to the length of resigning from the Baldwin Cabinet (a step which nearly proved fatal to his career) owing to his firm opposition to even a Conservative measure of liberalism on the Indian issue. Enoch Powell, much later to become Shadow Minister of Defence under Edward

[1] *In the Path of Mahatma Gandhi* (Macdonald, London; Regnery, New York), 1948.

Heath, held yet more extreme views, such that even Churchill was to come to doubt his balance of judgement. Much more moderate men, such as Halifax with the experience of a Viceroy, felt that the midst of a desperate war was surely not the right timing for instant Home Rule. There was not unnaturally resentment by those whose minds were obsessed by the struggle against Hitler, who seemed incarnate evil, that, while many respected Indians such as Noon and the elder Sapru, whom later I visited, held to what may be called a Redmondite position, others (including Gandhi) could think it to be a patriotic duty to see, albeit reluctantly, in Britain's distresses India's opportunities. At one stage Gandhi was here under pressure from Subhas Bose. Gandhi would have received the invading Japanese with peaceful non-cooperation and non-violent resistance. Subhas Bose was prepared, with as much Japanese cooperation as he could get, to accept the slogan of "Asia for the Asians" and to spearhead armed revolt.

Within the Labour Party itself and its National and Parliamentary Executive Committees, there were divisions of view. Some here also felt that the issue was best delayed to some time more propitious but in an unspecified future. Some were prepared to favour an immediate declaration of support for Home Rule for India. A very few—among whom I count myself one—felt this to be inadequate; and that India must not just be offered a constitution by Westminster, but feel totally free to follow her own route at her own choice: to be independent outside the Commonwealth or (as we hoped) within the multi-racial Commonwealth. I had very much at heart the failure of the Irish negotiations, because the generous offer was never made at the right stage but always one stage too late. (Today nothing is more heart-warming than, thanks to Independence, the vast improvement over forty years in Anglo-Irish affairs—now sadly in jeopardy.) We were convinced that India, for a satisfactory solution, must not only have complete freedom of choice at the end of the War, assuming Allied victory, but be seen and felt by herself to have this.

In politics much lies in the manipulation of an agenda. Resolutions on India tended to be placed at the end of the agenda at Labour Party Conferences, where the fate of three-and-a-half hundred million people had to compete with the closure of the Conference, the trains to be caught by delegates, the votes of thanks to the local mayor, heavy jocular commendations of the good boys of the Press and, finally, the singing of *The Red Flag* and *Auld Lang Syne* by those so nostalgically inclined. For all I cared, I would have been as much inclined to sing *God Save the King* (a proper sentiment) and *Land of Hope and Glory*, with views in which I strongly believed—and with the expectation that the hope would be gratified, if only the delegates would attend to Indian business and to the affairs of a *raj* for which, like it or not, they were responsible. Kipling's great *Recessional*, with its modest attitude to rule, might be sung occasionally, *con amore*. It is not discreditable to the England that produced it and, like that by Spring-Rice, gives a perspective to Victorian imperialism.

What mattered to me was that the Labour Party delegates should get down to discussing, along with domestic bread and butter, these vast overseas responsibilities. I was shocked that too often they did not, and I was converted to Tagore's view that one nation, "democratic to itself alone", should never autocratically control the affairs of another. Stable power could not be founded on such a hybrid basis.

Indian freedom was one of the three major activities in my life, with which I had now become immensely concerned. Stafford Cripps had led his South-East Bristol Labour party to move a strong resolution on India. I, still an official, had got the Chelsea Party to second it. But Laski, as Party Conference chairman, cut me down to a five minutes speech instead of the regulation ten, in order to get on to the routine votes of thanks. After all, India or no, the comrades did want both to sing and to catch their trains. I did not readily forgive Laski.

I believe in a positive patriotism, which makes its contribution to the international community of men. This was also Mazzini's oft-stated belief. Emphatically it was the belief of Rabindranath Tagore, *poeta divino* and good humanist (on whose centenary I delivered, by invitation of four Royal Societies in London, a published address)—and it was the belief of Gandhi. Incidentally, during my second visit to India I went up to Tagore's old home at Santiniketan, where Sudhir Ghosh met me, which, fortunately, had not yet been too emphatically converted into a shrine almost comparable to the temple at Belur.

Without despising Macaulay's contribution to Indian culture and administration—or the contribution of Britons to the establishment of Congress itself—I agreed emphatically with Tagore that the democracy of the United Kingdom was no more democratically entitled to impose its pattern of life and its administration and economic (and military) control upon the Indian Empire than the Athenian democracy had been entitled to impose itself upon Melos. A home democracy cannot run an extended empire. It was true that the *raj* had, for the first time in Indian history, presented India with a union of the whole sub-continent; and it was true that, administratively, the *raj* had much to its credit.

Yet the rule of one nation by another—by the voters of Bradford and Greenwich, preoccupied with their own wages and local drains—was an intolerable one, save as transitional. It was a repetition of the old error of 1776. Whereas the Roman Empire, where finally every subject was also a full citizen, was a true imperialism, enforcing peace, this was a pseudo-imperialism. Indeed no philosophy of Empire—or of Commonwealth—had ever been worked out, even by the Victorians. The citizens of Birmingham and Bootle were left, as "the sovereign people", in unchallenged control. In Rome their opposite numbers were not. All were equal—under Caesar Augustus.

In the British Empire the United Kingdom electors remained sovereign. They didn't even count—here more reactionary than the French—the representatives of Malta or Gibraltar within the walls of their fossilised Parliament. In the Roman Empire the *proles Romuli* were put firmly into their small place. Whereas New England and New Zealand were examples of true and beneficial colonisation, this in India—with its *sahibs* and *mem-sahibs*, so often desiring to return "home"—was a pseudo-colonialism. As the Sardar Panikker pointed out to me, in a striking phrase which stuck in my mind, "for a century India has been governed by Knights Commander"—not indeed by knights in armour but by the Orders of Chivalry of the Knights of the Star of India and Knights of the Indian Empire, all arranged from London, and in twill or striped pants.

Assuredly it was no purpose of mine, when we had rolled up the Empire, to reduce the Commonwealth. Despite Churchill, "jewels" might be misplaced; but my object was to re-form and extend the Commonwealth. The inclusion of India ensured that it would remain multi-racial. Just as the enforced importation of the Negro sets a problem for the United States which Providence will not allow it, as the mills grind on, to escape, so the years of military rule and profit over non-Nordic or non-Caucasian peoples (the Brahmins are purest Aryan) set a problem for us that to this day the voter in Lewisham or Paddington must not be allowed to evade, however he squeal or talk of his own bread and butter. The problem was to solve it in a cast of magnitude, grandeur and dignity.

§ ii

In September 1945, I introduced P. B. Seal, who had earlier been secretary of the London branch of the National Indian Congress, to Arthur Greenwood, then Privy Seal and Deputy Leader of the Labour Party. The suggestion was made that a

Parliamentary delegation (if successful, to be followed by a Cabinet mission) should go to India to meet Congress leaders. Encouraged by Arthur Greenwood, a probing telegram was sent to India which brought in reply a cable, of 10th September, to Seal from Allahabad:

"Your cable to Gandhiji. British friends always welcome here but delegation hardly opportune. Now it is for British Government to state clearly policy regarding Indian Independence and not merely make vague statements or encourage goodwill missions. Jawaharlal Nehru."

Greenwood was at this stage in consultation with Attlee. A further cable went from London which, following a meeting of the working committee of Congress, produced a reply of 25th September from Poona, to Seal:

"Your cable. British friends coming on their own initiative for helping mutual understanding always welcome. Jawaharlal Nehru."

This last cable was formally considered, not without consequences, by the British Cabinet sub-committee on India.

In 1946 I received, in conjunction with P. B. Seal, an invitation from the President of Congress, Maulana Azad, to come to India where I might be of help with advice. This was at the time when the British Governmental Commission of Cripps, A. V. Alexander and Pethick-Lawrence would be there. Woodrow Wyatt, a brisk young man and great social success, not much heard of earlier, accompanied Cripps, although himself scarcely a Crippsian character. My friend John (later Lord) Wilmot told me that Alexander had seriously thought of inviting me to accompany him, but that it was in the end thought that I was too closely associated with the Bose family. (Actually the relations of Sarat Chandra Bose, the "boss" of Calcutta, and Subhas Bose, although fraternal, were by no means unduly close.) On reflection I hold that maybe things were better as they were, with myself entirely independent. As Ellen Wilkinson said to me: "I admire the fact that, instead of fussing around asking advice, you went on your own." Incidentally all of this cost private money and I was not rich.

Merely to go, of itself, was not easy. Air-travel was still restricted. I here appealed to Ivor Bulmer-Thomas and, as Under-Secretary for Civil Aviation, he was generous enough to secure me, Seal, and one other, under the special orders of A. V. Alexander, a priority passage. I was met at Delhi by Sarat Chandra Bose in his white, priestly, Bengali robe. (It recalls the ancient Egyptian, but has the disadvantage that one garment leg too frequently hangs lower than the other.) Within an hour I was

hustled in to meet Nehru, yet again, and Azad. Both Bose and
Azad were later to be my guests at 2 Cheyne Walk. Nehru's sister
"Nan", Mrs. V. L. Pandit, who was to become one of our closest
friends, I had already met at the San Francisco Conference, in
1945.

Later, when the British Commission moved to Simla, I took a
car and went up there, staying at the Wilson Hotel. Agatha
Harrison was already in Simla. I still recall the pricking of the
nose from the high altitude, the jangle of the rapid rickshaw bells
and, above all, waking one morning to see, instead of clouds, the
long, vast range Tibet-wards of the snow-clad Himalayas. Not
less, I recall the mixture of brown corrugated iron roofing and of
Streatham-like villas in Simla, and also taking tea in an Indian
restaurant, gazing at two oleographs of—the Bay of Naples. Very
odd. In Simla I met Gandhi for the third time and also Jinnah's
sister. Meanwhile I settled down to the serious job of drafting, by
request, a memorandum for Maulana Azad.

The row with the Moslem League and about a secessionist
policy for Pakistan was already on; my own thought ran in terms
of a united India. With one Moslem view, expressed to me in
Aligarh, I had not much sympathy. "We were in charge when you
British came to India. Why do you not leave us in charge?" I have
seldom seen the point made, but one secret of Hindu–Moslem
friction is precisely that the Moslems represent the yet-older
Moghul invading and colonial power.

In my memorandum to the Maulana I suggested that attention
should be turned away from legalistic discussion of the sovereignty
of Delhi; that legitimate local demands should be accommodated
within a federal and decentralised system; but that full attention
should be given to objective power, as distinct from juristic claims
—to actual federal control of communications, railways, waterways and irrigation, the Ganges and Indus. In turning attention
from legal abstractions to actual powers I was following a political
principle which I had consistently held. In turning attention to the
waterways I did not fail to have in mind the fashion in which a
constitutional claim over navigable waterways had enabled the
Federal authority in the United States to establish in Tennessee
the monumental Tennessee Valley Authority under Franklin
Roosevelt. In India irrigation especially mattered and who held the
water.

In the following year, 1947, I was again invited out to India,
as always by Congress but this time by Mrs Naidu, the President of
the Inter-Asian Conference, then to take place in Delhi. In Delhi,
in March, apart from talks with Nehru and hearing the Mahatma

enjoin those delegates who wished to understand India to visit the Indian village, I also heard that remarkable woman, Mrs Naidu, deliver a presidential speech with better oratory than Lloyd George and in such beautiful English that it would stand comparison with an address by any British native. It could have been printed as delivered, and was an outstanding performance.

I also observed my wartime friend, George Yeh, who was later Foreign Minister and was now leading the Chinese Delegation, obtain ladder and paint-pot and firmly draw the Chinese frontier, on a wall-map, round the outside of Tibet. The Tibetan delegates, with their turquoise-studded crowns, were magnificent, silent fellows, like figures of satin-wood—silent until I heard one say to his secretary: "O.K. See you in the morning." I congratulated their interpreter on their knowledge of English. "Why not? I was educated at Rugby." I received an invitation to visit Lhasa but, expense apart, it then involved more days on mule-back than I had to spare. I congratulated an Indian diplomat upon being appointed to that post where he could visit the Potala. "Very interesting for the first week," was the reply.

On this occasion I had come on to Delhi from Calcutta, where I was the guest for a week of Sarat Chandra Bose. Before I left, Bose told me that, in the very week of my stay, conferences had been taking place in the house with a view to maintaining, on the basis of communal representation acceptable to both Moslems and Hindus, a united Bengal with what must be called a species of "Ulster autonomy". The comparison was indeed apt.

The joint signators of this memorandum were Sarat Chandra Bose, K. S. Roy, S. R. Babai (Hindu), Suhrawardy, Abul Hashim and Mohammed Ali (Moslem). Bose wished me to carry this memorandum up to Delhi and personally to give it to the new Viceroy Lord Mountbatten (whose Durbar I attended). To Delhi, therefore, I went. I favoured the integrity of Bengal as I favoured the integrity of India, although I consistently said that it lay in the very nature of independence that this was for Indians themselves to decide. It was certainly not my business to interfere or to be more than a useful messenger. Gandhi was ambiguous in his attitude to the plan. Azad favoured it. Mountbatten thought it had something in its favour. Jinnah was against it, unless he got the Eastern Punjab in compensation. This plan, hence, could mean that Congress would lose direct control of both the Eastern Punjab and of Western Bengal. Not unnaturally, both Nehru and Patel were opposed; and the plan came to nothing.

As I write this, the Bengalis' Eastern Pakistan, that artificial area so uneconomically divorced from West Bengal, are "dying

like flies" from cholera or are fleeing in thousands from Eastern
Bengal, following "the restoration of order by military means" in
the land. I am aware that the political structure of Northern
Ireland offers no perfect model for other countries, although both
Westminster and Dublin contrive to endure it. I am also aware that
linguistic separation constitutes a threat to the political unity of
India, and that, if Bengali popular nationalism offers a direct
threat to rule from Karachi, it no less presents its difficulties for the
authorities in New Delhi. I have always refrained, for example
over Kashmir, from expressing views over the internal affairs of
the sub-continent. Nevertheless, I cannot but regret that the
confidential and indeed secret proposals which I carried that
spring, from Calcutta to the Viceroy in Delhi, were not implemented. Much good for many millions might have resulted. The
desperate horrors of the flight across the border, which continue
at this moment, might not have occurred.

My dear friend, the late Dr Humayun Kabir, Moslem, sometime Minister of Culture in Delhi, told me that, actually at the
same time as Sarat Chandra Bose's *démarche*, a plan was well
advanced in which he and the Hindu Speaker of the Bengal
Legislature were jointly involved, which could have produced a
sovereign and united Bengal, affiliated to Pakistan but with a
defence treaty with India; and that this plan was approved by
Jinnah, Nehru and Gandhi. According to him it was destroyed by
Bose's premature publicity. I do not know enough to record a
judgement, but I was aware that there was some prejudice against
Suhrawardy and any proposals by him.

In retrospect it is possible to regard the failure of these joint
communal proposals for a united but federated Bengal as a
historic disaster. It was such, even although one can see that their
acceptance would have involved a sacrifice for Pakistan, such that
Jinnah asked for the Eastern Punjab as compensation, and for
India, which would have lost some measure of direct control (or
indirect control through Indian Calcutta) over Western Bengal.
It is regrettable that these "compensations" or "losses" were
regarded as too much to pay. In September 1971, by invitation I
returned once more, and for the fifth time, to Delhi to hear once
again about the human problems of Bangla Desh.

When "the Irish question", which one had felt had been, at
least temporarily, settled by partition in Lloyd George's day,
blazed up again, I advised the Leader of the Opposition, Harold
Wilson, in August 1971 to come out with a dual statement: of a
Declaration of Minority Civil Rights to which both Ulster and the
Irish Republic might accede, and a Declaration of Intent, in

British policy, to regard all Ireland as one country, with probably a federal provincial settlement for Ulster. In the alternative, and before we plunged into all the terrors and atrocities of another Vietnam War which, justly or unjustly, would blacken the name of the British military and, internationally, the British name, I submitted that every British soldier should be withdrawn without delay. I did this, not only against the terrifying experience of Vietnam "slow involvement" but, no less, against the fear that the province of Ulster would reproduce the sad experience of the Province of Bengal. Deplorable that Irish heads should be cracked, in a Belfast "as English as Glasgow or Cardiff": but if they had to be, better that the sectarian Irish should be seen to do the cracking themselves.

That urgent decision on Indian Independence had to be made I do not doubt. The explosive situation certainly did not admit of British delay (whatever may be said today)—nor is there a particle of justice in the suggestion that Cyril Radcliffe, brought in by the Viceroy as a respected judge, drew the frontier (whatever incautious and premature disclosures, prior to finalisation, may have been made at a lower level to the Governor of the Punjab, Jenkins) in any fashion other than of the strictest impartiality. There were threats of assassination of Jinnah—so that the Viceroy, with extraordinary personal courage, chose to ride with him in the same carriage through the streets of Karachi. Both the Punjab and Bengal were on the verge of civil war. The latter situation determined the decision of Gandhi, in consultation with and on the advice of Mountbatten, to go and sit the days out—and the "nights of the long knives"—in Calcutta along with the Moslem leaders, especially Suhrawardy.

In Hyderabad Sir Walter Monckton at least got an agreement out of the Nizam which Patel, in an emotional interview, initialled as a sign of personal affection for Sir Walter—but which the Nizam's advisers, to their own cost, were foolish enough to tear up. Neither the Nizam nor the dithering Maharaja of Kashmir displayed any quality of statesmanship.

I was on the tarmac when the Viceroy's plane first came in to Delhi. Lord Louis invited me to stay with him and Edwina Mountbatten at Viceregal Lodge for a week, on my return from China. It was interesting to watch the game of social chess firmly played by Edwina Mountbatten as hostess, thanks to which Jinnah and the Sikh leader, the Maharaja of Patiala, were moved on to the same sofa in the hope that they would agree on some acceptable political formula. On the third day after his arrival, Lord Louis invited me alone to his private study to discuss the political situation and, especially, the Mahatma.

I expressed the view that most men are best judged by what is known about their attitudes in their youth. The Mahatma was a lawyer and, once one moved on to the discussion of legal details, nothing but an obstinate wrangle was to be expected. However, as a young man in South Africa, Gandhi had been beaten up in a colour-bar row in Durban. No other than Joseph Chamberlain, by cable from Westminster, had ordered the arrest of his assailants. The Mahatma was a three-times war-*décoré* and I was confident that he was emotionally pro-British. I was also sure that the great little man had much on his chest, and if Lord Louis invited him to unburden himself, even to the extent of recalling his life-story, and only then put to him the essential questions, I was certain that Lord Louis would get the answers he wanted.

The Viceroy listened with that kind of instant attention which recalled Roosevelt. Naval officer, film-star, royal, executive to the finger-tips, I had no particle of doubt that Lord Louis was a very great man and entirely after my own heart. When I returned from China, to stay with him, he commented: "Well, I took your advice. It was quite true that we had to listen to the whole story of his life, but in the end we got the agreement we wanted." It was one manifestation of Lord Louis' heart-warming generosity that he gave me credit (others may perchance have made the same general proposal) for the critical suggestion. In a recent luncheon conversation at Romsey I have re-confirmed the general outline of this episode. I have not observed that all statesmen are equally generous: they tend to listen to good ideas and then discover these were all along their own.

The Mahatma I met five times in all. I was deeply concerned, as I had been before the war, with the assessment of pacifism as politically valid. Especially I wanted to discover how far he was himself an absolute pacifist. I met him in Simla, along with Rajkumari; in his *ashram* in Delhi, when I accompanied him to his prayer-meeting in the Maidan; and, finally—the fifth time in all— I was summoned to him by telegram to meet him in 1947, at his rooms in the sweepers' quarters. The telegram ran: "Going Delhi Sunday morning. There four days and return here. Catch me any point. Gandhiji."

The telephones in that quarter of Delhi did not operate, so I took a taxi and chanced the convenience of the time. Miss Slade met me and told me the Mahatma was that day very busy. He had to receive a formal Tibetan delegation from the Dalai Lama and then, Dr Radhakrishnan, later President of India. But he wanted to see me alone and she would consult. She came back. Would I mind talking to the Mahatma as he took his bath? It was the best chance. (I have always found this an effective answer to those who said they were "too busy to talk.") I accepted. We talked for about ten minutes and I left him in the midst of his Tibetans giving them a moral exhortation, and with Sir Sarvepalli Radhakrishnan waiting audience in the garden. Among other gifts, rolls of silk, the Calcutta photo of the Dalai Lama and the rest, the Tibetan delegation presented some figurines, clothed in tinsel national costume. "Tell your great little Lama, I call him great because of his office and little because he is young enough to be my grandson," he preached to the goggling Tibetans, "that the Buddha came, a poor man and humble, without tinsel. Beware of tinsel."

It was on the occasion of this visit of 1947 that I was also given, on the introduction of Sir Francis Rose, the opportunity of meeting Shri Aurobindo, the third member with Tagore and Gandhi of the Indian founding trinity. I was indeed aware of the story of the young and retiring Gandhi going, in the early days, to pay his respects to Aurobindo, then enjoying the free air of French-ruled Pondicherry. After a long and deferential pause, Gandhi asked the *guru*: "What shall we do to restore the glory of India?" Aurobindo, without looking up, laconically commented: "India is already in its glory." He then continued his reading of *The Times* newspaper. Hence I was not totally surprised when I received from Aurobindo's French wife a summons which read to the effect that Shri Aurobindo would be giving a *darshan*—shall we say, "a ceremonial manifestation" as of the Host or of de Gaulle?—at a given date, but that, at such a *darshan*, "there would be no discussion".

I meditated and then replied, expressing my thanks, recording that I had "just come on from Rome where"—as I shall tell later— "I had spent half an hour in private discussion with the Sovereign Pontiff, Pius XII", and adding that I now had an appointment, at the time mentioned, to meet in Calcutta "that very humble and great man, Mahatma Gandhi. Therefore, with extreme regret, I should not be able . . .", etc. etc. I heard no more.

Some of my good Quaker friends were, I believe, rather shocked that I was so persistent in trying to ascertain (shall I say, precisely as a political scientist?) the exact nature of Gandhi's pacifism. I was told that I "was trying to draw truth out of a well with a hook": the Mahatma's views were more mystical than precise. I do not myself know why truth should not be drawn out of a well, if it chances to be there, and I do not like an evasive piety on matters of such high human importance. But I have already described these interchanges in my *In the Path of Mahatma Gandhi*, and have no need to repeat them here.

Briefly, to the question whether, supposing a Kantian impartial world tribunal to exist and that such a tribunal gave a judgement, the Mahatma approved *police action* to support its execution, Gandhi's answer was "Yes". This statement was later confirmed by a message in writing through Rajkumari Amrit Kaur. Later attempts, in some Indian quarters, to show that the Mahatma was only concerned with civil resistance inside India, I believe to be invalid. He had a wider view. *The New Statesman*, reshaped by Martin, took to praising Nehru as the secular progressive and to a snide view of Gandhi—prominent although Kingsley Martin made himself at Gandhi's funeral—as a religious reactionary. This also was invalid. But this qualification of his (a very wise one) on his doctrine seems to me of the highest importance. Absolute pacifist he was not. What he did say—and I regarded this as at least questionable—was that it would be easier to convert all the world to an organised pacifism, a non-violent resistance, than to convert world tribunals of lawyers to professional impartiality in politics. I disagreed; but Gandhi had a case.

The real trouble, as I have said earlier, with Pacifism as an absolute philosophy (as distinct from the vocational duty of physician or priest) is that it offers no deterrent means, beyond appeal to conscience, for halting an aggressive tyranny and, despising "the secular sword", has no dialogue or recommendation to make about how the rule of law and peace shall be enforced. The virtue of justice is sacrificed to a virtue, more emotional than rational, of charity. In older but still valid terms, the problem was and is how to confront the original sin of man without grace—or, if one prefers the style, the passions of the ape-cousin without reason but sustained by power. It must be emphasised that there is no predestination of men to damnation; nothing that prevents them, without themselves being gods, to be made in the rational image of God; no necessary absence of grace nor are they "in general, vicious". They are not; but some are.

In theory, proposals for world government and even for regional government have more to offer. In practice, pacifism finds its justification in scepticism about how many of the world's so-called "just wars", without tribunal, are indeed just. (Kant said "none".) What we can say is that today the claims of any self-styled "Absolute Sovereign State" to break Natural Law are, by definition, unjust and to be non-violently resisted by its citizens.

Thanks to the Viceroy (and his car) I visited Jaipur, "the rose-red city" with its French-inspired street planning; and, thanks to

Sir C. P. Ramaswami Aiyar, I visited Travancore and stood on the point of Cape Cormorin. In Trivandrum I met that quite remarkable man, who became my close personal friend, Archbishop Mar Ivanios. The very ancient Church of St Thomas was a Christian Church before the English or Scots or even the Irish were converted. The Christian community in India, it is seldom remembered, is larger than the Sikh and far larger than the Parsee—although enjoying less publicity as a distinctive pressure group. (If all Christians wore turbans and beards it might be different.) Mar Ivanios told me of his hope to build a new college; and showed me the still cobra-infested field, with the trenches outlined, where he hoped to build it. He asked for my help and I promised it.

In 1952 I returned, nominally as Provost of that College, but actually to give advice on finance and policy. This enabled me to see India, not from air or train, but intimately, travelling from village to village and staying the night. They paid me a sum so large in their terms that I was ashamed; but it yet left me so far in debt that I had to go to the University of California to recuperate financially. My advice was that Indian students were too "literary", too fond of acquiring Arts degrees. What India needed was, above all, to develop agriculture; and I recommended the College to strengthen itself in biology and the chemistry and sciences of soils. I added that I thought they might find some of the great Foundations—alack! more likely American than British—to be interested. Incidentally, such farm work, although not Brahmin, was very consistent with the great Christian Benedictine tradition. I hope and believe my advice was good.

Incidentally, I always recall the pretty story of the present Archbishop of Canterbury, Dr Michael Ramsey, causing speculation about why, unlike so many British colonels, he seemed to prefer the Hindus to the Moslems. His chaplain explained that the reason for the preference was quite simple: "More High Church. . . ."

In 1949, my wife, still smarting from being refused an exit visa for the India Women's Conference during the war, went to India to attend the World Pacifist Conference. In January 1963, we were both invited as guests of the Government of India; stayed with Nan Pandit, then Governor of Bombay (about whom Vera wrote a book), and with Miss Naidu, Sarojini's daughter, Governor of Bengal. We learned that the gravel, outside the (then British) Governor's House was imported so that the footsteps of any trespasser, or even would-be assassin, in the night, might the more readily be heard. We were received by President Radhakrishnan, and attended the Republic Day parade. It was impressive, if

w

lengthy. The elephants did not come on parade until lunchtime;
but Nehru had made it, in best May Day style, a kind of general
demonstration of the people. I also had a quite lengthy talk at the
American Embassy with Ambassador John Kenneth Galbraith.

When I was staying with S. C. Bose in Calcutta, the recently
appointed (1946) Governor of Bengal—who left in 1947—was Sir
Frederick Burrows, an ex-railwayman. He did not entirely earn
Bose's commendation and there were some mutterings about my
becoming Governor. (However, Bose added that he was limited to
recommending Indians). Galbraith was mundanely more lucky.
Canadian born, he probably knew less about India than I did—
but for all that he became Ambassador, and indeed, wrote a book
about the fact. The Average Adjuster may suggest that I should
have taken Schlesinger's advice and myself become an American.
Anyhow, I didn't. Outside the Embassy was a notice requesting
visitors "not to molest the ducks" on the duckpond. . . We
endeavoured not to do this.

The *Indian Express* of Madras, was good enough to write, "Vera
Brittain and her husband, Professor George Catlin, are what
Sidney and Beatrice Webb are to Fabianism. If the Webbs have
done more through just one book to popularise the socialist sixth
of the world than the torrent of propagandist tracts, the Catlins
have done for India more than most Indians can claim to have
done." It was very flattering. Whether it was true or not is another
matter.

As myself a Victorian, and proud to be such—as a child I saw
an open carriage and, within it, a black lace bonnet and an old lady
leave Buckingham Palace: "*That* is the Queen"—I noted with
interest the statue of Victoria, Queen-Empress, still regnant in
Calcutta. She may have been a little woman but as, on any
reckoning, the mother of all her peoples, she was also a great
queen. It is some proof of Indian maturity and of the adult
recognition of the values of tradition and continuity in history that
the statue still remains. There is something profoundly uncultured
in destroying statues (as did the Vandals) and in a mob frivolity in
the changing of names. Let us hope that "the Square of the
Heavenly Peace" remains such. Quotations from what Victoria
said about freedom and responsibility are cut in stone on the
portals of Lutyens' great redstone House of the Legislature; and
their message remains.

It was, however, the Republic Day Parade which recalled to me
the sixteen-year-earlier experience of leaving Viceregal Lodge to
see the immense reception given in its gardens by the Last of the
Viceroys. In those gardens I watched the sun go down; the

magnificent, turbanned Sikh bodyguard at attention as on parade; the flag, soon to be replaced by that of India's freedom, still flying. It was the end of the *Raj*, the end of the *Kaiser-i-Hind*. With all its defects, it was the end of an era neither mean nor ignoble, and many had given dedicated lives to its service. The *Raj* had, for the first time, united all India and it had contributed something to the good and the civil peace of India. In that I continue to feel pride.

Lord Attlee has written that it is almost unique for a great power, in full possession of a vast rule, to yield it without bloodshed. The Commonwealth replaced the Empire, and of that Commonwealth the Queen still remains head. The story is something of which to be proud, without regret. Let others be busy writing about the sunset of Empire; my concern is about the sunrise that comes, whatever defeatists may predict from their books. I know that Pulin Seal now proposes a book in which he will show that Gandhi was in error and Nehru wrong, and that the true hero of Indian nationalism was the Japanese ally, Subhas Bose. Hence, the secret of the British withdrawal was really incapacity to rule due, not just to financial strain, but to the cessation of army loyalty. It was this challenge by Subhas Bose which brought the end. Even were these arguments substantial (and the history has still to be written), it yet fails to explain the means and method of transfer.

Of itself it fails to explain "the nights of the long knives" in Calcutta and the unfortunate division of India. It also treats as negligible those very principles, not trivial in politics, which led Cripps and others (including myself) to seek, and seek successfully, to carry the British Government under Attlee with them in a peaceful transfer of power to a free and free-choosing Indian authority. Principles and morale, for the cynical, are unimportant in politics; but they are not that unimportant. It has indeed happened that there are now two Governments in the Indian subcontinent. The Pakistan Minister of Information, Dr Khorashi at that time, invited me to Karachi. I was happy to know that I was not unacceptable in either State.

I prefer rather to dwell, as I have written elsewhere, on that strange love-affair which still exists between the English and the whole great sub-continent and its peoples. (I say English because the Celts, Irish, Welsh and Highland Scots, who have contributed so much, are yet something else again.) The English discovered in the pattern and subtlety of the Indian mind, somewhat imperfectly illustrated by E. M. Forster, something fascinatingly different from its own. The Indians discovered in the English certain downright and sober qualities which it is perhaps not

entirely an impertinence to name Roman. Both gained. I leave it to
journalists such as Mr Anthony Lewis, of the *Herald Tribune*, to
discern that we were xenophobic.

§ iii

At the Delhi Inter-Asian Conference, my Chinese friend of
wartime London, George Yeh was along. It was one of Nehru's
main hopes that the next Conference would be held in Nanking,
although he also hoped to make Delhi the focal point of Asia. In
the early war-days first Chiang (supported by Stalin) had opposed
Japan and Haile Selassie had opposed Mussolini; and then (after
some delay) Britain had "stood alone", opposed to Hitler. I recall
seeing later, in the house of an innocent tea-planter in Travancore,
at the back of his dinner-table, a framed picture of four wartime
allied heroes: Roosevelt, Churchill, Stalin, Chiang. A very
embarrassing static in the moving film-show of history. George Yeh
asked me whether I would be interested in going to China. At that
time Under-Secretary for Foreign Affairs in Nanking and later
Foreign Secretary of Nationalist China, George made immediate
arrangements thanks to which I was flown out to Shanghai.

There was an unwonted thrill in boarding the plane bearing the
Chinese symbols which told that it belonged to "the Middle
Kingdom", at Dum-dum Airport, Calcutta (where I later saw my
first jet-plane). It was long since I had felt the same sense of fresh
delight as when, having flown over the lower Himalayan ranges
and the route of the Burma Road, Brahmaputra, Irrawaddy and
Mekong, I arrived to breakfast outside the Yunnan walled city of
Kunming. While I have loved many countries, or at least some
few, no country has had for me the same fascination as China and
few people more than the Chinese—until recent "cultural developments" so industrious, so "common-sense", so much natural
gentlemen, with so neat a sense of humour; so well-mannered at all
levels (unlike those parts of the democratic West where individual
independence and boorish manners are identified); with so
magnificent a cultural tradition; a civilization literally the oldest in
the world. No country has more reverenced the scholar or been
more charactised by respect and dignity. If I were Chinese, I also
would be xenophobic and regard outsiders as vulgarian.

I always recall recommending to some visiting Chinese pub-
lishers in wartime to publish a collection of the Chinese classics in
English for British libraries. "Why in English? They should learn
Chinese." There is another side, indeed, to this coin which few
Chinese will forget. The story is of a formal dinner at which some
Occidental man of business found himself seated next to a Chinese.

For conversation, when the soup was served, he commented: "Likee soupee?" The Chinese bowed in affirmation. Later, the same Chinese, Dr Alfred Sze, the distinguished Ambassador, was called upon to speak which he did in impeccable English. When he sat down, he turned to his neighbour and remarked: "Likee speechee?" Incidentally, this may give a clue to why British consuls are frog-marched around. I also recall a story, told me by the American Vice-Consul in Shanghai about his Chinese friend, a wealthy merchant and man of humour, following a visit by U.S. Senators and Congressmen. The Vice-Consul waited for the comment to come. "Are most of your legislators like that?" "Probably." "Ah! I see that in your country a successful man becomes a Senator and travels around the world. Here he takes another wife."

If it comes to pass in the course of the centuries that only one people could dominate the world, since it could not be the Italians, even from the Vatican, I would prefer it to be the Chinese, who are natural humanists. (The French are far too chauvinist to be tolerable.) All this does not in the least convert me into a Maoist. Dr Hu Shih told me that Mao, poet, librarian and scholar, was one of the finest students he had ever had. Nevertheless, it is my conviction that, within two centuries, the fanaticisms of Mao— himself, be it said, no *apparatchik* or organisation man—will be as much rejected as the French would like to reject Marat and Robespierre. The grand tradition of historic China will reassert itself, with its twin bases in the family and in scholarly merito- cracy, not mediocracy.

In Nanking I saw not only the Prime Minister and Foreign Minister but also, amid surroundings of puritanical austerity, the Generalissimo (who presented me with a photograph of himself beautifully inscribed in Chinese characters). I travelled to Peking —my cablegram there from Delhi had been returned to me "town unknown": the Post Office only recognised "Peiping"—in a military plane with bucket-seats. In transit my nose was assaulted by the sharp smell of chemicals. It could have been some bomb. Then I identified it: it was my own suitcase. My medical bottle of ammonia had blown its cork. I spoke no Chinese. It could have been a very nasty incident. However, it passed off cheerfully.

I delivered a brief set of lectures in the University of Peking under the chairmanship of the Rector, my old Cornell friend, the very distinguished humanist, Dr Hu Shih. Dr Hu, in terms of his work in Chinese vernacular poetry, has been saluted as "the Dante of Modern China"—more as author of *De Vulgari Eloquentia* than of any Chinese *Divina Commedia*. In Peking, escorted by Hu

Shih, I viewed the Temple of Heaven and the exquisite Temple of Agriculture; called on the Cardinal of Peking, Archbishop John Tsien; wandered beneath the walls of the Forbidden City; and wrote a few poems. I looked at the paintings by a French Jesuit (pressed to do so by my infinitely courteous rickshaw driver) of the Emperor Chi'en Lung, in black armour, and of his favoured concubine with powdered Pompadour "hair-do". The square of the Gate of the Heavenly Peace was indeed busy; but there was peace by the water lilies in the moats and even on the side-streets, where one could find dromedaries asleep.

Most peaceful of all was to drink tea with my hosts on a small boat, floating on the great lake at Hangchow, where at fourteen points on the shore the same Emperor Chi'en Lung had put up stones or steles inscribed with his own poems, to indicate to the traveller what, in the view of the Celestial Emperor, were the best places from which to appreciate the beauties of the lake. It somehow does not occur to me that the Greater London Council would do that or, even in committee, compose poems.

The lectures were perhaps of more than trifling importance, since they were the germ of a pattern of argument which was later developed in my *Systematic Politics*. Dr Hu congratulated me on my courage in criticising Marxism to a student audience in Peking. The truth is, nevertheless, that Marx, an *émigré* to France and to England, was too much the child of the nineteenth century ever fully to understand (far less to explain) the nature of community, although he was "*the* scientific Communist", or to note its dangers, including the dangers of emotional and insurgent nationalism. The materio-economic interpretation was not enough. Marx, thoroughly urban, would have scarcely understood "the thoughts of Mao" on peasant revolution or the almost Anarchist quality of the Great Proletarian Cultural Revolution, where a thousand flowers ought to bloom—a thought worthy of Lao-Tze himself. I have not seen it elsewhere noted that "to study the thoughts of Mao" is entirely in the good Chinese tradition of studying (and being examined in) the thoughts of Confucius. Mao indeed is himself an anti-Confucian. But it is therefore the more probable that no little of his inspiration comes from the rival Chinese philosophy of Anarchist spontaneity and hatred of organising bureaucracy—the philosophy of Taoism and of Lao-tze. Some years later I was to visit Hu Shih's tomb in Taipeh—a simple but soaring monument like the man himself. He was a great scholar and a great man. Always I had revered Chinese humanism—something sharply different from occidental scientific humanism. Hu Shih was Confucian to the bone.

It can yet prove to have been a catastrophic misfortune for the West that, at a critical moment in post-war history in 1947, General George C. Marshall, Secretary of State, was an ill man and, like many a retired general, much in search of pacific solutions, which liberal and doubtless well-intentioned advisers were prepared to outline for him. One of these was that the Government of Chiang, our earliest ally, was thoroughly corrupt and that the wave of the future and the "mandate of Heaven" lay elsewhere. Churchill was temperamentally (and indeed provincially) unable to believe that any Chinaman could be of political importance. Edgar Snow, in *Red Star over China*, had romanticised Mao and his comrades, so that the contention of the government of China that it could not, in a civil war, negotiate with rebels with arms in their hands, when it had also to withstand the Japanese, fell flat. Anti-Chiang Chinese lectured around in Britain. In London I saw something of the Wellington Koos, who were our guests as we were theirs at the Chinese Embassy. Dorothy Woodman, a mental *apparatchik*, seemed to be of considerable influence there.

In Peking I said frankly to Hu Shih that the charge against his Government, which alienated support, was that it was alleged to be thoroughly corrupt. Hu's reply was that a fully representative sample of these Chinese civil servants had been his own students; that the value of the Chinese currency had fallen so far that, even to live, they had to take on supplementary work; but that, far from being corrupt, when compared with some European municipalities he was surprised how little corrupt they were. He was a most honourable man and I accepted his word for it against interested propagandists, which included a London *Times* correspondent, a most indiscreet person fellow-travelling in enthusiasm for Mao, with whom I shared a hotel room in Hong Kong. Once again I looked at the pervert sources from which the unhappy British public was getting its information.

The British Ambassador in Nanking, very recently arrived from Belgrade, pointed to a map of China and assured me, on his ambassadorial word, that in the near future all China would break up under rival provincial governors, *tachuns*, and war-lords. He seemed to regard this not without satisfaction. The great foreign merchant houses such as Jardine Matheson, bitterly resenting the new nationalism of the Kuo-min-tang which pressed China's sovereign rights against foreign concessionaires, were of the same rosy view. China would break up. As the lesser evil, one could even do a deal with the Communists, who would be weak, local and inoffensive. Even Chiang's own American military subordinate, General Stilwell, with singular loyalty habitually referred to his chief as "the pin-head".

The conduct, moreover, of some European Shanghai merchants did not cause them to be regarded with affection by the Chinese. The admirable Agatha Harrison told me how child workers were to be found dead from exhaustion or malnutrition, outside Shanghai factory gates; and how, when she saw the European factory management about it, the managers disclaimed responsibility. "Business was business." Unofficial maps existed and circulated of how the carcase of China was to be divided up between the vulture powers, France, Britain and Russia. The Russians, in Outer Mongolia, did not remain content with "spheres of influence". *They* were the great colonial imperialists. Indeed the conquest by them of Russian Turkestan is quite recent, Tashkent falling in 1865.

The prophesies of H.M. Ambassador and of the British merchant houses were indeed fantastically in error, although doubtless passed to Westminster as reliable information from "the man on the spot". It is hence not remarkable that today the Peking Government should loathe the very bones of the Westerners. What is more remarkable is that Chiang and his remarkable wife have not supported that view, even before 1948. There is, further, an irony in the fact that the United States, which alone had a fair record of "the Open Door" and devoted its share of the Boxer Indemnity to bringing Chinese students to American universities, and which alone kept its hands clean in the bloody matter of the professed carve-up of China, has been until recently the peculiar target of Peking animosity. However, if "peculiar", yet no longer "alone". In what Winston Churchill called "the symmetry of mutual invective", the Kremlin today declares that the dictator Mao will be answerable to the Chinese people for crimes such that the regime of Chiang is less reactionary, while the Maoists denounce "the fascist excesses" of "the Soviet swine". What ironic fun for a man from Mars.

China, most numerous in population, is one of the world's greatest civilisations, as well as perhaps of all the most ancient. Its Confucianism is a human and pacific model. Nevertheless, in our own days we have seen great European countries, proud of their culture, go mad in the mass. It is sad that from Peking should come such doctrinaire drivel. Mao perchance is more Taoist than organisation man, with some semi-anarchist belief in spontaneity. But in the land of Confucius we have adolescents marching in the name of "the Great Proletarian Cultural Revolution". (Also we have had the Komsomols and the Hitler-junge and other manifestations of "youth") "Burn Chou". Ironically the

Communist Party *apparatchiks* and the very workers of Nanking are denounced by Red Guards as "the instrument of the bourgeois and reactionary Communist Party Committee of the province" (*Sunday Times*, 8th January 1967). And then following, after the anarchist schoolboys comes the army. Where stands "the Chairman" on all this? Where will lie the Mandate of Heaven? In the end, I suggest, the immemorial tradition will prevail. The Russians will remain Russians. And the Celestial Empire, as ever proud in its contempt for the hairy barbarians, will remain Chinese. I wish it well.

In 1963, on George Yeh's renewed invitation, my wife and I were able to visit Taiwan going on from India, and I had the joy, anticipated from early childhood, of myself seeing the Feast of Lanterns; we met the ever-beautiful "Missima", Sun Yat-sen's sister-in-law Sung May-ling, Mme Chiang; and I was able to report back to my Indian friends (who had encouraged me to go) about the degree of improbability of some new, armed Chinese intervention into India on the Brahmaputra. I hope my information in a critical matter was helpful; at least it was accurate. Prosperous Formosa was not ill-informed.

In 1959 I was the guest at the Indian Embassy in Paris of the Ambassador, the late Sardar K. M. Panikkar, a man of brilliant ability and a rare sense of humour, a joy in conversation, who had earlier been India's ambassador in Cairo and Peking. A distinguished scholar of Christ Church, Oxford, an emphatic Indian nationalist, not without aspirations as a poet and a historian of merit, I shall venture to call him my close friend. For hours we discussed the strategy of the Indian Ocean and the need for India and Pakistan to assume the naval responsibilities from Aden to Singapore, once carried by the *Raj*. Ruby ring on finger, he was famous for his Lenin-like beard. He had not always worn it. Premier of an Indian Maharaja at a very young age, he had complained that he was never put on delegations going outside the State. "But you are so young," replied the Maharaja. "If I may venture to say so, Your Highness, you are younger." "Ah! my dear Panikkar, but I have a beard." The Sardar grew his beard. Nevertheless, when I met him, in about 1950 in the Hotel Gotham, New York, in the days of the Indian troubles, he was clean-visaged as a babe. "You did not comment that I have shaved my beard?" "I did not like to—but why?" The response was very Panikkar. "Well, I am perfectly orthodox Hindu and, with all these disturbances, I see no reason to be assassinated on the supposition that I am a Moslem."

The Sardar's daughter married a Kerala Communist and he

certainly had no anti-Communist prejudice. One of his comments, made in Paris and of the more importance owing to this detachment, I shall not forget. "If George Marshall had not been a sick man, and if the Americans had been prepared to continue all-out aid to Chiang, for historical reasons Chiang could have continued until this day to control all China south of the Yang-tze." Although this might have reduced the contemporary pressure upon Russia to look for co-existence with the West, had Chiang thus remained in charge, the history of today's affairs would certainly be remarkably different.

In 1953 I was invited by the British Foreign Office to speak in Bangkok, Rangoon, pagoda'ed Mandalay, Singapore and Djakarta. Having visited from the Golden Gate in San Francisco shadowed by Tamalpais, to the Long Bar in Shanghai; from cloudy Reykjavik to bright Blomfontein; from Anacapri to Haiti of the Zombies; to Santa Domingo to meet the almost blind Archbishop of the oldest cathedral of the New World, I added Bali. In Singapore I had the opportunity to meet Malcolm Macdonald. I was also invited to Hanoi; but this invitation was later cancelled "owing to disturbances".

I have a planned ignorance of Middle Eastern affairs. For the most part policy here seems to reveal the ghost of Anthony Eden, crowned and sitting on the grave thereof. What recent events do show indeed is the folly of abandoning—or, in humiliating fashion, attempting to abandon—an "East of Suez" policy (is not Palestine east of Suez?) or underestimating Hong Kong, Singapore, Cyprus, Malta, and Gibraltar. Here I basically disagree with the "little Europeanism" (not even good for Europe) of Enoch Powell and Christopher Mayhew. I believe in a wide naval policy. A little more might be spent on the Navy and the nurses and a little less on Modern Art.

As to South-East Asia, since I have not visited Vietnam, I do not wish here to express opinions about it. I can only say that there may be a case in Vietnam for a negotiation which will "let the water find its own level".

There is a case, for a decade or more, for "the enclave plan", at Cam Ran and Pleiku, as advocated by General Gavin (who has been "on the spot" and knows what he is talking about) or on the Ben-hai—as in the American naval base on Cuba—for American military enclaves as cities of refuge for those who will otherwise be murdered. Every country, even the Congo, is entitled to its own civil war—but there are limits to international Great Power toleration. Further, it can be argued that, just as Eden's preoccupation, in collusion with the French and Israelis, with the

Suez Canal (in part, a matter of getting the French "off the hook" in Algeria), diverted attention from the Hungarian Revolt, so American concentration on Vietnam tends to leave a void and a doubt on positive policy about the radically more important continent of Europe. That the United States is "primarily a Pacific Power" is a myth and a distortion which ignores the permanent elements in Russian policy.

The American airmen fly low, at their risk, into flak to pin-point specifically military targets, and it should be said that America and the President deserve some credit for deliberately fighting a "limited war" which, were it an "unlimited war", it is arguable that they could win tomorrow. All war is yet very dirty, nasty, immoral. It is not for those who indulged in "massacre by bombing" of industrial workers, or in burning women and children in Dresden and Hamburg, to talk. At least they should give the Australians and New Zealanders, who are under fire, the opportunity to speak first.

It is a fact little known that, under the original arrangements of 1945, British troops were sent to pacify Vietnam. However, on Chiang's representations, as I am reminded by Lord Mountbatten, the British were limited to south of the sixteenth parallel (not seventeenth) and Chinese divisions were sent in to the north. Ho Chi-Minh's forces were built up in resistance to the Chinese occupation. This is a fact worth pondering. Further, those who denounce American bombing in Vietnam must say whether they support or denounce "positive action" in Suez and Palestine, where napalm has been used (*not* by the Americans). On whom does Israel depend? The reliable French? Will Israel never bomb an Arab child? Conversely, should we be consistent pacifists, whatever happens to Israel? The critics (except on the thesis that "America is always wrong") cannot both eat their cake and keep it.

Whether the *New York Times* has advanced American prestige by publishing the "Pentagon Papers" or whether the American Congress has not shown cowardice (while passing the dubious Tonking Resolution) by declining to exercise its own rights under the Constitution of declaring—or refusing to declare—war, there is not space to discuss here. There is a fascinating parallel between the American Vietnam war—unlike Cuba, "too far from base for success," as Chairman Mao sagely observed to Edgar Snow—and the British Boer War, with the reservation that the Boers were united in opposition while it is of the essence of the matter that the Vietnamese are not. In both cases a world power endeavours to beat down a small, poor army, of which the tactics do not conform with expected military standards in warfare; and the technically superior army suffers local defeats and the others, as "under-dogs", arouse international sympathy.

The Boer War terminated in a Treaty which, in the long run, was to prove most advantageous to the Boers. Granted changed relations with Peking (for quite other reasons in the international chess-board), whereas a patent and explicit American defeat could so far upset—as with the Russians cut up by the Japanese at Port Arthur—the world balance of power and encourage Soviet militancy, it is not clear that an American withdrawal in Vietnam, short of "cut and run" would leave American prestige permanently damaged. That war itself, be it in the Germany of the Thirty Years War or in Vietnam or in Ulster, sacrifices truth to lies, involves atrocities and leaves historic scars is one of those basic facts of political life which makes the quest for stable world peace—did we know how—a moral imperative.

I had campaigned for the independence of India, not from any belief in nationalism greater than Tagore's own—Tagore and Gandhi, like Mazzini, were both internationalists—and certainly *not* from any desire to disrupt the Commonwealth. I had cam-paigned precisely because I did not believe in the right of any one democracy, like Athens in its worst moments, to direct the pattern of life of another people or nation. The same principle of freedom would also apply, against an even more diverse background, as *Uhuru* in Africa; the same principle of mutual respect. When I wrote a brief "life" of Jefferson, for Barratt Brown's symposium, nothing I came across caused me more pleasure than the story of the Negro farm-hand opening the gate for Thomas Jefferson and his son-in-law, Randolph, on horseback. The farm-hand raised his hat. The Third President raised his. "Why did you do that?" asked Randolph. "Because," replied Jefferson, "I should be sorry to think that a Negro farm-hand was a better gentleman than myself."

The ever-energetic Sylvia Pankhurst had roped me in, as she roped in Lord Winster and the Earl of Stamford, to be patrons of the Princess Tsahai Hospital in Addis Ababa—as a consequence of which I very briefly met that most remarkable man, the Emperor Haile Selassie, the Lion of Judah. In connection with Creech Jones's organisation, the Friends of Africa (of which I was for a while treasurer), I had met Seretse Khama. In London I met Bishop Trevor Huddleston, then of the Masai and now of Stepney. I regret that I have not met Kenyatta. On the one occasion that I met Nkrumah, he was arrogantly rude to his devoted admirer, Fenner Brockway, and I concluded that he was suffering badly from swollen head. A brief experience in Haiti, land of Zombies, voodoo

THE INDEPENDENCE OF INDIA 339

and the gods of Benin, did not encourage roseate dreams. I would
have wished to see much of central Africa; but it did not turn out
that way.

Morocco we visited several times; and saw in the amethystine
twilight the Tower of Marrakesh. One visit had an amusing and
unpremeditated side effect. In Rabat, as guest of the Pakistani
ambassador, I had the opportunity of talking with several members
of the diplomatic corps at a time when, by the merest chance, it
happened that the disappearance of Ben Barka in Paris was the
affaire scandaleuse of the moment. The Paris argument was that,
in the best James Bond tradition, the Minister of the Interior of
Morocco had chosen personally to visit France to supervise the
murder of a rival. Some thought that the French *Sécurité*, with
its mixed and dubious composition, was not guiltless. But any
French involvement was, at the time, contemptuously described by
the French President as "a subordinate and sordid affair", to be
dismissed from mind as incompatible with the known purity of
French politics. Actually the French para-military security forces
have been often sordid and vicious, and seldom pure. In the end,
it was the head of the Paris police who moved out of office to other
pastures.

The Friends of Africa organisation was primarily concerned
with S. Africa and the Protectorates. I have already mentioned
Winifred Holtby's preoccupation with the development of multi-
racial trades unionism there; and the work of Margaret and
William Ballinger and, in Kenya, of Dr Norman Keys. My only
effective visit, going on beyond the African coast-line in circum-
navigation from Casablanca and Teneriffe to Mombasa and Mog-
hadishu, was in 1964. Along with Julian Huxley, Richard Hillary,
Vivian Fuchs, Lawrens van der Post and others, Vera and I were
invited to Durban by the Vice-Chancellor of the University of
Natal, to speak on the occasion of the Jubilee of that University.
We also visited Cape Town, going on to Durban by the coast
route, Blomfontein, Pretoria and Johannesburg; and talked to
people in the widest possible spectrum of political opinion, from
supporters of Verwoerd and from de Graaf Villiers to Nobel-
prizeman Chief Luthuli in his prison. Some years later, having met
Dr Martin Luther King several times and in the most diverse
places and very much approving of his Gandhian, determined but
non-violent approach to racial problems, I was honoured to
become a Sponsor of the Martin Luther King Foundation. He
himself met the same fate as Gandhi—and Lincoln.

The core of the trouble in South Africa is the Broederbund.
Peace-aspiring English Liberals chose to forget that the Boers,

who typically believed that the Old Testament sanctioned slavery, had trekked up into the Transvaal precisely to get away from the British on the Cape who did not approve of their pristine, if not Neanderthal, *Rassen-theorie*. The Boers do not forget—although of the family of Jan Steyn in Blomfontein I have most pleasant memories.

We did not go up into Rhodesia. General de Gaulle did not treat his kith and kin kindly in Algeria—indeed, as a consequence, they wished to assassinate him. It is arguable —and I amused myself by playing with the idea—that the Prime Minister should have arrested Ian Smith (a more moderate man than some) in Downing Street on a charge of suspicion of complicity in treason against Her Majesty and Her forces, relying here on the impartiality of Her Majesty's judges. . . It would have got some Conservative army support. This would have brought the central issue of conspiracy or treasonous rebellion out into the front with a flaming clarity. Instead we have economic sanctions. Emphatically it is now a matter for the United Nations.

It is arguable that today the legal position is not clear; nor do the performances of Mr Kaunda or of the Nigerians improve the political position. The opinions of Dr Hastings Banda, Premier of Malawi, about Southern Africa and what is political "realism", have to be taken into account. Rhodesia is no more "a threat to peace" than Israel in the eyes of the Arab-Islamic world, the Arabs in the eyes of the Israelis, or the Pakistanis and Indians in each other's eyes. The fundamental issue is, hence, that of the status of Rhodesia as less than an independent dominion, free to shape its own constitution, but more than a Crown Colony. It would seem to be *de jure* not an independent political entity, guaranteed under the U.N. Charter (just as the earlier League guaranteed even Hitler's treatment of his German citizens), but *de facto* treated as self-governing. We live in a legal twilight thanks to a hesitant, indecisive and short-sighted British policy, which has its nemesis.

If a policy of "collective security" is to be taken seriously, then there is (as I have said) a case for "maintaining a presence" in the Far East, which links up strategically with Australasia. How far we can expend men and means effectively on a "South of Suez" policy is today more open to doubt, especially where there is no strong metropolitan sentiment of like-mindedness. One of our misfortunes is that the British have never worked out a philosophy of Commonwealth any more than, unlike the Romans, they did of Empire.

The courageous Vice-Chancellor in Natal, Dr Malesherbe, and his vivacious and high-principled wife, wished to see the University

Jubilee marked by a blow struck for liberalism. On the first night, when I had to speak, H.M. Governor-General, Mr Swart (later President of the Republic), explained in his opening speech that education and politics were necessarily interlocked; and that South Africans (white) were fully competent, without alien advice, to manage their own affairs. This somewhat ill-chosen gambit freed the way for an obvious follow-up. I could not but agree with the Governor-General about this interlocking; and I did not presume to interpret South African opinion. Likewise South Africans were not in a position to say what British opinion was, unless it was explained to them from the mother-country. (Incidentally, as I learned from the Dutch Ambassador, "the Netherlanders" were a peculiar target of Boer wrath.) I then did explain, succinctly and for the record, what this opinion was, especially on *apartheid* in education. Dr Malesherbe was pleased. Mr Swart was not.

I may not have contributed much on that platform in Durban, anymore than I may have as a Sponsor of the Martin Luther King Foundation. But at least I had yet more clearly defined my own position: emphatically and consistently a Commonwealth position. However, the relation to "the New Commonwealth" and the relation to "the Old Commonwealth" are historically different and can carry different consequences.

XV

HOBBY HORSES

IN the second chapter of this book I raised the problem of how far contemporary Western civilisation had any common public philosophy. The answer there was that Western civilisation did not have such a philosophy, save in so far as denial of its existence was itself a common philosophy. It had indeed a "climate"—permissive, valuing the transient as such, anarchist in fundamentals. It is the culture of the anti-hero and of anti-dignity, the age of poor youth put in the saddle by a calculating commerce, the age of the charlatan and the sophist.

As Malcolm Muggeridge has commented, we have the cult of "the broiler-house Bardot"—"Never, I should suppose, have human beings been so bombarded with sex as they are today on our side of the Iron Curtain." We have an architecture, in "commercial vernacular", parading as a new form of art what is indeed the miserly result of a cost economy. We have a new sculpture which broadly divides into Gruyère and Camembert types, full of holes or deliquescent. We have a poetry of crosswords and puns, which conspicuously fails to communicate meaning or to please with its music. We have painting where the painters seek to "buffalo" their patrons, whether art dealers or stockbrokers seeking good investments in novelty. Acceptable art is defined as being, not that which exalts the traditional into new masterpieces, but that which is "novel" by any standards. Of literature, William Faulkner's brother has recorded that at first Faulkner's books did not sell, so he deliberately peppered them with pornographic incident—and the sales followed. For the little known author or publisher who produces a *Last Exit to Brooklyn*, there is (sometimes) money in it.

Of some writers it can be said, as was said of Maupassant, "M. de Maupassant est en train de s'animaliser." We have a commercial world of ponces and panders, catering to the taste of the adolescent and talking about "freedom". We have a rhetorical praise of "freedom" and "free choice" which never asks itself the social question: What do we choose? There is much rhetoric, fundamentally the hypocrisy of the age, about human dignity; and, in the name of "realism", little respect for it. There is a reaction against reason in the name of the exalted passions—the

Platonic charioteer overthrown by the horses—or whoreses. We have a fence-sitting negative philosophy of "it is not our job to give any specific answers"—a neutral cloud of intelligent indecision. We have, in Paul Goodman's phrase, a civilisation "growing up absurd".

One of the very few merits of de Gaulle's régime was that in France, in some measure, national dignity has replaced vulgarity. It is not regarded as a proof of wisdom to have just laid aside diapers. Marxist scholars may have limited views but, in Communist countries, it is their views, not those of the light entertainment industry, that are sought. They have something there. The incoming tide of radical reform of manners, in the cycle of human affairs, will come and is fully due.

Our culture may not indeed be as vulgar as that of the Edwardians or of "the Gilded Age" in the States; it may conceivably be better than that about which the Emperors Tiberius and Decius lamented. But it is a distasteful one of *trompe l'oeil*, of commercial, profit-hunting advertising and of promotional "bogus", of which the soul is profit and its worship a golden calf superimposed on the tower of Babel. Unless watched, censored, controlled, a civilisation of the vulgar and bogus, with often a deliberate and evil cult of the ugly, inflamed by sensationalism, greed and the Caliban inferiority complex, will squander, amongst much else, the irreplaceable resources of civilisation and even of nature. In a poor choice, any day I prefer the communism of Esdraelon to beatnik anarchism—Marx to Spencer. In the rhythm of affairs the tide of permissiveness has almost reached high water-mark and will soon be due to ebb. The folly is nearly over. My own idea of the "good society", which I must leave for discussion elsewhere, would be a replica of neither extreme. Maybe Thomas More would be its patron or, perhaps, Confucius.

In October 1967, in Urbana, Illinois, a "voice" rang me up. "Scotland Yard speaking." I later discovered that it was in fact the voice of the Federal Bureau of Investigation (F.B.I.) "standing in" for Scotland Yard. "Will you go to Bow Street Police Court? A case of obscenity." Having been called as an expert witness for the prosecution at Marlborough Street Police Court in the case of a book called *Last Exit to Brooklyn*, published by the firm of Calder and Boyars, and the book having been found by a London jury to be obscene but the court having only local jurisdiction, it emerged that a further prosecution, this time by the police and not on private complaint, would take place before a new jury and the Bow Street magistrate. I was in a somewhat strong position since, not only had I sociological experience not excluding

Brooklyn, but I had been on the solicitors' lists for the defence in both the case of Radcliffe Hall's *Well of Loneliness* and of D. H. Lawrence's *Lady Chatterley's Lover*.

The Metropolitan Police, I was told, would pay my fare for the mere six thousand miles journey. There was, however, some delay and debate with Thos. Cook and Co. (as I commented to both parties) on whether the credit of the Metropolitan Police was good enough for the costs. As a result I found myself suddenly told to leave for London in twenty-four hours when I was (on other business) actually in New York—and without my passport or visa. As a British citizen B.O.A.C. was prepared to ship me to London. As I told Scotland Yard, their job was to get me back to New York. They did, "as if we were with you ourselves". Indeed I could have imported a cwt. of bullion without impediment. In due course I swept through customs and immigration under New York Police escort—and so back to Urbana.

In those days the doctrine, acceptable in the cultivated Oxbridge circles of E. M. Forster and friends, was in circulation that "the permissive" is the civilised. (Permissive of what?) Indeed one might almost say that there were no "limits of pure toleration". I had heard all these moral arguments, *pro* and *con*, in the days of Prohibition; and the answer seemed to be, not dogmatic, but empiric. Admittedly any law whatsoever sets limits; but this can be urged, in some quarters, as an excellent argument for less law and less social obligation. Friends would conduct themselves, as Rabelais said, just on the principle of honour—although certainly a fanatic for free choice such as Sartre might doubt even that value. Socrates, however, declined, as a citizen, to escape punishment, even if the citizenry were wrong.

I am afraid that I leaned, here and elsewhere, to the cynicism of a Marxist explanation. What would not be tolerated or even permitted in a Communist society would be accepted in a profit-competitive capitalist one. As a *Herald Tribune* article writer has cogently said: Shades of Dr Samuel Johnson! What is wrong with making money, so why this humbug and hypocrisy? There is very big money in pornography, so (to meet demand) why not sell it? Many books are, in the words to me of George Weidenfeld, "not commercial propositions". But pornography is such a proposition —not perhaps with a particular book but for publicity; and, in the whole market, big money, very big capitalist money indeed. (So, too, is pop singing, under a skilful agent; spy stories; and the autobiographies of very notorious criminals.) As a B.B.C. man said to me: to make the headlines or the T.V. studios it is necessary "to be sensational or, preferably, notorious"—a criminal (sitting back to the viewers) or an unnamed sympathiser with the "Angry Brigade" bomb throwers. Vice is news; and novelty is the breath of profit.

It is a sociological probability, demanding research although clearly short of a lawyer's or a logician's "proof", that what people —and not solely the mentally unstable 11 per cent being the number of those who have been, are or will be in mental hospitals —read and see significantly affects what they want to read and see. What is overlooked is that irreverent men of reputation in quest of a career or of publicity in the world of letters, art and entertainment, not to speak of pressmen and cameramen, have a vested interest—greatly to their cash profit and "freedom"—in denying this, except when, "to stir things up" it is their pleasure to say otherwise. Plato knew better. And amid all the "Miltonian" protests, there is much ill-concealed hypocrisy.

The law in Britain and America is not friendly to pornography. It even says that there is such a thing. But recent British law itself provides an escape-hatch. If the book or writings in question are of high literary or scientific value, then this outbalances the possible damage of obscenity. Hence a high-minded tinge of fine literature has to be found by defence counsel. I myself had held that the total literary value of D. H. Lawrence's work—although the total work had an irrationalist and even proto-fascist tinge— outbalanced a few pages where he "powerfully" describes the effect of flowers in unusual female places. Likewise, the social discussion of Lesbianism could be argued to exonerate, as print-worthy, the very mild writing of Radcliffe Hall. There was a case. *Last Exit* I believed to be a different matter.

After being held by two juries of ordinary citizens to be "ob-scene", the publishers took the stance (against which Laski had elsewhere fought) that such a delicate matter of taste was some-thing for a "special jury" of the literary élite, not the vulgar majority. However, the Appeal Court quashed the conviction by jury on the ground that the Bow Street magistrate had failed to point out to the jury that a great moral case could be made—that *Last Exit* might not only gratify "the right of the public to know", in terms of "social realism" about Brooklyn but, further, could arouse the indignant moral sense of the citizens of London when (shades of Juvenal!) they read about the immoral goings-on of the proletariat of Brooklyn.

At Bow Street Professor Kermode, for the defence, explained at length to the jury how a work of art was a work of art; and how the Calder-Boyars' masterpiece was such. He also made plain the virtue of publishers. (It was not, of course, explained how the lovers of high art might offer their creations to the public "for art's sake" and without profit.) For myself I simply took the line that under existing law there was such a thing as obscenity in books; and this being so, in my judgement, if *Last Exit* could not be judged obscene it would be difficult to find any other book to be obscene.

Incidentally, it is a quirk of the law that an expert witness, presumably not hired like counsel, may yet not, as a professional, cite the jugement of other professionals, perhaps in quite recent and relevant research, since this, although on oath, is merely "hear say". (President Robert MacIver had recently cited to me research in New York on the effects of obscenity on delinquency.) One had to stand by one's personal experience. Unlike the *Oz* case of 1971, it was all very decorous. Clearly, as the libertines assert, people are "entitled to their own points of view". It is not a criminal offence to hold a point of view, although such can be adequate evidence of a muddled mind. But it can be an offence when the social consequences for others of the permissive conduct, in terms of delinquency, are harmful on the objective evidence available. The issue is how far they have any right whatsoever to intrude, whether or not for profit and gain, their point of view upon the majority of their fellow citizens in a fashion which that majority regards as, not merely offensive and deserving of a kick in the plutocratic rump of the "exploiters for profit", but specifically—if not in logical proof, at least in empiric probability—contributory to social damage and delinquency.

Apart from thinking that the law of libel might be extended to cartoonists who bring into "obliquity and contempt", I am inclined to the view that legal obscenity does require re-definition; and that it should include, not only excessive sexuality, but the description (doubtless "powerful" and literary) of acts of sadism, beyond mere violence. It would need careful drafting. I do not myself find either the Memoirs of Casanova or *Le Petit Parisien* peculiarly corrupting. However, *Last Exit* seemed to me to have no more literary merit than could be found in a tape-recording and was without sociological scientific value as being descriptive of quite abnormal episodes in some slum-selected Brooklyn life. It was not to promote sociology or art that it was likely to sell.

Sex plus sadism, as Aldous Huxley knew, is an old mixture, not to be encouraged among a youth that believes itself to be "opinion shapers". The author, artist, entertainer, comic and tragic poet (one recalls Plato on poets), as well as the dollar-chaser and headline-hunter—and it is a fact of life that some men would murder their mothers to gratify their exhibitionism and for a head-line—can claim that they have and should have influence on opinion and, hence, behaviour. If they acquire great wealth or, as the pre-Jagger Beatles claimed, were "better known than Jesus Christ", then they have a species of social power. A wealthy pop-singer may choose to be more than an "entertainer"; to immerse himself in politics; and to find that he is wooed by politicians. He may become a real "man of power" (maybe plus bodyguards). However, amid glorious freedom, they cannot claim, at the same moment, that they have also no influence on behaviour or no responsibility for the influence. Here it is for society to decide upon the reality and nature of the influence; the desirability, in any culture, of the power; and, in the words of Mr Justice Holmes, "the proximity of the danger". All that the political scientist can say is that, on the market, an excess of license leads to a demand for more authority; and an excess of discipline to a demand for more liberty.

It should be added that, a few weeks after the Appeal Court decision, the author of *Last Exit*, Mr Hubert Selby, not a party to the case, arrived in London. He blandly declared his indifference to the claim that he had tried to improve the morals of Britain by powerfully depicting the immoralities of New York. His position was simple and quite at variance with the law which the Appeal Court had sought to refine upon. If the law in Britain proposed censorship, he was against the law; he was against any kind of censorship at all. Pre-publication censorship, anathema to news-papers but an insurance to theatres—"Commit the offence first, after you have invested your money; and then the police will attend to you"—or post-publication censorship, he was against both. Maybe the law ought to be changed. Anyhow, if Mr Selby was right, then the Appeal Court's basis of judgement collapsed. "It is not what they want, it's what's good for them," said Milton's employer, the Lord Protector Oliver. "*That* is the question." It is. And, as to 'what's good for them", maybe it is not for Fellows of the Royal Society of Literature (like myself) but for the jury and for the majority to decide, except where reason speaks clear. Reason spoke for me.

The contemporary common purpose is to produce ever more and more, more and more quickly; and that admen should bring hesitant customers to the factory door, like Strasburg geese, to have their throats stuffed with goods as one stuffs geese to produce *pâté de foie*. As cultural accompaniment, the enemy of all funda-mental integrity of the character of the individual person, there is the contemptible passion to "be with it" and to accord with the momentary "temper of the times", so permissive except for those who withstand it. However, in the decade of Francis Chichester, the circumnavigator, we should beware of sweeping generalities whether about youth or age—or about "writing England off".

Discussion of these matters, of the bogus and "phoney for profit", of the Yahoo, and of "living it up" is the affair of another book. What is said here is more baldly political—that the issues of today between states are issues of peace and of power that can be accommodated. Ideologically, not only do Moscow and Peking differ, but the conflict of ideologies is beyond question, of itself, worth no war. Cardinal Spellman was here a kind of recusant cardinal. I am neither Marxist nor Leninist; but I would be prepared to affirm that, today, the popular morality (I do not mean the esoteric conspiracies) of the Communist world is not only more puritan but better than that of an anarchist West, be it of Paris or New York, and I applaud the good manners of a Confucian China. If that were the only issue, then it would command my vote.

If some sadism must needs be, then what a joy for the saints to see the commissars of Lenin and Mao descending, in the armour of socialist realism, and ordering the bright young men of "the new wave", of theatre and pen, to "community service" and to cracking rolling stones for new state highways in the virgin lands of the Hebrides.

A more lotus and poppy occupation could be found, for the men "made" by managers out of the primal clay, in the Services of the new Soviet "dictatorship of the people", or amid the flowers of the great cultural revolution. "Lack of restraints in sexual life", said Lenin, "is a bourgeois phenomenon." But permissive sadism is a graver "phenomenon" than pornography. And provision of a quite special kind would also have to be made for "Hell's Angels" from California. I would be happy to see Messrs Muggeridge and Levin installed as our Red Queens.

Jeremy Bentham was a good man, who yet made a bore of himself by having too many good ideas. I am sure also that my admired Goethe, with his great Renaissance ideal of the *uomo universale*, polymath, poet, playwright, man of science, Minister of Finance, Minister of Mines, had too many good ideas. Today the "universal man" is viewed with admiration on principle but yet with acute alarm by institutionalists and bureaucrats, for whom the followers of Goethe all were dilettanti. (One of my greatest honours was to be permitted to deliver in Heidelberg, the *Rector magnificus* in the chair, an address on the bicentenary of Goethe's birth.) In this chapter I am parading a motley crowd, not entirely sterile of results, even if they are only side-shows to my main campaigns.

Since about 1936 I have kept a day-by-day diary. Originally these were loose leaves, with notes for books I proposed to write, not least *Face of Revolution*. These sheets tended to get lost and hence, as a measure of precaution, were put as dated jottings between hard covers. The Diaries developed by mere force of accumulation and, to notes of conversations, passing comments (as in Jefferson's commonplace book) were added. There are now eighteen volumes. In an endeavour to waste no time that could be saved, in about 1954 I added night-diaries of the happenings on the coloured cinema film which nature was good enough to permit me to enjoy each night. I became a Beachcomber of Dreams. A dozen years of these records are, as I have mentioned, to be found stored by the Librarian's request in the University of Sheffield. I hope that some day the psychologists will rouse themselves, following a brief summary article of mine in *The International Journal of Social Psychiatry*, to utilise them.

I have, I am happy to say, never paid a penny to a psychoanalyst. One of these indeed told me that he would not be interested in the Diaries if their data conflicted with the Freudian system, upon which his income depended. I raised my eyebrows. I have always replied, to those who urged that "only psychoanalysis in depth" was of any scientific value, that if they could make no use of about four thousand five hundred specimens then their science must be in a poor way. Apart from points about colour, sound, the technique of reminiscence and the logical fallacy of those who, recalling no dreams, assert that they have not dreamt, I have profited by learning some facts about my own nature which it would be idle to seek to change.

It emerges clearly enough that I am highly gregarious; that I like to be surrounded (more myself as equal or adviser than as *primus*) by friends, colleagues, students; that I like visiting churches as tranquillisers, but with some aptitude for criticism; that I fear the frustration, especially by delay, of my purposes; and that I am far too profoundly political in my instincts for any other career to give me satisfaction. I often dream of my old university, but it is of Christ Church, Oxford, not New College, that I dream. Cornell remains always in my affections. Those whom I know best appear but seldom and the animosities (perhaps too fully indicated elsewhere) of my working life disturb my tranquil dreams little. Happiness for me lies in having a circle, a vital group, of half-a-dozen or so loyal and like-minded friends— those whose minds inspire me—who "raise a curtain", and who, in Winston Churchill's challenging phrase, are "with me". This is so different from the diurnal life of "one-damn-thing-after-

another". Nightmares are so few as to be negligible. I have no
premonitions, only an Elysian present enjoyment. It is all very
classical. The freedom of dreams is not "terrible" but more
pleasant than the ambitions of daytime actuality. There is here no
Shakespearian "rub". Dreams are good. Nirvana is best. Why
fear ?

Again, one of the more frightening things today is that man may
be mastered by his own scientific discoveries and machines. Any
fool can see that these may be beneficial. It does not follow that
they must be. From the "animate instruments" (in Aristotle's
words), the slaves of ancient civilisation, we have progressed to the
inanimate slaves, our machines. The machines, however, have
their own inherent logic—a consideration often ignored—and
these have to be controlled or over-ridden. Nor are our physicists,
technicians, even physicians—masters of the art of "passing the
buck" morally—entirely to be trusted to control "progress". This
logic is called "efficiency" or sometimes "economy".

There is the computer's "convenience" that human beings
should be set into equal slots, as "numbers". Like the button-
moulder's choice, in Ibsen's *Pier Gynt*, all the human buttons
would be strictly interchangeable, unoriginal, equal and in-
humanly dull. Professor Fred Hoyle has protested against "the
human species becoming subservient to machines" and against the
anti-human power-lust of the technocrat to subordinate everything
to pseudo-economic efficiency. It is the logic of material power
(*alias* "know-how"), instrumental and without inquiry into
"power-for-what". Within this much wider context it has interested me to note that the automobile and "the man in power
behind the wheel", with the logical demands for its and his
efficiency, have their own momentum in relation to the countryside, its beauty and its future. I am not friendly to him or it. I
would practice "economy" at their expense and put the savings
into more mobile defence and more efficient diplomacy, on which
the present power of nations rests. Remembering Soviet submarine power, perhaps "scrap all cars; and put the money into
the navy." Peacetime democracies, of course, do not like spending
money on defence (just as wartime democracies do not like
negotiating a fair peace), until they are themselves taken short.

In balance against spending money on the Navy, in my personal
capacity but as Vice-President of the World Academy of Art and
Science (patrons the King of Sweden and the sometime President
of India) I went a few years ago to see the head of the Ford
Foundation, McGeorge Bundy. I suggested that, in view of the
billions spent on national defence, perhaps 0.01 per cent might be

expended by the Ford Foundation on objective research into the actual conditions of peace for humanity. Some authors have recently written about a "science of peace". However this may be except as grounded on a systematic science of politics, nevertheless those engaged in the research must indeed be objective. They must not be guilty of the blasphemy against science of knowing the "right" answers before the research began. I suggested to Dr Bundy that, if only ten substantial conclusions were reached and only three of these valid, nevertheless the value of these in political life would make the expenditure well worthwhile. However, I found that the Ford Foundation had otherwise allocated its available monies.

In the little town of Pocatello, Idaho, I meditated upon the then quite novel use of the parking-meter. What America, in our engineer's culture does today, Britain will do ten years later. I ascertained that Pocatello paid for its entire police force from its parking-meter fees. I wrote to Hugh Gaitskell, who had been Chancellor of the Exchequer until 1951, about this desirable situation and proposed a similar usage. Having stood in Fifth Avenue in the rush hour, I further suggested later that within a three or five mile radius of cities of over a million inhabitants no private car should be permitted (except those of certified residents) but only public conveyances and, at given times, business trucks. The saving of space, economy on roads and increase of fluidity of transport would be immense. Also the annual murder rate by cars, in Britain alone, of around 7,000 a year might be cut.

Again, whereas there is no virtue in change in itself, some things require changing. I see no virtue in changing "Constantinople", in the English language, into a Greek patois word, Istanbul, *eisten-polin*—meaning "going to Town"—in the false belief that it is more Turkish; or in substituting for "Siam" the extraordinary hybrid "Thai-land". This is all smart journalistic "up-to-date-news". "Peking: town not known." How much more dignified "the Babylonian Ambassador" than "the Iraqui Ambassador". It took Sir Winston to return us to the common-sense and Biblical usage of "Persia". "Thus saith Cyrus, King of Persia." But equally I see no reason for retaining unchanged a clumsy mediaeval currency system which wastes months of schooltime and confuses accounts.

This problem of mathematics and of time-saving has mildly interested me. In some quarters the proposal for a British decimal currency, despite its advantages technical and in school and accountants' time, produced great dismay. For one thing, it was thought that it must upset the price system and would enable grocers to filch extra farthings from the poor. On the other hand, the over-clever designed entirely novel and new-fangled currencies. I saw no need for either.

British currency was already so nearly decimal. The essential things were (a) not to upset the housewife's price system, especially at the level of the family budget; and (b), so far as possible, not to produce confusion by merely arbitrary departures from custom at the whim of scarcely full-bright experts and green-eyed boffins.

In 1962 I wrote to Anthony Barber, then Financial Secretary to the Treasury, setting out suggestions requiring the minimum of change at levels only below the florin—one tenth of a pound, and received a very pleasant reply. But his advisers thought that the florin (larger in value than the franc or Deutschmark) was "too small" as a unit. They were wrong: the two shilling or ten new pence is one of the most used coins today. After an earlier brief word at Party Conference, I took the matter up again in 1966— on this occasion with James Callaghan, Chancellor of the Exchequer. I got a reply of 14th March 1966:

"My dear George,

Many thanks for your letter of 7th March 1966. I do indeed remember very well, and with pleasure, the chat that we had at Brighton, and enjoyed hearing your views on the taxation of betting as of course we felt alike on this.

You are quite right in your selection of price stability as one of the most important criteria for any decimal currency system which is introduced. This was one of the preoccupations of the Halsbury Committee, as you may recall, and it will certainly not be overlooked in whatever changes are finally decided on. I am grateful to you for recapitulating the ideas you presented to Barber, and have taken note of them.

One way in which we hope in due course to make the whole process of changing over a smooth one is by making a real effort to educate and instruct the public so that they will fully understand all the ins and outs of the new decimal system. One of my intentions, as perhaps you have seen, is to set up a Decimal Currency Board which will have this educational task as one of its main duties, and I am sure the task will be carried out effectively.

I appreciate your comment on aspects of the change over to the metrical system of weights and measures. This is by its nature going to be a long drawn out business, and I believe myself that, because the time factor is not too pressing, we shall be able to resolve any problems which arise in a generally satisfactory manner.

You might like to go into action in defence of the £1 as the unit—as I see there is some sniping about it. I have *not* done it for City reasons!

Yrs. James Callaghan."

In the end at least we won out on the pound as prime unit and in the focal retention of the florin (unimaginatively called "ten new pence"). What we did not get, and should have got, is twenty five pennies (one more) or *one hundred farthings* in the florin; the retention of the shilling (or half florin) and "bit" (or quarter florin) unchanged; and *no* change of household prices at all above the "bit" (old 6d). What we got from the gentlemen and boffins of the Treasury, however, was something not traditional or more convenient, but something gleefully complex, pretentious, new-fangled, inconvenient and expensively advertised, from taxes, to a reluctant public. This new strictly decimal system introduced to us such items as "seven-and-one-half" (or decimal o.5) pence in commerce; instead of the immemorial shilling we are told more briefly to refer to the "five new pence"; and the decimal-vulgar fraction of the "half-new-penny". It all may have the political merit of so confusing the mind of the ordinary housewife about prices that even the Common Market new costs will seem tolerable. But it is to be hoped that members of the Commission will receive no "golden (obsolete) handshake" for their work.

Of not dissimilar interest, for those concerned about the evil works of bureaucrats and boffins, is the problem set to the harassed human memory of the postal code numbers and the telephone code. The American postal code is far simpler; and the Manhattan telephone directory is unimpaired by numbers replacing letters. Without unconditional confidence that psychologists can agree among themselves, I suggested to Technology Minister Lord Snow ("C.P.") that he might set up a psychological sub-committee to discover just how many numbers the average (and possibly hurried) citizen could keep accurately in his memory at one time. I suspect seven.

Changes in the money system, which may end in swindles of the housewife or trader and lack of perception of price increases, changes in measurement contrary to public wish, changes in postal and telephone code names, are pushed forward on a bustled, hustled public by a small group of place-men.

The boffin and the bureaucrat their little games do play;
And reck not, in their merry rounds, of what the public say.

I did not plunge forward into other decimal or metric reforms (I still prefer Fahrenheit as more precise) or whether we should have a ten day week—it wasn't so successful in Russia—or, while abolishing Sunday and Monday, have (as the inimitable, but often imitated Max Beerbohm suggested) a Huxley-day, Marx-day and —yes, why not?—a Maximum Beerbohmday. Since we lack saints or heroes to give them names, I am indifferent whether the Bankers' Holy Days fall on Whit Monday or Black Friday.

One "gadget" change which is not, I think—certainly educationally—too trivial to mention is the desirability of issuing historical series of stamps, not least for abroad, carrying the faces of our great explorers, scientists, poets, philosophers, statesmen, and sea-captains, instead of (as at present) circulating the modest violet and our local weeds. It is typical of the down-beat of the decade that we present, not Chichester, but the yacht that carried him, and it is just here that there is something "rotten in the State of Denmark", with the stress on the impersonal and mechanical, and not on the dynamic and personal.

Whatever that notoriously anonymous figure, Chairman Mao, may say, a little more of "the cult of personality" will do no harm. We omit to commemorate the landing, in 1770, of Captain Cook in Australia or the centenary of the Confessor or of Alfred, the father of the nation, but we have a passion for commemorating defeats such as Hastings—won by the Norse-men who had previously thrashed the Kings of France and robbed them of their Northern duchy. We shall doubtless issue a stamp to commemorate Dunkirk and M. de Gaulle's arrival in Quebec. However, by 1971, we have at last arrived at commemorating—in series too short for the philatelist—the anniversaries of such literary figures as Scott and Keats, not to mention Gray, who is best known for a popular elegy in a graveyard.

Again, I have mentioned in earlier chapters such small but not perhaps trivial points as *son et lumière* for the magnificent Castle at Warwick, in the countryside with which I have a family connection; and there is to be a gift for 1976 from the People of Britain to the People of America, to be placed outside the White House in Washington, of a heroic statue of Chatham, who said all the right things during the War of Independence. "The Americans fight for the rights of every Englishman. . . . Had I been an American I would have taken up arms myself." I got encouragement of some enthusiasm for the idea from General Eisenhower, Ambassador David Bruce and Ambassador John Freeman. It would balance the statues of von Steuben, patron of the German-American Society, and of the nude lady looking up at that gift of French monarchic and national policy, Lafayette, and according to the irreverent exclaiming: "You give me back my robe and I'll give you back your sword." Such a bicentenary statue of Chatham would balance off the statues in London, in positions of prime prominence, of Abraham Lincoln outside Westminster Abbey and of Franklin Roosevelt in Grosvenor Square. (One to Eisenhower is missing and I will not cite that to George Washington in Trafalgar Square, so neatly sited as to be looking into the backside of George IV's horse.) I know that Ernie Bevin did not want a statue, since he said he didn't want the pigeons leaving their droppings on his head. But here Chatham is called on to serve a higher public cause. (However, my latest information is that, in gratitude for recent French policy, M. de Lafayette may be moved into a more central position, near the entry to the White House.)

On a different plane, I have already mentioned the suggestion of an annual Law Amendment Bill, comparable in regularity with the Budget, emerging from the Law Commission, for the most part technical rather than controversial and unlikely to occupy much parliamentary time but critical for efficient legislation. This would bring the law annually up to date in machinery and rules and in the light of technical changes, e.g. in the value of money, and the effect of fines.

I have given earlier the record of my attempts, begun over thirty years ago, to establish a National Economic Council and an academic Social Science Research Council of the United Kingdom. I have unremittingly campaigned for the status of the Social Services, Cinderellas for those whose feet do not fit the shoes.

One recent research suggestion, however, came to me from an outside source. The great Einstein had the vision of a World Academy of Art and Science, so as both to encourage research of high international priority and to concentrate the weight of the international opinion of scientists and *savants*. The project took some time to get off the ground but eventually the Academy was established, with secretariat in Israel and with King Gustav Adolphus of Sweden, not called "President" but "Hon. Member". Later addition was made of the then President of India, Sir S. Radhakrishnan. When I was invited to become a member, of the one hundred and twenty members, twenty were Nobel Prize-winners. On invitation I proposed that their tasks (including the desalinisation of water, appropriate for physicists and a project of immense importance with a sinking world water level) should include research into the problems of Conflict, Peace and War, already discussed at Pugwash Conferences and by the Myrdal Institute in Stockholm. I was invited to be chairman of this section and, in the presence of the then deputy premier of Israel, Dr Abba Eban, gave an address on it at the Academy's Rome Conference of 1965. The theme was close to my most profound interest since 1918 in the causes of war. I was also invited to be a vice-president of the World Academy, which I was honoured to accept. Here was indeed a central human theme, much more than any hobby or paragon.

Although I fear to plunge into domestic constitutional details beyond my ken, I had also a small but abiding interest in House of Lords Reform, since this had been the subject of my Oxford University Gladstone Prize of 1920. The House of Lords is, of course, like the seven-hundred-year-old British House of Commons, a medieval structure, with the disadvantages as well as the advantages of its antiquity. (The two-hundred year old American Constitution, with its jealousy of the executive and philosophy based on the individualism of John Locke and the Whigs, is not a much better case.) In most walks of life a seven-hundred-year-old structure, to function efficiently, demands radical reconstruction. This the Commons needs. It is only semi-democratic and is confused in its purposes. The trouble in the case of the Lords, however, is that almost any reform would strengthen this largely nominee House and of such a strengthening the Commons would be jealous.

It is a species of stock market calulation that, were the House abolished as some radicals want, the social and commercial value of a tontine of Peers, to whose numbers no one could add, would steadily increase. In Germany such functionless titles are now illegal but France and Italy are full of dukes who are called upon to perform no parliamentary function and who are quite irresponsible. Assuming even a modest social equalisation, this privilege without duties is intolerable. It does not at all follow that being a duke in France, whether adorning industry or promoting champagne, is without cash value.

I put forward to Lord Attlee, when premier, a proposal that by law no one (recognised courtesy titles apart) might assume a title unless he were "a lord in parliament". This has legal precedents. Further, that every peerage should decrease in honour by one stage, on succession to a deceased peer. This proposal would retain a limited but decreasing "ancient peerage"; but it would, at a stroke, make all barons life peers. Those anxious (on the Rignano system) to retain a grade of peerage for their heirs would have politically to work hard for it, so as to secure their own elevation by at least one stage. Otherwise the peerage would be on the road to lapse. I also added that far too many civil servants, today well-paid, while claiming the irresponsibility of the anonymous, on retiring blossomed forth into the full publicity of honours—and this far too easily and by routine.

I have two riders to what I then said. I would suggest that noblemen who decide to emigrate and live outside the country permanently should cease to be lords of Parliament, hence should lose their titles and should be liable to prosecution if, visiting the country, they continued to use them. On the other hand, there seems to me (as with bishops and law lords) to be a strong case for bringing certain people temporarily into the Upper House in view of their function, such as the Moderator of the Church of Scotland, the Catholic archbishops, maybe the Chief Rabbi, the chairman of the TUC, and the Lord Mayor of (at least) London (whose predecessor was indeed accounted one of King John's "barons"). Also, in order to avoid an overwhelmingly nominee House, there could be a case for giving the Lords a limited and proportionate power of co-option, comparable to the system of election of Scottish peers but going beyond the existing peerage ranks.

Lord Attlee viewed the proposal (as he did that of the Chatham statue) with considerable favour and told me that Arthur (Lord) Ponsonby had put forward a similar proposal. I took the matter up again with the succeeding Labour Prime Minister, Mr. Wilson, resubmitting the memorandum. I received, from 10 Downing Street, the following letter (which I am authorised to quote), dated 10th November 1966:

"Dear George,

Your old memorandum on the House of Lords reads very well—particularly its last paragraph since I implemented it the other day!

On the major issue of Lords reform I think we are primarily concerned at present with powers rather than with composition. All the same I like your neat device for making them climb faster and faster in order to keep on the same rung of the ladder.

Yours
Harold Wilson"

However, the Lords Reform Bill was, during the last Parliament under Labour, withdrawn by Home Secretary James Callaghan.

Again, during my years in Cornell I was in touch with a small-radius university broadcasting committee, of which the work was educational, chiefly for the benefit of local farmers. This kind of thing seemed to me to have great possibilities and, in long conversations with Hendrik van Loon (a sometime Cornell colleague of immense charm), in the Holly Hotel, Washington Square, when we talked of history and about "Hanny's" ingenious little illustrations, we also discussed the possibilities of "a University of the Air"—here primarily an extra-mural extension of an existing university. As myself a sometime Workers' Education Association tutor, this had quite especial interest for me.

After the Election of 1945 my good friend, Ellen Wilkinson, became Minister of Education. The Labour Party, following up on the Butler Education Act, had promised to do much for adult education, but there was financial austerity, and Cripps, to be faced. I suggested to her that this was precisely one of those cases where the bold use of new methods, techniques and media was warranted. The product might be crude and imperfect; but it would be much better than doing nothing. Why not take our leading *savants*, the Huxleys and Hogbens; get them to record and "can" sets of academic lectures; get these broadcast; and use the existing core of tutors (who could not be abruptly increased in numbers overnight—nor was there the money for this) to act in their tutorial capacity, commenting on the lectures so delivered? Primarily this was an "adult education" scheme, but it could also be a "refresher course" scheme. Degrees could be given to those who sat (long customary in London Universities) for the extra-mural examinations. It is also important to stress that, far from being an extravaganza, this was an economy measure.

I knew that some county education officers, to whom I had mentioned it, were enthusiastic. Ellen was highly sympathetic with the new idea as a help amid her own problems. Alas, she died so soon. It should perhaps be added, for the record, that these proposals, later of a very specific kind, were put forward by me to Ellen (and, afterwards, to Harold Wilson) before—to the best of my knowledge—Michael Young had put forward like ones. However, I took upon myself to go and see Mr (later Sir) George Barnes, of the BBC, about the proposals. He informed me briefly that they were technically impossible.

The BBC had origins strange and mysterious, duly recorded in Asa Briggs' history. In the beginning it was regarded as a piece of Heath-Robinson gadgetry by electrician "boffins". The Army was concerned that this new-fangled public broadcasting (the horror for them of television was yet to come) might interfere with Army signals. The Corps of Engineers was profoundly suspicious of this pop radio—national security; secrecy. It was perhaps for these reasons that a Tory Prime Minister, Stanley Baldwin, was responsible for introducing a vast measure of what was in effect nationalisation—and this, be it noted, in the very media of in-formation—by giving the British Broadcasting Corporation a national monopoly (which it still enjoys as to radio). If Smith and Jones wish to listen to ITV exclusively, they still have to pay— and here lies the outrage to the BBC of the much-denounced pirate "pops"—through the National Post Office a tax-subsidy to the BBC for the privilege of having a receiving set to listen to the rival company. Despite which, until recently, ITV attracted more viewers.

In the days of Lord Reith as Director—as the inscription on stone in Broadcasting House says, with a hint of ambiguity: *Deo omnipotenti Johanne Reith Rectore*—there was the tolerable excuse that the BBC was the nation's schoolmistress, reiterating the already quoted words of Cromwell, "It's not what they want, it's what's good for them—that is the question." There was something rather awesome and admirable about Reith's austere Puritanism. That defence assuredly no longer existed under Hugh Greene.

In June 1961, "out of the blue", I was invited by telegram by Lord Derby to become a vice-president of his newly formed Popular Television Association, of which Ronald Simms was secretary. The purpose was to set up independent television companies. There was no official Party line in the matter. Some Tories, such as Quintin Hogg, supported the BBC monopoly. Reginald Fletcher, Lord Winster, an earlier Labour M.P., came to sit with me on the PTA committee. Christopher Mayhew was passionately opposed to this commercialisation, sullying the purity of the BBC —a position that today has a certain delicious irony. The BBC monopoly was held by its enthusiasts to be the national cynosure of the world's eyes. Harold Nicolson, with an austere gesture of moral superiority, told me that he could not support my liberal thesis of "the freedom of the media of information", because "I am a Socialist". I knew that, by accepting this vice-presidency, I should incur the even more undying hostility of Herbert Morrison; but I was prepared to take this on.

I was no fanatical champion of the Whig doctrine of some absolute natural right in "the freedom of the Press". The freedom is conditional on serving the better functioning of democratic discussion and variety. The argument that "the public has a right to know"—demands to be titillated and tickled (as Plato said) and is to be satisfied by the "coups" of heavily competitive, capitalistic profit-seeking press proprietors—has singularly little to do with the communicating of unbiased and impartial information for the better working of democracy. (A newspaper, a British *Osservatore Romano* or *Christian Science Monitor*, run precisely on the lines of the admired BBC, with the same financial support from the Post Office, would be a fascinating experiment: no wicked adver-

Y

tisements.) There is a great deal of interested humbug in this matter. To adapt a famous phrase, the power of the BBC "had increased; was increasing; and should be diminished".

Nevertheless, the analogy—although furiously denied—of this freedom of the Press with the freedom and non-monopoly of other media of information seemed to me quite clear. Indeed television was to be far more influential than the Press. I favoured local stations, in most cases tied in with the local newspapers (for which I had high respect). I was against monopoly. We have had one frank admission at least of the satisfaction that sheer power gave. As Baldwin said, in a comparable connection, it is the satisfaction of the harlot. Politically it can be an oligarchic power, certainly "to make" and even "to break". It is most dangerous.

I made clear to Simms that I was primarily interested in possible ITV promotion (as promised) of an educational programme. He gave me pledges. Indeed at that time there seemed to be little chance to obtain any other effective route to push (as I was determined) the "University of the Air" proposal across. I accepted membership of the PTA executive committee and I campaigned. We changed a public opinion poll vote against changing the BBC monopoly into one in favour. This shaped the votes in Parliament.

There was much discussion of what was meant by "educational". Was it "academic" or did "our fine cultural programme" suffice? I began by thinking of an Educational Corporation, itself exclusively empowered to decide the educational priorities, but prepared to sustain itself by selling time in the hours it did not need. I ended by advocating an Educational Commission (ultimately permanent) surveying the entire educational field, BBC and commercial, with mandatory powers in the educational field. Moreover, just as I had great belief in the value of the local paper, so I had belief in the value of the local radio station, not BBC "homogenised"—with authentic diversity of approaches—but possibly tied to the local paper (giving mutual reinforcement) or using the talent of the local university. I had profound respect for Lord Reith, who had principles (even if mistaken), but much less for those whose aspiration was to be "with it" and for the fashion-hunters. For once I almost agreed with that remarkable Pascalian, Malcolm Muggeridge. I may add that I made not one penny of money by my advocacy.

In July 1960, I wrote an article, "The University of the Air" for the *Contemporary Review*. Subsequently, at a PTA Press Conference, on the spur of the moment I gave to the Press my proposal for "a University of the Air"; and the Press then picked up the phrase. It was, I believe, the first public mention by name of this proposal which I had been the first to put forward in Britain. When the PTA presented its report to the Pilkington Committee, I also presented a special memorandum on this theme. Subsequently, I learned that the Committee had not thought the theme to be worth discussing further. The Independent Television Authority, thanks in no small part to our efforts, came into existence.

When Harold Wilson was still leader of the Opposition in March 1963 I took the matter up with him at a Fawcett Society luncheon, some months before his speech, in November, in Glasgow which moved towards making the proposal part of official Party policy, although there was a shift of emphasis from adult education and refresher courses.

On Harold Wilson's suggestion, the papers seen by him were passed on to Dick Crossman. The theme entered the Election Manifesto, with subsequent references by the Prime Minister, the project being temporarily renamed "Open University", and including some of the long-established techniques, not especially original, of a "Correspondence College". Since Dick Crossman did not in fact become Minister of Education and Science, the proposal came to rest in the capable and energetic hands of Miss Jennie Lee. After, according to the press, her visit to Chicago University where much has been done along these lines, the term "University of the Air" was restored in press references.

Again, in the autumn of 1961 a letter appeared in *The Times* over the joint signatures of the Bishop of Southwark and myself, urging consideration of the future status of the teaching profession in the context of educational development. A committee was in fact set up, of which I became chairman since the Bishop of Southwark did not wish to be such. Its report, sent to the Robbins Committee, took a somewhat different shape, in its educational survey, from that originally intended. It had the advantages of counsel from two sometime Parliamentary Secretaries of the Ministry of Information, Lindsay and Hardiman. I was exclusively responsible for drafting the section on the role of television in education and largely responsible for that on higher education. It enabled me to express some of the views on education that I had entertained for long.

In Sheffield, it was within my experience that bursaries were awarded fairly easily to the sons of local people. These students were well in a position to pay for themselves during their long vacations. Some of the sons of local miners and railwaymen were not—although in WEA classes I had formed a high opinion of their fathers as excellent "educational material". At Cornell I had found that it was an entirely accepted thing (for which adjustments were made) for students "to work their way through". Such a man as young Elmhirst, now the owner of Dartington Hall, did this. I recall a shipboard conversation with Carritt, an Oxford don and lecturer on aesthetics, who was horrified by this unacademic and vulgar practice, this desertion of the ivory tower. He complained that, at Harvard, sometimes the young men did not need the money—President Coolidge's son, who went tobacco-picking, did not need the money—and, final scandal, they even bought themselves cars with the proceeds. I, on the contrary, saw here enterprising young students, determined "to go to college", even if it involved heavy work and long hours. I discussed the matter with Sir Alfred Zimmern, a wise man, and he with some passion agreed with me.

I would think that the first function of a Vice-Chancellor in a civic university would be to tell the city fathers that he wished the closest co-operation, not least with the industry of the town; and that he wanted this, not only for the benefit of the university, but in the employment of the students and for mutual advantage. I do not view with favour schools of technology, engineering, agriculture or even teacher-training being set up in a fashion isolated from the broader life of a university. No less, although I am not "an existentialist", do I disapprove of the intellectual snobbery of the "pure academic". A university radio station, along with extramural work, falls in to the same overall plan. So does a Business School.

On the other hand, there is an opposite error to be avoided. In the early days of the last century it was the belief of James Mill and of the Liberals that what we needed was "an educated democracy", and that the upper middle-classes, well aware of what "education" meant, would instruct the other orders. This belongs to the past. (In Scotland and Wales there was an almost religious enthusiasm for education as the answer to most problems.) Today there is debate about what we mean by "education" and there is special public praise for the youth who, leaving school at fifteen, becomes a world-known pop-singer or a tycoon. The easiest escape route in the world from teasing moral problems is to call for "more education". But just what do we here mean by education?

There is a risk that "democracy" will insist that *it* will tell the teachers what is to be meant, for the future, by "education", and, although popular, this will certainly not be academic in its standards. "A good education", in the older sense, now almost blotting a child's record as "class conscious", may become something to be concealed like bad breath. The really clever boy will leave school "and all that jazz" at an early age, in pursuit of cash success. (Why indeed go to a university at all and end as an unemployed graduate?)

The older Liberals talked of "dignity" and "excellence"—and, for the Goethean, there is the rule of "classic order". But such aspirations can be resented by the modern libertarian as "snobbish"—Professor Higgins is a snob—whereas the airs put on by the beatnik do not equally offend against the manner of "our street" and of Mr Dolittle. Shaw who, like Marx, had little use for the egalitarian *Lumpen-proletariat* was all wrong. Maybe he was. Maybe "excellence" is undemocratic—although the fundamentally aristocratic Communists do not think so. And maybe, moreover, "a liberal education" (*pace* Mill) is fundamentally nonutilitarian—and even anti-utilitarian.

The British press (*Evening Standard*, Sept. 1, 1971) is already asserting editorially that "universities can no longer decide for themselves what type of graduate student they want to produce. They must bend to the wants of their customers—be they students or employers." Accustomed hitherto, in the last century, to "universities for gentlemen" and unaccustomed to the wide demands of those who demand a "higher education" for all (whatever "higher" means) and to the American (and even European) prevalence of vast student bodies, there is a general fear of the "unemployed graduate" (not uncommon in Africa and Asia) who may become the "unemployable graduate".

The university student may be unable to decide whether he is a member of a privileged "intelligentsia", entitled to be given a job by "a just society". Or he may feel himself to be a non-privileged ordinary fellow, who yet expects to get rather more technical training than his neighbours as a reward for being bright in examinations. He is, in brief, "the consumer" telling the universities (as commerce tells him) what training he needs. In effect an uneducated fellow, in the older sense, he yet can give business what it wants and beat his neighbour to it. Maybe inspired educationalists can here mix in—in educating such technicians as physicians, dentists and lawyers—some elements of a liberal education. Or our student may just be someone who, with wider opportunities than ever before to absorb, even if critically, the traditional culture of high civilisation, is adjudged capable of making, by his gifts, a special contribution to the service of the community (not excluding, as in China and among Benedictine monks, farm work), expecting reward, not in competition, but "according to what society sees to be his needs?"

The controversial issue here is of the permanence of values in a humane, liberal or Confucian education. Perhaps training in being models or pop-singers—both most remunerative—is what the electorate really wants. The popular pressure at the present time for the light-weight, "with it", entertaining and easily intelligible is immense. The education of the future will, it seems, not be visual or even literate, as it has been since the days, not (*pace* McLuhan) of Gutenberg, but of the Egyptians and Phoenicians; but audio-tactile, fixated on Big Brother's goggle-box, impinging (as with monkeys) on the finger and, also, on the ear—the louder din the better. This will swing. There will be "audio-tactile" higher mathematics. For myself, I await the coming of the Communist, intolerant (within "limits"), aristocratic, puritan revolution, which today appears over the horizon. There is much democratic virtue in the American "comprehensive" or "high school", about which I know a little. It is yet sometimes thought to be the weakest link in the American educational system. Theoretically, and often indeed in practice, it can instil a "classless sense of community", like its predecessor, "the little red school house" with its "melting pot". Too often over-large, it lacks discipline and, in some localities—not slums—what may emerge is the intimidating thug rule of old "bully", modern "young thug", over juniors.

Alas! the "schools of humane letters" based on Latin and Greek, can no longer give us the liberal and humane education we want. It once was an education for the clergy, and then for squires and civil servants. The privileged and leisured days of "the young gentleman", when "meritocracy" was an unknown word, have gone by. What today *is* a liberal education? What *do* we want? How far should it be "useful" or, like the law and divinity and medicine, at least vocational? Or, as technology, useful to the country and to the armed forces? I myself have a prejudice. I hold that the teaching in universities of political theory, ranging from the political philosophy which connects with the humanities to the political and social sciences, which share many of the methods of the other sciences, provides the educational buckle we require, replacing *litterae humaniores*, between what Lord Snow chooses to call "the two cultures" of the humanities and of the natural sciences.

Although it is unpopular to say so, I regard with suspicion any excessive stress on physical science and technology. I suspect an *arrière-pensée*; either to train our magnificent men to produce bigger and better bombs for the destruction of humanity or to train our engineers to produce, in competition with other tribal peoples, ever more goods (as Professor Kenneth Galbraith says) for the advertisers to sell to a public which does not want them. Reduction of population would be a better route. The major problem of the twenty-first century will be that of vastly increased leisure for the more Sybarite nations. The social consequences can well be more boredom, more fornicating, more violence, more war. It is precisely as a check upon this that, not a "scientific" or technical only, but a well-considered liberal education is required, an education in discipline, authority and manners—a Confucian education from childhood. I do not wish to be thought to condemn technology—I do not—or the morally controlled pursuit of power over nature, man reaching to the stars. This last indeed is the millennial material destiny of humanity. But it is not the vocation of the common citizen, Aristotle's "man of judgement".

Even in the technical field the popular argument is weak. I recall the personnel manager of a large industry in Minneapolis explaining that, in choosing men for executive promotion, he chose men who had had some training in philosophy, preferably logic. "For executive posts the technicians fall flat on their faces." British educationalists today, like reformed prostitutes, seem to be over-enthusiastic for new ways. The old pleasures may be better. Education indeed is expensive and cannot afford to be wasteful. My duty, as chairman of a large department in McGill, was to report to a university-employed firm of efficiency experts just how many cubic feet of space the classes of the department occupied, on what hours and days of the week and in what weeks of the year. It would give me malicious pleasure to watch some Oxford or Cambridge don getting down on the floor, with a foot-measure, to make the same economy survey.

The truly grave matter is the number of young students who, by any intellectual test, merit a university education. Some of these merit the best education that the country affords. They will not, in fact, get it. Indeed, in the 1960s, only 2 per cent did. This was my motivation in pushing the idea of an extra-mural University of the Air. It is probably too generous a statement to say that Oxford and Cambridge between them are not geared to take more than twenty-five thousand students. What, then, of the rest? I have advocated the enlargement of existing universities, despite the protest that "the more means the worse". The universities must be larger. Although it may be a brave experiment, the venture of establishing universities for a few hundred choice spirits, as at Keele, is too expensive in overheads for Britain at the moment. The University of Paris, which is not unknown or of mean reputation, has more students than any British university.

It may indeed involve some lowering of classic standards (and increase of utility) if, further, the number of the universities themselves is increased, although this policy is expensive. I have yet advocated it. Ministering to the needs of a region, they should be able to rely upon local pride. I would like to see a University at Lincoln for example, with departments of history, agriculture, education and engineering, such that a Lincolnshire man would be glad to graduate from it.

However, it is patent that one major requirement of the present, as a sheer matter of increasing numerical capacity, is at least one more "great university", entitled to *ad eundem gradum* degrees with Oxford and Cambridge. (Lord Murray of Newhaven tells me we need two.) The patent first choice should be York, with its history as ancient capital of Britain, its local wealth and its loyal north country population. It is sad that its present new university plan is so conventional, with a mild flurry into fashionable science courses rather than the humanities.

Certainly one does not wish such a university to be a pale copy of Oxford or Cambridge, It should be an experiment in matters new but needed. Two developments are required in Britain. The one is the development, thanks to the condition of contemporary studies, of major and semi-autonomous Graduate Schools, until recently neglected by Oxford and Cambridge faculties which were historically geared to tutoring the undergraduate. ("Doing what we do well".) The other is a great Law School, which would do much, as is done on the Continent, to give English lawyers more coherent grounding in jurisprudence and make their training, unlike dentists, less purely vocational. Further, something at York comparable to the Harvard Business School, whatever pure economists might think, would do no harm.

I had spent some months, in 1965, in the unremunerated hard work of composing a Fabian Pamphlet, *The Creation of the Atlantic Community*. Since I was well aware that anything I said would make little impression in Oxford, I decided merely to enjoy myself for a few mornings by quickly putting together a memorandum on Oxford University reform, which I sent, in due course, to Lord Frank's Commission, in accordance with the general and public request of the Commission.

One of the first things needed in Oxbridge—Oxford a university by "custom" and Cambridge by papal decree—universities primarily designed to give highly specialised tutorship on a three year course to undergraduates straight up from school, was not merely provision for graduate students but the separation of graduate studies, under their own Dean, from the various under-

graduate faculty tutors, with some incitement to Fellows to join—
perhaps for research, which is not at all the same as the skill of a
competent lecturer—the Graduate School. The gilded amateurism
of the elegant art student is indeed an excellent thing; but he
should not suppose that it is professionally enough. Further, while
paying all homage to the debating prowess of the Oxford and
Cambridge Unions (in a witty style no longer so much in demand
by the democratised House of Commons as it was), nevertheless
student Councils were also required, which should carry a considerable measure of constitutional responsibility, not to be
limited to Masters of Arts or Hebdominal Council alone, in the
shaping of community life, although, unlike the students of the
mediaeval university of Bologna or even certain Scottish universities, they should not believe themselves to have the authority to
run the place.

The professors should themselves take more of the tutorial load
off the shoulders of Fellows and tutors. Not only chairs of psychology, anthropology, political philosophy and political science were
needed, but also a Regius chair of sociology, in one faculty. The
numerous university chapels should be ecumenicised in proportion to demand, instead of asking for money for new chapels. All
Souls should be held to its trust deed; and Mass should be
celebrated there, in Chichele's chapel, by the Cardinal Archbishop
or other, on St Crispin's and on All Souls Day—since the Angli-
cans and other dissenters cannot say mass for the dead. While not
seeking to tamper with the sacrocanct College system ("which
makes us what we are"), for the convenience of wandering scholars
who cannot readily make contact with College *savants* and
Fellows, for whom it is almost a matter of pride not to know each
other (impossible to talk over Trinity College wall to next door
Balliol), a central university faculty union should be built, which
would provide an alternative for the studious to college cuisine.
Women graduates should be admitted to the facilities of Colleges
(such as my own) which have the daring already to admit to
College premises (albeit separated by a six foot stone wall) the
wives of male graduates. Hot water baths ought not to be found
chiefly in converted College mediaeval stables.

I fear that this was in no sense a humble or modest document.
It is no adequate excuse that I was seized by a sudden Carnaby
Street desire "to have fun". There was even a touch of arson in it.
I can fully sympathise with the Cambridge don who described me
(or, rather, my work) as "intolerable". Perhaps I regret my intrusion, because it conflicts with my own profound and Confucian
respect for good manners. I am almost a traditionalist and my

normal habits are well-behaved. There is yet an exception—and it implies a compliment to Oxford. I am well-behaved except where I do, in fact, care a great deal. I still retain some of the old love. My anger is not against Oxford's friends but against those who do harm.

I understand that it was said in Oxford Common-rooms that it was no longer necessary to go to London to visit nightclubs; one could get as good fun by reading the contributions to the Franks Commission. However, I was not so naive as to entrust my memorandum, however casual, solely to the volumes of material for the Franks Report. I sent a copy to 10 Downing Street. I got back a very prompt personal note from the Prime Minister (who once was bursar at University College, Oxford): the Memorandum contained many good ideas and the Prime Minister was much interested. So far as I could do it, I had done my job. I had been my "think-tank".

XVI

THE UNITY OF EUROPE AND THE ATLANTIC COMMUNITY

§ i. *Beginnings*

In January 1948, I was in Luxemburg. I can date the event precisely because the Mahatma was assassinated in Delhi during those days, and the Press in Luxemburg asked me for comment. The occasion of the Luxemburg Conference was an international meeting of the *Nouvelles Equipes Internationales*, one of the six voluntary organisations then working for the Union of Europe. Alone among these in being supported semi-officially by political parties—the Christian Democratic Parties of Italy and West Germany and the M.R.P. of France, led by the chairman of the French Resistance, Georges Bidault—the N.E.I. was the most influential of the Six.

In the previous year the British Occupation authorities, with some German journalistic collaboration, had arranged for me to visit Germany and to talk in the Universities of Heidelberg and of Göttingen, as well as in Kiel, Hamburg, Essen and Hanover. In talking to student and youth groups I had been impressed that discussion of democracy only produced the feeling among them that they were "being lectured to", but that what was going to be called "democracy" depended upon whether it was Russians, French, Americans or British addressing them. The figure of democracy had a rubber nose. But, when I spoke of Victor Hugo's and Stresemann's, Briand's and Coudenhove's dream of a United Europe, I got an immediate spark of response and the feeling that here was a new hope for Germany, the best and creative way, without lapsing into national defeatism, to turn one's back on the recent past.

I have already mentioned the little compilation, *Above all Nations*, edited by my wife, Sheila Hughes and myself, which put on record deeds done during the war, by people of different nations, which held up the candle of civilised and humane behaviour even while the war was still on. I have also mentioned my Goethe bi-centenary address in Heidelberg University. As a consequence I was host in our London house to Herr Grimmer, then Minister of Education for Lower Saxony, in connection

with the Goethe Celebration dinner in London. It seemed a pity
that this should end with cigar smoke and empty wine bottles.
The Goethe Centenary struck the right note for an attempt to
bring Germany back into the main stream of European comity.
I found that Gilbert Murray and G. P. Gooch shared my view.
Although the Foreign Office was hesitant about the time being
opportune, a small group of us met in 2 Cheyne Walk, including
Victor Gollancz, Violet Bonham Carter and Harold Nicolson.
We were much encouraged by John Hynd, Chancellor of the
Duchy of Lancaster and, then, Minister for German Affairs; by
Lord Longford, subsequently Chancellor; and by the new head
of the German Diplomatic Delegation, Herr Schlange-Schoen-
ingen. After some delays the new Anglo-German Association
took shape in 1951. The Federal Republic expressed its appreciation by the award of high honours to Alexander of Tunis, our
president; to Frank Longford, our chairman; as well as by the
award of a Commander, Grand Cross, of the Order of Merit, to
myself. I believe the Association, of which I have the honour to
be a Vice-President, has contributed significantly to good Anglo-
German relations.

It is crucial to the understanding of what follows that the
position at the time be recalled. Thanks to the mutual agreement
of three (or four) old men, recently enemies, a miracle seemed
possible. Whether "federal" or "functional", a "pooling of
sovereignty", beginning in the economic area of coal and steel,
with its "Sovereign High Authorities" might be practicable in a
Europe devastated down to our own day by the civil wars of
Bourbon and Hapsburg, French and German. A model might be
seen to work, unexpectedly institutionally superior to that of the
Commonwealth; and more effective than anything, at that moment,
likely to be practicable between even the Senate of the United
States and the Parliament of Ottawa (although both North
American) or that of Westminster.

Hence even sacrifice of the immemorial British policy of
detachment, and of holding the balance of power against any
union of Europe—Imperial, Bourbon, Napoleonic or Hitlerite—
might be considered. Of course Louis XIV, Napoleon and Hitler
had detested England as the especial enemy. But this perchance
also might be superseded. The design could clearly be an historic
move forward in the everlasting quest for stable peace for Europe
and the world. If successful in the Western European area, it
might be extended to Britain and even, perchance—I had written
a war-time pamphlet on the subject—to Poland. It could provide a
working model for the whole world—at least for the Atlantic

World. It was a great adventure. It assumed that this European plan would be very firmly placed within the framework of the earlier Atlantic plan.

In these transitional days I was (and still am, as ideal) a supporter of the goal of world government, even if it were no more than "a horizon ideal", with all the practical difficulties in the foreground. Clement Attlee gave it the weight of his support, and Gilbert McAllister, a former Member of Parliament, became Secretary General. A Charter was signed in Versailles and one of the earliest European Conferences was in Monaco. However, despite the warm personal reception given to us by Princess Grace and Prince Rainier, the only observable result was that the devoted Gilbert McAllister died, before we left Monaco, of over-work.

The French delegation at Luxemburg was led by Maurice Schumann, whom I was to count as a personal friend, then known best in London as a broadcaster for the Free French, later Minister and today Foreign Minister. The old German Centrum had a representative, Herr Carl Spiecker, who had some support from the British Foreign Office, but much the more numerous German delegation was that of the new Christian Democratic Party. It was led by a man fairly unknown outside the Rhineland, except to experts, an ex-mayor of Cologne who had been dismissed by a British brigadier for "incompetence". General Templar had confirmed the dismissal by Brigadier Barraclough and lost one chance of military promotion as a consequence. The name of the leader of this German delegation was Conrad Adenauer, later German Chancellor.

The scratch British delegation—"scratch" because there were in Britain no confessional parties and it had necessarily to be composed of European-minded individuals—was led by myself. Barbara Barclay Carter, secretary of the British group and translator of the works of Don Sturzo, founder of the Italian *Partito Popolare*, requested me to take this function on, since the Duchess of Atholl, sometime Under Secretary of State for Education, who would normally have led the delegation as chairman, did not wish to do it. Hence, to my own surprise, I found myself "opposite number" to Adenauer and Schumann.

Despite some keen and even emotional objections from the Belgian Delegation at this early date after the war, a formula, which I well recall, was agreed upon by the Conference as an *ad hoc* aim of policy: "a federal and united Germany in a federal and united Europe." Whether Britain was included was left undiscussed. I was to see Dr Adenauer again in the Federal Parliament in Bonn; and Robert Schuman on several occasions—last at a

conference in Bruges, where I also had the chance of breakfast
conversation with George Brown, then dipping his feet into the
waters of the European movement, and with his most pleasant
wife. We were, in sentiment, "all good Europeans". At the first
Hague Conference of the N.E.I., subsequent to Luxemburg,
Katherine Atholl was present. On that occasion I brought along
our daughter, Shirley Williams, who overslept and delayed the
duchess's car to her Grace's ill-concealed annoyance. Here she
too was first introduced into the European Movement. Years later
she became chairman of the Labour Party's Parliamentary
European Group.

The second *Nouvelles Equipes* Hague conference was merged
with that of the European Movement as a whole. Winston
Churchill came over to speak. As a member of the N.E.I. international executive committee, I was a substitute delegate (my
senior, however, did not appear) for the organisation of this
conference. I breakfasted as the guest of Paul van Zeeland, ex-
Premier and Foreign Minister of Belgium, to discuss arrangements. I was embarrassed by having in my pocket at that moment a
circular letter from Morgan Phillips, then National Secretary of
the Labour Party, instructing recipients as Party members to
dissociate themselves from the Conference.

According to a report of what had happened in the Cabinet,
which reached me through a Parliamentary source, Clement
Attlee, as Prime Minister, had conditionally promised Churchill a
measure of support in the Conference enterprise. Churchill, in his
famous Zürich speech balancing his Fulton one, was concerned to
bless the European movement, although whether with Britain in
the European Union or with Britain outside but benevolent, was
ambiguous. A reversal of historical English policy could indeed be
involved. One "power", may be the European Commission,
would dominate Europe, something always the object of British
policy to avoid—but a peaceful and friendly power, not Eyre-
Crowe's bugaboo. In Cabinet Attlee had expected endorsement of
this attitude, but Aneurin Bevan (who regarded it as "Churchill's
show"), here supported by Hugh Dalton, vigorously opposed.
Both followed a narrow and ideological Party line. The majority of
the Cabinet seemed to concur. In turn the Party supported what they
wrongly supposed to be a unanimous negative Cabinet decision.
Hence the circular letter—"typical Aneurin" and very deplorable.

The breakfast with Paul van Zeeland over, I packed my bags,
took a look in at this historical Conference assembly and, in
accordance with instructions, caught the next train and boat for
London. That "good European", my friend Harry Hynd, M.P.,

rebuked me later for my action or inaction. However, I maintained and maintain that, with some diplomatic correctitude, I carried out my obligations both to the Conference and to the Party. What issued from the Conference was the decision to establish the Council of Europe at Strasburg. The late Lord Layton brought me in to the national and voluntary Council of the European Movement in London; and I signed various round-robin circular letters which they promoted. I still maintain, without change, the position I then held.

On the great occasion of the Council of Europe's inauguration at Strasburg, I had the privilege of being placed in a position directly across the street from where Winston Churchill was to address the citizen crowd below. The hour came and, after a pause, a window opened in the house facing. This was followed by a puff of smoke and, following the cigar, the well-remembered face displayed in photographs in the place of honour in almost every hotel foyer in Western Europe. Churchill spoke in his own distinctive Anglo-French. "Messieurs et mesdames, au-jour-d'hui jer parle fran-çais; et quan-d jer parle fran-çais, prenez garde." I had seen Churchill on several occasions as a public speaker and once briefly talked with him in the Commons—as I had also briefly met and heard Lloyd George in 1939. But this was, even for him, one of his great hours.

The Council was established and, at first, the Consultative Assembly adopted a form of seating and discussion quite unique in the fashion in which it ignored national and party divisions. It was strictly alphabetical. It had ironic consequences—when William Whiteley, British Labour Chief Party Whip, wished to instruct Mr Ungoed Thomas seated two away, he had to whisper across the front of Mr de Valera, firmly placed under the letter "V". Churchill, as a House of Commons man, initiated an important campaign to assert the authority of the European Consultative Assembly over the more limited Council of Ministers speaking for national governments. Nationalism and Party spirit, however, and the old claims of constitutional responsibility were too strong. The attempt failed and the Council of Europe began to wither on the vine as anything more than a debating forum. The spirit of an integrated Europe, federal or functional, receded at this time steadily from the early ideal. Later, in Westminster, far from prepounding the policy of instant entry, Churchill was to encounter a comparable resistance to change, not least from Anthony Eden, once "a Geneva man". "The Party machine wash too shtrong for me."

For that ideal of a United Europe I was myself an enthusiast, if a circumspect one. The final goal indeed was the establishment of stable peace in the world; the proximate step was the widest regional integration and what Michael Stewart has called "the blurring of sovereignties". Two "civil wars" in Europe in a life-time were more than enough. Whether Britain were in or were only benevolent in encouragement (as the United States is today), the Union of Western Europe could be an invaluable experiment, a pilot experiment in integration for the western world in what could be done in getting away from archaic political and lawyers' prejudice and old military enmities into what Field-Marshal Montgomery has called "pooling sovereignty" for peace. It was to be *pro tanto* functional, not least in defence.

Furthermore—and this was of the highest importance—in these early days I found the French, Maurice Schumann, Bichet and the rest, quite receptive to the idea that Britain had peculiar Common-wealth commitments. They tended to add that *they* also had *la France d'Outremer*—although I found the implied analogies between Canada or Australia and French Indo-China or the Gabon somewhat irksome. (I had failed to think of *la Nouvelle France*, waving the flag of the fleur-de-lys inside Canada.) They also accepted on basic principle the essential importance of the Atlantic Community framework—although more as an agreed goal than as present condition and means. It might be—and even be welcomed as—"a second step". Incidentally "the organic union", which I had proposed in 1940, with its plan for normalised meetings, not only of heads of government, but at lower depart-mental meetings, was exceedingly similar to the contemporary proposals of Christian Fouchet.

Briefly, the prospect seemed fair for such a unification of Europe as would contribute to the stabilisation of peace; would end these civil wars which had devastated Europe and weakened its power twice in the century; and would permit Britain, herself (be it noted) secure in the wider Atlantic framework, at long last to abandon that deliberate policy of calculated detachment and of balance of power traditional since the days of Cardinal Wolsey without fear of a Franco-German *entente*. This international "break-through" in diplomacy would be limited in region but real in substance.

On 8th May 1963, my wife and I were in St Peter's for what proved to be the last public audience and almost the last public appearance of one of the most remarkable men of our age, John XXIII—in the words of Nikita Khrushchev's son-in-law, "a true Pope". A man who radiated goodness of heart, the Holy Father also had a neat sense of humour. Fast advance in international affairs is seldom possible, but Pope John's wry comment on those of the Curia who retarded his policy is a memorable joy: "Io sono solamente il Papa"—"merely the Pope". It would not be inaccurate to say that ideological East–West *détente* dates from his time and that the new slant given to Vatican policy in its world mission and in its practical re-interpretation of impassioned ideological differences was peculiarly his work. It is well that such great men as Pope John of blessed memory are still to be found, great in vision and down-to-earth in experience, among those who play a major role in world politics. In the reported words of Nikita Khrushchev, "Now that Pope John and John Kennedy are dead, with whom can I talk about world peace?"

However, my personal contact (thanks to friends in London), was more extensive with Pope John's predecessor. The reputation of Pius XII has been traduced by the playwright Hochuth in his play, *The Representative*. One can only say that Pius XII was officially thanked by the Israeli Foreign Office for his work for Jewish refugees and that the Vatican archives show that, short of overtly preaching sedition against a government diplomatically recognised by Secular Powers as legitimate, there was little the Pope could have done which was not done. Some of this actual resistance is documented in our book *Above All Nations*, to which I have referred. "A more courageous policy" was indeed pursued by the Catholics in Holland. The direct consequence, as in the case of Anne Frank, was an even more ferocious Nazi persecution of the Jews than occurred in other non-German, occupied countries. It was a desperate choice, in which more zealot ideal counsels could have been Masada counsels of suicide. Nor could the Pope have gone further in denouncing Hitler "with burning anxiety" (the title of his predecessor's Brief) without discussing the other monster, Stalin, who boasted massacres yet more numerous counted out in millions on his fingers.

The present successor of Pius, Paul VI, has indeed courageously demanded a cease-fire in Vietnam today, as did Benedict XV in Europe in 1916; but the gratitude the Pontiff has received for this intervention seems to have been a muted one. It was the Sardar K. M. Panikkar who described the Papacy to me as "the sole sovereign that had increased its dignity" during the Second World war—a statement reiterated almost verbatim by the Pakistani High Commissioner in London, Mohammad Ikramullah.

I had an appointment with Pius XII at Castel Gondolfo. Fortunately I had mentioned my appointment, on the previous evening, to members of the British Embassy. In the morning my booked car failed to arrive at my hotel. "My miserable country-men," wailed the head porter. Transport in Italy, in 1947, was not easy to obtain. In desperation I rang the Embassy. "Yes, after it has delivered the Embassy children to school, it will call for you." Three quarters of an hour late for my appointment, seldom can any car or noble Roman have torn down the route of the *Via Appia Antiqua* more furiously than ours. However, on arrival I was relieved to discover that this delay was regarded by officials as not unusual.

I expected to wait and to pass from ante-chamber to ante-chamber. On the contrary, a door was opened and I found myself precipitated direct into the papal presence. We talked totally informally, in a mixture of English and French. We talked *à deux*, chiefly about a project of mine to promote the European cause through a newspaper to be printed on available Luxemburg presses in French, German and English and dedicated to the European Union cause. Pius, a man of remarkable profile and with a full face dominated by his eyes, was another of those few who gave all of his attention intimately to the person to whom he was talking or listening at the time. There was no peremptory haste but more the thoughtful interest of a parish priest. Simplicity. At the end of our talk he presented me with some medallions, one of which I gave to Gandhi. After I had bowed out, I looked at the Castel Gandolfo clock. I had had precisely twenty-five minutes of special audience.

Less enthusiastic days followed. With the decline in power of the M.R.P. in France, the importance of the *Nouvelles Equipes* also withered. With the defeat of the proposal for a European Defence Community, for which disaster Mendès-France and Anthony Eden must share responsibility, the European tide began to ebb. "To govern is to choose," said Mendès-France. They chose wrongly. Later came de Gaulle and the idealist era of Robert Schuman, Adenauer and de Gasperi, the original trinity applauded by Churchill, faded away. No longer was it *"Union Européene"* but *"Union des patries"* and later that enigmatic (but surely anti-American) concept, "European Europe". An entirely new project, with its own problems, arose.

The British Government in the 'Fifties displayed no great enthusiasm for "entry into Europe". Initially it expected the whole scheme to collapse when faced with the traditional political realities. When this defeatism proved to be itself, not "realism", but an economically dangerous self-delusion, a counterbalancing plan was pieced together, not least thanks to the skill of Reginald Maudling. Less strenuous in its conditions than those of the

Treaty of Rome, it envisaged a Free Trade Area including our Scandinavian friends, with Austria and "our oldest ally", Portugal. Economically successful, it yet contained the danger that Europe was to be, literally, "at Sixes and Sevens". It was not until a yet later date that Harold Macmillan was swung by the winds of change to accept the desirability of most urgent entry and to use Edward Heath to negotiate the detail, about which more later. (I could not agree with Mr Macmillan more than with his recorded belief that the failure, earlier in the century, to establish a Parliament in Westminster, representing the peoples of all the Dominions—not just Malta or Gibraltar—because of disloyalty to party whips or the like, was a monumental catastrophe.) It was a different chapter; and spelled more personally a different chapter in my own life. Initially my new fears and my new view, despite encouragement from Attlee and Gaitskell—and, for that matter, Rockefeller and Eisenhower—had almost no official support. I had to carry on very much alone.

What followed was what Macmillan himself described in the words, "the door was brutally slammed" by Brigadier de Gaulle, later President of France, who held domestic powers wider and more autocratic than those of the President of the United States. (In international power, he was of course not in the same category.) It is regrettable that the Foreign Office under Eden, that Galahad of a long-distant Geneva League of Nations, did not push Winston Churchill forward towards entry going beyond his position of benevolence towards the close union of others, rather than retard Churchill's personal efforts and desire to move—a movement which gave the best chance ever of what (rather controversially) has been called "British leadership". Here Eden and Dalton in effect joined hands. In those early days, under Churchill, there would have been no question at all of "going cap in hand". On the contrary, Continental Europe, if not leaderless, was still diffident of its own power and ready for a British lead. In the words of an eminent Spanish physician, Dr Trueta, whom I met in Basque-Catalan society, "Britain was the hope of a tortured continent of Europe!" (including Spain).

It cannot be over-emphasised that the arrival of de Gaulle and of the Gaullists on the scene and de Gaulle's subsequent traditionally French interpretation, not only of the Treaty of Rome but of the entire European project, vitally changed the situation. "To enter Europe" meant, henceforth, not one plan, but any one of two, if not three—and these plans not merely different but basically contradictory.

As I have said earlier, one can learn most about some new

emergent political star, if one takes the trouble—so few do—to
read what this leader said or wrote in his youth and then note it
seriously. *Mein Kampf* and Gandhi's autobiography were alike
illuminating for those who could read. *Vers l'Armée de Métier* and
Le Fil de l'Epée (1932) are no less important as a guide to the
would-be "Constable of France's" thinking. The reader must not
be bored or put off because de Gaulle is here preoccupied, in the
first book, with the role of a professional army and, in the second,
like Captain Sir Basil Liddell-Hart, with tanks. Assuredly I was
startled to hear from Lord Alexander of Tunis that he had not
read them. Passages in the book reveal the workings of de Gaulle's
mind; emphasise his admiration for the intransigent military
spirit; his contempt for the politician's character—but yet his very
clear notion of how the effective politician should behave. For the
soldier—

"... *la guerre est, bel et bleu, leur raison d'être, la carrière ou ils
se deploient et, comme dit Gustave Lanson, 'leur chance' (sic) ...*
"*La force fait la loi aux peuples et leur règle, leur destin.*"

However, in contrasting politician and soldier:

"*Celui-là gagne le but par les couverts: celui-ci y court tout droit.
L'un, qui porte au loin une vue troublée, juge les réalitiés complexes
et s'applique à les saisir par la ruse et par le calcul; l'autre, qui voit
clair, mais de près, les trouve simples et croit qu'on les domine pour
peu qu'on y soit résolu. Dans le fait du moment le premier pense à
ce qu'on va dire, tandis que le second consulte des principes.*"

"*Aussi la politique met-elle tout son art à la séduire, dissimulant
suivant l'heure, n'affirmant qu'opportunément. Pour devenir le
maître, il se pose en serviteur et fait avec ses rivaux enchère
d'assurances. Enfin, par mille intrigues et serments, voici qu'il l'a
conquise: elle lui donne le pouvoir. A présent, va-t'il agir sans
feindre? Mais non: Il lui fait plaire encore, convaincre le prince
ou le parlement, flatter les passions, tenir en haleine les intérêts. Sa
puissance, si étendue qu'elle soit, demeure précaire.*

*A quoi tient l'empire du politique? Une cabale de cour, une
intrigue de conseil, un mouvement d'assemblée le lui arrachent dans
l'instant.*

*Toute sa vie, toute son oeuvre ont un caractère instable, agité,
tumultueux qui les oppose à celles du soldat.*

*Politiques ou soldats, les meilleurs serviteurs de l'Etat sont
rarement les plus plastiques. Il faut que les maîtres aient des âmes
de maîtres.*

*Disraeli s'accoutumait de l'adolescence à penser en premier
ministre.*"[1]

---

[1] from *Métier des Armes* (Plon, Paris).

The picture is clear enough for the most naive. And what will be noted is that de Gaulle was a politician. His conduct must be expected to conform to his own outline of what this career requires. I have no space here to comment on the tergiversations in Algeria which nevertheless led, with a France threatened by civil war, to his own accession to power on 1st June 1958. For the rest, on the fly-leaf of *Le Fil de l'Epée* is inscribed the epigraph, quoted from *Hamlet*, but more emphatic in the French:

"*Etre grand, c'est soutenir une grande querelle.*"

It may be. One is happy to oblige the General.

I had occasion to hear Dutch deputies in London imploring Britain to make a firm "declaration of intention" of British entry *in order* to confront de Gaulle and what he stood for. On the other hand, Edward Heath seemed to put such stress upon entry that, in conclusion, he sought to draw ever closer to de Gaulle and his anti-American policies, if not "to play the poodle". In France the gossip circulated that de Gaulle thought that Macmillan and Home (by now Sir Alec Douglas-Home) would be succeeded by Wilson (as they were): that a Labour Government would, to French advantage, speedily collapse: and that "Then I shall only have Heath to deal with." (Mr. Reginald Maudling is a quite different story). How to handle "the off-shore island" indeed still presented a difficulty; but would be easier.

The distinctive view expressed by Harold Wilson as Prime Minister has been that there were indeed several "European Communities" (not one)—respectively organised as that of Steel and Coal (with its Sovereign High Authority); that of Atomic Energy; that of a purely economic and commercial E.E.C.; and also that of a potential and advocated Technological Community. Admittedly this introduces a new meaning into the semantics of the word "Community".

Another view, expressed by the Dutch, by Paul-Henri Spaak in Belgium and, less specifically, by the Germans and Italians, remains the traditional one; that there will be one authentic Community, with marked political overtones and pooling of sovereignty (here comparable to NATO, if with a different function and in a more limited area). They have been desirous of seeing Britain entering into this economico-political entity; tolerant of the addition of other countries, such as the Scandinavian and Ireland; aware of Commonwealth ties; and themselves quite prepared to give substance to the wider notion of an Atlantic Community as "second step". Dr Hallstein, like Robert Schuman before him, was clear that the proposal was not solely functional and economic but was ultimately profoundly political and social.

In the days of Macmillan these political aspects of the plan were pooh-poohed and played down. Today they are freely admitted, although, for an indefinite present, not in any federal sense. M Pompidou's chosen phrase for the structure is "confederal".

The third policy, articulated by de Gaulle, unflinchingly affirmed to the point of reaction and contempt for internationalists as *Jean-foutres*, visualised a loose confederation of Europe effective, on the Rome terms, on a strictly economic level. It was to stretch even "to the Urals" (why not beyond—or was the U.S.S.R. to be split?) and was to be marked by a French language culture which emphatically found leadership in Paris. This policy fluctuated between support of the Franco-German alliance which Adenauer had made his life-work, and a revival of the Franco-Russian alliance. Here I would personally put my money, despite Adenauer's admirable effort, on the selection of the Franco-Russian alternative. As both parties are well aware, this is traditional French policy and hence appealing. De Gaulle normally preferred traditional French policies, the glories of which can be retrospectively contemplated.

The General's doubt was whether the wedge between the parts of the Anglo-Saxon world ("Anglo-Saxony")—Britain and America, Australia and New Zealand—could be driven home. The abomination here is the concept of the Atlantic Community.

My own views here were emphatic and at a focal point of my whole effort. A veteran supporter of European union (if I may so describe myself), thanks to the Gaullist reinterpretation of the Rome Treaty, not federal but politically as Paris-centred as in French traditional diplomatic policy, a totally new situation had to be examined and confronted with courage. Further I did not personally believe that a "successful" Gaullism would come to an end if the Brigadier could be ousted from office. Others were— in my view, rashly—more optimist. With M de Gaulle taken up, in a new Assumption, to the throne of Zeus all, they felt, would be well.

As the European movement became embroiled by de Gaulle in difficulties and reactionary trends—as Frank Giles of the *Sunday Times*, said: "The European clock is turned back to the seventeenth or eighteenth century"—the older, wider and more powerful Atlantic Community concept swung again into the foreground it alone had occupied in 1941. To that campaign I propose to turn in the final chapter of this book.

Although Mr Duncan Sandys has provided certain significant hints about what he meant by miscalled "partnership", the political game was most explicitly given away in a *Daily Mail* editorial

(11th December 1966). "Europe", (i.e. Germany, France, Belgium etc.) "needs our technology if the Community is to build up an effective industrial *rivalry* to the U.S." The cat was out of the bag. The alternative then, for this pious "partnership of equals" is a pretty deadly trade war—not "partnership" but "rivalry", based on stark fear of united Anglo-Saxon power. Against this Britain might usefully set the ancient maxim: "If you can't beat them, join them"—join what is a high standard of wage and higher standard of living bloc, an Atlantic Free Trade area, rather than (in some areas) a lower. Aid to the underdeveloped depends upon one's own economic wellbeing.

There has, indeed, been some inauspicious and even rather silly talk about "a new Marshall Aid". More wisely, there has been stress upon European technological "lag". It seems that even the pooled and cartelised resources of North-Western Europe, in the judgement of some, are not equal to America's. There is not the money and they are too split-up and laggard. Here Britain can indeed under any circumstances, in or out of E.E.C., make a contribution much needed by the Continent in electronics, computers, aircraft and the rest. (It will be noted that a significant part of the components of *Concorde* have, on the basis of competitive tenders, been supplied by American firms.) As I have re-emphasised, I welcome British entry into E.E.C., granted political safeguards and with a political status somewhat higher than Nigeria. But I do not counsel England joining in a last stand, *le Défi*, in the anti-American ditch, where "The Community" precisely spells defiance of "the Atlantic Community" as an incompatible. This could be the Great Betrayal.

§ ii. *Interim*

In the charter of the North Atlantic Treaty Organisation, itself issuing from the Atlantic Charter signed by Roosevelt and Churchill in Placentia Bay, Newfoundland, there was a clause, pushed in by the Danes and Norwegians, and by Canada, stating that among the functions of the organisation would be that of promoting economic and even cultural measures for the better nurturing of democracy.

In 1948, thanks to the courtesy of one of my sometime students, Harvey Mansfield, now a professor in Columbia University and then chairman of department in Ohio State University, I was lecturing in Columbus, Ohio. General Eisenhower was at this time President of Columbia University. I took the opportunity of establishing a connection and, thanks to an introduction from Mrs Eleanor Roosevelt, of spending half an hour with him, on 9th

June in New York. I met General Eisenhower in the Administration Building of what had been King's College, New York, George II's foundation, now Columbia University. The blue flag with the white royal crown, the flag of the University, waved in front. The University President, relaxed but still sheltered by an army staff, was learning his new duties but was already being canvassed as possible President of the United States—for which Party was not yet clear. General Lucius Clay's task of converting to Republicanism a national hero, who was yet essentially a non-party figure, was not yet complete.

We discussed the confrontation of the recently victorious West by the renascent power of Stalin, and the disillusionment that had followed from the West's failure to secure, for Russian strategic reasons, free elections in a Poland Chamberlain had pledged the West to aid against tyranny even by world war. No one (except a few Poles living the miserable life of exiles) thought that the war could or should be renewed. They had been betrayed; and that was the end of it, as someday it will probably be the end of the Taiwan Chinese. Nevertheless free Poland had gone; the Baltic States had gone; fighting Finland had had to compromise; the Western world had, at last, been shocked to the bone by the assassination or suicide of that good friend of the West, Jan Masaryk, whom I personally knew.

Whatever military counterbalance might be built up, the issue was certainly not one of arms alone but of psychology, propaganda, of having common ideas around the defence of which the minds of the people of the West could cohere. I could not forget the declaration of Victor Hugo: "No army can withstand the strength of an idea when its time has come." Was there indeed any such common, fighting belief? Could there be? Later I was to reach the conclusion that—despite Walter Lippmann's valiant attempt—the only "public philosophy" of America is that it has no public philosophy. And upon this view feeds a parasitic anarchism which is America's greatest weakness, despite all the Lockean theology of the Supreme Court.

Ideas are to be met not only, or chiefly, from the outside by the strategy of arms and physical pressure. Nor can they be "sold" to others like detergents. Like an atomic bomb, they have to be exploded by fission from within and by the innate force of the more lucid and persuasive idea—a force, in the case of the great religious movements, almost hypnotic and instinct with conviction.

The well-known geniality of face departed. The quick choleric temper of the General, famous in the army, which I had noted when he was dealing with critical journalists in Chicago, came on top. "When America goes into the field of propaganda she takes an awful panning." "This has got to cease." The General rose from his chair behind the large desk and paced the room as I talked. "This subject that you talk about to me—there is no subject in which I am more interested and more concerned." The half-hour passed quickly. There were certain eminent Americans, academicians, heads of colleges, I presumed to suggest bringing along for a second meeting. An hour was allocated for a further talk. I felt that the interview had been encouraging and the time most well spent.

For this interview with the General I had travelled up, at my own expense, from Ohio. Any allocation of sterling, to cover expenses, in the Crippsian and post-Crippsian days of rigid British economy was out of the question. Even the British Delegation to the UN went to an hotel which I could afford myself in New York. This meant that the time required for appointments and talks which seemed to me to be not without importance was fairly rigorously curtailed. Exiguous reserves to back entirely private and personal plans were supplemented in my case by an offer, both generous and of a totally unexpected and chance nature. I have never myself been a conspicuous worshipper of Mammon. However, as a Regent of a Long Island University explained to me, there are uses, not least for the Goulds. In retrospect I perhaps ought to have given them more attention. Public service seldom has, from a lazy public, significant reward and can easily end in private bankruptcy.

Anna Gould, Duchesse de Talleyrand, at a luncheon party in Irvington-on-Hudson, a very solemn and ceremonious affair with white-gloved waiters, knowing that I suffered from the urgencies of still unfinished business (nor was there hope that the British Treasury would give any relaxation to a private person, not engaged in exporting tooth-brushes or like articles of commerce) suggested that I should stay at her place as a guest and catch a later boat home.

The daughter of the "robber baron" railway magnate, Jay Gould, it was of her that the rhyme ran:

> I am Anna Gould, Anna Gould,
> And before I die, before I die,
> I shall ride on the Santa Fé, the Santa Fé.

She died in splendour, but not, however, owner of the Santa Fé Railroad. When she divorced the Marquis de Castillane, the opposing French lawyer asked: "Madame, can you expect to do better?" The owner of the pink Chateau de Chaillot in Paris replied that she certainly could. In status she did. She married Talleyrand.

She had earlier entertained at her estate on the Hudson the young Hapsburg princes, until the early noise of their motorcycles had interfered with her morning rest. Experience has taught me that, with millionaires, any hesitation about accepting their hospitality as extravagant is regarded quite without favour. They expect themselves, as of right, to make extravagant offers. I, therefore, promptly accepted. My sole obligation was to dine with my hostess each evening. It was a most generous gesture of hospitality.

This visit meant, not only that I was provided with my own butler, housemaid and chauffeur in my own private chalet in the grounds, while dogs and keepers kept their watch by night outside, but that I woke each morning to gaze at not one but several pictures, photogravures, aquatints, of Charles Louis de Périgord, Bishop of Autun, Duc de Talleyrand, Prince de Benevente and Foreign Minister of France. In 1940 I had had an introduction and an invitation to visit Hearst's stupendous American castle of St. Simeon, described by Aldous Huxley, at San Luis Obispo in California and had passed it up. But this was the next best thing. As it were nude in a mere black tie, I attended my hostess in the Diamond Horseshoe at the *première* in the Metropolitan Opera. There bejewelled ladies who had come rather to be seen than to hear—the opera was *Fidelio*, which I had last heard in Munich, with Adolf Hitler in the front row—dozed with their feet on the balcony brass rails. Sinatra was also along that night with some party of his.

Alack! Eisenhower left for Washington on the affairs of his Republican candidature, which at that stage he was refusing; the arranged hour's talk was postponed, never to take place; and I sailed for home.

The theme of our successful talk, nevertheless, continued to preoccupy me. When Dwight Eisenhower became President, he appointed a Time-Life-Fortune man, C. D. Jackson, to head the U.S. Central Office of Information. I had briefly met both Harry and Clare Booth Luce and I had more respect than some people for the dynamism of Luce. All the same, the gospel of the nuclear-based "American century" seemed no adequate answer to my questions. C. D. Jackson was, unlike Ed Murrow, a "yes-man" who did not seem equipped to provide an answer to so profound a spiritual issue for the distracted West. Nor did I think the Scottish Presbyterian lawyer, John Foster Dulles, for all his undoubted integrity of purpose, had the answers—not even if Nikita Khrushchev did describe him (to the horror of some of the devout) as the American Secretary of State who had impressed him most:

"He knew his business."

In December 1950, when SHAPE was still SHAFE and NATO still to come, General Eisenhower had only arrived a few days earlier in Paris when I wrote to him again suggesting that I might be of use at headquarters in developing the civilian function mentioned in the NATO Charter. Sometimes these personal decisions arise from chance and from what Horace Walpole called "serendipity"; sometimes they are sudden inspirations, arising from incessant brooding on a personal determination. Later I was to discuss the same NATO issue in correspondence with Lester Pearson and with John Diefenbaker in the Prime Minister's office in Ottawa. The reply to my letter personally signed "Dwight D. Eisenhower", was friendly and encouraging. After all I had been professor of politics in one of the more eminent of America's "Ivy League" universities for eleven years.

In retrospect I can see that, not consulting anyone's convenience, I should forthwith have taken plane and gone over myself to see the General. Instead of imposing myself uninvited, I wrote again saying what I should like to do. The answer stated, rather more formally, that any appointment would have to be recommended from Westminster. I did indeed consult Lord Mountbatten of Burma and "Lord Louis", with that immense generosity and personal warmth that has always characterised him, advised me that, since a negative from the Prime Minister would be final, I had better first write to the minister in charge in London, Herbert Morrison, Lord President of the Council.

At a cocktail party some years later, in the American Embassy in Ottawa, where the matter happened to crop up, a British staff officer, whisky glass in hand, told me he had been the "buck-passer", the artisan of the official trip-wire who had referred me back to the British authorities in accordance with protocol. (It had never been my experience that either Americans or Canadians found elaboration of this procedure necessary, even as a circumlocution for *verboten*.) He was perceptibly put out when, in turn, I informed him of my source of advice.

However, despite the somewhat brisk "snaps to you" attitude which tends to characterise British negativity in middle official echelons, I can make no technical complaint about the procedure. The question was whether Herbert Morrison was prepared to play. He was not. I received a note to say that a small NATO information office might indeed be set up in London, but that no such civilian development at headquarters (in accordance with the Canadian–Scandinavian proposals) as I seemed to visualise would in fact be developed. NATO was military. My only feeling at the time about the Lord President's comment was "So much the worse." It did not convert me to the view that nothing needed to be done. I merely thought that Morrison had, as usual, got himself submerged in routine details and routine advice. My present judgement about this negativity to the civilian aspects of NATO is that it was and is a disaster.

I was to see Eisenhower briefly again in Chicago when he was nominated, on 11th July 1952, as the Republican presidential candidate at the Convention I attended there, when everyone wore "I like Ike" buttons. The hullabaloo of nominating Party Candidates, and of parading with banners in the aisles, has become far less during the time that I can recall. Even so, a small circus elephant was outside the Convention doors, symbol of the Republican circus within. I again saw the General, for rather longer, in the Brown House Hotel, Denver, to congratulate him on his nomination. That occasion I chiefly recall in terms of talks with that quite remarkable and dedicated man, Russell Davenport, who had been Wendell Willkie's campaign manager; and of how, if almost from idleness, I walked around the interior gallery, which characterised that unusual hotel, from General Eisenhower's suite to that of Jim Hagerty, his Press Secretary.

After the usual courtesies I hazarded the view to Hagerty that public opinion polls, even in other countries, were not quite without comparative value; that the contemporary British polls showed the Conservatives leading on every point save national health policy, and that if the Republican Party, out of office many years, wished to remain in power once Eisenhower had been elected, they might do well to introduce a strong "medicare bill", which appealed to the voter afraid of a long illness and in pursuit of security. Human beings, even voters, are afraid about their health, want some assurance within their means and fear lest the excessive bills which the philanthropic medical profession could charge for attending their mother's last illness would leave them confronted with harpy morticians, and with no spare money to bury the old lady.

Hagerty reacted by saying that this was not at all the Republican philosophy. He recited the customary American Medical Association arguments about the nobility of a free profession. It occurs to me that, had Hagerty and his fellows been more receptive to my view, with a few million extra votes the Republicans would have been returned in 1960, depriving the Democrats of their narrow majority for the benefit of Richard Nixon, and throwing out John F. Kennedy. The impartial historian will probably comment that this would have been a bad thing—but scarcely such from the point of view of Republican policy, from 1960 on progressively ossified for some years.

Later still I was to see Eisenhower on several occasions, primarily to talk about Atlantic affairs. But the immediate opportunity to get ahead with the work that preoccupied me seemed to come from another quarter.

I have campaigned all my life on the supposition that luck could be twisted to a purpose. Can sheer will, courage alone, prevail? Perhaps courage or will-power is the only weapon against luck. The man who thinks he is beaten is beaten already.

During the Second World War by chance I met H. J. Jordan, a bluff and honest man, son of a Kentish policeman, High Commissioner in London for New Zealand. Of the little 1940 book of mine on the hopes of the Atlantic Community, sent to him because I suspected a common interest, he wrote to me: "Before the day of the post-war conference, I hope you will express to me some of your opinions, as I am sure that they will be worthwhile putting forward at such a conference. . . . Anything which comes from your pen can be read with advantage by all." I was flattered by the comment, although sceptical—very rightly—that "all", or even my own countrymen, would appreciate the advantage offered to them.

It was not then just luck, but as a consequence of these talks and letters, that I was introduced to Jordan's fellow High Commissioner, later Sir Eric Harrison, Deputy Prime Minister of Australia. Because of this, in the network of events I was introduced to Sir Percy Spender, Australia's Minister for External Affairs and later Ambassador in Washington.

I have a keen memory of an exciting, sunny afternoon, after the war, in London at Claridges. Sir Percy there introduced me to his novelist wife, a lady of considerable drive, and discussed the possibility of my joining the Australian delegation to the United Nations, just as years earlier Gilbert Murray, himself Australian-born, had played a role in the South African delegation to the League of Nations. "Vansittart's commendation of you is good enough for me." However, constitutional questions were raised by the etiquette-minded among the members of the delegation Sir Percy headed, and Canberra was not encouraging.

In 1952, Sir Eric Harrison arranged, as it fell out, for me to come on from Jakarta to visit Australia, thanks to financial arrangements which he proposed with the Australian Broadcasting Company and the *Sydney Morning Herald*. The notion that I might be associated with Australian political affairs still persisted and the Deputy Premier met me in his car at the airport at Canberra and arranged for me to meet the current Minister of External Affairs, now Lord Casey, who himself had not refrained from taking a British *raj* Governorship, of Bengal, from Winston Churchill—a man who was not too timid to cross national boundaries of citizenship for his own purposes.

Canberra has been described as seven villages in search of a town. More exactly its roads were transferred from straight lines on a drawing-board to a countryside made funereal by sad eucalyptus trees. The consequent impression, not least on a wet day, was of avenues of crematorial gloom, recalling Brookwood Necropolis. Part of my hotel was unheated and the independent-minded taxi-drivers were sparing in their attention. To visit Mr Casey, I walked to and from the hotel in the rain. Although later rescued by Lindsay Nicholas, the millionaire of Aspro fame, then husband of Hephzibah Menuhin, with whom I later stayed on his ranch in the Western District of Victoria, I nearly caught pneumonia that day in Canberra from the chill. Today Canberra, I understand, is a different place.

Lord Casey was not on the warmest party fraternal terms with Sir Percy and his reception was not encouraging. Hephzibah gave me domestic messages for her brother, whom I had met inspecting elephant wild-life from the safe range of a launch on a lake in remoter Travancore. Thanks to the good Victor Kaufmans, from the perspective of an apartment overlooking the magnificence of Sydney Harbour I saw Sydney, with its ginger-bread iron balconies and its suburban streets where large men in short sleeves and woollen socks talked over the garden fence with their neighbours. But the Spender proposal to put me on the Australian delegation to the U.N. was still-born.

The net consequence of these events was that I had the scarcely world-shaking fortune of seeing Sydney Bridge, which Australians come from afar to worship, bringing their seventeen dolls; and also of visiting friendly, steak-eating Melbourne, under the amiable guidance of Sir Ian Potter. However, I did not see as much as I should have liked of the Irish there or of their devotion to Archbishop Mannix. An Irishman, we are told, had acquired some money and before leaving his home had fitted it up with a fine toilet. On his return a year later he found the toilet lid missing. "The chiney seat is very cold for us old folks," complained his mother. "But, granny, before I left I fitted it up fine." "Ach, son, you wouldn't be thinking I'd waste that mahogany seat on such? I used it to frame Archbishop Mannix's portrait."

There was also the unexpected bi-product of my visit that,

having spoken in Bangkok, in hyacinth-laden Mandalay—where my chairman painfully recited a *Who's Who* entry from date of my birth to final flourish of clubs: however, better that than in Phoenix, Arizona, where the State Lieutenant Governor forgot my name . . . —in Singapore and Jakarta, on my route westwards, I celebrated the spring feast of Vishnu (as I had done earlier in Kerala with Raymond Mortimer of the *Sunday Times*) amid the gossamer-delicate paradise of ever-memorable Bali.

Even so, in this heaven also there was comedy. It was amazing how quickly one got accustomed to bare-bosomed women in the main street (after all in Travancore it used to be a status symbol, a sign of aristocracy). However, bill-boards outside both airport and hotel, six foot by three, read: "Anyone photographing, intentionally or unintentionally, women nude or without breastcovering are liable to arrest and fine, as insulting Balinese womanhood and the sovereignty of the Indonesian Republic." Especially I appreciated the legal subtlety of "unintentionally" and the drum-roll of magnificence in the reference to Indonesian sovereignty under the aegis of Bung Karno. One brash young journalist I learned had approached a senior Indonesian statesman. The legal regulations about nudity, he said, were not being observed in Indonesia. What had the Hadji to say? "In Indonesia," replied the Hadji, "there are forty million women. The textile mills of Indonesia are not enough to provide covering for all. Good morning."

I remained in correspondence with Sir Percy Spender, who later became President of the International Court of Justice. Owing to an unfortunate experience he attached importance to words and names. The great project for aid to underdeveloped countries, had been his especial foster-child. It was then called the Spender Plan. But, in connection with large expenditure of tax-payers' money on aid, those with a sixth sense for publicity had felt "Spender" to be unfortunate. He was out of luck. The project became known as "The Colombo Plan".

I hold a letter from him in which he wrote to me: "I am surprised that you attribute the phrase, 'the battle for the minds of men', to President Truman. I used it in a public speech before he did. And you should know this because it was you who suggested the phrase to me."

I later checked up on this phrase with Senator William Benton, now editor of the *Encyclopaedia Britannica*, who was at that time President Truman's speech-writer. The phrase was indubitably also his: but we remained undecided who used it first. The truth is that, as with "evolution", in circumstances which invite a certain phrase or certain research, many are likely to arrive at the

discovery or at the *mot juste* at about the same time. And George
Creel had, in fact, used almost the same phrase in the Great War.
It merely said—what Marx, the dogmatic materialist, had
super-abundantly, if quite inconsistently, demonstrated—that ideas
matter and can even make or destroy the morale of peoples and
armies as those ideas march incarnate, angels or microbes, in men's
minds. Indeed it is by incarnating such ideas or forms that men
chiefly achieve their individual vital immortality in the record of
history. They may even, as Voltaire said, come to have in them
"more of that spirit which all men have than most men have."

What mattered was the issue and that political attention should
be given to the issue. It was and is not possible (as Secretary
McNamara so truly said in Montreal) to fight by bombs and
purely military means what is now called an "ideology", a word
meaning different things to different people, a mental attitude
which yet amounts in effect to a rigorous and almost religious
doctrine, pluming itself on the logic of its "theory". Let us admit
that the French Inquisition at Toulouse had extinguished by its
penal methods (aided by the elder Simon de Montfort) the heresy
of the Albigenses and, in our own day, Stalin had extinguished the
theories along with the persons of so many of the Mensheviks, if
not of the Trotskyites, by liquidation of heretics. Force had
indeed thrown back Islam at Tours and at Lepanto. But yet
"ideas", together with the human desire for self-preservation, had
seeped away the morale and strength alike of the vast armies of the
Czar and of those of the Western-oriented Chiang Kai-shek.

In the late 'Forties and early 'Fifties, there was a dearth (after
Laski's death) of Western political theorists of weight, who were
more than recorders of other men's thoughts and institutions, or
learned critics of other men's positive constructions, so that the
glory of the English tradition from Bacon to Mill had been dimmed
by mediocrity or irrelevance. There have been of course distinguished exceptions although these, such as Sir Isaiah Berlin, have
mostly been sparing in writing. I had yet dared, when there were
all too few companions, fool-hardily to throw myself into this
"battle for the minds of men". Perchance there were armed
Goliaths of the mind, brave Montmorencies, on my side but I did
not see them in the array. The problem was how to make any
constructive proposals of my own stick. However, my considered
conclusion was that, perhaps fortunately, the flux of power
decides more than the intransigencies of ideologies, which can
even end as mere propaganda tools of power. What pragmatically
matters is how men behave at the time, even if it is their ideas,
their philosophies (often unconscious), their religion, which shape

their culture.

Australia, where democracy holds aloft the dubious banner with a strange device "Anything goes", may be geologically the oldest continent, but it has a civilisation proud to be without aristocracy or "vanguard". These remarks are made in sorrow, recalling how I watched strong men drinking, in rows three deep in the stone-flagged bars of Sydney's best hotels—but yet with hope. They are not made in any such superior mood as that of Clemenceau when he enjoined Lloyd George, "Bring out your barbarians, Monsieur George." A continent in itself, who shall set limits to Australia's vast potentialities, especially if its population increases ? Nevertheless, if one were battling for the mind of Western civilisation, Australia was a remote fulcrum for such an axis or pivot for such a lever as I needed.

I was never a "cold-war warrior" of military commitment. I merely felt that purposelessness in the West would no more outwit purposefulness in the Soviet East than a gold-laden camel could pass through the needle's eye of resolute determination.

My own views on Anglo-American relations from 1925 until I acted professionally as technical adviser to Wendell Willkie (without losing my connection with the Roosevelt family), and during the war, in contact with Arthur Greenwood but also working through the America and British Commonwealth Association, which I co-founded, I have already described in earlier chapters. I have mentioned how, in a last attempt to galvanise action on Anglo-American relations before A.B.C.A. was merged in the non-political E.S.U., I went to Washington and saw Vice-President Alban Barkley on New Year's Day, 1950. I first explored the realism, in the contemporary scene, of Herbert Agar's federal unionist views and then put forward proposals to check anti-British propaganda in America and anti-American propaganda in Britain. "That seems to me commonsense, reasonable and what we want," commented the Vice-President—who had courteously given me time, although he was that day swearing in the Senate.

It was on this Christmastide trip on S.S. Queen Elizabeth, that I discovered that Walter Lippmann, an acquaintance of over twenty years, was on board. However, Walter was tired and told me that he would not be free for a talk until the end of the voyage. I also received a flattering request to cocktails, along with a *Time-Life* representative, *à quatre* with my sometime sovereign leige lord, Edward VIII, now Duke of Windsor, and his Duchess. The Duke looked youthful and well and, with pleasing informality, served cocktails and carried his wife's dogs. He was affable and she was gracious, most elegant and as charming as

Marina of Kent. Not wishing to disturb so eminent a journalist, I did not tell Walter.

I also persuaded Arthur Greenwood to chair a small committee in a room in the Houses of Parliament to consider the development of this Anglo-American theme. However, those who supported it seldom came, whereas William Warbey, M.P., an extreme left-winger, was assiduous in attendance.

Before going to Washington and still valiantly aided by Captain Beaumont, Labour M.P. for Uxbridge, a strong United Nations man, and by Albert Braithwaite, Conservative M.P. for the Buckrose Division of Yorkshire, we got together a large and indeed expensive dinner at the Dorchester Hotel to discuss next steps. I had earlier discussed with them the setting up (since it did not yet exist) of an Anglo-American Parliamentary Committee. At first the Foreign Office was not keen, but later changed its mind. Braithwaite became the honorary treasurer. There were two honorary secretaries. I heard with wry amusement Sir Percy Harris, M.P., Liberal, tell me that he had proposed Aneurin Bevan for one of these posts—"He knows so much about America, don't you think?"

The company at the dinner was diverse, ranging from Herbert Agar, who wanted nothing less than "union now", to Sir Alfred Swanson-Taylor (Lord Grantchester) who stood his ground on a United Nations approach. As too often happens on such occasions, little was decided. Since I had no official post, I was highly conscious that I was in a weak personal position, without public weight. However, I drove through a resolution to set up a sub-committee for action of about five persons. Since I knew that Frank Darvall, then Director of the E.S.U., a member, was favourable to what I had in mind, I was surprised that so little progress seemed to be made—the more so as we had taken the precaution of putting a leading official of the Foreign Office, indeed the occupant of "the American desk" and son of a sometime Liberal Leader, on to our sub-committee. Later Frank said to me: "He was such a nice fellow: I just can't understand what happened." Lord Strang was more cagey. I, however, had quite ceased to be surprised by our lack of progress. The name of the Foreign Office official was Donald MacLean, the Russian defector. My belief that, in matters of public policy, one must always be guided by Foreign Office officials, waned.

This line having proved abortive, despite constituency work in Bury and North Hendon and lectures in the University of California at Berkeley, I felt I must give my attention to securing the closer and expert consideration of detailed consequences, not only of the Union of Europe, as I have already described, but of parallel development in the framework of the wider Atlantic Community.

In 1960 I was invited "from the blue" by my sometime student, Dean (later Vice-Principal) Noel Fieldhouse to occupy a foundation chair at McGill—in *la grande ville de Montréal*—which has always claimed to be the senior Canadian university. Since this gave me the opportunity to return for a while to "establishment" academic life, I accepted. I had, indeed, since I resigned from Cornell, earned my income year by year, "professing". The Dean was, by an almost blasphemous hyperbole, good enough to describe my availability as "as gift from Heaven". Shortly afterwards the Vice-Chancellor of McGill invited me to become chairman of the joint department of economics and political science, a department of fourteen professors, one the future Finance Minister of Quebec. I objected that this would involve stopping all work on my *Systematic Politics*, which was to be the definitive instalment of my work in political theory, and immersing myself in committees. (Modern institutionalism had entirely outpaced the happy Cornell days when committee business was quickly decided *à deux* by a swift conversation in a corridor.) It was represented to me that it was my civic duty to take on the post. I did so. It was, I believe, a happy enough department during my tenure. At least I was happy. Incidentally, the original project for the New Democratic Party of Canada was, in 1959, drafted in my office (although in my absence) at McGill.

One trouble in Montreal was that, despite the heroic efforts of James McGill, founder of the university, there were in it three separate communities, scarcely intercommunicating. There was the wealthy but small Jewish community, living *"d'outre mont"*; the out-going but still socially prominent Scottish community, which used to have commercial control, and which lived "West of Bloor Street"; and the French *habitant* community, newly moving into control, "East of Bloor Street". A girl who married "West of Bloor Street" ceased to be acceptable "East of Bloor Street". During my brief time at McGill one of the few places where one might meet with Mr Arnold Steinberg, of the Jewish community, the President of *l'Université de Montréal* and a Governor of McGill University, was in our appartment in Côte des Neiges.

One of my economic colleagues was an archaic liberal, otherwise called an economic conservative. I passed over to him a book by the Archduke Otto, *Soziale Ordnung von Morgen*, sent to me by the author. Its theme was that the poisons of our contemporary life were Marxism and capitalism (a very Cecilian–Hapsburg proposition). My colleague objected that the book was "no good". I pressed him on his judgement and he reiterated it. "You mean, David, that you find the Hapsburgs too radical for you?"

I also recall with pleasure the story told me by my legal colleague, Professor Frank Scott, the defence lawyer in the case, of protests by the local Mohawk Indians against having one end of a vast bridge across the St Lawrence coming down in their reservation. A Minister had come from Ottawa to explain the advantages. Chief Poking-the-Fire and Lady Poking-the-Fire sat watching. "And what," enquired the chief, "is that plot of land there to be used for?" "This," remarked the Minister, "is space for a great step in modern progress—a sewage works." With grave and forbidding solemnity Lady Poking-the-Fire replied as in a declaration of Uhuru, "White man's ways. Not red man's way."

In 1960 I resigned from McGill, my *Systematic Politics* complete. Montreal was, I found, too far from Westminster. But this period in the senior dominion was helpful in putting some variety of experience behind my own views. I crossed Canada twice, experiencing the bitter cold of Grand Portage, Winnipeg, and the echoing magnificence of the Hotel Bessborough, Saskatoon. In all I travelled from Halifax to Vancouver. John Buchan, Lord Tweedsmuir, unfortunately died before I had the opportunity to visit him. However, I did visit his successor as Governor General, Vincent Massey, who had become a strong exponent of Anglo-French partnership and of all Canada becoming bilingual. The later stringing up, on the Heights of Abraham, of a stuffed dummy, labelled "Wolfe", with its throat cut, did not seem to me very encouraging.

Prophecy and crystal-gazing are no part of the role of a political scientist. Nevertheless, were indeed—and I hope the contrary—Britain intent to become a homogenised part of a 'European Europe", I would see little future for Canada, if it is to avoid the miserable fate of Belgium, except for its Provinces to become (as Goldwyn Smith had been persecuted for suggesting) States of the American Union—part of a true "United North America" (just like Europe . . .)—with a "Free Quebec", an independent sovereign State, probably (despite the Monroe Doctrine) in military alliance with France.

To develop my notion that a research centre was wanted, to make an entire census and to map the economic and technical situation involved in any authentic Atlantic "partnership", with all its Commonwealth implications—and the Atlantic Community, taken without geographic pedantry, *would* include the Commonwealth, whereas European Union, unqualified, would not—I raised Canadian money for the purpose. I went up to Ottawa and persuaded the Permanent Secretary, Ministry of External Affairs, that Canada had an interest in this. Some people in Philadelphia also had a concern. (Lester Pearson, then in Opposition, I saw several times in Montreal. I have had the pleasure of keeping in touch with him ever since.) A little later and this proposal was to be an item on the agenda of a Conference to take place in London, in October 1959.

There was indeed some British objection to any such Atlantic Community Institute on the ground of duplication of the work of the existing Atlantic Treaty Committee (a NATO auxiliary organisation). A Canadian delegation, resolved on support, was to attend the Conference. I went up to Ottawa again and, this time, saw the Prime Minister, John Diefenbaker. It was suggested that I should join the Canadians. Mr Diefenbaker asked me to write him a letter, putting the proposal into words. "Just go into the next room and dictate it to my private secretary." I did, and was put onto the Canadian delegation, by the Canadian Prime Minister personally. After all, I was in North America where things happen. With memories of my experiences with Eisenhower and then with Australia, I had the haunting feeling: "Here we go again."

Sometimes indeed I did have to wait. I was summoned from Boston up to Ottawa by Mr Diefenbaker one Friday. On arrival I learned from his secretary that Mr Duncan Sandys was there; that the Prime Minister was at that time unfortunately too busy to see him; and that, hence, he also could not see me. I foresaw a dreary week-end ahead of me before leaving on the Monday. The reformers had so arranged that Ottawa was a "dispensing area" for liquor. My needs were most modest—perhaps four cocktails over two days. However, under law the Hotel Frontenac could supply nothing on Sunday and the dispensary declined to supply me, also by law, with anything less than an entire bottle of Bourbon—a fiscal discouragement of a debauch. Since my air-baggage was limited, after divine service I was compelled to spend a Sunday alone in Ottawa with this Bourbon as the sole solace and, for literature, *My Wicked, Wicked Life* by Errol Flynn. I arranged for a photograph by the great Karsh for the Monday morning before leaving. I hope and believe that it gives no impression of excess.

When I finally left the great city of Montreal, on a Canadian Pacific boat, my wife and I happened to share a table with the sometime Governor-General, Earl Alexander of Tunis. I learned that the Field-Marshal was greatly interested in Anglo-German relations. On my return I pressed that he should be invited to be President of the Anglo-German Association. And he became President. I have had reason to be profoundly indebted to this great man and soldier on more occasions than one.

One memorable morning, over the breakfast table, I enquired: "Lord Alexander of Tunis, what do you think about Tunis?" I received a reply a comment on the whole Maghreb and the French colonial regime there which, by its boldness, roused my full attention. Field Marshal Alexander was an Irishman; and I do not know how he would have commented on the singularly nasty form of colonialism, by Presbyterian Scots in Ulster under James I, for the unholy purpose of, by expropriation, holding down "the bog Irish". However, what he said was that the French *colons* had appropriated the best land, leaving the lean to the Arabs. And then—I leave the logistics to a master of military science—he added: "What should be done is to put the whole lot of the *colons* onto ships, and ship them back to France."

The projected Institute of Atlantic Affairs was established. I went twice (at my own expense) to Brussels to work with five others on the draft of its proposed constitution. It was to be located in London or perhaps Milan, not Paris. Yet, in the end it was placed in Paris; proceeded chiefly to regurgitate the old E.E.C. arguments with which one was so familiar; and the word "Atlantic" as distinct from "European", was not much heard in the land. However, it did valuable research work in connection with the European Common Market, which was the primary "Community" considered by it. Later its director, Henry Cabot Lodge, departed (much to his own disadvantage) to Vietnam.

At the time I wrote my small book of 1941, the Soviet Union was in the toils of the Ribbentrop–Molotov Pact; Germany and Italy were enemy countries; the official Head of State of France was Marshal Pétain; de Gaulle had been condemned to be shot. It was out of the question then to write in terms, not of the power-triangle of Washington–Westminster–Ottawa, but to spin hopes about Bonn–Paris–Rome. A united Europe was Hitler's idea, as it had been Napoleon's. However, I re-read the book and decided that I still agreed with what it said. The reprint (with a new chapter added), *The Atlantic Community*,[1] took full account of the north-western European fringe of the great Eurasian continent.

In 1966, the Pergamon Press published my *Grandeur of England and the Atlantic Community*.[2] It was a strict development of the

[1] *The Atlantic Community* (Coram: Macmillan Co. of Canada), 1959.
[2] *The Grandeur of England and the Atlantic Community* (Pergamon Press), 1966.

EUROPE AND THE ATLANTIC COMMUNITY   397

argument on policy in my earlier political books. Some of the
preliminary detailed work had been put, as I have said, into shape
as a Fabian pamphlet, *The Creation of the Atlantic Community*.
The book itself was first offered to the publishing house of
Macmillan; but they replied, very courteously, that it seemed to be
about current affairs and these changed so rapidly, as it were *de
jour en jour*, that they felt unable to undertake publication. The
temptation to make an obvious reply was too great and so I wrote:
"The grandeur of England does not change."

The book, when published, received admirable notices in local
papers in the north of England which stressed what journalists call
its "human interest". Its focus was on the westward-looking
history of England. Its message was that statesmanship lay in
noting the essence of a people's tradition and its genius, not in
flouting but making the most of this genius and destiny. England
had one massive unique historical advantage, shared by no other
European country: it was not the most powerful but it was the
senior member of the global English-speaking world; and here lay
the true development from the earlier imperial position. It was
only her enemies who would recommend cutting the painter of this
special relationship. Earl Attlee was good enough to write a notice
of it as "most thought-provoking", backed by "a wealth of
practical experience"; and the Minister for Defence to comment
that it was "most impressive". Lord Mountbatten wished it "a
wide sale". However, perhaps because it was first published as a
paperback, not much notice (what little there was was laudatory
enough) was taken in the national Press. It was followed by a small
Penguin book, *The Atlantic Commonwealth*—a title which I stole
by permission from Henry Kissinger—chiefly concerned with
Atlantic Free Trade Area proposals.[1]

Earlier, in 1957, I delivered the Weil Lectures, *On Political
Goals*[2] in the pleasant University of N. Carolina; and in 1964 I had
delivered in Seattle the Walker Ames Lectures, subsequently
published as *Applications*[3] and also translated into Japanese.

In 1964, in Washington, D.C., on personal introduction from
Harold Wilson, and to discuss the picture of Atlantic and Common
Market affairs, I had met Harland Cleveland, later U.S. Ambassa-
dor to NATO. I also met Ambassador Schaetzel and Ernest
Lindley in the Department of State; Arthur Schlesinger in the

[1] *The Atlantic Commonwealth* (Penguin Special), 1969.
[2] *On Political Goals* (St Martin's Press, New York), 1957; published
as *What Does the West Want?* (Phoenix House, London), 1957.
[3] *Political and Sociological Theory and its Applications* (University of
Michigan Press, Ann Arbor, U.S.A.; Moritsu Bunkasha, Tokyo), 1965.

White House; ex-Secretary of State Christian Herter; ex-Secretary of State Dean Acheson for an hour; Senators Fulbright and Millee and Vice-President Hubert Humphrey. I had met the Vice-President several times before (he had once been a professor of political science in a college where I had lectured), and it gave me much pleasure to receive a letter of 10th November 1966 which read in part: "I look forward to your letters and the chance to share your thoughts". (A memorandum was sent on 30th May 1967.) In Independence, Missouri, I talked, not for the first time—as I have told earlier—with ex-President Harry Truman, and we had shaken hands on the policy of support for the Atlantic Community—with certain drastic remarks by Mr Truman about M. de Gaulle thrown in.

A few days later I spent a most profitable hour with ex-President Eisenhower in Palm Springs, California, and saw him again for half an hour the following year in Gettysburg. I submitted various suggestions for the title of the American edition of *Grandeur* and, with his usual generous courtesy, he took time on the matter. Of the title *The Stronger Community* he commented: "That seems a most excellent title; it would certainly interest me." So, for the American edition, this was the title I chose for a book which was to state my fighting beliefs in the campaign on which I had spent almost a lifetime.

Again, in Gettysburg, I met President Eisenhower, on 16th October 1967. He went to hospital the following afternoon—but I do not think that I was responsible. ... By way of additional introduction I sent him a copy of one from Lord Attlee, surely among the last Clem Attlee wrote. A laconic man, not at all easy to know, in his last years I had broken the silence barrier and he was kindness itself to me. He had written that he looked forward to reading my autobiography, and his letter of 30th August (he died on 8th October) ran:

"Dear George,

It was a pleasure to see you yesterday, and I am glad to learn that you will be seeing General Eisenhower shortly.

Would you be good enough to tell him how pleased I was to know that he is better again, and give him my warmest regards and very best wishes.

I hope that you will have a pleasant journey.

Yours ever,

Clem."

The General looked deceptively well when I met him in the remembered office. He expressed his views on his sometime subordinate officer, General de Gaulle, with reference to his visit in the *Colbert* to Québec and his procession down *le Chemin du Roi*, in downright and colloquial language, even more emphatic than that used by ex-President Truman four years earlier in Independence, Missouri. The General was good enough to describe my own work as "important", and to that last conversation I shall return.

He gave me introductions to Governor Nelson Rockefeller and David Rockefeller in New York, and I met both. The Governor received me (at a time when his own house was being picketed by strikers, so that he had every excuse for not doing so) not merely with courtesy but cordiality. Our agreement on Atlantic affairs was wide and emphatic. In conclusion—he had forgotten that, in 1940, Karsh had taken a photograph of him—he signed my Karsh photo with the words "from his newest friend, Nelson A. Rockefeller", a gesture not so much political (whatever the Communist comrades may say) as showing the outgoing nature of a remarkable American.

XVII

AGAINST THE BREAK-UP[1]

§ i. *The Quest for a Rôle.*

Having lost an Empire, and that the most wide flung in the world's history, Britain is "in search of a role". So, for that matter, is the United States. The famous phrase is that of a major statesman and not unadmiring critic, sometime Secretary of State Mr Dean Acheson, who honoured me with correspondence, despite failing eye-sight, as late as early in 1971. In the case of France and even of the old German Empire, a trauma was left, a wound to the national pride. In the case of England, as Winston Churchill boasted, it could not be conquered by Shickelgruber. But what was to come next? The policy of Pompidou? The contemporary pain is surprisingly small, precisely because there is a national confidence that answers will be given to the question, although they are not yet there. The Irish, knowing that Queen Anne is dead but not Dutch William, fight out their own answers among themselves. Scottish and Welsh secessionists are not yet a problem to disturb the night's sleep. Whither yet Britain?

The Empire was a fact without a philosophy such as Rome had. The liberally conceived Commonwealth never had a considered philosophy. Suspended between nationalist follies and internationalist hopes, groping towards institutional form, it was described by the more enthusiastically "trendy" of Fleet Street journalists as "a yawn". We have to give these journalist songsters something to choke their guts with, assuming that they have any. Maybe the United Kingdom is itself merely "a yawn";

[1] This chapter, in an early draft, was first printed and privately circulated in March 1971. It received some praise from Mr Harold Wilson; was described by Mr Denis Healey, sometime Minister of Defence, as "admirable"; and received even more emphatic approval from Mr James Callaghan, sometime Chancellor of the Exchequer and Home Secretary. The views stated differ rather emphatically from those recently expressed by my daughter, Mrs Shirley Williams, Shadow Secretary of State, Home Office. It may be that, in a famous phrase, "the Suez Canal runs through our front room", although party unity was a prime factor on which we agreed—and the difference certainly did not affect our human relation. Nevertheless for neither of us was the issue one where we shaped our judgement as mere journalistic observers or as uninformed outsiders. As M. de Gaulle observed in a characteristic phrase: "Etre grand il faut épouser une grande querelle."

and we have but an England or Wales floating in some Irish
stew called Europe. The question, posed by Acheson, remains.
What answer shall be given by patriot and realist? What vision in
world affairs is going to prove indeed the best realism? I essayed
an answer thirty years ago. I still believe that answer to be true.

Some of us have, since then, enlarged an Anglo-American
policy, alone viable in war-time, into a more profound Atlantic
policy by working after about 1943 for the Unity of Europe. We
were indeed rebuked at the highest party level for our pains. We
wanted to see how far an imaginative experiment, not merely
national but of functional "sovereign high authorities", involving
(as Field Marshal Montgomery suggested) a certain erosion of the
old legal intransigence of "absolute sovereignties", could be
pushed successfully in the comparatively small experimental area
of Western Europe. These "high authorities" excellently illustrated the hopeful road of functional and experimental advance.
Transport and water-ways could well have been next on the list,
as well as technological and health regulations. Not only might
this achieve the miracle of ending the centuries' old Franco-
German feud, tracing down from Bourbon and Hapsburg. Indeed,
in my pamphlet, *The Union of Europe*, published by the Polish
Government-in-Exile in 1943, I had suggested the inclusion of
Poland. If the plan operatively succeeded, then it could be applied
over the whole "free world", in a fashion more acceptable than
Empire and more institutional than Commonwealth.

In 1963 President de Gaulle "brutally slammed the door".
Harold Macmillan as Prime Minister had indeed, in succession,
had three policies. The first, inherited from Anthony Eden, was
one of benevolent but sceptical detachment towards the Messina-
Rome project. In return for an Indo-China (Vietnam) deal with
Russia, Mendès-France had ended the dream of a European
Defence Community; and the Economic Community might go the
same way. In fairness to Harold Macmillan be it said that, in the
House of Commons, he had been violently attacked by Left Wing
extremist William Warbey, MP, for designing a much closer
connection with the United States, which Winston Churchill had
advocated in his Fulton and Virginia Addresses of 1946. The
second phase was one of Sixes and Sevens in Europe. Instead of a
Common Market entry, a more politically acceptable, if not
economically very impressive, EFTA Seven had been welded
together by Reginald Maudling. The third phase, held to be
electorally a possible Tory winner, its agent Edward Heath,
proposed not merely a Churchillian benevolence to European
Union but an actual entry by Britain into Europe, which went

beyond anything to which Churchill had specifically committed himself. It had Commonwealth implications which could turn the stomach of true Tories, but it might attract the new floater voter, his yacht veering to the wind of change.

Maybe Winston Churchill attached more importance to what he said at Fulton in 1946, than to what he said at Zürich. Sir Alec Douglas-Home may insist, as the Foreign Office has always tended to insist, that EEC has no serious political implications, nothing more as touching sovereignty than is already involved in the UN and NATO—but this emphatically is not the view of many of his Continental colleagues; and it does not accord with Mr Heath's announced dreams of unifying Europe in a fashion of which a more intelligent Napoleon or Hitler might have approved. For M. Pompidou (8th July 1971) there is not only "a decisive act in turning toward the Continent" but "a political finality", issuing in political integration. De Gaulle, on the other hand, could say that "the time will come when the British will thank me for keeping them out". The Anglo-Saxons, the English and their culture, did not really belong in a Europe which was firmly to be shaped by French policy; a Francophone Europe, Paris its Mecca. The very association of *les Pouvoirs anglosaxons* was a menace to Europe, France, and Parisian prestige. The door was slammed and a chapter, that of Robert Schuman, of de Gasperi, even of Adenauer, ended. A new chapter had to be begun. Nor was that new chapter itself to be finished with the death of Charles de Gaulle. As Chancellor of the Exchequer Roy Jenkins said in New York: "Gaullism does not end with the death of de Gaulle."

It was Winston Churchill who said of de Gaulle that "he was a great enemy of the English-speaking peoples". For those, "the diminishers", who do not believe that the English-speaking peoples have much in common anyhow (and seek so to persuade the merely social English-Speaking Union) this is, of course, no very serious charge. Two recent British Prime Ministers, not the least eminent, had American mothers—a third was Canadian. Certainly de Gaulle had no such ancestry. His was Alsatian. Let us admit that de Gaulle was "a great man and good for France". This is an argument that has to be used with caution, since it has also been applied, by his admirers, if with less truth, to Mussolini. I honour, as I admire, de Gaulle's obstinate pertinacity against his critics. It is a rare human quality. Were I a Frenchman I might even be seduced by his appeal to the French glory of an earlier age. I do not happen to be French.

Churchill's comment applies, not only to the very young de Gaulle lecturing his father about how the French ought to have

won at Agincourt, but to those later days when Charles de Gaulle
had to swallow the bolus of patronage and to express gratitude to
the British Government who, by heavy investment, had built this
"outsider acting brigadier" up against senior rivals. To acknow-
ledge his actual dependent position on Britain was to destroy his
own appeal in France. It was surely odd and psychologically naive
for General Spears to be surprised by a vindictive ingratitude. It
was perhaps even more unpleasant to express gratitude to the
Anglo-Saxon in Britain than to express detestation of Roosevelt
and those of the other *Pouvoir anglosaxon*, which had little use for
him and his tantrums. Historic fate here condemned de Gaulle
to be devious, vindictive, ungrateful. It was indeed not the
Liberation, but (by methods also devious) his termination of the
French Empire in Algiers, which established his position.

At least, with no wish to be "modern", de Gaulle understood
the continuity of history and the meaning of tradition, and that
France would not be France if she tore up her roots. Would that
others understand this as well. His final dramatic satisfaction
could be found in a situation which left the colossus to die and
be buried in self-chosen detachment at Columbey. In the words
of the heroic Cyrano, "Puisqu'elle est en chemin, je l'attendrai
debout ... et l'épée à la main". Meanwhile the smaller men of
pomp—and the President of the United States well to the side in
order of juniority, and the British heir to the throne precisely
placed behind the Shah of Persia—were perforce gathered to pay
him homage a hundred miles away in Paris. How delicate a revenge
for how arrogant a hero. However,

> "Je ne suis pas de Gaulle,
> Si vous donnez mon nom,
> Un son méchant ou drôle" ...

A critical view of de Gaulle and his chauvinism does not
involve a condemnation of France. Sometimes indeed the stomach
is turned when an eminent general of the French air force can
publicly suggest in London that, at a crunch, the Americans cannot
be trusted to come to European support were New York
threatened, but that, whatever the threat to Paris, the French
could be trusted to defend Bonn and London. What effrontery!
Nevertheless, not only reverence for M. Robert Schuman, but
many meetings with M. Maurice Schumann, convinced me that
here were men liberal, humane, and of more than merely European continental outlook. When I congratulated Maurice Schumann on becoming Foreign Minister of France, I read with
warmth the telegraphed reply (ironically reaching me, labelled

"Overseas Cables"): "Vifs remerciements, fidèle amitié, Maurice Schumann, Etat priorité, 4.ii.69."

After the great de Gaulle, Pompidou—as the cartoonist McLachlan put its, "That damned, elusive Pompidou". For all of this the policy of M. Pompidou, less downright, perhaps better bottomed, perhaps more subtle, than that of de Gaulle, remains typical. It is that of defence of French interests, not least agricultural; of an uncommitted hand in reasserting French influence and power, through French diplomatic leadership, in Europe but also in Moscow and the Middle East; economic aid to ex-French colonies; to retain the old colonial "Community" links (no "yawn" this); sale of arms to any willing buyers; and claiming the cultural primacy of French civilisation, even outside Europe, even in North America, a claim which seeks for itself the right to define what is "a good European". It is a claim from which England, maritime and looking West, has no less traditionally consistently dissociated herself.

It may be that it would be better, as de Gaulle hoped, to allow France, without interference, to shape the policies of a United European Community. The limits of French military power and even diplomatic influence render this dubious. The more prudent course would be to insist on that policy of OECD (which Australia also has recently joined) and of the North Atlantic Treaty Organisation, acceptable hitherto to Western Germany, from which France, at much cost to others, has chosen to detach herself. (Modern missiles transcend even continental limits, over-shooting Europe; but for regional secondary arrangements within NATO, with interchangeable weapons, there might be a case.) The calculated departure of France from NATO, while keeping a diplomatic finger in the pie of the Atlantic Treaty, has deplorable strategic consequences, which EEC will not remedy and may accentuate. If, for example, the United States sought to support Israel, by withdrawing emergency troops by air from the Rhineland, it is a conceivable Pentagon calculation that France might and maybe would wreck the operation by refusing over-flight permission.

On the contrary, the defence qualities of NATO are not destroyed by a new emphasis—complementary to or absorbing OECD (Organisation for Economic Co-operation and Development), while making global its own too limited and 'North Atlantic' area—on the "civilisation" of NATO, along the lines of the Atlantic Free Trade Area, including the economic, political and cultural elements of Clause 2 of its own Charter. Such a "civilisation" is welcomed by Signor Brosio, its recent Secretary

General, and almost certainly would be welcome in Washington.

In 1940, as mentioned earlier, I urged as a principle "organic consultation", later rephrased as Organic Union, a principle taken up and quoted from me with approval by Walter Lippmann, in his *US War Aims*. This means, not only building institutions and organisations (necessary as these are if one is to go beyond the uncertain foundations of public sentiment), but normal and habitual personal meetings of the like-minded and exchanges and inter-minglings at the summit level and also at all department levels, economic, health, transport, environment, defence and diplomatic. In the words of Senator J. K. Javits, in the *New York Times* and *Herald Tribune* (18th June 1971), "ministerial meetings need to be put on a regular basis. . . . In short, we in the United States must go forward much more intensively to establish the Atlantic Community rather than to fractionalize and run away from it." Here regional European integration is in no wise necessarily or desirably incompatible, granted the right statesmanship, with a concurrent wider institutional and policy development. These are the specific objective lines which policy, moving towards an Atlantic Commonwealth embracing Western Europe, should take.

The reshaping of NATO, so as to leave an open door for détente with the Warsaw Pact countries, does not invalidate the need for the structure. A highly integrated, centralised Western Europe, including Western Germany and with economic and transport focus in the Ruhr, is likely to be less, not more, amenable than an Atlantic Free Trade Area to negotiation with the Warsaw Pact countries. The American Senate will not construe NATO as abrogating national rights of decision. A non-elective Brussels Commission with an "integrated defence and foreign policy", might be less respectful to the rights of the British Parliament on the cardinal issues of peace and war. As for Russia, nostalgic for Rapallo but almost pathologically fearing German power, the Soviet Union respects NATO power while intriguing against it and fostering Atlantic divisions, and consistently respects power as such. The flaw in French policy and in French jealousy is that it encourages such divisions.

As for Britain, developed from England into the United Kingdom, and from the Kingdom into the world-wide Commonwealth, it has been my consistent view that its historic development and destiny, at the next stage, lies in the multi-racial but still coherent Atlantic Commonwealth, to which perchance Europe also will adhere—even the enemies, now friends, of 1939–45. I am not a "continentalist"; and I do not approve of a restricted, provincial continentalism. I do not approve of such a continentalism, even were it to include all Europe—to include the Soviet Union—so long as it maintained, as at least one very distinguished Polish Communist Minister has maintained, that this would yet be an area in which "the Americans have no interests", not being Europeans. The Soviets remain part of the area. The North Americans (including the Canadians) do not. What, rather, is required is, not a "security system" of Europe, but for Europe.

The Anglo-Saxon tradition is in antithesis to this continentalist obsession. The sound maxim is the union of the widest practicable region, not of some alliance of jealous or envious Second-rate Powers, such as appeals to timid and second-rate personalities.

If the various countries of North Western Europe from Luxemburg up, repeatedly victims of defeat, do not share a British position dissimilar in basis from that of the Continent, a position unique in history of intimate association with one of the world's two Super-Powers—so that Secretary of State George Marshall spoke to the Pilgrims in London of "the mother country", a phrase deleted by timid men from the printed record—the fault lies under Providence, not in their demerits, but in their stars. As well may a Polish general wish that Poland was a hilly country.

The danger is most real of constituting, in the world of international affairs, an envious "Third Force". We can concede that, unlike the downright General de Gaulle, M. Pompidou disclaims with emphasis any such intention; and, indeed, the new Third Force concept is not the old one of Aneurin Bevan and his friends of a dream Socialist Europe (without electoral change) interposed between the poles of a "Communist" Russia and a "Capitalist" America. Nevertheless, the economic, strategic, political and cultural actuality and danger of a self-identified "European Europe" remains.

It can do little but harm to the cause of stable peace. Whatever may be said for sub-regional arrangements, an Anglo-French joint nuclear atomic deterrent, "doing its own thing", is a contribution to peace both undesirable and ineffective. When some of us worked for the pioneer experiment of a "united Europe", with novel supra-national institutions having quite specific governmental functions, assuredly we did not work to build up such a Third Force. Rather we were suspicious of the seductive "Two Steps" doctrine, not of pragmatic simultaneous advance as opportunity offered, but of "the European step first". (And the second step when and whither?) The second step may change direction and looks likely to be a deliberate one backwards in an anti-Atlantic, "Little Europe"—more exactly "Little N.W. Europe"—direction.

What should be the true goal? We fought the policy of Aneurin Bevan and his fellows, for a Socialist Europe standing ideologically between a capitalist America and a totalitarian Russia, not because we were capitalists or Leninists, enamoured of one of either supposed alternative, but because we thought the political analysis faulty and unrealistic. However, a Third Force prepared to dicker with both Moscow—which, be it noted, is "also European"— and with Washington, while seeking to gain petty power by holding the balance, disliking Communism but deeply envious of and inimical to American power, is not unrealistic. Merely it is a menace.

In his memoirs, *Le Renouveau*, de Gaulle records a conversation with Prime Minister Harold Macmillan, then in the first phase of his European policy. An economic integration, Macmillan suggested, would lead on, as both Robert Schuman and the European Commission under Professor Hallstein asserted, to political union. If such a Europe pursued a determined political policy, and one which could conflict with the rest of the Atlantic Community and with the United States, could not the result be "war"—and, finally, not just trade war? With talk today of a trade war, alike by a European organisation seeking to exercise pressure in support of its own protectionism, and with a Senate in Washington being lobbied for a protectionist defence at a time of recession, Macmillan's question still has an unhappy relevance.

When it comes to Europe, competition we are told is a fine thing. Britain will profit. Assuredly in 1971 Britain has had, under the fierce, healthy wind of competition, as prophesied by Enoch Powell and subscribed to by others, a startling crop of bankruptcies, possibly reducing costs, without price controls, but (as in accordance with classical *laissez-faire* economics) certainly increasing unemployment. The brilliant journalist, Bernard Levin, has explained in the *International Herald Tribune*, that the British economy needed "a jolt". It is receiving it. When it comes to American competition however, this fever is not so fine a thing, and some (not all) British industrialists, especially in the newer and weaker industries, flee for protection. Some British banking and City interests approve. Is protectionism, not Free Trade, what we want? Is it war, with political undertones—which we were warned by Macmillan, may become political overtones—which indeed we want? Is the right way to build an Atlantic Community to build up what Servan-Schreiber calls *le Défi*?

It is indeed urged that, not only will Britain have the benefits of a healthy competition, including the side-effects of unemployment and an EEC immigration so free that, although an Australian will be excluded, a Guadeloupe West Indian (being, under French law, a full French citizen) can of right come in, but Britain will also have the advantage, by European co-operation, of a great technological leap-forward. Admittedly this will be protective against American technological superiorities and, hence, takes-over and competition, but it will be, it is urged, patently a progressive thing, a good thing for the well-being of mankind. I can only comment that, if aid to the underdeveloped countries and human advance depends upon new technological enterprise—which to some (limited) degree it does—to substitute for world technological discovery that of the co-operation of relatively weak European technologies to the exclusion of that most effective, seems to me to be a most odd way of going about procuring this boon for human progress. On the contrary, the proposal seems to be, not merely protectionist, but reactionary.

The danger may not be deadly for the continental mainlanders, who have another history. It is lethal for the common policy of the English-speaking world. Why sacrifice the values, "the solid foundation", which we have? "Pull out the red telephone connection between Westminster and Washington", says M. Pompidou. We will not.

§ ii. *The Posture of the Parties.*

The Willkieite ideal of 1941 of a common citizenship of the United States and the British Commonwealth (which also, Churchill had said, might include a France then staggering to defeat) was politically swamped, in the mid-'Forties, by the Rooseveltian version of One World as one of a universalism that would issue in the United Nations, not indeed as an organisation to enforce peace but as a forum for the argument of differences. (For the Russians and even for the American Senate it meant Great Power Veto.) The Rooseveltian policy (here a Wilsonian derivation) did indeed issue in the Atlantic Charter, signed in Placentia Bay, from which (despite the sardonic signature of Stalin), rather than from any atlas concept of geography, the phrase "the Atlantic Community" derives. According to Wilcox and Haviland, in their *The Atlantic Community*, the idea and name was put into circulation at about this time by Streit, Lippmann and myself.

When the glamourisation of Great Power harmony as a basis

for the United Nations began to tarnish—remarkably quickly and first in Polish affairs—the tide of idealism moved over, secondly, to a movement, not indeed for that world democratic federation, for which such entirely worthy men, ahead of their times, as Clarence Streit, US Senator Joseph H. Ball of Wisconsin, State Senator Humber, Mr Justice Roberts, Clayton and others, Americans all, had worked, but for a more regional Union of Europe. This accorded well with the aspirations of German youth hoping for readmission to the Concert of Europe, and of French politicians—both working under the smart of humiliation rather than the exhilaration of victory. It was a congress of the victims of war, over whom loomed the force of the new Great Powers holding peace in their hands. Just what will concretely shape from this regional movement, what channels, what limits, remains the great problem to this present day.

The movement has come to oscillate between intense resentment of the power of the new Great Powers by the old, and the aspiration by muting differences jointly to become a Third (or Fourth) Super-Power itself. Provincialism more and more discarded the international aspiration towards stable peace under world government, even as a utopia. There might be a revival of neo-Fascism in Italy (an E.E.C. state) but the passion for authentic internationalism abated, thanks to a more paltry grocer's business vision, such as Edmund Burke once dismissed as no true basis for community.

American idealism, as ever moralistic, welcomed this peaceful advance, which might (it was then thought in the early years) even in the end follow the federal constitutional example and "great experiment" of the United States itself. The ever present temptations of isolationism also beckoned, with the prospect that "Europe would be able now to defend itself and the American tax-payer's pocket be saved". What in Britain was presented as "a vision", in America could be supported as a popular, hard-boiled, if short-sighted, calculation for the tax-payer's benefit—which, in turn, tends in fact to lead to extraordinary aberrations in grand policy. It was conveniently forgotten that Soviet Great Power business was with the citizenry of the United States itself, and not with Europe. The disastrous myth even grew that the United States was after all "a Pacific Ocean Power", concerned to watch the back-door of the Russian bear and of the Chinese dragon. The "development of Europe" by Europeans was indeed to become "the strategic down-grading of Europe" by Americans—and, be it added, the political down-grading of America by Europe. In President Nixon's words, in Kansas City

(July, 1971), "Vietnam has almost totally obscured our vision of the world".

The euphoric optimism about America and far-flung protective treaties (even if resting on a dogged Presbyterian pessimism about others) of John Foster Dulles, was followed by the unhappy strategic miscalculation of, and obsession with, commitment to not-so-like-minded friends in Vietnam, fundamentally a strategic side-show. Even so, the American electorate (whatever the generals might say) was not prepared to take the strategic consequences of an all-out drive to win the war. Upon it Chairman Mao made, of this future Eastern Yugoslavia, the perceptive comment to Snow, of *Red Star over China*, that, unlike Cuba, for the Americans it was "too far from base". "To win in war the first thing is not to be fated to lose it."

Alliances come and go. That at least was recognised. But the costs of any effective Community could frighten the Senate and their electors. Hence the soporific phrase, in Euro-American relations, was "Partnership". John F. Kennedy had the vision to say in many speeches including that in the Paulus-Kirche in Frankfurt on 25th June 1963;

"We must also look—and even more closely—to our trans-Atlantic ties. The Atlantic Community will not soon become a single over-reaching super-state. But practical steps towards a common purpose are well within our grasp."

In Naples he spoke of "the unity of the West"; and in Bonn (24th June) he said (italics mine):

"I think Western Europe *and* the United States, Canada, Great Britain and the Commonwealth have a major role in saving us the centre of the core of a great effort throughout this world to maintain freedom."[1]

President Kennedy had the vision to use the word "Community" (not just of "Europe")—but also the diplomatic discretion to use the word "Partnership". American democracy politically (whatever may be the case industrially) by ingrained tradition untrained in empire, even when placarded by propaganda as "imperialist", always shrinks from the suggestion that it should assume the responsibility of being "world gendarme". And here indeed lies the guarantee of an organic Community based on dialogue, consultation, co-operation, and not on dictatorship or even on centralisation around some continental capital.

What then of the American "Partnership"? Mr Duncan Sandys more bluntly says, "rivalry". Partnership is indeed a foxy

[1] *Vide* my *The Atlantic Commonwealth* (Penguin Special, 1969). pp. 49–50.

word and we risk being foxed. Not all partners in a business have equal shares. What is "a partnership" where mutual trust is lacking? The ambiguity of the word has recently been well illustrated by Mr Kosygin, commenting on the present arms reduction conferences with the United States. "We are prepared to cover our part of the road to agreement and, if our partners are prepared to do the same, the problem will be solved" (3rd Jan. 1971). A Kosygin-style partnership, however, with Washington is not what Westminster has at present under consideration. But M. Debré and others seek to measure matters out on a goldsmith's balance. For them, England must come into Europe so that this Association of Second Class States may exactly weigh up as equal to the United States. (Of course Moscow could provide decisive overweight.)

Other terms than "partnership" came into circulation, such as the "dumbell" illustration which Paul Nitze used perhaps in irony— a dumbell being a gymnastic instrument, heavy and powerful at the ends but joined by an iron of inferior thickness. More favoured was the example of "Two Pillars", although this is a figure intelligible in architecture when it supports something, such as NATO, but otherwise chiefly associated with ruins. The vigour of American vision had become dimmed, hesitant, tentative, liberally optimistic until shocked into a new look by Franklin Roosevelt's bugaboo, de Gaulle. The American moralists retreated into inert but offended disillusionment. America could not be the world-constable. Rebuffed, America complained that she was not loved.

America was called upon by the objective logic of history to be a Super-Power. The problem was whether the American electorate, burdened with the enshrined Whiggery of the Constitution, had any appetite either for this power or for the attendant political duties and responsibilities. Its youth might pursue happiness better amid the permissive smoke of drugs, while the Kremlin watched the anarchy and waited. Perchance America would make *il gran rifiuto*.

In Britain the position was different—patently from the American one but also, by history, tradition and strategy, from that of the non-Anglo-Saxon continental Europeans. After the distant days when the Plantagenets ruled most of France, consistently England endeavoured to detach herself, with periodic intervention to crack the head of the more flagrant aggressor, Spanish, French, German, even Russian. As M. Pompidou (24th Feb. 1970) has recently reminded us, Winston Churchill remarked: "if I have to choose between Europe and the sea, I

choose the sea". Piously M. Pompidou deplores the historic
choice. He himself, at least, has no option. Mr Heath and his
various English supporters, when Churchill is no longer alive to
bite them in the bottom, applaud. For myself, if we have to choose
between North America and France, without hesitation I choose
North America. To enter into Europe for all purposes or even for
economic, fiscal and financial purposes, and not merely for specific
ad hoc functional purposes such as affairs of coal and steel,
involves a radical departure from traditional English wisdom in
foreign affairs from the epoch of Cardinal Wolsey to that of the
Eyre-Crowe Memorandum of 1907.

The Liberal Party indeed, limited in numbers, were always
distinguished as kite-fliers of brilliantly coloured ideas, among
which Entry into Europe almost ranked with Proportional Representation. It had and has a record of honourable consistency in
advocacy, from the days of the Liberal members of the old
Federal Union group onwards.

The Conservative Party, on the contrary, has had a more
variant range in its policy. Roughly it is a matter of, as I have said,
three phases—from the time of Sir Anthony Eden, who declared
that he "was not a European animal", and from the days when the
British Foreign Office regarded the Messina Conference as
concerned with a pipe-dream of which the smoke would soon
vanish in the colder air of reality, to those of the building of
EFTA; and then, again, to the days of Edward Heath's instant
enthusiasm for Entry, which became an issue of personal prestige
for himself and as removing doubts, in the words of the *Daily
Mail*, that he was and is "a politician of strength" and even of
obstinacy. There is, indeed, no reason to tax Mr Heath with any
unusual personal conceit in his attachment to a cause which first
made his name, as Harold Macmillan's emissary, distinguishable.
Many eminent men have had the same view, although it is dangerous to number the author of the Fulton Address, Winston
Churchill, in any unconditional fashion among them. The evidence
is to the contrary.

Having had earlier correspondence with President Kennedy,
on the introduction of Eleanor Roosevelt and of the Duke of
Devonshire, and having only missed a personal conversation by
misfortune of timing, I welcomed the opportunity in 1967 of a
meeting in Washington with his brother, Senator Robert Kennedy. The Senator's view then of British policy and of America's
attitude was incisive, but also *simpliciste*. "We want to see a
strong Britain. The leaders of all your Parties tell us that entry
into Europe will strengthen you. What, then, do you wish us to

do?" This downrightness failed to allow for the subtleties and nuances which resulted in an almost total change of direction, if not by all Tories, at least in official Conservative policy. It also failed to allow for the actual position of the Labour Prime Minister.

On this issue, the history of the British Labour Party is far less one of black and white simplicity than the Senator seemed to suppose. Lord Attlee wrote to me on 20th March 1967:

"My dear George,

Thank you for your letter. I don't think that Stanley Baldwin had any enemies at the time of the abdication. He asked my opinion and I told him not to think only of London, but to understand the Yorkshire and Lancashire and other provincial views. I told him the reactions of our members from these areas.

I hope you have an interesting time in U.S.A. De Gaulle had a pretty close shave in the French Elections. I don't see him lasting much longer. If he stops our joining the Common Market, he will have repaid what he owes us.

Yours ever, Clem."

Earlier than this, Hugh Gaitskell, Attlee's successor as Leader of the Labour Party, had written to me:

"Dear George,

Thanks so much for your charming letter which I greatly appreciate.

Like you, I am not an unconditional anti-Marketeer, but the present terms simply are not good enough and break the Government's pledges in the most flagrant manner.

I hope you will write to the American press on all this. They are woefully misinformed.

Yours, Hugh."

In his early speeches and writings Prime Minister Harold Wilson declared himself as very much a "Commonwealth man" since 1947. However, when Britain is necessarily seeking a larger market, the problem with this policy is whether the Commonwealth, without its geographical centre-piece in the United States, is economically viable by itself and as providing the crucial market. It may be that the Prime Minister was intellectually converted to accord with the Common Marketeer push by economic arguments which yet quite outstandingly failed to convince such of his chief expert economic advisers as Lord Balogh and Professor Kaldor. Under such ambiguous circumstances it would not be unexpected that he should yield to George Brown's known and ardent desire to go to the Foreign Office. Lord Attlee has commented in writing, in his laconic style, on a like ambition of "the little man", Herbert Morrison. If George Brown succeeded, it was a gain; if he lost, nothing much was lost. It is ironic that those journalists who sought to denigrate Harold Wilson for so long "sitting on the fence" later proceeded to attack him in July 1971 for "abandoning his known principles" and for coming down on what, for themselves, was "the wrong side".

I have a profound and not unwarranted suspicion that the Prime Minister, as ever desiring "to keep his options open" and his Party united, was never intuitively convinced by the Marketeers. To decline to take the politically inspired "no" of de Gaulle as a final answer and to assert that, if the Cabinets of the Six were prepared to sit down and to talk terms they should not be met by some comparable crude rebuff, is not to say that it is the obligation of a statesman to accept any terms that Britain may be offered or that it would be a reversal of declared policy by Harold Wilson if he refused to do this. Certainly, "a great move forward in political unity" is needed. But what? George Brown had his own highly personal policy ebullient for instant Entry at almost any cost, even for entry first and to complete the negotiations later—all this with an enthusiasm which almost outdid Mr Heath's own.

Admittedly many persons have taken up a particular stand, even for some years—with obdurate consistency, as I have myself—and would find it unpleasant to change their public view. Nevertheless, the greatest affairs of nations are not to be decided in these terms of personal biography. Nor, although personal consistency is a virtue, is it to be placed ahead of an open mind about facts affecting the national interest. Statesmen from Peel to Churchill have been prepared to change. Not only polls but Party Conferences have been known notoriously to change.

The further assumption that, nevertheless, reiterated public opinion should be "led" in a way that flouts its declared judgment —that there is, for leaders, no duty "to follow public opinion"— is an élitist view certainly contrary to what, for example, Lincoln believed to be democracy. It raises the issue of Party and Leader *versus* People.

The issue of Britain's Entry into Europe is not fundamentally one of being for or against the Common Market. On the record I have in the past been in favour of it. The opinion expressed to me, and reiterated in print, of Lord Harlech that "we do not want by narrowing the English Channel to widen the Atlantic Ocean" (the former, I may add, so vitally strategically wide and the latter so technologically narrow) is an admirable maxim with which there can be basic agreement. Since this balanced view is easily distorted or misrepresented on the "yes or no"—"when did you stop beating your wife?"—principle, it is well to emphasise it beyond ambiguity.

Assuredly there must be continuity of our national foreign policy which cannot be totally reshaped, after four centuries, by some sudden wind of change in 1962. The line of advance is through the Atlantic Commonwealth and the affirmation, beyond ambiguity, of Atlantic solidarity (as against, for example, some renewed American isolationism). The objection, let us re-iterate, is not to some economic Common Market in and with Europe as such or along with associated Members. It is political. It is to any political institutions or guide-lines which, in actuality, will lead away from the Atlantic solidarity and to the substitution of a smaller for a greater emotion and diplomatic plan. And before Britain commits itself to European merger of any species, it is only fair that "the Six" should be told this unambiguously and, moreover, should explicitly accept it. As of this moment, M. Pompidou does not.

The issue is one of *what kind* of Common Market; of the centralising and non-democratic elements of the Rome Treaty; of how far this "Europe" is to be an exclusive and protectionist segment of the whole of Europe. It is not one of whether, in M. Pompidou's words, we are to be "closer to France". (And, maybe, further from Germany.) Naturally, if Britain becomes closer to French policy, British Entry will be very acceptable to Paris. The issue is whether in all respects we are to cut our ties and to drift further from North America and from what in fact has been the greatest of all of our sometime Colonies. Again in M. Pompidou's words, are we to "pull out the red telephone wire" to Washington? That is the policy issue. And are we to re-engage ourselves in the European Balance of Power?

This issue can be stated with even more polemic vigour. Edward Heath stated (19th May 1971) that "we . . . face at this moment a momentous [*sic*] test of will. . . . We owe it to our friends in other parts of the world to minimise the problems these changes may create for them. . . . Do we have the wisdom to achieve by construction and co-operation what Napoleon and Hitler failed to achieve by destruction and conquest?" In brief, Napoleon and Hitler had the right idea and grand design. Merely they were stupid in the means which they adopted; and Mr Heath and his friends can find better. British policy in so often opposing the Grand Design was all a great mistake. Heath knew better. There is indeed a Grand Design, which includes our allies of two World

Wars; but it is not Mr Heath's. The point here and its implications are emphasised by a recent and notorious speech by M. Pompidou on 17th May 1971 to which I shall return.

As I have said, there is no intrinsic reason why there should not be a regional Western European integration, dealing locally with its own problems—*but* firmly placed within a consultative and co-operative framework, NATO, O.E.C.D., "Atlantic", of which North America and Australasia would also be part. The crucial point is that this is not the same plan as that of M. Pompidou's "European Europe". The latter is the opposite plan.

The situation has been stated excellently by *The Washington Post* of 12th May 1971:

"In actuality the issue is whether Britain can project itself as enough of a 'European'—by starting *to reduce both its special ties to the Commonwealth and its special relationship with the United States*—to become acceptable to France, whose continuing thrust is to make France *an ever more effective challenge to American influence* on the Continent." (Italics mine.)

Let us be clear. The target of our criticism must be neither Schuman nor Adenauer, neither Germany nor indeed the regional Common Market in principle and in itself. The unrelenting target of attack must be French policy, French aspirations and French national philosophy as expressed by de Gaulle and in persistent Gaullism, although assuredly not limited to them.

It can indeed be urged, and this by some English politicians of sincerity that, once the United Kingdom is in the E.E.C. it will take the lead; certainly not accept a French hegemony; "dispose" of Pompidou; and maybe also check any anti-American policy. It will all be wonderful for Britain since, far from being merely "European European", it is she who will play the leading role in Europe and hence in the world. Frank Giles has a paean to this effect in the *Sunday Times* (27th June 1971). Indeed the perfect "Trojan horse", which de Gaulle feared ... This purpose for Britain has been explicitly stated. Assuming, as one must, a fierce French opposition, I fail to find this to be a sound basis for some happy future Community feeling of all "Little Europeans". Also it assumes a far stronger Britain that is supposed in the general stock-in-trade of most E.E.C. supporters.

It is true that in the early post-war days of Churchill's premiership there was, not only a vacant chair, but a vacant chairmanship. This is so no longer. I can conceive of few policies more calculated to produce a blaze of enmity or to involve Britain inextricably in those Continental feuds from which it has been, in her history, consistent British policy to avoid, or less calculated to build up a happy, new apocalyptic Community for the good of mankind, than straight away to become the supporter of Germany against French claims of leadership or of an economically weak France against a re-nascent Germany.

It is essential to repeat that the objection (at least for me) is not to all kinds of Common Market or like functional international institution. It is to any policy which does not place itself firmly within the framework of something available and larger, a larger market and a larger defence, a larger Atlantic Community or Commonwealth. It is a matter of Atlantic solidarity. It is specifically a fundamental objection to the announced French (or Gaullist) policy and philosophy of "a European Europe". That is the sticking point.

Three times and more the opinion of the electorate of England has been polled and three times they have polled massively against European Entry on the terms at present known. In October 1970, affirming previous results, to the question, "Do you approve of Britain entering the Common Market?", the National Opinion Poll showed 24% in favour and 61% against. To that same question in a poll of March 1971, the returns were: 22% approve; 66% disapprove; and 12% "don't know". (A straw vote among its readers by a Nottingham journal yielded 95% against.) According to a Gallup Poll of 15th July 1971 taken subsequently to publication of the terms secured by Britain for Entry, the vote in favour of Labour against Heath rose to a 21.5% lead. (However, an Opinion Research Poll carried out, significantly on behalf of the European Movement at a critical moment, was deviant, support for Entry rising from 27% in two weeks to 37%.) The final Opinion Research Centre Poll, taken on 17th October and published on 24th October, before the Parliamentary vote of 28th October, 1971, showed 47% against Entry and only 32% in favour. The Harris Poll was not less emphatic.

There could be no pretence of "massive public Support" about which Prime Minister Heath had talked. Instead of standing by his own word, the Prime Minister chose to stand on the technicalities of the British Parliamentary system which to date has, rightly or wrongly, found no place for a referendum or current vote *ad hoc* of the electorate. Democracy or not, the need for mandate from the electorate could be ignored. (No wonder there has been persistent complaint in some youthful quarters that "bourgeois democracy" is "bogus democracy".) The mandate could be ignored even when the issue was one of Parliamentary surrender, in taxation and foreign affairs, of Parliament's own powers. What the polls did yet show was, first, a fatalistic belief of the electorate that their Government could in fact push the country into Entry, whether the country willed it or not; and, secondly, that "the decision on principle" taken, interest could lapse in a protracted Parliamentary fight. Wearily they turned back to see what the Government could do on prices and unemployment.

Altogether apart from whether "Entry into Europe" on the terms of the Rome Treaty is right or wrong, contemptuously to flout the majority will, repeatedly expressed in the only way constitutionally practicable to express it, is to flout electoral democracy in the name of people who think they know better, advised by "experts" whose expert opinions are radically challenged by others no less expert. It is an effrontery, stimulated by conceit. Moreover, in terms of the last General Election, the present Government has no electoral mandate for Entry as such. It is certainly something very different from what de Gaulle called "the silent but imperative call of France".

There may be a "strong man's" hustled decision attempted, with Parliament confronted with "obligations in honour" to support the conclusions reached privately by the Government negotiators, sweating so long and so hard to reach agreements over their cognac. Or, if this hustle is thought imprudent, every resource of propaganda unsuccessfully employed to persuade the public over the last nine years may be brought into play again to "brainwash" and to hypnotise the voter about his unalterable "destiny", so that a confidence trick appears as "a vision".

A referendum (despite Balfour, Churchill and Baldwin) may be held to be unconstitutional in Britain or it may be regarded with high favour, as by the Foreign Office about the citizens of Gibraltar. Norway, Denmark and Ireland will all conduct referenda on Entry. Nevertheless the situation remains as stated by so eminent a journalist as Robert Carvel. There will be a demand for a Referendum. But it will not be granted. For why? Because the Government would be defeated. There will be a Parliamentary demand for a General Election. But it will not be granted. For why? Because the Government, here also, would be defeated. Indeed in a House of Commons of 630 members, defeat for the Conservative Party in a mere fourteen by-elections could turn Edward Heath out. This is one of those cases where it can be the duty of the Opposition on principle to oppose.

Throughout the Western World today there is resentment against our present democratic forms of Government because so many electors feel that, despite their vote, they have in affect no power. I can imagine nothing more calculated to bring

Parliamentary and like institutions into disrepute than so flagrant and disgraceful a contempt for the actual popular will.

Nor is this disillusionment appeased if democracy is to be denied the necessary information, upon which to base a vote and a vital judgement, because all the media of official propaganda present only one side and, on the record, the leading newspapers and television and radio extend few or no invitations for the statement of the opposed case.

Voters, it may be admitted, are capable of changing their minds, be it in polls, referenda or even before and after General Elections. It is one of the accepted perils of democracy. And pollsters can only record opinion at a given moment, with such indications of the future as are found adequate, for example, in industrial polls. Nevertheless, not only have the people the right to judge, both in Parliament and (to the extent of not being flouted or treated with contempt) outside Parliament. The People—and here not just Parliament—in peace time has the democratic "right to know" and hence to be informed, not just by one side, but in open national debate so that it can make an objective democratic decision. This is what democracy means. It cannot be done by a hustled, heavily financed and privately organised campaign of governmental brain-washing.

It has indeed been blandly suggested that once the wolf has swallowed the lamb, "in five years' time" the lamblike public may —with no provision for "opting out"—poll in favour of digestion. Maybe England will last on only in terms of its language and its law—and, in a Common Market dominated by the Civil Law, even the latter is dubious. The question is whether the present Prime Minister, leading a Party in Parliament so far divided that he only carried his motion by the aid of Opposition Members, and without electoral mandate except to "explore the conditions", is entitled to say "we shall enter" and to override the electoral and democratic majority on the vital future of the nation and indeed on whether, in the old sense, it is to remain a nation at all.

§ iii. *Mr Heath's Economics.*

It has been urged that the benefits of Entry will be so demonstrably beneficial as to justify even conduct so strange. In the last days of the Macmillan period the economic advantages alone were stressed. These were suggested to be so immediate that sterling itself would collapse unless there were instant entry. There was no entry; and sterling did not collapse, except in that modest sense in which the French franc did so also. At this moment there is, as yet, no Entry—but we are told of an economic boom in Britain (without it) already on the horizon. The economic "miracles" of continental revival—in the case of Germany under Erhardt perhaps not so remarkable, Germany (like Japan) being without the burden of a Defence budget—became not more but less outstanding with time. The Common Market had its worst year in 1970—"an all-time low"—for prices and incomes since it was formed in 1957; and its own economic experts add: "the Commission feels that the slow-down in economic growth, which started in 1970, will probably continue into 1971". Perchance we might some day share in the high standards of living of Southern Italy and indeed of an aspirant Spain or even a courted Roumania.

David Blake, in the London *Sunday Times* (a pro-Market journal) of 31st October (just after the Parliamentary vote of the 28th), wrote: "The Common Market is probably in a more sorry shape now than at any time since its creation", and that it "had brought guaranteed prosperity to Western Europe is being questioned more and more". Editorially, the *Sunday Times* then wrote: "realism compels the admission that Six Power Europe is at present a sickly animal" ... "there is a real danger of [an intra-European] trade war", while the *Guardian* comments on, in E.E.C., "an increase in the number of the unemployed".

The finances of Germany, while giving pleasure to Germans, do not today induce general European harmony. The agriculture of France (with its large Communist Party) and the economy of Italy (with its larger Communist Party) scarcely encourage euphoria. Or shall we put our trust in the Irish veto under the unanimity rule?

If indeed wages in, for example, Italy in the first ten years of the Common Market rose by 55%, whereas in Britain this growth rate was only 20%, then (as with Soviet statistics) we have to ask for the zero line—"rose from what?" It is relevant that, in the same period, in the United States the hourly index earnings of the worker in the manufacturing industries stood, in 1957, at 5.4 in cash or 1.6 in "real value" balanced against costs; and in 1967 (1957–59 basis) at 4.0 or 1.3. It would seem to follow: How unhappy is the American wage-earner compared with the Italian. Incidentally, one of the highest standards of living, in terms of real wages, in the world is that of Australia—a country which, thanks to modern transport, has never been closer to us; and a country for which to be drawn into the Japanese "Asian Co-Prosperity Scheme" would be the reverse of healthy.

The weakness of economic growth in Britain may be easier to explain by the epidemic of strikes than, with present success in the British balance of payments, by any disaster of non-entry. Entry provides no automatic guarantee of an end to strikes—unless the country is to be flooded by immigrant strike-breakers under the new regulations.

The most varied estimates have been given of immediate cost of Entry to the British elector, the more ardent "Marketeers" reducing this, very questionably, to 1% rise for the first five years—some adding that this last year 1970–71, in part since the Election, has seen as much as an 8% general (pre-entry) rise in costs. As Mr Jonathan Aitken, a Conservative, has written in the *Evening Standard*, discussing the Heath policy of *Europa über Alles*, "in the short run" the housewife, the old age pensioner, the working man, "will be broke". One does not have to be a Machiavelli to entertain the suspicion that the present Government's ineffectiveness in price control, and indeed repudiation of such controls, may not be unallied with Edward Heath's private "revolution" for changing the status of the British nation behind its back. If domestic prices rise sufficiently agonisingly, the pain of the final operation of Entry will be clearly, as a relative matter, much reduced.

When it comes to the question of the touted "economic advantages", the British people when polled appeared to be "confused", we were told, even after seven years of explanation by experts with all the resources of propaganda at their disposal. The public had their excuse. Thanks to the incisive work of the ex-President of the Board of Trade, Douglas Jay, in his book *After the Common Market* (1968), followed by *New Trade Strategy for the World Economy*, edited by Professor H. G. Johnson, and *Destiny or Delusion*, edited by Sir Roy Harrod, the myth of short-range economic benefit, as distinct from crushing costs, was exploded. This study was preceded by *The Alliance of Necessity* (1966), by a well-known Canadian advocate of the above anti–Market policy, Mr Lionel Gelber. These findings have been supported by a series of expert economic pamphlets from The British–North American Committee and the Atlantic Trade Study (beginning in 1966), as well as from the Canadian–American Economic Committee, including an old Montreal friend of mine, Mr Robert Fowler. With these groups Sir Michael Wright has been associated.[1] The advocacy of these groups has been for the organisation of an Atlantic Free Trade

[1] Sir Michael Wright: *The Problems of 1971–2*, 1971, published by the Committee of the Atlantic Trade Study, 6 Buckingham Street, London, WC2. W. Randolph Burgess and James R. Huntley: *Europe and America*, 1970 (Walker & Co., New York).

Area which would not only include Europe, but which, it is arguable, by associating in its framework Britain with Europe could prevent the Common Market itself from the danger (as Denis Healey has suggested) of dissolving.

"If you can't beat them, join them" is a maxim (which the Scots have learned) that applies alike to wealth, to standards of living and to power. Even the Concorde aircraft adventure becomes a very trivial charge by comparison with the costs of Entry. For the costs almost to be equalised out, the Government must by its own policy encourage the people's food prices to rise, and to go on rising— to the level that Entry demands in terms of price raising, not price reducing. This process is taking place now. Nor is the argument other than confused or disingenuous which urges, since the Federation which set up the United States has been so successful, not that we should extend this principle of a wide, free-trade domestic market, but that we should set up some rival, if weaker, Federal Union of Europe.

Hence it is not without excuse that the Conservative London *Evening Standard* writes (1st Jan., 1971): "The past year has seen successive reports, both from governmental and independent sources, suggesting that membership [of E.E.C.] would entail economic consequences varying from the temporarily crippling to the catastrophic." Believing as I do that a fervent patriotism and a principled internationalism—the last the cause of my early differences with Mosley even in the glamour of his Socialist days— are not incompatible, I do not often find myself in political agreement with Mr Enoch Powell, whom I suspect of being "a little Englander". Nevertheless I cannot refrain from quoting with agreement his comment, also of January 1971: "If there is one thing that millions of British people would be glad to see dead, buried and forgotten before 1971 is out, it is British entry into the Common Market."

The Market argument was later shifted to the assertion that, although the short-range economic costs were indeed heavy and tax regulation from Brussels was less than a pleasant prospect, nevertheless it was still the case that Entry would produce for Britain inestimable benefits "in the long run". Admittedly, according to the chief British negotiator at Brussels, Sir Con O'Neill himself, fiscal arrangements which took the form of "value-added tax" would add 100% to the British consumer's expenditure. However, the incompetent electorate still remained deplorably "confused", despite its busy mentors of Whitehall, B.B.C. and Fleet Street; and maybe even reflects, in Keynes' famous phrase, that "in the long run we shall all be dead".

The trouble was that, from the very nature of the case, these long-range benefits lay in the future, were undemonstrable and inestimable. (According to *The Sunday Times* "Business News" of 17th Jan., 1971, "Britain will be obliged from 1980 onwards to pay about 22.23% of the total Common Market budget"—larger than that of France, which naturally views this bonus with favour.) This is not to deny that there may be capitalist pickings in the European markets, not least for the aircraft and automobile industries, and for the City of London and the banks. Before negotiations are finalised this disadvantage may be increased. There has been indeed an effort to produce an atmosphere of robust confidence and unshakable faith. But when the Minister in charge, Mr Geoffrey Rippon, referred in Parliament to a period, not "if we enter", but "when we enter", the "we" for whom he spoke represented little more than his fellow believers. This assurance was about an issue on which Rippon was, in the terms of the Conservative Election Manifesto (by a *volte face* being little more than a copy of the Labour Manifesto) and Election mandate, only authorised to ascertain facts. "Our sole commitment is to negotiate, no more and no less"—which presumably was to be regarded as an honourable commitment and not "just a joke". Edward Heath went further by declaring that what would be required for Entry would be the electorate's "whole-hearted approval". Shall we say, charitably, that the statement was little else than an act of faith or, to use current jargon, the issue is that of the Credibility of Edward Heath.

§ iv. *Cosa Nostra.*

However, by now the final shift of ground has taken place. The recorded truth of the Treasury's ground for recommending Entry has emerged in public. This is not economic. As so vigorous a "Marketeer" as Sir Tufton Beamish, a Member of Parliament with French, German and even Italian family affiliations, has rightly said: "This is a question about the national survival: it is not about the price of groceries." Despite the endeavour of certain journals to suggest the contrary, the issue is not some trivial and maybe almost childish one of meat and butter, sugar and pepper, Kangaroo tails and like "low concerns". It is indeed very much one of "high affairs of state".

The issue is political. This is quite basic and needs to be underlined, the more so as, for tactical reasons, there has been a cloud of hypocrisy and indeed a miasma of dishonesty in this matter. Tactically, for the Market policy to succeed it was thought best to direct the public mind to the "small economic costs" (in fact,

large) of Entry to what was emphasised to be "just a market"
and to the vision of "vast benefits" in Kingdom-come; and to
direct attention away from the political costs which, it was quite
rightly thought, would be unpleasant and might even be
unacceptable.

In apocalyptic style, reminiscent of Lloyd George exhorting us
to turn our eyes to the mountain heights of his native Wales,
Edward Heath (17th May, 1971) spoke of "a prosperity which
none of us—in Scotland, Britain or Europe—[not hitherto
Europe, even under years of the Common Market?]—which
none of us has known before. . . . For me, if there is once again
to be a great future for Europe [*sic*], it lies in creating that unity
of which we have *got* to be a part" (italics mine). A hypnotic
effect. And indeed, to use Edward Heath's own words, he has
"minimised the difficulties". But since, to repeat, the basic issue
is political as now admitted, I object to democracy being hood-
winked by having its attention disproportionately limited and
distracted to this economic technicolor panorama—or phantas-
magoria.

One major negotiator, when point-blank asked to refresh our
memories on what the great political advantages might be, has
explained that this political advantage is "cultural". It is one of
association, maybe, with Mediterranean civilisation and of dissociation from the colonial "sticks", however European in heritage. ("Europa" according to Greek myth, was an Asian lady
raped, while in flight to Crete, by Zeus in the form of a bull.)
Europe, of course, is not "the cradle of our civilisation". The
Mediterranean is. The culture of which we treasure the tradition
stems from Rome, Athens, Asian Ephesus, African Alexandria
and, maybe, from Jerusalem. It does not trace from Latvia or
Finland or even from Iceland nor, in general, evenly from the
whole Western peninsula (not the so-called "heartland") of the
EurAsian continent.

Nor, despite the phrase *la civilisation c'est la France*, and the roll
of Gallic rhetoric—or even the assertion by a certain Professor
André Brousson that Britain and the United States are "intellectually underdeveloped countries"—will an internationalist
accept that, all talk of the East apart, our present culture (and this
not only of Anglo-Saxon lands) owes outstandingly more to
Racine, Molière and Fragonard or David than to Dante and
Goethe, Michelangelo, Titian, Shakespeare, Milton and Beethoven. Our heritage is not only that of Louis Quatorze, whose
plans were rebuffed at Blenheim. In the field of war the final
victors did not come from France. In the field of peace, John

XXIII was not French. My object here is not to minimise but to make proportionate. Even Jesus Christ was not a Frenchman—and not a European (although Lincoln was).

This passing comment may seem to carry us a long way from discussion of pear farmers and apple growers, lamb, mutton, butter and molasses—as Burke said, "pepper and calico"—and from claims of French peasants and of German industrialists and the views of Zürich bankers on sterling. However, when we are discussing the real factors, the deeper motivations, in politics—call them sentimental or traditional or merely loyal, if one will—this is not entirely true. As General de Gaulle had the wisdom to see, the shaping of politics cannot be divorced from those of economics, trade and profit. For him—and rightly—the former held the master cards. Even such a remote subject as language (as any Welshman or Irishman or, indeed, Zionist can testify) is, despite English laziness, insensitivity or pragmatism here, not irrelevant to the political dynamic. In the summer of 1942 I spent my days in an endeavour, as already mentioned, to get an Institute for the Nurture of the English Language financed. By a close margin I failed. But the French Government has not been hesitant about spending sums only to be called vast on the propaganda of the French language. It is well for patriots to recall that the contemporary Czecho-Slovak State sprang from a nationalist movement in Bohemia, brought into being by scholars, historians and politicians who demanded a revival of the Czech language and who were tired of Germanisation or Europeanisation.

In these "cultural affairs", it may seem most innocent, natural and convenient that M. Pompidou, President of France, should urge, as said earlier, the use of French as "the working language"—English, Dutch and the like (maybe Welsh someday) being "official languages"—in the conclaves of a truly "European Europe". It would seem petty, parochial and troublesome to object. Furthermore, M. Pompidou cannot himself speak English whereas Mr Heath makes a gallant attempt at French with a pronunciation which, to avoid misunderstanding, involves television men in re-takes. (Winston Churchill, of course, spoke a superbly English French when addressing the French, even in Strasburg, where election manifestoes are printed in German. Ernest Bevin, no inconsiderable statesman, did not get beyond "*bon jour*".)

M. Pompidou cannot fail to recall that French was indeed the universal language of diplomacy until the time Woodrow Wilson and Lloyd George preferred, for good reason, to speak English. The "*Que dit-il?*" of de Gaulle in such situations cuts no ice.

M. Pompidou will also be aware that this prevalence of French as the language of polite diplomacy was itself due to the fact that Louis XIV had the educational misfortune of being unable to command the preceding international language of diplomacy, Hapsburg Latin.

To quibble on all this would seem to be to display precisely those prejudices of a narrow and reactionary nationalism—or have Welsh and Zionists and other nationalists a better case?— were it not that M. Pompidou, in an evil moment, confided to the world a comment which threw a most revealing and even lurid light on the implications. Suddenly a modest and common-sense proposal, suitable for secretaries, took on all the tones of the "Yankee, go home" movement. On 17th May, 1971, after stating his useful reasons for French being the language of committee discussion M. Pompidou went on to a further statement, according to press report (*Herald Tribune*, 18th May):

"I do hope that this rôle of French will be recognised within the Community. After all, English is also the language of the United States; and, if Europe wishes to be truly itself, *it must be distinct* from the United States." (Italics mine).

M. Pompidou subsequently explained that he did not here mean that Europe should "sever" relations with N. America, as one might sever diplomatic relations with the Bolsheviki—there were indeed "all kinds of relationships"—but only that a "European Europe", in search, Pirandello-like, of its own "identity" (as well it might be, considering that Moscow is also in Europe) would "find itself" by contradistinction from the Americas. It was rather a question of symbolism, of finding identity (as an "inadequate" patient might seek to do on a psychoanalyst's couch), of "differentiation". In brief, with all its strategic implications, a wedge was to be driven in with a hammer between what the French themselves used to call the Anglo-Saxon Powers. Personally, I would rather emigrate to Idaho than accept this detestable betrayal.

In a speech at Southampton on 26th May, 1971, James Callaghan, of the Labour Front Bench and sometime Chancellor of the Exchequer and Home Secretary, said:

"M. Pompidou is wholly opposed to any alteration in the fundamental character of the E.E.C. He intends that even its language, its relations with the United States, the Commonwealth, Africa and Asia shall be determined by the French Continental-European approach. He is no less clear that so far as British history, our political ideas, and our links with the world differ from those of the French-dominated E.E.C., then

Britain must subordinate them to the extent of a complete rupture with our identity. ... Millions of people in Britain have been surprised to learn that the language of Chaucer, Shakespeare and Milton must in future be regarded as an American import from which we must protect ourselves if we are to build a new Europe ... we are obstinately Atlantic Europeans."

There can, of course, be a Gadarene hysteria among trendy fellows about the fated, predestined course—as it were a stampede of cattle after seeing the wraith of a vision and scenting the smell of success. However, if we are to attend to history, and not to some wind of fresh change blowing in all directions, then the history of the British people, their political tradition, what has seemed to them the inevitable policy as an island and later as an empire, from the days of Cardinal Wolsey until the arrival of Mr Heath, points in the exact opposite direction to the helpful designs of Napoleon and of Hitler. To say otherwise is, as A. J. P. Taylor has pointed out, quite unblushingly to falsify history.

The English have no desire to join in Napoleon Worship in the Place Vendôme. In the past, British statesmen have proposed to maintain the balance of power in Europe, not in order to interfere amid the land armies of the Continent but, guaranteed against a dangerous aggression by Spaniard, Frenchman or German, in order to keep their hands free, not in splendid isolation but as a maritime and naval power which, according to the destiny of their history, looked westward and overseas. Not unnaturally M. Pompidou has, as I have said, expressed his disagreement with Winston Churchill on this point. I prefer the Churchill outlook.

However, on the political issue it can be urged that there is here a misunderstanding. On the surface M. Pompidou's policy would seem to be in that Gaullist tradition, consistent since the days of Louis XIV, of French-centred diplomatic pre-eminence, without restraints inconvenient to full sovereign decision, which the General adopted and developed with the insight of genius and the firmness of national tradition.

Certainly—to some satisfaction in the British Foreign Office— Gaullists did not contemplate "any erosion of essential national interests". Some functional "merger of sovereignty" in specific utility affairs of coal and steel was a minor matter. "Confederation" could be the new and prudent phrase. The demolition of what was called the British Commonwealth (prior to Nehru) could be one hell of a big matter of political and constitutional change; but in legal technicality it did not affect local sovereignty, whether "essential" or not. "Interdependence" could be a word of many meanings.

This interpretation, it may yet be held, is misleading. The facts are not so. The whole new policy of inviting English entry, whatever the rhetorical façade, issues not from French strength but from French weakness. There is alarm at the threat of German predominance, financial, economic and ultimately of a revived Reich (which can also play the cards of a pro-Russian, "Rapallo" policy: Russia has so much to offer). Britain is being wooed, not to support a renascent W. Germany against Gaullist *gloire*, but seduced to comfort France against Germany in war and peace.

Were this argument sound (as it undoubtedly is in at least some measure), then what emerges behind the apocalyptic veils of the gospel of "*The* Community" (i.e. "European Europe"), object of our new loyalty and dedication, is the fact of the old, old rivalry— not the spirit of the Franco-German Mass of goodwill in Notre Dame or of the equestrian statue of Charlemagne, outside the great Cathedral, but the desire to get England committed, as she has always sought not to be committed, to taking sides in the secular Continental rivalry. Profoundly I distrust a tactic which so limits our political freedom, contrary to diplomatic precedent, and which can only incite German suspicion and enmity. The so-called Community cracks from the beginning if we look beyond the hypocrisy of talk of union. We shall be wiser to consider the preservation of our own historical heritage.

§ v. *The Break-Up.*

There is yet one more facet in political presentation. It can be urged, and has been urged by Edward Heath, that Western Europe, despite or because of its large Continental Communist Parties, has to be saved from the Communists; and that Britain's entry into Europe will, in some significant fashion, contribute to this end. It is perhaps not too uncharitable to describe in the vernacular this argument as "guff" or, to use the phrase of Samuel Johnson, "cant". A "cold war" argument may here appeal in some quarters but, to be realistic, it has today to be recast.

Mr Heath indeed has had to be adaptable. In his address to the American Bar Association (19th July, 1971) he sought to rally all to a common front against Communism in the mass and of all kinds, Soviet and Chinese alike—"Communist ambitions have not changed". Hence Europe must unite and—a fine hypnotic touch—British entry is "inevitable". But, confronted by the sudden news of President's Nixon's future visit to Peking and rising to the occasion, Mr Heath continued that this last event only served to confirm the united rally, because "the means by which we in the West handle" the Communists "has undergone a change". It surely has.

There is yet one programme of policy which requires profound attention. It goes far beyond any mere cautious pessimism, alike about the prospects of Russian-Western détente or disbelief that the best results are likely to be achieved from the direct negotiations of Washington and of the Kremlin. It is unmoved by the French weakening of NATO and, *pro tanto*, of the Atlantic Treaty relationship in the West, since it believes that NATO, except in the remote and tentative form of some alliance relationship, is actually a dead organisation of the past. It is not preoccupied with the economic structure of E.E.C.—far from it, save as re-enforcement.

It is indeed preoccupied with the political structure of Western Europe. But it cares neither for some past Utopian dream for federal union of Europe nor even for "political integration" and the European Commission and the Rome Treaty (with, as de Gaulle discovered, so many possible re-interpretations). It regards them as illusory political "guff"—all idealistic dream or bogey. The sovereign nations of Western Europe, some minor regulations apart, will remain sovereign as before. The N. Americans will all be "out". There will be a vacuum of power. The actualities of military and especially bombing arrangements will fill it. There will be, with all the appropriate ribbons and trappings, a Dual Entente, sealed in Paris. This is the destiny; and this is what is going to happen.

In view of the visit of 1971 of Mr Brezhnev to Paris, it may be supposed that this will be, as at the beginning of this century and recorded by me in the first chapter of this book, a Franco-Russian Entente. That, after all, was the old beginning. It would accord well with the historic French dreams of a French diplomatic hegemony over the land powers of Europe, aided by Russian co-operation in its own area of Eastern supremacy. Against whom, then, would it be directed? As originally, not least against Britain? Certainly not. Against Germany? Also not, although if the Germans preferred to look rather to American protection than to French aid, this folly would be viewed with a Russian displeasure that the French would understand. Anyhow Russia would have the immense satisfaction of seeing the break-up of an antique NATO and, more important, the end of the American presence and of that Anglo-American unity which Hitler had so rightly feared.

However, this Franco-Russian notion also is superficial and wrong. The Triple Entente is not yet. Let, it is suggested, the

Germans do (more or less) what they like—even in *Ost-politik*.
The proposed new Dual Entente is one, primarily military—"to
fill the power vacuum"—between Britain and France. Mr Sam
White of the *Evening Standard* may know every politician of
sophistication and every lady of elegance and wit in France but,
it may be said, he is not a political heavyweight. Nevertheless, I
do him the honour of taking his report (19th Sept., 1971)
seriously. It is neat, even elegant.

Basically, the plan is directed against Soviet dominance—
and also American. Europe (N.W.) hereby discovers its identity.
Subsidiarily, on the one side it has strategic merits as covering
the 1939-40 time gap (if it could recur) and, on the other side,
of treating the Anglo-American "special relation" as not only
objectionable ("with a non-European Power") but as dead and
the policy, hence, not too displeasing for the moment to Russian
anti-American central strategy. It would be the United States
which would be just "an isolated country", flanked by a not-over-
loving South America and Canada (including Québec). The
sheet-anchor of the policy, however, is the conviction that there
must be American withdrawal from Europe within the next
decade. It takes as its gospel leaves from the books of Senator
Mansfield and of the disillusioned Senator Fulbright. The
evidence comes from student and other electoral protest against
the well-intentioned but misbegotten Vietnam war in remoter
Asia, which has distorted the proportions of American policy.

In a further report in the *Evening Standard*, this time from the
Azores Conference (December 1971), Mr Sam White suggested,
not indeed that the United States, suffering from the sin (of
which London used to be accused) of "gigantism", should be
encircled in the south by Mexico, but the proposals were abroad
that, in the north, Canada should become an Associate State of
the European Community ("*The* Community"), which would, of
course, not include the United States. French sentiment and
Quebec influence could move Canada, "from sea to sea", into
this Paris orbit. . . This could outdistance even de Gaulle. In
connection with the Azores Conference some resentment was
reported in the press that France was presenting herself as a
spokesman for "the entirety of Western Europe", and, to use a
French phrase of delicacy, might merit a kick in the *pompi*. However, the latest report was that, in these negotiations, it was
Mr Anthony Barber who appeared as "*plus royaliste que Giscard
d'Estaing soi-meme*" (*Sunday Times*, 19 December 1971).

One can but repeat that the road to world peace leads (despite
the disclaimers of the Chinese for their own leadership purposes)

through the consultative accord, where practicable, of the Super-Powers and not through the multiplication of egocentric Mini-Powers, seeking to bestride the Balance.

The Bermuda "Summit" (Anglo-American) Conference followed the Azores "Summit" (Franco-American) Conference. Reporting from Bermuda (21 December 1971), Robert Carvel stated that Edward Heath expressed there, "if not a mild form of anti-Americanism, at least the strongest assertion of how he expects Britain and the rest of Europe to take over as the strongest economic unit in the world bar none". Moscow will be delighted to hear Mr Heath's boast. President Nixon, on the contrary, said in Bermuda that "I can reassure you that that special relationship, special in the sense of a dedication to principles that are inalienable and indestructible, is as strong now and ever more necessary now than ever before because, as the world changes, it is even more vital to maintain those principles to which our nation and the British people have been directed throughout *our* (*sic*) history". I agree with the President.

On December 22, in Paris on television, Mr Heath's comrade, ex-banker M. Pompidou, stated, chiefly with reference to finance, that "the United States has been forced to admit that Europe is an economic equal and the proof of this, he said, is that Washington now 'fears' European economic power and competivity". However, here CAP, quite peculiarly objectionable to Britain, is central. "Let me tell you that, if the Common Market for Agriculture is weakened, at that moment there will be no further prospects for political union". The French farmer will not give ground.

The basic policy assumption throughout is that America is "inevitably" moving into isolationism; that American power is moving into permanent eclipse; and (here the comrades may disagree) that French diplomatic power will take over and fill the vacuum. Macmillan's prognostications of danger—of "war" with America—were not wrong. Pompidou's farmers have to be told "No". The present issue of this moment, in principle, of British politics, involving the whole future of this country, is whether we agree with this resonant "No", and get Heath out, or whether we do not.

In his Nobel Prize speech in Oslo, Chancellor Brandt maintained that Europe and America could not be separated. On the same day it was reported, on the Common Market negotiators in Brussels (*Herald Tribune*, 12 December 1971), that "France rejects the implication that the United States should have the right to help determine the EEC's cause", not least with reference to Agricultural policy. As invariably, the egocentric policy of

France is the fly in the ointment, although the smell of it does not disturb Mr Heath's enthusiasms, any more than do Mr Rippon's fish concessions. Aloft, amid the environment, in Concorde, there is no smell—only costs.

However, the protest of the White House and of a Republican President against this isolationist policy has already been mentioned. It is worthy of notice that a Democratic President, Lyndon B. Johnson, made one of his rare recent public appearances (15th November, 1971) to say that a formidable isolationist coalition, capable of irreparable damage to world order, appeared to be forming in the United States. It could wrongly be mistaken for majority opinion. "There is no safety for this country in oceans of isolation . . . If we fall into isolationism, we are the ones who are isolated. We cannot afford to repeat the tragic mistakes of the past."

Whenever it comes to a crunch the endemic American isolationism can always be revealed as being precisely such as the President Johnson said—minoritarian. Nevertheless, those of us who were directly involved would feel it to be sad indeed if the work of 1935–40, in rescuing the United States from this philosophy, had to be done all over again. Either the "new policy" described above rests on a dangerous error of fact or, alternatively, it should not be agreed to but fought further, relentlessly and savagely. Otherwise the philosophy of Western defeatism will become self-fulfilling. Nor will the multiplication of nostalgic sovereignties nor of mini-Super Powers nor of Unions of the Frightened and Jealous contribute to peace. They are inimical to peace.

However, to balance this stress on Anglo-French or E.E.C. "independence", it is correct to say that Europe, amid such talk of "European power" wants to conduct its own defence on the cheap for electioneering reasons. In the words of Denis Healey (3rd October, 1971) there is "a great disparity between what America is doing to defend Europe and what the 'Europeans', especially since the divisive French walk-out on NATO, 'are doing to defend themselves' ". "President Pompidou appears to survive the imminent disaster with a complacent *Schadenfreude*." (Healey, *Sunday Times*, 21st November.) The precise and most alarming opposite emphasis to this was that of Edward Heath in his Party Conference speech of 16th October, of which the *Herald Tribune* reports: "He warned against the possibility of a 'protectionist trade war', (presumably initially and chiefly waged by the United States). And he said that Britain must work with the Common Market, which it is about to join, 'to protect West

European interests'." So much for "solidarity"....

While authentically seeking détente, the dangers of "objective" Soviet imperialism cannot indeed be safely ignored. The problem, as said earlier, is one not of ideology but of history and of power. If indeed a military danger is visualised, then it is the divisive policy of France and the French chauvinist decision to quit NATO which have uncompromisingly to be condemned. We do not want support for some weak local bombing arrangement. Professor Raymond Aron, in *Figaro*, expressed his fears about Soviet hegemony. This is not the way to allay them. If indeed the Continental Europeans simply cannot get together among themselves, whatever their danger, this is their misfortune which the accession of Britain will not cure.

If the doctrinal and credal faith of Khrushchev in Communist conquest "in time" of Europe, America and the world were to become fact, the cause would not be the march of Russian legions. As Nikita Khrushchev stated in admirable words, "One cannot build civilisation on a radio-active ash heap". Rather the cause would be the infection of the whole West by an anarchist philosophy, parasitic or "permissivist", which neurotic defeatism would make resistance, in ideas or in arms, impracticable. A general "back-lash" towards discipline and authority, even Kremlin-style, would then become acceptable as a "lesser evil" for thinking men. Then indeed we might see, not in Chile alone or in the large Italian and French Communist Parties alone, the shape of a World Communism to come. Here indeed lies the future danger for the West. The remedy lies at home in a new positive philosophy of life and in a better concept of duty and of authority as guarantor of any socially acceptable liberty.

The advantage springing from the Treaty of Rome is more frequently stated as being that Europe will be able "to speak with one voice" (maybe along with M. Pompidou on Israel); will make clear that this Francophone voice is identifiably different from any American voice; will exercise its full and eminent influence; and that the English and Irish will together stand in with Europe against the outsiders. A variant on this theme is that since two World Wars "have arisen in Europe" (a statement which overlooks Ethiopia and Japan), therefore it is necessary to look to that unhappy area, being on the record not peace-minded, to establish exclusively the beginnings of a stable world peace. No imposed peace by the Super Powers (who alone have the power it takes), whether in Europe—or in the Middle East. . . . By the same logic it can be argued that, many recent wars having been started in the Balkans, it must be left exclusively to the Balkans to initiate peace.

Mr Enoch Powell is not unjustified in stigmatising the whole position as dishonest—and hence dishonourable. At one time the public was cozened with the assertion that the plan was merely an economic, marketing arrangement and that all political and, on the record, federal plans for union were far from us. Now the theme is (quite truly) that economic integration will lead on into political integration. At the Atlantic Treaty Association London Conference (Sept. 1971), Signor Colonna di Paliano, *rapporteur*, demanded a "positive integration" of "The Community", as a full "political entity". Alternatively, "The Community" would, he asserted, wither. It would be interesting to know whether Sir Alec Douglas-Home agrees. In fairness to Sir Alec it should be said that, on the record, it appears that he does not. "The Community" here is not, of course, that of Atlantic solidarity, but the N.W. European parochial one, including monetary union. Enthusiasts, and those who have adopted, not internationalism but a diminished European provincialism as a religion exclaim that we must forthwith "go into Europe". They then, the next moment and by a muddle-headed logic, say that "we are already part of Europe, always have been in Europe". (Strange aberration of our forbears to think otherwise.) This is, like schoolchildren, to accept the fallacy of cartographers. Is not all Europe—for that matter including Muscovy—coloured green? Therefore we must belong to "the Greens". Incidentally the British Empire including the United Kingdom used to be coloured red.

Mr Heath assures the reluctant Commonwealth that "we must stand on our own feet", as sovereign. Based on the Statute of Westminster, that is good enough for them. At the next moment, talk of sovereignty muted, we are to base ourselves on the Treaty of Rome and are to stand on our European feet. Which is it to be? These shufflings are just not good enough, in logic or in politics.

The United Kingdom must be dissociated from the United States—and from the overseas Commonwealth—in order to be associated with Paris and Brussels. According to the comment in *The Financial Times* (26th Jan., 1971), the temper at the Singapore Conference tended to the view "let the devil take the Commonwealth".

This direction of policy can only be regarded as a betrayal of all British achievements and development. We cannot become a Sweden if we wish and it would be sad if we became a Portugal. The British are on the whole a decent and loyal people and I known no reason why they should be pushed around against their will. Britain (although not Scotland) and each of the British Dominions are indeed sovereign; but there are other ties, more profound than institutions, which hold countries together in peace and war.

As a Canadian Senator recently said to me with ironic bitterness: "Well, our ways now part: very pleased to have met you." Other comment is yet more downright. The Australians say, more dangerously, that there is a British disloyalty of sentiment they will neither forget nor forgive. Australian opinion is outspoken, downright, negative and as obstinate as the British Prime Minister Mr Edward Heath himself. The Heath policy means the effective end of the Commonwealth as hitherto understood. Here he can be attacked on better grounds than de Gaulle ever was for ending the French Empire.

The New Zealand correspondent of the "pro-Common Market" *Sunday Times* (20th June, 1971) selects for quotation the remark of a representative farmer there. "Look, if Britain wants to sell us out, that's her business." This comment comes from a spokesman of those who, in September 1939, declared: "We are with you to the last penny and the last man."

This is no haggle about mutton or butter. It is the expression of the emotion, enduring until jilted, of a people upon which their policy, their loyalty and their sacrifice could be built.

There is indeed agreement by all on the affirmation of sovereign rights of decision. But there is no agreement that these decisions should take a form which flaunts indifference to Commonwealth consensus, such as might be expected even in the most ephemeral of military alliances. Mr Edward Heath may have "won his long fight to show once and for all that other Commonwealth countries have no right to tell Britain what she can do"—*can* do, not should do. Let Mr Heath give the same reply to the European Commission at Brussels, when it seeks to impose supranational obligations under that Rome Treaty which, with extraordinary lack of consistency, Edward Heath loves so well.

The strategy of the Indian Ocean is one (which I have discussed elsewhere) as complex in its nature as that of America's role as a Power in the Pacific. Whether Britain should have any policy "South of Suez" is no less complex. But it is not this that is the issue. The issue is that of flexibility, good temper, accommodation, common loyalty. The philosophy of Commonwealth, with its anomalies, may have been even less thought out than that of Empire. Many mistakes about citizenship were made, not least by Mr Duncan Sandys, with his hasty pledges to Asians later expelled from Africa. There is yet some residue of agreement on this consensus. The Commonwealth structure must not be treated with contempt as by some berserk builder's demolition worker.

Edward Heath, "the most committed of all" (*Sunday Times* 24th Jan., 1971), may be so obsessed with his personal involvement in the Common Market, where he may see history beckoning him to a private niche, that he can regard the Commonwealth as a bore. But his Commonwealth colleagues may take a very different view. The result of all this fine statesmanship is that "the Commonwealth can never be the same again"—that in the end there was at Singapore in January 1971 what Robert Carvel describes as "the ferocity of the extraordinary Commonwealth punch up", Asian, Australian and African, with M. Trudeau acting as the broker of a last minute verbal formula. The states-men at the Congress of Vienna did not indulge in a "punch up". Nor is this any way to confront Russia in Africa.

Mr John McEwen, until recently Australian Minister of Trade, has raised the issue whether Edward Heath has any international legal right under GATT to enter the Common Market in a fashion which involves violation by imposing new barriers to trade for the benefit of the N.W. European "closed shop". A country, of which 90% of her population is of British stock, resents its people being treated as unwanted aliens and resents a newly arrived Prime Minister appearing to be hell-bent on wrecking ancient community ties. What odd socialism. (Admit-tedly Mr Heath never claims that.) What even odder conservatism.

Blatant dissociation is a bizarre independence policy for a Government (not even here supported by its own polled people) to follow in what is, it would seem, only ironically called a Commonwealth. The issue is no mere grocer's account. It is one of whether a human contract of the past shall be perpetuated to the days of our grandchildren, a contract of peoples with one common royal Head, a contract of centuries sealed in the blood of many wars, a contract which neither local nationalism nor independent policies of commerce or of a mean jealousy should dissolve. To regard it otherwise is contemptible.

We destroy what we have. We present the Commonwealth on public platforms (as, alas! did Mr Michael Stewart) as some kind of Kiwani club of like-minded good fellows, indeed sharing values —but add nervously, looking over our shoulders to Paris, that these values are not so valuable as to differentiate ourselves from the notoriously democratic Germans and the altruistic French. We destroy what we have known; and build we know not quite what. Paris alone knows.

General de Gaulle's honourable goal was *une union des patries*, which excellently and traditionally permitted the European primacy of French diplomacy. Nevertheless, a major danger of his very success was always that he could awake dreams of some German de Gaulle. Herr Franz Josef Strauss, stronger in Germany than Mr Enoch Powell in Britain, stands in the wings to assume this role. He yet, by contrast with the General, asserts his belief in a federal union of Europe in the fullest sense. There are, he says, not to be many Foreign Ministers of the States of Europe, but one Foreign Minister; not many Defence Ministers but one (maybe Herr Strauss). Presumably Great Britain will maintain a High Commissioner in Paris or Brussels. Certainly it is not the President of the United States who will be chairman—it appears that Mr Arthur Schlesinger, jnr., by an unfortunate speech in Chicago, destroyed that dream for Herr Strauss. Nor are there to be many Heads of State; but one Head of State, one President.

Many eminent Englishmen, listening to Herr Strauss in London, I saw nodding their heads when he spoke, in enthusiastic assent. They were dazzled by the notion of being bridegroom in an indissoluble marriage to have the six brides of the Continent. The time was when they might have lost their heads for treason. Clearly the various monarchs of Europe become redundant, embarrassments in the one council chamber, "fifth wheels" to the European coach. Clearly a British Premier, being of lower protocol status, must be embarrassed to sit at a council table with a French President, and not offer to the latter the vacant chair. . . . Clearly, on principle and for the desired future, the Queen is being invited to abdicate.

In the entire English-speaking world, America included, the Queen has an unchallenged social precedence, and as Head of the Commonwealth an indubitable role. But in this new Europe, what? For myself, I say that this is not the moment—nor will it be so long as any English-speaking world is a reality—to speculate about abolishing the monarchy, which is yet the final logic of Brussels, and of Mr Edward Heath.

If indeed one is to accept the full romantic creed of what is called, not "the West", not "the Free World", not NATO or SEATO, but "*The* Community", then there are certain clear consequences. The true "European European" will regard those legally of this grouping, that is of the little provincial exclusive North Western Europe, including by French law a few Negro denizens of West Indian Guadeloupe and the like, as his countrymen whose interests he will "take to heart". Patently the rest, not being "European European", will be "foreigners". The final break-up of *les Pouvoirs anglosaxons* will doubtless cause bonfires in the Place Vendôme and beneath the Arc de Triomphe which records only certain victories, not Waterloo or Blenheim. Maybe

Trafalgar Square will be re-named "Concorde".

To this mass-emotion or what is called "vision", compared with which, in the words of journalist Mr Anthony Lewis, the Commonwealth was always "a myth"—odd that Royal Commonwealth Societies and the like never announced it—there are certainly legal and constitutional consequences. The Queen's distinctive position is not the same as that of the Queen of Holland, the King of Belgium or other Low Country dignitaries. Her distinctive position, which relates to that of Britain herself, is that of Queen of lands overseas and Head of State. Admittedly, if the Commonwealth is "a myth", then the monarchy as symbol is a myth. But the Commonwealth (whatever the position of local sovereignty) is not a myth unless Britain chooses to make it so.[1]

To all this the Marketeers have one final reply—the risks of displaying disunion in their respective parties apart. (And is not the whole future of the nation important enough for the division bells?) It is a wail of despair. "*What* alternative is there? There is none." We must have a wider market than the fifty million home market of Britain—or present world Free Trade—provides. This statement that there is "no alternative" happens to be grossly fake. It is the criminal error of British diplomacy that the alternatives have not been officially explored. "There are difficulties." Of course there are difficulties. "Tell me not of the difficulties, but of how to overcome the difficulties."

Is there not, however, a far wider market available than even the North-Western section of the European peninsula—available in the Atlantic Free Trade Area?[1] "This policy", runs the reply, "is not a runner. It has been revealed to us and we know it." A dogmatic negative, never probed or firmly explored in British diplomacy. How do they know? When Defence Ministers explore as routine a hundred plans, hypotheses and alterations in military relations, there is something criminal in a refusal to explore in the Foreign Office, diplomatically and officially, the available alternatives in Atlantic Free Trade Area, O.E.C.D., NATO quarters—because, as a matter of Party policy, there is a calculated wish to play these alternatives down.[2]

[1] In fairness to Mr Lewis, I should add that his article, "The End of the Lane" (*Herald Tribune*, 17th Aug., 1971) on the future of London, was one of the wisest and most charming that I have read for a long while. I would put alongside with it, Mr Alfred Friendly's leave-taking article on Britain, "The Unique Society" (*Herald Tribune*, 27 December, 1971).
[2] George Catlin: *The Atlantic Commonwealth*, 1969, Penguin. (Discussion of AFTA). *The Grandeur of England and the Atlantic Community*, 1967, Pergamon.

There are some, as I have said, who regard citizenship of Europe almost with the fervour of a new religion. Unlike Palmerston, they are proud to cease to be English, Scottish or Welsh. There are others, perhaps more dangerous, who (frequently as journalists) find it "modern", tough and trendy, not only to write with *Schadenfreude* about the Twilight of Empire and of the transition of the Commonwealth from Disillusion to Dissolution, but to repeat in the name of realism that Britain must be "cut down to size" and learn to adjust herself as a small island to the position of being a second or third-rate power. It is a neat idea, comparable to the frivolity of the New York hostess who, having twice introduced the Swedish Ambassador as the Swiss Ambassador, remarked gaily when the Swede expostulated: "I'm so sorry, but I can never understand why all you small nations don't join up." The "diminishers" are so clever as to share the mood of the pseudo-realists of 1940, inaugurators of "the Age of the Anti-Hero" and of the mediocre spirit, who thought that Britain would surely "have her neck wrung". The Channel, they urge, has since Dunkirk become a negligible ditch. It is to the eternal credit of de Gaulle, great patriot that he was, that he thrashed the like defeatists in France and they remained thrashed. Even the man from Broadstairs will scarcely survive.

The Senate of the United States is a loosely organised body of varying moods and views, ranging from the world federalist plans of Senator Joseph H. Ball, of Wisconsin (so different from Under Secretary George Ball) and of Senator Kefauver of Tennessee, to the rankest isolationism. In 1970 voting against the Protectionist Mills Bill, the Senate can still haver over whether to provide protection against Japanese textile competition—and, by remoter implication, Common Market protectionism on other matters. Such business competitions, or what de Gaulle called "affairs of the bourse", are part of the normal texture of politics. Internally Massachusetts and the Carolinas have been for decades in like competition on textiles. De Gaulle was right in denying that they or oil or gold should shape the face of politics and the destiny of nations.

If, in a Senate of recent years normally favouring and still favouring GATT and Free Trade, the protectionists voice resentment against Common Market tariffs, it is because no other than the Europeans, in defiance, first chose to plan the offensive. But although in the last resort the Senate may veto progress (as advocates of the League of Nations found), it is not to the Senate that one has to look for the shaping of American policy. It is an executive task. In my last conversation with President

Eisenhower, he deplored the danger of protectionist demands from the U.S. steel-masters. However, contemporary policy has been stated (30th Dec., 1970) by President Richard Nixon in his Message to Congress: "This Administration remains committed to the objective of expanding mutually advantageous world trade."

The Department of State is not the White House. And such sometime spokesmen of the Department as French-connected ex-Under Secretary George Ball belong to a previous Administration and are out of date as the voice of the present one. Those who assert that "there is no alternative to E.E.C." (for example in AFTA) do yet, in fact, have their negativism aided by a Department of State hitherto obsessed by the Vietnam war and too busy to worry about Europe, a Department conscious of the popularity of reducing tax expenditure and the direction of manpower to European defence. "Let the Europeans defend themselves" is an obvious slogan. Confronted by the permanent factor of Moscow such pseudo-realist isolationism can be quite unrealistic—but it is electorally attractive. There is a certain sluggishness in national policies, call it inertia or tradition, which infects alike the Department of State and the British Foreign Office—a "departmental view". Incidentally it ignores the virulence of anti-Americanism, envious, resentful, snobbish, in certain European cultural quarters.

Nevertheless, when the Department of State repeats the gramophone record dating from Churchill's day (when it made sense), "Britain should go into Europe"—the chairman's chair then being vacant—without safeguards and despite the most real danger of the anti-American Frankenstein of a "Third Force" being created, one is entitled to ask that the record be thrown away as cracked.

Mr George Ball, an earnest and indefatigable advocate of pushing a protesting Britain into Europe, has indeed the modesty to declare "I do not think Soviet Intelligence is so stupid as to report ... that I speak with tacit Administration support". Nevertheless, the ground of this advocacy, in some quarters resented, by an American of the highest ability is basically the old fear of the growing powers of Germany. Of Mr George Kennan the great Mr Secretary Acheson wrote that he had "no sense for power". Mr Ball has a distorted sense. Inside the Third Force Balance there is to be an inner balance, whereby Britain adds its weight to a France liable to be dominated by a Germany which, for reunification, might turn to a "Rapallo" pro-Moscow policy. I suggest that getting Britain to balance off Chancellor Brandt is not the happiest auspice for mutual confidence in this new and better community, which can cut the painter of those NATO–Atlantic commitments which hitherto have held a pro-American Germany from adventurism. The problem of Berlin will be solved by solution of the problem of the two Germanies; and this again will be solved in terms of Washington-Moscow relations (not Paris–Moscow "Dual Entente" or exclusively Bonn–Moscow relations), where unilateral interference by Paris, Bonn—or even London—is merely mischievous.

George Ball's answer is one of the oldest answers, from which we had hoped that at least de Gaulle and Adenauer had rescued us; a bad answer; a pre-1914 answer, in which on the record I have no part. If balance is needed, let America do its own work.

This itch on the part of some few Americans to push Britain for her good is likewise to be discovered in the London correspondent of the *International Herald Tribune*. Mr Lewis, after having spent much powder and shot in firing at the White House, and later in gunning for Mr Wilson, has more lately found that, if Britain does not enter E.E.C., its government will be "without friends in Europe, mocked around the world, powerless to save Britain from being ground between the millstones of the great trading powers". Is that indeed so? The danger cited by the *Washington Post* of a Moscow policy "to split Europe off from the United States" is not mentioned. The voice of Mr Lewis here seems to recall that of a certain Ambassador of America to Britain of long ago, who sought to alarm Roosevelt by dyspeptic cries of "Woe".

"Hallelujah, the America era is ending" is now the call. But it is not ending. It is being re-shaped. The constructive and positive views of the senior Senator for New York State, Senator Jarvis, I have already cited. And the destiny of Britain does not lie, as some suppose, in reversing its history. It does not even lie, as Mr Heath has amazingly suggested, in so reversing traditional policy as to repeat the Continental designs of Napoleon and Hitler in some quieter way. It lies in the world beyond the seas, westwards, and in the growth from "the old Commonwealth" to the Atlantic Commonwealth.

Dr H. Malmgren, an economic adviser to President Nixon, in the London *Times* of 5th July 1971, has stated the solid grounds for economic fears, for the United States, in a European protectionism—fears which, in discussion with Chancellor Brandt, M. Pompidou has already begun to appreciate. An even greater danger lies in the potential growth of an isolationism which, in 1938–9, it took immense political effort to overcome. Should indeed the atrocious catastrophe of war come again, those who contribute to this, directly or indirectly, will be signing their own death-warrant. Here one can agree with Dean Rusk that a main job of our civilisation is to prevent this trend.

More importance should be attached to the advocacy by President Nixon's closest adviser, Henry Kissinger, of "an Atlantic Commonwealth", than to ex-Under Secretary Ball's views or to anything that came out of the Department of State during the "Vietnam period". On my quotation of his argument, Kissinger was good enough to send me a note in 1970, saying that he was happy with my citation of his work here.

As to the CAP arrangement and its agricultural policy, Senator Hubert H. Humphrey, sometime Vice President, stated in London, after reference to the vision of President John F. Kennedy, that this policy "has become a major disruptive force in world agricultural markets. These activities are contrary to the principles agreed in the General Agreement on Tariffs and Trade (GATT)", so far that persistence in them "can only be damaging to U.S. relations". Described by the *Herald Tribune* as "a ferocious attack", but indeed a most diplomatic speech solely expressing American policy, the comment of the still titular chief of the Democratic Party took, on that Friday, 30th July, 1971, the myth that all America wanted British "Entry" into E.E.C. on Heath-Rippon terms; set fire to it; and exploded it in Mr Heath's face. The dismay of the Heathite press, including sourly bundling the speech into two inches in *The Times*, was marvellous to note.

However, what can readily happen is that a fiscal and trade war between the United States and the Common Market countries can develop—in the words of the *Sunday Times* (Business News, 22nd August, 1971), "a dreadful, escalating confrontation", with Britain finding itself on the wrong side of the line for its own advantage.

An edge and a precision has to be given to John F. Kennedy's talks in the Paulus-Kirche and elsewhere, about an Atlantic Community as the necessary framework for all lesser regional arrangements—as itself the plan for "the widest practical area for peace", which N.W. Europe assuredly is not. Advocacy of the Atlantic Commonwealth represents the next step in advance. It is within this that the older British Commonwealth makes strategic, economic and political sense. The periphery of either Commonwealth should be multi-racial and multi-national. But in 1940, the focus of power lay in Washington, Westminster, Ottawa, and until terms for lasting peace are reached with Moscow, it will still lie there. The Atlantic Commonwealth, in practical terms, involves economic steps in accord with the present U.S.

economic bonus to industries investing inside the U.S.A. It no less involves positive development, cultural and political. The second clause of the NATO charter, the existing multi-national Organisation for Economic Cooperation and Development, the normal interchange of personnel and coordination of plans and policies in so many fields, based on tested mutual confidence, which I termed during the last war "Organic Union", can all (as Senator Javits has truly said) be bricks in the structure.

On 9th January, 1971, I ventured to write to the Governor of New York, Nelson Rockefeller, to whom I had been introduced by a telephoned message from President Eisenhower in 1967. I wrote in part: "Humbly I suggest that what is needed is some strong American voice and American vision which will make a declaration—even using the words "Atlantic Commonwealth": as yet it is in no public document—which will replace earlier routine replies belonging to the period of Vietnam preoccupation."

A weakness of the United States, it can be argued, is a traditional reluctance to assume political responsibilities in accordance with its power. As a nation it is by temperament immeasurably less imperialistic than the Russian, whether of the Czars or of the Soviets—although I would regard the Warsaw Pact as far more liable to explosion than NATO. The characteristic comment, earlier quoted, made by Mr Dean Acheson on George Kennan— "He has no sense of power"—can be applied more widely. There is a tendency in America, encouraged by the enshrined Whiggery of the Constitution, to accept the philosophy: "Every man his own President", with President-baiting, after baseball, as the national sport. Although NATO has modified this the tendency of America, unlike the Soviet Union, far from being towards imperialist domination is much more likely to show itself as a minority demand for retreat within the boundaries of "Fortress America". An American chairmanship and "democratic dialogue" are the best that politically (as distinct from strategically) can be anticipated.

I recall one-time Foreign Secretary Patrick Gordon Walker advising me that the term "natural and historical interest" might be a better one. In 1965 I tried the phrase out on President Truman, in Independence, Mo. After praise of the Atlantic Community, the ex-President would have none of the new coined term. "Let us be honest. There *is* a special interest, isn't there?" Rightly, no American Administration and particularly no Democrat Administration, with its universalist and Wilsonian tradition, is prepared to confine its policy and limit its commitments to some exclusive national favouritism. But this does not evacuate the phrase "special interest" of meaning in an English-speaking world or in an Atlantic Commonwealth which can, by Europe's own choice, include much of Europe. The Japanese and French are ready enough to use the same phrase at their convenience on their polite visits to Washington. Indeed, it may be, as Mr Denis Healy suggests (*Sunday Times*, 21st Nov., 1971) precisely now a period of "bilateral arrangements with individual countries".

Taught by Mr Truman, when I delivered the Winston Churchill Memorial Address at Westminster College, Fulton, in October 1968, I discarded this spinsterish caution.[1]

For those who demand a market, it is by developing a vigorous sentiment—and sentiments are the basis of political action and the deepest realities—that we may move into AFTA and to the largest market of all. However much we may deplore with Lord Harlech and with Roy Jenkins, as I do, any policy which creates a divorce between the lesser Community of part of Europe and an Atlantic Community which can include it, one cannot ignore the kind of situation where the Director of the British Council of the European Movement (Mr E. Wistrich), in replying to an article of mine following up my Fulton Address, entitles his article, "We Must Avoid the Atlantic Menace". The conflict of policies is stark and uncompromising.

It may be, as Edward Taylor, sometime Under Secretary for Scotland under Edward Heath, remarks that "many support the Common Market because they have lost faith in Britain". About these men with cold feet it may be added that they have also become credulous that "an era is over" (presumably to the advantage of Moscow and beckoning to holocaust); that the United States lacks credibility, economic, strategic, political; and that the other great Anglo-Saxon Power, America, has, from now forth, ceased to be—as indeed some secretly always wished—a world Great Power. It is a view which encourages isolationism and is, objectively, a view of the enemies of this country.

Hence it was with delight I noted that on 3rd May 1971, Mr Harold Wilson in addressing the Legislature of Texas in joint session of Senate and Representatives in Austin, discarded the phrase "special interest" as inadequate and said that a close relationship between the United Kingdom and the United States is

". . . an *essential, indispensable, vital factor* in world affairs . . . for good or evil and we must make it for good in world affairs" (italics mine).

[1] George Catlin, *Atlanticism*, Fulton Address, 1969 (Blackwell, Oxford).

A more direct slap in the face for M. Pompidou's theme about a "European Europe", when Westminster will "pull out" the red line to Washington, could scarcely be phrased.

I would not wish, following the example of that rightly revered man, M. Jean Monnet, to arrogate any journalistic title of "Mr Atlantic Community". Some time ago *The Guardian* exaggerated, by describing me as "the founder of the [movement for] the close union of the United States and the British Commonwealth". Union has many meanings and my proposals were "open-ended". As *The New York Times* said, I was "one of the pioneers of the Atlantic idea"; but *The Atlantic Community* (Brookings Institution), already quoted, also named Walter Lippmann and Clarence Streit. Whether my proposals, in Lord Sankey's phrase, "deserved well of two hemispheres" is for others to judge and recognise. At least my advocacy has been consistent and unconditional. It still stands.

§ vi. *Affirmation.*

I have referred to the defeatist mood of self-denigration which has infected this generation in Britain, just as an inchoate anarchism in philosophy has until recently infected a younger generation in America. Respectable bankers, such as Mr David Montague, are scarcely able to exaggerate their mis-cast confidence that either Britain must "go into Europe" or, naturally, "go down the drain". (In passing be it said that the most expert economic opinion that has come my way discusses this national denigration with contempt.) It is either frivolous or hysterical to suggest, as the director of the Hudson, N.Y., "think-tank" or Institute has recently done, that Britain needs to be revolutionarily stirred by even deeper economic crises or by a war or like disaster or "by a new religion". It is to be hoped that democracy can provide a leadership of vision, courage, pertinacity, at once patriotic and international, without having to evoke from the depths an autocracy of a new de Gaulle. Nevertheless, what is required is a statesman (or, in homage to Mrs Meir, perhaps one should add a stateswoman) who is competent to provide that conjunction of vision and commonsense which will be adequate to the age. There is, indeed, a "wider vision" needed. It is the vision of the widest available area, for the sake of the peace of the world, to be integrated. Compared with it, a N.W. European "vision" which, "European European" and even European chauvinist, proposes to remain only such, is provincial. The wider vision is that Atlantic one which has always been peculiarly compatible with the British outlook. Nor will history "leave us out". It is foolery, as great as that of "Little Englanders", to suggest it.

I have commented on the significant damage to Atlantic solidarity and Western unity done by the French "walk-out" from NATO. I have commented on the weakening, and indeed quite deliberate moving away from, those English-speaking bonds which have served us so well, all grander matters apart, in concrete military terms in the two great wars of my life-time. I have commented with aversion on that break-up of the Commonwealth, both Old and New, not indeed initiated but signalised by Mr Heath at Singapore, which spelled the end of the earlier view, to which I was attached. This was of a European pragmatically experimental area, more extensive than merely Steel and Coal Authorities, which was yet to be most firmly placed in a context—in a political solidarity, not just of passing alliance but of community—wider than a merely North Western European or than the embrace of France. Finally, while expecting the entry with us of the Irish Republic into this Europe (with, we are told, "a common foreign policy" and maybe instructions from Brussels about its enforcement), it would, I hold, be well if we first attended to peace, union and statesmanship within the British Isles themselves, instead of awaiting civil war.

The I.R.A. is an illegal organisation, so described in the Irish Republic; and the internment of suspects without trial has British precedent during the Second World War. I do not overlook the possibility that there may be certain elements in the Provisional I.R.A. who are uninterested in the good of Ireland and who are only interested in their own fanatical and revolutionary purposes (not that they are alone in being fanatics). The Vietcong in S. Vietnam are illegal and violent men. So certainly were the Algerian armed rebels confronting the *colons*, resident in Algeria for generations, and the French army. None, however inspired by sentiments of a violent patriotism, probably short-sighted and wrong-headed, regarded themselves—or were even regarded by world opinion—as just criminals and thugs. Nor was confidence in army "victory" enough. No Orangeman could outstrip the loyalty of the Algerian *colons* to metropolitan France, so that they were even ready to contemplate the assassination of their French opponents. No one doubts the like intransigent loyalty—and, as in Rhodesia, loyalty can suffocate—of Orangemen who are descendants of the Scottish plantation colonists sent in by James I (some rewarded with baronetcies) to hold down, by colonialism, the "bog Irish". Maybe the situation requires some major states-man, perceiving that there will be no military victory any more than in Vietnam but only a political victory, to go to Belfast and to say: "We understand what you mean." He will save the ancient and basic relationship of England, Ireland, Scotland and Wales. The story of the "Black and Tans" and the records in Tom Jones' Diaries is a sorry story, a shameful story.

Maybe what is required, as I wrote to ex-Home Secretary James Callaghan, on 27th October, 1971, with copy to the ex-Prime Minister, Harold Wilson, is for the British Government to make a dual declaration: (a) that the British Isles, even to the Hebrides, are an entity; have so been since the Twelfth Century and that the Government regards "all Ireland as a country", as much as Scotland or Wales; and (b) that a Declaration of Human and Minority Rights (which, in Ireland is the minority?) shall be drawn up by lawyers of both sides, accepted by the Irish Republic and imposed in the United Kingdom. It was time, I suggested, for the Opposition to get off the fence. Maybe this could forestall the situation when the British electorate, as tired as the American, will say: "This is an Irish quarrel. Let the world see it to be such— and, if the Northern and Southern Irish wish to crack each other's heads, it is their fight. Not another British soldier nor another British gun."

To those who are not bone-head fanatics or bigots, I commend the words in President Franklin Roosevelt's Inaugural Address of 1936, so often quoted by President John F. Kennedy: "Better the occasional faults of a government [and people] living in the spirit of charity than the consistent omissions of a government frozen in the ice of its own indifference"—and static formulae. The opposite of official or sectarian intransigence is an unremitting search for a settlement.

If such are indeed the negative and deplorable results reached from these recent developments of policy under Mr Heath, then one can only say that, great though my personal respect may be for such men as Hailsham, Home and Maudling, the sooner Edward Heath is pushed off the boat and forced to resign, the better for the country. The Queen is head of the Commonwealth, Queen of Canada, of Australia and of New Zealand. It is not for her at Singapore to be bundled out of this great position by one of her many Prime Ministers, the one most recently arrived and most untried, just because he happens to be a prisoner of his private ideological obsessions. According to the recent judgement made by "Rab", Lord Butler, "Heath is an extremely ruthless man". The comment has to be that of Leo Amery to a mulish man of his day, Neville Chamberlain: "Go. For God's sake, go."

I have had the honour of being in touch, in some modest

measure, with Mr Harold Wilson since 1963. In recent years this had meant correspondence and messages of increasing frequency, especially on Atlanticism and the concept of a "European Europe". The first privately printed draft (printed 1st March, 1971) of this present chapter, as well as my earlier Fulton Address, had been sent to him, at that time, and had received his comment. I certainly could not claim the peculiar advisory status of Harvard-bred Dr Henry Kissinger. I had to trust my own "hunches" on the political situation. But I did not feel—and I was right—that the following letter, written on 24th June, 1971 and sent by hand on Monday, 28th June, would be resented. At least it was one week ahead of the *New Statesman's* editorial comment. It was also repeated by me, in much abbreviated form, in a letter of 7th July, 1971 in the *Herald Tribune.*

"I hope you will pardon these jottings:

"Under the British constitutional system one cannot get out a Prime Minister, save by his own choice or under five years, except (a) by the loss of his majority by bye-elections. In the present case this could mean 14 bye-elections lost [by the Heathite Conservatives], not a large number out of 630 M.P's. but still far too optimistic about the achievement of quick results. (b) By a revolt, as with Neville Chamberlain (who yet had a tidy majority had he chosen to persist), among his own majority. This indeed is today present and decisively present, unless Heath is kept in office by Labour M.P.'s. (Abstention won't be enough.) The Tory disarray is critical and abnormal; but how many Labour M.P.'s can be prepared to break Party unity I don't know.

"There is, however, a third route, in the past used by the Tories themselves against steel nationalisation. It is for the Leader of the Opposition to declare that the Government lacks any clear mandate and that, hence, returned to power, the Labour Party will re-negotiate the whole issue. And this *before* any Parliamentary decision is taken which—like a Communist Party election—is here irreversible. ... I doubt whether the Six will, at this stage, abandon negotiations—there is too much advantage for *them* in it—but a General Election (I overlook referendum) will at this stage be forced.

"I see no reason to attack the Common Market as such. I note that Henry Kissinger is here; and I doubt whether such an attack would in fact even please Washington. Many of the economic conditions may be excellent; and I also doubt whether the country can be aroused over particular (and complex) economic stipulations. They are more interested in prices and unemployment. What is true is that the country will be much happier if the negotiations are in some other hands than Heath/Rippon. The central issue is political. (Even Washington cannot be happy about Gaullist policy.) And it has to be made beyond peradventure plain (a) that the whole plan has to be finally placed within a wider, forward-going, non-protectionist, non-exclusive framework (e.g. NATO cl. 2; O.E.C.D., etc.); and, hence, (b) that the Pompidou view of a "European Europe" is regarded by the Government of this country with suspicion, if not explicitly repudiated. We will not tolerate a divorce in the Atlantic Community. In fairness even to the French there should be no misunderstanding.

"Heath will now go out on a top-powered campaign, not to inform (which a democracy demands) but to propagate, by every instrument of press, radio, T.V. The B.B.C. has got to be compelled to give strictly equal time to the other case, and no nonsense. In an Election this can be insisted upon. It will be necessary to spike the Tory campaign for a "heroic" Election—in a later year.

"I am aware that all this is highly controversial. Hence I should think it improper to ask for or indeed to expect any reply. But, equally, I could not excuse myself if I did not write this.

"'Prices' and 'unemployment' can be quite decisive issues if and when one has a General Election. But neither (on which the Tories can be united: 'give us another four years') can provoke an Election *now*, while they are in disarray and when 'getting Heath out' can unite the Labour Party. Further, under democracy, the public has a right to judge, know and be informed. And 'informed' they will not be by a hustled, brain-washing, one-Party campaign.

With all regards and loyalty,
As ever,
George Catlin."

In writing this letter, the crucial principle—the opposite of George Brown's—was that only an E.E.C. publicly and un-mistakeably placed in an open Atlantic context is acceptable—which is a plain repudiation of M. Pompidou's vision of an exclusive "European Europe". The pragmatic tactic, however, was to produce a Parliamentary situation which would be effective means to the end of compelling the calling of a General Election in order to give a people's mandate, even if the vote might also be cast on unemployment and price issues.

On Monday, 17th July, 1971, the Labour Party "Special Conference" took place in London. The view of the delegates (there was no formal vote) indicated what was to be the judgement of the Brighton Party Conference in October—a decisive vote of the Party Conference and of its National Executive Committee against "Entry" on the terms as then stipulated in the Brussels negotiations and in conversations in Paris. After the morning meeting of Monday, the 17th, the Leader of the Opposition, Harold Wilson, on the platform turned and said to me: "I expect my speech gave you more pleasure than you expected."

At 10 p.m. on Thursday, 28th October, 1971, Edward Heath's policy nevertheless won approval in the Commons on the issue of "principle" (indeed rather of future political pattern than of political ethic) by 112 votes, with 39 of his own Party going into the Opposition lobby. In all (and with 20 abstentions) 69 Labour Party Members defied the "three-line-whip" of their own Party, affirmed in both Party Conference and Parliamentary Executive meeting, and voted with Heath. This transfer from the one lobby to the other gave the Heath Government the advantage of 138 votes. If they had been cast in accordance with Party loyalty (in what was not, for the Labour Members, "a free vote"), then the pro-Heath vote would have been 69 less and the Opposition 69 votes more, i.e., the pro-Heath vote would have been 28 short of a bare majority. The Labour Members voting were, in their private motivation, assuredly not supporters of Mr Heath's Government or general policy. Nevertheless, "objectively" it goes down on the historical record that twenty eight Labour Members that night kept Heath in power. The best that can be said is that, in the final shaping of policy, maybe he becomes their captive. . . .

The vital points are that N.W. European arrangements, of which the political aspects have been stressed by President Pompidou and Chancellor Brandt themselves, should be firmly placed beyond misunderstanding in the context of a dynamic Atlantic Commonwealth; and that the apparent implications, political and cultural as much as economic and technological, of M. Pompidou's provincial philosophy of "a European Europe" should be firmly and unambiguously repudiated for Britain. Regional economic and defence arrangements and pioneer experiments in merger, explicitly compatible with the wider context, are another and acceptable matter. There is indeed need for a "great adventure"; but it must be the right adventure and the right design.

The issue, as stated above, is indeed one of power and political handling. It is, however, far from being one merely of party politics and of counting Parliamentary heads to gain a head's length win about the whole future of the nation. It is one of principle, of framework and friendship, and of commitments that must shape the role of the nation for centuries to come. And clearly, in fairness to European statesmen, not a refusal to negotiate, but national reservations on where we are going politically must be stated now before, not after, any irreversible signature. If the Government's negotiations have much exceeded their publicly announced instructions by improper commitment, lest we be accused of perfidy the present is the time to state this. As for the Heath-shaped justificatory "White Paper" of July 1971, I content myself with the comment of *The Guardian*:

> "The White Paper ... is a disappointing document. It is politically timid, economically complacent, and vague on some vital points."

On the Community Agricultural Policy (C.A.P.) which sharply divides the negotiations of 1967 from the novel situation of today, it is almost silent. It only states the case for the great sell-out.

I have already explained that, while understanding the emotion against England being advised to go around cap in hand, which motivated Lord Attlee's downright condemnation, I did not and do not myself take so negative a view of the contribution in Europe which Britain might take, granted firm affirmation of the Atlantic framework as basic. Likewise, I would not wish to narrow myself, off-hand, quite as much as General Eisenhower did to me in the last of our several conversations in Gettysberg in October 1967. I might have wished to add (as Willkie did) reference to the entire Commonwealth. President Eisenhower's initial warning on the dangers of a protectionist isolationism has since been re-enforced by President Nixon's attack on the same minoritarian Mansfield-Fulbright policy, as late as 29th September, 1971: "There is a growing and disturbing isolationism ... these are not views that I share ... a strong United States will continue to play a responsible role in the world". Dwight Eisenhower's own view was clear. What mattered was the momentous importance of the implications of that great man's words. It was a judgement affirmative and brave.

Not, as earlier, in the informality of his Palm Springs house but seated behind his desk, the American flag on his right, the Thirty-fourth President, General of the Army which jointly liberated Europe, received me for a talk which must have lasted, like its predecessors, for half an hour. His words I shall never forget.

"What I have always wanted is a political union, no holds barred, of the United States, the United Kingdom, Canada, Australasia, EFTA—and perhaps the Germans." As I rose to go, he added: "Keep the idea alive." I have tried to execute the command.

INDEX

1 Figures in bold type indicate that the subject is discussed in some detail, or is of particular significance.

2 Relationships to Sir George Catlin (GC) are shown in square brackets following the name.

464   INDEX